Merry Christmas

Nancy & Jim

Birds of the New York Area

BIRDS OF THE

by *John Bull*

Scientific Assistant, Department of Ornithology,
American Museum of Natural History

NEW YORK AREA

DOVER PUBLICATIONS, INC., NEW YORK

International Standard Book Number: 0-486-23222-0
Library of Congress Catalog Card Number: 75-16037

Manufactured in the United States of America
Dover Publications, Inc.
180 Varick Street
New York, N.Y. 10014

To Edith

Contents

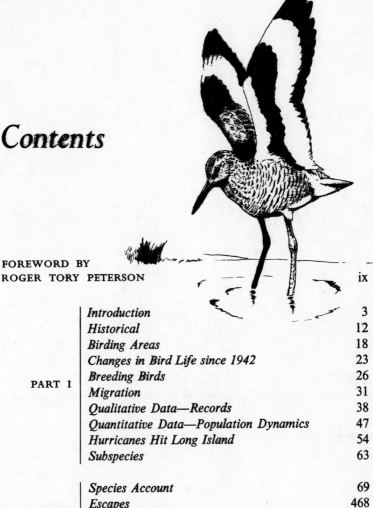

Contents

Foreword

by Roger Tory Peterson

In most parts of North America local ornithology has enjoyed only a brief history. There still are states that have never had the benefit of a comprehensive state bird book, and there are innumerable lesser, but important, areas that have not been published on at all.

Not so the New York City region. This is to be expected of the world's greatest metropolis, with its long history of human occupancy. Perhaps the only other regions in America that can boast such a long, unbroken record of active amateur field work are the Philadelphia area, where ornithological history goes back to the days of Wilson, Audubon, and Bonaparte; and Concord, Mass., with its tradition of Thoreau, Brewster and, in later days, Griscom and his cohorts.

A regional publication, embracing any one region, should be brought up to date every twenty or twenty-five years; there should be a new book for each generation of birdwatchers. This treatise by John Bull is the fourth work in less than a century to cover the New

York City region. The first was Frank Chapman's *Birds of the Vicinity of New York City*, published in 1906. This embraced 337 species. Seventeen years later (1923) Ludlow Griscom's erudite *Birds of the New York City Region* ushered in the era of field-glass ornithology. It was Griscom who showed the older generation that sight records, to be acceptable, need not always be made through the sights of shotguns. As the dean of field ornithologists, he schooled the remarkable group of young men who made up the original Bronx County Bird Club, sons of sidewalk and pavement who found pleasure in searching out the birds of the vacant lots, dumps, and waterfronts of their borough. Not to be confined, they soon extended their field of operation to the entire greater New York City region. At least two of the original group—Joseph Hickey and Allan Cruickshank—are now known to nearly everyone who watches birds. I was the first non-Bronx member of the club.

Griscom's *Birds of the New York City Region*, which covered 363 species, became our bible. We hung on his every word and at the slightest opportunity could quote chapter and verse from the book. Rivalry was intense. But whereas Griscom could draw on the resources of scarcely more than a dozen major contributors in compiling his great work, expert field observers proliferated like mushrooms during the next two decades and an avalanche of information accumulated. My own *Field Guides* were a direct result of Ludlow Griscom's teaching.

Fine binoculars became available to everyone, and automobile travel made it possible to probe every out-of-the-way spot, every back road. This mobility modified our knowledge of the birds of the greater New York area from year to year. Meanwhile the actual status of certain birds was changing. Years of protective laws were having their inevitable result: the return of species that had not been seen near New York City for a generation. To offset these gains, other species went into a decline because of attrition of the habitat around the ever growing metropolis. This deterioration continues, although remnants of wilderness will always be preserved even at the city's doorstep.

It was inevitable that one of the leaders of the Bronx County Bird Club, Allan Cruickshank, should carry the ball and nineteen years later produce the successor to Griscom's book—entitled *Birds Around New York City* (1942). Inasmuch as he is one of the top bird photographers of all time, his book was embellished with some of the finest examples of his portraiture.

By now the number of species recorded for the New York region (which covered an area slightly larger than that in Griscom's book) had climbed to 375, and Cruickshank was able to evaluate frequency of occurrence in his own way. For example, under the Cape May Warbler he states: "I have seen as many as twenty-one during a vigorous day of birding in Westchester County." However, an active day for Allan Cruickshank would be enough to incapacitate the average man; but even so, these statements do offer some measure, some yardstick by which future generations may judge whether a given species has increased or declined over the decades. Of course, the only accurate measure of bird population is something like the National Audubon Society's breeding-bird censuses. Unfortunately, too few of these have been taken in the New York City area. Even though this situation may be corrected, and many censuses taken in the future, we shall never have a really accurate check against the past because of the lack of earlier work of this sort.

After the passage of twenty-two years we now see the publication of this book by John Bull, also a member of the Bronx County Bird Club, but a bit younger than the original eight or ten men who made up that well-knit group. No one is better qualified than John Bull to have undertaken this assignment, for he is perhaps the most active link in the New York City area between the post-Griscom era and the present. No one knows the region and the trends more thoroughly. He has also worked for some years with the world collection of birds at the American Museum of Natural History in New York City, and this has given him a breadth of background that the regional field student often lacks.

During these last twenty-two years the number of species recorded in the New York City region has jumped again, this time to 412 species. As Joseph Grinnell once remarked about California, given enough time, nearly every migrant bird in North America might occur in a region, for birds have wings and they are subject to wind-drift. Immature birds, particularly, often seem to suffer errors of navigation.

Accidentals are added to the avifauna of most states nearly every year, and although it is becoming increasingly difficult for an observer to spot a "first" in the metropolitan area, new birds will continue to show up for years to come.

One of the stickiest problems for the author of a regional book is to decide whether a sight record is "good" or not. In the old days no record was considered worth anything unless it was backed by a specimen. Although collecting is still necessary in a few instances, it is no longer easy or advisable to collect birds in the heart of a big city or on its outskirts (with certain exceptions, of course). If a person were to attempt to pot a rare gull at Jones Beach, he would be quickly herded in by the state troopers regardless of state or federal collecting permits. Recently, however, because of the fine equipment now available to photographers, many records have been substantiated by recognizable photographs, both stills and movies. Banders, catching rarities in their mist nets, have also produced acceptable records, which are usually documented photographically. Even the use of tape-recording equipment may be a tool for the verification of rare vagrants. Recently the song of a Western Meadowlark that had established residence in Massachusetts was recorded on tape for the benefit of the doubting Thomases.

What should be the criteria for the acceptance of other sight records? In some states, a well-documented account by at least two competent observers gives credence to such a record; in others, sight records are never accepted. However, we are reaching the time when the latter point of view can no longer be sustained. In fact, the acquisition of one specimen for a region does not mean that all the succeeding sight records are any better than they would have been had the specimen not existed. Their validity still depends on the quality of the observer, and that is where the author of such a work as this must be a wise arbiter. No one would question a sight record of a male Vermilion Flycatcher in good plumage, but a sight record of a Bell's Vireo along the eastern seaboard, even by the best of observers, is something else again.

Regional bird books should make comparisons with the past as much as possible. In this book John Bull attempts to do this, for there have been many changes during the two short decades since 1942.

Birds that were virtually unknown as summer residents in the New York City region twenty-five or thirty years ago now breed regularly. This reflects in part the national protection they now enjoy. But another factor is the creation of such areas as the Jamaica Bay Wildlife Refuge on Long Island, where a "prairie" pond with its fresh-water vegetation has been produced adjacent to salt water. Here one finds breeding Glossy Ibises, Snowy Egrets, Common Egrets, Little Blue Herons, and Louisiana Herons (one record)—species that were not known to breed on Long Island in Griscom's day or during the period of which Cruickshank wrote. In addition, migrant ducks that normally breed in the prairie regions far to the west have recently remained to nest: the Shoveler, Gadwall, Ruddy Duck, Green-winged Teal, Baldpate, and Pintail. Shortly after my arrival in the New York City region in 1925 the Least Tern returned to breed. Within the next ten years the Herring Gull moved southward to Long Island, to overlap the breeding range of the Black Skimmer pushing northward from New Jersey beaches; another ten years saw the establishment of nesting Great Black-backed Gulls on eastern Long Island.

The sandpipers and plovers, pulling out of their deep depression of the early years of this century, have recovered because of the cessation of shorebird shooting. Some species, such as the godwits, once extremely rare in the northeast, are now almost commonplace during migration.

In the years ahead, because of the widespread use of pesticides, especially in heavily populated areas, we may lose many of our birds. The drastic drop in the Osprey population since 1950 around eastern Long Island and Gardiner's Island can almost certainly be attributed to the residual effects of toxic chemicals passed on through the food chain. Small fish ingesting the poisons fall easier prey to larger fish which in turn transmit the stable poisons in their tissues to the Ospreys, which in recent years have been hatching only a minority of their eggs. Without replacement by young birds we may well lose our last Ospreys before the successor to this book is written.

The Peregrine Falcon, finest of all birds, is gone from nearly every eyrie in the Hudson Valley and its environs, where as late as 1950 a dozen or more pairs existed. Could this too be the end result of pesticides? We don't know.

It would seem to me that among the most important projects that the field birders of the New York City area could undertake are population studies: censuses of spray-free habitats as well as of contaminated areas; censuses of heronries, and a careful record of the nesting successes and failures of the birds of prey. To combat the forces of destruction we must have facts, measurable facts; impressions are not enough. This new book by John Bull, which admirably sums up our current knowledge of the status of birds of the New York City region, should be used as a springboard.

Part One

Introduction

The purpose of this book is to present a detailed account of the bird life of greater New York and vicinity, with emphasis on faunal changes during the past twenty years. Since the turn of the century three books have been written on the bird life of this region: Chapman (1906), Griscom (1923), and Cruickshank (1942). Many changes have taken place in the local avifauna within the past two decades, just as they had in earlier years and will in the future, for the bird life of a region is never static.

While numerous migrants still pour through this region each spring and fall, a number of breeding species have been adversely affected by the alteration or obliteration of former nesting haunts. An exploding human population that has reached approximately 17,000,000 in and around one of the world's largest cities, necessitating increased housing and industrial development, has been the prime factor in eliminating many habitats for birds. Nevertheless, certain other areas have been set aside to provide protection for birds. An excellent example of the latter is the recently created Jamaica Bay Wildlife Refuge on Long Island. This unique area, in view of the Manhattan skyline, adjacent to Idlewild Airport, and within walking distance of a subway, lies wholly within New York City. Despite the noise of jet airliners and trains, this wildlife sanctuary contains a great variety and abundance of birds at all seasons.

EXTENT OF AREA

The New York City region as here understood, is somewhat greater than that encompassed by Cruickshank's book; but has not changed since publication of my pamphlet (Birds of the New York City Area, 1958). The region as now defined (see map, p. 506) includes the following *new* territory since 1942: (*a*) Connecticut—that portion of southwestern Fairfield County east on Long Island Sound to Westport, and inland to the towns of Wilton and Weston. (*b*) New York—all of Putnam County, and the southern half of Orange County north to an east–west line running through Cornwall, Goshen, and Port Jervis. (*c*) New Jersey—down the coast to Manasquan Inlet, including the town of Point Pleasant, and along the Delaware River to Frenchtown. For the southern limits inland between Point Pleasant and Frenchtown, see map. While the size of this region is considerably larger than before, only one breeding species has been added within the new territory: Yellow-bellied Sapsucker; and only one nonbreeding species—Fieldfare. The offshore limits are considered to be approximately thirty miles, as this is the usual extent of travel by the commercial fishing boats.

TOPOGRAPHY AND ECOLOGY

The large map (see p. 506) indicates the more important topographical features to be found in the area. The ecological characteristics of the New York City region are varied. Ranging from sea level to over 1800 feet in northwestern New Jersey, many different ecological

4

niches or habitats are present and contain a great variety of birds. Formerly much of this area was covered with a fine hardwood forest, of which only small portions remain. Much of the woodland today is second growth and consists primarily of oak, beech, maple, and hickory on the interior uplands where the soil is rich. In the sandy areas of the coastal plain pitch pine and several species of "scrub" oak are the dominant trees. The formerly extensive areas of pine barrens have been much reduced by cutting and burning, and this is particularly true on eastern Long Island. The unique prairielike region on western Long Island, known as the Hempstead Plains, is nearly destroyed, with only pitifully small remnants today.

Just back from the ocean lie the barrier beaches with their sand dunes and scattered patches of dense thickets. On the bay side of the barrier beaches are numerous inlets and lagoons, mud and sand flats, and salt marshes. Much of this area is threatened by draining and filling. The once wild and unspoiled ocean beaches are gradually being taken over for summer resorts.

Most of the forests had been cleared for farmland by the 1850s. Shortly after World War I agriculture declined and many farms and orchards were abandoned. These areas were later replaced by housing developments, particularly after World War II. Open country, consisting chiefly of grassy fields and meadows, has suffered extensively and has been overrun with numerous shopping centers as well as industrial and housing sites. Other former farm sites have grown to scrub. Fresh-water marshes, swamps, and bogs are becoming fewer and fewer each year.

Except for parks and sanctuaries, the only remaining relatively unspoiled sections are found in the wooded highlands of the interior where the land is either too steep or too rocky for cultivation. There are numerous ponds, lakes, and reservoirs within the area. Small streams, and large rivers like the Hudson and the Delaware, still provide resting and feeding places for birds, but pollution has rendered some undesirable and others uninhabitable.

GENERAL TREATMENT

The annotated list (pp. 69 ff.) is based on (*a*) specimens examined in collections, both public and private, (*b*) the published literature which today is vast and scattered, some of it in little-known periodicals, (*c*) a voluminous mass of unpublished notes by many field workers, and, (*d*) the writer's own field experience covering a period of more than thirty years.

Particular emphasis is placed on ecological associations (especially those of breeding species), population trends and fluctuations, relative abundance, seasonal occurrence, and local geographical distribution. To a lesser extent little-published notes on characters that may facilitate field identification are discussed; and in the relatively few cases applicable, taxonomic relationship, chiefly at the subspecies level, is included.

Throughout this work the "species approach," rather than the "ecological approach," is used. Each breeding-species write-up includes local habitats known for that species, which eliminates much of the duplication that results from grouping the species under habitat headings. The method of listing tables of seasonal occurrence for each species, and of listing accidentals, casuals, winter visitants, etc., has been abandoned.

The chief reason for omitting these tables is that many species "fit" into several categories. For instance, it would be misleading to assign the Peregrine Falcon to a particular category when, in fact, it belongs in several. As a species it is found every month of the year and, therefore, is a "permanent resident." It breeds locally and rarely and, as such, is a "summer resident." It occurs most frequently and in largest numbers in fall along the outer beaches, thus it is a "fall transient." Furthermore, in view of the foregoing, it would be hopeless to hazard a guess as to when its "normal" or "average" arrival and departure take place in spring and fall because we have already seen that it winters and summers. The only thing definite about it is that during fall migration its maximum numbers on a particular day can be stated, the so-called peak date.

The foregoing terms are in quotation marks because it is felt that more meaningful and definitive substitutes are warranted. The following terminology is suggested instead:

Resident—rather than "permanent resident." Resident itself implies permanency.

Breeder—rather than "summer resident." This is greatly preferred as the avian nesting season does not always coincide with our

6

summer season. The Great Horned Owl, which nests as early as February with snow still on the ground, can hardly be called a "summer resident."

Migrant—rather than "transient." The words "migrant" and "transient" are not synonymous; transient implies impermanency, not periodic movement from one area to another. (And "migrant" seems more fitting with "migration.")

Winter Visitant—rather than "winter resident." There is nothing permanent about the Brown Creeper in winter. It may be with us for only a small portion of the winter, so why call it a "winter resident"?

Because of much yearly variation in migration dates, the so-called "normal" or "average" dates are deliberately omitted as misleading. Furthermore, with the exception of those late April and May migrants, which are more or less regular in their spring arrival, the vast majority of migrants, and winter and summer visitants as well, have irregular arrival and departure periods. As a substitute, the words "rare before" or "rare after" such and such a time are used for a relatively broad period rather than the completely misleading fixed date—for example, May 12. No species can be "guaranteed" to arrive or depart year after year on the same day. It just does not work that way. The following time periods are used here: "early May" for May 1–10; "mid-May" for May 11–20; and "late May" for May 21–31. The same time periods apply to any month. As an example, the Olive-sided Flycatcher in spring is rare before late May (i.e., May 21–31), and in fall is rare after early September (i.e., Sept. 1–10). This method, while somewhat indefinite, is more realistic than selecting an "exact" date which can never be wholly correct.

The so-called "extreme" dates of many species are being exceeded by earlier and later dates almost every year, so that too much importance should not be attached to these happenings. However, these dates do have some value when correlated with immediate or long-range weather conditions, as well as indicating certain trends.

For both maximum counts and early and late dates, the names of observers are omitted unless the counts and dates are of exceptional nature.

Another problem is attempting to determine *spring departure* and *fall arrival*, as well as maximum numbers, of the commoner breeding

7

species during the migration periods. The Ovenbird serves as a good example. The *spring arrival* and *fall departure* of this common species are easily ascertained anywhere in our area. However, it is hopeless to establish *spring departure* or *fall arrival* in the surrounding woodlands where the Ovenbird nests commonly, because it is impossible (except in the few instances of banded birds) to differentiate migrant individuals from the local breeding population. This applies to maximum numbers as well. On the other hand, this problem does not exist in city parks and along the outer coast, in which areas Ovenbirds do *not* breed. If we see twenty-five Ovenbirds in woodland at a New Jersey locality inland on May 15, separating the migrants from the local breeders is impossible, but if twenty-five Ovenbirds are seen in Central Park or at Jones Beach on May 15, then we can be certain that *all* are migrants. This is why maximum numbers are given for such species only at localities where they do *not* breed.

Information on "egg dates" is taken from Cruickshank (1942), who in turn secured much of his data from the large egg collection in the American Museum, the data compiled by Dr. Dean Amadon, together with additional data accumulated since, the latter primarily of those species found breeding for the "first" time in our area.

The rarer species are included as breeders only when satisfactory evidence of breeding is obtained, such as nest under construction, nest with eggs or young, or when *flightless* young out of the nest are under parental care. This last point is stressed because, among certain water birds, notably terns, "*flying* young being fed by parents" does not necessarily constitute on-the-spot breeding. They may have bred at a considerable distance from where feeding was observed.

For the *rarer* species, singing males present during the breeding season or those birds with gonads in an "advanced" condition—such as testes or ovaries enlarged—do not per se constitute breeding evidence, and are excluded from the breeding category.

For the *commoner* species, repeated occurrences of adults during the nesting season is ordinarily sufficient to establish breeding. However, this does not apply to certain ducks, herons, shorebirds, gulls, terns, etc., which are noted for their wandering tendencies and are sometimes present in numbers during the nesting season without actually having bred.

8

Regarding terms used, although there is much to be said for the terminology of Humphrey and Parkes (1959) concerning molts and plumages, their system is nevertheless radically different from that used in most of the literature. Dwight's terminology (1900), with certain modifications, is used here. In order to avoid confusion, and at the risk of oversimplification, the terms "breeding plumage" or "nonbreeding plumage" are used here. For age categories, adult, sub-adult, immature, and nestling or fledgling are stated.

With three exceptions, the scientific names in the annotated list follow those of the A.O.U. *Check-list* (1957). The three exceptions are: (1) *Camptorhynchus labradorius* (not *labradorium*), see Mayr (Auk, 75: 225, 1958); (2) *Bombycilla garrulus* (not *garrula*), see Parkes (Auk, 75: 479, 1958); (3) *Turdus iliacus* (not *T. musicus*), for which see explanation under *Turdus iliacus*.

The vernacular names herein also follow those of the A.O.U. *Check-list* (1957), with the exception of three species having the singularly inappropriate and misleading appellation "Common." More meaningful names have been substituted, which are believed to be of greater significance and usefulness. The three name changes affect the "Common" Egret, "Common" Teal, and "Common" Scoter. Reasons for these name changes are discussed under the "Remarks" sections for these three species. Wood Stork is also used in preference to Wood Ibis, for which see explanation under that species.

Sequence of species follows that of the A.O.U. *Check-list* (1957) with the exception of the teal-shoveler complex and the phalaropes. Reasons for changes within these two "groups" are found in the annotated list.

Extralimital ranges affecting local status are given in abridged form for those birds whose usual breeding limits, winter limits, or migration routes occur outside the greater New York area. The reader thus has the opportunity of ascertaining in these pages information which would otherwise be found in *detail* only in the A.O.U. *Check-list* (1957).

Records are included through the breeding season of 1962, with the exception of important information altering the status of certain species; also specimens obtained of three species "new" to the

9

region—Red-billed Tropicbird, Fulvous Tree Duck, and Boreal Owl —as well as satisfactory evidence of a Bullock's Oriole in December 1963. In no instances are any records included after December 31, 1963.

ACKNOWLEDGEMENTS

This is, in reality, a cooperative effort. For without the enthusiastic help of several hundred contributors, this work would have been quite impossible. It is out of the question to thank each one here individually, but their names may be found in the species accounts. Their aid is gratefully acknowledged.

There are a number of persons who went out of their way to assist the writer with innumerable problems and questions. The following were of especial help: New Jersey—Irving H. Black and Joseph R. Jehl, Jr.; Staten Island—Howard H. Cleaves; mainland New York —Stanley O. Grierson, Michael Oboiko, John C. Orth, and Edward D. Treacy; Connecticut—Richard L. Burdsall, William B. Cook, and Paul C. Spofford; Long Island—Irwin M. Alperin, John J. Elliott, Edmund Morgan, Eugene T. Mudge, and Gilbert S. Raynor; entire region—Robert S. Arbib, Jr., Paul A. Buckley, George Komorowski, Peter W. Post, and Frank E. Watson.

I am particularly indebted to the following for permission to examine collections or to those who answered numerous queries concerning specimens: H. Lee Ferguson, Jr., Dr. A. K. Fisher, Dr. William T. Helmuth, Paul G. Howes, Roy Latham, and Dr. Alexander Wetmore (see also Chapter 2—Historical).

To the members of the scientific staff of the Department of Ornithology, American Museum of Natural History, I owe a special debt of gratitude for their services and assistance in many ways, but notably to Dr. Dean Amadon, Chairman and Curator of Birds, who gave much of his time reading the manuscript and offering many valuable criticisms and much needed advice; also to Charles E. O'Brien, Assistant Curator, who was of immeasurable help in "running down" many rare and important specimens.

Geoffrey Carleton and Eugene Eisenmann have critically read the manuscript in its entirety and made innumerable suggestions. The former kept in touch with the many active field observers and

10

forwarded their latest information to me, and helped with difficult "borderline" sight reports. The latter was of inestimable help by virtue of his technical and editorial experience. Indeed, Eisenmann has constantly given encouragement in completion of this work.

The writer owes much to Harry N. Darrow for assistance in compilation of numerous records on a projected, but never completed, work on the birds of Westchester County; and in later years much valuable information on field data from coastal Long Island.

To both Richard E. Harrison and George Colbert for the superlative map, and to Cornelius J. Ward for the attractive and very lifelike drawings, the writer is particularly indebted.

For their infinite patience in seeing this volume through to completion, I owe much to Richard B. McAdoo and John Macrae, editors of Harper & Row; also to Miss Lisa McGaw and Miss Pace Barnes for editorial assistance.

To my sister-in-law, Miss Doris Hellman, of the Los Angeles County Museum, for editorial suggestions on the manuscript, I am very grateful.

Finally, if it were not for my wife's typing and critical proofreading of the entire manuscript, together with much forebearance and encouragement, this book would not have been possible. To her, I owe much for suffering through a long and arduous undertaking.

Not to forget our young daughter, Doris—too often neglected.

Any errors of omission or commission are, however, the writer's.

Historical

With the exception of old-time accounts of game birds and waterfowl shot in colonial days, the ornithological record in the New York City region began in a serious way around 1830. The first book of any consequence dealing with this region was that about Long Island birds by Jacob P. Giraud (1844). Little or nothing of major importance was written for approximately the next sixty years.

For many years subsequent to 1830, records of most rare birds had to be substantiated by specimens before they were given credence by ornithologists. Some of the earliest specimens collected from the 1830s to the 1860s were taken by Giraud, Pike, and others. Most of these specimens were housed in the Long Island Historical Society in Brooklyn, founded in 1863. The bulk of this collection was deposited at a later date in the Brooklyn Museum and ultimately in the American Museum of Natural History. In the American Museum there is a specimen of Royal Tern collected at Raynor South (now Freeport), Long Island, on August 27, 1831, by a man named Ward. This specimen is unique. It is quite possibly the oldest specimen taken in the local region still in existence with fairly detailed label data. This is remarkable in itself as most specimens collected prior to the 1870s have very little data, usually only a vague locality, such as "Long Island," or sometimes just locality and year. Prior to 1944 it was the only published local record *known* of Royal Tern for over a century.

Many of Giraud's specimens went to Vassar College and some of these finally to the American Museum. The largest part of the Long Island Historical Society collection was from Colonel Nicholas Pike. He started a collection of Long Island birds early in the 1830s. Nearly all of Pike's specimens were mounted by John Akhurst, a taxidermist who also collected birds on Long Island for over fifty years. Many other birds in this collection were obtained from professional gunners (usually market hunters) and from Fulton Market—formerly the center for much of the sale of produce and game taken on Long Island. One of Akhurst's chief rivals in getting the rarities at Fulton Market was John G. Bell, another well-known taxidermist of that day, who collected in Rockland County also. Many an early morning visit to the market was made to see who could beat the other to the choicest specimens. Bell was noted for having taken the "last" Labrador Duck on Long Island in 1875, in fact the last known specimen from anywhere.

The 1870s to about 1900 marked the height of the collecting period. During this time the three largest local collections were amassed by George N. Lawrence, William Dutcher, and Jonathan Dwight. These men did little collecting themselves, but hired professional collectors. Dwight had birds collected for him until the early 1920s. Most of the Lawrence, Dutcher, and Dwight specimens are now at the American Museum and are estimated to total well over 15,000 from the New York City region alone. The Lawrence and Dwight specimens were obtained throughout this area, while those of Dutcher were almost all taken on Long Island.

Smaller but important collections now in the American Museum are: from Long Island—Braislin, Cherrie, Hendrickson, Howell, Thurston, and Worthington, and in later years, Griscom and Murphy; from Staten Island—Chapin; from New Jersey—Chapman, W. de W. Miller, Van Rensselaer, von Lengerke (chiefly hawks), and Weber (many of his specimens also in the United States National Museum, Washington, D.C., *fide* Wetmore); from mainland New York—

13

Bicknell and Mearns (the latter chiefly U.S.N.M. collection, *fide* Wetmore). I have examined all of the above in the A.M.N.H. collection, while some of the rarities contained in the Mearns and Weber collections in the U.S.N.M. were kindly verified by Dr. Alexander Wetmore.

Two important collections made in our portion of Connecticut are those of Paul G. Howes in the Bruce Museum, Greenwich (examined by me) and William H. Hoyt, formerly in the Stamford Museum, but now in the Yale Peabody Museum, New Haven (reported in detail by Sage *et al.*, 1913).

One of the larger local collections was made in Westchester County at Sing Sing (now Ossining) and the Croton Point area by A. K. Fisher. The bulk of this material is in the Museum of Comparative Zoology, Cambridge, Mass. (M.C.Z.), and was examined in its entirety by me. It contains well over 1000 specimens. Other Fisher specimens are in the A.M.N.H. collection.

One of the most important local collections is that of Arthur H. Helme. Most of his specimens (over 1000) were taken on Long Island at Miller Place, a few at Port Jefferson, and others at Montauk. A number of specimens are of great rarity—some of these at the A.M.N.H. and others in the private collection of the late Harold H. Bailey of Goshen, Va. Mrs. Bailey kindly verified the existence of some of the records, all of which have been published.

Some of the local specimens of note mentioned in Eaton's great work (1910 and 1914) are in the New York State Museum at Albany (N.Y.S.M.). There are also a number of specimens in the Cornell University Museum. Both of these collections were examined by the writer. The latter specimens, for the most part, were taken in recent years chiefly by students.

A few important collections in later years (1900–20, some up to the 1940s) were made by private collectors, chiefly on eastern Long Island. Henry L. Ferguson (Fisher's Island) did considerable collecting, especially hawks—the stomach and crop contents being used by A. K. Fisher in his hawk and owl studies. Many of Ferguson's specimens, particularly the rare species, were sent to Frank M. Chapman for verification and the records were published from time to time. These specimens are now in the Henry L. Ferguson Museum (private), founded in the summer of 1960 and cared for by his son, H. Lee Ferguson, Jr., who was most helpful to me in all ornithological matters concerning Fisher's Island.

For a number of years LeRoy Wilcox of Speonk, L.I., has made important collections in the Moriches–Shinnecock area and the identification of most of his rarer specimens was confirmed by various authorities in the American Museum.

The late Dr. William T. Helmuth of Easthampton spent more than thirty-five years collecting many valuable birds principally from Mecox Bay to Montauk. While I examined most of his collection over ten years ago, its present whereabouts appears to be unknown. However, I was fortunate in securing from Mrs. Helmuth, through the efforts of Geoffrey Carleton, thirty-four volumes of detailed field notes amassed from 1908–51. Some of the records, including those of specimens taken prior to 1942, are published here for the first time.

Of all the private local collections seen by me, that of Roy Latham of Orient, L.I., is second to none. His collection of more than 1200 bird specimens (skins and mounts) is carefully labeled with much detailed data appended. He also has an extensive nest and egg collection. A busy potato farmer by vocation, Latham is a naturalist of the old school. For a half century or more during his spare time he has amassed an enormous natural history collection ranging from mammals and birds to insects and other invertebrates, plus numerous botanical specimens and many interesting archaeological items. What makes it unique, however, is that nearly all of it was obtained on the Orient peninsula, much of it within a few miles of his farm. His bird collection contains much of value, not only many rarities, but also small series of the commoner species, all of which I examined. Latham explained to me that he identified the great majority of his specimens without any outside aid, only with the books he had on hand. A few difficult species and some subspecies were sent to the American Museum for determination. Some of the records of the very rare species, including a few taken many years ago, are published here for the first time. His numerous records and observations formed the basis of the "Orient Region" in Griscom's work of 1923.

It should be emphasized here that a number of Long Island water birds published as taken at such localities as Freeport, Merrick,

Amityville, Babylon, Islip, Patchogue, and other south shore points were actually collected opposite these towns on the barrier beach (either along the ocean or on the bay side). For example, a specimen labeled "Amityville, Braislin" was, in fact, taken at Jones Beach by Andrew Chichester (a collector for Braislin).

The writer has made an extensive search for old specimens of great rarity and has succeeded in finding the great majority. However, a number could not be found. Their present whereabouts are unknown.

With the gradual decline in local collecting by the 1920s, due mainly to protective bird laws, a new era with a different emphasis evolved, namely field observation. The field glass took the place of the shotgun. The influence of Chapman in the early 1900s in popularizing study of the bird in life, and especially his initiation of the annual Christmas Census, together with the vast experience of Griscom in the techniques of field ornithology by means of sight identification and the publication of his book in 1923, all contributed to the development of bird study for the amateur. Sumptuous state bird books with beautiful colored plates, such as those of Eaton (1910 and 1914) and Forbush (1925–29) replaced, to a large extent, the old-style technical works with their necessarily detailed plumage-and-structural descriptions. With the advent of the Peterson and Pough field guides in the 1930s and 1940s, as well as Cruickshank's book in 1942, and with the appearance of modern prism binoculars and telescopes, the hobby of bird watching grew by leaps and bounds in the New York City area from probably less than 100 observers in 1920 to thousands today. Greatly improved methods of transportation and the superhighways developed within the past thirty years have made it possible for the field ornithologist to reach many areas previously somewhat inaccessible. As with the binocular and telescope, the camera too has largely replaced the gun and is used extensively for "shooting" birds. For the few who banded birds prior to 1930, there are now hundreds. There has also been a large increase in feeding stations, and many a rare bird has appeared at feeders in recent years. Recent techniques in radar studies of migratory birds have projected ornithology to the threshold of the space age. Finally, the ornithological literature of today is so vast and scattered that the reader interested in all of its various aspects will find that much time is spent in merely perusing

16

the literature, to say nothing of trying to absorb it. Not the least important have been the wise conservation laws enacted through the years which have brought to us increased numbers of certain species that were formerly on the brink of extinction, and of others that had become dangerously reduced in numbers.

Birding Areas

Some of the best localities for bird watching are listed below. They are arranged geographically, section by section, and may be found on the large map. No attempt is made here to tell *how* one may reach these places. Good up-to-date road maps are readily available. Inquiry about how, when, and where to go may be made at the National Audubon Society and through such local bird clubs as the Linnaean Society of New York. Certain localities are noted especially for rarities or particular groups of birds which are indicated below. The best time of year varies with each bird and that information will be found under the species accounts.

I. Long Island (east to west, south shore)

    A. Montauk (at the Point unless otherwise stated): Cory's Shearwater, Gannet, Great Cormorant (on jetties at entrance to Lake Montauk), Harlequin Duck, Common Eider, King Eider, Black-legged Kittiwake, Razorbill, Thick-billed Murre, Dovekie; Rough-legged Hawk and Northern Shrike in open areas; land birds in fall in vicinity of lighthouse.

    B. Hook Pond (Easthampton), Georgica Pond, Sagaponack, Watermill Pond, Mecox Bay: all are excellent for various water birds; Watermill for ducks, especially Redhead.

18

C. Shinnecock Inlet to Moriches Inlet: the inlets are especially good after storms for possible jaegers and phalaropes, and occasionally shearwaters; the "dune" road paralleling the ocean and stretching from inlet to inlet is worthwhile traversing in fall for land birds.

D. Moriches Bay: the flats and marshes in the vicinity of the inlet are famous for the variety and abundance of shorebirds; Whimbrels, Willets, and both godwits are regular and the Oystercatcher (one pair) breeds in the vicinity, as well as numbers of nesting Black Skimmers and Roseate Terns. Occasionally Royal and Caspian Terns are present.

E. Jones Beach (Tobay Pond to Jones Inlet)
   1. Tobay: Herons (Louisiana Heron regular), waterfowl (including nesting Gadwall), shorebirds, and Black Tern. Entry permit must be obtained from Town Clerk, Oyster Bay, N.Y. (parking area at rear of Tobay Pond).
   2. Zachs Bay (west end) and lawns and shrubbery in the vicinity of water tower and bathhouses, as well as the fishing station nearby: excellent place for migrant land birds (Red-headed Woodpecker, Western Kingbird, Mockingbird, Loggerhead Shrike, Blue Grosbeak, Dickcissel, Lark Sparrow, and Clay-colored Sparrow in fall).
   3. Short Beach to Jones Inlet: migrant land birds from police barracks to coastguard station; the inlet and adjacent beaches for shorebirds, gulls, terns and Skimmers, and waterfowl, especially Brant. All inlets should be visited after storms. Birders should be careful to park *only* in designated parking fields in the entire Jones Beach area. Stopping along the highways is unlawful and one does so at his own risk.

F. Jamaica Bay Refuge: the east and west ponds (parking field at latter) adjacent to Cross Bay Boulevard are excellent all year around, and a "must" for any birder—one of the best places in the entire region due mainly to the efforts of Herbert Johnson, the refuge manager. Entry permit must be obtained from Department of Parks, Arsenal, Central Park, New York City. The main attraction is the variety of breeding water birds, notably American Coot, Common

Gallinule, Pied-billed Grebe, Ruddy Duck, other waterfowl in lesser numbers, Great Egret, Snowy Egret, Little Blue Heron (rarely), and best of all—Glossy Ibis; also a good tern and Skimmer colony. This is the place *par excellence* for those rare Old World shorebirds, the Curlew Sandpiper and the Ruff. The former should be looked for in late May on the tidal flats at the west end of the west pond (preferably on an incoming tide) the latter is possibly regular each year anywhere from April to early fall and prefers the pond shores and grassy areas rather than the flats. The ponds are also good for Wilson's Phalarope, as well as many other shorebirds. Also noteworthy is the variety of ducks and geese in season, and it is one of the better localities for Snow and Blue Geese. During the winter months Ipswich Sparrows, Lapland Longspurs, and Snow Buntings occupy the sandy grassy areas that are the summer nesting grounds of the tern colony.

G. Riis Park: migrant land birds, especially in fall; the same species listed under Jones Beach (2) above. The introduced House Finch breeds chiefly at the east edge of the park and in the nearby residential areas.

Note: A new bridge under construction (completion expected by early spring, 1964) will connect Captree State Park with Fire Island State Park. This will provide birdwatchers easy access to a once relatively remote area that will well repay the field investigator at all times of year. Fire Island is especially productive in fall.

II. Long Island (other than areas under "I")

A. Prospect Park (Brooklyn): migrant land birds, particularly in spring.

B. Mill Neck (north shore): nesting land birds.

III. New York City parks (Manhattan and Bronx)

A. Central Park (Manhattan): one of the best areas for migrant passerines and noteworthy for its warblers; the best portion is the "Ramble" between 72nd and 81st streets.

B. Bronx, Van Cortlandt, and Pelham Bay Parks (all in Bronx County): the first named is good for migrant land birds and in winter for owls in the evergreen groves; the last named is perhaps the best locality in the region for owls, all of the regular woodland species having been recorded in a single winter. It is also one of the better localities near the city for bay ducks; Van Cortlandt Park has nesting marsh birds and is an ideal locality for breeding Traill's Flycatcher and Warbling Vireo. The nearby ridges are good in fall for migrant hawks.

IV. Staten Island

Wolfe's Pond, the shore opposite Raritan Bay, and the garbage dumps in the Fresh Kills section should be searched for rare gulls. In recent years those regular Old World species, the Little and Black-headed Gulls have been reported frequently, chiefly at sewer outlets. On the dumps in winter look for Glaucous and Iceland Gulls, as well as the very rare Lesser Black-backed Gull, another wanderer from Europe.

V. Connecticut and mainland New York

Excellent areas for nesting land birds are the Audubon Nature Center in Fairfield County, Mianus Gorge and Poundridge Reservation in Westchester County, Fahnestock Park in Putnam County, and Bear Mountain and Harriman Parks in adjoining Rockland and Orange counties. The best place to see wintering Bald Eagles is on the Hudson River at Croton Point, preferably when there is ice in the river.

VI. New Jersey

A. Troy Meadows (Morris County): the best fresh-water marsh in the entire region, seen to best advantage by traversing the elevated boardwalk. Here one may find Sora and Virginia Rails, both bitterns, Wood Ducks, and other marsh-loving birds. Nearby Boonton Reservoir is good for ducks, and the Boonton hills for migrant and nesting land birds.

B. Greenbrook Sanctuary (Bergen County): on the Palisades and overlooking the Hudson; this is very good for breeding land birds, as well as occasional Bald Eagles and Peregrine Falcons.

21

C. Sandy Hook (Monmouth County): recently made a state park, it has nesting herons and egrets, and should prove to be an excellent locality for migrant land birds. The sewer outlets in nearby Raritan Bay are good places for the rare gulls mentioned under Staten Island.

D. Manasquan Inlet (Monmouth County): like the inlets along the coast of Long Island, this locality should be visited for sea birds especially after storms.

E. High Point State Park and nearby Stokes State Forest (Sussex County): excellent for nesting land birds, and a good area for the northern breeding warblers and other "Canadian Zone" species. Autumn hawk flights may be observed on the more exposed ridges.

Changes in Bird Life since 1942

There have been numerous changes in the avifauna within the New York City area during the past two decades. Some species have increased, while others have decreased. Details of these changes may be found under the species accounts. Only a listing is presented here with a few remarks on the breeding species. Those marked with an asterisk are extremely rare as *breeders* in our area.

I. Increases

A. "Southern" element

1. *Breeding:* Great Egret, Snowy Egret, Louisiana Heron*, Yellow-crowned Night Heron, Glossy Ibis*, Turkey Vulture, American Oystercatcher*, Black Skimmer, Tufted Titmouse, Mockingbird, Blue-gray Gnatcatcher, Prothonotary Warbler, Cerulean Warbler, Cardinal, Blue Grosbeak*.

2. *Nonbreeding:* Cattle Egret, Royal Tern, Red-bellied Woodpecker, Yellow-throated Warbler, Summer Tanager.

   It has been suggested that amelioration of the climate has been a factor in the northward spread of these species. There may be certain cyclical and ecological factors involved also, as well as population overflow.

B. "Western" element

1. *Breeding:* Gadwall, Pintail*, Shoveler*, American Widgeon*, Ruddy Duck. The successful breeding of these primarily western ducks in the east is perhaps due to drainage of marshes and drought in the west. Creation of waterfowl refuges along the Atlantic coast possibly simulates their natural breeding grounds and provides suitable nesting areas.

2. *Nonbreeding:* Western Kingbird, Dickcissel (formerly breeding), Lark Sparrow, Clay-colored Sparrow.

C. "Northern" element

1. *Breeding:* Great Black-backed Gull, Herring Gull, Traill's Flycatcher, Brown Creeper, Evening Grosbeak*. The flycatcher and creeper have been steadily breeding farther south in the Appalachian Mountains and along the coastal plain within the past dozen years or so. The Evening Grosbeak might well be placed in the "Western" category, as it has been spreading eastward as a breeder for over forty years, and has reached New Brunswick and Maine, south to Massachusetts. In 1962 it ranged as far south as Connecticut and New Jersey.

2. *Nonbreeding:* Great Cormorant, Brant, Common Eider, Ring-billed Gull, Boreal Chickadee.

D. Widespread species

1. *Breeding:* Pied-billed Grebe, Great Blue Heron (local), American Coot, Pileated Woodpecker (local). The grebe and coot have increased in the same localities as the ducks.

2. *Nonbreeding:* No marked changes reported.

II. Decreases (breeding species only)

A. "Southern" element: Little Blue Heron*, Acadian Flycatcher, Kentucky Warbler, Orchard Oriole. The flycatcher and warbler have declined greatly during the past half-century and have, for the most part, withdrawn from the northern sections of our area since 1942.

B. "Northern" element: Green-winged Teal*, Bobolink.

Both the Little Blue Heron and Green-winged Teal present anomalies. Despite the fact that they have decreased locally during the past twenty years, nevertheless, they were first noted as nesting in our area in the late 1950s. This local decrease may prove to be temporary.

C. Widespread species: Peregrine Falcon, Bobwhite, Upland Plover, Cliff Swallow, Short-billed Marsh Wren, Warbling Vireo, Parula Warbler, Pine Warbler, Eastern Meadowlark, Grasshopper Sparrow, Henslow's Sparrow, Vesper Sparrow. The plover, Bobolink, Meadowlark, and the three sparrows, all open-country grassland species, have decreased for the same reason—rapid disappearance of their habitat for building purposes. A general reduction in agricultural areas has been a contributing factor also. These birds were formerly common on the vast Hempstead Plains, this unique prairielike region, now all but completely obliterated.

Breeding Birds

Due to the varied terrain of the New York area, an altitudinal variation ranging from sea level to over 1800 feet, and its location within three faunal life zones, at least 190 species of birds [46 per cent of the total fauna (412)] have been reliably reported as breeding at one time or another. Of great interest is the fact that this region is the "meeting" place of a number of northern and southern forms, some of which breed at or near the extremity of their ranges. The Great Black-backed Gull and Glossy Ibis on Long Island are at their present extreme southern and northern breeding limits respectively. Instead of the outmoded and somewhat arbitrary "Canadian," "Transition," and "Carolinian" life zones, suggested replacements (in that order) are "northern," "neutral," and "southern" elements, with a small number of species (five ducks) belonging to a "western" element. The so-called "neutral" element comprises those widespread species occupying a more or less extensive breeding range from Canada to the southern states or, in a number of

26

instances, ranging even as far as South America. Other species in this "neutral" category are more local in distribution, but nevertheless nest to the north and south of us. The majority of breeders (104) fall into the "neutral" category. The "northern" (35) and "southern" (37) elements are about equally divided. Introduced species (9) are listed separately.

Although Long Island has always been notable for its breeding water birds, the adjacent mainland has a much greater variety of nesting land birds. The breeding land bird element on the north shore of Long Island (glaciated) is more closely related to that of the mainland (glaciated) than it is to the breeding land birds of the south shore (unglaciated). This is true, to a large extent, of the flora also. However, a number of the more common breeding mainland land birds are either quite rare or very local on Long Island's north side and are almost unknown as breeders on the coastal plain south of the terminal moraine. Staten Island presents an anomaly. Although politically part of New York, it is more closely related to New Jersey than it is to Long Island, as evidenced by much of its fauna and flora, and particularly by the presence of certain forms that are either rare or lacking on Long Island, with the exception of those forms occurring on the coastal plain of both islands. The following breeding species are widespread or locally common in northern New Jersey, mainland New York, and/or adjacent Connecticut, but rare or very local as nesting species on Long Island and to a lesser extent on Staten Island. Those species marked with an asterisk are unknown as breeders *anywhere* on Long Island and Staten Island. Turkey Vulture*, Red-shouldered Hawk, Barred Owl, Pileated Woodpecker*, Least Flycatcher, Cliff Swallow* (formerly on Long Island, now greatly reduced on the mainland), Tufted Titmouse, Blue-gray Gnatcatcher, Yellow-throated Vireo, Worm-eating Warbler, Golden-winged Warbler* (mainly in the interior highlands), Louisiana Waterthrush, Hooded Warbler, Orchard Oriole, and Rose-breasted Grosbeak.

A number of nesting species are restricted to the interior highlands and are extremely rare at lower elevations: Solitary Vireo, Nashville Warbler, Magnolia Warbler, Black-throated Blue Warbler, Blackburnian Warbler, Northern Waterthrush, and Canada Warbler. Four other species with northern affinities, but breeding rarely or locally on the coastal plain are Traill's Flycatcher, Brown Creeper, Hermit Thrush, and Purple Finch.

Nevertheless there are a number of nesting "land" birds that are rare or local away from the coast: Marsh Hawk, Osprey, Short-eared Owl (much reduced), Horned Lark, Pine Warbler, Savannah Sparrow, Sharp-tailed Sparrow, and Seaside Sparrow (last two species restricted to salt marshes).

NEUTRAL ELEMENT   (104)

Pied-billed Grebe; Great Blue Heron (local); Green Heron; Black-crowned Night Heron; American Bittern; Least Bittern; Mallard (mostly semidomesticated); Black Duck; Blue-winged Teal (local); Wood Duck; Hooded Merganser (once); Sharp-shinned Hawk; Cooper's Hawk; Red-tailed Hawk; Red-shouldered Hawk; Broad-winged Hawk; Bald Eagle (very rare); Marsh Hawk; Osprey; Peregrine Falcon (local); Sparrow Hawk; Ruffed Grouse; Heath Hen (extinct, eastern race only); Bobwhite; Turkey (extirpated, re-established locally); Virginia Rail; Common Gallinule; American Coot (local); Piping Plover; Killdeer; American Woodcock; Upland Plover (local); Spotted Sandpiper; Laughing Gull (formerly); Common Tern; Roseate Tern (local); Mourning Dove; Yellow-billed Cuckoo; Black-billed Cuckoo; Screech Owl; Great Horned Owl; Barred Owl; Long-eared Owl (rare); Short-eared Owl (local); Whip-poor-will; Common Nighthawk; Chimney Swift; Ruby-throated Hummingbird; Belted Kingfisher; Yellow-shafted Flicker; Pileated Woodpecker (local); Hairy Woodpecker; Downy Woodpecker; Eastern Kingbird; Great Crested Flycatcher; Eastern Phoebe; Eastern Wood Pewee; Horned Lark; Tree Swallow; Bank Swallow; Barn Swallow; Cliff Swallow (local); Purple Martin (local); Blue Jay; Common Crow; White-breasted Nuthatch; House Wren; Long-billed Marsh Wren; Short-billed Marsh Wren (local); Catbird; Brown Thrasher; Robin; Wood Thrush; Eastern Bluebird; Cedar Waxwing; Loggerhead Shrike (twice); Yellow-throated Vireo; Red-eyed Vireo; Warbling Vireo (local); Black and White Warbler; Parula Warbler (now rare); Yellow Warbler; Black-throated Green Warbler; Pine Warbler; Ovenbird; Yellowthroat; American Redstart; Eastern

Meadowlark; Red-winged Blackbird; Baltimore Oriole; Common Grackle; Brown-headed Cowbird; Scarlet Tanager; Indigo Bunting; Dickcissel (formerly); American Goldfinch; Rufous-sided Towhee; Grasshopper Sparrow; Henslow's Sparrow (local); Sharp-tailed Sparrow; Vesper Sparrow; Chipping Sparrow; Field Sparrow; Song Sparrow.

NORTHERN ELEMENT (35)

Canada Goose (semidomesticated); Green-winged Teal (very rare); Red-breasted Merganser (rare); Sora; Common Snipe (very rare); Great Black-backed Gull (local); Herring Gull; Passenger Pigeon (extinct, south in mountains); Saw-whet Owl (once); Yellow-bellied Sapsucker (once); Traill's Flycatcher (south in mountains); Least Flycatcher (south in mountains); Black-capped Chickadee (south in mountains); Brown Creeper (local); Winter Wren (twice); Hermit Thrush (local); Veery (south in mountains); Solitary Vireo (local); Golden-winged Warbler (local, south in mountains); Nashville Warbler (local); Magnolia Warbler (local); Black-throated Blue Warbler (local, south in mountains); Blackburnian Warbler (local, south in mountains); Chestnut-sided Warbler (south in mountains); Northern Waterthrush (local); Canada Warbler (local, south in mountains); Bobolink (south in mountains); Rose-breasted Grosbeak (south in mountains); Evening Grosbeak (twice); Purple Finch (local); Pine Siskin (twice); Red Crossbill (twice); Savannah Sparrow; Slate-colored Junco (twice); Swamp Sparrow.

SOUTHERN ELEMENT (37)

Little Blue Heron (rare); Great Egret (local); Snowy Egret (local); Louisiana Heron (once); Yellow-crowned Night Heron (local); Glossy Ibis (rare); Turkey Vulture (local); King Rail (local); Clapper Rail; Black Rail (very rare, overlooked?); American Oystercatcher (rare); Least Tern; Black Skimmer; Barn Owl (local); Red-headed Woodpecker (local); Acadian Flycatcher (local); Rough-winged Swallow (north in valleys); Fish Crow; Carolina Chickadee (N.J. only); Tufted Titmouse (on L.I. only twice); Carolina Wren; Mockingbird (local); Blue-gray Gnatcatcher (local—twice on L.I.); White-eyed Vireo; Prothonotary Warbler (rare); Worm-eating Warbler;

29

Blue-winged Warbler; Cerulean Warbler (local); Prairie Warbler; Louisiana Waterthrush; Kentucky Warbler (local); Yellow-breasted Chat; Hooded Warbler; Orchard Oriole; Cardinal; Blue Grosbeak (twice); Seaside Sparrow.

WESTERN ELEMENT (5)

Gadwall (local); Pintail (once); Shoveler (very rare); American Widgeon (twice); Ruddy Duck (local).

INTRODUCED (9)

Mute Swan; Gray Partridge (extirpated); Ring-necked Pheasant; Rock Dove; Skylark (local, extirpated); Starling; House Sparrow; House Finch; European Goldfinch (extirpated).

It is remarkable that in such a well-worked area as ours *seven* additional breeding species were found just within three years (1960–62): Glossy Ibis, Pintail, Green-winged Teal, American Widgeon, Hooded Merganser, Winter Wren, and Evening Grosbeak. Note that four of these are ducks.

It may be of interest to list those species that have been found breeding for the "first" time since 1942 within the New York City area.

Little Blue Heron	Ruddy Duck
Great Egret	Hooded Merganser
Snowy Egret (also 1885)	American Oystercatcher
Louisiana Heron	Great Black-backed Gull
Glossy Ibis	Winter Wren
Gadwall	Cerulean Warbler
Pintail	Blue Grosbeak
Green-winged Teal	Evening Grosbeak
Shoveler	House Finch
Baldpate	Slate-colored Junco

Note that of the 20 foregoing species, there are 7 ducks and 4 herons. Only one species reported as breeding between 1923 and 1942 has not been found breeding since 1942—Black Rail. However, it is probable that this secretive species has been overlooked.

The exact local breeding status of a number of species remains to be worked out in detail on a widespread co-operative basis and deserves further study.

30

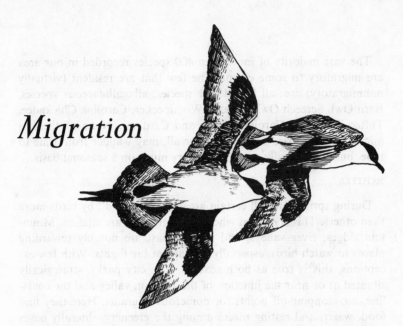

Migration

Of all the phenomena dealing with birds, probably none arouses the interest and curiosity of the field ornithologist and excites the bird-watcher quite as much as migration. Insofar as the greater New York area is concerned, virtually no month of the year is without some dispersal or movement of birds. Through December and into early January, many waterfowl emigrate to warmer climes to escape the ice-bound waters. During mild winters some birds return northward as early as mid-February or even before. Again, in late spring and well into June, many northbound insectivorous birds are still passing through. By early July the first shorebirds are on their southward flight, some migrating tremendous distances from tundra breeding areas to winter quarters in the tropics or even further south to the pampas.

It is during May and September, however, that the greatest variety of birds is to be found in our area. These are the times that birders are out in the field *en masse*. Given the "right" weather conditions and knowing where and when to go, a birdwatcher can run up a list of well over 100 species a day during either month. Although May has the reputation for producing the largest lists per day, September has just as diversified a variety per day.

The vast majority of more than 400 species recorded in our area are migratory to some extent. The few that are resident (virtually nonmigratory) are: all introduced species, all gallinaceous species, Barn Owl, Screech Owl, Pileated Woodpecker, Carolina Chickadee, Tufted Titmouse, Carolina Wren, and Cardinal. None of these is migratory in a strict sense. Some, or all, may wander from time to time, but do not really move about very much on a seasonal basis.

ROUTES

During spring and fall certain areas are "favored" by birds more than others. This is evident when the migrations are studied. Mountain ridges, river valleys, and the seacoast are notably rewarding places to watch birds, especially on days of big flights. With few exceptions, this is true at both seasons. The city parks, strategically situated at or near the junction of the Hudson valley and the coastline, are stopping-off points for numerous migrants. Here they find food, water, and resting places among the greenery—literally oases surrounded by a vast desert of steel and concrete. These city parks, being small compact areas, often have great concentrations of birds, while the adjacent countryside has them scattered over a wide area.

The New York City region is but a small portion of the much-used Atlantic flyway. Within our area three main routes are traversed each year by multitudes of birds: (1) the two inland waterways along the Delaware and Hudson valleys; (2) the outer route along the Atlantic coast of New Jersey and Long Island; and (3) the inner shores of Connecticut–New York–Long Island. The inland ridges, too, are frequented by many birds. It should not be assumed, however, that between these routes there is little or no migration—far from it. There are no places where at least some movement does not occur. Birds travel over a broad front. It is just that in certain localities one will find birds more concentrated than in others.

WEATHER

At the risk of oversimplification, the "ideal" weather in *spring* for a flight of land-bird migrants may be described as a rise in temperature with accompanying southwest winds. Whether the flight materializes to the satisfaction of the observer depends upon the weather itself,

32

that is whether there is a sudden occlusion of two fronts. The warm (usually moist) southerly air mass coming into contact with cool dry air will probably result in fog, or more often precipitation in the form of showers, thus causing the birds to descend. If the weather is continually cool or continually warm, birds tend to trickle through. If cold rainy weather persists, migration on a large scale is suspended until the next warm air mass approaches.

In *fall* the prevailing winds are from the northwest, particularly as the season advances. A drop in temperature, accompanied by northwest winds, is favorable for a flight. If the wind is strong enough many of the land birds will "pile up" along the outer coast where they may be seen to advantage in the low shrubbery and on the ground.

The spring migration of land birds is completed within a relatively short period. The bulk of the migrants (at least as to species) in these latitudes pass through in late April and especially in May, as they hasten to the breeding grounds. On the other hand, the fall migration is much more protracted, extending from late July or early August until well into October when the first hard frosts ordinarily terminate the migration of many species.

Water birds are not affected by climatic changes to the same degree as land birds; clear skies and temperature changes do not necessarily precipitate flights. In fact many water birds arrive in numbers during or after spells of bad weather. Storms, periods of easterly winds often accompanied by rain or fog, frequently produce the biggest flights of waterfowl, shorebirds, and the like. The best time for the observer to be on the coast, regardless of season, is during or after bad weather with strong onshore winds.

MORTALITY

The hazards of migration are clearly reflected in the numbers of dead birds reported annually. Many of these birds come to grief by hitting obstructions, especially during inclement weather; others are lost at sea; still others perish as a result of out-of-season snow and ice storms.

Although referring primarily to accidentals, Braislin (1907: 99), stated: "The number of birds lost in migrations is illustrated by such waifs and stragglers, comparatively few of which ever fall under the

33

observation of the ornithologist. Those destroyed at sea or lost on land probably reach an annual aggregate of large proportions, for observers are so few and the area each can explore so small, that the waifs actually recorded must be only a minute fraction of the total number."

These words apply today despite a great increase in observers on the lookout for rarities and nonrarities alike, and with many more localities visited nowadays than in 1907. When it is realized that nearly all observers are in the field chiefly on weekends, it will be appreciated that the number of unreported strays and migrants occurring the rest of the week, must be sizable indeed.

Obstructions such as lighthouses, tall buildings, television and radio towers, airport ceilometers, and other structures are responsible for the deaths of many birds, especially during migration. In former years most of the lighthouses along the coast were very destructive to birds, this being due to the fact that they were equipped either with fixed light beams or with flashing white lights. During periods of overcast or foggy weather particularly, these bright lights proved to be irresistible attractions to birds. Nowadays most lighthouses possess slower revolving beams which apparently are not as alluring to birds. At any rate fewer birds are reported killed at lighthouses now than formerly.

Many of our records of birds killed at lighthouses came to be known through the interest and efforts of William Dutcher, who persuaded the lighthouse keepers to save dead birds for him during the 1880s and 1890s. Many of these birds are now specimens in the American Museum.

Some of the biggest "kills" took place at the Fire Island light. The fall of 1883 was a notably late migration. On the night of Sept. 30 a great destruction of birds took place. The wind was variable north to east with periods of thick fog and rain. The next morning a "bushel basketful of birds" was picked up at the base of the lighthouse, the outstanding being: Black-poll Warbler, 230; Veery, 29; White-eyed Vireo, 20; Connecticut Warbler, 16; Black-billed Cuckoo, 9; Scarlet Tanager, 7. On Oct. 12 of that year, with a fresh northeast wind and stormy weather, the following were picked up: Black-throated Blue Warbler, 48; Connecticut Warbler, 18; Scarlet Tanager, 7.

On the night of Sept. 23, 1887 (weather not stated), there was terrific mortality; a total of 595 birds struck the light, among which were: Black-poll Warbler, 356; Red-eyed Vireo, 91; Connecticut Warbler, 57; Blackburnian Warbler, 6; Indigo Bunting, 6. On May 19, 1891—231 birds killed, 20 species represented, including 133 Yellowthroats and 42 Ovenbirds.

Shinnecock light, Sept. 17, 1890—outstanding were: Ovenbird, 39; Northern Waterthrush, 28.

In recent years, the Empire State building proved to be a deathtrap until the management shut off the stationary all-night beacon during migrations. On the night of Sept. 11, 1948, 212 individuals representing 30 species were recovered, including the following: Ovenbird, 78; Connecticut Warbler, 10; Chestnut-sided Warbler, 8; Yellow-breasted Chat, 5.

After the rainy night of Sept. 22, 1953, the following were represented among others: Bay-breasted Warbler, 63; Tennessee Warbler, 42; Magnolia Warbler, 32.

Possibly the biggest "kill" reported in recent years occurred at the Westhampton Air Force Base tower on Oct. 5, 1954. The weather was overcast with much fog and drizzle. There were 596 birds of 47 species, the following being noteworthy: Black-poll Warbler, 114; Yellowthroat, 63; Swamp Sparrow, 46; Red-eyed Vireo, 39; Northern Waterthrush, 38; Parula Warbler, 34; Redstart, 25; Scarlet Tanager, 24; Ovenbird, 22; Connecticut Warbler, 13; Yellow-breasted Chat, 3.

RECENT STUDIES

Within the past five or six years banding by means of mist-netting has shown that certain species, formerly thought of as being quite rare, are actually not uncommon at all. This applies principally to those shy or secretive birds inhabiting thickets and undergrowth, such as the Yellow-breasted Chat and the Connecticut Warbler.

Radar studies of night migrants, both spring and fall, indicate that numerous passerines do not always stop at the coastline and travel parallel to it, but continue out over the ocean. This is confirmed by the arrival of many migrants at Bermuda in good weather, and is not necessarily attributable to storms.

For the student interested in the fascinating aspects of migration and its relation to weather, banding, radar studies, and ground observations, see the accounts by Bagg (1955), Baird *et al.* (1958, 1959, 1960), Lack (1959), and especially that of Drury and Keith (1962). This last paper cites the extensive literature dealing with migration and related topics.

MIGRATION TABLE

The following "calendar" or migration table is presented to indicate extent of the spring migration. Only spring arrivals are included as they are considered of greatest interest to the average migration watcher, and especially to the beginner, who wishes to know which species *arrive* at certain times. More than any other time of year, April and particularly May are noted for the more or less regular "pattern" regarding arrival of northbound migrants. Most of the insectivorous species especially, arrive like "clockwork"—some within a few days of the same date each year. But depending upon the vagaries of the weather, the early portion of the spring migration—from late February to mid-April—is anything but regular, some species varying as much as several weeks in their migration schedule.

No species common and widespread throughout the year or more numerous during winter is included in the table, nor are rarities or irregular and very local species included.

Late February—Feb. 21-28 (29): Canada Goose; Red-winged Blackbird; Common Grackle.

Early March—March 1-10: Pied-billed Grebe; Wood Duck; Killdeer; Woodcock; Robin; Eastern Bluebird; Rusty Blackbird; Fox Sparrow; Song Sparrow.

Mid-March—March 11-20: Gannet; Black-crowned Night Heron; Snow Goose; Turkey Vulture; Piping Plover; Common Snipe; Mourning Dove; Belted Kingfisher; Yellow-shafted Flicker; Eastern Phoebe; Fish Crow; Water Pipit; Eastern Meadowlark; Brown-headed Cowbird.

Late March—March 21-31: Double-crested Cormorant; Osprey; Greater Yellowlegs; Laughing Gull; Tree Swallow; Golden-crowned Kinglet; Savannah Sparrow; Vesper Sparrow; Field Sparrow.

Early April—Apr. 1-10: Great Blue Heron; Great Egret; American Bittern; Blue-winged Teal; Broad-winged Hawk; Pigeon Hawk; Pectoral Sandpiper; Yellow-bellied Sapsucker; Brown Creeper;

Hermit Thrush; Ruby-crowned Kinglet; Pine Warbler; "Yellow" Palm Warbler; Rufous-sided Towhee; Chipping Sparrow; White-throated Sparrow; Swamp Sparrow.

Mid-April—Apr. 11–20: Snowy Egret; Green Heron; Yellow-crowned Night Heron; Clapper Rail; Virginia Rail; Sora; Upland Plover; Rough-winged Swallow; Barn Swallow; Purple Martin; Blue-gray Gnatcatcher; Myrtle Warbler; Louisiana Waterthrush.

Late April—Apr. 21–30: Little Blue Heron; Common Gallinule; Semipalmated Plover; Black-bellied Plover; Whimbrel; Spotted Sandpiper; Solitary Sandpiper; Least Sandpiper; Dunlin; Semipalmated Sandpiper; Whip-poor-will; Chimney Swift; Bank Swallow; Cliff Swallow; House Wren; Brown Thrasher; Solitary Vireo; Black and White Warbler; Worm-eating Warbler; Nashville Warbler; Parula Warbler; Yellow Warbler; Black-throated Green Warbler; Prairie Warbler; Grasshopper Sparrow; Sharp-tailed Sparrow; Seaside Sparrow.

Early May—May 1–10: Least Bittern; Ruddy Turnstone; Willet; Short-billed Dowitcher; Common Tern; Least Tern; Ruby-throated Hummingbird; Eastern Kingbird; Great Crested Flycatcher; Least Flycatcher; Long-billed Marsh Wren; Catbird; Wood Thrush; Veery; White-eyed Vireo; Yellow-throated Vireo; Warbling Vireo; Golden-winged Warbler; Blue-winged Warbler; Black-throated Blue Warbler; Chestnut-sided Warbler; Ovenbird; Northern Waterthrush; Yellowthroat; Hooded Warbler; American Redstart; Bobolink; Orchard Oriole; Baltimore Oriole; Scarlet Tanager; Rose-breasted Grosbeak.

Mid-May—May 11–20: Knot; White-rumped Sandpiper; Roseate Tern; Black Skimmer; Yellow-billed Cuckoo; Black-billed Cuckoo; Common Nighthawk; Eastern Wood Pewee; Swainson's Thrush; Gray-cheeked Thrush; Cedar Waxwing; Red-eyed Vireo; Tennessee Warbler; Magnolia Warbler; Cape May Warbler; Blackburnian Warbler; Bay-breasted Warbler; Black-poll Warbler; Yellow-breasted Chat; Wilson's Warbler; Canada Warbler; Indigo Bunting; White-crowned Sparrow; Lincoln's Sparrow.

Late May—May 21–31: Sooty Shearwater; Wilson's Petrel; Black Tern; Yellow-bellied Flycatcher; Traill's Flycatcher; Olive-sided Flycatcher; Mourning Warbler.

37

Qualitative Data—Records

SPECIMENS

Despite the fact that we are in the era of binoculars, telescope, and field guide, the museum specimen still is of paramount importance. There is much truth to Van Tyne's statement (1956: 65), "Though a specimen record may involve an error in identification, the specimen remains as a basis for correction." When a very rare bird or one difficult to identify is seen in the field and the observer is unable to establish its identity by means of color plates or by descriptions in the literature, a visit to a museum is a necessity, especially if one is near a large museum like the American Museum of Natural History. While the need for general collecting is a thing of the past, the American Museum and similar institutions still desire to obtain specimens of certain birds. Although most of the common species are represented by large series of study skins, certain rare species are lacking, or deficient in collections. Moreover, dead birds may be useful in other ways. In many instances individuals of even the commonest species may be valuable as skeletal material or alcoholic specimens. Specialists need birds for anatomical studies, for examining their internal organs, musculature, plumage details, stomach contents, parasites, diseases, etc. When submitting specimens of dead birds, it is important to include the *date, locality,* and *collector.* Without these necessary data, specimens are practically useless.

Valuable specimens may be picked up dead in various places. During spring and fall migrations particularly, birds strike many obstructions such as picture windows, skyscrapers, telephone wires, lighthouses, airport ceilometers, radio and television towers, and bridges. More than one rare bird has been washed up on the beach during periods of inclement weather, principally after tropical storms. Dead birds are frequently found among debris along the line of "drift" at the high-tide mark. The important thing to remember is to save dead birds. Possibly the dead bird you save may be rarer than you realize and may even represent a first record; also, a dead bird may be banded—always look for bands.

Not a small number of species (and "critical" subspecies) recorded for the New York City region are based on specimens only, in some cases on only a single specimen. The following species are known only from specimen records (figures in parentheses represent number of specimens): Yellow-billed Loon (1); Black-capped Petrel (1), Red-billed Tropicbird (1), White Ibis (3), American Flamingo (2), Barnacle Goose (4+), Fulvous Tree Duck (1), Corn Crake (5), Lapwing (3), European Woodcock (1), Eurasian Curlew (1), Bar-tailed Godwit (1), Arctic Tern (2), White-winged Dove (1), Burrowing Owl (1), Great Gray Owl (2), Boreal Owl (1), Chuck-will's-widow (1), Red-cockaded Woodpecker (1), Fieldfare (1), Townsend's Solitaire (1), Brambling (1), Hoary Redpoll (2).

The words "specimen(s) not extant" appear in the species accounts. This means that a specimen no longer available has been previously examined and verified by a competent ornithologist and, for the purpose of this book, is almost as acceptable as a specimen still in existence.

While on the subject of specimens in general, and collecting in particular, it is highly desirable to state that collecting on a *limited* scale is still necessary *today* to document the occurrence of certain species of birds; this is true despite the undeniable fact that there are a number of well-meaning but misinformed persons who would put a stop to any and all collecting. I can do no better than to quote from that eminent ornithologist, L. L. Snyder, Curator, Department of Ornithology, Royal Ontario Museum, Toronto, on the merits of collecting. The following is taken from his paper in the *Oriole*, 24: 21–25, 1959, which all are urged to read in full.

There are some people who object to the collecting of birds. They are inclined to believe that this procedure is unnecessary and inconsistent with the urgency of conservation. I wish to state that it *is* necessary, and it has a negligible effect on bird populations. Frederick C. Lincoln (Auk, 48: 540, 1931) presents a list of the known causes of death among banded birds, giving the agencies in the order of frequency. Next to the bottom, immediately before miscellaneous causes which includes being struck down by golf balls, we find scientific collectors. He shows that this cause of death amounts to .000015 of 1 per cent of all known causes, and we can be sure that all such cases were reported.

Specimens collected, preserved, labelled, and carefully housed in a research collection are perpetually useful. A research collection is not unlike a library of books or a bureau of standards. Specimens are not expendable in the ordinary sense and can be referred to during the development of new ideas or re-examined for verification or rejection of established concepts.

In this history of bird conservation in the United States many of the most earnest proponents were, or are, scientific collectors. To mention but a few, we have Chapman, Griscom, ... Undoubtedly birds, as well as the study of them, profited from their collecting. [To this I would like to add the name of William Dutcher, a founder of the National Audubon Society, and in his earlier days an avid collector of birds. One of the largest local collections was amassed by Dutcher. J.B.]

Without the background of knowledge based on collected specimens, no adequate bird protection law could be framed, and no authoritative bird book could be written.

An erratic bird [accidental wanderer] collected, labelled, and preserved proves beyond all doubt, . . . that a representative of a given species did occur extra-limitally at a certain time. No other evidence is as absolute, and the specimen can be referred to again and again.

A specimen taken extra-limitally often marks the occasion when some biological event is taking place far away in the heart of the range of the species involved. The specimen is simply an undeniable basis for correlation, now or at some time in the future.

A regional rarity is not always a waif or stray. It may prove to be a pioneer of range change, and thus a collected specimen becomes historically important. Certainly the collecting of a pioneer will not thwart population expansion if it is underway, any more than Indian massacres stopped the settlement of this continent.

It is well known that many waifs and strays do not survive displacement. A specimen in a research collection will be useful for an estimated thousand years or more. Its remains on a beach or field make small contribution to the scavenger or soil.

There is also a "code" for collectors included in Snyder's article, concerning moral as well as legal obligations which collectors should heed.

In passing the writer would like to add that those few who violently object to any form of collecting are among the first to "rush" to a museum and examine specimens of the rarity they have just observed in the field. It is primarily to these people that the foregoing remarks are directed.

PHOTOGRAPHS

Next to specimen records, recognizable photographs, preferably in color, are most useful in substantiating the occurrence of many rare birds. The following species, each known to have occurred only once in our region, were color-photographed: Yellow-nosed Albatross, Sage Thrasher, Redwing (thrush), Bullock's Oriole, Black-throated Sparrow.

It should be emphasized that only for those species which are distinct in appearance from other species, or are ordinarily identifiable in the field, may photographs serve for purposes of establishing *bona fide* records of rarities. Photographs of species extremely difficult to identify are not accepted as evidence of occurrence of the species. Only a specimen is satisfactory evidence in such an instance.

BANDING DATA

Much valuable information has been accumulated through the years by means of banded birds. In addition to ascertaining longevity, and determining time and extent of migration, bird banding indicates whether individual birds are resident or migratory and establishes relative abundance of different species at stated localities. Other data can be obtained only by handling live birds. By examining birds in the hand such information as age, sex, weight, fat deposition, color of soft parts, and ectoparasites (such as bird lice or *Mallophaga*) are determined.

Banding today is done on a much larger scale than formerly. First of all, there are now many more banders. Second, in addition to traps for capturing birds, mist nets have come into increased use. Mist-netting, in particular, has produced more individuals of certain rare species than was realized, especially those not easily observed in the field. Secretive species or those inhabiting undergrowth are often netted or trapped, but seldom seen in the field—or at least rarely seen in numbers. Difficult groups, like the *Empidonax* flycatchers, may be examined minutely and measured. This should not be interpreted to mean that *every* individual bird captured alive is identifiable as to species—far from it. The bander, if unable to identify a bird or doubtful as to its identity, should either get someone more experienced to verify the identification, or color-photograph the bird, or better still compare the bird with museum skins if possible. If none of these is possible, one should release the bird *unbanded*, without guessing at its specific identity. Collecting the bird requires a special permit. Above all, with few exceptions, birds should not be banded on a *subspecific* basis. It cannot be done by the amateur and should be left for the specialist.

SIGHT REPORTS

The most difficult task of a compiler of ornithological data is to judge sight reports. While many species are easily identified in the

42

field, there are others that are difficult and a few that are impossible. Still others are relatively easy to identify as adults, but not as immatures, and some may be differentiated in breeding plumage, but not in nonbreeding plumage.

The rarer a species, the more difficult its identification or the more out of place or off-season its occurrence, the more questionable a field observation becomes. All of these factors must be considered before including or rejecting a report. But the biggest factor is the personal equation. The more experienced, the more reliable, the more competent an observer is, the more the personal factor gains in stature. Conversely, the beginner with but limited experience and training has little or no chance of having his report accepted— subject of course to the rarity of a bird and the difficulty of identification. This is why it is extremely important that a rarity seen by a beginner be corroborated by an experienced observer or substantiated by means of specimen or photographic evidence. A collected specimen of an accidental species does not mean that prior or subsequent sight reports of that species are necessarily valid. In other words, a first collected specimen does not automatically establish presumptive correctness of previous or subsequent sight reports. Each bird, whether collected, photographed, banded, or merely observed, stands on its own merits. The evidence for each report must be carefully weighed before inclusion or rejection. The reader should also realize that in a few instances sight reports of certain species of extreme rarity have been omitted here, either because of lack of confirmation or because of absence of published details. An accidental or a bird very difficult to identify in the field is not included here, regardless of the competence and experience of an observer, unless satisfactory details have been submitted or, better still, have been published in one of the leading journals. Too often reports of rare birds are buried in the field observer's notes or appear in obscure and little-known publications.

Unfortunately not a few erroneous sight reports are accepted by bird clubs as "good records," and worst of all these "records" are published and perpetuated. Sometimes little or no attempt is made to screen these observations or even to question the report. One wonders why such observations are allowed to appear in print.

In some instances rarities reported are without details and relegated to the commonplace. The unlucky compiler, often has no way of knowing whether an observer is competent, and thus faces the problem of evaluating the observation. This necessitates much correspondence and time.

Of all published reports in need of scrutiny, those of the annual Christmas counts are in a class by themselves. The Christmas counts have become increasingly popular and in the aggregate are worthwhile and reliable in indicating population trends. However, individual reports of rarities are open to question in a number of cases. Why is it that many rarities reported on Christmas counts are mysteriously absent just prior to or subsequent to the counts? The truth of the matter is that these counts are run on a highly competitive basis, the urge to run up as large a list as possible is present, and the rare and unusual are emphasized; all these tend to cast doubt on many observations. Where does one draw the line between the accepted and the rejected report? In the final analysis the compiler must judge each report on its own merits, weigh the pros and cons, and hope for the best. No matter what happens he leaves himself open to criticism for including certain "records" and excluding others.

Below is a partial list of groups of species similar in appearance and frequently confused with each other on Christmas counts. More often than not the rarer species is erroneously identified when it is probably the commoner bird that is present. Lack of knowledge on the part of the inexperienced observer regarding seasonal status of the species involved, as well as unfamiliarity with the critical field marks, leads to publication in the Christmas count reports of certain rarities that should have been omitted. It is this writer's belief that too many of these rarities are included on Christmas counts and that they are out of proportion to the known facts. This is why the Christmas count is considered by some to be a sport and unscientific; see especially the remarks of Hickey (Wilson Bull., 67: 144–145, 1955), Van Tyne (1956), and Cruickshank (Audubon Field Notes, 10: 66, 1956, and 11: 70, 1957).

The species in the left-hand column are those rarities that are reported, while those in the right-hand column are, for the most part, the probable species misidentified as the rarer ones. In each case the "reported species" is much rarer than the "probable species" in our area.

REPORTED SPECIES	PROBABLE SPECIES
Yellow-crowned Night Heron (immature)	Black-crowned Night Heron (immature)
*Lesser Scaup	Greater Scaup
Goshawk (immature)	Cooper's Hawk (immature)
Broad-winged Hawk	Red-shouldered Hawk (immature)
Gyrfalcon (dark phase)	Peregrine Falcon (immature) or Rough-legged Hawk (dark phase)
Pigeon Hawk	Sparrow Hawk ("sooty" individuals) or Sharp-shinned Hawk
Kittiwake (adult)	Ring-billed Gull (adult)
House Wren	Winter Wren
Oregon Junco (female)	Slate-colored Junco (female)
Chipping Sparrow	Tree Sparrow
Lincoln's Sparrow	Swamp Sparrow (immature) or Song Sparrow

* Beginners mistakenly assume that any scaup seen on fresh water inland must be Lesser Scaup. This is often not the case.

The following species are also confused with each other, but differ from the previous grouping in that both species *may* be present. In some instances both species are reported on the Christmas count merely to "pad" the list, even though there is some element of doubt attached to the correctness of the identification. Needless to say, this is an unwarranted and careless practice.

Great Cormorant	Double-crested Cormorant
Common Eider (female and immature)	King Eider (female and immature)
Glaucous Gull	Iceland Gull
Northern Shrike	Loggerhead Shrike
Purple Finch	House Finch

Additional species, similar in appearance and occurring at other seasons, are discussed in the annotated list (species account). It should be remembered that, although the vast majority of species found in our area can be identified by means of field guides alone, field guides tend to oversimplify identification of a few of the really difficult species without emphasizing that individual variation exists —a fact that will be appreciated only by examining specimens. The beginner will learn that not every individual bird seen in the field can be instantly recognized and that, on occasion, it cannot be recognized at all.

The experienced observer is familiar with these problems. The foregoing discussion is intended primarily for the neophyte, the inexperienced, who should understand that it is *experience* and *knowledge*, not truthfulness, that is being questioned. An observer's integrity is assumed; his competence is not.

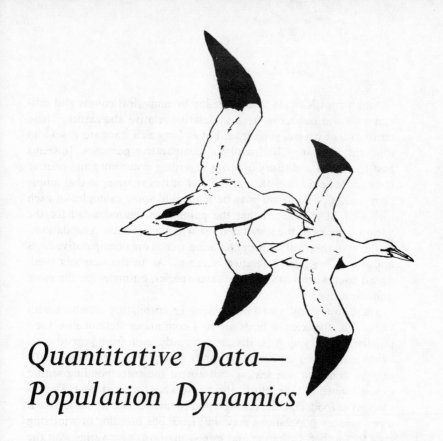

Quantitative Data—
Population Dynamics

RELATIVE ABUNDANCE

Reading through the ornithological literature, one often wonders about the meaning of the vague terms "abundant," "common," and "rare." No two readers interpret the meaning of these highly subjective terms in *exactly* the same way. For example, in a bird book of the mid-nineteenth century is the statement, "The —— is not very abundant." Does any reader have the faintest idea what is actually meant here? "Not very abundant" might be interpreted as abundant, very common, common, uncommon, or perhaps even rare. Even recent works on birds use a terminology—common, not common, rare, etc.—without *precisely* defining the terms. What the word "common" or "rare" means to one person may be entirely different from what it means to someone else.

An attempt is made here to define by numerical counts and estimates the various terms used to describe relative abundance. These terms are, of course, subjective, but as long as a standard is set and followed, they may be useful for comparative purposes. It seems best to present a glossary of terms regarding occurrence and relative abundance here rather than at the end of this volume, so that ample clarification of the terms may be made and some examples of each discussed. It is believed that the population figures stated for the various species in the annotated list will aid in future compilations. In this way they will reflect population trends on a comparative basis and act as a guide to relative numbers. As to the numbers used, actual counts are stated for the rarer species, estimates for the more numerous ones.

There are many variables present in correlating numbers with terms. Most species of birds are in a continuous state of flux, their populations varying from decade to decade, even from year to year. What is common now may be rare a few years hence. Some birds may be common one season, but absent the corresponding season of the following year. Birds also move about a great deal. Due to changes in food, climate, ecology, and to interference by man, partial or even entire populations may shift from one breeding or wintering area to another. Counting and estimating birds also varies with the observer, depending primarily upon his length of experience.

The important point to stress here is that some sort of stability and consistency should be maintained. It matters little whether the figure "40" represents common, very common, or rare. What does matter is that the figure "40" be used to represent a certain category of relative abundance throughout the species account, regardless of the species involved, thus standardizing usage of "actual" numbers with their representative terms. In other words, if a particular species is stated to be merely "common," there is little or nothing to go by. This does not inform us what is intended by the vague term "common." However, there is not the slightest doubt what is meant when the figure "40" is used to mean "common."

Perhaps one of the most difficult problems to resolve in preparing this book was the treatment of species that flock in large numbers and that may be numerous only in one or two localities, or numerous

48

only at brief intervals during a particular season, as compared with species that do not, or very rarely, occur in flocks, but are relatively more numerous over a wide area. Three examples will suffice.

No one will deny the fact that the Red-eyed Vireo, ordinarily a nonflocking species occupying a vast breeding range from the Atlantic to the Pacific and extending, in the east, from northern Ontario and Nova Scotia to Florida and other Gulf states, is numerically superior to the Gannet, a flocking species restricted on the American side, to a few islands in the North Atlantic Ocean during the nesting season and limited to a marine environment in migration and winter. And yet while one may see from 200 to 500 Gannets passing Montauk Point within a half day, or even within a few hours, it would be utterly impossible to see 500 Red-eyed Vireos in one day of birding, even if one were to cover all the "best" spots.

A competent field worker would have no great difficulty in locating 20 breeding pairs of Scarlet Tanagers in suitable woodland during the course of a day over a large area. He would be extremely fortunate, however, if a half dozen pairs of nesting Broad-winged Hawks were found within a day over a similarly large area. Nonetheless, during the height of migration, 2000 or more Broad-winged Hawks may be observed in favorable territory in a day, but no one could hope to see 2000 Scarlet Tanagers during the course of an entire spring and fall migration combined.

One thinks of owls as solitary creatures and sparrows as flocking birds, but there are exceptions: the Short-eared Owl has occurred in loose groups up to 40 individuals; it would be very unlikely for one to see more than three or four Lincoln's Sparrows together.

There may be some objection to using these comparisons as criteria for relative abundance, species by species. However, if certain qualifying words are used, the exact meaning becomes clear. For instance, the Common Redpoll is "absent" during some winters in our area and present in flocks or concentrations of from 500 to more than 1000 in others. Hence this species would be termed "*occasionally* very abundant," signifying that at times it does occur in very large numbers. The Gadwall is a very scarce and local species over most of our area, but is *locally* common in favorable localities, occurring in groups of up to 50 or more.

It has been suggested, and not without some merit, that two separate sets of figures be stated for relative abundance—one set for flocking birds, the other for nonflocking birds. Such a system would involve too many categories and become very complicated. It therefore seems advisable to confine numerical data to a single set of figures, for the sake of simplicity and uniformity.

OCCURRENCE

Going to the other extreme, we find a number of species that have occurred on only one or two occasions, or at the most, nine or ten times. Here usage of the terms "accidental" and "casual" is meaningful provided they are defined numerically, just as the more numerous species were defined under Relative Abundance. Even here certain species change radically from decade to decade.

Ten years ago the Cattle Egret would have been listed as accidental in the New York City region. The first report of this species was in 1953, the second in 1954. In the spring of 1962 there were nearly 100 individuals reported from various sections of this area, one group of about 40 seen on eastern Long Island alone. Within ten years the Cattle Egret has "changed" its status from "accidental" to "locally common." At its present rate of expansion it may become "abundant" within a few years, and even settle down to nest.

Prior to 1950 the Royal Tern was classed as "accidental," but by the mid-1950s it occurred as a "locally rare but regular" summer visitant, occasionally even "very common" after hurricanes.

FREQUENCY

The frequency with which a species *may* be observed is one thing, the *actual* frequency of the same species is quite another matter. How often a species is observed depends partly on the observer and partly on whether a bird is conspicuous or not. The weekend birder may not see a single Philadelphia Vireo during the entire fall if it is an "off" year for that species, or at the most he will see but one or two. An observer who gets into the field daily, or nearly so, from late August to early October may see as many as a half dozen per season, or even more in "good" years. However, thanks to modern methods of mist-netting, as many as nine Philadelphia Vireos have been banded in *one day* at a single coastal netting station. This proves that some species are actually more numerous than had been realized.

We might select another example—a secretive thicket-inhabiting species like the Connecticut Warbler. Although ordinarily much more difficult to observe than the Philadelphia Vireo, the former is numerically more prevalent in our region. An active observer may see from two to four Connecticut Warblers per day in "good" years in the proper places. And yet these numbers are insignificant when compared to the numbers that hit obstructions during the fall migration—as many as 57 hitting the Fire Island lighthouse one night and 13 hitting the Empire State building another night.

The terms "accidental," "casual," and "very rare" are automatically classed with "irregular" by their definition. The terms "rare" to "very abundant" are usually classed with "regular," but there are exceptions. These terms should not be interpreted too literally. Species in the categories from rare to very abundant are subject to fluctuations from time to time, and thus may "shift" from one category to another. The chief purpose of these terms is to act as a guide rather than to be a rigid concept of arithmetical conversion. Their values are relative only.

The following glossary of terms relating to occurrence, frequency, and relative abundance is intended as a guide for the active, competent observer who is likely to find certain species in suitable habitats at the proper seasons, and for the beginner who may find the glossary helpful for comparative purposes.

1.	Very abundant	over 1000 individuals per day per locality (often in large flocks)
2.	Abundant	201–1000 individuals per day per locality
3.	Very common	51–200 individuals per day per locality
4.	Common	21–50 individuals per day per locality
5.	Fairly common	7–20 individuals per day per locality
6.	Uncommon	1–6 individuals per day per locality
7.	Rare	1–6 individuals per season
8.	Very rare	over 12 records, but of very infrequent occurrence
9.	Casual	7–12 records
10.	Accidental	1–6 records
	Regular	reported annually (applies to 1–7 above)
	Irregular	not reported annually (applies to 8–10 above)

Some examples of species rated according to this glossary are:

1.	Greater Scaup	1.	Red-winged Blackbird
2.	Great Black-backed Gull	2.	Slate-colored Junco
3.	Ruddy Turnstone	3.	Redstart
4.	Great Blue Heron	4.	Brown Thrasher
5.	Common Gallinule	5.	Solitary Vireo
6.	Rough-legged Hawk	6.	Olive-sided Flycatcher
7.	Royal Tern	7.	Summer Tanager
8.	Black Guillemot	8.	Boreal Chickadee
9.	White Pelican	9.	Varied Thrush
10.	Arctic Loon	10.	Hoary Redpoll

It should be emphasized that inclusion of more than one maximum count or estimate in the species writeups indicates *relative abundance* and not the norm, but it may be helpful in pointing out *when* and *where* a species is most numerous and thus more likely to be found. The maximum numbers listed for *every* species in the categories "very abundant" to "rare" reflect extraordinary conditions, conditions that in many cases may never be equaled again. It is of the greatest importance, therefore, that these "maxima" not be misinterpreted. They merely represent exceptionally high numbers, *not* what one is likely to see in the field. Not a few species have only one "maxima" listed. This means that this one "maxima" was the only one available to the writer. It also means that more information is needed to determine variation in numbers for these species. In this way we will be better able to ascertain their relative numerical status. Those species that contain the greatest number of "maxima" are naturally "better known" numerically than those that contain only one or two "maxima."

It is to be hoped that in the future observers will state actual numbers, or at least estimated numbers for each species observed rather than the vague terms "abundant," "common," "rare," etc. If this had been done in the past we would have a more accurate picture of the status of each species from the time of Giraud down to the present, and we would know whether birds have increased or decreased and by how much.

The reader is referred to the important paper by Arbib (Audubon Field Notes, 11: 63–64, 1957) relative to suggested criteria of abundance, etc., for the proposed New York State bird book. An excellent set of standards is listed in this paper and, for the most part, the criteria used are similar to those employed in the present work, with minor modifications. The main difference in the two systems is the evaluation of breeding data. Arbib has listed a scale of breeding abundance based on density figures, namely, so many pairs per acre, per square mile, etc. This has been used successfully on several occasions—notably in Maryland by Stewart and Robbins (1958)—but it was carried out by trained professional ornithologists. It has not been found expedient to use this system in the present work simply for the reason that very little counting by this method has been, or is likely to be, employed by the majority of amateur observers in the New York City region.

Hurricanes Hit Long Island

A glance at a map indicates why many storms of tropical origin hit, or veer close to, the shores of Long Island. Extending eastward from the mainland well over 100 miles into the Atlantic Ocean, Long Island is the southernmost land area of considerable size, north of Florida, which lies in the path of the so-called West Indian hurricanes. From 1878 to the present time, 16 tropical storms worthy of the name hurricane (winds of 75 miles per hour or over) have lashed the Long Island coast. Fifteen of these, however, occurred from 1924 to 1960—seven of them from 1954 to 1960. Apparently the hurricanes of 1876, 1879, 1893, 1898, and hurricane

54

Hazel of Oct. 15, 1954, which struck some of the northeastern states, but not Long Island, carried no "exotic" birds to the New York City area. At least none was reported during those years.

Except for the hurricanes of 1938 and 1944, most recent tropical disturbances after leaving the Caribbean or West Indian region centered their course toward Florida or other South Atlantic and Gulf states. Of 11 hurricanes that visited the southern states from 1900 to 1954, only those of 1938 and 1944 reached the Long Island and New England areas and inflicted heavy damage to those two regions. However, in three years alone (1954–56) six hurricanes veered away from Florida and traveled north toward the northeastern coastal states.

In discussing these hurricanes specifically, it is well to consider certain important aspects. Their relation to "exotic" birds driven ashore will be treated in detail later. No attempt is made to describe the physical characteristics of each hurricane, other than to trace its origin and route when known.

Most hurricanes occur in the months of August and September, although the season extends from June to November. Almost without exception, they originate in the region between 10 and 20 degrees north latitude. Supposedly, the majority are born off the west coast of Africa, somewhere in the vicinity of the Cape Verde Islands. This area, extending west to the northern extremity of the Caribbean Sea, is known as the doldrums. This region of quiescence, linked with high temperatures and high humidity, produces a combination favorable for setting such storms in motion. Thus, following a "normal" course westward toward the West Indies, these storms usually head for the Gulf of Mexico, the United States, or swing northward into the open ocean, depending upon the prevalence of low-pressure areas. High-pressure or anti-cyclonic areas may divert hurricanes elsewhere. A characteristic of these storms is that they increase in intensity as long as they travel over water, until cold air currents are encountered. Once they come into contact with large land masses there is a tendency for them to dissipate.

The highly efficient hurricane-alert system, which is in use today, was lacking in 1938. Warning of that hurricane arrived at the East

55

Moriches Coast Guard station only an hour before the storm struck and the unprepared island suffered frightful damage. Nowadays, the Weather Bureau, with assistance from the Navy and Coast Guard, has an elaborate system for spotting and tracking hurricanes while the storms are still far from land. Planes equipped with the latest instruments are dispatched to possible trouble areas, radio balloons are sent aloft, and a radar network of stations scattered along the coast can watch the storms as far as 250 miles offshore. The space age has brought with it satellites that photograph storms from far above the earth.

Few storms in Long Island's history have been as well documented as the great hurricane of September 21, 1938, which scored a direct hit on Long Island, and few, if any, exceeded its intensity. On Sept. 18, it was reported centered due east of the Bahama Islands, and by late afternoon of Sept. 20 was not far off Cape Hatteras.

After passing off Cape Hatteras the hurricane would have continued its "normal" movements in a generally northeast direction, possibly well out to sea, but for two high-pressure areas, one over land from the Carolinas to southern New Jersey, the other over the ocean just beyond the hurricane. With a low-pressure area in between, the great storm headed directly for Long Island. During the early evening of Sept. 21, the time of the highest tides of the year (the autumnal equinox), together with winds in excess of 180 miles per hour at the storm's center, and amidst torrential rains, the great hurricane unleashed all its fury upon the unprotected barrier beaches of the south shore. It struck first and hardest at Westhampton Beach, as a 20-foot tidal wave rose out of the Atlantic and washed away 150 homes. The storm concentrated also on Fire Island, ocean waters pounding through the beach at three different spots. It continued northward through a relatively wide area across Long Island and into western New England, finally spending itself in southern Ontario.

Prior to the storm the late Dr. William T. Helmuth was constantly afield. His observations are so pertinent that his remarks are here quoted in part (Helmuth, 1954): "The actual onset of the hurricane was preceded by at least two weeks of definitely abnormal weather." For several days before the hurricane itself, he states, "the sea had

56

grown progressively more turbulent. Instead of hard, southerly winds, there had been recumbent periods of still and oppressive air, often accompanied by brief, but torrential downpours of warm rain. There were also frequent periods of heavy fog. The intervals of flat calm occasionally alternated with strong gusts of wind, mostly from the south or southeast. On September 19th and 20th, my son and I made rather thorough surveys of the whole coastal region from Montauk Point to Moriches Inlet. It was obvious to us, on the afternoon of the 20th, that something truly unusual was brewing, although we did not in any way anticipate the violence of the storm that was to come."

Covering the same area immediately after the hurricane, Helmuth stated, "On the following morning [September 22nd], the wind still blew violently. We were in the field at daybreak, filled with expectations of discovering all sorts of exotic birds blown northward from tropical or sub-tropical regions. It was, however, often difficult to reach many local areas normally well-frequented by birds, and our attention was all too often diverted by the amount of devastation caused by the hurricane, or by the necessity of helping many of its victims. As regards 'exotic waifs', this survey was extremely disappointing."

On the other side of Long Island, Roy Latham (Proc. Linnaean Soc. N.Y., 50, 51: 68, 1940) speaking of the Orient peninsula the day after the hurricane said, "The marine tide had reached a point inland approximately one-half mile farther than any previous record established within the memory of living man. The whole southern border paralleling the salt marshes was flooded and water stood from four to ten feet deep over all the salt meadows."

Alteration in the shore line at certain points was brought about by the 1938 hurricane. The topographical maps issued by the Coast and Geodetic Survey had to be changed as far as the coastline was concerned. The area affected extended from Cape Cod to Cape May. All the fresh and brackish ponds became salt, killing off the vegetation. Off Montauk Point the great clam and mussel beds were either destroyed or shifted elsewhere, and Oldsquaws, scoters, eiders, and alcids became scarce and remained so for many months. The magnificent stand of primeval oak-beech-maple forest on

Gardiner's Island was almost entirely destroyed. Many birds that had been washed ashore or had died from exhaustion were found buried beneath the shifting sands and scattered debris weeks and even months later.

Relatively few accidentals were encountered in 1938 and 1944. Indeed, most of the strays were carried well inland to northern New England, particularly after the 1938 blow. More rarities have been found after hurricanes that brushed the edge of the New York City region, as was evidenced by the later storms of the mid-1950s and 1960. This applies to live birds that survived as well as to dead ones cast ashore or picked up farther inland. However, it should be realized that now there are many more observers afield and more areas accessible than prior to 1954.

The following is a chronology of tropical storms in relation to the ornithological record. Brief mention is made of the species affected. Full details for each species may be found in the annotated list.

1878, Sept. 12. One of the most southerly hurricanes on record with the center over Trinidad on Sept. 1, then moving northwestward across the Caribbean, reaching Haiti on Sept. 4, traversing the length of Cuba, thence veering abruptly northward through Florida on Sept. 9 and traveling along the eastern seaboard on Sept. 11, then turning inland well west of Long Island on Sept. 12, and finally northeastward into the Canadian maritime provinces on Sept. 13. The only species of note was the Sooty Tern with five specimens picked up: two on Long Island, two in Orange County, N.Y., and one on the Connecticut coast in Fairfield County.

1924, Aug. 26. No details as to the exact course of this storm except that it struck Florida on Aug. 24 and traveled northeastward out to sea. The only bird reports are those of an Oystercatcher in eastern Suffolk County, 14 Black Skimmers at Mecox Bay, and another Skimmer on the Bronx County shore.

1928, Sept. 19. A particularly vicious hurricane which devastated Puerto Rico and swept over parts of Florida and other Gulf states, then traveled northward through Pennsylvania and western New York into the Great Lakes region. Only a two-day northeaster on Long Island, with strong tides, but it produced the largest flight of

Sooty Terns in our area on record: total of 16—ten collected and six others seen—most of these occurring on eastern Long Island from Moriches to Montauk. Also reported were big flights of Forster's Terns, the largest flocks at Mecox Bay (200) and Newark Bay (230) and even occurring inland on the Hudson River at Croton Point (7).

1933, Aug. 22. This storm, like the last, after moving up the east coast pushed inland to the west of us. The only strays reported were two Wilson's Plovers in the Easthampton area.

1934, Sept. 1. This hurricane, which hit the Florida area, moved northeastward out to sea. However, a Magnificent Frigatebird was reported from eastern Long Island and at least four Gull-billed Terns, one at Jones Beach, one at Sagaponack, and two at Mecox Bay. The first big flight of Black Skimmers appeared on Long Island, with 110 at Jones Beach, and one seen over the Hudson River at Englewood.

1936, Aug. 27. Another Florida coastal storm that produced the following: Brown Booby, two seen off the beach at Mecox Bay; a Long-tailed Jaeger in the Georgica area; a Royal Tern (the first record since 1831) at Mecox; and 50 Skimmers on Moriches Bay.

1938, Sept. 21 (for details see above). Of 15 Cory's Shearwaters picked up dead after the hurricane, one was determined to be the nominate race, *diomedea.* The only Long Island records of White-tailed Tropicbirds were: three picked up dead on the beach in the Easthampton area, the remains of another at Montauk, and one seen flying at Jones Beach. Also reported were: one Wilson's Plover at Jones Inlet, a Sooty Tern at Manorville, and another flight of Skimmers at several places along the south shore.

1944, Sept. 14. Next to the great hurricane of 1938, this was the most violent tropical storm to hit our coast in recent years. However, it was less destructive, partly because it moved along the immediate seacoast until it reached eastern New England, and partly because we were "prepared" for this storm. Nevertheless, the eastern portion of Long Island was hard hit. The following species were affected: Leach's Petrel, four picked up dead at different points on extreme eastern Long Island, including one at Orient; three Oyster-catchers observed on the south shore; two Sabine's Gulls seen at

59

Easthampton. The largest flight known of Forster's Terns occurred in the region between Easthampton and Montauk, where 700 or more were reported. The first big movement of Royal Terns to reach Long Island took place along various south-shore points, particularly near the east end, with a maximum of 16 observed between Mecox Bay and Easthampton. The Black Skimmer was reported on Long Island in the largest numbers up to that time, "hundreds" being seen all along the south shore, and a number of records for the north shore including a group of seven at Little Neck Bay. Numbers of this species remained as late as January 1945. It is well to emphasize that this species nested in inconsequential numbers on Long Island prior to the late 1940s. Finally, a Fork-tailed Flycatcher was reported at East Quogue.

1949, Aug. 29. A hurricane that swept through the Bahamas, skirted the Florida Keys and east coast, and passed northeastward out to sea was probably responsible for a Brown Booby reported off Moriches, and a Great White Heron at Jones Beach, seen later at Mecox Bay.

In 1954 and 1955, no less than four hurricanes struck the northeastern states. Although these storms did not create much damage on Long Island, as they were mainly offshore, the number of species and individuals discovered was phenomenal indeed. Particularly in 1954, a long list of rarities was found in Massachussetts, Long Island, and New Jersey. Only the outstanding birds that occurred in our area will be mentioned.

1954, Aug. 31 (hurricane Carol) and *Sept. 11* (hurricane Edna). White Pelican, Shinnecock Inlet; four Brown Pelicans, Jones Inlet; at least seven Oystercatchers from Jones Inlet to Shinnecock Inlet; seven or more Wilson's Plovers in the same general area and one at Wreck Pond on the New Jersey coast; two Gull-billed Terns at Fire Island Inlet; very big flight of Royal Terns, possibly as many as 60 at various south-shore points and along the Jersey shore; Bridled Tern, Manasquan Inlet; Boat-tailed Grackle, Raritan Bay area and Brookhaven. The two Boat-tailed Grackles represent the only reliable reports for the New York City region. For more details on these two hurricanes, see Boyajian (1955).

1955, Aug. 12 (hurricane Connie) and *Aug. 19* (hurricane Diane).

Outstanding was an Audubon's Shearwater on the Staten Island shore. This year was notable for another Sooty Tern incursion with at least ten reported. One was seen on the Hudson River at West Point, another inland on the Commonwealth Reservoir, Essex County, N.J. Large numbers of Caspian Terns and especially Black Skimmers were reported. As in 1944, Skimmers lingered into early winter.

1956, Sept. 29 (hurricane Flossie). This storm, too, moved out to sea before arriving in the Long Island area. Only two species of note, both at Fire Island: adult Long-tailed Jaeger and Sooty Tern.

1957, June 27 (hurricane Audrey). Devastated the Gulf coast of Louisiana and Texas, and moved northeastward through Tennessee and Kentucky. By June 30 it had passed through western New York into Canada. This storm probably contributed our first record of a Sandwich or Cabot's Tern.

1960, Sept. 12 (hurricane Donna). This hurricane, reported to have originated more than 1000 miles east of Puerto Rico, traveled west northwest through the Leeward Islands, brushed the north coast of Puerto Rico, ripped through the southern Bahamas and the Florida Keys, and swung northward along the southwest coast of Florida, inflicting severe damage en route. It then proceeded northeastward over the Florida mainland toward the east coast below Jacksonville, and then moved up the Atlantic coast just off-shore until it finally lessened in intensity as it neared Nova Scotia.

As far as Long Island was concerned it brought many rarities to the coastal areas including ten species of terns, the following being phenomenal: Gull-billed Tern—28 from Jones Inlet to Sagaponack with more than half of these in the Jones Inlet area; Sandwich Tern—9 from Jones Beach to Sagaponack; more than 300 Royal Terns and probably well over 400 Caspian Terns along the south shore; also noteworthy were 12 Sooty Terns. Although both the Bridled Tern and Noddy Tern were recorded from the New Jersey coast south of our region and the latter species on Block Island, just 12 miles east of Montauk Point, neither of these was reported on Long Island. Indeed, the Noddy Tern (*Anous stolidus*) has never been known to occur within the New York City area. It should be looked for after future storms.

Other outstanding rarities reported from Long Island's south shore were: three Leach's Petrels; a Magnificent Frigatebird seen flying over West Islip; 12 Oystercatchers; a Sabine's Gull at Jones Beach; and a Gray Kingbird at Westhampton Beach. As usual there were large numbers of Black Skimmers, at least 1200 being estimated. For a more detailed account of hurricane Donna, see Buckley (1960).

In conclusion, it should be pointed out that of the tropical and subtropical representatives (Audubon's Shearwater, Magnificent Frigatebird, Brown Booby, Great White Heron, White-tailed Tropicbird, Sooty and Bridled Terns, Gray Kingbird, and Fork-tailed Flycatcher), only the Sooty Tern was represented in more than two hurricanes; it occurred in at least six. This is not surprising, as this species is widespread, abundant, and wanders long distances far from land, and is thus most likely to be caught in the path of a hurricane.

Of the "southern" species, Black Skimmers have been reported in numbers in nearly every hurricane year. Even before they nested commonly on the south shore, they would appear each summer, late in the season. However, it was after hurricanes that Skimmers were present in the largest concentrations.

Subspecies

In modern ornithology the species is the basic unit. The subspecies, or geographical race, is a subordinate, often an arbitrary subdivision. One of the outstanding improvements of the recent A.O.U. *Check-list* (1957) over previous *Check-lists* was the elimination of subspecific vernacular names, thus simplifying things for the amateur field worker. The subspecies is a category essential or convenient to the professional ornithologist and, with few exceptions, is best disregarded by the amateur.

Moreover, the vast majority of subspecies are indistinguishable in the field to the birdwatcher and in the hand to the bird bander. Even in those few subspecies that are identifiable certain individuals may be intermediate in appearance and, therefore, not determinable. In view of this, the amateur should not attempt to identify every individual subspecifically because this is often impossible. Most birdwatchers are unaware of the extent of variation existing within each subspecies. For an important discussion, see Tucker (1949).

The following few subspecies occurring in our region are considered separable in the field *under favorable circumstances:*

Iceland Gull, *L. g. glaucoides* and *L. g. kumlieni* (adults only);
Horned Lark, *E. a. alpestris* and *E. a. praticola* (but not *hoyti*);
Robin, *T. m. migratorius* and *T. m. nigrideus* (males only);
Palm Warbler, *D. p. palmarum* and *D. p. hypochrysea*;
Common Grackle, *Q. q. stonei* and *Q. q. versicolor* (males only);
Rufous-sided Towhee, *P. e. erythrophthalmus* and *P. e. arcticus*.

Many races are exceedingly difficult to differentiate even in the skin, and only by critical study of large museum series is it possible to assign individual specimens to a subspecific population with some degree of certainty. Some races considered by taxonomists as "microsubspecies" are nothing more than minor variations unworthy of designated subspecific names. Many individual specimens cannot be assigned to a subspecific population because of slightly varying morphological characters (color, size, etc.). These characters often show a blending or gradual change from one extremity of the bird's geographical range to the other. This situation is known as a cline.

Another difficulty arises when fresh material is compared with old museum skins, the latter having faded or "foxed" (become brownish) due to age. *Post-mortem* color changes take place also. Seasonal variation due to molts, and variation in sex, age, and polymorphism often make identification of subspecies a difficult task.

For the more advanced student interested in subspecific determination of specimens and the complexities involved, the papers by Rand (1948), Amadon (1949), Rand and Traylor (1950), and especially Mayr *et al.* (1953) are recommended.

The writer was fortunate in having had access to the large study skin collections in several museums, notably the very fine local collection in the American Museum of Natural History, New York, together with a vast amount of literature available in the library of that institution. This combination of large series of study skins and the extensive literature was necessary to determine the various subspecies present in our region.

In the New York City area a total of 32 *additional* races or subspecies of polytypic species have been reliably recorded, in each instance based on critically identified specimens.

In the Species Account, the discussion of subspecies occurring within our area is placed at the end of each polytypic species account. Under polytypic species the nominate form is not stated trinomially if it is the *only* form recorded from our area. If, however, the nominate form occurs together with additional forms, then trinomials are used in all instances.

Part Two

Species Account

In the New York City area, 412 recent species (Regular List plus "Escape" List) are considered to have actually occurred. An additional 23 species fall into two categories: Hypothetical List—19; Fossil List—4.

REGULAR LIST—404

The Regular List includes those 404 species that are supported by the following evidence: (a) specimens—386; (b)* color photographs—6 (Yellow-nosed Albatross, Sage Thrasher, Bell's Vireo, Black-headed Grosbeak, Green-tailed Towhee, Black-throated Sparrow); (c) sight reports—12 (Western Grebe, Heath Hen, Turkey, Franklin's Gull, Lewis' Woodpecker, Bewick's Wren, Swainson's Warbler, Townsend's Warbler, Western Meadowlark, Brewer's Sparrow, Harris' Sparrow, Golden-crowned Sparrow). As to Heath Hen and Turkey, no *known* local specimens exist, despite the fact that they formerly occurred in numbers.

Divisions (a) and (b) are self-explanatory. The sight reports (c) are based on creditable observations by three or more competent and experienced people for at least one observation of each of the 12 species. If there are less than three observers, the report is included in the Hypothetical List. It is felt that by requiring three or more reliable and experienced observers *per observation*, personal bias is reduced to a minimum and confirmation of the observation is more fully realized. This is admittedly an arbitrary viewpoint, but

* Since the above was written, Bullock's Oriole has been added, but information was received too late to include in the above totals.

in the case of an area such as the New York City region in which portions of three states are included, the usual treatment of requiring one specimen per state as proof of occurrence is eliminated. Moreover, all but one of the 12 species have been collected in adjacent states; and the one exception, Swainson's Warbler, has been taken nearby (Maryland).

Each species in the Regular List supported by a specimen has an asterisk after its name. In addition those that have bred within the region have the letter B after the name.

"ESCAPE" LIST—8

The "Escape" List includes those eight species, the origin of which is in doubt. The identity of four of them is beyond reproach as they are substantiated by specimens, and the remaining four have been well seen by numerous observers. All eight are of questionable origin because of the uncertainty about whether they were genuine wild vagrants, or had escaped from captivity. Each one is discussed in detail in the annotated list. See also discussion under Escapes (pp. 468 ff.).

HYPOTHETICAL LIST—19

The Hypothetical List includes those 19 species, the evidence for which is considered either unsatisfactory (14) or insufficient (5). The latter (Great White Heron, Fork-tailed Flycatcher, Say's Phoebe, Black-throated Gray Warbler, Boat-tailed Grackle) although observed by reputable people with details of the observations submitted, had less than the required three observers per observation. Double asterisks after the names of these five species indicate that the identifications are considered reliable.

FOSSIL LIST—4

The Fossil List includes those four species, the remains of which were found in ancient deposits. Only one of these (Sandhill Crane) still survives, but has not been reported from our area to date.

Recapitulation: Regulars—404; "Escapes"—8; Hypotheticals—19; Fossils—4. This makes a total of 435 species.

LOONS: GAVIIDAE

COMMON LOON (*Gavia immer*)*

Range: Holarctic species, breeding south to the northern portions of New York and New England; casually to Pennsylvania, Massachusetts, and Connecticut.

Status: Common to abundant migrant and winter visitant along the coast. Most numerous on the ocean. Numbers fluctuate from year to year and from month to month. Reported every month of the year. Regularly observed flying overland in late April and May.

Occurrence and maxima: Due to its summering occasionally, the fall arrival and spring departure of the Common Loon are difficult to determine. The spring migration is greatly protracted. Usually most widespread and numerous in April, May, and November.

Maxima: *Winter*—200, Montauk, Jan. 1, 1921. *Spring*—300, Long Beach, Apr. 11, 1933; 70, Swartswood Lake, N.J., Apr. 28, 1953; 50, Prospect Park, May 7, 1950; 42, Montclair, N.J., May 9, 1930; 250, Jones Beach, May 20, 1950. *Summer*—16, Montauk to Easthampton, July 20, 1939. *Fall*—470, same area, Nov. 6, 1949.

Although occasionally reported in summer on inland lakes in the New York City region, there is no confirmed breeding within our area. This includes birds that summered on a small reservoir in Orange County in 1962 and 1963.

YELLOW-BILLED LOON (*Gavia adamsii*)*

Accidental: A northern Palearctic and northwestern Nearctic species of high latitudes, breeding east to western Keewatin (Canada). Winters primarily within the breeding range, the Palearctic population ranging commonly west to Norway. Snyder (1957) suggests that the American breeding population probably migrates west along the Arctic coast to the Pacific coast of Alaska where it winters. Accidental anywhere in the North Atlantic quadrant, even in Greenland.

One local record: The remains of a specimen picked up on the beach, but only the mandible preserved; eastern Long Island, "early" 1930 (G. H. Thayer), A.M.N.H. No. 4005. Identified by Zimmer (Auk, 64: 145–146, 1947), and corroborated by Wetmore. As this record was not published until 1947, it does not appear in Cruickshank (1942).

71

ARCTIC LOON (*Gavia arctica*)*

Accidental: Holarctic species; breeds commonly on the Pacific coast of Alaska, in lesser numbers east to southern Baffin Island, Labrador (casually), and south to northern Ontario (Hudson Bay). Winters commonly along the Pacific coast, but apparently very rarely in the western Atlantic. The eastern American breeding population is, perhaps, partially sedentary, but many individuals probably migrate west to the Pacific coast. Accidental on the Atlantic coast of Quebec, New Hampshire, and Long Island.

The race *pacifica* has been collected once in our area; adult male in breeding plumage, Sand's Point, L.I., Apr. 29, 1893 (G. Merritt), A.M.N.H. No. 10980.

The following sight reports of adults in breeding plumage, with full details submitted, are believed correct: Montauk Point, March 30, 1941 (Helmuth); Shark River Inlet, N.J., Apr. 14, 1956 (Ryan), sketch on file.

Sight reports of birds in nonbreeding plumage are not reliable. Individuals in this and transitional plumages are not easily differentiated from other species, despite published field marks. General size, size and shape of bill, and coloration depend on age or on stage of molt, and are subject to considerable variation. Several specimens collected or picked up dead, thought to be this species have proved, upon examination of skins, to be either Red-throated Loons or immature Common Loons. The student who believes that *G. arctica* is easily identified in the field should consult Witherby *et al.* (1940) and Griscom (1943).

RED-THROATED LOON (*Gavia stellata*)*

Range: Holarctic species, breeding south to James Bay and Newfoundland.

Status: Common to very common migrant and winter visitant on the ocean, but highly variable in numbers; some years scarce. Much less numerous, but regular elsewhere on salt water. Rare inland (including some oiled birds). Reported every month of the year, but very rare in summer.

Occurrence and maxima: In fall occurs chiefly in November and December; in spring chiefly in April. Sometimes outnumbers the Common Loon.

Maxima: *Fall*—78, Montauk, Nov. 6, 1949; 100, Rockaway Point, Nov. 24, 1948. *Winter*—480, Easthampton to Montauk, Dec. 28, 1941 (Helmuth). *Spring*—75, Jones Beach, Apr. 23, 1950; 9 in breeding plumage, Eaton's Neck, L.I., May 15, 1936 (Cruickshank), an unusual occurrence.

The adult Red-throated Loon in breeding plumage is seldom observed in our area, in contrast to the Common Loon which is often seen in breeding plumage.

72

GREBES: PODICIPEDIDAE

RED-NECKED GREBE (*Podiceps grisegena*)*

Range: Holarctic species, the race *holböllii* breeds south to Ontario and Quebec.

Status: Uncommon to fairly common migrant and irregular winter visitant, chiefly along the coast; occasionally more numerous after severe weather when it appears in large numbers. Rare inland, where sometimes found trapped in icebound ponds. Erratic and variable in numbers.

Occurrence and maxima: The Red-necked Grebe occurs chiefly in March and April, again in late fall or early winter. Reported in every month except August. Rare before October and after April.

Maxima: *Winter*—25, Montauk Point, Dec. 31, 1936; 35, Bayville, L.I., March 5, 1933. *Spring*—115, Easthampton to Montauk, Apr. 7, 1940; 64, Point Lookout, L.I., Apr. 11, 1939.

During the great winter irruption of late February 1934, when a severe freeze closed the Great Lakes, large numbers of Red-necked Grebes were reported both dead and alive along the coast of Long Island. On Feb. 22, while visiting the Montauk area, L. Breslau counted 225 dead—frozen carcasses chiefly on the ocean beaches. He estimated at least another 150 alive, but in very weakened condition, including 14 waddling about on the main street of Montauk village. On the same day at Long Beach, Sedwitz saw 50 alive; also eight dead there on March 18. A specimen was caught alive in a snow drift at Ramsey, N.J., on Feb. 23 (A.M.N.H.).

Casual in midsummer: One in breeding plumage, Newark Bay, July 8, 1934 (W. Eaton and Rose), perhaps a survivor from the severe weather of the previous February.

During the early spring of 1959, after a series of easterly gales, there was a considerable incursion along the north Jersey coast, Staten Island, and western Long Island. This species even appeared in "unprecedented" numbers on inland lakes, where it is usually rare. On Apr. 5 in northern New Jersey, Black and Niosi counted at least 64 between Boonton Reservoir and Culver's Lake; the maximum seen was 17 on Swartswood Lake.

HORNED GREBE (*Podiceps auritus*)*

Range: Holarctic species, the race *cornutus* breeds south sporadically to southern Ontario and the Gulf of St. Lawrence.

Status: Very common migrant and abundant winter visitant along the coast. Regular in migration in small numbers on inland lakes and ponds.

73

Occurrence and maxima: In fall occurs chiefly from mid-October on; in spring until late April. Rare in summer.

Maxima: *Fall*—250, Shinnecock and Mecox bays, Oct. 21, 1924. *Winter*—1200, Montauk Point to Ditch Plains, Dec. 28, 1957; 1000, Atlantic Beach to Point Lookout, March 8, 1959. *Spring*—70, Tod's Neck, Conn., Apr. 18, 1934; 48, Fort Salonga, L.I., Apr. 28, 1934 (both localities on Long Island Sound). *Summer*—10, Greenwich (harbor), Conn., summer of 1953; 4, Jamaica Bay, summer of 1954.

The late winter of 1934 produced a large flight (see Red-necked Grebe). In the Montauk area on Feb. 22, Breslau estimated 350 dead—frozen carcasses chiefly on the Sound beaches—and another 300 alive, but in very weakened condition. Note the numbers reported above in April of the same year on Long Island Sound.

Horned Grebes in breeding plumage are frequently seen in spring.

EARED GREBE (*Podiceps caspicus*)*

Very rare visitant: An African, Palearctic, and western Nearctic species, breeding east to southern Manitoba and central Minnesota. In our area a coastal visitant from the west, occurring chiefly in winter.

An adult male of the race *californicus* was collected at Wreck Pond, N.J., Feb. 16, 1955 (Woolfenden), specimen in the University of Kansas Museum, No. 32994 (Wilson Bull., 69: 181–182, 1957).

The following 13 sight reports, including one or two that were color-photographed, were studied intensively by competent observers and are in all probability correct: Long Beach, Jan. 9–16, 1938 (Janvrin and Sedwitz); Jones Beach, March 16, 1941 (Allyn and Sedwitz); Manasquan Inlet, N.J., all Jan. to early March 1948 (many observers); Lawrence, L.I., Feb. 12–29, 1948 (color-photographed by Komorowski and seen by many observers); Long Beach, Dec. 1, 1949 to March 11, 1950; Shark River, N.J., March 9–23, 1952; Jamaica Bay, Jan. 21–28, 1953; Long Branch, N.J., Jan. 2, 1956; Jones Beach, Dec. 29, 1957; Rockaway Beach, Dec. 30, 1957 to Jan. 1, 1958; Sandy Hook, Jan. 19, 1958; Great Kills, Staten Island, March 8–15, 1958; Spring Lake, N.J., Feb. 12, 1961 (Black and Wolfarth). All sight reports in the 1950s were corroborated by competent observers.

Extreme dates: Dec. 1 to March 23. Reliably reported by numerous observers as arriving at the Jamaica Bay Refuge as early as the second week in October—both in 1962 and 1963.

The species is not unmistakable in life. A number of sight reports are not reliable and at least one specimen collected, and identified in life by many observers, proved to be a Horned Grebe. Oiled birds and especially individuals in changing plumage are particularly difficult to identify, the two species then resembling each other very closely.

WESTERN GREBE (*Aechmophorus occidentalis*)

Accidental: A western Nearctic species, breeding east to southern Manitoba and southwestern Minnesota. Winters mainly on the Pacific coast. Not collected on the northeastern seaboard, but specimens have been taken in western Pennsylvania and in South Carolina.

Four sight reports from the coast of Long Island, and one off Connecticut, all with details submitted, are believed correct: Long Beach, May 21, 1916 (Fleisher, Hix, and Rogers); Acabonack, L.I., Nov. 19, 1949 (Helmuth); Zachs Bay, Jones Beach, Dec. 3, 1949 (M. Gordon, Levine, and Ryan). This last report, together with a sketch, was submitted shortly after the observation [see Linnaean News-Letter, 3 (8): Jan. 1950]. It is possible that the 1949 individuals were the same bird. The other two reports are as follows: one in direct comparison with Red-throated Loons off Compo Beach, Westport, Conn., Jan. 2, 1955 (Cook, Spofford *et al.*); one seen at very close range, Greenport, L.I., Jan. 13, 1962 (Yeaton and Lamoreaux); this individual was also with Red-throated Loons. A bird reported as a Western Grebe outside our area, on the New London, Conn., shore opposite Greenport, Dec. 30, 1961, was possibly the same individual.

The Western Grebe should be identified with extreme care and collected if possible. It resembles closely the nonbreeding plumage of *Podiceps cristatus*, the Great Crested Grebe of the Old World. The occurrence of the latter on the American side of the Atlantic is possible. There are even instances where Red-throated Loons have been misidentified as Western Grebes.

PIED-BILLED GREBE (*Podilymbus podiceps*)*B

Range: A wide-ranging American species, breeding from Canada to Argentina. The nominate race occurs in our area.

Status: Fairly common to very common migrant. Uncommon in winter along the coast. Local breeder.

Migration: Most numerous in fall—50, Easthampton, Sept. 14, 1913; 65, Shinnecock Bay, Sept. 24, 1952; 125, Easthampton to Southampton, Oct. 15, 1949 (Helmuth). These numbers are exceptional, as flocks of 10 to 15 are the rule. Usually arrives in early March.

Breeding: The Pied-billed Grebe prefers quiet ponds and marshes where the aquatic vegetation is not too dense. A nesting survey in 1940 revealed at least 33 scattered pairs in 25 localities: 12 localities in New Jersey, 8 on Long Island, and 5 in Westchester County.

Egg dates: Apr. 22 to June 26.

Change in status: This species has increased in recent years, wintering in larger numbers along the coast in ponds and on the bays. It was formerly

75

considered rare in winter. In late December 1949, nearly 50 were reported from Easthampton to Brooklyn and along the Staten Island and north Jersey shores. Note the large numbers reported above in October of the same year. On the combined Christmas counts in 1953–54, about 350 were reported, of which nearly 250 were from Long Island alone. This is perhaps due, in part, to a succession of mild winters and may represent a trend similar to that of another species wintering in greater numbers than formerly, viz. the Ring-billed Gull.

The breeding population has also increased despite reduction in marshland acreage. Creation of wildfowl refuges has probably helped this species to become more numerous; and, in one instance, flooding the marsh by damming a river was a favorable factor. On a canoe trip through the Hackensack Meadows in the summer of 1958, Wolfarth and Jehl found at least 15 nesting pairs and believed that "many" more were probably breeding. At the Jamaica Bay Refuge seven pairs nested in 1959. At the latter locality in 1961 Johnson estimated at least 40 pairs with young.

ALBATROSSES: DIOMEDEIDAE

YELLOW-NOSED ALBATROSS (*Diomedea chlororhynchos*)

Accidental: An oceanic species breeding, so far as known, only on Tristan da Cunha and Gough Islands, South Atlantic Ocean, and St. Paul Island, Indian Ocean. In the nonbreeding season wanders widely through the South Atlantic and Indian Oceans. Accidental in Quebec, New Brunswick, Maine, and off Long Island.

One local record, the first for New York State: Adult seen and color-photographed about two miles off Jones Beach, May 29, 1960, by numerous observers (see Bull, 1960; also Bull, Auk, 78: 425–426, 1961).

SHEARWATERS, PETRELS: PROCELLARIIDAE

FULMAR (*Fulmarus glacialis*)*

Accidental: Holarctic species, breeding south to west-central Greenland and Baffin Island. Pelagic in winter, ranging south to the Grand Banks off Newfoundland; very rarely to Massachusetts; casually farther south. The great increase of the Fulmar within the past century has not been reflected in American waters south of the Newfoundland Grand Banks, where it is still an extremely rare bird.

There are five occurrences in our area, four of these in the light phase. One was picked up alive after a storm, Oradell, N.J., December 1892 (J. Lozier), A.M.N.H. No. 64081; the date given in the literature as early December 1891 is erroneous.

The sight reports are: One off Mecox Bay, Oct. 3, 1930 (Helmuth); Rockaway Point, Oct. 13, 1937 (Mayer); one picked up alive, Ramsey, N.J., Jan. 7, 1956 (S. Thomas); photographed, banded, and released on the Hudson River at Alpine, Jan. 9 (Dater and C. K. Nichols). A dark-phased individual was reported well-seen at close range off Riis Park, Nov. 4, 1961 (Mayer and Rose).

As the above specimen is unsexed and the bill intermediate in length between *F. g. glacialis* and *F. g. minor*, subspecific determination is not possible. Witherby *et al.* (1940) and Hellmayr and Conover (1948) do not recognize *minor*; Fisher (1952) considers *minor* as the intermediate population in a cline between nominate *glacialis* of Europe and the Pacific *rodgersii*. Vaurie (in press), too, does not recognize *minor*.

CORY'S SHEARWATER (*Puffinus diomeda*)*

Range: The distribution of this southwestern Palearctic species is very different from that of the Sooty and Greater Shearwaters, both of which breed in the southern hemisphere and spend their winter (our summer) in the northern hemisphere. The Cory's Shearwater breeds on islands— Azores, Madeira, Canaries, etc.—in the eastern Atlantic (race *borealis*), and on islands in the Mediterranean (nominate race), and after the breeding season migrates into the western Atlantic north to Newfoundland, returning to the eastern Atlantic in late fall.

Status: Common to abundant late summer and fall visitant off eastern Long Island; much less numerous off the western end, and off our section of New Jersey.

Occurrence and maxima: The late Dr. W. T. Helmuth had much experience with this species in the region between Easthampton and Montauk. The following summary, extracted from his journals, will give an idea of this bird's extraordinary numbers at times in that area. Although usually occurring in greatest numbers from the latter half of August until late in October, the year 1939 witnessed an early flight, with as many as 120 individuals on July 6 and continuing numerously the remainder of the season. During 1936 this species occurred in the largest numbers reported to date: 120 between Montauk and Block Island as early as July 10; from 150 to 300, off Montauk Point, Aug. 27 to 31; 500, Sept. 8; 700, Oct. 2; 750, Oct. 11; 500, Oct. 25; 125, Nov. 2 (when his observations ceased for the year). In 1949 they arrived late in the season with numbers increasing in mid-October; on both Oct. 29 (250) and Nov. 6 (300), the birds were seen to accompany whales as the latter drove fish to the surface. Thirty were seen there as late as Nov. 20. The same year, on Nov. 13, Darrow and the writer saw as many as 200 at Montauk Point.

That Cory's Shearwaters have been recorded near New York City on occasion, is attested to by the fact that Murphy collected five specimens near Ambrose lightship on Sept. 9, 1918 (A.M.N.H.).

Extreme dates: The latest fall dates are Nov. 29 (specimen), Dec. 1, and 3, the last reported in 1950 off Lake Como, N.J. (Edwards). The earliest prior summer date was June 26, 1937 (J. T. Nichols), when two birds were seen off Mastic, L.I., but this species is ordinarily very rare before the first week in July. However, there are two exceptional recent reports much earlier at this season: 4, Shinnecock Inlet, June 5, 1954 (Wilcox); and 2, about five miles off Jones Beach, May 29, 1960 (Linnaean Society field trip; see Bull, 1960).

Rare before July and after mid-November.

Subspecies: The nominate race (*P. d. diomedea*) has been collected three times in our region: 2, Jones Beach, Oct. 4, 1902 (Chichester), A.M.N.H.; 2, Montauk Point, Aug. 15, 1907 (Braislin collection), A.M.N.H.; 1 picked up dead, Montauk Point, Sept. 22, 1938, after the hurricane of Sept. 21 (Helmuth), specimen in his collection. All five specimens were verified as this race by R. C. Murphy.

GREATER SHEARWATER (*Puffinus gravis*)*

Range: A pelagic species breeding, so far as known, only on Tristan da Cunha Island, South Atlantic Ocean. Ranges north after the breeding season, through the western Atlantic to Labrador and Greenland, then migrating eastward out to sea toward the eastern Atlantic in fall.

Status: Regular summer visitant offshore, ocasionally common at the east end of Long Island. Usually rare but sometimes seen from the beaches.

Occurrence and maxima: This species, like the Sooty Shearwater, arrives in numbers off our coast in late May and early June, but is present in numbers later in the season (late June and July) than the latter. Both species are frequently found together offshore. The Greater Shearwater occurs inshore in lesser numbers than the Sooty Shearwater and is greatly exceeded in numbers by the Cory's Shearwater.

Helmuth, who had considerable field experience with shearwaters on eastern Long Island, observed the following concentrations: 20, Easthampton, May 23, 1937; 40, same area, June 23, 1916; 25, Montauk Point, July 6, 1939. Also noteworthy are: 50, Jones Beach, June 8, 1957 (several observers); at least 150 from Moriches to Shinnecock the following day (Grant *et al.*), the latter an unusually large number; 100 off Mecox Bay, Sept. 23, 1918 (Helmuth).

Murphy's statement (1936: 661), "They are common, too, at times in the Lower Bay of New York," is apparently not the case in recent years,

78

as I have been unable to find any recent reports from this area, despite an ever increasing number of observers.

Extreme dates: 3, Easthampton, May 4, 1937 (Helmuth), exceptionally early; May 11, 16, and 23 to Oct. 25 and Nov. 6. Rare before late May and after early October.

SOOTY SHEARWATER *(Puffinus griseus)**

Range: A pelagic species, breeding on islands in the southern hemisphere including those off southern South America. Ranges widely at sea after the breeding season, north through the western Atlantic to Canada, Labrador, and southern Greenland, then migrating eastward out to sea toward the eastern Atlantic in late summer.

Status: Regular summer visitant offshore, occasionally very common to abundant at the east end of Long Island. Usually rare, but regularly seen from the beaches.

Occurrence and maxima: The Sooty Shearwater is present in maximum numbers in our waters in late May and early June, apparently soon after arrival. It is relatively rare after June, numbers decreasing markedly although little is known about its movements and numbers during late summer in our area. In certain years this species is seen in considerable numbers, but in some seasons only a few are found.

Helmuth, who had considerable field experience with this species on eastern Long Island, observed large flocks as follows: 50, Easthampton, May 23, 1937; 250, same area, June 2, 1928; 350, Easthampton to Montauk, June 1, 1939. There were 280 seen between Moriches and Shinnecock inlets, June 4, 1955 (Puleston and Raynor). On June 1, 1957, between Mecox and Moriches bays, several observers saw over 300 individuals, with one flock containing not less than 160; several birds were picked up dead and others were even seen to fly into the inlet (Moriches) and settle on the water. Also observed were 25, off Easthampton, Aug. 20, 1913 (Helmuth).

Extreme dates: May 11, 18; summer stragglers; Oct. 16, 24 (no later dates confirmed). Rare before late May and after mid-September.

MANX SHEARWATER *(Puffinus puffinus)**

Accidental: A western Palearctic species; breeding also on islands off the Pacific coast of Mexico. Formerly nested on Bermuda, but not since 1884. The nominate race breeds on islands off the west coast of Europe and off northwestern Africa. Accidental in Massachusetts and Long Island (specimens).

One definite local record: One picked up dead after a storm, Ocean Beach, Fire Island, Aug. 30, 1917 (Thurston), skin and skeleton preserved, A.M.N.H. No. 349273; identity verified by W. de W. Miller and J. T. Nichols.

A bird well seen and color-photographed about five miles southeast of the Jones Beach tower, May 27, 1962 (Linnaean Society pelagic trip), was probably this species. Color photos taken by N. Levine and P. Post were submitted to R. C. Murphy who states (*in litt.*), ". . . have examined kodachromes and believe the bird to be a Manx Shearwater."

AUDUBON'S SHEARWATER (*Puffinus lherminieri*)*

Accidental: A pan-tropical species, breeding on a number of islands (chiefly oceanic) throughout the world. The nominate race nests on Bermuda, the Bahamas, and some of the smaller West Indian islands. Wanders north along the Atlantic coast to Long Island; once to Martha's Vineyard, Mass. (specimen).

Four specimens have been taken in our region, all from Long Island. One collected opposite Bellport, Great South Bay, Aug. 1887 (Dutcher collection), A.M.N.H. No. 64714. One picked up dead, Point Lookout, July 24, 1938 (Lind and Rorden), identified by J. T. Nichols; the skin was too far gone, but the skeleton was preserved, A.M.N.H. No. 4110. Two individuals picked up dead in 1951 (E. Costich), are in the Tackapausha Museum on Long Island. The first was taken at Dix Hills, July 31, and preserved as a skeleton; the second, at Cedar Beach, Sept. 4, was made into a skin; the writer subsequently examined and identified them.

A live individual seen and photographed close inshore at Oakwood Beach, Staten Island, Aug. 14, 1955 (C. Redjives)—two days after hurricane Connie—was probably, but not positively, an Audubon's Shearwater; photo shown to R. C. Murphy.

Remarks: There have been several recent sight reports (May 25 to Sept. 5) of small black-and-white shearwaters observed from the beaches on the south shore of Long Island and from boats offshore, but specific identification in the field is difficult in such a critical group. Size is deceptive, unless the two species (*puffinus* and *lherminieri*) are together, and color differences are unreliable except in the hand. For the difficulties involved, see Griscom and Snyder (1955) and Gordon (1955).

To add to the difficulties, a third species—the Little Shearwater (*P. assimilis*), primarily an Old World form, and considered by some authorities to be conspecific with *P. lherminieri*—has been collected in Nova Scotia and South Carolina and is a possibility in our waters. These two birds would be virtually impossible to differentiate in the field.

80

BLACK-CAPPED PETREL (*Pterodroma hasitata*)*

Accidental: West Indian species, breeding or formerly breeding on certain islands of the Greater Antilles, has been very rare for many years. Recently discovered breeding locally in the mountains of Hispaniola by David Wingate. Recorded after hurricanes north to Ontario, New Hampshire, Connecticut, and New York (all specimens).

One local record: remains of a specimen, Quogue, L.I., July 1850 (Lawrence collection), A.M.N.H. No. 46145 (only foot and bill saved).

Just outside our region, an oiled, dead individual was picked up at Fairfield Beach, Conn., Oct. 7, 1938 (after the great hurricane of Sept. 21), and is now mounted in the Fairfield Museum. This specimen, originally identified as a Greater Shearwater, was reidentified as an adult female *P. hasitata* by Murphy (Auk, 69: 459–460, 1952). This illustrates how unfamiliarity with museum specimens may lead to misidentification in this group of birds.

STORM PETRELS: HYDROBATIDAE

LEACH'S PETREL (*Oceanodroma leucorhoa*)*

Range: A widespread pelagic species, breeding on offshore islands both in the North Pacific and North Atlantic oceans, the nominate race nesting south to Maine; also on Penikese Island, Mass., at the entrance to Buzzards Bay.

Status: Very rare visitant inshore, perhaps regular offshore, but status little known.

Occurrence: In our region dead Leach's Petrels have been recorded more often, picked up either after storms or after crashing into lighthouses. There are relatively few reports of living birds. This is not surprising as this species is known to be nocturnal much of the time, particularly during the nesting season. At least four specimens taken locally struck lighthouses (see below). Gross (1935) reports, "At this same colony [off Maine] I found that the lighthouse was responsible for the deaths of considerable numbers of birds." He noticed the absence of Leach's Petrels at sea during the day, and seldom did he see one on the fishing banks, while Wilson's Petrels came to the boats frequently. Gordon (1955), referring to the area off the southern New England coast, stated, "... also from my own observations of large amounts of nocturnal activity among Leach's Petrels at sea ..."

There are at least 15 specimens collected in the New York City area, of which nine are known to be extant. Four of the latter in the American

81

Museum are: one picked up dead, Hoboken, N.J., Nov. 3, 1861 (W. Cooper), No. 45793; one hit the Fire Island light, May 4, 1888 (Dutcher collection), No. 64718; two hit the Montauk Point light, one on May 30 1889, No. 64719, the other on June 15, 1890, No. 64720 (both Dutcher collection). Cruickshank (1942) lists six more specimens recorded up to that time, including one that hit the Montauk light, July 27, 1889 (Gurnett); also an individual picked up dead at New Rochelle, N.Y., July 28, 1938 (Rich). These two July specimens may represent individuals that wandered from the nearby Penikese Island nesting colony or perhaps were summering nonbreeding birds. Wynne-Edwards (1935) stated that many pass the entire summer at sea without breeding and that these may be birds in their first year.

After the hurricane of Sept. 14, 1944, four birds were picked up dead on the beach: one at Orient, Sept. 17 (Latham), specimen in his collection; one each at Georgica and Sagaponack, both on Sept. 15, and another at Montauk Point, Oct.22 (all by Helmuth), specimens in his collection.

After hurricane Donna of Sept. 12, 1960, three Leach's Petrels were reported on the south shore of Long Island: one seen alive at Babylon (Alperin); one captured alive, banded, and released at Speonk (Wilcox); one picked up dead near Shinnecock Inlet (Post).

On two pelagic trips, Leach's Petrels were observed as follows: 12 off Montauk, Oct. 1, 1932 (Helmuth); four off Jones Beach, May 29, 1960 (numerous observers).

Extreme dates: May 4 (specimen) to Nov. 8 (specimen).

Remarks: As Murphy (1936) has pointed out, this species is very similar to *O. castro* (Harcourt's Petrel). The latter species, a pan-tropical form, has occurred several times in eastern North America after tropical storms and is a possibility in our region. It would be very important to submit any individual collected for proper identification. All local specimens of the genus *Oceanodroma* seen by Murphy were determined by him to be *O. leucorhoa.*

WILSON'S PETREL (*Oceanites oceanicus*)*

Range: An Antarctic and sub-Antarctic species, breeding north to islands off southern South America. Ranging in the Atlantic Ocean after the breeding season, north to Labrador.

Status: Somewhat erratic and variable in numbers, but usually common to occasionally very abundant summer visitant offshore. Sometimes found in large numbers in New York harbor but apparently less frequently than in former years. Rarely seen from the beaches except after storms.

Occurrence and maxima: From late May until the latter half of August, anywhere from several individuals to concentrations estimated in the "thousands" have been seen off the coast and in the waters adjacent to New York City, in the latter area chiefly during June. However, it should be noted that many a trip on a Staten Island ferry or on a fishing boat offshore has not produced a single Wilson's Petrel.

This species is rare before May 20 and very infrequent in September. The earliest date is May 11, 1930, when 25 were seen off the north Jersey coast (Helmuth). One observed at Orient, Sept. 29, 1933 (Latham) is very late. However, Helmuth picked up a dead specimen at Montauk Point on Oct. 22, 1944, which Murphy confirmed as this species. It may have been a victim of the hurricane of Sept. 14 as the specimen was in poor condition.

A few individuals have been reported in Long Island Sound; also up the Hudson River, once as far as Irvington, N.Y., Aug. 27, 1933 (A. Thomas).

TROPICBIRDS: PHAËTHONTIDAE

RED-BILLED TROPICBIRD (*Phaëthon aethereus*)*

Accidental: A pan-tropical species, the race *mesonauta* breeding locally in the Lesser Antilles north to the Virgin Islands. In the nonbreeding season ranges widely in the Caribbean Sea and tropical Atlantic, but the northward limits little known—at least to lat. 23° N. (off the Bahamas). The statement in the A.O.U. *Check-list* (1957: 27), "casually north to the Newfoundland Banks," is based on an old unsubstantiated sight report.

The following Long Island record of the Red-billed Tropicbird is the first known occurrence for continental eastern North America: Immature female found dead along the shore of Bergen Beach, Jamaica Bay (Kings County), June 10, 1963, by Walter J. Lynch—specimen in A.M.N.H. collection, No. 776556.

The record is of such importance that the following interesting notes are taken from a letter to me by the collector, Lynch: "The bird lay on the sand at the high-tide mark among the usual flotsam and jetsam of the Bay. Had the bird not been lying prone, I would not have seen the barred plumage and would undoubtedly have passed it by as a dead gull."

The U.S. Weather Bureau reported a tropical disturbance of less than hurricane strength centered between the Bahamas and the Virgin Islands on June 2, which passed northward offshore, but fairly close to the east coast of the United States, finally decreasing in intensity on June 4 between the latitude of Virginia and Pennsylvania. This tropical storm, passing through the area the species inhabits, very likely "brought" this vagrant to our shores.

Only adults possess red bills, immatures having yellow bills. In this respect this and the next species are alike.

WHITE-TAILED TROPICBIRD (*Phaëthon lepturus*)*

Accidental: A pan-tropical species, the race *catesbyi* breeding not only on many West Indian islands, including the Bahamas, but also on Bermuda. Recorded north to New York, Massachusetts, and Nova Scotia.

The only known occurrences in our area were after the great hurricane of Sept. 21, 1938: One seen flying over Jones Beach, Sept. 25 (Brennan, Tengwall, and Russell); three picked up dead at Easthampton—two on Sept. 22, one on Oct. 3 (Helmuth); and the remains of one at Montauk, Jan. 1, 1939 (Helmuth), specimens in his collection.

Sometimes known as the Yellow-billed Tropicbird, only the immatures have bills this color, the adults apparently acquiring a red bill by the third year.

PELICANS: PELECANIDAE

WHITE PELICAN (*Pelecanus erythrorhynchos*)*

Casual: A western Nearctic species, breeding east to southwestern Ontario. Winters east to the Gulf States, commonly in southwestern Florida; occasionally summering in the latter state (nonbreeding birds). Wanders rarely to the Atlantic seaboard in migration.

In our area there are at least seven reports, all from Long Island. Only two specimens have been collected, and only one apparently extant: one taken at Canarsie Bay "many years ago," formerly in the Long Island Historical Society collection; the other taken at Roslyn, May 11, 1885 (West), is A.M.N.H. No. 11579. The sight reports are as follows: flock of six, Shelter Island, Oct. 12, 1926 (Worthington); two seen flying over Baldwin (D. Cooper) and Massapequa (Aronoff and P. Murphy) on May 20, 1944, observations made independently and perhaps the same birds as they were seen flying in an easterly direction—the species was also observed about this time in Connecticut; Jones Inlet, Oct. 12–17, 1946 (several observers), and possibly the same bird at Moriches Inlet Oct. 28–30 1946 (Wilcox and Elliott); Mastic, Sept. 15, 1948 (Nichols) and Moriches Bay, Oct. 10, 1948 (Darrow and Wilcox), perhaps the same individual; Shinnecock Inlet, Sept. 2, 1954 (Wilcox) following hurricane Carol of Aug. 31. It is conceivable that this individual was carried up from Florida.

The lone bird present at Mill Neck, L.I., for nearly two years from mid-June 1952 through April 1954 was almost certainly an escape. There was, at least, one large aviary in that area.

BROWN PELICAN *(Pelecanus occidentalis)**

Casual: An American species, ranging on the Pacific coast from British Columbia to Chile; more restricted on the Atlantic side, ranging south only to the Guianas, the race *carolinensis* breeding north to South Carolina, rarely to North Carolina. Reported north to Nova Scotia.

There are ten local reports, only one a specimen—no longer extant. It was collected off Sandy Hook in 1837 (*fide* DeKay). The sight reports are as follows: East Marion, L.I., Aug. 28, 1902 (Latham); Oak Beach, May 26, 1912 (Johnson and Griscom); Montauk, July 30, 1927, and Southold, L.I., Sept. 1, 1932 (both by Latham); Rockaway Point, May 10, 1936 (J. F. Buske *et al.*); Easthampton, Sept. 12, 1949 (Helmuth); Keansburg, N.J., Sept. 4, 1950 (Eisenmann); a group of four flying into Jones Inlet, Sept. 7, 1954 (Bull), after hurricane Carol of Aug. 31; flock of five off the beach at Fire Island (opposite Bellport), July 6, 1962 (Alperin).

BOOBIES, GANNETS: SULIDAE

BROWN BOOBY *(Sula leucogaster)**

Accidental: A pan-tropical species, the nominate race breeding in the West Indies, including the Bahamas. Occasionally driven by hurricanes north to Massachusetts.

There are three local occurrences. An immature was collected on Moriches Bay "many years ago," formerly in the Long Island Historical Society collection (examined by Dutcher), the specimen apparently not extant. Two sight reports made by experienced observers with details submitted are worthy of consideration: two seen off the beach close inshore at Mecox Bay, Sept. 2, 1936 (Helmuth), following strong southerly winds from a Florida hurricane, published here for the first time; one seen off Moriches Inlet, Sept. 3, 1949 (Mayer and Rose), following a hurricane on Aug. 29.

GANNET *(Morus bassanus)**

Range: A species of the north Atlantic Ocean of limited breeding distribution, nesting exclusively on coastal islands: Palearctic region, off the British Isles and Iceland; Nearctic region, confined to islands in the Gulf of St. Lawrence, but formerly south to Gannet Rock off southern Nova

85

Scotia. Summers (nonbreeding) offshore south to Maine; more rarely to Massachusetts.

Status: Common to abundant offshore migrant, less numerous in winter, usually in large numbers only at the eastern end of Long Island. Regularly seen from the beaches.

Occurrence and maxima: Gannets are most numerous off Montauk Point. Peak numbers occur from late October to early December and from late March to mid-May.

Maxima: *Fall*—500, Montauk Point, Oct. 28, 1924; 200 in one hour, Jones Beach, Nov. 3, 1956; 200, Point Pleasant, N.J., Nov. 12, 1927; 300, Montauk, Dec. 8, 1944. *Winter*—220, Easthampton to Montauk, Dec. 31, 1949; 125, Montauk, Feb. 7, 1937. *Spring*—300 in a half-hour, off Mecox Bay, Apr. 16, 1953; 200 (only four adults), Jones Beach, May 15, 1949; 150 (mostly immatures), same locality, May 20, 1950; 30, Moriches, May 30, 1956. These latter figures would seem to indicate that adults migrate to the breeding grounds early in the season, while immatures form the bulk of the later May flight.

*"Extreme" dates: Early September to late May or very early June. Very rare in summer: several late June, two July, and four August occurrences. An adult picked up dead on the beach, Easthampton, July 4, 1936 (Helmuth), is in his collection. Another adult found dead at Westhampton Beach, July 13, 1949 (R. Staniford), A.M.N.H. collection. Frequent pelagic trips might reveal that this species occurs less rarely in summer. Usually arrives in mid-March.

Remarks: Occasionally driven to inside waters by strong gales, and reported by reliable and experienced observers at such places as Rye, N.Y. (twice), Newark Bay, and on the Hudson River at Englewood and Riverdale (twice). Accidental inland: Immature picked up alive, but injured, on a hillside after a severe easterly storm, North White Plains, N.Y., November 1947 (W. Townsend) and sent to the Staten Island Zoo (*fide* Darrow).

CORMORANTS: PHALACROCORACIDAE

GREAT CORMORANT (*Phalacrocorax carbo*)*

Range: A widespread species in the Old World, but of very limited distribution in the Western Hemisphere, being confined to the northeastern portion of the Atlantic coast. The nominate race breeds south to northern Nova Scotia. Winters south to New Jersey, very rarely farther.

Status: Uncommon to locally very common winter visitant along the coast, but rare in many areas. Great increase in recent years.

* "Extreme" dates mean that exact dates are not known.

Change in status: This species has become more numerous throughout the northeast since the early 1940s, probably due to its recent success on the northern breeding grounds. This increase is clearly reflected by its occurrence in many "new" localities and by its greater numbers in the New York City region than when Cruickshank (1942) summarized its status.

Occurrence and maxima: The Great Cormorant is an inhabitant of rocky coasts and is purely casual along sandy shores. It is thus most regularly seen at such places as the Montauk area, the rocky islands and jetties of Long Island Sound (both shores), and the northern sections of the New Jersey coast. It is most often observed from December through March and regularly from late October through April.

The chief wintering grounds are off the Rhode Island coast, Martha's Vineyard, and islands in Buzzard's Bay, Mass., where 200 to 300 birds are present annually at each of those areas; as many as 700 at Martha's Vineyard, Jan. 25, 1953 (see Griscom and Snyder, 1955).

Maxima for the New York City area listed by section: (*a*) Montauk—27 (13 adults, 14 immatures), Feb. 22, 1942; 52, Feb. 23, 1948; (*b*) western Long Island Sound: Larchmont, N.Y.—30 (6 adults, 24 immatures), Feb. 20, 1944; 40, Jan. 23, 1953; Sands Point, L.I.—30 (mostly adults in breeding plumage), Feb. 13, 1954; (*c*) north Jersey coast: Long Branch—90, Jan 2 to Feb. 25, 1955 (Edwards); Sea Bright—100+, March 3, 1959 (Jehl *et al.*). These New Jersey coastal birds are commonly seen offshore perched on fish weirs, where they spend all or part of the winter. Prior to 1953 they had been listed as Double-crested Cormorants on the Christmas counts until members of the Urner Club ascertained that very few were of that species (see Jehl, 1961). These fish weirs were reported as destroyed by a severe coastal storm in March 1962.

Extreme dates: Sept. 14 (specimen) to May 3. There are no summer occurrences supported by specimens and no confirmed sight reports earlier in fall or later in spring than those listed.

Specimen data: There are five specimens taken locally, all from Long Island prior to 1942. I have examined all of these: immature, Little Gull Island, Sept. 24, 1888 (Dutcher collection), A.M.N.H.; immature, Amagansett, Oct. 15, 1904 (Mulford), A.M.N.H.; immature, Orient, Sept. 14, 1929 (Latham), in his collection; immature picked up dead, Sagaponack, Oct. 1, 1939 (Helmuth); adult in breeding plumage, also found dead, Easthampton, early February 1940 (Helmuth), both in his collection. As far as I know, the 1929, 1939, and 1940 specimen records are published here for the first time.

Remarks: No inland reports are accepted, as confirmation is lacking. This species is accidental inland in the northeastern United States. Palmer (1949) knew of only a single record in Maine, based on a specimen, and Griscom and Snyder (1955) mention none from Massachusetts. The statement in *Birds of Rockland County* (1959), "rare and occasional fall transient," is unsatisfactory.

It is well to emphasize the difficulties involved in field identification of *P. carbo*. Size is deceptive unless the two cormorants are side by side. Flying birds are particularly difficult to identify unless direct size comparison is available. The adult in breeding plumage, with white throat and flank patches (acquired as early as late January), is relatively easy to identify, but adults in fall must be told by size. The identification of immatures presents an even more difficult problem when based on plumage characters alone. Immature specimens of *P. carbo* are clear white from breast to undertail coverts only at certain times of year, when they can be identified. However, as the birds advance in age, they go through molts until the dark adult plumage is attained. In other words, immatures become darker as they get older, just as *P. auritus* does, and then the two species are indistinguishable as regards color.

DOUBLE-CRESTED CORMORANT (*Phalacrocorax auritus*)*

Range: Nearctic species, widely distributed, but local. As a breeder unreported on the Atlantic coast between Massachusetts and North Carolina. The nominate race breeds on the coast south to the Weepecket Islands, off southern Massachusetts (since 1946); and inland south to islands in eastern Lake Ontario (since 1945). Winters north to Maryland, but rare farther north.

Status: Common to very abundant coastal migrant. Regular summer visitant on eastern Long Island. Rare in winter along the coast. Usually uncommon inland, but regular in spring, occasionally in flocks.

Occurrence and maxima: The Double-crested Cormorant may be seen flying along the coast in very large flocks both spring and fall, but the largest concentrations occur at the east end of Long Island. Helmuth stated in his diary that it sometimes roosted by the thousands on the shoals in Gardiner's Bay between Cartwright and Ram Islands, particularly in September and October, and it may still do so.

Maxima: *Fall*—450, Moriches Inlet, Aug. 17, 1946; 900, same locality, Sept. 2, 1951; 5500, Ram Island Shoals, Sept. 13, 1935; 15,000, Easthampton to Montauk, Oct. 18, 1930 (Helmuth); 1000, Gardiner's Bay, Nov. 8, 1949. *Spring*—5000, Jones Beach, Apr. 22, 1934; 2000, Mecox Bay, May 7, 1932; 400, Jones Beach, May 23, 1948. *Summer*—nonbreeders regular on eastern Long Island, as follows: 220, Montauk to Acabonack, June 20, 1936; 100, Gardiner's Bay, July 13, 1939; 300, Moriches Bay, July 23, 1949; 30, same locality, all summer of 1955.

Inland it is usually observed in very small numbers, from one to four seen perched on pilings or rocks in the Hudson River, but occasionally

88

flocks are observed flying overhead, especially in *Spring*—110, Woodridge, N.J., Apr. 26, 1959; 160, Tuckahoe, N.Y., May 15, 1935. *Fall*—95, Bear Mountain, Sept. 22, 1949.

Remarks: Reports of flocks seen in winter are almost certainly the previous species, *P. carbo*. Contrary to what is generally believed, the Doublecrested Cormorant is rare in our area before late March and after November, although a few are seen with *P. carbo* during the winter months. There is no winter specimen of *P. auritus* from our region in the American Museum collection.

FRIGATEBIRDS: FREGATIDAE

MAGNIFICENT FRIGATEBIRD *(Fregata magnificens)**

Accidental: A tropical species, the race *rothschildi* breeding in the West Indies, including the Bahamas; regular, not uncommon, nonbreeder in south Florida waters. Recorded after tropical storms north to Newfoundland.

There are four occurrences in our area. Adult female collected on Gardiner's Island, Aug. 4, 1886 (J. P. Miller), A.M.N.H. No. 11705. Three sight reports, with details submitted, are worthy of consideration: Easthampton, Sept. 5, 1934 (John Helmuth), following a tropical storm off Florida; an immature or female at Jones Inlet, May 19, 1959 (Gilbert and Richard Rogin), and the same or another individual seen off Middletown, R.I., the following day by J. Baird; one flying over West Islip, L.I., Sept. 15, 1960 (Alperin), three days after hurricane Donna.

The much published specimen taken on Faulkner's Island (in Connecticut waters) is outside the New York City region.

HERONS, BITTERNS: ARDEIDAE

GREAT BLUE HERON *(Ardea herodias)**B

Range: A widespread but local American species, breeding from Alaska and Canada to Mexico and the West Indies; also Bermuda and the Galapagos Islands. The nominate race occurs in our area.

Status: Common, occasionally very common coastal migrant; lesser numbers in winter; regular nonbreeding summer visitant. Very local breeder.

Nonbreeding: Inland, Great Blue Herons usually arrive in early April.

Maxima: *Migration*—75, Lawrence to Hewlett (by boat), Aug. 28, 1949; 46 in a single flock, flying over, Easthampton, Sept. 24, 1921; 200, Easthampton to Montauk, Sept. 24, 1929 (Helmuth). *Winter*—38, Jones Beach, Jan. 1, 1958; 100, Jones Beach to Jamaica Bay, winter 1951–52. Regular at Playland Lake, Rye, N.Y.—20 to 30 birds each winter.

In *summer*—Great Blue Herons may be found singly or in small scattered groups on the salt marshes of Long Island, but they are strictly nonbreeding individuals.

Breeding (see map): This species is local over much of its range, requiring remote or undisturbed areas for nesting. Consequently, it is very sporadic in the New York City region as a breeding bird. The few inland colonies are found in wooded swamps, the birds nesting in tall trees. On the coast they have been reported to nest in mixed colonies of other herons and egrets, with the nests lower down in dense growth of small trees, bushes, and vines.

On Long Island, it has been known to nest only on Gardiner's Island, but not since 1900. In New Jersey a colony of 12 pairs was found in Sussex County in 1940 (Brown).

Change in breeding status: In the past decade (1952–62) there seems to have been a substantial increase, as the species has been found nesting in at least four different localities: In 1952 and 1953 several pairs were noted in a mixed heronry at Sandy Hook, Monmouth County (G. Stout); this colony was reported to have increased to nearly 100 pairs in 1957; at the newly created Sandy Hook State Park, 30+ pairs were reported breeding in 1962 by park naturalist, R. Cole. The Sandy Hook breeding colony was situated in a "good-sized" stand of American Holly (*Ilex opaca*), according to Stout.

In 1955, three additional nesting sites were reported: 30 or more pairs with nests containing eggs and young, Lafayette, Sussex County (M. Ferguson and G. Johnson), perhaps the same locality that was reported in 1940; 42 nests, some with eggs, Wickham Lake, near Warwick, Orange County (Treacy *et al.*), but colony abandoned in 1960; a single pair at nest, edge of a wooded swamp, Fahnestock State Park, Putnam County (Nolan, Thurston, *et al.*).

Egg dates: Apr. 17 to June 11.

GREEN HERON (*Butorides virescens*)*B

Range: A wide-ranging American species, breeding from southern Canada to extreme northern South America. The nominate race occurs in our area.

Status: Fairly common to locally abundant migrant and breeder.

Migration and summer: Most numerous at roosts and in fall—143 going

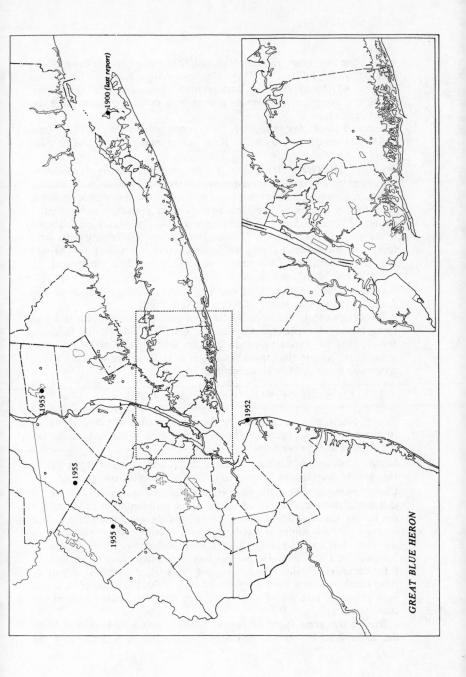

1900 (last report)

1955

1955

1955

1952

GREAT BLUE HERON

to roost in one hour between 7:30 and 8:30 P.M., Far Rockaway, L.I., July 31, 1949 (Bull); 200, Troy Meadows, Aug. 5, 1929 (Urner and Walsh); 60, Mecox Bay to Easthampton, Sept. 28, 1928 (Helmuth). These are exceptional, however, groups of a dozen or more being the usual number.

Extreme dates: Apr. 1 to Nov. 26, exceptionally to Dec. 4, 12, 17 (one picked up dead), and Dec. 21. Rare before mid-April and after mid-October.

Breeding: The Green Heron is widely distributed in the breeding season, usually nesting in small scattered groups in trees and bushes in the vicinity of water. However, it sometimes nests in colonies in considerable numbers. In a former colony at Far Rockaway, now a housing development, I counted 37 occupied nests in the summer of 1949 and Mayer banded some of the young. In 1955 at the Jamaica Bay Refuge, 136 nesting pairs were found by Meyerriecks (1960) while conducting a breeding survey and behavior studies. Six of the nests were actually found on the ground.

Egg dates: May 2 to July 15.

Remarks: This species winters north to South Carolina. Casual at this season north to Maryland and southern New York.

In our area there are three winter sight reports on the south shore of Long Island: Arverne, Queens County, Dec. 29, 1948 (Bull); Baldwin, Jan. 2, 1954 (G. Peters); an individual spent the winter of 1961–62 in a creek near Quogue (Puleston, Wilcox, *et al.*). There are no local winter specimens in the A.M.N.H. collection.

LITTLE BLUE HERON (*Florida caerulea*)*B

Range: Neotropical and southern Nearctic species, breeding north to southern New Jersey; rarely to Long Island (since 1958), and casually in Massachusetts (1940 and 1941).

Status: Uncommon summer visitant, more numerous in flight years. Has greatly decreased in recent years. Very rare breeder on the coast.

Change in status: The Little Blue Heron is indeed an anomaly. With the increase of most herons in the south after the prohibition of collecting for the feather trade, all three native "white" herons wandered north in late summer after the southern breeding season. From the late 1920s through the 1930s this species greatly outnumbered both native egrets combined, because the Little Blue Heron was less persecuted, its feathers having little commercial value. While primarily coastal, it occurred inland in large numbers during the flight years of 1929, 1930, 1933, and 1936. It has been relatively rare inland since then, and decidedly uncommon on the coast.

During the great flight of native "white" herons in 1948 and 1949, the Little Blue Heron was definitely in the minority, especially in the latter year. Except for one concentration in 1952, it has been relatively scarce in our region since 1949. This local decrease may prove to be temporary.

As it nests numerously in Maryland and southern New Jersey, I am at a loss to account for its scarcity today in the New York City area. I do not believe that it is overlooked among the large flocks of egrets, as has been suggested. While counting herons arriving at evening roosts in several localities on the south shore of Long Island during the late 1940s and early 1950s, I paid particular attention to the relative abundance of each species and invariably noted that the Little Blue Heron was greatly outnumbered by all of the "commoner" herons.

What is perhaps most surprising, however, is the fact that the Little Blue Heron did not nest in our region until 1958. This situation is the opposite of what happened in southern New Jersey where all three native "white" herons are common breeders. According to Stone (1937) the Little Blue Heron bred there first in 1935, preceded by the Great Egret in 1928. But the Snowy Egret did not nest there until 1939 (*fide* Potter). On Long Island, however, they appeared as breeding species in the following order: 1949—Snowy Egret; 1953—Great Egret; 1958—Little Blue Heron.

Nonbreeding: A peculiarity of this species in our region is the fact that the adults predominate in spring. All seven spring specimens collected between April 3 and 24 are in the adult blue plumage. The white immature, however, greatly exceeds the adult in late summer, Cruickshank (1942) estimating that less than 5 per cent were adults at that season. Singularly, the intermediate "pied" plumage is very rare in the New York City region.

This species is at maximum abundance in August and early September.

Usually it is confined to the coast—inhabiting salt marshes, mud flats, and ponds, especially in spring. During the large postbreeding flights of the 1930s it was locally common to abundant inland, a characteristic species of fresh marshes, ponds, and wooded swamps and streams.

Maxima: *Inland*—100+ (only 10 adults), Troy Meadows, Aug. 7, 1929 (Urner and Walsh); 54, Iona Island, Hudson River, Sept. 6, 1936 (Orth). *Coastal*—50, Easthampton to Mecox Bay, Aug. 30, 1948 (Helmuth), his only sizable count since 1930; 60 (all immatures), South Amboy, N.J., Aug. 17, 1952 (Seeley), the "only" large concentration reported within the past decade; on Sept. 4, 1949, my wife and I counted "white" herons going to roost at Tobay Pond (Jones Beach), the following being noteworthy: Great Egret—280; Snowy Egret—37; Little Blue Heron—only 12 (1 adult).

In the summer of 1930 the largest known flight in local history occurred—a widespread movement throughout the northeast. Charles Urner located a very large roost in a locust grove at Bound Creek, Newark Meadows. The site of this roost was subsequently destroyed to make way for the Newark airport. His estimates indicate the following fluctuations, building up to a peak in late August: 102, July 31; 145, Aug. 7; 253 (only 6 adults), Aug. 30; 239, Sept. 3; 86, Sept. 13; 11, Sept. 21. On Aug. 20 Helmuth counted 123 between Easthampton and Shinnecock Bay.

Extreme dates: March 30, 31, and Apr. 3 (specimen) to Oct. 22 (specimen), Oct. 27, and Nov. 6. The date of March 19 listed by Cruickshank (1942) is an error. It should be April 19. Note that this species arrives later and departs much earlier than either of the native egrets. Rare before late April and after September.

Breeding: While visiting the mixed heronry at Tobay Pond on July 18, 1958, the writer discovered an adult feeding two young just off the nest. There were possibly two pairs nesting in the vicinity, but of this I could not be sure. This is the first reported nesting of this species in New York State. The Little Blue Heron nested subsequently on Canarsie Pol, Jamaica Bay, one pair each in 1960 and 1961 (Buckley, Post, and Restivo), and three pairs at Lawrence, Nassau County, in 1961 (Post). In 1962 the number of nesting pairs doubled at the latter localities: two pairs at Canarsie Pol; six pairs at Lawrence (Post).

Egg dates: No data.

Remarks: This species is treated binomially here as is done by most authorities. The morphological differences are too slight to warrant separation into two subspecies.

CATTLE EGRET (*Bubulcus ibis*)*

Range: A widespread species in the warmer parts of the Old World; the nominate race presumably crossing the Atlantic Ocean from Africa to northern South America around 1930, thence spreading elsewhere in various parts of the American tropics. In recent years (since 1952) becoming locally established in Middle America, the West Indies, Florida (locally abundant), and more recently in other southern states. Numerous recent records in the northeast north to Newfoundland, the first specimen for North America taken in Massachusetts in 1952. First found breeding in New Jersey (Cape May County) in 1958, nesting as far north as Stone Harbor; at least 20 pairs reported in the latter locality during the summer of 1960. Found breeding in southern Ontario in 1962.

Status: First reported in 1953. Accidental until 1958, when it became regular (see above for first nesting in southern New Jersey the same year). Big flight in 1962, becoming locally common.

Occurrence and maxima: The Cattle Egret is in the process of further expanding its range and, at its current rate, may be found breeding within our area in the next few years, as witness the 1962 Ontario breeding (see above). Unlike most other herons, the Cattle Egret prefers grassy fields.

Often, but not always, associates with cattle and other livestock; these animals stir up insects upon which the birds feed.

First occurrence—1953: One remained at West Long Branch, N.J., from Nov. 28 to Dec. 7 (Black and Seeley), and was observed eating partly frozen grasshoppers; possibly the same bird seen at Eatontown, N.J., Dec. 9 (Ryan); one at the Lukert farm, East Moriches, L.I., May 17–27, 1954 (Wilcox *et al.*), in the company of half-grown white turkeys, was hard to pick out because of similar size and color; one, Brookhaven, L.I., Oct. 20–25, 1956 (many observers).

Each year from 1958 to 1961, two or more individuals were reported in our region. During the spring of 1962, an unprecedented flight took place. A conservative estimate for the entire region was 200 individuals. Some birds in New Jersey were reported in freshly plowed fields, feeding with Ring-billed Gulls. Single birds were even observed in Van Cortlandt, Pelham Bay, and Prospect Parks, all on May 23.

Maxima, 1962: 40, Remsenburg, L.I., May 2–5 (Wilcox *et al.*); 23, Wyckoff, N.J., May 7 (F. McLaughlin); 20 near Morristown, N.J., May 11 (numerous observers).

Extreme dates: Apr. 4 to Dec. 9.

Specimen data: Immature collected near New Brunswick, N.J., May 12, 1960 (T. Crebbs), specimen in the Rutgers University Museum (*fide* B. Murray).

Remarks: What happens to all of our Cattle Egrets in spring? Do they disperse and leave the region entirely, or do a few remain in summer? Irving Black (*in litt.*) states, "I know of no Cattle Egrets in northern New Jersey since the spring [1962] flight."

GREAT EGRET (*Casmerodius albus*)*B

Range: A nearly cosmopolitan species, the race *egretta* breeding north along the Atlantic coast to Long Island (1953 on); much more rarely to Massachusetts (1954 on), and casually on the coast of Maine (1961). Winters north to North Carolina; more rarely to southern New Jersey, and very rarely to Long Island.

Status: Common to locally abundant summer visitant along the coast and a less common and very local breeder. Very rare in winter. Relatively uncommon to rare and irregular inland. Great increase in recent years.

Change in status: The Great Egret has always been most numerous on the broad salt marshes along the south shore of Long Island and also on the coastal ponds. Prior to the 1870s it was an occasional summer visitor, but due to persecution by feather hunters it was nearly wiped out by 1910. With the passage of protective laws in 1913 a slow but steady recovery was made and by the early 1920s it was again a regular summer visitant in small numbers. On eastern Long Island Helmuth reported it as "extremely rare" prior to 1928 and "rarely recorded" in spring before 1940. By 1942 Cruickshank stated that it was a "locally common to uncommon summer visitant" with 50 or more in a day along the Jones Beach strip.

After 1942 this species had increased so much that large concentrations were seen each summer and it was not long before it began to nest on the coast. A marked characteristic of the "southern" herons is their northward postbreeding dispersal, and the Great Egret is no exception. This northward wandering takes place in late summer and is at its height in September. The reason for this dispersal is believed to be drought conditions occurring in southern breeding colonies, thus lowering water levels and resulting in depletion of the food supply. It is at this season that the Great Egret has shown a very great increase, especially since 1942. This increase can be best illustrated by indicating maxima under separate headings—nonbreeding and breeding.

Nonbreeding: Always most numerous and widespread.

Maxima: 165 coming into evening roost at Tobay Pond, Jones Beach, Sept. 14, 1947 (Bull), and Sept. 4, 1949, when my wife and I counted at least 280 arriving just before sunset, continuing until dark. This was a most impressive sight.

In 1959 the weather remained mild and open until very late in fall. At the Jamaica Bay Refuge Herbert Johnson estimated at least 70 individuals as late as Nov. 23 and the writer saw 20 or more there on the east pond up to Dec. 20, but by Dec. 23 they had all cleared out after a snowstorm and severe cold wave. (See Snowy Egret for comparative numbers in 1959.)

Breeding (see map): According to Stone (1937), first found definitely breeding in southern New Jersey in 1928. Urner found a pair nesting in a Great Blue Heron rookery at Tuckerton in 1936, the northernmost known breeding record at that time. But it was not until 1952 that this species was found breeding in the New York City region. Its history in our area follows in chronological sequence according to locality, with numbers representing known breeding pairs or nests actually occupied:

1952–Sandy Hook, Monmouth Co. (Stout)	6 pairs and young
1953–Sandy Hook, Monmouth Co. (Stout)	12 pairs
1953–Fisher's Island, Suffolk Co. (Ferguson)	3 pairs (first for L.I.)
1954–Fisher's Island, Suffolk Co. (Ferguson)	8 pairs
1957–Fisher's Island, Suffolk Co. (Ferguson)	17 nests
1956–Tobay Pond, Nassau Co. (Alperin, Bull *et al.*)	15 pairs
1961–Tobay Pond, Nassau Co. (Elliott)	20 pairs
1961–Lawrence, Nassau Co. (Levine and Post)	4 pairs
1962–Lawrence, Nassau Co. (Post)	8 pairs

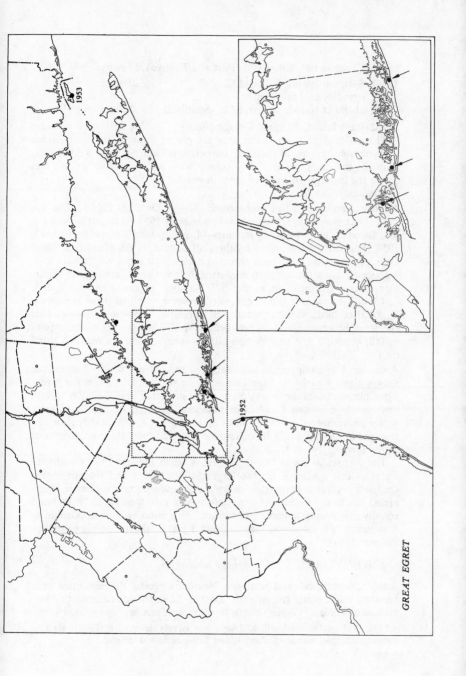

GREAT EGRET

1960–Canarsie Pol, Kings Co. (Post and Restivo) 25 pairs

*1961–Sheffield Island, Fairfield Co.   20 nests
  (Bradley and Spofford)

1962–Sheffield Island, Fairfield Co. (Spofford) 2 nests only

1962–Ram Island, Fairfield Co. (Spofford) 14 nests with young

The majority of nests in our area are placed in dense scrub of almost impenetrable tangles of catbrier, bayberry, poison ivy, and wild cherry. Some of the nests in the Tobay colony were as low as four or five feet above the ground. Others had nests in pines.

Egg dates: No data.

Winter: First reported at Smithtown, L.I.—1, Dec. 23, 1944 to Jan. 15, 1945 (Fischer *et al.*); 3, Sandy Hook, winter of 1952–53 (Stout)—note the first breeding record above; maxima—4, Hempstead Reservoir, Feb. 13, 1954 (Phelan), and 4, same locality, all January 1956 (Guthrie). Since 1956, one or more have been reported each winter along the coast.

Extreme dates: Owing to its wintering in recent years, arrival and departure dates are difficult to ascertain. It has been reported on March 2, 5, 8, 10, etc., in various years, but whether some or all of these are spring migrants or birds wintering nearby is, of course, impossible to state. This species is, however, generally rare before April. The same condition applies in fall, although it is *usually* rare after November, but see maxima listed on Dec. 20, 1959, above.

Remarks: For comparative abundance of the native "white" herons, see Snowy Egret and Little Blue Heron. Prior to the early 1950s the Great Egret outnumbered the Snowy 50 to 1, but since that time the latter species has greatly exceeded *C. albus* in numbers. Both egrets combined were vastly outnumbered by Little Blues up to the 1930s, but the situation has reversed itself—the Little Blue Heron is now decidedly the least numerous of the three.

The vernacular name "Great" Egret is much preferred to "Common" Egret as this species is (*a*) the largest of the egrets and (*b*) not *always* the most numerous egret (the Snowy is now the common species in many areas); the term "Common" is an unfortunate substitute for its former and equally inappropriate name "American," this latter being inapplicable as it is nearly worldwide in range. Great Egret is the name also used by Palmer (1962).

SNOWY EGRET (*Leucophoyx thula*)*B

Range: Neotropical and southern Nearctic species, the nominate race breeding north along the Atlantic coast to Long Island; casually to Massachusetts (1955). Wanders north to southern Canada

*The 1961 colony on Sheffield Island was largely deserted in 1962 owing to human disturbance, nearby Ram Island being occupied instead.

Status: Common to abundant, but local summer visitant and breeder on the south shore of Long Island. Has greatly increased in recent years. Very rare inland.

Change in status: The Snowy Egret, like the previous species, is most often found in or near extensive salt meadows on the coast. It occurs in lesser numbers along the bays, tidal estuaries, and coastal ponds, uncommon to rare anywhere else, and the rarest of the native "white" herons inland. An individual collected at the mouth of the Croton River, Westchester County, summer of 1880 (Fisher) is our only known inland specimen, M.C.Z. collection. The first inland report in recent years was of an individual seen at Troy Meadows, Aug. 5, 1929 (Urner and Walsh). Even today rarely more than three or four individuals are seen inland.

The history of this species in our area is so interesting that details are worth mentioning. Giraud (1844) stated that "on Long Island it is not abundant, though by no means uncommon." With the advent of the millinery trade in the 1870s, this species was valued most highly for its ornamental plumes and consequently suffered severely. As late as 1879 Helme shot one from a group of 18 at Mount Sinai, L.I., on Aug. 4. By the early 1900s it had almost become exterminated throughout its North American range and was placed on the "extirpated" list by Griscom (1923). With complete protection by 1913 it began to recover in the south. By 1942 Cruickshank remarked that "today it must be regarded as an uncommon but regular summer visitant" and stated that flocks up to 12 were seen. His prediction that it might breed on Long Island within a decade has been fulfilled.

Only those active observers who have been in the field for the past 30 years or so can appreciate the phenomenal comeback this heron has made. Even as recently as the early 1930s the report of a Snowy Egret in the New York City region was enough to send an observer rushing to the spot in hopes of seeing it. Today the Snowy is the most numerous of the native "white" herons, at least on the outer coast, and is more deserving of the appellation "common" than its larger relative. Potter (Audubon Field Notes, 1959) stated, "It is by far the most common heron in coastal New Jersey." He and others estimated that out of a total of 3000 herons at the Stone Harbor roost 2000 were Snowy Egrets.

Nonbreeding: Helmuth (diary) stated that on eastern Long Island the Snowy Egret was extremely rare prior to 1938 (his first record was at Sagaponack, Aug. 25, 1933), but by 1948 it greatly outnumbered the Little Blue Heron. This applies today anywhere on the coast of our area.

Maxima: Like other "southern" herons, most numerous in late summer, especially in September—first "large" flock, Jones Beach, Sept. 4, 1949 (Mr. and Mrs. Bull), 37 coming into evening roost at Tobay Pond with Great Egrets (see that species for comparative numbers); 85, same locality, Sept. 3, 1953 (Bull), arrival at evening roost. It should be emphasized that up to that time these numbers were unprecedented so far north, and that these figures represented postbreeding wanderers from farther south, as by 1953 this species was barely established as a nesting bird on Long Island.

Big flight in 1959—locally abundant breeder on western Long Island—the following figures undoubtedly represent both local breeding stock and individuals from more southerly nesting areas: 100, Jamaica Bay Refuge, Aug. 23 (numerous observers); 288, Moriches and Shinnecock bays, Sept. 4 (Wilcox), a previously unheard-of number so far east on Long Island; 50, Captree State Park, Oct. 11 (several observers); 40, Jamaica Bay Refuge, Nov. 23 (Johnson), unprecedented numbers for so late; 20 still present there (east pond), Dec. 20 (Bull), but all had cleared out after the severe cold wave and snow storm of Dec. 23 (see Great Egret).

Extreme dates: March 15 and 25 to Dec. 20. Generally rare before mid-April and after October.

Breeding (see map): Giraud (1844) said nothing of its breeding on Long Island. Griscom (1923) stated tersely, "undoubtedly bred," but gave no details. The only report of definite nesting in early years that I have seen is that of a "pair building a nest in an extensive pine and cedar swamp" on Great South Beach (Fire Island), opposite Sayville, May 30, 1885 (Dutcher and Foster).

The first recent nesting in southern New Jersey was in 1939 (*fide* Potter). This species re-established itself as a breeder on Long Island in 1949 when Heathcote Kimball discovered two nests with young in a Black-crowned Night Heron colony at Oak Beach. The second nesting reported was of a pair that successfully raised young at Jones Beach, near Tobay Pond in July 1951 (Komorowski). The third nesting was of two pairs at the Jamaica Bay Refuge in 1953 (Alperin). The first reported breeding for northern New Jersey was that of a nest with five young at Sandy Hook, Monmouth County, summer of 1955 (Stout).

The following Table indicates breeding adults (pairs) or nests from 1956.

1956–Tobay Pond, Nassau Co. (Alperin, Bull *et al.*)	80–90 (plus 320 young)
1958–Tobay Pond, Nassau Co. (Guthrie)	50+
1961–Tobay Pond, Nassau Co. (Elliott)	50
1958–Meadowbrook Causeway, Nassau Co. (Levine)	50
1959–Meadowbrook Causeway, Nassau Co. (Levine)	100+
1961–Lawrence, Nassau Co. (Post)	20
1960–Canarsie Pol, Kings Co. (Post and Restivo)	90
1961–Sheffield Island, Fairfield Co. (Bradley and Spofford)	8 (with young)

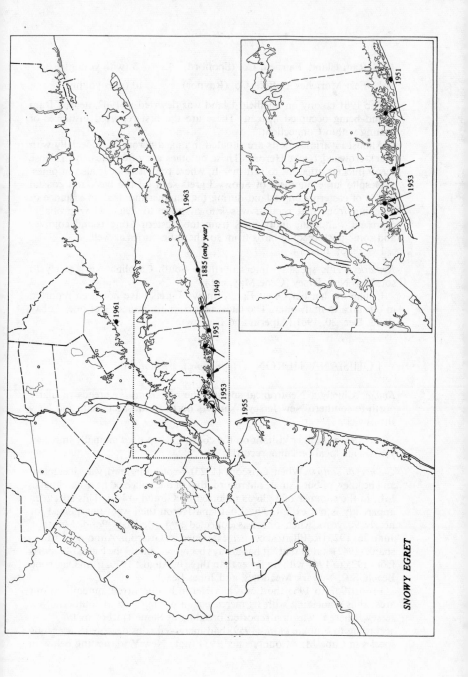

SNOWY EGRET

1962–Ram Island, Fairfield Co. (Spofford)   3 (with young)

1963–East Moriches, Suffolk Co. (Raynor)   10 (plus young)

The 1961 colony on Sheffield Island was deserted in 1962, nearby Ram Island being occupied instead. These are the first reported instances of nesting within Connecticut.

Almost invariably nests are situated in mixed heronries, especially with Black-crowned Night Herons. These colonies are often located in dense scrub thickets adjacent to salt marsh, where the birds feed; also in pines.

Despite large numbers of Snowy Egrets seen on the bays and coastal ponds of eastern Long Island during the summer months, no instance of breeding from that section was known prior to 1963. They probably represent wandering individuals from the western Long Island colonies and some postbreeding birds from southern heronries as well.

Egg date: June 14.

Remarks: This species winters north to South Carolina; very rarely to southern New Jersey (Cape May, etc.).

Unlike the hardier Great Egret, Snowy Egrets have not been reported in our area in midwinter. The latest report in our region is of one, Tobay Pond, Dec. 30, 1961 (Alperin and Darrow).

LOUISIANA HERON (*Hydranassa tricolor*)*B

Range: Chiefly a Neotropical species, the race *ruficollis* breeds regularly north to southern New Jersey. Wanders north to Massachusetts and New Brunswick.

Status: Rare summer visitant on the coast, but reported annually in recent years. One local breeding record.

Change in status: When Griscom (1923) wrote, this bird was accidental and he knew of but a single old record, that of one collected near Patchogue, L.I., in the summer of 1836 as reported by Giraud (1844). This specimen apparently is not extant. The Louisiana Heron then went unreported for nearly 90 years when one was collected at Little Reed Pond, Montauk June 26, 1925 (R. Ellis); specimen examined by Griscom. Although Cruickshank (1942) stated that "it has always been accidental," he listed 14 reports from 1925 to 1941 with no fewer than three in August 1930, from Oakwood Beach, S.I., Newark Meadows, and Jones Beach.

From 1953 to 1963 the Louisiana Heron has occurred annually in our area, thus coinciding with its increase as a nesting bird in southern New Jersey, where it was first reported breeding at Stone Harbor in 1948, and according to Kunkle *et al.* (1959) had increased considerably as a nesting species in Cape May County since 1954 (note New York nesting below in

102

1955). In 1958 a total of 210 were reported in three colonies in southern New Jersey.

Of more than 40 reports in our region, nearly half have come from Jones Beach and the Jamaica Bay area. Mostly one or two individuals per locality have been reported, but four adults were noted on May 13, 1955, at the Jamaica Bay Refuge by A. Meyerriecks. He saw the first individual on April 19 and was fortunate to discover a nest containing three eggs on May 17. However, due possibly to Fish Crow predation, the nesting was unsuccessful. This represents the only known breeding north of southern New Jersey (Wilson Bull., 67: 184–185, 1957). Its suspected nesting at Jones Beach in recent years has not been proved so far. Although two birds were present in a heronry on Canarsie Pol, Jamaica Bay in 1963, actual breeding was not established. No nest or young was found.

Egg date: May 17.

Maxima: as many as eight were seen at various south shore localities on Long Island the day after hurricane Donna of Sept. 12, 1960.

Extreme dates: March 22 and April 1 to Oct. 23; casual, Dec. 1, 1940, Orient (Latham).

This species is confined chiefly to the outer coast in our area, with the following occurrences elsewhere: Two reports from Newark Meadows (1930 and 1933); one from Little Neck Bay, L.I. (1948); and one on Ram Island, Norwalk, Conn. (1962). There are no confirmed inland occurrences.

BLACK-CROWNED NIGHT HERON (*Nycticorax nycticorax*)*B

Range: A nearly cosmopolitan species, the race *hoactli* occurring in our area.

Status: Locally common to abundant resident near the coast, least numerous in winter. Uncommon to rare inland, except near tidewater and the larger lakes.

Migration and winter: Black-crowned Night Herons are often heard calling as they fly over at night, especially during migration. Migrants usually arrive in mid-March. The largest concentrations are reported during and after the breeding season. Numerous summering nonbreeders at roosts are often mistaken for nesting birds. Like most herons, many individuals of this species participate in postbreeding dispersals from more southern nesting colonies, as proved by banding.

In winter confined mainly to the coast where roosts of up to 150 birds have been reported at several localities.

Breeding: This species nests in colonies—in swampy woodland, often of red maple; in dry areas of both deciduous and coniferous growth near water; and in scrub thickets of mixed vegetation in sandy areas adjacent to the ocean.

103

There are fewer large colonies now than in former years. For an account of its breeding distribution on Long Island prior to 1942, see Allen (1938a). Two of the largest colonies in recent years have been situated close to New York City: (*a*) Great Neck, Nassau County—approximately 1000 nests in 1934 (Beals); much reduced by 1951, 600 nests (Meyerriecks); the present status of that colony is uncertain and should be investigated; (*b*) Sandy Hook, Monmouth County—at least 700 nesting pairs reported in 1957 (Stout).

Egg dates: Apr. 7 to July 7.

YELLOW-CROWNED NIGHT HERON (*Nyctanassa violacea*)*B

Range: Neotropical and southern Nearctic species, the nominate race breeding locally along the Atlantic coast north to New Jersey and Long Island, rarely to Connecticut and Massachusetts.

Status: Local and uncommon, occasionally common visitant and breeder along the coast, chiefly on Long Island. Great increase in recent years. Very rare inland.

Change in status: The Yellow-crowned Night Heron was called a casual visitant by Griscom (1923), and he knew of only nine occurrences. Cruickshank (1942) stated that it had increased considerably and was uncommon but regular in late summer. He discovered four nesting pairs at Massapequa, Nassau County, in 1938, the first known breeding for New York State. He also listed one breeding pair at Great Neck, Nassau County, in 1941.

Since 1947, 13 new breeding localities have been reported on Long Island, three in Connecticut, and one in Bronx County (see Table, p.106). Usually these have been located in mixed heronries, especially with Black-crowned Night Herons. All nest sites have been situated on or near tidewater (see map).

As with other "southern" herons, this species is no exception to the rule of wandering northward after the breeding season in late summer, and it is at such times that they are ordinarily reported in largest numbers. However, within the past decade maximum numbers of the Yellow-crowned Night Heron have occurred at breeding colonies.

The following Table summarizes the history of breeding within the New York City region, and emphasizes increase and spread since 1947. Maximum numbers are indicated by nests or breeding pairs:

Nassau County		*Nassau County* (continued)	
1938–Massapequa	4	1950–Woodmere Woods	4
1941–Great Neck	1	1951–Tobay Pond	5
1947–Woodmere Woods	2	1956–Tobay Pond	30+

104

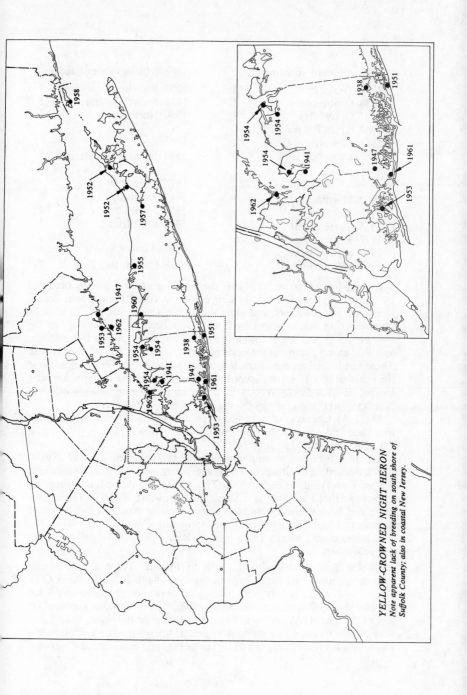

YELLOW-CROWNED NIGHT HERON
Note apparent lack of breeding on south shore of
Suffolk County; also in coastal New Jersey.

Nassau County (continued)		Suffolk County (continued)	
1958–Tobay Pond	15	1957–Riverhead	1
1954–Centre Island	4	1958–Fisher's Island	1
1954–Oyster Bay	3	1960–Northport	2
1954–Sands Point	6		
1961–Lawrence	4	*Queens County*	
1962–Lawrence	10	1953–Jamaica Bay Refuge	1
Suffolk County		*Fairfield County*	
1952–Mattituck	1	1947–Westport	6
1952–Southold	1	1953–Norwalk	4
1955–Mount Sinai	3	1962–Ram Island	2
1957–Mount Sinai	6		
1959–Mount Sinai	4	*Bronx County*	
1960–Mount Sinai	5	1962–Pelham Bay Park	2

As may be seen from the above, the breeding sites are usually occupied by one to six pairs. The 1956 nesting colony at Tobay Pond (Jones Beach) is unique. Six observers, including the writer, found this species actually outnumbering Black-crowns by 2 to 1. This heronry was situated in the midst of an almost impenetrable growth of bayberry, poison ivy, catbrier, and wild cherry, many of the nests placed less than six feet off the ground. These scrub thickets are characteristic of the sandy barrier beaches along the outer coast. A very different habitat was that of the heronry formerly located at Woodmere Woods in a red maple swamp; and another at Northport in deciduous woods, the nests found in tall oaks.

The 1953 Connecticut nest site listed above was the first reported for that state and possibly the only one up to that time.

Egg dates: May 6 to June 14.

The first breeding in southern New Jersey occurred in 1927 (Stone, 1937). According to Cruickshank (1942), young were raised at Rutherford, Bergen County, in the early 1900s! This species should be found breeding at Sandy Hook, as there is a large Black-crowned Night Heron colony there and both native egrets have nested there in recent years. It should be searched for elsewhere in coastal Monmouth County.

Extreme dates: March 19 to Nov. 1. Rare before mid-April and after early October.

Remarks: This species winters north to Florida. There are no winter records reported for South Carolina (Sprunt, 1949), although the A.O.U. *Check-list* (1957: 51) lists it as occasional there, nor are there any listed for Maryland (Stewart and Robbins, 1958). There are none reported on any of the Christmas counts at either Cape May or Barnegat, N.J.

It therefore comes as a surprise to find at least *five* reliable winter sight identifications from Long Island by competent and experienced observers.

All birds are adults, to my knowledge: Idlewild, Feb. 22, 1942 (Mayer); Lindenhurst, Jan. 14, 1956 (M. A. Nichols); Jones Beach, Dec. 30, 1956 to Jan. 6, 1957 (Arbib and Skaar); Mount Sinai, all January and February 1958 (Raynor); Hewlett, March 2, 1959 (Berliner).

Several reports of immatures on Christmas counts by inexperienced people are not considered satisfactory. There is too much chance of confusion with the immature Black-crowned Night Heron. This applies also to immatures reported by beginners at various inland localities during other seasons.

AMERICAN BITTERN (*Botaurus lentiginosus*)*B

Range: Nearctic species, breeding south to Maryland; casually to Florida. Winters regularly north to Delaware, more rarely to Massachusetts.

Status: Locally common breeder. Rare, but regular in winter in recent years.

Migration and winter: Most numerous in fall; on a trip from Shinnecock Bay to Montauk, Oct. 9, 1932, Helmuth saw no less than 29 individuals. Because it breeds and winters, arrival and departure dates are difficult to determine, but it usually arrives in early April.

Cruickshank (1942) listed this species as "decidedly rare in winter." In recent years it has been present regularly in small numbers at this season on the coastal marshes, and in 1953–54, on all Christmas counts combined, 22 were noted. This may be due, in part, to a much greater number of observers.

Breeding: The American Bittern nests throughout the area in fresh-water marshes, but is relatively rare in brackish and salt marshes. The number of breeding pairs naturally depends on the size of the marsh. On June 1, 1947, the Urner Club found 13 nesting pairs at Troy Meadows.

Egg dates: Apr. 26 to June 12.

LEAST BITTERN (*Ixobrychus exilis*)*B

Range: An American species, breeding from southern Canada (rarely) to tropical South America. The nominate race occurs in our area.

Status: Uncommon to rare, local breeder; occasionally locally common.

Migration: This generally secretive bird is rarely reported as a migrant. A specimen in the American Museum was picked up dead at the corner of Bank and Washington streets lower Manhattan, May 8, 1950 (J. E. Taylor).

Extreme dates: Apr. 16, 17 (specimen) to Oct. 2; possibly later. Casual at Jamaica Bay Refuge, Nov. 19, 1960 (Johnson). Rare before May and after September.

Breeding: The Least Bittern nests locally in fresh-water marshes, chiefly in cattails; more rarely in coastal brackish marshes. Often overlooked. During a survey of Troy Meadows on June 1, 1947, the Urner Club found at least ten nesting pairs and, during the same summer, four pairs were present at Idlewild (Mayer). In 1949 Helmuth found Least Bitterns breeding in eight localities from Montauk to Mecox Bay, the latter locality being a brackish marsh.

Recent maxima: Six nesting pairs, Jamaica Bay Refuge, 1960 (Johnson *et al.*); at least ten breeding pairs, Hackensack Meadows, 1962 (Black and Jehl). This latter locality is a partially tidal, brackish marsh.

Egg dates: May 17 to July 16.

Remarks: This species winters north to central Florida; casually to Maryland, New York (specimens), and Massachusetts. In our area, there are two winter specimens and two reliable sight reports: Long Island City, Dec. 12, 1895 (Hendrickson), A.M.N.H.; one picked up alive, Lido Beach, L.I., Feb. 17, 1949 (Elliott), died the next day, specimen in the Tackapausha (Seaford) Museum; one seen at Lawrence, L.I., Jan. 28, 1950 (Boyajian and Ryan); one present at Iona Island, Hudson River, Feb. 3 to March 3, 1952 (Orth *et al.*).

STORKS: CICONIIDAE

WOOD STORK (*Mycteria americana*)*

Casual: Neotropical species, breeding north to coastal South Carolina. Wanders widely after the breeding season, recorded north to southern Canada.

A specimen was shot in a wooded swamp at East Marion, Suffolk County, June 21, 1890 (C. Schellinger, *fide* Latham). Most remarkably, 65 years later, Latham himself saw an individual in this very same swamp on June 23, 1955. By coincidence, a flock of 10 was observed in the same area flying over East Marion, Aug. 17, 1958 (E. Morgan), and the next day perhaps the same group (13) was seen over Orient (Latham), and later over East Marion (Morgan) and Riverhead (P. Stoutenberg). Still another individual was seen and color-photographed at Moriches Bay, Aug. 30 and 31 by several observers. A flock of 11 was observed flying over the Jamaica Bay Refuge, June 10, 1961 (Johnson). Another flock of 15, with about 100 Snowy Egrets and 35 Great Egrets, were carefully observed as they alighted on the salt meadows north of Jones Beach, Apr. 2, 1962

(Alperin). It is believed that these birds accompanied the egrets, the latter having "just arrived" from the south.

It seems remarkable that there was only the one record of a single individual in over a century and that suddenly within five years *flocks* of Wood Storks have been reported within three of those years. A possible explanation may be the fact that in recent years drainage and drought on the southern nesting grounds have forced the Wood Stork to go elsewhere to find food.

This species is more properly called Wood Stork because it is not an ibis. This name is also used by Palmer (1962).

IBISES, SPOONBILLS: THRESKIORNITHIDAE

GLOSSY IBIS (*Plegadis falcinellus*)*B

Range: A widespread species in the warmer portions of the Old World, but of very local and discontinuous distribution in the American tropics; also, southeastern United States. The nominate race breeds north to southern New Jersey (since 1955); rarely to Long Island (since 1961).

Status: Very rare visitant formerly, but has greatly increased in recent years to locally fairly common on the coast. Very rare breeder.

Change in status: Cruickshank (1942) called this species an accidental visitant and listed only five records, all single individuals. In addition to specimens taken at Southampton, L.I., Sept. 12, 1847, and Canarsie, L.I., Oct. 10, 1848, neither of which is apparently extant, there is an earlier specimen not published previously: adult, Great South Bay, 1840 (N. Pike), A.M.N.H. No. 436089. Despite the fact that these three records occurred within a period of nine years, the species went unreported for nearly 90 years, the first recent reports being those of individuals seen in the spring of 1935 at Van Cortlandt Park and Troy Meadows.

Nonbreeding: Since 1944 the Glossy Ibis has been reported almost annually.

Most of the reports prior to 1959 were of single birds, occasionally groups of four or five. A flock of 11 was observed flying over the Loop Causeway north of Short Beach, July 12, 1959 (Levine). That same year was notable for the largest incursion into this region up to then; as early as Apr. 18, five arrived at the Jamaica Bay Refuge and remained the entire summer. This influx coincided with the spread of the species in southern New Jersey where, according to Kunkle *et al.* (1959), it first nested in Cape May County in 1955 and in Atlantic County in 1957, with a total of 12 nesting pairs in three colonies in 1958. At Stone Harbor on Aug. 14, 1958, no fewer than 122 were counted at the rookery. For its spread northward in recent years, see Hailman (1959).

109

In our area a big flight occurred in 1962: 22, Jamaica Bay Refuge, May 16 (G. Tudor), an exceptional number; 10, Hackensack Meadows, May 30 (Black and Jehl).

Extreme dates: Apr. 14 to Oct. 10 (specimen) and Nov. 9, 1959, Oyster Bay, L.I. (many observers)—present since September. An individual remained at Jamaica Bay Refuge until Dec. 12, 1963, an exceptionally late date (several observers).

Breeding: During the summer of 1961 the first known nesting for New York State occurred, when three nests containing eggs were found at the Jamaica Bay Refuge (Johnson, Post, and Buckley). At least six pairs nested there in 1962 (Johnson and Post). The same year five Glossy Ibis were noted in the heron colony at Lawrence, L.I., but no breeding evidence was obtained. For a summary of nesting in our area, see Post (1962).

Egg dates: June 25 to July 1.

Remarks: Some authorities consider this species conspecific with the White-faced Ibis (*Plegadis chihi*).

WHITE IBIS (*Eudocimus albus*)*

Accidental: Neotropical species, breeding north to coastal South Carolina; more rarely to North Carolina (1951). Accidental north to Quebec and Vermont.

There are three records in our area, specimens taken many years ago, but apparently only one is extant: Raynor South (Freeport), summer of 1836 (*fide* Giraud); adult, Great South Bay, 1840 (Pike), A.M.N.H. No. 442374; Moriches, early March 1843 (*fide* Giraud). The Great South Bay specimen has apparently never been published. It seems extraordinary that three individuals occurred within eight years and that there have been no reports of the species from our area in nearly 120 years, but such appears to be the case.

Outside the New York City region, however, the White Ibis has been observed in southern New Jersey and Connecticut in recent years. Individuals were seen at Stone Harbor, N.J., in August 1951 and during the fall of 1958; another in July 1961 at Litchfield, Conn.

SWANS, GEESE, DUCKS: ANATIDAE

MUTE SWAN (*Cygnus olor*)*B

Introduced: Palearctic species, common to locally abundant on our coast. Apparently first introduced in southern New York in 1910 in the lower

Hudson Valley (near Rhinebeck, Dutchess County) just north of our area, and in 1912 both on eastern Long Island at Southampton and farther west near Oakdale. It has become established throughout the New York City region, but is most numerous on the bays and ponds of eastern Long Island and least common in inland areas. It is primarily resident wherever found, but wanders somewhat in fall and spring.

Regarding Long Island, Helmuth (*in litt.*) says, "Once known only at Lake Agawam, Southampton. Very rare on the bays prior to 1926, but a few could always be found in the ponds." Apparently it had increased in that area shortly thereafter. Some of his maximum numbers are: 187, Easthampton to Mecox Bay, Dec. 2, 1937; 275, same area, Dec. 31, 1949.

As to New Jersey, Stone (1937) quoting Urner says, "Since about 1916 it has become completely naturalized and a number of pairs breed in a wild state in suitable ponds along the coast from the vicinity of Asbury Park to below Point Pleasant." Urner had fall maxima of flocks up to 35.

Some maxima since 1950 are: 175, South Haven, L.I., Dec. 9, 1950; 40, Westport, Conn. area, late December 1954; 40, Boonton Reservoir, Oct. 21, 1955, a very unusual number inland. In mid-July 1958, Elliott estimated 60 adults at Mill Neck, L.I., and 155 adults at Fort Pond, Montauk. Out of a total of about 570 on the Long Island waterfowl census, Jan. 17, 1959, 315 were reported on Shinnecock and Moriches bays. Over 500 were reported on Moriches Bay, Dec. 26, 1959.

Nests along the shores of shallow ponds and in marshes, mainly along the coast.

Egg dates: March 30 to June 12.

WHISTLING SWAN (*Olor columbianus*)*

Range: Nearctic species, breeding south to the Belcher Islands (Hudson Bay). Winters on the Atlantic coast chiefly from Chesapeake Bay, Md., to Currituck Sound, N.C.; rarely north to New Jersey and Long Island. This eastern population presumably migrates overland by way of the Great Lakes, as it is relatively rare on the Atlantic coast north of Maryland.

Status: Uncommon to rare migrant and winter visitant, chiefly along the coast; at rare intervals locally common. Occasional inland.

Occurrence and maxima: The Whistling Swan frequents the coastal ponds and bays and occasionally associates with the introduced Mute Swan, at which times the two species may be readily compared. Great care must be exercised, however, in identifying flying birds, as Mute Swans wander somewhat, and quick identification of swans flying offshore or overhead as "Whistlers" is, needless to say, a careless practice. The trumpetlike flight call of the latter species is diagnostic.

Maxima: *Fall*—unprecedented coastal flight down the New Jersey shore on Oct. 28, 1951,. three or more flocks totaling at least 100 between Belmar and Manasquan Inlet (Urner Club); 8, Port Monmouth, Nov. 4 (same year). *Spring*—13, Atlantic Beach, Apr. 1, 1951, perhaps the same flock seen later that day at Jones Beach. *Winter*—6, South Haven, L.I., late January to Feb. 22, 1942; 9, Mecox Bay, present all winter of 1960.

Extreme dates: Oct. 21 (specimen) to Apr. 13. September and May dates are unconfirmed, confusion with the Mute Swan being likely.

Specimen data: The only local specimen seen by me is that of an adult collected at Shinnecock Bay, Nov. 26, 1886 (Dutcher collection), A.M.N.H. No. 64819 (head only).

Note: Regarding the Trumpeter Swan (*O. buccinator*) there is no evidence for the vague statement made in the A.O.U. *Check-list* (1957: 60), "Formerly ... on the Atlantic seaboard to North Carolina." There are no specimens from this range and one supposedly taken in Maine is regarded by Palmer (1949) as unsatisfactory. None of the more recent works on birds from Newfoundland to North Carolina include this species. The Trumpeter Swan is easily confused with the Whistling Swan, as proved time and again by misidentified specimens.

CANADA GOOSE (*Branta canadensis*)*B

Range: Nearctic species, the nominate race breeds south along the Atlantic coast to Newfoundland, occasionally to Massachusetts.

Status: Abundant to very abundant migrant and winter visitant along the coast. Less numerous inland in migration, but flocks regularly seen and heard flying overhead.

Occurrence and maxima: The Canada Goose frequents coastal bays and estuaries. At times it is found in large flocks feeding on the grain fields of eastern Long Island. Impressive numbers are often seen flying over, both inland and along the coast. Canada Geese are also commonly heard at night because they are nocturnal as well as diurnal in migration.

Maxima: *Spring*—12,000, Easthampton to Mecox, March 9, 1945; 8000, same area, Apr. 2, 1949. *Fall*—4000, Jones Beach, Nov. 5, 1950. *Winter*—5000, Shinnecock Bay, Jan. 1, 1922; 5000, Mecox Bay, Feb. 5, 1950. *Inland*—500, Hudson River near Bear Mountain, Oct. 25, 1949; 1000, same locality, Nov. 26, 1956; 1000, near West Nyack, N.Y., March 31, 1962.

The statement in the A.O.U. *Check-list* (1957: 60), "on migration confined to the seaboard," is misleading in view of its regular occurrence inland. The hawk watchers see this species annually along the inland ridges.

As Canada Geese are commonly raised in captivity and escapes are frequent, it is difficult to give arrival and departure dates. Semidomesticated birds are found the year around and breed throughout the region. The numerous small flocks seen on inland ponds are for the most part descendants of captive birds.

Egg dates: Apr. 3 to May 24.

Subspecies: This polytypic species is so variable in coloration, pattern, and especially size, that no fewer than ten subspecies are currently recognized (A.O.U. *Check-list*, 1957). With such variation present, it is no wonder that confusion was rampant in the older literature, some of which prevails to the present day. The chief trouble stems from the fact that the *B. canadensis* complex is subject to considerable individual variation due to differences in age, sex, and season within the various subspecies (see Delacour, 1951).

If specimens in museums are difficult to assign to certain populations, it goes without saying that sight reports of small Canada Geese as "Hutchins'" and other races—including some unfortunately published— are unreliable.

While the races *hutchinsii* (breeding south to Baffin and Southampton Islands) and *parvipes* (breeding southeast to northern Manitoba) have been reported as collected on the Atlantic coast of the United States, other than nominate *canadensis*, only *interior* (breeding southeast to Michigan) has been taken in our area, so far as is known. This would invalidate the statement in the A.O.U. *Check-list* (1957: 61) concerning *interior*, "Not recorded from the Atlantic coast north of Maryland."

Three specimens of *B. c. interior* were collected on Long Island and identified by Parkes (1952). These three, which I have examined, are in the American Museum collection and are from Montauk Point. Two were obtained on March 14, 1902 (Nos. 350133 and 350134), the other on Dec. 3, 1909 (No. 350131). The "best" character distinguishing *B. c. canadensis* from *B. c. interior* is the sharply defined dark neck and pale mantle in *canadensis*, in contrast to the gradual merging of the dark neck and slightly lighter mantle in *interior*. In other words, the neck and mantle coloration is very abrupt in *canadensis*, whereas there is a blending of these colors in *interior*.

In no case has the nearly extinct race *leucopareia* of the Aleutian Islands been reliably reported from eastern North America. Its inclusion in the New Jersey list by Fables (1955) is unjustified. The report by Woolfenden (1957) of a specimen taken by him at Point Pleasant, N.J., Dec. 22, 1954, in the collection of the University of Kansas Museum, and identified as *leucopareia*, is almost certainly referable to some other subspecies and should be re-examined.

BRANT (*Branta bernicla*)*

Range: Palearctic and eastern Nearctic species of high latitudes, the race *hrota* breeding south to Baffin and Southampton Islands. Winters chiefly from Long Island to Chesapeake Bay, more especially from Barnegat Bay to Brigantine.

Status: Abundant to very abundant migrant and winter visitant on the south shore of western Long Island. Variously rare to common elsewhere. Has greatly increased in recent years. Reported every month of the year.

Change in status: (a) Prior to 1931—Griscom (1923) considered it a common migrant, uncommon in winter. (b) 1931 to 1949—big decrease everywhere; Cruickshank (1942) stated that it was a generally uncommon migrant and rare in winter. Both Griscom and Cruickshank (*op. cit.*) knew of very few occurrences inland, where it was practically unknown. Continued scarce up to 1949, except in migration when locally numerous. (c) 1949 to 1962—gradual increase to unprecedented numbers from 1953 on; a few individuals now summer annually on the coast and flocks regularly seen flying over inland in migration.

The Brant is essentially a marine goose. It always was and is now best known as a characteristic species of the ocean front and the shallow bays and flats back of the barrier beaches. Among the most impressive sights in recent years have been the enormous numbers present along the coast, particularly from Great South Bay to Jamaica Bay. The spectacle of thousands in the air wheeling about in a dense mass is not soon forgotten.

The favorite food of the Brant is the eel grass (*Zostera marina*), a marine alga. In 1931 this plant, found on both sides of the Atlantic, was attacked by a parasitic organism known as *Labyrinthula* (see Salomonsen, 1958). The eel grass disappeared from many places and the Brant became scarce over much of its winter range. This was indicated by estimates made just south of our area on Barnegat Bay, N.J., before and after the blight. On Feb. 22, 1925, there were at least 80,000 present. During the winter of 1932–33, only 1800 could be found. For an account of the decrease in eel grass and its effect on Brant, see Urner (1934a). The eel grass continued scarce for many years, but by the mid-1940s Brant began returning in larger numbers. They had found food substitutes in two other marine algae known as sea lettuce (*Ulva lactuca* and *Enteromorpha* sp.). By 1949, Brant were approaching their former numbers.

In some areas eel grass has recovered and it is reappearing in others. It remains to be seen whether Brant will revert to this former diet.

Meanwhile, the Brant had almost completely changed its migration habits as well as its food. As mentioned previously, prior to 1949 the Brant was essentially a migrant, generally uncommon in winter, very rare in summer, and virtually unknown inland.

114

Since 1951, it has become very abundant in winter, lingers later in spring than ever before, summers regularly in small numbers, and is reported frequently inland, where it very rarely alights except by accident. The summering birds probably represent oiled, sterile, or immature individuals.

Coastal maxima (1949 to 1962): *Winter*—10,000, Jones Inlet to Long Beach, winter of 1953–54; 20,000, Woodmere and Hewlett bays, L.I., Jan. 10, 1960 (Bull), three flocks flushed by a helicopter; on March 13, the same year, my wife and I estimated at least 3000 grazing on the Woodmere golf course directly adjacent to the salt marsh. *Spring*—10,000, Jamaica Bay, Apr. 27, 1957; 4000, same area, May 20, 1956; 500, Point Lookout, L.I., June 4, 1950, with a few stragglers there in July and August. *Summer*—11, Point Lookout, July 31, 1948; 5, Shinnecock Bay, summer of 1954; 40, Jamaica Bay, summer of 1961. *Fall*—no large numbers comparable to spring, possibly due to its lingering later in spring in recent years and perhaps nesting later on its Arctic breeding grounds. At any rate, really large concentrations do not occur until December when the wintering population builds up.

Inland maxima (1949 to 1962): Regularly flying overhead, chiefly along the Hudson Valley, 1950 on, with notably late spring flights—flocks from 500 to 2000 or more seen, May 18–31, various years. Much less numerous in fall and more irregular, although occasionally reported by hawk watchers along the ridges.

BLACK BRANT (*Branta nigricans*)*

Accidental: An eastern Palearctic and western Nearctic species, breeding in high latitudes east to Melville Island, northern Canada. The American population winters chiefly on the Pacific coast south to Baja California. Casual or accidental on the Atlantic coast from Massachusetts to Virginia.

The type specimen of *B. nigricans* (Lawrence), an adult male, A.M.N.H. No. 3211 was taken at Egg Harbor, N.J. (outside our area) in January 1846. Two more specimens were collected there in the spring of the same year, one of which, taken on March 18, is still in the Lawrence collection, A.M.N.H. No. 45893.

As for our area, the Black Brant has been reported only from Long Island, a total of five occurrences, three of them specimens, none apparently extant: the first record is that of a specimen collected prior to the type, Islip, 1840 (*fide* Dutcher); Babylon, spring, 1889 (Dutcher); Babylon, March 31, 1908 (Herrick). The other two occurrences are sight reports made by direct comparison with *B. bernicla:* Merrick Bay, March 30, 1946 (Bull and Komorowski), well seen with more than 2000 Brant, both on an exposed mud flat and in flight; an individual observed on the beach at Mattituck, Oct. 25, 1959 (E. Morgan), full details submitted. For sight

115

reports in Massachusetts under similar circumstances, see Griscom and Snyder (1955).

Some authorities consider this species conspecific with *Branta bernicla*. The relationship of dark-breasted birds taken on the American side of the Atlantic coast is considerably confused. For discussion of their taxonomy and nomenclature, see Delacour and Zimmer (1952) and Manning *et al.* (1956).

BARNACLE GOOSE (*Branta leucopsis*)*

Accidental: A western Palearctic species breeding west to eastern Greenland and wintering in northwestern Europe. Recorded in eastern North America from Baffin Island and Labrador to North Carolina.

The status in our region is the same as that given by Cruickshank (1942). The writer is in agreement with him that some of the "present-day" records are probably escapes from aviaries or zoos. The species is not unusual in captivity (Delacour, 1954). The following three records listed by Cruickshank (*op. cit.*) are suspected of being escapes either because of their tameness or because of their proximity to aviaries: Farmingdale, L.I., 1922; Overpeck Creek, N.J., 1926; Little Neck Bay, L.I., 1933.

The following four records are all collected specimens, none apparently extant: Jamaica Bay, Oct. 20, 1876 (Lawrence collection); adult, Money Island, Fire Islands, Great South Bay, Oct. 16, 1919 (G. V. Hollis), first seen Oct. 12; Orient, Dec. 11, 1926 (*fide* Latham); one taken with a flock of Canada Geese, Shinnecock Bay, December 1926 (*fide* Latham). These four specimens were all taken during the hunting season at coastal points. While there is no proof as to their origin, the likelihood exists that some or all were wild vagrants from the Old World. Barnacle Geese have been taken in such places as Baffin Island and Labrador.

WHITE-FRONTED GOOSE (*Anser albifrons*)*

Casual: Palearctic and western Nearctic species; breeding also in western Greenland. In North America winters and migrates chiefly west of the Mississippi River. Very rare or casual on the Atlantic coast, where recorded from Labrador to Georgia.

The status of this species in the eastern United States is very confused for two reasons: (*a*) The subspecies (*A. albifrons frontalis* and *A. a. flavirostris*) are in doubt, as most specimens collected are no longer extant, all five taken on Long Island apparently having disappeared (see below). (*b*) There is the possibility that two allied Old World species (*A. fabalis*, the Bean or Pink-footed Goose, and *A. erythropus*, the Lesser White-fronted

116

Goose) might occur. Some of the sight reports, particularly those in recent years, may have been escapes of these Old World species which resemble *A. albifrons*, and are frequently kept in captivity (see Delacour, 1954). An individual of *A. erythropus*, present at Islip, L.I. all fall of 1960 into the winter of 1961 was almost surely an escape, as this species is chiefly east European and west Asiatic in range and has not been recorded from North America.

However, insofar as our area is concerned, all reports of White-fronted Geese are from coastal points, eight of the nine from Long Island, the other from New Jersey. It is, therefore, likely that some or all migrated to or from the Arctic.

There are five early specimens and an old sight report from Long Island as follows: Babylon, year not stated (Giraud); Great South Bay, November 1846; Islip, March 18, 1849; Montauk, March 2, 1872 (all formerly in Dutcher collection); Sag Harbor, Oct. 18, 1889 (formerly in Braislin collection); also a flock of 11 seen at Miller Place, Apr. 5, 1883 (Helme).

There are three recent reliable sight reports: adult with several Canada Geese, Hook Pond, Easthampton, Apr. 14, 1944 (Helmuth); another adult with three Snow Geese and many Canada Geese, feeding in a rye field, Water Mill, Dec. 31, 1948 (Helmuth); one with a flock of Canada Geese, Lake Como, N.J., Sept. 30, 1953 (several observers).

SNOW GOOSE *(Chen hyperborea)**

Range: Nearctic species (for details, see Subspecies).

Status: Variously uncommon to very abundant migrant, both inland and along the coast. Rare to uncommon in midwinter.

Occurrence and maxima: In our area the Snow Goose is essentially a spring and fall migrant en route to and from the breeding and wintering grounds. Large flocks seldom alight in our region. Occasionally small groups drop down and stay a short time. At such times they frequent coastal ponds and bays, and occasionally are observed on fields and golf courses near the coast. The nearest regular stop-off places for the spectacular concentrations are situated on the lower St. Lawrence River not far from the city of Quebec, and on the New Jersey side of Delaware Bay.

The fall flight is primarily coastal, the largest flocks reported chiefly during the second half of November and the first half of December. Apparently the spring flight is mainly inland, as there have been no large flocks reported on the coast east of Babylon and Jones Beach. Perhaps the birds turn inland and fly across Long Island to New England, and then overland to the St. Lawrence Valley. Good-sized flocks are reported flying by way of the Hudson Valley and are probably regular along the ridges, as they have been reported frequently by hawk watchers. Peak of the spring flight is during the last week of March and the first two weeks of April.

Maxima: *Fall*—big flight in 1948. 5500+, south shore of Long Island, Dec. 12 (annual waterfowl census, several flocks up to 700, and one over 1000; 2200, Idlewild [Mayer]); also 2000, Raritan Bay, N.J., Dec. 13 (Black *et al.*). This latter flock lit on the bay, unusual for so many in this region. On Nov. 16, 1958, after a heavy easterly storm, big flocks were noted inland: 1000, Dover, Morris County, N.J. (Thorsell); 250, Stony Point, and 200, Nyack, both in Rockland County, N.Y. (several observers). *Spring*—Apr. 14, 1936; 300, Woodmere, and 750, Lake Success, both in Nassau County, L.I.; 900, Paterson, N.J., Apr. 13, 1941; Jones Beach, 1950—150, Apr. 5, and 100, Apr. 15; the following flight on Apr. 5, 1959, indicates a split inland and coastal movement with flocks at widely separated locations—200, Carmel, Putnam County, N.Y., and 125, Suffern, Rockland County, N.Y.; also 700, Babylon, Suffolk County (Alperin)— three separate flocks of 200, 300, and 200 within a fifteen-minute period around 5:00 P.M. In 1962 at Mount Kisco, Westchester County, N.Y., 800 were seen on Apr. 4, and 460 on Apr. 5.

Extreme dates: Sept. 21 (earliest specimen, Sept. 28) to May 17 and 24. Rare before mid-October and after April. Usually arrives in mid-March and departs by late December.

Generally rare in midwinter, not more than four per locality.

Casual in summer: Seven immatures, Spring Creek, Jamaica Bay, entire summer of 1961 (many observers). These birds were often seen feeding on grassy upland fill, and at other times in ponds at the nearby Jamaica Bay Refuge.

Subspecies: The Snow Goose is a Nearctic species divided into two subspecies.

1. The larger northern race, *atlantica*, is confined to high latitudes, breeding in a limited area from northwestern Greenland south only as far as northern Baffin Island. Its migration routes have been discussed above. Winters primarily along the Atlantic coast from Chesapeake Bay to North Carolina; less commonly north to Delaware Bay. This is presumably the dominant form in our area.

At least nine specimens have been shot locally, but apparently only three are extant (in the American Museum collection).

2. The smaller western and southern nominate race has a much more extensive range than *C. h. atlantica*. The nominate race breeds from extreme northeastern Siberia and northern Alaska east to southern Baffin Island and Southampton Island; occasionally south to the Hudson Bay coast of extreme northern Ontario. The eastern population of nominate *hyperborea* migrates along the west coast of Hudson Bay and primarily west of the Mississippi River to its winter quarters along the Gulf of Mexico from eastern Mexico to northwestern Florida, but principally along the coast of Louisiana and eastern Texas.

Recorded as occurring (specimens) on the Atlantic coast from Quebec to South Carolina.

In our region four specimens have been collected, three of them extant and examined by me: Immature, Shinnecock Bay, Oct. 8, 1881 (Dutcher collection), A.M.N.H. No. 64812; immature, Montauk Point, Oct. 29, 1888 (Dutcher collection), A.M.N.H. No. 64813; Newark Meadows, Oct. 29, 1917 (Urner), only the wing preserved and measured by him; I do not know the whereabouts of this specimen; adult, Shelter Island, Oct. 29, 1933 (Latham), in his collection.

Wing length, the criterion most often used in separating specimens of the two subspecies, is fairly reliable, but with some overlap present. The best character is the length and depth of bill, which is much smaller in nominate *hyperborea.*

Remarks: No sight reports accepted as to subspecies. Whether the "Lesser" Snow Goose, as the nominate race was formerly called, is as rare in our region as reported, is not known. Unlike its close relative, the Blue Goose, the former would be easily overlooked among flocks of Snow Geese. Moreover, the four specimens listed above indicate that it is not strictly accidental. For example, only two local specimens of the Blue Goose— known to occur regularly—are believed to be extant. (See discussion under Blue Goose.)

BLUE GOOSE (*Chen caerulescens*)*

Range: A central Nearctic "species" of very limited breeding and wintering range, the distribution quite similar to that of the eastern population of *A. h. hyperborea* ("Lesser" Snow Goose). The Blue Goose breeds from southwestern Baffin Island and Southampton Island, south sparingly along the west coast of Hudson Bay, and recently (1956) to the extreme northern coast of Ontario (Hudson Bay). Migrates chiefly by way of Hudson Bay (both coasts) and the Mississippi Valley. Winters primarily on the coast of Louisiana. Recorded on the Atlantic coast from Maine to Florida.

Status: Uncommon to rare, but regular coastal migrant; occasionally fairly common. Very rare in midwinter.

Occurrence and maxima: Blue Geese almost invariably associate with Snow Geese; the gray, white-headed adults stand out very conspicuously from their more numerous relatives. They may be seen on coastal ponds, occasionally feeding in short grassy areas such as golf courses and cut-over grain fields in company with Canada Geese. This is particularly true in the open agricultural region of eastern Long Island near the coast. However, sometimes during migration, they do not alight, but pass over-head in big flocks of Snow Geese.

Casual inland—only seven reports at hand.

Maxima: *Fall*—"big" flight in 1934, as mentioned by Cruickshank (1942): 9, Moriches Bay, Nov. 8, and 4, Shinnecock Bay, Nov. 15; altogether at least 20 reported on eastern Long Island from Nov. 1 to early December, several of which were shot. Also, 5, Bridgehampton, L.I., Oct. 15, 1953; 6, Orient, Nov. 2, 1951; 13, Jamaica Bay Refuge, Nov. 5, 1960; 5, same locality, Nov. 16 to Dec. 1, 1956. *Spring*—12 near Red Bank, N.J., March 21, 1954; flock of 10, Miller Place, L.I., Apr. 28, 1883 (Helme), late for so many.

Unusual were three that spent most of the winter of 1950–51 on the fields and in the marsh near Mecox Bay. Two were frequently observed at Baisley Pond Park, near Idlewild, winter of 1959–60.

Extreme dates: Oct. 9 to May 17. Rare after April.

The individual listed by Cruickshank (1942) at Mill Neck, that remained from Sept. 21, 1936, to June 8, 1937, was very likely an escape. There are several waterfowl aviaries in the vicinity and a number of species have escaped from time to time according to the gamekeepers. I have seen tame Blue Geese in several ornamental waterfowl preserves. This is one of many of the family Anatidae that is kept in captivity (see Delacour, 1954).

Of the dozen or so Blue Geese shot in our area very few have been preserved. I have examined only two: adult female, Jones Beach, Nov. 22, 1893 (Chichester), A.M.N.H. No. 64815; immature, Orient, March 14, 1929 (Latham), in his collection.

Remarks: The Blue Goose is perhaps conspecific with the Snow Goose and probably a color phase as believed by some authorities. Arguments have persisted for years as to whether the two forms are different species or the same.

Both Sutton (1931) and Soper (1946) maintain their specific distinctness, but for different reasons. The former believed them to be hybrid populations on the basis of their interbreeding on Southampton Island, while the latter found "no evidence of hybridization" on Baffin Island, the two forms being segregated during the breeding season.

Manning's view (1942), that they are subspecies, is untenable on the grounds that the two forms are sympatric over a relatively broad breeding area.

However, Cooch (1961) believes them to be color phases and states that "pairing between phases is common, but not random." He also stresses what has been known for a long time, namely, that their breeding, migration, and winter schedule are synchronous both as to time and place.

His arguments are strengthened by the fact that a great similarity exists between the two forms on morphological grounds, with the exception of color. Both are alike in other respects: (*a*) they are the same size and (*b*) bill structure is practically identical. In addition, voice and behavior are considered the same.

120

Summary status of Snow Goose and Blue Goose in the New York City region: There is the possibility that the "Lesser" Snow Goose may not be as rare here as generally believed. It would be much more easily overlooked in Snow Goose flocks than the Blue Goose, the latter conspicuously obvious both to the hunter and birdwatcher. This is borne out by the fact that of 13 specimens of the Snow Goose taken in our area, of which only seven are extant, *four* of the seven belong to the smaller, nominate subspecies. Of 13 local specimens of the Blue Goose, only two are believed extant. That as many Blue Geese (13) have been shot as both races of Snow Geese combined (13) is significant. The hunter, who is relatively familiar with the more numerous Snow Goose (races not distinguished), would naturally regard the Blue Goose as a novelty and be more inclined to shoot it.

The writer believes that while the Blue Goose and the "Lesser" Snow Goose are of equal size and while both are smaller than the "Greater" Snow Goose, nevertheless it would be extremely difficult to differentiate the two Snow Geese in the field (unless side by side) and be absolutely certain of identification. Therefore, no sight reports of "Lesser" Snow Geese are accepted. There are intermediate specimens in collections indicating a certain amount of variation.

FULVOUS TREE DUCK (*Dendrocygna bicolor*)*

Accidental: A tropical and subtropical species, with an extraordinary *discontinuous* distribution—breeding in five widely separated areas: (*a*) from central California, southeastern Texas, and southern Louisiana, locally through Mexico, south to Guatemala and Honduras; (*b*) from Colombia and Peru east to Venezuela, Trinidad, and the Guianas; (*c*) from central Brazil to northern Argentina; (*d*) eastern Africa from the Sudan and Ethiopia (Abyssinia) south to Natal, and the island of Madagascar; (*e*) India and Ceylon.

The race *helva* occurs in North America and, since 1955, has wandered widely in the nonbreeding season east to Florida and north along the Atlantic coast to North Carolina; since 1960 to Maryland, southern New Jersey (Brigantine Refuge)—and most remarkably, in *flocks* during late fall and the *winter* months in 1961 and 1962 to Long Island, Rhode Island, Massachusetts, and even New Brunswick! The largest concentrations occurred in New Brunswick (flock of 21, Nov. 4, 1961) and Rhode Island (30, Dec. 23, 1961).

Perhaps most extraordinary of all were identically sized flocks occurring on Martha's Vineyard (Mass.) and Long Island on the same day—Dec. 22, 1962; one shot from a flock of six to eight in the former locality, and three shot from the same-sized flock in the latter area.

121

Of the three secured by duck hunters on Long Island, one was eaten, one was mounted, and the third was preserved as a specimen—adult male, A.M.N.H. collection, No. 781279, taken on Sexton Island, Great South Bay (Suffolk County), collected by Adam Kopf.

These Sexton Island birds represent the first known record for New York State.

MALLARD (*Anas platyrhynchos*)*B

Range: Holarctic species, the nominate race breeds south to Virginia.

Status: Resident throughout (chiefly semidomesticated stock), and a common to locally abundant late fall migrant and winter visitant. It has increased in recent years.

Migration and winter: The status of the Mallard in our area is difficult to determine because of releases of captive birds from time to time. While most of the truly wild population nests far to the north and west of us, the local birds are greatly augmented by many individuals from other areas, chiefly in late fall and winter. They often associate with Black Ducks during migration and winter. In recent years, especially since the late 1930s, the Mallard has increased in the northeast. The largest winter concentrations are found along the coast where the weather is milder.

Maxima: 450, South Haven, L.I., Feb. 18, 1938; 135, Scarsdale Reservoir, N.Y., Dec. 28, 1941; 2500, all Christmas counts combined, 1949–50; 4000, all counts combined, 1953–54.

Breeding: Mallards nest on the ground in and near marshes and along ponds and streams.

Egg dates: March 25 to June 30.

BLACK DUCK (*Anas rubripes*)*B

Range: An eastern Nearctic species, breeding south to North Carolina.

Status: Abundant to very abundant fall migrant, and common to abundant winter visitant on the coast. Fairly common to locally common breeder.

Migration and winter: Our most widely distributed duck, occurring in flocks even on the ocean during severe winter weather.

Maxima: 5000, Shinnecock Bay, Oct. 16, 1924; 4700, Troy Meadows, Oct. 28, 1933; 25,000, all Christmas counts combined, 1953–54, the majority along the south shore of Long Island.

Breeding: The Black Duck is among the most adaptable of waterfowl, nesting in fresh-water marshes, coastal salt marshes, along the shores of

122

Swans, Geese, Ducks: Anatidae

lakes, ponds, and streams, and even in scrub fields or open woodland some distance from water.

During the summer of 1949 in the Jamaica Bay area, Mayer found 34 breeding pairs with an estimated total of 260 young.

Egg dates: March 9 to July 16.

GADWALL (*Anas strepera*)*B

Range: Holarctic species, breeding commonly east to Manitoba and Wisconsin; locally inland east to northwestern Pennsylvania and western New York; and very local on the coast from Long Island to South Carolina (chiefly since the mid-1940s). Winters north to Maryland, less frequently to Long Island.

Status: Locally common to very common migrant and winter visitant along the south shore of Long Island. Relatively uncommon to rare elsewhere. Local breeder since 1947.

Change in status: (1) Nonbreeding. The Gadwall is most numerous on the fresh water ponds from Valley Stream east to South Haven, but according to Vogt (1935) was a rare migrant at Tobay Pond. During the winter months, it seems to prefer those ponds that are at least partially wooded, which would explain its relative scarcity at Tobay (before it bred in 1947) and the Jamaica Bay Refuge. This species has increased considerably since 1942, when Cruickshank considered it as uncommon, but regular in migration and winter.

Maxima: 50, South Haven, Nov. 15, 1952; 55, same locality, Dec. 13, 1940, an exceptional number for that period; 37, Oakdale, Jan. 6, 1951; 100, Valley Stream State Park, March 5, 1959; 77, East Patchogue, March 24, 1956; 62, Babylon, Apr. 18, 1960.

Extreme dates (nonbreeders): Aug. 25 to May 24.

(2) Breeding. With the recent spread eastward of this species, it has bred at scattered localities along the Atlantic coast, especially since the development of waterfowl refuges.

During the summer of 1947, Gadwalls were found nesting at Tobay Pond for our first known breeding record. For a description of the bird's ecology and numerical status as a breeder at this locality, see Sedwitz, Alperin, and Jacobson (1948 and 1951), and Sedwitz (1958a). A partial summary of nesting results is presented below. It should be emphasized that a number of adults present were apparently nonbreeders, as the following estimates include more females seen than broods of young or actual nests found. The breeding population fluctuates from year to year.

1947—5 to 8 pairs with 60 to 80 young.
1950—85 adults, 118 young (many adults, nonbreeders).
1952—40 adults, 93 young (some adults, nonbreeders).

123

1955—7 pairs, at least 2 broods of young and 1 nest.

1959—40 adults, only 4 broods of young.

Since 1952, they have decreased, possibly due to an increase in the giant reed (*Phragmites*).

In 1961, three pairs nested at the Jamaica Bay Refuge (Johnson and Norse), the second known breeding locality in our area.

Egg dates: June 12 to July 10.

PINTAIL (*Anas acuta*)*B

Range: Holarctic species, breeding south to Quebec and New Brunswick; more rarely to northwestern Pennsylvania; also northern and western New York (1945 and 1959 respectively), and Long Island (1962).

Status: Abundant to very abundant spring migrant in inland New Jersey and a much less numerous fall migrant and winter visitant on the south shore of Long Island. Has greatly increased in recent years. One breeding record.

Migration and winter: This is one of few ducks that is more plentiful in New Jersey than on Long Island. It is especially numerous in the large fresh-water marshes such as Troy Meadows and adjacent areas.

The Pintail, formerly a rare duck in the northeast, has increased markedly since the early 1920s. As with many other "fresh-water" ducks, it favors large marshy ponds and lakes, and is relatively rare on the deep-water reservoirs inland. It is also at home on coastal brackish ponds and estuaries, especially in winter.

Maxima: *Spring*—500, Overpeck Creek, N.J., March 22, 1924; 3000, Troy Meadows, March 15, 1942; 3000, same area, Apr. 3, 1937. *Fall*—200, South Haven, L.I., Nov. 1, 1945. *Winter*—600, same locality, Dec. 26, 1934; 250, Tobay Pond, Jones Beach, Jan. 14, 1962.

"Extreme" dates: Mid-August to late May; several June and July reports; also three individuals that spent virtually the entire summer of 1929 at Easthampton (Helmuth).

Breeding: The first and only known breeding report for our area is that of a pair with downy young at the Jamaica Bay Refuge in June 1962 (Johnson).

EURASIAN TEAL (*Anas crecca*)*

Range: Palearctic species, the nominate race breeding west to Iceland. Recorded on the Atlantic coast of North America from Labrador to South Carolina.

Status: Variously uncommon to very rare winter visitant on Long Island. Casual elsewhere.

124

Change in status: In our area this species almost invariably associates with Green-winged Teal to which it is very closely related and considered conspecific by some authorities.

Griscom (1923) considered it accidental. There are two adult males in the American Museum collection, the only two from the New York City area, as far as I know, that are extant: one labeled only "Long Island" (no date), A.M.N.H. No. 3646, may be one of those taken on Long Island in 1858 or earlier by J. G. Bell. The other was collected at Merrick, L.I., Dec. 19, 1900 (Braislin collection), A.M.N.H. No. 350739—one of two shot from a flock of Green-winged Teal. There seem to be no records between 1858 and 1900 and apparently none between the latter year and 1932. It was "rediscovered" Feb. 27, 1932, at Boonton Reservoir (Edwards).

Cruickshank (1942) stated that from 1932 on, it was a rare, but regular visitant to Long Island. As may be seen from the following maxima, the Eurasian Teal had decreased by the early 1940s.

Maxima (1932 to 1942)—adult males in all instances: 4, South Haven, Nov. 26, 1935; 5, Hempstead Reservoir, March 15, 1936; 6, same locality, Apr. 16, 1937 and Dec. 11, 1938.

Maxima (1943 to 1962): Never more than 2 per day at one locality and more often only 1; a few years (1950s) it was missed entirely.

Casual away from Long Island, only 5 or 6 reliable occurrences: Boonton Reservoir and Troy Meadows (1932), possibly the same bird; Newark Bay (1935); Croton Point (1936); Central Park (1947); Pelham Bay Park (1956).

Extreme dates: Late November to May 1, 5, and 13. Cruickshank (1942) listed the earliest fall date as Oct. 13, but the validity of any sight report before late November is questionable for the following reasons: (*a*) both *A. crecca* and *A. carolinensis* males assume eclipse plumage by June or at the latest by early August; (*b*) the eclipse plumage is retained until at least the latter part of November; (*c*) the black-and-white scapulars of *A. crecca* are the "last" feathers to reappear before complete molt is attained (see Kortright, 1942).

The writer has examined more than 70 fall males of *A. crecca* in the American Museum collection. Specimens taken on Sept. 28, Oct. 5, 11, 12, 17, Nov. 4, 8 (2), 11, and 14 were *all* in eclipse plumage; in other words, the white horizontal scapular stripes were lacking—the one and only satisfactory field mark in distinguishing *A. crecca* from *A. carolinensis*. The earliest male examined in "full" plumage was collected Nov. 28! Females of the two forms are indistinguishable in the field.

Griscom and Snyder (1955) accepted *no* records prior to Nov. 22, and stated, ". . . note the absence of reports when teal are in eclipse plumage."

A possible explanation of the Oct. 13 sight report may be that a male teal was observed lacking the vertical white patch of *A. carolinensis*, and was assumed to be *A. crecca*.

Remarks: The question of whether local records of this species represent truly wild birds (strays from European waters) or escapes from captivity has never been answered conclusively. See especially Phillips (1928), Hickey (1951), and Griscom and Snyder (1955).

Phillips stated: "The [Eurasian] Teal has become commonly imported, often from hand-reared stock, and doubtless has sometimes made its escape."

Griscom and Snyder: "The species has occurred suspiciously often for an 'accidental straggler,' and this may be another case where records are discredited by escapes from game farms. . . ."

Hickey stated the pros and cons regarding the possibility of escapes, but one of his arguments does not appear to support the known facts. Regarding possible escapes he stated that, "The most telling arguments in support of . . . hypothesis are (1) the nearly complete absence of current North American records of *A. crecca* outside of the New York City region." This is contradicted by both old and recent records of *A. crecca* occurring in Labrador, Newfoundland, Nova Scotia, Maine, Massachusetts, Connecticut, Pennsylvania, Ohio, Maryland, Virginia, and both Carolinas, as well as in New York and New Jersey. The Eurasian Teal has occurred much too often over a wide range in the northeast for *all* of the individuals to be escapes. Moreover, an individual banded in England, Nov. 9, 1952, was captured in Newfoundland less than a month later—Dec. 5, 1952 (see British Birds, 46: 297, 1953).

Hickey's strongest argument favors the theory that this species derived from captive stock during the 1930s, when it was least rare: "(2) the fact that the sudden regularity of [Eurasian] Teal in New Jersey and Long Island coincided with the importation of this species by dealers."

His statement on ". . . the complete absence of local records between mid-May and mid-October," is only true because males are *not* identifiable during most of this season, as discussed previously under plumages.

It is quite impossible to state even an approximate percentage of the Eurasian Teal occurrences in North America that are of wild stock. Very likely, they are both wild and captive, as is true of many waterfowl.

The A.O.U. *Check-list* (1957) name of "Common" Teal is completely misleading, as the species is listed there as "accidental" in North America. It is most certainly not strictly accidental in view of the foregoing discussion. Moreover, the *common* teal in North America is the Green-winged Teal. Eurasian Teal is the most appropriate name as this form breeds from Iceland east throughout Eurasia to the Pacific coast of Siberia and Japan.

GREEN-WINGED TEAL (*Anas carolinensis*)*B

Range: Nearctic species, breeding southeast to Ontario, northwestern Pennsylvania, western New York, and recently to Maine. Since 1950, it has expanded its nesting range south as follows: 1953—southeastern Pennsylvania (Tinicum Marshes); 1954—eastern Massachusetts; 1956—Virginia; 1960—southern New Jersey (Brigantine) and Long Island; 1962—northern New Jersey.

Status: Variously common to abundant migrant on Long Island and locally in New Jersey; less numerous in winter. Four recent breeding records.

Change in status: 1. Nonbreeding—this species has fluctuated in numbers through the years. It was considered common prior to 1910, then was very scarce until about the mid-1920s, when it again became numerous, but has decreased once more since the early 1950s, and is now (1962) rarely reported in flocks up to 100. It frequents marshy ponds, both fresh and brackish, and shallow lakes; also coastal bays and estuaries in winter.

Maxima: *Fall*—40, Jones Beach, Aug. 28, 1946; 210, Easthampton, Sept. 25, 1949; 200, Jones Beach, Nov. 17, 1934; 450, same locality, Dec. 11, 1949. *Spring*—450, Hempstead Reservoir, Apr. 3, 1938; 250, Jones Beach, Apr. 7, 1937. Occurs chiefly from late August to early May. Casual in *summer*, but there are several June and July reports; one individual summered in 1938 at Tobay Pond.

2. Breeding—although the Green-winged Teal has decreased within the past ten or more years in our area, the first known breeding here occurred in 1960. Its breeding range, like certain primarily "western" ducks, has spread south and east. It is suggested that creation of waterfowl refuges in recent years in the northeast has been instrumental in providing suitable nesting situations. The great majority of breeding records since 1950 (see above under Range) have been located in wildlife refuges.

The local breeding records are: Female flushed off nest containing ten eggs, Easthampton, June 18, 1960 (McKeever), the eggs later disappeared, perhaps eaten by a raccoon; one pair, possibly two pairs with downy young, Jamaica Bay Refuge, summers of 1961 and 1962 (Johnson *et al.*); about four breeding pairs, including one nest with four eggs, Hackensack Meadows, summer of 1962 (Black and Jehl)—the eggs, however, did not hatch.

Egg dates: June 18 to July 8.

Remarks: By some authorities considered conspecific with the Eurasian Teal (*A. crecca*).

BLUE-WINGED TEAL (*Anas discors*)*B

Range: Nearctic species, in the east breeding from southern Canada to North Carolina.

Status: Locally common to abundant fall migrant on the south shore of Long Island, less common in New Jersey and relatively rare elsewhere. Much less common in spring. Local breeder. Casual in winter.

Migration: This species is most numerous on the coastal ponds, and brackish creeks and estuaries. It is one of the earliest ducks to arrive and leave in fall. In spring it is one of the later ducks to arrive and remains into May, but it is erratic and unpredictable at this latter season. Rare before April and after early November.

Fall maxima: 150, Mastic, Aug. 20, 1952; 250, Tobay Pond, Sept. 7, 1941; 115, Sagaponack, Oct. 8, 1939.

Winter: The Blue-winged Teal is one of the rarest of ducks at this season. It winters regularly as far north as southern Maryland, but is rare to casual farther north. In the New York City area there are scarcely a dozen reliable midwinter reports (single individuals in all cases); there are no specimens taken locally at this season to my knowledge.

Breeding (see map): According to Giraud (1844), "This species breeds on Long Island. At Fort Pond, Montauk, it is said a few are found breeding every season." No further reports of breeding occurred for many years and Griscom (1923) knew of none. Cruickshank (1942) reported it breeding on Long Island at Orient, Speonk, and East Moriches, and in New Jersey at Troy Meadows, Morristown, and South Plainfield.

The following recent breeding records are: Nest and eggs, Orient, 1948; pair with young, Hook Pond, Easthampton, 1949; nest and eggs—later destroyed—Baldwin, 1949; pair with two half-grown young, Franklin, Sussex County, 1950; one pair nested in a small marshy pond, Great Kills, Staten Island, from 1949 to 1953; pair with four young, Lake DeForest, Rockland County, summer of 1957. At the Jamaica Bay Refuge one pair nested in 1956, and as many as six pairs in 1960 and 1961 (Johnson *et al.*). During the summer of 1962 at least 20 pairs were estimated on the Hackensack Meadows, although only five broods of young were observed (Black and Jehl).

Egg dates: Apr. 30 to June 7.

Subspecies: This species is currently divided into two subspecies, the nominate race, primarily an inland population, breeding east to southern Quebec, western New York, and West Virginia, and the race *orphna*, a dark coastal population breeding in tidal brackish marshes from Nova Scotia and New Brunswick south to Pea Island, N.C.

Presumably this latter race breeds in our coastal areas of Long Island, as well as in the marshes of southern New Jersey (Barnegat, Brigantine, Delaware Bay, etc.).

Whether the breeding birds reported at inland localities, such as Troy Meadows, represent an intermediate population is not known, as no breeding specimens have been examined from these inland areas.

SHOVELER (*Spatula clypeata*)*B

Range: Holarctic species—in North America widespread in the west, but rare and local in the east, breeding at widely separated localities—(*a*) inland

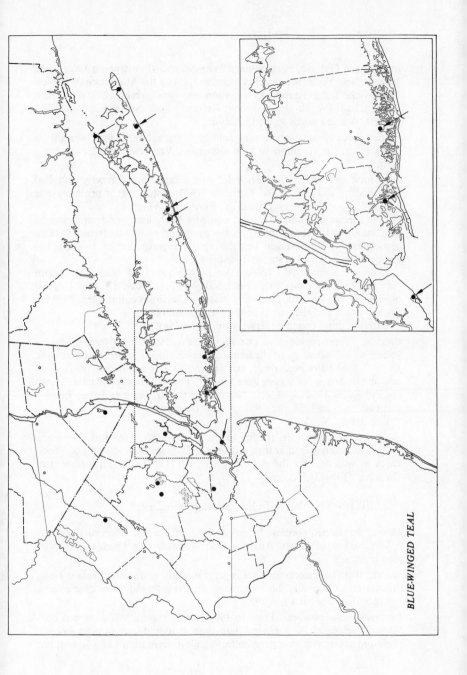

BLUE-WINGED TEAL

in southern Ontario, northwestern Pennsylvania (Pymatuning Lake), and western New York (Montezuma Marshes); (b) on the Atlantic coast in New Brunswick, Long Island (1956), southern New Jersey (Delaware Bay, 1950), Delaware (Bombay Hook Refuge), and North Carolina (Pea Island). Winters north to Long Island.

Status: Locally common to very common migrant and winter visitant on Long Island; uncommon to rare elsewhere. Very rare breeder on Long Island.

Migration and winter: The Shoveler was a rare duck formerly, but had increased by the mid-1920s. Griscom (1923) stated that it probably was of less frequent occurrence than the European Widgeon.

This species is found in largest numbers in shallow ponds and marshy lagoons along the coast, chiefly on the south shore of Long Island. It often associates with Blue-winged Teal during the warmer months. Inland it has always been relatively rare, and is still so.

Maxima: *Spring*—70, Tobay Pond, Apr. 8, 1961. *Fall*—35, South Haven, Nov. 15, 1940; 200, Jamaica Bay Refuge, Nov. 17, 1963 (several observers). *Winter*—100, southern Nassau Christmas count, Dec. 28, 1952 (Tobay Pond and the ponds in the Hempstead area).

Extreme dates (nonbreeders): Aug. 11 to May 27.

Breeding: First reported in our region in 1956, when a female and 11 young were discovered at the Jamaica Bay Refuge (numerous observers). In 1957, two pairs bred there, but apparently not again until 1960 when one or two broods of young were found. They were not reported as breeding in 1961 or 1962 (Johnson). Nested and raised young at Tobay Pond— one pair each in 1958 and 1962 (several observers).

Egg dates: No data.

Remarks: The Shoveler, related to the Blue-winged Teal and Cinnamon Teal, is placed here rather than between the American Widgeon and Wood Duck as was done in the A.O.U. *Check-list* (1957). The arrangement of Delacour (1956) is followed.

EUROPEAN WIDGEON (*Mareca penelope*)*

Range: Palearctic species, breeding west to Iceland. Recorded on the Atlantic coast of North America from Labrador to Florida and more locally inland.

Status: Rare to uncommon, but regular migrant and winter visitant along the coast; occasionally fairly common on Long Island. Very rare inland. Decreased somewhat since 1953.

Occurrence and maxima: Prior to 1900, the European Widgeon was considered accidental in our area, less than a half dozen records known. Eight old specimens have been collected, all from eastern Long Island, but only two appear to be extant: adult female, Center Moriches, Nov. 7, 1903 (Braislin collection), A.M.N.H. No. 350643; adult male, Springs (near Three Mile Harbor), Dec. 3, 1906 (Dwight collection), A.M.N.H. No. 350603.

This species almost invariably associates with Baldpate (American Widgeon). Although the latter has shown a very great increase, the European Widgeon is reported much less frequently nowadays than it was from the 1930s to 1953. This is particularly true on Long Island. Curiously enough it is less rare now on the coastal ponds of New Jersey, although not occurring in the numbers once reported on Long Island.

Maxima (1930 to 1953): 14, South Haven, Nov. 3, 1935 (Cruickshank *et al.*), an unusually large number; 6, Hempstead Reservoir, Nov. 6, 1938; 7, Rockville Centre, Dec. 7, 1947; 4, wintered, Point Pleasant, 1948–49; 4, Hempstead Reservoir, Jan. 2, 1950; total of 11 from Tobay Pond to Valley Stream, Dec. 20, 1952; 5 on ponds along the New Jersey coast from Belmar to Point Pleasant, Dec. 30, 1953.

Maxima (1954 to 1960): Never more than 2 per day at any one locality.

Extreme dates: Sept. 4 and 12 to Apr. 29 and May 14. Rare before October and after March.

Reported inland as far as Boonton Reservoir and Troy Meadows, N.J., and Jones Point, Rockland County, N.Y.

Remarks: The question has often been asked why the European Widgeon is such a widespread and regular species in North America when it is supposed to breed only in the Old World. Several ornithologists believe that there may be a small breeding population somewhere in the vast reaches of the Canadian Arctic. Hasbrouck (1944) is of this opinion, stating:

(1) "A definite southerly migration extends along the entire Atlantic coast in the fall and winter months as far as east-central Florida."

(2) "A marked northerly spring migration occurs up the Mississippi flyway mostly in April and May in company with other wildfowl."

(3) "The species is found not only singly or in pairs, but also in small flocks by itself or often in company with its near relative, *M. americana*."

Hasbrouck's hypothesis sounds plausible. After all, we did not even know the location of the breeding grounds of *Limnodromus griseus griseus*, which is an abundant bird, until 1960, when dowitchers were discovered nesting in the wilds of northern Quebec.

However, there is no doubt that some North American individuals of European Widgeon do originate in Europe, as proved by the following evidence.

Donker (1959) states that birds banded in Iceland during the breeding season were recovered in six eastern North American localities in fall, all along the seaboard—from Newfoundland, Prince Edward Island, Nova Scotia, Massachusetts, Maryland, and North Carolina. These birds were taken in September, October, November (twice), and December (twice).

AMERICAN WIDGEON (*Mareca americana*)*B

Range: Nearctic species, breeding regularly south and east to Wisconsin and southern Ontario; occasionally to northwestern Pennsylvania (Pymatuning Lake). In recent years spreading eastward and southward: 1957—Nova Scotia; 1958—Prince Edward Island; 1959—western New York (Montezuma Marshes); 1960—northern New York (Massena); 1961—Long Island.

Status: Locally common to very abundant migrant and winter visitant on the coast. Uncommon to locally common inland. Great increase in recent years. Two breeding records.

Occurrence and maxima: The Baldpate, as it is familiarly known, occurs most frequently along the coast in ponds, brackish meadows, and shallow bays, especially in winter. In former years, it was reported numerous only at the eastern end of Long Island: 1000, Gardiner's Island, Dec. 3, 1911; 1200, Shinnecock Bay, Oct. 21, 1924; 2000, Montauk area, Nov. 23, same year. Much less numerous in spring inland: 300, Troy Meadows, March 23, 1940. It arrived in late August and departed by early May. Casual in summer, including several June and July reports.

Change in status: 1. Nonbreeding—since the mid-1950s this species has increased tremendously in the northeast, and like other primarily western breeding ducks, has been found nesting in a number of eastern localities.

Recent maxima: 2500, Mecox Bay, Jan. 11, 1957; Jamaica Bay Refuge, 1959—3000, Oct. 18 and 8000, Nov. 13 (Johnson and Bull); 1960—5000, late September; also 3000, Shark River, N.J., Jan. 29, 1961.

2. Breeding—during the summer of 1961 American Widgeon were reported breeding on western Long Island in two localities: two or three pairs with broods of downy young, Jamaica Bay Refuge (Johnson *et al.*); one pair with young, Flushing Meadow Park (R. Cohen). No definite breeding evidence in 1962.

Egg dates: No data.

WOOD DUCK (*Aix sponsa*)*B

Range: A widespread but local Nearctic species; in the east breeding from southern Canada to Florida; also in Cuba. Winters north to Maryland; rarely to southern New York and New England.

Status: Occasionally common to very common fall migrant, both inland and along the coast. Local breeder. Usually rare in winter.

Migration: In fall this species is sometimes seen in fairly large numbers on the coastal fresh-water ponds, as well as in the more wooded inland areas.

132

Fall maxima: 72, Bridgehampton, L.I., Aug. 11, 1930; 90, Katonah, N.Y., Sept. 1, 1958; 54, Raritan River, N.J., Sept. 30, 1952; 117, Easthampton, Oct. 5, 1937; 42, Van Cortlandt Park, Oct. 24, 1925; 50, Iona Island, Hudson River, Nov. 3, 1961. Cruickshank (1942) stated that over 200 were present in the Smithtown, L.I., ponds in the fall of 1932.

On an all-day canoe trip through Troy Meadows, Oct. 21, 1961, Black and Thorsell estimated the astounding total of 1000 Wood Ducks. Black states (*in litt.*) that they "estimated 700 in one flock and 300 in another," and further states that Thorsell "says that this is a more or less 'normal' situation in Troy [Meadows] in mid fall." This number is unprecedented for the New York City region as I have not heard of anything remotely resembling such a concentration in our area. Penetration by boat into the heart of this swamp is the best method to cover such a vast area. By comparison, a count from the boardwalk would produce only a small fraction of this number.

No comparable numbers in spring, as Wood Ducks resort to the breeding grounds almost immediately after arrival.

Generally rare before March and after mid-November.

Winter: Wood Ducks are ordinarily quite rare at this season, but during the winter of 1933–34, there were 18 in Bronx Park; most of these had become quite tame through artificial feeding. This number is, however, unusual—1 to 4 being the usual maximum.

Breeding: The Wood Duck breeds chiefly in wooded swamps and in the vicinity of ponds and streams. A hole-nesting species, laying its eggs in hollow trees and stumps; also in bird boxes.

In 1940 a nesting survey in the New York City region revealed at least 115 pairs in 39 localities. In the Bear Mountain section alone, 22 nests were found.

A current breeding survey would be most desirable. Destruction of habitat in recent years has eliminated many of its former nesting haunts.

Egg dates: Apr. 4 to June 10.

REDHEAD (*Aythya americana*)*

Range: A western Nearctic species, breeding east to eastern Michigan; rare breeder farther east—northwestern Pennsylvania (Pymatuning Lake), Ontario, and New Brunswick. In the east, winters chiefly in the Chesapeake Bay region.

Status: Locally common winter visitant on eastern Long Island, where formerly abundant. Uncommon to rare and local elsewhere.

Occurrence and maxima: The Redhead was formerly numerous on eastern Long Island, but after 1928 it had greatly decreased. Its early abundance

133

there coincided with an even greater abundance on the island of Martha's Vineyard, where at times concentrations of over 12,000 birds could be found, chiefly during the periods 1900–10, and 1922–28 (see Forbush, 1925). After 1928, for reasons apparently unknown, it diminished markedly in both areas.

This species has always been much less common on the west end of Long Island. It is generally uncommon in coastal New Jersey (north portion) and is relatively rare inland.

The Redhead associates with Canvasbacks and scaup. It was formerly more numerous than the Canvasback, but since 1928 has been much rarer than that species. Redheads frequent fresh or brackish coastal ponds, such as are found in the Montauk area and on Gardiner's Island, as well as saline waters of bays and estuaries along the coast.

Maxima: Early period (1900–28)—2000, Moriches Bay, Nov. 17, 1905 (Dutcher), never reported as numerous before or since; 300, Gardiners' Island, Dec. 3, 1911; 600, Great Pond, Montauk, Jan. 5, 1924; 300, Fort Pond, Montauk, Dec. 9, 1928, ". . . last record of a big flock, never really common again" (Helmuth, diary).

Maxima: Recent period (since 1928)—80, Easthampton area (Hook and Georgica ponds), Sept. 28, 1933 (Helmuth), unusually early for so many; 160, Water Mill, Dec. 2, 1950, and 100, Dec. 20, 1952; 70, South Haven, Feb. 12, 1956; 50, Jamaica Bay Refuge, Nov. 25, 1956 (many observers), an unusually large number for western Long Island. However, some of these may represent introduced birds (see Remarks).

Two facts are obvious from the above estimates: (a) the much larger numbers present in the early period; (b) the absence of spring concentrations. Note that all of the maxima above are during fall and early winter (latest Jan. 5).

Possible explanations of (b) may be that the Redhead migrates in fall partly in a west–east direction toward the coast, as proved by banding; that the wintering population moves to more southerly points, especially in severe winters, to Chesapeake Bay, etc.; and that the spring migration may be chiefly via an inland route to the western breeding grounds.

Extreme dates: Sept. 6 and 18 to May 22, 31, and June 5. Rare before October and after April. No July or August occurrences of "wild" birds.

Remarks: The New York State Conservation Department liberated this species on several occasions within recent years. One of these liberations took place in 1953 in western New York (Montezuma Marshes). Foley (1960), referring to northern New York stated, "We have tried to establish the Redhead on certain good quality marshes, and in 1960 they bred at four sites." One of these sites was near Massena in the St. Lawrence valley. He did not mention the location of the three other sites.

In 1960 Redheads were introduced at the Jamaica Bay Refuge. During the summer of 1961, one brood of young of this stock was reared successfully, and in 1962 two, possibly three broods (Johnson). If this species becomes established here, then it should be added to the breeding list.

RING-NECKED DUCK (*Aythya collaris*)*

Range: Nearctic species, breeding south to northwestern Pennsylvania and the northern portions of New Hampshire and Maine; in recent years to northern New York (Adirondacks, 1946) and northeastern Massachusetts (1951).

Status: Locally common to abundant migrant and winter visitant. Great increase in recent years.

Occurrence and maxima: More than any other species of this genus, the Ring-necked Duck frequents the deep fresh-water areas such as the inland lakes and reservoirs, and the deeper ponds on Long Island. It is relatively scarce in coastal shallow-water localities like Tobay Pond and Jamaica Bay Refuge.

That this species was formerly exceedingly scarce in the New York City region is indicated by the fact that there are only two local specimens in the American Museum: Adult female, Long Island, no date (Elliot collection), A.M.N.H. No. 3659; immature male, Jones Beach, Nov. 3, 1898 (Chichester), A.M.N.H. No. 351190. It certainly was not overlooked by the old time hunters, who knew and shot both scaup ("broadbill"). Moreover, Giraud (1844) mentioned that the gunners of that day were familiar with the Ring-necked Duck and knew it by the name of "Bastard Broadbill." Griscom (1923) considered it such a rarity that he stated, "It most certainly cannot be regarded as strictly accidental. . . ."

At any rate, the species had spread and increased over the whole northeast by the early 1930s, both as a migrant and locally as a breeder. This great increase has been well documented by Griscom (1939), and particularly by Mendall (1958). Foley (1960) tells of its rapid gains as a nesting bird in the Adirondack region.

Maxima: *Fall*—240, Boonton Reservoir, Nov. 9, 1941; 230, Water Mill, Nov. 13, 1948. *Winter*—260, Titicus Reservoir, N.Y., Jan. 15, 1955; 150, Smithtown, Jan. 25, 1942; 340, Kensico Reservoir, Feb. 5, 1950; 300, South Haven, Feb. 12, 1941. *Spring*—300, Swartswood Lake, Apr. 2, 1958.

It is difficult to comprehend Cruickshank's statement (1942), ". . . at present it is a much more common duck in our region than the Canvasback." Judging from comparable numbers this is certainly not the case (see Maxima under Canvasback), although the Ring-necked Duck is perhaps more widespread at times.

Extreme dates: Sept. 20 to late May and June 7. Rare before late October and after mid-April. Reported in every month except August. Casual in midsummer: Bear Mountain, July 19–20, 1947 (Grierson and Orth);

135

4, Boonton Reservoir, June 26, 1949 (Urner Club); adult male, Babylon, July 4–17, 1954 (Elliott).

CANVASBACK (*Aythya valisineria*)*

Range: A western Nearctic species, breeding southeast to northern Minnesota. In the east winters chiefly in the Chesapeake Bay area.

Status: Common to locally very abundant winter visitant.

Occurrence and maxima: In our area the Canvasback is primarily a saltwater duck, preferring the bays and estuaries, and at times the Hudson River. Local on inland lakes. Prior to the 1920s, it was much rarer than the Redhead, but since then it has increased tremendously, whereas the Redhead has become very scarce in most places. Regarding the Canvasback, Cruickshank's statement (1942), ". . . none of our waterfowl shows more irregularity in its movements, its numbers, and its points of concentration . . ." is applicable today.

Maxima: First known big flight year—1924, at widely separated localities—800, Hunt's Point, Bronx County, Feb. 3; 140, Newark Bay, early March; 400, Mastic, Feb. 23; 500, Orient, March 1; 1000, Montauk area, Dec. 4–12, Helmuth (diary) stating that it was "never as numerous at Montauk before or since" (1908–51). Other high counts at various localities—1925–1942—2000, Hunt's Point, Jan. 22, 1926; 500, Croton Point, March 3, 1929; 5000, Raritan Bay, Dec. 3, 1939. Since 1942—5300, Flushing and Little Neck bays, Jan. 15, 1954; 1500, Stony Point, Hudson River, Dec. 3, 1958.

Extreme dates: Sept. 28 to May 7, 15, and 22. Rare before November and after early April.

Casual in summer: Shinnecock Bay, Aug. 2, 1929 (Helmuth and Wilcox); Idlewild, July 13, 1946 (Mayer); 2, Jamaica Bay Refuge, June 19 to July 18, 1956 (many observers).

GREATER SCAUP (*Aythya marila*)*

Range: Holarctic species, the race *nearctica* breeds south to northern Ontario and central Quebec; casually to the Gulf of St. Lawrence.

Status: Very abundant winter visitant on Long Island Sound and adjacent bays; also on bays along the outer coast. Regular inland.

Occurrence and maxima: This species is by far the most numerous and widespread of our winter ducks, sometimes outnumbering all other species combined.

Maxima: Big flight in 1929—75,000, Shinnecock and Mecox bays, Oct. 24; 250,000, Great South Bay, Dec. 3 (Helmuth); also—40,000, Flushing and Little Neck bays, Dec. 20, 1952; 85,000, Pelham Bay and

136

Long Island Sound east to Stamford, Conn., Dec. 31, 1953; 23,000, Jamaica Bay, Jan. 15, 1956. Fables (1955) mentions estimates of 50,000 for Raritan and Sandy Hook bays, but does not give dates.

The Greater Scaup is found also in small numbers on inland waters. It has been reported every month of the year; at least nine summered at the Jamaica Bay Refuge during 1956.

LESSER SCAUP (*Aythya affinis*)*

Range: A western Nearctic species, breeding southeast to the west shore of Hudson Bay (Manitoba); very rarely east to southern Ontario; also northern Ohio (1954). In the east winters chiefly from Chesapeake Bay to Florida.

Status: Because of great similarity to the previous species, it is impossible to state the exact status of the Lesser Scaup in our area. It is, however, primarily a bird of fresh-water inland and coastal ponds. Relatively infrequent on salt-water bays. It is a fairly common spring migrant, but usually rare in midwinter. Fall status little known because of its wariness at that season.

On rare occasions when the two species of scaup are found together and offer a ready comparison, or when males of the Lesser Scaup are observed close enough for the critical characters to be noted, the latter species may be recognized in small flocks. Females are virtually indistinguishable in the field.

Because of the difficulties involved and the likelihood of error in identification, maximum numbers are omitted. Both species of scaup occur together on inland lakes and along the coast in both fresh and brackish water, but separating the two on a percentage basis is impossible. Undoubtedly there are often a number of Lesser Scaup present with large flocks of Greater Scaup, particularly during migration.

There are several summer records based on old specimens. Three males summered with Greater Scaup, Jamaica Bay Refuge, 1956; direct comparison was obtained.

COMMON GOLDENEYE (*Bucephala clangula*)*

Range: Holarctic species, the race *americana* breeding south to the northern portions of New York (Adirondacks) and New England.

Status: Common to very abundant winter visitant on Long Island Sound and the adjacent bays, and on the ocean at the east end of Long Island during frigid weather; in lesser numbers on the bays elsewhere and on the Hudson River. Regular in small flocks on the larger inland lakes and reservoirs.

Occurrence and maxima: This species is most numerous when the winters are at their severest, particularly during long cold spells. When the weather moderates in late March, their numbers disappear rapidly. Usually rare before November and after early April. Reported every month of the year, but only vagrants during summer, including an adult male collected at Englewood, N.J., July 28, 1911 (Weber).

Maxima: *Coastal*—8000, Orient, Dec. 26, 1924 (Latham); 10,000, Gardiner's Bay, March 24, 1910 (Griscom); 4000, Montauk, March 15, 1945 (Helmuth). *Inland*—1000, Croton Point, Feb. 24, 1929 (F. E. Watson).

BARROW'S GOLDENEYE (*Bucephala islandica*)*

Casual or very rare winter visitant: Nearctic species; also breeds in Iceland. Nests south to northern Labrador and northeastern Quebec. Winters (a few) on the Atlantic coast regularly south to Massachusetts, but only casually to Long Island.

In our area there are two specimen records and less than a dozen credible sight reports. Several other reports, including one or two from inland areas, are without substantiating details and are omitted. Females are particularly difficult to identify. The specimen records are: adult female taken on Long Island "many years ago" (Elliot collection), A.M.N.H. No. 3683; adult male shot on Great South Bay near Oakdale, Dec. 3, 1959 (J. Strong), specimen examined by Elliott, Levine, and Ward. The validity of the latter specimen as a wild bird is open to question for the following reasons: (*a*) It was secured in shallow water "inside" on the bay, a highly unlikely place for a wild Barrow's Goldeneye, a species normally inhabiting relatively deep water along rocky coasts; (*b*) the keeper of a waterfowl aviary near Patchogue (only six miles from Oakdale where the bird was shot) not only raises Barrow's Goldeneyes, but reported that several had escaped *prior* to the time of the collected specimen.

The following Long Island sight reports, all except one being adult males, are believed well authenticated: Orient—6, Jan. 5, 1909; 1, Mar. 3, 1918; 3, Feb. 1, 1935 (all by Latham); Montauk Point—Jan. 29, 1939; Mar. 15, 1945; Georgica Pond, Dec. 31, 1948 (all by Helmuth), the last after a severe gale from the southeast the day before. Adult female well seen and described in detail, Atlantic Beach, Feb. 11–13, 1961 (Mayer, Rose, Carleton, Eisenmann *et al.*); Orient, Feb. 22, 1961 (Elliott). The following two reports of adult males are from New Jersey: Keansburg, Jan. 5, 1936 (Urner); Leonardo, Feb. 5, 1939 (Brown, Edwards, and Wolfarth). There are only five occurrences since 1942, although judging from the number of individuals observed at Orient, this species may occur there less rarely than supposed. For recent status of this species in New York State, see Elliott (1961).

Extreme dates: Dec. 3 and 31 to March 15.

138

BUFFLEHEAD *(Bucephala albeola)**

Range: A western Nearctic species, breeding southeast to western Ontario.

Status: Locally common to abundant winter visitant.

Occurrence and maxima: The Bufflehead is found in the largest concentrations on coastal bays and estuaries; locally numerous on inland lakes and reservoirs.

Maxima: *Coastal*—500, Jamaica Bay Refuge, Dec. 11, 1959; 500, Orient, Dec. 25, 1912; 80, Great Pond, Montauk, March 15, 1945; Jamaica Bay, 1956—25 on May 5, and 5 on May 20. *Inland*—200, Forest Lake, near White Plains, N.Y., Nov. 8, 1949.

"Extreme" dates: Sept. 16 and 23 to late May. Rare before mid-October and after April. Very rarely, summering stragglers are reported: several June dates, twice in July (6 and 8) and once in late August.

OLDSQUAW *(Clangula hyemalis)**

Range: Holarctic species, breeding south to northern Ontario, central Quebec, and northern Newfoundland.

Status: Common to occasionally very abundant winter visitant on Long Island Sound, particularly at the east end and on the nearby bays; in lesser numbers on the ocean and in the inlets along the south shore. Very rare inland.

Occurrence and maxima: Although rarely as numerous as in Massachusetts, such as off Cape Cod, this species is sometimes found in impressive numbers at the east end of Long Island. Helmuth (diary) states that it is most numerous after severe cold waves on the shoals between Montauk and Gardiner's Island.

Maxima: 2500, Montauk, Jan. 1, 1930; 1250, Orient, Jan. 15, 1954; 5000, Gardiner's Bay, March 24, 1910 (Griscom); 1100, Fire Island Inlet, March 30, 1953.

Generally uncommon before late October and after April. Reported every month of the year. Oiled and sterile birds are not infrequent in midsummer. Adult male collected at Oyster Bay, July 12, 1884 (Berier).

Remarks: The supposed "breeding" record near Little Gull Island in 1886, mentioned by Sage *et al.* (1913), was an unwarranted inference based on the presence of summering birds in changing plumage.

HARLEQUIN DUCK *(Histrionicus histrionicus)**

Range: Nearctic and eastern Palearctic species; also breeding in Iceland. Breeds south to northeastern Quebec and central Labrador. Winters on

139

the Atlantic coast south to Long Island; more rarely to New Jersey, but has increased in recent years (1950 on).

Status: **Rare** to **uncommon** but regular winter visitant at Montauk and vicinity. Rare and irregular elsewhere on the outer coast.

Occurrence and maxima: The Harlequin Duck frequents rocky coasts almost exclusively and is casual along sandy shores. It is thus least rare in and around such areas as Montauk and Orient Points, and occurs occasionally in the immediate vicinity of rock jetties along the ocean, especially those jetties situated at the entrance to inlets.

Maxima: 7, Montauk Point, Feb. 4, 1956; 5 (2 males and 3 females), Atlantic Beach, Jan. 28, 1961. These numbers are exceptional—usually only one or two are seen at a time.

Extreme dates: Nov. 2 and 10 (specimen) to Apr. 11 (specimen), Apr.12, 16, and 18.

Casual on Long Island Sound: Adult male shot by a hunter near Little Captain Island, off Greenwich, Conn., Nov. 15, 1946 (specimen in collection of M. Oboiko).

No inland reports are properly verified.

Remarks: The report listed in Cruickshank (1942) from Ellis Island, Sept. 7, 1913, is unsatisfactory. The date is nearly two months too early and no ornithologist examined the specimen.

LABRADOR DUCK (*Camptorhynchus labradorius*)*

Extinct: Breeding range unknown; supposedly nested in Labrador. Occurred in winter on the Atlantic coast south to Long Island and possibly New Jersey. Stone (1937), however, stated that there were no definite records on the New Jersey coast, several specimens in the Philadelphia Academy of Natural Sciences having no data. At least 15 specimens taken on Long Island were listed by Dutcher (1891 and 1894) as being extant. Five of these are in the American Museum, the remainder in other collections, including the last recorded specimen (U.S.N.M. No. 77126, collected on Long Island in the fall of 1875 by J. G. Bell). Most of the specimens have little data except the year, and almost never the locality, other than Long Island.

Very little is known of this bird's habits. Greenway (1958) states: "The mature male was always rare, even during the first half of the nineteenth century when the birds could sometimes be found in the markets of New York. In winter the birds were found in sandy bays and estuaries. The reasons for its extinction are not known." This species was called the Sand Shoal Duck, a name attributed to its preference for sand bars where it was reputed to feed on shellfish. It was also known as the Pied Duck, and as the Skunk Duck on Long Island, both these names referring to its coloration.

COMMON EIDER (*Somateria mollissima*)*

Range: Holarctic species, the race *dresseri* breeding along the coast south to southwestern Maine (Casco Bay). Winters south to eastern Long Island; rarely to New Jersey.

Status: Uncommon to occasionally very common winter visitant in the Montauk area. Rare and local elsewhere.

Change in status: The Common Eider is exclusively a marine duck and is purely casual elsewhere.

Griscom (1923) considered it very much rarer than the King Eider. Cruickshank (1942), referring to the Montauk region, stated, "It appears that one to six birds are to be found there every winter."

It has increased greatly since 1942. The breeding population on the Maine coast at Muscongus Bay rose from 800 birds in 1949 to over 6000 in 1959 (*fide* J. Cadbury). Its chief wintering grounds are on the shoals between Cape Cod and Nantucket, and west to Martha's Vineyard. Griscom and Snyder (1955) estimated that the main wintering group off Monomoy increased from 15,000 in 1940 to about a half million in 1951.

This increase has been reflected off Montauk Point where, since the early 1940s, it has become more numerous, although its numbers are insignificant when compared to the vast flocks in Massachusetts waters.

Recent Montauk maxima: 1947, off Montauk Point—32, Jan. 1 (Helmuth), and over 140, Feb. 23 (Helmuth). He stated (diary) that this latter flock was "composed of at least 40 adult males, the balance consisting chiefly of this species, with a few King Eiders"; 1950, from the Point to Ditch Plains—42 (9 adult males), Dec. 10 (Eisenmann and Grant), and about 115 (30 adult males), Dec. 31 (Grant and Komorowski).

After a severe cold wave Sedwitz reported 4 (including 2 males) at Atlantic Beach, Jan. 1, 1948.

Extreme dates: Nov. 8 (specimen) to March 27 (specimen); rarely to Apr. 20, 1946, Montauk Point (Aronoff and Wells), 4 adult males. Reported casually at Montauk Point, Sept. 2, 1940 (Helmuth and Sedwitz).

Accidental inland; adult female collected, Ossining, N.Y., Dec. 14, 1894 (Fisher), M.C.Z. collection No. 300372; specimen examined.

Subspecies: The more northern race *borealis* winters south to the coast of Maine; very rarely to Massachusetts. Helmuth (diary) reports an adult female collected at Montauk, Dec. 15, 1945, by S. Lester; specimen examined by J. T. Nichols, but I have not seen it.

KING EIDER (*Somateria spectabilis*)*

Range: Holarctic species, breeding south to northern Labrador; occasionally to James Bay. Winters south to eastern Long Island; more rarely to New Jersey.

Status: Uncommon to fairly common winter visitant in the Montauk area, but local and irregular elsewhere along a rocky coast.

Occurrence and maxima: The King Eider, like the previous species, is most frequently recorded in the Montauk area, but in much smaller numbers. Unlike that species, however, it is more widely distributed, being found occasionally in Long Island Sound, although rare at the west end; twice on the Hudson River at Riverdale (Cruickshank)—this is not surprising as King Eiders are occasionally reported on the Great Lakes. At times they are found in small flocks in the vicinity of rock jetties on the south shore of Long Island and along the coast of New Jersey.

Maxima, Montauk area: Dutcher (1888) tells of a flight during the winter of 1887, ". . . especially on the shoals from one-quarter to one-half mile out." Flocks up to 20 were seen, and on Apr. 8, a maximum of about 30 were noted, of which at least 10 were adult males. Maxima, Montauk in recent years: 7 adult males, Dec. 18, 1945; 22, Feb. 2 to March 16, 1958 (at least 8 adult males). Maxima elsewhere: Atlantic Beach—8, Dec. 29, 1957 to Jan. 30, 1958; 8, March 23, 1952; Long Branch, N.J.,—5, Dec. 24, 1936; 14, all January 1957.

Extreme dates: Sept. 30 and "early" October (specimen) to Apr. 27 (specimen), May 15 and 31. Rare before November and after early April. Stragglers in summer: Long Beach, June 8, 1924 (Janvrin and Rogers); male in breeding plumage, Oyster Pond, Montauk, entire summer of 1938 (Helmuth *et al.*); 3 females and 1 immature, Atlantic Beach to Short Beach, July 9–30, 1960 (Bull, Walsh *et al.*), two of these badly oiled; during the summer of 1961, single individuals were noted at Jamaica Bay and Short Beach, and 3 at Great Gull Island (various observers). Probably most of these summering vagrants were either oiled, crippled, or immature.

Specimen data: Whereas there are only two local specimens of *S. mollissima* in the American Museum, there are 32 of *S. spectabilis*, all taken on Long Island, and all but 9 from Montauk. Only 4 are adult males, the remainder females and immatures, the latter in various stages of plumage. More recently an adult male was picked up dead at Atlantic Beach, Dec. 10, 1948 (Berliner).

Remarks: It should be noted that while adult males of both species are easily recognized, and adult females may be distinguished at close range, many immatures cannot be identified. The maximum numbers listed under each species undoubtedly have both kinds present on occasion.

Formerly the King Eider occurred more regularly than the Common Eider off Montauk. Today, although the King Eider has probably not decreased, the Common Eider has definitely increased and is the more numerous species.

Swans, Geese, Ducks: Anatidae

WHITE-WINGED SCOTER (*Melanitta deglandi*)*

Range: Nearctic species, the nominate race breeding southeast to southern Manitoba and northwestern Ontario.

Status: Very abundant migrant and winter visitant on the ocean and Long Island Sound.

Occurrence and maxima: This species is the most numerous of the scoters although occasionally locally outnumbered by the Surf Scoter. At times occurs in spectacular numbers off Montauk Point.

Maxima: Montauk, 1930–75,000, Jan. 1; 180,000, March 16 (Helmuth); 90,000, Jones Beach, Dec. 7, 1952; 25,000, Mount Sinai, Dec. 25, 1910. Large flocks occur from October to April, and a few are always present each summer—14, Orient, summer of 1916; 150, three miles off Mount Sinai, June 28, 1955.

Rare, but regular inland, often seen flying overhead during migration, sometimes in small flocks.

Remarks: Very closely related to the Palearctic *M. fusca*, the Velvet Scoter, and perhaps conspecific with it; treated as such by Witherby *et al.* (1939) and Delacour (1959).

SURF SCOTER (*Melanitta perspicillata*)*

Range: Nearctic species, breeding south sparingly to northern Saskatchewan, islands in James Bay, and central Labrador.

Status: Common to very abundant migrant and winter visitant on the ocean, and on Long Island Sound, particularly at the eastern end.

Occurrence and maxima: The second most numerous of the scoters off Montauk, occasionally locally outnumbering the White-winged Scoter, but apparently the least numerous species at the west end of Long Island.

Maxima: Montauk, 1930—25,000, Jan. 1; 120,000, March 16 (Helmuth); 5000, Jones Beach, Dec. 7, 1952. Large numbers occur from October to April. Stragglers in summer—50, three miles off Mount Sinai, June 28, 1955.

Occasional on the larger bays. Rarest of the scoters inland.

BLACK SCOTER (*Oidemia nigra*)*

Range: Palearctic and western Nearctic species, the race *americara* breeding from central Siberia east to western Alaska; found in summer, but not reported as breeding, south and east to James Bay and Newfoundland.

143

Status: Common to locally very abundant migrant and winter visitant on the ocean and Long Island Sound, but generally much less numerous than the other scoters, although sometimes outnumbering the Surf Scoter at the western end of Long Island.

Occurrence and maxima: 10,000, Montauk, Jan. 3 and March 16, 1930; 18,000, Jones Beach, Apr. 5, 1936; 600, same area, Sept. 25, 1955.

Numerous from late September to late April. Summer stragglers are rare, but reported in every month. Very rare inland.

Remarks: Called Common Scoter in A.O.U. *Check-list* (1957). The least common of the three species over most of its American range. The name Black Scoter is much more appropriate, as indicated by its technical specific name, and because the male is the only scoter with entirely black plumage. This name is also used by Eisenmann (1955) and Delacour (1959).

RUDDY DUCK (*Oxyura jamaicensis*)*B

Range: Primarily a western Nearctic species; local in the Neotropical region. The race *rubida* breeds east to Manitoba, Iowa, and Illinois; sporadically east to central New York, and very rarely in eastern Massachusetts. First reported breeding on Long Island in 1955 and in northern New Jersey in 1958.

Status: Common to locally abundant fall migrant and winter visitant. Great increase in recent years. Very local breeder.

Change in status: The Ruddy Duck frequents coastal ponds, marshes, brackish estuaries, and shallow bays; also inland lakes and ponds. Prior to 1930 it was reported numerous only at Water Mill and nearby ponds on eastern Long Island, where it was found in concentrations up to 400. This still remains a favorite area.

Since the mid-1940s this species has increased considerably and has been found in large numbers in other localities as well.

Migration and winter: *Coastal maxima*—1200, Mecox Bay, all October 1957; 400, Jamaica Bay Refuge, Nov. 15, 1958; 2000, Water Mill and Mecox Bay, Dec. 13, 1948; 480, Easthampton area, Dec. 31, 1949; 900, Long Branch, N.J., area, all January 1958. *Inland maxima*—750, Hudson River near Nyack, N.Y., Nov. 1, 1955; 200, Jerome Reservoir, Bronx County, Nov. 11, 1956. There are no comparable spring concentrations except at the breeding areas.

Summer: The Ruddy Duck has sometimes remained during the summer months at such places as Tobay Pond, and in 1954 nine individuals summered on Mecox Bay, but in no instance was nesting evidence obtained.

Breeding: In 1955 two nests were built at the Jamaica Bay Refuge, but they were later found destroyed. The following year at least seven pairs nested there. By 1961 it was estimated that 25 broods of young were raised (Johnson, Mayer, *et al.*), and in 1963 an actual count of 40 broods was made (H. Hays). To date (1963) this is the only locality on Long Island where breeding has been confirmed. In the summer of 1958 Wolfarth and Jehl found 30 or more adults on the Hackensack Meadows and on July 27 they discovered several half-grown young. This constitutes the first reported nesting in New Jersey. In 1962 approximately 100 adults were seen at the latter locality, but on July 15 only seven broods of young were counted (Black and Jehl).

Egg dates: No data; however, on the basis of downy young observed in early June, nests with eggs should be found from early to mid-May (incubation about 23 days). This information was kindly furnished by Miss Helen Hays, currently engaged in life-history studies of the Ruddy Duck.

HOODED MERGANSER *(Lophodytes cucullatus)**B

Range: This Nearctic species, although widely distributed in the breeding season from southern Canada to Florida and Louisiana, is nevertheless rare and local in the east during this season south of the northern portions of New York and New England. A number of eastern states are without any breeding records. For example, the following is a summary of the known nesting reports from Massachusetts to Maryland: Massachusetts (four breeding occurrences, 1936–52); Connecticut (one old nesting—also 1937); Rhode Island (none); New York (nearest known breeding, Catskill area); New Jersey (Cape May County, 1949, and see below); Pennsylvania (several old nestings); Maryland (1946 and 1954).

Status: Locally common to very common migrant and winter visitant on the larger ponds, lakes, and reservoirs, both inland and coastal. Great increase since about 1920. One recent breeding record.

Occurrence and maxima: This species, decidedly the least numerous of the mergansers, is essentially a fresh-water duck, but resorts to brackish creeks and coastal ponds during freeze-up periods.

Maxima: 110, Playland Lake, Rye, N.Y., Dec. 5, 1942; 135, Smith's Pond, Rockville Centre, L.I., Dec. 5, 1959; 100, Jamaica Bay Refuge, Dec. 11, 1959.

Usually rare before October and after April.

Remarks: Despite the nearby nesting locations listed above, there was no known breeding record of Hooded Merganser in the New York City area prior to 1962, although there have been several June and July occurrences in wooded swamps in situations similar to those frequented by Wood Ducks. These two species are hole nesters, occupying bird boxes as well as hollow trees and tree holes.

A female and six flightless young were found on a small pond north of Blairstown, Warren County, N.J., June 23, 1962 (Abraitys, Drinkwater, and Edwards).

COMMON MERGANSER (*Mergus merganser*)*

Range: Holarctic species, the race *americanus* breeds south to the central portions of New York and New England (rarely); casually to Pennsylvania and Massachusetts.

Status: Abundant winter visitant on the wider stretches of the Hudson River, and very common on the largest inland lakes and reservoirs. Least numerous on Long Island. Occasional in salt water during severe freezes.

Occurrence and maxima: Primarily a fresh-water species, it is seldom numerous before cold weather sets in around December. Departs in numbers by April after the ice goes out of the inland waters. In recent years, however, it has lingered much later in spring than formerly (prior to 1900), and there are several instances of stragglers remaining into June and even early July. No proof of breeding in our area. Rare before late October.

Maxima: 1500 (70 per cent males), Croton Point, March 15, 1936 (Cruickshank); 2300, Hudson River between Haverstraw and Tomkins Cove—a distance of about four miles—Feb. 24, 1952. On both occasions there was much ice in the Hudson. Other maxima: 500, Kensico Reservoir, Dec. 22, 1935; 140, Central Park Reservoir, Dec. 23, 1945; 175, Water Mill, Feb. 19, 1949; 250, Hempstead Reservoir, March 13, 1949.

Remarks: The name "Goosander" is less confusing than the misleading name "Common." It is the most common merganser on fresh water, but is much less numerous than the Red-breasted Merganser on the coast. Goosander is the name used by Witherby *et al.* (1939) and Delacour (1959). However, it is an unfamiliar name in America.

RED-BREASTED MERGANSER (*Mergus serrator*)*B

Range: Holarctic species, the nominate race breeds south to northern New York (Adirondacks) and the coast of southern Maine; very rarely to the coasts of Massachusetts and Long Island, and casually to New Jersey (Barnegat Bay).

Status: Common to very abundant coastal migrant and winter visitant. Usually rare inland. Regular in summer on the coast (nonbreeders). Very rare breeder.

Migration and winter: This species occurs in the largest numbers in ocean waters of the Montauk area, in Long Island Sound, and on the larger bays. It is occasionally found in small groups in spring on the Hudson River and the larger inland lakes. There are indications that the Red-breasted Merganser is less numerous in our area than it was twenty years ago, when the largest concentrations occurred.

Maxima: *Outer coast*—10,000 Montauk area (Napeague, around the Point, and west to Ditch Plains), Nov. 23, 1937 (Helmuth); "unprecedented" flight, Montauk to Easthampton, late November 1941 (Helmuth) —25,000 on Nov. 27, and at least 40,000 on Nov. 30; 1500, Reynolds Channel, Atlantic Beach, March 11, 1950. *Inner coast*—800, Stony Brook, L.I., Dec. 31, 1939. *Inland*—50, Croton Point, N.Y., March 15, 1936 (big flight of *M. merganser*); 27, Pompton Lakes, N.J., Apr. 21, 1940 (Edwards, Eynon, and Wolfarth).

Breeding: Although this species frequently summers along the coast, there are very few instances of *proved* breeding. Griscom (1923) knew of none. Cruickshank (1942) listed several breeding occurrences on eastern Long Island, based on nests or "very small" young: Fisher's Island (1933 [Ferguson]); Gardiner's Island; Oyster Pond (Montauk); Shinnecock Bay (1912 [Helmuth]); and Mastic.

Since 1942 I have been able to find only one instance of definite breeding: adult female and four young, Jones Inlet (Short Beach), Aug. 3, 1953 (Cantor and Norse)—the first reported nesting on western Long Island.

Egg dates: No data.

AMERICAN VULTURES: CATHARTIDAE

TURKEY VULTURE (*Cathartes aura*)*B

Range: Neotropical and southern Nearctic species, the race *septentrionalis* breeding northeast to central New York, Connecticut, and southwestern Massachusetts. Winters commonly north to Maryland and southern New Jersey; more rarely to the New York City region.

Status: Variously common to uncommon migrant or even resident; wintering locally. Most numerous and widespread west of the Hudson River, but locally fairly common (since 1950) east of the Hudson in Putnam County, N.Y., and Fairfield County, Conn.; rare but regular spring migrant on Long Island. Local breeder.

Change in status: The Turkey Vulture, formerly uncommon to rare over much of the northeast, has increased greatly in recent years, especially since about 1950. This increase has been reflected within the New York City area, except on Long Island where it is still rare. The Turkey Vulture is found most frequently in the interior highlands and is rare and local near the coast, except in Monmouth County, New Jersey.

Migration: Arrives in mid-March and departs by late November. While

147

locally resident in New Jersey, it is essentially a migrant. There is a definite movement in spring and fall, most noticeable on the inland ridges. Migration is heaviest during the fall hawk flights west of the Hudson River.

Maxima: *Fall*—40, Ringwood, N.J., Sept. 2, 1952; 35, Bear Mountain, N.Y., Sept. 21, 1952. *Spring*—9, Mohansic Lake, N.Y., March 29, 1949.

Roosts: The following numbers are very unusual in our area and were unheard of prior to 1954. These roosts are occupied at various times of the year, so that certain populations may be resident, although there has been considerable dispersal observed at several localities. Numbers fluctuate seasonally, but more observation is needed to determine when a given roost is at maximum and minimum.

Maxima: New Jersey—35, near Wanaque Reservoir, Passaic County, early July 1954 (Waldron); 100, Waterloo, Morris County, all March 1958 (Black); New York State—30, near Cornwall, Orange County, Feb. 24, 1955 (Treacy); 127 in hemlock grove, Fahnestock State Park, Putnam County, March 30, 1955 (Brech and Odell).

Other concentrations: New Jersey—up to 15, town dump, Hackensack, Bergen County, winter of 1954 (various observers); Connecticut—up to 20, dump between Wilton and Weston, Fairfield County, same winter (Long).

Breeding: While it breeds locally throughout the mainland areas of our region (chiefly in hilly country), actual nesting sites have been found on very few occasions. The bird nests on the ground—in forested areas, among rocks, in caves, and at the base of hollow trees.

The only definite breeding records that I am aware of are: young in nests near Boonton and Denville, Morris County, N.J., prior to 1923 (Carter, in Griscom, 1923); two eggs and one young in cave (photographed), Lewisboro, Westchester County, N.Y., June 8, 1925 (Howes, 1926), the first nesting reported in New York State; pair at nest in abandoned privy, Andover, Sussex County, N.J., early May 1946 (Thorsell); two eggs in a small cave situated on talus slope, near Bear Mountain, Rockland County, N.Y., May 4, 1955 (Orth); pair nested in a cave near Blooming Grove, Orange County, N.Y., in the late 1950s (M. Earl). There may be others, but nests are difficult to find.

Egg dates: May 4 to June 12.

Remarks: Two possible factors in the recent spread and increase of the Turkey Vulture are suggested: (*a*) great increase in the deer population—during recent winters starvation and disease because of overpopulation has supplied more deer carcasses; (*b*) construction of many new highways with an upsurge of speeding traffic, resulting in the killing of numerous small mammals, reptiles, etc., has provided another source of food.

Not to be overlooked is the amelioration of the climate within recent years that has possibly resulted in a northward dispersal of this and other species belonging to the "southern" element.

148

BLACK VULTURE (*Coragyps atratus*)*

Very rare visitant: Primarily a Neotropical species; resident through much of its breeding range. Locally common through much of the south, but less numerous than the Turkey Vulture in most areas. Breeds as far north as southern Ohio and Maryland; nested in southern Pennsylvania (near Gettysburg) in 1952. Wanders north to southern Canada.

In our area the Black Vulture is a possibility at any time of year, having been reported in every month but January and November, although more than half of the 24 reports have occurred in spring. All occurrences have been of single individuals. Of the following four specimens taken, only one is apparently extant: Sandy Hook, spring 1877 (Lawrence collection), shot while feeding on a pig carcass; Coney Island, 1881 (Le Berier), picked up dead on the beach; Plum Island, May 19 or 20, 1896 (Braislin collection), shot while feeding on a dead sheep; Shelter Island, Dec. 22, 1925 (Latham), specimen in his collection. Over the years Latham has observed this species on six occasions in the Orient area, four times in June and twice in May, all in different years.

HAWKS: ACCIPITRIDAE

SWALLOW-TAILED KITE (*Elanoïdes forficatus*)*

Casual: Primarily a Neotropical species, the nominate race breeding north to South Carolina. Wanders north very rarely to southern Canada and northern New England.

Only two of ten local reports are supported by specimens, neither apparently extant: Raynor South (now Freeport), 1837 (Giraud) and Chatham, N.J., 1873 (Herrick). The following two reports were of birds seen (not collected, as erroneously stated in the literature): south shore, Long Island, 1845 (Akhurst), who spent an unsuccessful day trying to secure it (Bull. Nuttall Ornith. Club, 6: 126, 1881); Piermont, N.Y., Aug. 22, 1900 (Nicholas), bird seen, observer previously familiar with the species in the south (Auk, 17: 386, 1900). The following six observations were made by experienced people: Stamford, Conn., May 2, 1907 (Howes); Orient, May 28, 1927 (Latham); Chappaqua, N.Y., Oct. 2, 1927 (Pangburn); University Heights, Bronx County, Apr. 30, 1928 (Hickey and Cruickshank); Raritan River marshes between Fords and Nixon, May 19, 1940 (Cant, Fables, and Rapp); Jamaica Bay Refuge, Sept. 2, 1956 (Mayer).

For a recent paper on this species, see Rapp (1944). In this account he omitted the Orient observation and included a Morristown, N.J., report which Griscom (1923) considered unsatisfactory.

GOSHAWK (*Accipiter gentilis*)*

Range: Holarctic species, the race *atricapillus* breeds south to the mountainous portions of Massachusetts, New York, and Pennsylvania; casually to northwestern Connecticut and western Maryland.

Status: Rare and irregular winter visitant; uncommon, but regular fall migrant along the inland ridges. At long intervals fairly common in flight years, both inland and along the inside coast.

Occurrence and maxima: Goshawks are occasionally numerous from late October through December, when many are shot around game farms and by hunters. Within the present century there have been several marked flights, that of 1926 being the largest by far.

Maxima, *flight years:* fall of 1917—16 shot, Fisher's Island (Ferguson); 16 killed, Stag Lake, N.J. (Von Lengerke); 1926—over 50 shot at the latter locality, Oct. 10 to early Dec. (*fide* Von Lengerke)—with a total of 9 adults between Nov. 4 and 28, all in A.M.N.H. collection; 5 adults shot on Fisher's Island between Dec. 7 and 10 (Ferguson), all in the A.M.N.H.; 1944—8 or 9 reported shot in northern Westchester County, late fall (*fide* Townsend), and according to Grierson (*in litt.*) at least 12 killed in the White Plains area.

Maxima, *non-flight years:* 5, "Raccoon Ridge," N.J., Oct. 27, 1940; 3, same locality, Nov. 6, 1951.

Extreme dates: Oct. 3 and 7 (specimen) to Apr. 19 (specimen) and Apr. 29. While earlier fall and later spring reports are possibly correct, no adequate confirmation was available. Confusion of immature Goshawks with immature Cooper's Hawks is likely. Rare before late October and after March.

SHARP-SHINNED HAWK (*Accipiter striatus*)*B

Range: Nearctic and northern Neotropical species, breeding from Alaska and Canada to Mexico and the West Indies. The race *velox* occurs in our area.

Status: Common to occasionally abundant fall migrant. Generally rare in winter. Uncommon breeder. Formerly more numerous.

Migration: The Sharp-shinned Hawk is usually found in the largest numbers along the inland ridges, lesser flights occurring on the coast (but see below).

Maxima: *Inland*—110, Van Cortlandt Park, Bronx County, Sept. 18, 1951; 230, Montclair, N.J., Sept. 21, 1948; 140, "Raccoon Ridge," N.J., Oct. 15, 1939. *Coastal*—50, Far Rockaway, L.I., Sept. 24, 1950. No comparable spring maxima at hand.

The following data indicate that this species was more numerous at one time. Ferguson (*in litt.*) states that on Fisher's Island this species was, "Formerly a very common fall transient, now much rarer. Huge flights used to occur in September." In the days of hawk-shooting, owl decoys were used for these "shoots." Large numbers of Sharp-shins were shot from 1917 to 1921, but in 1919 and 1920 unprecedented numbers were taken. In the former year 472 were killed, and in the latter year the astounding total of 850. The maximum numbers per day were 406 shot on Sept. 19, 1920. It is not surprising that it has decreased within the last forty years.

Breeding: This species breeds in forested areas. It usually nests in conifers, preferably in pine and hemlock, rarely in deciduous trees. It is scarcer than the Cooper's Hawk as a breeding species, although greatly outnumbering the latter on migration.

Egg dates: May 5 to June 11.

COOPER'S HAWK (*Accipiter cooperii*)*B

Range: Nearctic species, breeding from southern Canada to northern Mexico and the Gulf states.

Status: Fairly common to common fall migrant. Uncommon to rare, but regular in winter. Fairly common breeder. Compared to the Sharp-shinned Hawk, it is more widespread in summer, less rare in winter, but much less numerous in migration.

Migration: Height of the fall migration is during October. Cruickshank (1942) stated that it is unusual to see over 50 in a day on the ridges of New Jersey. I have no significant data more recent for our area. Broun (1935) lists a maximum of 42 at Hawk Mountain, Penn., Oct. 8, 1934. It is certainly the least numerous of the regular hawks of the *Accipiter* and *Buteo* types that fly along the ridges.

Breeding: The Cooper's Hawk is found chiefly in low, alluvial woodlands, nesting most frequently in deciduous trees—often in old crow nests—but commonly building its own nest. It is found in the same type of country frequented by the Red-shouldered Hawk.

Egg dates: Apr. 16 to June 12.

RED-TAILED HAWK (*Buteo jamaicensis*)*B

Range: Nearctic and northern Neotropical species, breeding from Alaska and Canada to Panama and the West Indies. The race *borealis* breeds in our area.

Status: Common to abundant fall migrant, less numerous in spring; locally common in winter. Local breeder.

Migration: One of the features of the *fall* migration is the spectacular flights of this species in late October and November along the inland ridges: 450, "Raccoon Ridge," N.J., Nov. 4, 1952 (Darrow and Herbert); 150, Bear Mountain, N.Y., Nov. 6, 1951. Much less numerous in *spring:* coastal flight in 1943—30, Prospect Park, March 20; 24, Orient, March, 26.

Winter: Rare inland, but locally common in the large marshes on the mainland, frequenting rat-infested garbage dumps: 24, Pelham Bay area, Dec. 27, 1942; 14, Hackensack Meadows, Dec. 30, 1945. These numbers were taken from the Audubon Christmas counts and there is the possibility of some duplication involved, as Red-tails cover a lot of territory.

Breeding: The Red-tailed Hawk has decreased considerably in the past thirty years or so. It breeds in the wilder sections of the interior highlands and in the pine and oak barrens of eastern Long Island. Breeding distribution is similar to that of the Great Horned Owl.

In the Long Island pine barrens, Helmuth (diary) called it a common breeder prior to 1930, nesting pairs present at Hither Woods, Northwest Woods, and between Georgica and Poxabogue; has greatly decreased since; still to be found in the pine barrens farther west.

Latham (1957), speaking of the north fluke of Long Island, stated that they nest mainly in large oaks, also pines. Formerly breeding at Orient and Greenport, now confined to the wildest sections.

On the mainland, occurs chiefly in the highlands of northern New Jersey, less common elsewhere.

Egg dates: March 17 to May 6.

Subspecies: This species is polymorphic, especially in the west, exhibiting a great deal of individual variation, as well as being geographically variable. The race *calurus*, breeding north and west of *B. j. borealis*, has occurred in Pennsylvania, New Jersey, and New York.

Several specimens have been reported from our area. Friedmann (1950) lists a specimen from Andover, N.J. (date not stated). Parkes (1952) examined three specimens of *B. j. abieticola* (= *calurus*) taken in New York: adult male, Huntington, L.I., Feb. 10, 1922, A.M.N.H. No. 168728; adult male, West Point, March 20, 1927, U.S.N.M. No. 307938; adult female, Ossining, Nov. 5, 1921, Cornell University Museum No. 966.

RED-SHOULDERED HAWK (*Buteo lineatus*)*B

Range: Nearctic species, breeding from Nebraska and southern Quebec to northern Mexico and the Gulf states; also in California. The nominate race breeds in our area.

Status: Common to locally abundant migrant inland; rare to uncommon in winter. Fairly common breeder in the lowlands of the interior, but rare any time on Long Island.

Migration: Although regular in some numbers on migration along the inland ridges, the available evidence indicates that the bulk of migrants occur just in from the coast on the mainland. Indeed in Maryland, Stewart and Robbins (1958) state, "During migration in the fall this species tends to concentrate along the fall line of the Piedmont Section."

The same thing is true in our area, the birds being most numerous near the shoreline of Connecticut and Westchester County, N.Y., and in the lowlands of New Jersey southeast of the Piedmont. The species usually avoids the entire coastal plain, however, where it is very rare. Thus at Cape May, N.J., during the autumn of 1935, Stone (1937) mentions a total of only 12 Red-shoulders as against 50 Red-tails and hundreds of Broad-wings.

That Red-shouldered Hawks are most numerous along the inside coast and relatively uncommon on the ridges of the interior is indicated by the following maxima: *Spring*—290, Rutherford, N.J., March 18, 1944. *Fall*—122, Tuckahoe, N.Y., Oct. 29, 1944 (80 of these in one hour, and all but 2 of the 122, adults); only 45, "Raccoon Ridge," N.J., Oct. 15, 1939 (compared with 140 Red-tails).

Breeding: The Red-shouldered Hawk is most prevalent in lowland forests and wooded swamps on the mainland. It is rare and local at higher elevations, on the north shore of Long Island, and nearly absent from the entire coastal plain. However, it was formerly common on Staten Island, no fewer than 13 nesting pairs found in 1908 (Chapin and Cleaves). The breeding distribution is similar to that of the Barred Owl.

Egg dates: March 28 to June 12.

BROAD-WINGED HAWK *(Buteo platypterus)**B

Range: Essentially an eastern Nearctic species, breeding from Alberta and New Brunswick to Texas and Florida; also in the West Indies. The nominate race breeds in our area.

Status: Abundant, occasionally very abundant fall migrant inland; much less numerous in spring. Local breeder.

Migration: The Broad-winged Hawk occurs in spectacular fall flights inland, chiefly during the latter half of September, and is unquestionably our most numerous migrant hawk. These flights occur on a fairly broad front and are by no means confined to the ridges. Very rarely small flights occur along the coast, but they are exceptional. The spring movements are always on a much smaller scale and take place in April or early May.

Maxima: *Fall*—4300, "Raccoon Ridge," N.J., Sept. 20, 1952; big flight on Sept. 21, 1948—Van Cortlandt Park, N.Y. (2500) and Montclair, N.J. (2100); another large flight in New Jersey on Sept. 16, 1945—Paterson

(2000), Montclair (1500), Hackensack (400); on Sept. 22, 1945—Montclair, N.J. (2000) and Van Cortlandt Park, N.Y. (2700). Small coastal flight on Sept. 24, 1950—Prospect Park (200) and Far Rockaway, L.I. (40, with 15 in one flock). *Spring*—80, Paterson, Apr. 11, 1953; 380, Montclair, Apr. 19, 1947; 100, Ridgewood, Apr. 26, 1944; 30, Prospect Park, May 6, 1946.

"Extreme" dates: early April to late October: collected at Point Pleasant, N.J., Nov. 1, 1875 (A.M.N.H.).

Breeding: The breeding distribution of this species is similar to that of the Red-tailed Hawk, the species being most prevalent in the higher sections of the interior and in the pine-oak barrens of eastern Long Island. Being more inconspicuous than the latter species the Broad-winged Hawk has not decreased as much through persecution.

Speaking of eastern Long Island, Helmuth (diary) said, "From six to eight pairs nest between Easthampton and Sag Harbor, and today [1947] it is much more generally distributed as a summer resident than the Red-tail." Latham (1957), referring to the same general area, stated that it nests "sociably" with Red-tails on occasion.

Egg dates: May 4 to June 17.

Remarks: This species winters chiefly in northern South America from Brazil to Peru; casually north to the Mexican states of Veracruz and Sinaloa (see A.O.U. *Check-list*, 1957). It is very rarely reported in winter in southern Florida. Sprunt (1949) lists only one winter specimen for South Carolina and perhaps one or two "good" sight reports. Stewart and Robbins (1958) do not mention any winter occurrences for Maryland, and Griscom and Snyder (1955) have accepted none for Massachusetts. Stone (1937) stated that published winter reports for New Jersey may refer to Red-shouldered Hawks.

In view of this it is impossible to believe the rash of sight reports from the New York City region, the vast majority within the past 25 years. Most of these are completely worthless.

Actually there is one known winter specimen reported from this area: immature collected at Stamford, Conn., Jan. 12, 1929 (D. Shipley), identification confirmed by J. T. Nichols (Auk, 47: 417, 1930). This merely proves that the species has definitely occurred *once* in our area in winter. There are two sight reports of individuals, with the details known, which are probably correct: a badly crippled bird near a garbage dump, Van Cortlandt Park, Dec. 7, 1933 to Feb. 7, 1934 (Cruickshank, and many others); a very sluggish individual, suspected of being sick or injured, Troy Meadows, Dec. 23, 1951 (Edwards), was not reported later and perhaps did not survive.

Readers are referred to Griscom's excellent account (1923) on the difficulties of identification. The writer has come across more than two dozen winter "reports," including a number published, especially those on Christmas counts. None, except for the two sight reports mentioned

154

above, was adequately confirmed or had details published. Furthermore, most sight reports were made by beginners.

In short, the winter reports are out of all proportion to the known facts.

SWAINSON'S HAWK (*Buteo swainsoni*)*

Accidental: A western Nearctic species, breeding east to western Minnesota; rarely to Illinois. Winters mainly in Argentina, but in recent years (1952 on) fairly common in southern Florida, indeed an anomaly. Casual in migration in the northeast, but at least four specimens taken in Massachusetts and two in northern New York.

In our area an adult was collected at Cornwall, N.Y., Oct. 14, 1892, specimen identified by Howell (Dutcher, Auk, 10: 83, 1893). The present whereabouts of this specimen is not known. There is also a recent sight report, probably correct: adult, Oradell, N.J., Oct. 22, 1947 (C. K. Nichols, familiar with the species in the west).

ROUGH-LEGGED HAWK (*Buteo lagopus*)*

Range: Holarctic species, the race *sancti-johannis* breeds south to southeastern Quebec and Newfoundland.

Status: Uncommon to rare and irregular winter visitant.

Occurrence and maxima: The Rough-legged Hawk is found most frequently on the larger coastal and tidal river marshes, often near garbage dumps, where it is attracted by large rodent populations. During most seasons only one or two are reported, chiefly at the east end of Long Island, but in flight years this species is more widespread. Rare along the inland ridges.

Maxima, *outer coast:* 7, Montauk, Nov. 25, 1934; 9, Gardiner's Island, Dec. 23, 1924. Maxima, *elsewhere:* 6, Pelham Bay area, Dec. 23, 1951; 6, Hackensack Meadows, Dec. 30, 1945.

Extreme dates: Oct. 6 to May 13. Rare before late October and after mid-April.

Remarks: As is well known, this species has two basic color phases—light and dark—although intermediates do occur. Examination of skins in the American Museum taken locally reveals that the light phase predominates. Of 24 specimens, only four are in the dark phase, one of these from Stag Lake, N.J., Nov. 13, 1926 (Von Lengerke), the only known inland specimen from our area. Three out of four taken at Montauk between Dec. 6 and 15, 1897, are in the light phase.

155

GOLDEN EAGLE (*Aquila chrysaëtos*)*

Range: Holarctic species, the race *canadensis* breeds east and south to the northern portions of Ontario and Quebec; very rarely and locally to northern New York, northern New England, and—until recently—in the more remote mountainous areas south to North Carolina and Tennessee.

Status: Rare to locally uncommon, but regular migrant along the inland ridges. Casual elsewhere.

Occurrence and maxima: The Golden Eagle occurs most frequently during the latter half of October and November in the mountainous sections of northwestern New Jersey—"Raccoon Ridge" in the Kittatinny Mountains being a particularly favorable place to see it. The famous Hawk Mountain in Pennsylvania is, more or less, a continuation of this ridge (the Kittatinnies), where Golden Eagles are observed in some numbers each fall.

Maxima: "Raccoon Ridge"—8, Oct. 22, 1944 (Urner Club); 8, including 5 adults, Nov. 5, 1946 (Darrow and Herbert); on the latter date at Hawk Mountain, 13 were reported (Broun, 1948).

Extreme dates: Sept. 18 and 22 (specimen) to March 2. Excessively rare in spring—Apr. 19, 1950, Great Swamp, N.J. (Cant and Hunn). In view of these dates it is difficult to understand the statement of Cruickshank (1942) that it "... has been *seen* in every month except July, but summer records are very few. ..." (Italics mine.) I am afraid that these "summer records" are based on misidentifications of inexperienced observers confused by immature Bald Eagles with white in the plumage. Moreover, no Golden Eagles have been reported by reliable and competent observers between April and September within the past twenty years, nor are there any local specimens taken at that season.

Specimen data: Of 16 specimens taken locally (there may be others), at least seven are known to be extant—three from inland areas and four from Long Island: adult, Katonah, N.Y., early winter of 1912 (*fide* Wheeler), mounted specimen in the Poundridge Reservation Museum; adult female, Culver's Gap, N.J., Nov. 27, 1918 (Von Lengerke) A.M.N.H. No. 142875; adult, Bear Mountain, N.Y., Dec. 31, 1941 (Carr) A.M.N.H. No. 308895; adult, Long Island, no date (Lawrence collection) A.M.N.H. No. 54064; Fisher's Island, Suffolk County—Oct. 12, 1924, Oct. 12, 1926, and Nov. 20, 1954 (Ferguson), all immatures, in his collection.

Remarks: While this species was supposed to have bred in our area at one time, and possibly did so, there is uncertainty regarding its nesting. Griscom (1923) merely stated, "... apparently bred in the Hudson Highlands," and he more than likely based this information on Mearns (1878). The latter remarked, "Formerly quite characteristic of this wild mountainous area, is now becoming quite scarce. Formerly *known* to nest on the cliffs on the west side of the Hudson, north of West Point, and perhaps

156

at least one pair still does, although I have *never actually found* a nest. However, I occasionally see it in winter." (Italics mine.)

BALD EAGLE (*Haliaeetus leucocephalus*)*B

Range: Nearctic species, breeding from Alaska and Canada to Baja California, the Gulf states, and Florida.

Status: Generally rare, but locally fairly common winter visitant and fall migrant; rare summer visitant. Very rare breeder. Reported every month of the year.

Nonbreeding: The Bald Eagle was much more numerous and widespread in former years. Giraud (1844) tells of 60 to 70 individuals having been shot on Long Island during one winter season. Mearns (1878) stated, "In early spring when the ice breaks up, I have counted more than twenty-five that were in view at once." He was referring to the Hudson River near Cornwall, N.Y.

The continued decrease in the east for many years has been due to (*a*) shooting, trapping, and egging—although protected by federal law for some time; (*b*) removal of nest trees; and (*c*) very likely an increased use of insecticides, suspected of indirectly causing sterility in adult eagles by their feeding on "contaminated" fish.

Bald Eagles are largely restricted to lakes, rivers, and coastal estuaries, although during the migrations they occur also along mountain ridges.

Maxima: *Winter*—18, Croton Point, Feb 11, 1951 (Darrow), "much ice in Hudson River"; one to six birds are usually observed here. This is by far the best place in winter to observe Bald Eagles. They may be seen close up—perched in trees at the tip of the point or on ice cakes in the river; during mild winters few if any are seen. *Fall*—17, "Raccoon Ridge," Sept. 11, 1939; 16, Montclair, Sept. 10–21, 1941; good flight in 1950— 6, Van Cortlandt Park, Sept. 17, and 5 more there Sept. 24; 5, Idlewild, latter date (Mayer)—an unusual number for the coast. It should be pointed out that the winter maxima listed above represent a count of birds in view at *one time*, whereas the fall maxima represent a count for the *entire day*.

Breeding: Nests inland in the vicinity of mountain lakes; more rarely along the coast near tidal estuaries—in former years especially in the Shrewsbury section of New Jersey. Fisher found it breeding locally near the Hudson River in the vicinity of Ossining from the 1870s to the 1890s. It undoubtedly bred in the more remote areas of New Jersey, Long Island, and elsewhere, but we have little information regarding this.

In more recent years, it nested on Gardiner's Island, off Long Island, until 1930 (*fide* Latham). Fables (1955) stated for New Jersey, "It formerly bred near Delaware Water Gap, Warren County and Greenwood Lake,

Passaic County, and in 1952 nested near Splitrock Pond in Morris County. There are records also for Red Bank, Monmouth County. . . ." As recently as the spring of 1957, one "active" nest was located in Monmouth County (Russell Peterson). In 1957 at least 15 nests were reported in southern New Jersey, south of our area (*fide* Potter), but by 1961 only one out of seven nests contained young, according to F. McLaughlin (see comments above for decrease).

Egg dates: No data.

Subspecies: The smaller, southern nominate race supposedly breeds as far north as Virginia; see A.O.U. *Check-list* (1957, footnote, pp. 113–114), indicating uncertainty as to the breeding limits of the two subspecies. It is possible that our region is in the zone of intermediacy between nominate *leucocephalus* and the larger, northern subspecies *alascanus* insofar as breeding birds are concerned. *H. l. alascanus* is alleged to breed south to Pennsylvania, New Jersey, and Maryland, but this is questionable.

At any rate, individuals of the southern population from as far south as Florida regularly wander north after the breeding season, chiefly in late spring and summer. This has been proved by banding. These eagles were mostly immatures, which returned south in early fall.

On the other hand, some of the winter individuals on the Hudson River may well be *H. l. alascanus* from the north. There are two local specimens, apparently this form, in the American Museum collection: immature male, Highland Falls, N.Y., March 27, 1883 (Mearns), A.M.N.H. No. 54767; immature female, Southampton, L.I., Jan. 2, 1885 (E. A. Green), A.M.N.H. No. 98726. The wing measurement (chord) of the male is 605 mm., that of the female, 637 mm., both of which are well within the limits of *H. l. alascanus*, according to Friedmann (1950).

Friedmann (*op. cit.*) and Brown and Amadon (in press), although recognizing two forms, are of the opinion that there is a gradual north—south cline diminishing in size over a broad area from Alaska to Florida.

MARSH HAWK (*Circus cyaneus*)*B

Range: Holarctic species, the race *hudsonius* breeds south to Virginia.

Status: Fairly common to common fall migrant and winter visitant on the outer coast. Much less numerous inland. Has decreased as a breeder—now relatively rare and local.

Migration: Regular inland in small numbers, even along the ridges. Marsh Hawks are most numerous in the vicinity of coastal marshes.

Fall maxima—45, Fire Island Inlet, Sept. 27, 1952 (Darrow); 46 shot on Fisher's Island, Oct. 5, 1921 (Ferguson); 24, Easthampton, Oct. 9, 1932.

Winter: 15, Troy Meadows, Dec. 23, 1951, a mild, open season; 40, Brooklyn to Montauk, 1953 Christmas counts. A roost of nearly 50 was reported in an open meadow near Flemington, N.J., winter of 1961–62 (Abraitys), a most unusual occurrence.

Breeding: The Marsh Hawk, as its name implies, nests in the larger marshes, chiefly along the outer coast of Long Island and New Jersey, and to a lesser extent on the larger tidal marshes of Newark Bay, the Hackensack Meadows, and the Hudson River; also in the inland marshes, such as Troy Meadows, Great Swamp, and adjacent areas, but has greatly decreased. Latham (1957), referring to eastern Long Island, found that nearly all nests were situated in cattails.

Egg dates: Apr. 25 to June 16.

OSPREYS: PANDIONIDAE

OSPREY (*Pandion haliaetus*)*B

Range: Nearly cosmopolitan species, but not reported to breed in America south of British Honduras. The race *carolinensis* occurs in our area.

Status: Fairly common to common migrant, especially along the coast; usually uncommon inland, but occasionally common (see maximum numbers below). Locally common to formerly very common breeder on extreme eastern Long Island, but has decreased considerably of late years; uncommon to rare elsewhere.

Migration: Ospreys occur chiefly in the vicinity of water, but may be seen flying overhead almost anywhere during migration.

Maxima: *Spring*—50, Orient, Apr. 1, 1944; 47, Montclair, Apr. 19, 1947 (Eynon). *Fall*—135, Mecox to Shinnecock bays, Sept. 2, 1929 (Helmuth); 44, Sherwood Island, off Westport, Conn., Sept. 12, 1954; 42, Montclair, Sept. 17, 1944 (Urner Club); 21, Far Rockaway, Oct. 13, 1950. The above numbers at Montclair, N.J., would seem to indicate that, at times, there is considerable movement inland.

Extreme dates: March 10 and 16 to Dec. 7. Rare before late March and after early November.

Breeding: The Osprey, or Fish Hawk, nests in a variety of places such as trees, the tops of telephone poles, old buildings, and elevated platforms; and even in low bushes, and on the ground.

Formerly a numerous breeder on the islands at the east end of Long Island, it has recently become much less numerous, supposedly due to interference from Herring Gulls which have greatly increased of late years. However, Ospreys nest in some places where Herring Gulls do not breed, and it is possible that the use of insecticides has been a cause of decrease in Ospreys—that is, sterility in adult Ospreys from feeding on "contaminated" fish.

The largest and best-known colony is located on Gardiner's Island. According to Chapman (1908) at least 300 nests were present there in the early nineteenth century and in 1908 he estimated between 150 and 200 nests. It was considered the largest Osprey colony in the world. Most of the nest sites were in trees, with at least ten nests on the ground. Wilcox (*in litt.*), who banded about 1000 Ospreys on Long Island between 1935 and 1950, stated that as recently as 1958 there were as many as 60 ground nests on Gardiner's Island, but that by 1961 only 2 occupied nests were located there. However, in 1962 at least 21 "active" nests were counted on the north end of the island.

The Osprey has decreased also at Orient Point (25 nests in 1951), and on Shelter Island, at which latter locality in 1961 there were 30 active nests. On Fisher's Island there were six nests in 1961 (Ferguson).

Elsewhere on the coast it is decidedly rare and local—practically unknown on Long Island west of Peconic Bay, although one pair nested at Mastic in 1945 (J. T. Nichols). On the north shore it has been found much farther west. Bred at Mill Neck in 1960 and 1962, and in the latter year also at Oyster Bay (Yeaton). On the north Jersey coast it still nests on Sandy Hook, the exact number of pairs not reported. In 1946, 12 nests were located from Belmar to Manasquan.

A very poor season was reported in 1963 on eastern Long Island and along the coast of northern New Jersey; very few eggs hatched—perhaps due to pesticides.

Inland it has always been very rare, and perhaps a few may still breed in the vicinity of lakes and rivers.

Egg dates: Apr. 18 to June 12.

Remarks: This species winters north to central Florida; rarely to South Carolina, and very rarely to Maryland.

In the New York City area it has been reported every month! Occurrences on Dec. 16, 22, 25, and 27, and as early as March 1 may represent stragglers that wintered not far to the south of us. There are two midwinter sight reports of birds well observed on Long Island and probably correct: Smithtown, Feb. 14, 1926 (L. Turrell); one seen perched on a dead tree stub, Hither Hills, Montauk, Jan. 12, 1957 (M. Russak).

FALCONS: FALCONIDAE

GYRFALCON (*Falco rusticolus*)*

Very rare winter visitant: Holarctic species of high latitudes, the race *obsoletus* breeds south to northern Quebec and northern Labrador. Mainly resident, but winters south very irregularly to southern New England and Long Island. No definite evidence of occurrence (specimens) south of Long Island.

To avoid confusion, the color terms used here for this polymorphic species include only dark and light phases. The terminology in the older literature, such as white, light, "normal," gray, dark, and black, has been used indiscriminately and interchangeably. Actually there is no such thing as a "black" gyrfalcon. Adults range from pure white to dark gray. Dark immatures are sooty brown, not unlike first-year Herring Gulls. As Friedmann (1950) has indicated, a wide range of variation occurs and birds of different color phases may be found in the same nest, although he recognizes the form *obsoletus*. Vaurie (Amer. Mus. Novitates, 2038: 3–8, 1961), and Brown and Amadon (in press), would treat *F. rusticolus* as monotypic, stating that variation is of individual rather than of geographical nature in most of the range.

Of 11 local specimens taken, *all* are reported to be in the dark phase; the whereabouts of six are unknown. Griscom (1923) listed four Long Island specimens taken in 1856, 1875, 1877, and 1899; and one collected in Westchester County, N.Y., in 1879. Cruickshank (1942) in addition, listed one from Oceanside, L.I., "about" 1929.

The five known local extant specimens are: One taken at Stamford, Conn., fall of 1888 (C. E. Rowell), A.M.N.H. No. 750415—this specimen is not mentioned by Sage *et al.* (1913), Forbush (1927), or Howes (1928), and is published here for the first time; four shot on Fisher's Island by Ferguson are in his collection: one taken on Oct. 15, 1915, was examined by Chapman; the others were taken on Oct. 28, 1925, Oct. 30, 1926, and Oct. 12, 1929. Ferguson (*in litt.*) states that all were "shot as they came to owl decoys." These Fisher's Island specimen records are published here for the first time. It is surprising that in view of nine Long Island specimens, there is no *proved* occurrence for New Jersey or farther south.

Out of a total of more than 20 sight reports, only three are of the light phase, the so-called "White" Gyrfalcon: (*a*) an old report from Miller Place, L.I. (date not stated) by Helme, who was unable to secure the specimen; (*b*) Jones Inlet, Jan. 8, 1939 (Pough), the same day a dark-phase bird was observed by Cruickshank only a half-mile away; (*c*) Montauk Point, Jan. 23, 1939 (Helmuth), perhaps the same individual seen at Jones Inlet.

Extreme dates: Oct. 8 and 12 (specimen) to mid-March. Earlier fall and later spring dates lack confirmation and several published inland reports are without adequate details. In addition there are several unsatisfactory Christmas count reports made by inexperienced observers.

While the field guides and the literature emphasize a similarity between this species and the immature Peregrine Falcon, many observers are unaware that the dark-phase Rough-legged Hawk bears a superficial resemblance to the Gyrfalcon, especially when perched. While their flight is somewhat different, the relative proportions of the two are similar. First of all, many dark Rough-legs lack the white patch at the base of the tail; second, both species have relatively short wings and long tails. In view of this, it is believed that a number of sight reports attributed to be Gyrfalcons may be nothing more than Peregrine Falcons or Rough-legged Hawks.

When Gyrfalcon "flights" occur, as during the winters of 1938–39 and 1944–45, individuals were reported by reliable observers, in some instances confirmed by several competent people. These "flights" may contain as many as three or four different individuals, but Gyrfalcons cover a lot of territory and allowance should be made for possible duplication. An unfortunate situation arises following the "genuine" observations, when a rash of sight reports made by persons unfamiliar with this species and lacking experience with the other raptors confused with it leads the writer to believe that probably less than half the Gyrfalcon reports are worthy of acceptance.

PEREGRINE FALCON (*Falco peregrinus*)*B

Range: A nearly cosmopolitan species, the race *anatum* occurs in our area.

Status: Fairly common fall migrant on the outer coast. Rare, local resident and breeder.

Migration and winter: This species may be seen at any time of the year. During the colder months it roosts on tall buildings in cities and large towns, feeding on or chasing the all-too-numerous pigeons and starlings.

It is along the beaches of the outer coast in fall, however, where they occur in numbers, especially from mid-September to late October.

Maxima: 12, Fisher's Island, Oct. 4, 1920; 10, Far Rockaway, Oct. 13, 1950. On Oct. 10, 1959, at Jones Beach, C. Ward observed 18 within a six-hour period, and a total of 33 between Oct. 2 and 12 of the same year. Twelve were shot on Fisher's Island, Oct. 28, 1921 (Ferguson). Ordinarily up to six are seen in a day.

Breeding: The Peregrine Falcon, or Duck Hawk as it was formerly called, nests on the few precipitous cliffs available along the Hudson River. From six to eight or more eyries have been occupied from time to time on the Palisades and in the Hudson Highlands and one or more elsewhere, but disturbance by eggers, falconers, and picnickers has resulted in desertion of several sites. In addition to these cliff nesting sites, the species has attempted to nest on a bridge, and on the ledge of a mid-Manhattan skyscraper, although in the latter instance a pair actually bred on the St. Regis Hotel in 1943 (*fide* Herbert), the young were killed later.

For a detailed account of its former breeding status in the east, see Hickey (1942).

162

In 1958 a female laid eggs on the steel framework at the west end of the Bear Mountain bridge. The eggs, placed on the bare metal, invariably cracked as a result of excessive heat from the sun. (E. Treacy, *in litt.*)

A current survey of local eyries would be most desirable.

Egg dates: March 28 to June 12.

PIGEON HAWK (*Falco columbarius*)*

Range: Holarctic species, the nominate race breeds south to northern Michigan, southern Ontario, New Brunswick, and Nova Scotia. Reported as breeding south to "northern New York, New Hampshire (probably), Maine" (A.O.U. *Check-list,* 1957: 121), but actual nesting in these states questioned by Eaton (1914), Forbush (1927), and Palmer (1949).

Status: Common to very common fall migrant on the outer coast. Much less numerous in spring. Uncommon to rare inland.

Occurrence and maxima: The Pigeon Hawk, or Merlin, is most frequently observed along the beaches during September and the first half of October.

Maxima: *Fall*—66 shot on Fisher's Island, Sept. 13, 1921 (Ferguson); 40 in four hours, Far Rockaway, Sept. 16, 1950; 60, Easthampton, Sept. 18, 1930; 35 in one hour, Westhampton to Shinnecock Inlet, Sept. 21, 1955; 30, Saltaire, Fire Island, Sept. 30, 1956; 40, Jones Beach, Oct. 9, 1961; 25, Jones Beach, Oct. 17, 1935. *Spring*—12, Sandy Hook, Apr. 11, 1953.

"Extreme" dates: *Fall*—Aug. 5, 12, and various later dates, Sept. 2. (specimen) to late October, Nov. 1 (specimen), and exceptionally to Nov. 22 (specimen). *Spring*—late March and early April to May 21 (specimen), May 26, and 28. Rare before April and after October.

Remarks: This species winters primarily from Mexico to northern South America; occasionally north to the southern portions of Texas, Louisiana, Florida, etc.; very rarely to South Carolina. Casual north to Long Island (specimen) and Massachusetts (specimen).

In our area there is one definite winter record: One collected at Mount Sinai, L.I., Dec. 31, 1903, by Murphy (Griscom, 1923). Of more than 800 collected on Fisher's Island between 1914 and 1928, *none* was ever taken in winter (Ferguson, *in litt.*). Although there are several midwinter sight reports by reliable and experienced observers, including one that was seen at Canarsie, L.I., from Jan. 25 to Feb. 23, 1948 (Amadon), I suspect that many others were based on misidentified "sooty" Sparrow Hawks and immature Sharp-shinned Hawks.

As to alleged summer occurrences, Cruickshank (1942) stated that ". . . there are *apparently* reliable records of non-breeding individuals that remained throughout the summer." (Italics mine.) In my opinion the remarks on identification, under winter status above are also applicable to

163

June and July "occurrences." There are no specimens or other adequate evidence to confirm that this species summers, although it is possible that a few individuals might occur in early June.

SPARROW HAWK (*Falco sparverius*)*B

Range: A widespread American species, ranging from Alaska and Canada to extreme southern South America. The nominate race occurs in our area.

Status: Common to abundant coastal migrant; regular inland in small numbers. Widely distributed, but usually an uncommon breeder. Least numerous in winter.

Migration: Most numerous along the beaches of the outer coast; in spring —chiefly in April; in fall—last half of September and first half of October.
  Maxima: *Spring*—227 in one and one-half hours, Sandy Hook, N.J., Apr. 11, 1953 (G. Stout), an unusual number at this season; 25, Montauk, Apr. 28, 1935. *Fall*—60, Far Rockaway, Sept. 16, 1950; 43, Van Cortlandt Park, Sept. 22, 1953 (Komorowski), a large number for an inland locality; 500, Riis Park, Oct. 1, 1956; 550, Fire Island Inlet, Oct. 1, 1960; 100, same locality, Oct. 16, 1961.

Breeding: The adaptable Sparrow Hawk, or American Kestrel, although most prevalent in open country and in agricultural areas, may be found breeding in our largest cities. Thus it is found in such places as Central and Prospect Parks. It nests in tree holes, telephone poles, bird boxes, and building crevices.
  Egg dates: April 9 to June 3.

GROUSE: TETRAONIDAE

RUFFED GROUSE (*Bonasa umbellus*)*B

Range: Nearctic species, the nominate race (eastern population) occurring from central Connecticut and southeastern New York to eastern Pennsylvania and southern New Jersey.

Status: Resident in the wilder portions where variously fairly common to uncommon, but rare in many areas.

Occurrence: The Ruffed Grouse is an inhabitant of forest clearings and cut-over tracts of extensive second-growth woodland. It is equally at home on the mountainous ridges of northwestern New Jersey and in the pine-oak barrens of eastern Long Island. It nests on the ground at the base of a tree, near fallen timber, and among rock crevices in wooded areas.

164

The species is subject to marked fluctuations at irregular intervals, increasing and declining from time to time, but is virtually nonmigratory. While grouse may be seen in the most unexpected places at times, particularly during the colder months, they are found most readily where least hunted. From one to six per day are usually seen; rarely up to 20 in the better localities. Among the best areas to observe them near New York City are protected preserves such as Bear Mountain and Harriman Parks, Fahnestock State Park, Poundridge Reservation, and the Watchung Reservation.

Egg dates: Apr. 14 to July 20.

Subspecies: Aldrich and Friedmann (1943) stated that Long Island specimens are intermediate between nominate *umbellus* and the more northern race *togata*, but that the nominate race is the form present in the lower Hudson valley. However, introduced stock from other sections of the country have been liberated from time to time, so it is not surprising that birds of mixed blood occur in certain parts of the New York City region.

GREATER PRAIRIE CHICKEN or HEATH HEN
(*Tympanuchus cupido*)B

Extinct (eastern subspecies only): A central and eastern Nearctic species, the nominate race—known as the Heath Hen—now extinct, was resident mainly in areas of sandy soil along the coastal plain from Massachusetts to Virginia and locally inland to eastern Pennsylvania (Pocono plateau). Occurred as recently as 1932 on Martha's Vineyard.

Formerly a common species of the more open pine barrens of Long Island, especially wherever there was a scrub growth of pine and oak. It avoided forest. Reported most numerous in Suffolk County, but occurred rarely as far west as the Hempstead Plains. It apparently became extinct on Long Island in the late 1830s or early 1840s.

In southern New Jersey, it was well known in the "barrens," but was wiped out by the late 1860s. It may have extended as far north as the pine lands of Monmouth County, but of this we have no definite information. It was also reported to have occurred in the sandy region of Schooley's Mountain in the extreme southwestern portion of Morris County.

Very little is known of this bird's disappearance within our area. Not one local specimen exists to my knowledge; the American Museum of Natural History has none containing any data with reference to the New York City region.

Its ultimate extinction was supposedly due to excessive shooting and uncontrolled fires. According to Phillips (1928), many individuals of the western population (*pinnatus*) were introduced from time to time up to

1893, but these birds did not survive long. After the Heath Hen had become extinct, subsequent reports proved to be of Ruffed Grouse.

QUAILS, PHEASANTS: PHASIANIDAE

BOBWHITE (*Colinus virginianus*)*B

Range: A southern Nearctic and northern Neotropical species, the nominate race occurring in our area.

Status: Uncommon to rare resident, having decreased greatly in recent years.

Occurrence: Whereas the Ruffed Grouse has managed to hold on quite well in its woodland haunts, the Bobwhite has been much less fortunate. It has suffered greatly through a combination of five unfavorable factors: (*a*) decline of agriculture; (*b*) rapid destruction and subsequent development of open country; (*c*) excessive hunting; (*d*) severe winter killing; (*e*) introduction of southern and western stock, thereby reducing the vitality of the original native population.

This species was formerly common and widely distributed, particularly at lower elevations—especially numerous on the coastal plain. It was always relatively uncommon in the interior highlands.

Bobwhites favor farmland, brushy fields, hedgerows and thickets, and in winter, edges of swamps in open country. The nest is situated on the ground wherever suitable cover is available.

Egg dates: May 7 to Aug. 25.

An idea of its former abundance and its present scarcity may be seen from the following:

1. Mackay (1929) in his *Shooting Journal* complained of poor hunting due to the ground "pretty well shot over." This was in the vicinity of Bridgehampton, L.I., during the early 1870s. On Nov. 16, 1870, he shot 30, with a total of 87 for the week of Nov. 14–20. In 1871, he killed at least 60 in a three-day period in late October, with 23 birds shot in one day.

2. During the 1940s and 1950s nearly 90 per cent of the areas reporting on the Christmas counts did not list a single Bobwhite, in some cases none for years at a time, the remaining 10 per cent rarely more than a dozen individuals per area. These latter birds were seen chiefly near the coast in New Jersey and on Long Island. And this despite a vast increase in the number of observers.

GRAY PARTRIDGE (*Perdix perdix*)*B

Introduced: Palearctic species, the nominate race widely introduced into North America, chiefly in southern Canada and the northern United States.

166

Although the introduction of the "Hungarian" Partridge, as it is sometimes called, was unsuccessful insofar as the New York City area is concerned, it deserves to be included among the avifauna as much as the Skylark and European Goldfinch. Following is its brief history in our area.

Only two specimens are extant: both are adult males shot on Fisher's Island, Dec. 7, 1923 (Ferguson collection). Ferguson (*in litt.*) stated that, "There was no record of when these were stocked by Fisher's Island Sportsmen's Club."

Speaking of the Stamford, Conn., region, Howes (1928) stated that it was released in large numbers in 1910. At first seemingly successful, it had largely disappeared after 1912 and the latest report was that of a pair seen on April 28, 1928.

Just outside our area in Dutchess County, N.Y., Griscom (1933) mentioned a similar history.

Fables (1955) stated that individuals were released in New Jersey about 1900, but that they did not long survive. He remarked that Urner recorded a covey near Elizabeth in 1912.

The only other report of the species occurring in our area was that of a "number" introduced into Rockland County, N.Y., from time to time by sportsmen's groups, but not established. Reported by Deed *et al.* (1959) as seen in "recent" years.

Egg dates: No data.

RING-NECKED PHEASANT (*Phasianus colchicus*)*B

Introduced: An eastern Palearctic species, widely introduced into various parts of the world. The treatment here in using a binomial follows the A.O.U. *Check-list* (1957, footnote, p. 146): "The pheasants now established in our limits have come from China, supposedly *Phasianus colchicus torquatus* and from England, where the races *colchicus*, *torquatus*, and some others have been introduced and have mingled. The North American bird, being a composite of several subspecies, is included, therefore, only under the specific name."

As far as can be determined this species was introduced and naturalized in the New York City area by the early 1890s, although there were a number of earlier unsuccessful introductions.

The species is now well established as a result of frequent restocking. It is most numerous at lower elevations in open country, wherever there are fields interspersed with bushes and vines, and areas adjacent to swampy thickets. In many places this species has survived occasional heavy snows and hunting pressure. It has become a familiar sight in winter around

167

feeding stations both in rural and in suburban areas where it is attracted to corn.

Egg dates: Apr. 16 to July 6.

TURKEYS: MELEAGRIDIDAE

TURKEY (*Meleagris gallopavo*)B

Extirpated: A southern Nearctic and northern Neotropical species, the race *silvestris* formerly occurring as a resident north to southern Ontario, New York, and the southern portions of Vermont, New Hampshire, and Maine. It disappeared from much of this region, and now is found "native" in reduced numbers only as far north as northern Pennsylvania. Introduced and re-established in recent years, and spreading into adjacent New York and northwestern New Jersey.

Turkeys were formerly numerous throughout much of the northeast, especially in heavily forested areas, but had become extirpated from the New York City region probably by the early nineteenth century. According to old reports they were still found in the mountains of Sussex County, N.J. as late as 1825, and a few were to be seen in the more remote areas of Orange and Rockland counties, N.Y., until about 1840. Lumbering and overshooting were the probable causes of extirpation. There are no local specimens of the original stock in existence.

To what extent the population in Pennsylvania is wholly or partly wild is not known, but the probability is that the present-day make-up is of mixed stock. Birds from the south and southwest and even some domestic stock have been introduced at various times. Street (1956) stated that birds were restocked in the Poconos in the early 1950s and had increased by 1953.

At any rate, Turkeys have crossed the Delaware River at various places and have been reported in our area in New Jersey within the past decade as follows: 1954—one observed near Wallpack, Sussex County (*fide* C. K. Nichols), and 11 seen in nearby High Point State Park, early 1960; 1956— several in the Stokes State Forest, Sussex County (*fide* C. K. Nichols); 1959—three separate flocks totaling 42 birds, Millbrook, Warren County (G. Johnson); 1960—"several broods" along the Delaware River in Warren County (*fide* J. A. Zamos).

In Putnam County, N.Y., according to M. Brech (*in litt.*), "42 Turkeys were released in and around Fahnestock State Park in the late spring of 1959." They have also been restocked in several localities in northern Westchester County.

It remains to be seen how successful the introduction of these birds will be.

Egg dates: No data.

RAILS, GALLINULES, COOTS: RALLIDAE

KING RAIL (*Rallus elegans*)*B

Range: A primarily eastern Nearctic species, the nominate race breeding north to extreme southern Ontario and New York; casually to the coasts of Connecticut and Massachusetts.

Status: Rare in late fall and winter, chiefly along the coast, but a little-known migrant. Very rare, local breeder.

Migration and winter: Of 21 known specimens taken locally, only 6 were collected during the migration period: 3 in April, 2 in October, and 1 in November. The remaining 15 were secured in winter: December (5), January (7), February (1), and the first week of March (2). Eleven of these were from coastal salt marshes. Seven were caught in muskrat traps. There are also reports of at least another 19 seen on the salt marshes, nearly all in December and January, including 2 feeding with a Clapper Rail on an exposed mud flat at Lawrence, Jan. 2, 1960 (Bull). Perhaps this species is less rare in winter on the coast than is realized; or possibly, due to lack of suitable cover, the birds are more conspicuous and not as secretive during the winter as they are during the nesting season or in the dense vegetation of inland marshes.

Breeding (see map p. 170): In the New York City region the King Rail is at or very near the northern limits of its range. It nests in fresh and occasionally in brackish marshes. There are two breeding records listed by Griscom (1923): Great Swamp, N.J., 1900, and a probable one near Astoria, Queens County, 1922. Two more were listed by Cruickshank (1942): Bayside, Queens County, 1924, and Van Cortlandt Park, 1927. There is also a previously unreported nesting at Greenport, L.I., where Latham found a nest in 1925 on June 5, and secured nine eggs for his collection.

Since 1942 the King Rail has been reported as definitely breeding four times on Long Island, and once in New Jersey: Nest with ten eggs, Reed Pond, Montauk, July 3, 1949 (Helmuth); nesting pair at Orient, summers of 1952 and 1954 (Latham); adults with downy young, Lawrence, Nassau County, June 1954 (Bull). In the last instance, although the nest was thought to be located in a small fresh-water marsh, the birds often fed in an adjacent brackish marsh—in turn separated by a dike from a tidal salt marsh, where Clapper Rails breed commonly. The one recent New Jersey report known to me for our area is that of an adult with eight young, Fair Haven, Monmouth County, summer of 1956 (G. D. Stout).

Latham's account (1954) of the 1952 nesting is of sufficient interest to quote in part: "The nest was on the bare ground in a potato field 150 yards from the margin of a salt marsh. The nest, found June 10, contained three eggs. The bird was flushed from the nest while an irrigation system

169

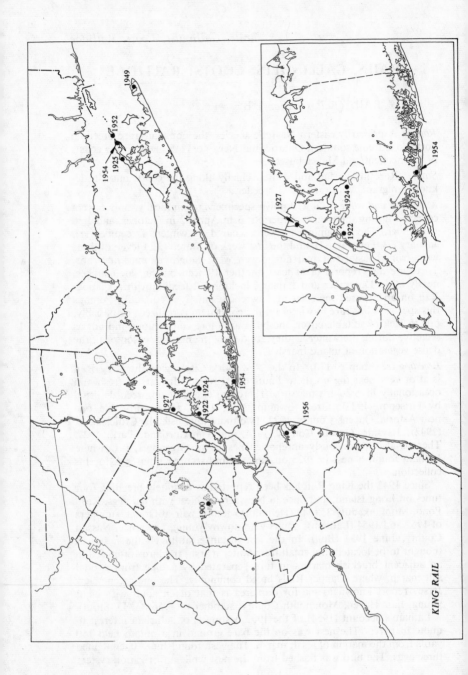

KING RAIL

was in operation. The nest was accidentally destroyed later by farm machinery. Clapper Rails were nesting at the time in the salt marsh 200 yards distant."

Egg dates: May 26 to July 3.

Remarks: Despite the fact that Cruickshank (1942) stated, ". . . undoubtedly *breeds* in the wild expanse of Troy Meadows where it is *heard* each year" (italics mine), it has never actually been proved to nest there. Although it should be found breeding in such an area and perhaps has done so, members of the Urner Club failed to find it on their breeding survey in 1947. Moreover, with so few King Rails reported nesting in the New York City area, this species could go undetected in such a vast expanse as Troy Meadows. In other localities, presumed breeding is based on the bird's presence, but this in itself is not conclusive proof of nesting.

As to the latter part of Cruickshank's statement, "where it is *heard* each year" (italics mine), this is a matter of opinion. I can only quote Brown (1947), ". . . by far the majority of Troy Meadow 'King Rail reports' that have been based solely upon call and noises are *extremely questionable*. Birds that are commonly seen in Troy Meadows such as Pied-billed Grebe, American Bittern, Least Bittern, Virginia Rail, Sora, and Gallinule, among them render such a bewildering profusion of calls, grunts, and noises that it becomes far easier to proclaim 'King Rail' than to prove it." In 16 years (1932–47) spent at Troy Meadows, Brown *saw* only *one* King Rail. Cruickshank himself, in noting the various calls of this species at the Van Cortlandt Park nest site in 1927, reported notes suggesting Virginia Rails, but "deeper in tone;" and other noises similar to those made by Least Bitterns and Common Gallinules.

That the notes of the King Rail may be confused with certain calls of the Virginia Rail was stated in an article by Potter (1926). In a marsh in southern New Jersey he *saw* and *heard* both species simultaneously. He claimed that ". . . the notes of one could not be distinguished from those of the other." Griscom (Bull. Mass. Audubon Soc., 28: 73–84, 1944) also remarked on the difficulty of differentiating certain vocalizations of King and Virginia Rails (see also Clapper Rail).

It is the writer's opinion that King Rails reported as occurring solely on the basis of "heard only," are not at all reliable. There are too many published reports of supposed King Rails based on alleged "known" call notes.

CLAPPER RAIL (*Rallus longirostris*)*B

Range: A widespread, but local American species, the race *crepitans* breeding exclusively in salt marshes north to Long Island and Connecticut; in 1956 to Massachusetts.

Status: Very common breeder on the coast, but rare and local on eastern Long Island. Regular, but uncommon to rare in winter.

Nonbreeding: Clapper Rails are regularly reported in winter on the south shore of Long Island. On the combined Christmas counts of the Nassau, Queens, Brooklyn areas in late December 1951, at least 55 were reported seen and heard.

The Clapper Rail is casual away from salt water. Carleton (1958) lists one report from Central Park and three from Prospect Park. In addition, two specimens—neither examined by me—were reported taken at Overpeck Creek, N.J. (G. C. Fisher) and Ossining, N.Y. (A. K. Fisher).

Breeding: Like the King Rail, the Clapper Rail is at the northern periphery of its range but, unlike that species, the Clapper Rail is locally numerous. The number of nesting pairs naturally depends upon the size of the marsh. Despite increased draining and filling of marshes, there are still large areas of relatively unspoiled salt meadows, particularly in southern Nassau County, where the breeding population is very large. How long much of this habitat will remain is dubious.

From the following estimates of nesting birds, it will be seen how numerous this species is in suitable localities. Even on the north shore of Long Island, where the Clapper Rail was formerly considered local, and where the salt marshes are much less extensive, there are good numbers reported: 12 pairs, Lattingtown, Nassau County, July 1954 (W. Post); at least 30 nesting pairs, Mount Sinai, Suffolk County, summer of 1942 (Murphy). But it is on the broad expanses of the south shore where it is really numerous. On a trip by boat (outboard motor) in the region from Lawrence to Hewlett Bay (about three miles) and from the latter area south to a point opposite Long Beach (about one and one-half miles), Darrow and the writer conservatively estimated not less than 120 pairs in the summer of 1950. These marshes are relatively small in size, as compared with the vast stretches of salt meadows that lie back of the Jones Beach strip. To my knowledge, these meadows have never been worked by boat, the best way to comprehend the numbers present on all sides. It is possible that the breeding population compares favorably with that of the southern New Jersey marshes, where Clapper Rails are found in very large numbers.

The easterly limit of the Clapper Rail on Long Island appears to be in the vicinity of Easthampton, where in more than 40 years of field work, Helmuth had only one breeding record, that of a nest with 14 eggs on June 17, 1944. Latham reports it rare on the Orient peninsula with very few nesting records. In our area in Connecticut several nests have been reported recently east to Westport (see Saunders, 1950). Outside our area, this species breeds at least as far east as Saybrook (mouth of the Connecticut River)—roughly on a north-south line with Orient and Easthampton.

On the tidal marshes away from the coast, the Clapper Rail is very

172

rarely reported. It formerly nested in the Harlem River marshes at Spuyten Duyvil until at least 1924 (*fide* Cruickshank). One recent breeding occurrence was that of a bird with young at Piermont, Rockland County, July 3, 1959 (Gamble).

Egg dates: May 3 to Aug. 7.

Remarks: There is no doubt that the King and Clapper Rails are very closely related and that they form a superspecies, at least. In size, pattern, coloration, and voice they are very similar. In the New York City region, they are geographically, but possibly *not* ecologically sympatric. Oberholser (1937) says, "There is little or no trenchant difference in behavior, voice, nest building or other habits between these two species." Lowery (1955), speaking of Louisiana, stated that "the King and Clapper Rails . . . are, for the most part simply ecological representatives of each other." He also mentioned a ". . . slight difference in the call notes of these obviously closely related species." Meanley (1957), referring to the same area, stated that "where the fresh water and brackish marshes meet, these species sometimes nest only a few yards apart" and further stated that "the mating call and several other calls uttered by the King Rail during the courtship period sounded identical to those given by the . . . Clapper Rail." However, Meanley and Wetherbee (1962) found both forms breeding "together" in a brackish marsh in Delaware, and collected a mated pair—the male a King Rail and the female a Clapper Rail. The five eggs, placed in an incubator, unfortunately did not hatch.

What was said on voice under the King Rail regarding caution as to field identification of individuals heard only, applies to the Clapper Rail as well. It is best not to attempt positive identification of rails heard, but not seen, in "atypical" habitat, because of similarity and variation of calls. This applies to many rails (see especially Yellow and Black Rails).

VIRGINIA RAIL (*Rallus limicola*)*B

Range: A widespread but local American species, the nominate race occurring in our area.

Status: Uncommon to fairly common fall migrant. Rare but regular in winter, chiefly along the coast. Locally common breeder.

Migration and winter: The Virginia Rail is regular in spring and fall, but as it occurs in summer and winter, it is difficult to give arrival and departure dates, though it is generally scarce before mid-April.

Fall maxima—7, Mecox and Shinnecock bays, Sept. 7, 1929 (Helmuth); 3 picked up dead at foot of Westhampton Air Force Base tower, Oct. 5, 1954 (Wilcox).

The Virginia Rail occurs regularly in winter as far north as Massachusetts. In our area Latham has taken it at least nine times at this season in the Orient region, four of which were picked up dead between Dec. 21 and 28, 1919, and two more collected on Feb. 1, 1920. Inland, Nolan observed four feeding together in a marsh on Constitution Island, in the Hudson River, Jan. 2, 1956. Thirteen were reported on all combined Christmas counts, 1953–54.

Breeding: Nests in fresh-water marshes, occasionally in coastal brackish marshes. Decreasing as suitable habitat is drained or filled. The maximum numbers are found in the largest marshes in New Jersey. On June 1, 1947, the Urner Club estimated at least 25 breeding pairs in Troy Meadows; at least 10 pairs were present in the Hackensack Meadows during the summer of 1962 (Black and Jehl).

Egg dates: May 4 to July 11.

SORA (*Porzana carolina*)*B

Range: Nearctic species, in the east breeding south to Pennsylvania and New Jersey; rarely to Maryland and West Virginia.

Status: Fairly common fall migrant, formerly more numerous. Very rare in winter. Local breeder inland, but rare on the coast.

Migration: Like the previous species, occurs the year around; migration dates, therefore, are difficult to determine, but usually rare before mid-April. The peak periods are in May and October.

Maxima: 6 hit the tower at the Westhampton Air Force Base, Oct. 5, 1954; 18, Mecox Bay, Oct. 11, 1930 (Helmuth). Formerly reported as numerous in fall in wild-rice marshes of the larger rivers, but no statistical data is at hand for our area.

Winter: The Sora winters north to South Carolina; much more rarely to Massachusetts. In our area it is much rarer at this season than the Virginia Rail. Only two known local specimens, both from Long Island: Seaford, Dec. 24, 1908 (Peavey); Wading River, Jan. 2, 1912 (Murphy). There are only two dozen winter sight reports, seldom more than one in a winter.

Breeding: Nests in fresh-water marshes, but because of draining and filling, it has decreased considerably. Fairly common only in Troy Meadows and nearby marshes. On June 1, 1947, the Urner Club found 14 breeding pairs at Troy Meadows. Rare on the coastal plain in the breeding season.

Egg dates: May 12 to July 17.

YELLOW RAIL (*Coturnicops noveboracensis*)*

Range: A northern Nearctic species of wide distribution, but rare and very local. The nominate race breeds south and east to Ontario, Quebec,

174

and New Brunswick; sporadically to northeastern Ohio. Alleged breeding records in the New England states listed by the A.O.U. *Check-list* (1957) are considered unsatisfactory: Maine (Palmer, 1949); Massachusetts (Griscom and Snyder, 1955); Connecticut (Sage *et al.*, 1913).

In winter this species ranges north to Florida, rarely to South Carolina; "accidental" on the coasts of Long Island (four specimens) and Rhode Island (one specimen).

Status: Rare, but perhaps a regular fall migrant, probably overlooked; very rare or casual in spring. Four winter records on the coast.

Occurrence: In our area there are 29 known specimens, of which 14 are in the American Museum collection, and another eight in private collections. The whereabouts of the other seven are unknown. There are at least 20 reports of birds *seen* by reliable observers.

The great majority of reports are from the coast of Long Island. Inland, Yellow Rails have been taken seven times, six of these in fall. There are two inland sight reports, both in May from Troy Meadows. In fact, most inland occurrences of this species are from this general region, having been collected once each at Whippany, Morris River, Troy Meadows, and Madison.

Of 21 fall specimens, eight were taken in September and eight in October. Four fall observations in each of the same two months are reported out of a total of 11. Thus it would appear that September and October are the principal months of occurrence for this species.

In spring, only four specimens are known, three in March and one in April, and six sight reports, with one in March, three in April, and two in May.

Extreme dates: *Fall*—Aug. 29 (specimen) to Dec. 4 (specimen). *Spring*—March 30 (specimen) to Apr. 29 (specimen), May 3 and 14.

Four winter records, all specimens from Long Island: Sayville, Jan. 17, 1894 (Dutcher collection), A.M.N.H.; Seaford, Jan. 10, 1909 (Peavey), A.M.N.H.; Islip, Feb. 22, 1929 (Ritchie), A.M.N.H.: Orient, Jan. 1, 1956 (Latham), in his collection.

So elusive and secretive is the Yellow Rail that many experienced observers have never seen it alive. Most of the local specimens and some of the observations were made with the help of rail dogs. Four specimens were picked up dead. Seldom reported by even the active field observer, it is found only by chance or after many years spent in the field. I was fortunate on one occasion to see an individual cross a road and then disappear into the marsh at Lawrence, L.I., Nov. 12, 1956.

In the Orient region Latham has collected it twice and seen it once. Helmuth observed it twice in the Easthampton area. Mayer has had the good fortune to come across Yellow Rails five times: on three occasions at Idlewild, once at the Jamaica Bay Refuge, and once at Lawrence. He describes two of these occurrences in an article written in a newspaper

175

("Nassau Daily Review-Star") column, "Long Island Bird Notes" (1950). Mayer had flushed two of these birds at Idlewild on Apr. 12, 1931, and March 30, 1936, both times after hearing the notes. The habitat, he says, ". . . in both cases was the extreme upland edge of the salt marshes, away from tide water, and the fresh water meadows flooded in part with pools of rainwater, and overgrown with short, fine grasses. In each case, there was a dry ditch nearby, covered with reeds and *Phragmites* and other growth, into which the bird retreated when approached too closely."

Inland, J. A. Weber used a rail dog. During the fall of 1920 in the Overpeck Creek, N.J., marshes, he flushed Yellow Rails four times between Oct. 4 and Nov. 25, collecting an individual on Oct. 11.

A number of reports—some published—of birds merely heard, but not seen, are considered unreliable. There is too great a chance of error. Other marsh birds, as well as rails, are a possibility and much remains to be determined regarding the voices of many of them. Certain call notes are probably very similar, and in some instances Yellow and Black Rails have been confused with each other. (See discussion under Black Rail.)

BLACK RAIL (*Laterallus jamaicensis*)*B

Range: This American species breeds locally in four widely separated areas: (*a*) along the Pacific coast of southern California and Baja California; (*b*) Pacific coast of Peru and Chile; (*c*) along the Atlantic coast from Florida to Connecticut, in salt or brackish marshes; (*d*) very rarely and locally in inland fresh-water marshes from Kansas east to Ohio, and in Florida. The Atlantic coast and inland populations belong to the nominate race. In most of its eastern range the Black Rail is reported as rare and very local even in Florida and South Carolina.

Status: Very rare visitant on the coast. Three breeding records on Long Island.

Nonbreeding: In our area this species has been found on relatively few occasions, nearly all on the south shore of Long Island; twice reported in northern New Jersey—once inland—Troy Meadows, Apr. 27, 1930 (Urner).

Extreme dates: Apr. 10, 19, and 29 to Oct. 29 and Nov. 1.

Helmuth saw this species on five separate occasions between 1937 and 1939, with dates ranging from Sept. 7 to Oct. 23—twice at Mecox Bay, once each at Sagaponack, Hook Pond, and Napeague. Whether the following two observations represent family groups that may have nested nearby, or were migrants, is difficult to state, as the Black Rail is extremely rare north of Long Island: ten flushed in less than an hour, Moriches Inlet, Sept. 9, 1939 (Cadbury and Cruickshank), and six at the same place, Sept. 12, 1953 (Grant).

176

Specimen data: Only four Black Rails have been reported as collected (cf. Yellow Rail, 29 specimens), all on Long Island: Jamaica (south of), spring of 1879 (R. B. Lawrence); Canarsie, spring of 1884 (C. Sargood); South Oyster Bay, near Gilgo Island, Aug. 1, 1884 (L. S. Foster); Napeague, Aug. 3, 1910 (Helmuth), specimen in his collection. This last record is published here for the first time and is apparently the only local specimen extant.

Breeding: Only in southern Maryland and southern New Jersey is the Black Rail reported as regular and locally numerous. In the latter state, Fables (1955) mentioned one man who examined 80 nests, and Stone (1937) another person who found 24 nests! It has been found breeding as far north as Tuckerton, N.J. (south of our region). North of this locality, records of only three nests are known on Long Island (see below), and two—outside our area— on the coast of eastern Connecticut (both at Saybrook). Two others listed in the A.O.U. *Check-list* (1957) are considered unsatisfactory: Hazardville, Conn. (Sage *et al.*, 1913), and Chatham, Mass. (Griscom and Snyder, 1955).

The only definite breeding evidence for our area is the same as that reported in Cruickshank (1942). A nest was located in "thick sedges and narrow-leaved cattail" at Oak Beach, June 20, 1937 (Carleton). The nest contained eight eggs, of which five hatched. The young were observed on June 27. On July 5, the deserted nest and three remaining eggs were collected, and are A.M.N.H. No. 454. At Long Beach during the same year four young were banded on June 30 (Mrs. Beals). Mayer found a nest with nine eggs at Lido Beach, July 12, 1940. These last two nests were situated in short-grass salt marsh (*Spartina patens*) resembling the habitat in southern New Jersey where numerous nests of Black Rails have been found. It seems remarkable that three nests were found in two years, and none before or since. The species has undoubtedly been overlooked.

Egg dates: June 20 to July 12.

Remarks: In view of its nesting in fresh-water marshes at several midwestern localities, it is not too surprising that there is an inland occurrence in our region. On Apr. 27, 1930, one was carefully studied at close range at Troy Meadows (Urner, Auk, 47: 560–561, 1930). This interesting article should be read in order to understand why rails may not always be identified positively, as they so often are, on the basis of voice alone. In brief, Urner stated that he *saw* a Black Rail and *thought* that this very same individual was calling, which is possible, although at no time did he *see* the bird calling. He apparently was puzzled about the call notes and, after consulting the literature, found them described as those of the Yellow Rail. However, both species have been reported at times to give similar calls.

In my opinion both Stone (1937) and Cruickshank (1942) erred when they listed Urner's observation under Yellow Rail without stating their reasons. Fables (1955) even went so far as to list it under both species!

One has only to read some of the accounts scattered in the literature to become confused regarding the vocalizations of these two rails. For sources, see Griscom and Snyder (1955: 84); see also Kellogg (1962). On the basis of the foregoing, reports of birds heard, but not seen, are not given credence. Other inland reports are without details and are rejected.

This species and the Yellow Rail are two of our most secretive birds, flushing only when almost stepped on. The best way of finding these birds is to visit suitable areas with a good rail dog. The second-best way is to have two or more observers spread out with a rope and "drag" the marsh. This latter method has proved successful on a number of occasions. The observer who hopes to see these elusive creatures merely by visiting the meadows will see very few, if any, unless he is extremely lucky.

CORN CRAKE (*Crex crex*)*

Accidental: Palearctic species that has been collected four times in our area, all on Long Island, three within a nine-year period; Oakdale, Nov. 2, 1880 (A. A. Fraser), A.M.N.H. No. 64859, "Shot at the foot of the uplands where they join the meadows in heavy cover"; Amagansett, Aug.15, 1885 (Dutcher collection), A.M.N.H. No. 64858, "Shot on dry upland with Meadowlarks"; Montauk, Nov. 1, 1888 (Dutcher collection), A.M.N.H. No. 64860, "Secured about three miles west of the Point in a meadow while shooting quail." The fourth specimen (no locality other than Long Island, and without date, collected by G. Smith) is A.M.N.H. No. 12537.

Also known as the Land Rail, this is primarily a bird of grasslands. It has decreased markedly in the past 60 years, particularly in the British Isles and to a lesser extent on the continent (Europe). According to Witherby *et al.* (1941), Norris (1947), and Haartman (1958), it has become scarce chiefly because of present-day methods of mowing by machine and mowing earlier in the season when the birds are nesting. In the few areas where mowing is still done by hand, the species is reported as flourishing.

Most of the dozen or so records along the northeastern seaboard, from Newfoundland to Maryland, were of individuals collected from 1857 to 1905. It is perhaps significant that these occurrences took place during the period when the species was common, and that only one specimen has been collected since, that of an individual taken at Orange, Conn., (outside our area) on Oct. 18, 1943 (Ball, Auk, 61: 471–472, 1944). In our area no sight reports have been confirmed, nor have details been published.

Since the above was written, Roy Latham (*in litt.*) states that a female Corn Crake was collected at Orient, Nov. 2, 1963. It was shot by a pheasant hunter, "in a field of young rye 200 yards from salt marsh." Specimen preserved in Latham's collection.

PURPLE GALLINULE (*Porphyrula martinica*)*

Very rare visitant: Primarily a Neotropical species, breeding north along the coast to South Carolina; locally inland to Tennessee. Wanders north to southern Canada.

In our area there are at least 18 occurrences, of which eight are specimens (4 known to be extant). Two old existing specimens, both adults, were taken on Great South Bay, dates unknown (Pike) and are A.M.N.H. Nos. 436536 and 436537. Another was collected at Middle Island, Suffolk County, in 1879 (*fide* Helme). Two specimens were collected at Stamford, Conn., in 1877 and 1884 (Sage *et al.*, 1913).

Cruickshank (1942) listed five sight reports between 1928 and 1939, including three on the south shore of Long Island and one each from Central Park and Peekskill, N.Y.

There have been eight additional occurrences since 1942, as follows: three specimen records—one found in a badly decomposed condition, Shinnecock Bay, June 18, 1948 (Wilcox); one picked up dead, Easthampton, Apr. 20, 1951 (S. Lester), in his collection—specimen examined by Helmuth; one found alive in weakened condition, but died later, Westhampton, Apr. 19, 1956 (Wilcox), in his collection.

The five recent sight reports are: Jamaica Bay Refuge, May 14–16, 1958 (several observers); Hewlett, May 17 to June 4, 1960 (Sloss and many others); Long Branch, N.J., May 20 to early June 1960 (Seeley *et al.*); one found exhausted at Bay Ridge, Brooklyn, Apr. 9, 1962 (S. Rifkin) and presented to the Prospect Park Zoo (*fide* Carleton); an adult captured in a garden at Manhasset, May 5, 1962 (J. Waite), and later the same day banded and released at the Jamaica Bay Refuge (*fide* Johnson and Mayer).

Extreme dates: Apr. 9 to July 27. It is a curious fact that *none* of the 18 local occurrences took place during the hurricane season of August and September, the period when many Purple Gallinules are reported outside our area, and the season when most of the "tropical" species occur in our latitudes.

COMMON GALLINULE (*Gallinula chloropus*)*B

Range: A nearly cosmopolitan species, but of somewhat local distribution. The race *cachinnans* occurs in our area.

Status: Regular fall migrant, sometimes fairly common, particularly near the coast. Rare, but regular in winter on the coast. Local breeder.

Migration: This species is occasionally fairly common in fall: Maxima—23, Mecox Bay to Easthampton, Oct. 10, 1929; 13, Easthampton to Montauk, Nov. 6, 1949. Because it summers and winters, arrival and departure dates are difficult to establish, but it is generally rare before mid-April and after mid-November.

Winter: This species winters north to Florida, more rarely to North Carolina; although very rare farther north, it is reported regularly on Long Island, at least in recent years.

In our area there is no winter specimen, but each year one or more are reported. Cruickshank (1942) stated that he knew of nine occurrences in winter. Since 1946 it has been reported regularly on Long Island, with a maximum of seven during the winter of 1954–55—five of these on the south shore from Brooklyn to Lawrence, and one each at Hempstead and Smithtown.

Breeding: Nests chiefly in fresh-water marshes with an abundance of cattails, pickerel weed, and other aquatic vegetation, but usually where open water is available.

In former years, the Newark Meadows was a favorite breeding area. In the summer of 1906, C. G. Abbott and others found 16 nests, some with eggs and young. By 1916 no nesting birds could be located, most of the meadows having become unsuitable because of drainage, filling, and industrial pollution.

On Long Island, the only colony known today is at the Jamaica Bay Refuge, where in 1959 about four pairs nested. By 1960 this colony had increased to at least eight breeding pairs, with a further slight increase in 1962.

During the summer of 1962 Black and Jehl estimated at least 200 pairs in the vast Hackensack Meadows, a truly phenomenal number. While this species has nested there for many years, it is believed that the "sudden" increase has been due to diking these tidal marshes, thereby creating a more favorable environment for them by reducing the salinity of the water.

Egg dates: May 14 to July 4.

AMERICAN COOT (*Fulica americana*)*B

Range: This widespread American species breeds from Canada to Ecuador, but it has a discontinuous distribution and in many parts of its range is local and sporadic. In fact, the nominate race is rare over much of its eastern range and a number of states are without a single definite breeding record: Maine (Palmer, 1949); Massachusetts (Griscom and Snyder, 1955); Maryland (Stewart and Robbins, 1958); only one for South Carolina (Sprunt, 1949). However, Todd (1940) reports it as breeding commonly at one locality in extreme western Pennsylvania, where it nests by the "hundreds" at Pymatuning Lake.

Status: Common to locally abundant fall migrant and winter visitant; occasionally more numerous. Very rare and local breeder prior to 1958; has increased greatly since.

180

Migration and winter: The distribution, relative abundance, and occurrence of the American Coot in our area has never been fully emphasized. Actually it has been reported as numerous in two periods: (*a*) from about 1900 to 1925; (*b*) from the late 1940s to 1962. Even during these two periods, the Coot fluctuated in numbers and was reported in large concentrations only on extreme eastern Long Island.

Maxima: *Early period*—1000, Great Pond, Montauk, November 1904; 2000, Moriches Bay, Nov. 17, 1905; 2000, Montauk, Dec. 20, 1924. *Recent period*—2300, Water Mill, Nov. 8, 1948; 750, Mecox Bay, Jan. 12, 1957.

Elsewhere in the region, flocks numbering from 50 to 400 or so are the rule. Inland maxima: 200, Boonton Reservoir, Oct. 25, 1941; 175, Kensico Reservoir, Dec. 7, 1941; 300, Croton Point, Nov. 28, 1943.

Change in breeding status (see map p. 183): The Coot prefers a type of marsh similar to that of the Common Gallinule, but requires extensive areas of open water.

Prior to 1958 this species was a very rare nesting bird in the New York City area, usually with only single pairs reported. Griscom (1923) listed one: Newark Meadows, 1907. Cruickshank (1942) called it a very rare breeder, listing four locations, two on Long Island and two in New Jersey: Dyker Beach, Brooklyn, 1924 and 1925; the other three, all in 1940 and 1941—Mill Neck, Troy Meadows, and Newton, Sussex County.

In 1950 one pair bred at Hewlett; in 1951 one pair bred at Alley Pond, Queens County; and in 1954 one pair nested at Mecox Bay, all on Long Island. These reports represent the only known breeding occurrences between 1941 and 1958.

Whether the following represents a temporary condition remains to be seen. At any rate, during a survey of the Hackensack Meadows in the summer of 1958, Wolfarth and Jehl found at least 100 nesting pairs, a truly phenomenal number. In 1962 about 300 pairs were reported, with "hundreds" of young seen (Black and Jehl). In 1959 more than 25 pairs were breeding at the Jamaica Bay Refuge. By 1961 this colony had doubled and about 50 pairs nested (Johnson). It will be of interest to ascertain whether Coots remain as numerous in these two areas, and whether they appear in any new localities.

Egg dates: May 20 to June 10.

OYSTERCATCHERS: HAEMATOPODIDAE

AMERICAN OYSTERCATCHER (*Haematopus palliatus*)*B

Range: A wide-ranging American species, but very local in distribution. The nominate race breeds along the Atlantic coast north to central New Jersey; very rarely to Long Island.

Status: Very rare visitant to the coast of Long Island, but has increased greatly in recent years and now regular each summer. Local breeder since 1957.

Change in status: 1. Nonbreeding—Giraud (1844) listed this bird as "rather scarce," but adds that "during summer a few are found on almost every beach along the whole extent of the sea coast." Griscom (1923) placed it on the "extirpated" list, and Cruickshank (1942) listed but seven additional occurrences.

Since then this species has occurred most often after hurricanes: 1944—two at Oak Beach, Sept. 23, and one at Moriches Inlet, Sept. 30. At least six individuals were reported after the late August and early September hurricanes of 1954 with three each at Moriches and Shinnecock Inlets. After hurricane Donna of Sept. 12, 1960, no fewer than 12 were observed from Jamaica Bay to Mecox Bay, five of which were at Moriches Bay. However, not all occurrences have been the result of storms. In late May and early June 1960, at least seven different individuals were reported along the south shore, excluding a nesting pair at Moriches Bay. In 1961 nonbreeding Oystercatchers were observed at Short Beach, Napeague, and on Gardiner's and Cartwright Islands. For its recent history in New York, see Post (1961b).

Extreme dates: May 9 to Oct. 22; also Nov. 11, 1951—one found dead at Moriches Inlet (many observers). An unusual date was that of one shot on the salt meadow back of the beach at Ponquogue, March 9, 1880 (*fide* Dutcher).

2. Breeding—According to Stone (1937), the American Oystercatcher was formerly a regular breeder on the south Jersey beaches, but had become very rare by the 1870s. The first recent nesting in southern New Jersey was in 1947 at Little Beach Island, Ocean County (*fide* Potter). According to Fables (1955) at least 11 nests were located in southern New Jersey in 1954.

First found nesting in our area in 1957 on Gardiner's Island where, on June 13, Wilcox discovered a nest with two eggs. During the summers of 1960, 1961, and 1962, Wilcox and others found single pairs nesting on an island in Moriches Bay and banded the young. On July 14, 1962, on Cartwright Island, Kallman observed a pair at their nest which contained five eggs; he saw six more adults there, but found no additional evidence of breeding. According to Walter Terry, a pair and nest were found at Tiana Beach, near Shinnecock Inlet, June 1963 (several observers).

Oystercatchers most often nest on the open sand, in situations similar to those frequented by Black Skimmers, Least Terns, and Piping Plovers.

Egg dates: June 13 to July 14.

Specimen data: Of 11 specimens taken in our area, only 6 are apparently extant: "South Side Meadows", Flatlands, Brooklyn, date not stated (Lawrence collection), A.M.N.H. No. 436555; Long Island, July 31, 1858

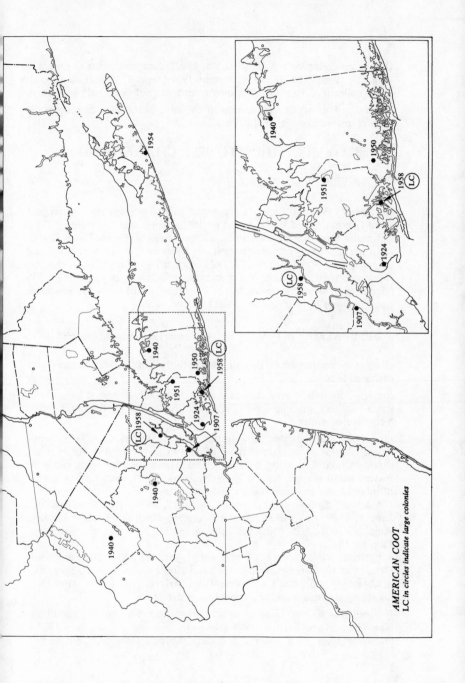

AMERICAN COOT
LC in circles indicate large colonies

(Lawrence collection), A.M.N.H. No. 45401; four specimens at Orient— Aug. 20, 1936; Sept. 16, 1939; August 1957; Sept. 8, 1959 (Latham), all in his collection. The 1939 specimen record was not previously published.

Remarks: This species is considered by some authorities as conspecific with *H. ostralegus* of the Old World.

PLOVERS, TURNSTONES: CHARADRIIDAE

LAPWING (*Vanellus vanellus*)*

Accidental: Palearctic species; recorded in the western Atlantic region from Greenland and Baffin Island to the Bahamas and Barbados.

Locally there are three records, all specimens taken on Long Island, only one apparently extant: The first was collected after a severe northeast snowstorm at Merrick, Dec. 27, 1883 (C. Lott) and another was shot at, but not secured; the other two specimens are—Mecox Bay, late fall, 1905 (*fide* Beebe); Bridgehampton, fall of 1910 (Eagleston), mounted specimen examined (see Reimann, Auk, 56: 332, 1939).

SEMIPALMATED PLOVER (*Charadrius semipalmatus*)*

Range: Nearctic species, breeding south to the Gulf of St. Lawrence and southern Nova Scotia.

Status: Common to very abundant coastal migrant. Reported annually in small numbers, on migration inland, and in summer on the outer coast. Very rare in winter.

Occurrence and maxima: Among our most numerous shorebirds, Semipalmated Plovers are found most often and in the largest numbers on extensive tidal flats along the outer coast. However, they occur singly or in very small groups, especially in dry years, on exposed muddy shores of inland lakes and reservoirs, chiefly in autumn.

Maxima: *Spring*—6000, Idlewild, May 17, 1939; 700, same locality, June 1, 1948. *Fall*—1000, Idlewild, Aug. 6, 1936; 4000, same locality, Aug. 24, 1951; 600, Moriches Inlet, Sept. 28, 1936; 50, Easthampton, Oct. 15, 1933.

Extreme dates: March 23 and early April to Nov. 20 (specimen), Dec. 7 and 10. Rare before late April and after October. A few summering nonbreeding individuals are present regularly on the coast; therefore, no spring departure and fall arrival dates are given.

Winter: This species winters north to South Carolina; rarely to southern New Jersey. There are no winter specimens for our area, but since 1950 a few individuals have lingered regularly through December. From late

184

December 1951 to Feb. 24, 1952, from one to three were present at Point Lookout, L.I. (several observers); two were reported at Jamaica Bay up to Jan. 2, 1954 (many observers); two more were observed at Jones Inlet, Dec. 29, 1957 (Buckley and Carleton).

Remarks: The Semipalmated, or Ring-necked Plover is closely related to *C. hiaticula*, the Ringed Plover, and considered conspecific by some authorities. The latter is a Palearctic and northeastern Nearctic form breeding west to Baffin Island where *C. semipalmatus* also breeds, but apparently not in the same areas. For a discussion, see Bock (1959).

PIPING PLOVER (*Charadrius melodus*)*B

Range: A central and eastern Nearctic species, the eastern population breeding along the coast south to Virginia.

Status: Locally common breeder on the outer coast, and occasionally a very common migrant there. Very rare in winter.

Migration: The Piping Plover is one of the first shorebirds to appear in spring. It departs very early, usually by early September.

Maxima: *Spring*—90, Moriches Inlet, March 26, 1948. *Fall*—150, Idlewild, Aug. 10, 1944.

Extreme dates: March 3 to Nov. 17, 30, and Dec. 10. Rare before mid-March and after September.

Casual inland: collected at Ossining in 1898 (Fisher), specimen in M.C.Z. collection.

Breeding: The Piping Plover breeds on the ocean beaches and filled-in areas near inlets and bays. Its nest is placed on the open sand where Least Terns also breed. Formerly common (prior to the 1890s), its numbers were decimated severely by heavy shooting, but with full protection in 1913, it recovered strongly by the 1920s.

Today it breeds wherever there are little-disturbed beaches, the number of pairs naturally depending upon the extent of unspoiled and undeveloped beachfront. Thus, many miles of Fire Island contain quite a few nesting pairs. Wilcox (1959b), who has banded a great many on eastern Long Island, stated that in the Moriches-Shinnecock-Mecox area, he examined 64, 55, and 50 nests in 1941, 1950, and 1958 respectively. These represented the maximum numbers in 23 years (1936–58) of banding. In June 1951, I estimated at least 75 pairs on the beach and sand fill in the Short Beach area.

Away from the ocean this species is rare. On the north shore of Long Island, it has been found nesting at Port Jefferson, where Komorowski found five nests with eggs during the summer of 1951. A nest with eggs was also reported at Oyster Bay in 1953, and three nesting pairs at Bayville in 1954. In 1959 one or more pairs were reported established on the

Connecticut shore at Westport (M. Brown), and during the summer of 1960 three pairs were reported nesting on Sherwood Island (off Westport). Perhaps they will be found breeding in other suitable areas on Long Island Sound.

Egg dates: Apr. 24 to July 16.

Winter: The Piping Plover winters north to South Carolina, rarely to Maryland and southern New Jersey; very rarely to Long Island and Massachusetts (3 specimens).

Not definitely reported in winter in our area prior to 1953. Since the winter of 1953–54, it has been reported on Long Island on eight occasions by qualified observers: 3, Montauk, Dec. 30, 1953 to Jan. 10, 1954; 1, Moriches Inlet, Jan. 1, 1954; 1, Tottenville, Staten Island, Jan. 15, 1956; 1, Point Lookout, Jan. 27, 1957; 1, Moriches Inlet, Jan. 4, 1958; 2, Montauk, Jan. 19, 1958, one of the latter collected, but not preserved; 2, Moriches Inlet, Dec. 26, 1959; 1, Fire Island Inlet, Jan. 7 and 8, 1961.

Remarks: Two apparently isolated breeding populations of this species occur: one nesting on coastal beaches from Quebec and Newfoundland south to Virginia; the other nesting on inland beaches from Alberta and Nebraska east to the shores of Lakes Erie and Ontario. This inland population is thought by many to represent a separate race, *circumcinctus*, the so-called "Belted" Piping Plover, and is currently included as a valid subspecies in the A.O.U. *Check-list* (1957). However, breeding studies made by Wilcox (1959b) on Long Island prove that individual variation is the main factor. Birds ranging from those with complete breast bands to those having broken or incomplete bands were found not only in the same nesting colony, but in the same nest. This condition prevails in many localities along the east coast and to a lesser extent inland, with much intergradation occurring (see Eaton, 1910, and especially Griscom and Snyder, 1955). The presence or absence of a breast band is, therefore, *not* correlated on geographical grounds. In view of this, the Piping Plover is treated here binomially, with no subspecies recognized.

WILSON'S PLOVER (*Charadrius wilsonia*)*

Very rare visitant: Primarily a Neotropical species, although the nominate race breeds along the Atlantic coast north to Virginia; more rarely to southern New Jersey. In the latter state it formerly bred regularly in Cape May County up to the 1820s, but was not found nesting again in southern New Jersey until 1935 at Brigantine, Atlantic County, and 1940 at Beach Haven, Ocean County, its most northerly known breeding station (Cant, 1941). Irregular breeder since (Fables, 1955).

In the New York City area Wilson's Plover has been reported principally on the south shore of Long Island. No inland reports are accepted,

186

as inexperienced observers confuse this species with immature Semipalmated Plovers having dark bills. Of more than two dozen reports in our area, eight have occurred in May and at least nine in September, the latter mostly after hurricanes.

There are nine local specimens, six of which are extant—these latter are: Flatlands, Brooklyn, no date or collector, A.M.N.H. No. 436592; Raynor South (now Freeport), April 24, 1833 (Lawrence collection), A.M.N.H. No. 45432; Shinnecock Bay, May 16, 1884 (Dutcher collection), A.M.N.H. No. 65099; Napeague, July 11, 1931 (Latham), in his collection; Mecox Bay, Sept. 17, 1932 (Helmuth), in his collection; Moriches Inlet, Sept. 19, 1954 (W. Bock), Cornell University collection.

Cruickshank (1942) listed about a dozen sight reports. Since then the species has been reported but rarely: several times in 1953; and after the two 1954 hurricanes when at least five individuals were seen between Moriches and Shinnecock Inlets on Sept. 3 and 4 (several observers); and one at Wreck Pond, N.J., Sept. 3–12.

Extreme dates: April 24 (specimen) to Sept. 22 and Oct. 2.

KILLDEER (*Charadrius vociferus*)*B

Range: Widespread, but local American species, the nominate race occurs in our area.

Status: Common to very common fall migrant both inland and coastal. In recent years, locally numerous in winter along the coast. Local breeder.

Migration and winter: Especially numerous in the fall migration, some years very common, in others less common. Since the early 1950s it has wintered in fairly large numbers, both on the south shore of Long Island and along the coast from Connecticut to Westchester and Bronx counties. Formerly less numerous in migration and winter.

Maxima: *Fall*—75, Lawrence, L.I., Aug. 9, 1952; 150, same locality, Oct. 5, 1948; 100, Hempstead Reservoir, Nov. 3, 1946; 75, Westhampton, Nov. 17, 1945. *Winter*—in late December 1952, 200 were reported from Bronx County to Westport, Conn., and 200 from Brooklyn to Jones Beach. On all Christmas counts combined—early January 1954—more than 700 were reported. Generally rare inland before March.

Breeding: The Killdeer nests locally throughout the New York City area in open fields, waste areas, fill, and on golf courses. The nest is placed either on pebbly ground or on bare ground where there are short-grass clumps, Fgg dates: Apr. 12 to July 31.

AMERICAN GOLDEN PLOVER (*Pluvialis dominica*)*

Range: Nearctic and eastern Palearctic species, the nominate race breeding south to northeastern Manitoba, Southampton Island, and southern

187

Baffin Island. Migrates in spring chiefly through the Mississippi Valley; in fall chiefly over the Atlantic Ocean (offshore).

Status: Regular, but uncommon to fairly common fall migrant on the coast, particularly on eastern Long Island; occasionally very common after easterly storms. Rare to uncommon, but regular in spring, at least in recent years (since 1947). Very rare inland.

Occurrence and maxima: The Golden Plover frequents burned-over salt meadows, short-grass and plowed fields, golf courses, and sand fill. Rare on mud flats where the Black-bellied Plover is numerous.

Formerly abundant, the Golden Plover was considered a great delicacy, and was shot in large numbers for the market. It had become very scarce by the early 1890s and remained so until the 1920s when, afforded protection, it reappeared again in small numbers.

Giraud (1844) stated, ". . . it frequents the Hempstead Plains, Shinnecock Hills, and Montauk. The Hempstead Plains are well adapted to its habits, and during some seasons it is quite abundant on this miniature prairie." Note the large numbers reported there in 1934 (see below). This habitat is now almost totally destroyed.

Helmuth, who was very active in the field on eastern Long Island, reported these birds in considerable numbers from the early 1920s to the late 1940s, particularly after prolonged easterly gales. The numbers given below for the Easthampton-Sagaponack region are taken from his diaries.

Another favorite place of these birds was the Newark Meadows, where in former years salt-marsh hay was cut and this, together with the burned-over meadows, was very attractive to Golden Plovers. When they started returning in flocks during the 1920s, Urner reported them until the early 1930s when the meadows "deteriorated" and were no longer suitable. Urner's numbers for the Newark Meadows area are given below. It is quite possible that some of the birds he reported at that locality came by way of an overland route. This species is known to leave its nesting grounds in the Hudson Bay area and proceed in a southeasterly direction, which might bring it to the Newark area, but this is purely conjectural. Easterly gales also may be responsible for the birds occurring there. For its former status in the Newark Meadows and a description of that locality, see Urner (1929).

Maxima: *Fall*—100, Sagaponack, Aug. 22, 1921; 40, Hempstead Plains, Sept. 10, 1934 (after easterly storm); 300, Newark Meadows, Sept. 15, 1932; 200, Easthampton, Sept. 16, 1944 (hurricane on Sept. 14); 150, Newark Meadows, Sept. 27, 1930; 60, Easthampton, Oct. 30, 1949 (notably late flight); 15, Mecox Bay, Nov. 9, 1929. *Spring*—5, Jamaica Bay, Apr. 16, 1955; 9, same area, Apr. 23, 1957; 6, Sagaponack, May 17, 1948; these numbers are, however, exceptional—usually only one or two birds reported each spring.

Extreme dates: *Fall*—July 9, 18, 24, 29, Aug. 1 and 4 to Nov. 28 and Dec. 4. Casual—a crippled bird at Jamaica Bay, near Broad Channel, remained to Dec. 30, 1956 (Mayer *et al.*). Rare before mid-August and after mid-November. *Spring*—March 31 and Apr. 5 to June 7 and 9. No summering individuals reported.

Specimen data: There are 15 local fall specimens in the American Museum collection, nearly all taken on Long Island; no extant specimens collected in spring, when it was formerly reported as irregular.

BLACK-BELLIED PLOVER (*Squatarola squatarola*)*

Range: Nearctic and eastern Palearctic species, breeding south to Southampton and Baffin Islands. Winters north to New Jersey, Long Island, and Massachusetts.

Status: Very common to abundant coastal migrant; occasionally more numerous. Regular in winter and summer (nonbreeders). Rare inland.

Occurrence and maxima: This species occurs in the largest numbers on mud flats and salt meadows. Largest flocks in spring (May), when more concentrated. Fall flight greatly protracted (August to November).

Maxima: *Spring*—1200, Idlewild, May 17, 1939; 6000, Hewlett to Oceanside, May 30, 1954 (Bull)—two miles of flats and salt meadows by boat. *Fall*—600, Idlewild, Sept. 2, 1946; 450, Mecox Bay, Oct. 17, 1936; 200, Idlewild, Nov. 5, 1944; 50, Jamaica Bay, Dec. 2, 1950. Migrants usually arrive in late April.

There are no *winter* specimens from our area in the large series in the American Museum, but it has increased greatly at this season in recent years. First *winter* report in 1929, and regular since then.

Maxima: 9, Idlewild, Jan. 9, 1949; 15, Fire Island Inlet, Jan. 23, 1949; 88 on all Long Island Christmas counts, late December 1952, the majority at the west end. The following winter (1953–54) on four censuses combined, 150 were reported from the Nassau-Queens-Brooklyn areas alone, and 63 in the Westport, Conn., area.

Black-bellied Plovers are regular in small numbers each *summer* along the outer coast. Maxima: as many as 25 were observed at Jones Beach, June 29, 1939; an individual was collected at Quogue, July 1, 1903.

Collected inland at Ossining, Sept. 1, 1885 (Fisher), M.C.Z. collection.

RUDDY TURNSTONE (*Arenaria interpres*)*

Range: Holarctic species, the race *morinella* breeds south to Southampton Island. Winters north to South Carolina; very rarely to Massachusetts (specimen).

189

Status: Very common to occasionally abundant coastal migrant. Uncommon but regular throughout summer (nonbreeding stragglers). Rare in winter, but has increased in recent years. Very rare inland.

Occurrence and maxima: This species favors sandy and pebbly beaches, rocky islands, and jetties, but is found also on mud and sand flats.

Maxima: *Spring*—500, Idlewild, May 24, 1946; 200, Long Beach, June 3, 1949. A few stragglers are regular each summer along the coast. *Fall*—75, Montauk, Aug. 7, 1930; 150, Idlewild, Aug. 24, 1951; 100, same locality, Sept. 17, 1944. Very unusual is a report of four seen inland at Lake DeForest, N.Y., May 19, 1957 (Steffens and Treacy).

Spring arrival and fall departure dates are difficult to determine because of its wintering, but it is generally rare before May and after mid-November. There are a number of reports through early December; several others in March and April may represent wintering birds.

First reported in *winter* during 1936–37 season when two individuals were observed, one spending the entire winter at Orient (Latham). In fact, these were the only winter reports known to Cruickshank (1942). Since then there have been more than a dozen occurrences, including one that remained until early February 1958 at Jamaica Bay (several observers). Reported in January on four occasions on Fisher's Island by Ferguson: 1956, 1957, 1959, 1961 (all singles). The maxima reported at this season are 9 at Montauk, Dec. 29, 1956 (Boyajian), an unusual number.

WOODCOCK, SNIPE, SANDPIPERS: SCOLOPACIDAE

AMERICAN WOODCOCK (*Philohela minor*)*B

Range: An eastern Nearctic species, ranging from southern Canada to Florida.

Status: Fairly common migrant. Rare in winter near the coast. Local breeder. Formerly (prior to about 1890) much more numerous.

Migration: The present-day observer can scarcely credit the former abundance of this species when, during the height of the fall flight in late October and November, hundreds were shot by hunters in a single day. Today, if the observer flushes a half-dozen Woodcock in a day, he calls it a flight. Of course, hunters with well-trained dogs will flush considerably more, but nothing like the numbers in past years.

In the 1870s, the open season started on July 1 and continued until Feb. 1. One hunter was reported to have shot 120 birds along the Passaic River near Chatham, N.J., July 4, 1878 (*fide* Herrick). According to Mackay (1929), he shot 77 at Bridgehampton, L.I., in less than a week in

190

early June 1870. In both instances, these were presumably local breeding birds—both adults and young—judging from the dates. Because this went on for decade after decade, it is no wonder that a great decrease had occurred by the early 1900s.

Eventually with a much shorter open season and reduced bag limits, Woodcock increased, but have not regained anything like their former numbers.

American Woodcock usually arive in our area by the first ten days of March, although they have been reported in late February during mild seasons. Recent maxima: *Spring*—9, Inwood Hill Park, Manhattan, March 28, 1950. *Fall*—18, Easthampton, Oct. 31, 1941 (Helmuth).

Winter: Though occurring at this season much more rarely than snipe, a few will occasionally be found in moist lowland areas near the coast, particularly if the season is mild and open. There is only one winter specimen in the large local series in the A.M.N.H. collection: Islip, L.I., Feb. 12, 1930 (H. W. Smith). As many as five were reported on the Staten Island Christmas count in 1961.

Breeding: Woodcock nest in moist or dry second-growth and cut-over woodland, adjacent to open fields and meadows. They are especially fond of alder and willow thickets. Today the best way to find Woodcock is to visit suitable breeding areas at dusk in early spring and watch them going through their aerial courtship performance.

Egg dates: March 14 to May 28.

EUROPEAN WOODCOCK (*Scolopax rusticola*)*

Accidental: Palearctic species, which has occurred as a straggler in eastern North America from Newfoundland to Alabama.

One local record: a specimen of the nominate race was collected near Shrewsbury, N.J., Dec. 6, 1859 (Lawrence collection), A.M.N.H. No. 45603.

COMMON SNIPE (*Capella gallinago*)*B

Range: Holarctic species, the race *delicata* breeds south rarely and locally to northern New Jersey, southeastern New York (Dutchess County), and central Connecticut.

Status: Variously uncommon to very common migrant. Uncommon to locally fairly common in winter on the coast. Casual breeder.

Migration and winter: This species frequents wet meadows and pastures, shallow marshes, and cultivated fields after rainstorms. Snipe fluctuate in numbers from time to time. They are rare in dry years and occasionally numerous after suitable areas become flooded. The spring flight is chiefly inland and occurs principally in April, while in fall the flight is primarily coastal with the peak in October.

Maxima: *Spring*—40, Carmel, N.Y., Apr. 3, 1959; 75, Chatham, N.J., Apr. 21, 1928; 65, Overpeck Creek, N.J., Apr. 25, 1946. *Fall*—23, Easthampton, Oct. 15, 1939. *Winter*—12, Mecox Bay, Jan. 9, 1940; 16, southern Nassau Christmas count, Jan. 2, 1956. In winter, Snipe are most often found in low areas where springs prevent freezing. There are but two known winter specimens in our area: Far Rockaway, Jan. 1, 1890 (A. Marshall), A.M.N.H.; Orient, Jan. 30, 1919 (Latham), in his collection.

Extreme dates: July 4, 10, and 16 (specimen) to May 24 and 31; a few nonbreeding stragglers in June. Usually rare before mid-March.

Breeding: Nests in bogs and marshy areas. In our region the Common Snipe has been reported to breed on only four occasions: two old vague occurrences—nested at Chatham, Morris County, "many years ago" (Herrick); a nest was found near Newfoundland, Passaic County, in the "early" 1900s (Dugmore). There are two known recent occurrences—(*a*) Adult and young, Franklin, Sussex County, summer of 1950 (E. B. Nixdorf), *fide* Fables (1955); this latter locality was visited again in June 1952 and 1954, and although birds were seen there, no breeding evidence was obtained. (*b*) According to Treacy (*in litt.*), "Mrs. M. Earl has reported courting adults every spring at Blooming Grove [Orange County] and has flushed them every summer since 1952. and on occasion has observed adults with young, but never found the nest."

Egg dates: No data.

LONG-BILLED CURLEW (*Numenius americanus*)*

Range: A western Nearctic species, breeding east to southern Manitoba; formerly to southern Wisconsin. Winters regularly in small numbers, and more rarely in summer (nonbreeders) on the coasts of South Carolina and Florida. Now accidental on the Atlantic coast north of South Carolina.

Status: No reliable record for our area in over 25 years (since 1938); this also applies to the coasts of Massachusetts and southern New Jersey. In the New York City area reported only from the coast of Long Island.

Occurrence: The "Sicklebill," as it was formerly called by the gunners, was a regular fall migrant on the coast of Long Island. Giraud (1844) stated that it was also regular in spring and that it occurred in autumn as late as mid-November. According to Pike (in Dutcher, 1887–94), he had shot "hundreds" in the 1840s when they were very plentiful, but by 1865 they seemed to have disappeared and he had not come across a single one since. However, N. T. Lawrence (in Dutcher, *op. cit.*) stated that in 1885 in the vicinity of Far Rockaway, it was more uncommon than the Eskimo Curlew, with only two records in 12 years, compared to four records in ten years for the latter species. According to Dutcher (*op. cit.*) a few were collected each year from the late 1870s until 1889 when the last known local specimen was taken at Montauk on Sept. 9. Griscom (1923) placed it on the extirpated list and called it a bird of the past, despite the fact that it was reported five times between 1889 and 1923. Cruickshank (1942) listed six sight reports between 1923 and 1938. The last known report for our area was of one seen at Georgica Pond, Aug. 11, 1938 (Helmuth). He saw the species on no fewer than five occasions between 1910 and 1938.

Extreme dates: *Spring*—Apr. 28 and May 5 (specimen) to June 15, 1922, Amagansett (*fide* Latham). *Fall*—July 10 and 21 to Sept. 12; Oct. 15, 1924, Sagaponack (Helmuth); to "mid-November" (*fide* Giraud).

The statement in Cruickshank (1942), "reported as accidental at Ossining years ago" is unsatisfactory. A. K. Fisher (*in litt.*) stated that he knew of no such occurrence.

Specimen data: There are at least 15 local specimens—4 extant in the American Museum as follows: 3 without date; 1 labeled "Long Island" (Arnold collection), No. 12567; 2, Rockaway "Meadows" (N. Pike), Nos. 436677 and 436678; the only known spring specimen is that of one shot at Montauk Point, May 5, 1877 (Dwight collection), No. 355723.

Subspecies: Treated here binomially, the poorly defined race *parvus*, although recognized by the A.O.U. *Check-list* (1957), is referred to in that work in a footnote, page 181, "There is some uncertainty in assigning older records to *N. a. americanus* or *N. a. parvus*. While there is an average size difference between the two, there is overlap, making the racial identification of specimens of unknown age and sex difficult." Neither Hellmayr and Conover (1948) nor Parkes (1952) recognize it.

Remarks: The Long-billed Curlew is somewhat of a mystery insofar as its "complete" absence for almost a quarter of a century in the northeast is concerned. Formerly reported to occur regularly, at least in fall, on portions of the eastern seaboard and recorded from New Brunswick to Florida, it is now virtually unknown north of South Carolina, where it is reported as regular by Sprunt (1949). With the exception of three individuals reported seen after a hurricane on the coast of North Carolina on Aug. 14, 1953, I am unaware of any reliable reports anywhere north of South Carolina since 1939, despite an enormous increase of observers on the lookout for it.

It has been suggested that the Long-billed Curlew has "changed" its migratory pattern over the years and that this has come about because the species has abandoned much of its former midwestern breeding range. In other words, its former regularity in fall along the eastern seaboard was the result of an annual overland migration of some individuals toward the east coast, but that since its withdrawal from most of its "eastern" range, the few individuals seen in recent years probably originate from the south Atlantic coast (Florida to South Carolina).

193

EURASIAN CURLEW (*Numenius arquata*)*

Accidental: Palearctic species, casual in Greenland.

Only one known record for continental North America: a specimen of the nominate race collected on Long Island in 1853 is in the New York State Museum, Albany, No. 324.

WHIMBREL (*Numenius phaeopus*)*

Range: Holarctic species, the race *hudsonicus*—formerly called Hudsonian Curlew—breeds south to northern Manitoba and northern Ontario.

Status: Variously rare to uncommon, but regular spring migrant, at infrequent intervals occurring in large numbers; common to very common fall migrant on the coast, but most flocks fly over without stopping.

Occurrence and maxima: This species is most frequently observed on salt meadows on the bay side of the outer coast and occurs less often on mud flats. However, being a wary bird, few alight, and seldom are large flocks seen on the ground. On Long Island, it never did, nor does it now, occur in very large numbers such as frequent the south Jersey coast. Moreover, most flocks of from 50 to 100 or more either pass overhead or fly offshore. These flying birds are often heard calling—their flight notes not too unlike those of Greater Yellowlegs. The spring flocks of up to 400 and the fall flights of 1000 or more are annual events in southern New Jersey, but if the observer sees 50 on Long Island he considers it a lucky day. Very likely many individuals bypass Long Island and migrate off the coast. However, in some years good-sized flocks do occur, especially in the early fall (July) flight.

Maxima: At Freeport, Thurston reported a flock of 150 on July 27, 1911, and Helmuth at Easthampton, a flock of 200 on July 30, 1922. There is often a smaller flight in late August and September. At this time, anywhere from a few birds up to 30 or so is the rule. A few are even reported on occasion from the inner coast (Connecticut and Rye to Baxter Creek, Bronx Co.), after strong easterly gales. The spring migration is almost always light and takes place chiefly at the east end of Long Island. An exceptionally large flight occurred at Easthampton in 1947 when Helmuth saw a flock of at least 250 on May 5, calling as they flew over.

Extreme dates: *Spring*—April 7, 12, and 20 (specimen) to May 31 and June 3. There are scattered reports all through June, but in no case is there a definite record of individuals summering although this is quite possible, as is true of many shorebirds. *Fall*—last week in June and first week in July to Nov. 10 and 15. Usually rare before late April and after early October.

194

Remarks: The Whimbrel winters chiefly in Middle and South America; rarely north to the coast of South Carolina.

Casual at Rockaway Beach, L.I., Dec. 24, 1912 (Bogardus), a bird picked up exhausted—died later, but not preserved. One carefully studied at Stony Brook harbor, L.I., Dec. 27, 1959 (W. Sabin). This latter individual was observed both at rest and in flight.

Subspecies: The first North American record of the Old World nominate race was that of an adult male shot at Jones Beach, Sept. 4, 1912 (S. Van Allen). It was in the company of two *N. p. hudsonicus*. The specimen is A.M.N.H. No. 11883 (see Miller, Auk, 32: 226, 1915).

Another specimen—the second known one—was collected in Labrador in 1948.

ESKIMO CURLEW (*Numenius borealis*)*

Extinct?: Formerly bred on the tundra of northern Mackenzie; migrated in fall to the Atlantic coast south to Long Island (chiefly offshore), and over the ocean to eastern South America; wintered from southern Brazil to Patagonia; in spring, migrated through the interior of North America.

The Eskimo Curlew was reported to be partial to dry upland fields adjacent to the seacoast, associating with Golden and Upland Plovers, generally avoiding the wet salt meadows and mud flats favored by Long-billed and Hudsonian Curlews. In clear weather Eskimo Curlews were rarely seen. After severe easterly storms, especially during early September, occasionally "hundreds" would be found on the fields.

Being esteemed as a delicacy for the table, great numbers of Eskimo Curlews were shot in the past for the market, both in the west on the north-bound flight and in the east on the return southward migration. This, together with constant hunting pressure on its wintering grounds in southern South America, caused this species to become virtually, if not entirely, extinct. Known by the hunters as Dough-bird (New England) and Fute (Long Island).

Despite the fact that there is one spring specimen for Maine and two for Massachusetts, there are no certain spring records for our area and no satisfactory occurrences any time in New Jersey. Stone (1937) stated, "Curiously enough we do not seem to have a single definite record of a specimen secured on the New Jersey coast." In fall it occurred only at the east end and on the south shore of Long Island, and then usually after sustained easterly gales in September.

Giraud (1844) reported that on Long Island it arrived in the latter part of August and remained until the first of November. He shot stragglers as late as Nov. 20. In later years (1875–91), however, the species was reported to occur from Sept. 7 to 30 (specimens in both cases) and this agrees with dates from the Massachusetts coast (Aug. 27 to Oct. 1).

The species was definitely recorded (specimens) only from Montauk, Good Ground (Hampton Bays), south of Amityville and Freeport, and in the vicinity of Far Rockaway. Of many local specimens reported taken, very few are in existence, and I have been able to find only three in the American Museum, all without dates: two mounts in the Lawrence collection, merely labeled Long Island, Nos. 3171 and 3348, and a skin in the Dwight collection, from Montauk Point, No. 355779. Two specimens in the Princeton University Museum were collected at Good Ground in 1880, and another in the University of Michigan, No. 121812, was shot near Amityville the same year on Sept. 11. The last known specimen from Long Island was taken at Montauk Point, Sept. 16, 1891 (Scott). The often published "record" of Aug. 3, 1893, was an unverified sight report (see Dutcher, 1887–94). The Aug. 3 date would appear to be about a month earlier than the earliest specimen.

The last recorded specimen was shot on the Labrador coast in the fall of 1932. While some recent sight reports of this species, including a few from the Texas coast, may be correct, none has been substantiated. Confusion with the Whimbrel is likely, as proved repeatedly by misidentified specimens. Although *N. minutus*, the Little Curlew—an eastern Palearctic species, breeding in Siberia and migrating along the Pacific coast of Asia to New Guinea, Australia, etc.—has never been taken in North America, it resembles the Eskimo Curlew very closely and would be indistinguishable from the latter except in the hand. Some authorities consider them to be conspecific.

A bird should be captured alive (federal law prohibits collecting) to answer the question whether the Eskimo Curlew is still in existence. The specimen should be examined critically by an expert, possibly color-photographed, and then released.

UPLAND PLOVER (*Bartramia longicauda*)*B

Range: Nearctic species, in the east breeding south to Virginia.

Status: Rare to uncommon migrant; formerly more numerous. Very local breeder.

Migration: On rare occasions Upland Plovers were found in considerable concentrations, but one to four is the number usually seen in our area today.

As to its former abundance in New Jersey, Stone (1937) mentions that C. S. Westcott shot "hundreds" in the 1860s in the fields near Long Branch, "mostly in potato fields and pastures right up to the edge of the bluff which rose fifteen to twenty feet above the surf."

Recent fall maxima: 25, Idlewild, July 14, 1935; 45, July 18, 1936 and 55, Aug. 11, 1934, both at Newark Meadows (Urner), some of these at the

196

latter locality possibly represent breeding birds; 27, Easthampton, Aug. 30, 1948. No comparable numbers in spring, the birds proceeding immediately to the breeding areas.

Extreme dates: Injured bird picked up, died later, Clason Point, Bronx County, March 18, 1933 (Kassoy), specimen in A.M.N.H., not published previously. March 25 and 28 to Oct. 28. Rare before mid-April and after mid-September.

Breeding: Formerly a widespread and locally common nesting bird in our area, the Upland Plover has greatly decreased within the past 60 years or so. Extensive shooting in earlier times, together with the decline in agriculture and widespread development of open country in recent decades has caused the decline of this species over most of the northeast. On eastern Long Island it was to be found at Montauk, Shinnecock Hills, Orient, and Gardiner's Island, but disappeared long ago as a breeder from most of these areas. However, on the Hempstead Plains this species survived until the mid-1940s. This isolated, nearly treeless prairie once extended from Floral Park east to Farmingdale (about 16 miles) and in a north–south direction at its widest from Jericho to the present Southern State Parkway (about 5 miles), and encompassed an area of about 60,000 acres. In the early 1920s, J. T. Nichols estimated at least 25 breeding pairs. With the near total destruction of this unique habitat after World War II, principally due to the vast building development of the area, the Upland Plover dwindled to no more than three or four pairs, which somehow have managed to hold on to the present time. Elsewhere on Long Island, single pairs have nested at Easthampton (1949), Syosset (1951), and Bohemia (1958); perhaps elsewhere.

It is unreported as a nesting bird in Westchester, Putnam, and Rockland counties, N.Y., but has bred in Orange County at Goshen and Washingtonville, and perhaps still does. The only known breeding report for our portion of Fairfield County, Conn., was a nest with eggs at Glenbrook in 1897 (Howes, 1928).

In New Jersey, it nested on the dry portions of the Newark Meadows until the late 1930s, but that area is now unsuitable. For many years it has bred at Lamington, Somerset County, and in adjacent Hunterdon County. Up to six pairs have been present in that area but in 1956 only two pairs were reported. According to Fables (1955), it nested recently near Red Bank, Monmouth County. In Middlesex County in the region between New Brunswick and South Plainfield, especially at Hadley Airport, as many as eight pairs were found in 1952, but by 1955 only two or three pairs were reported.

Aside from the short-grass prairie habitat (Hempstead Plains), the Upland Plover nests in extensive hay fields and pastures in our area.

Egg dates: May 2 to June 16.

197

SPOTTED SANDPIPER (*Actitis macularia*)*B

Range: Nearctic species, in the east—breeding on the coast south to Virginia and in the mountains to northern Alabama.

Status: Fairly common to occasionally common migrant. Widely distributed breeder.

Migration: The Spotted Sandpiper is an ubiquitous shorebird, being found from highland streams and ponds in the interior to salt marshes and muddy creeks along the coast. Although ordinarily seen in groups up to six, more have been found on occasion.

Maxima: *Spring*—32, Overpeck Creek, N.J., May 18, 1919. *Fall*—25, Jones Beach, Aug. 15, 1944.

Extreme dates: Apr. 3 and 8 to Nov. 14 and Dec. 3, 1943, Alpine, N.J. (Komorowski). Rare before late April and after mid-October.

Breeding: This species nests singly in fields, along ponds and streams, and in scattered groups in sand dunes where it is grassy. In this last habitat I estimated between 20 and 25 breeding pairs at Short Beach during the summer of 1951.

Egg dates: May 9 to June 27.

Remarks: Winters north to coastal South Carolina. Accidental at this season at Kensico Reservoir, Dec. 21, 1947 (Obioko and P. C. Spofford). This bird was studied carefully both at rest and in flight.

SOLITARY SANDPIPER (*Tringa solitaria*)*

Range: Nearctic species, the nominate race breeds south to the central portions of Ontario and Quebec. Reports of its nesting in the northern United States are not confirmed.

Status: Fairly common migrant.

Occurrence and maxima: The Solitary Sandpiper is ordinarily seen alone or in groups up to three or four, but on occasion more are observed.

Maxima: *Spring*—10, Dyker Beach, May 14, 1950; 12, Pocantico River, near Tarrytown, N.Y., May 20, 1949. *Fall*—9, Easthampton, Sept. 23, 1933. Although often referred to in the literature as being more numerous inland than on the coast, it is anything but rare in the latter environment, as may be seen by the aforementioned figures. It prefers fresh water, although rarely it may be observed on coastal mud flats or salt marshes. The two coastal localities mentioned above contain freshwater pools and small ponds. Whether the favored habitat is inland or coastal is immaterial.

Extreme dates: *Spring*—Apr. 7, 13, and 14 (specimen) to June 6. *Fall*—July 5 to Nov. 11, 16, and 18. Rare before late April and after mid-October. Regular the second week in July.

198

Remarks: The statement in *Birds of Rockland County* (Deed *et al.*, 1959) that it is "probably also a rare summer resident" is, of course, unfounded. As may be seen by the above dates, there is a one-month interval between spring departure and fall arrival—as is true of many migrant shorebirds.

WILLET (*Catoptrophorus semipalmatus*)*

Range: Nearctic species (for details, see Subspecies).

Status: Collectively the Willet (both subspecies) is a variously rare to common spring, and fairly common to occasionally very common fall coastal migrant. Subject to marked fluctuations, but has increased considerably in recent years.

Occurrence and maxima: This species delights in broad expanses of sand and mud flats. It frequently associates with Greater Yellowlegs and is often seen with godwits. In spring it is most numerous and regular at the east end of Long Island, but is more widespread in fall.

Maxima: *Spring*—19, Westhampton Beach, Apr. 28, 1937; 34, Shinnecock Bay, May 16, 1958; 50, Mecox Bay to Easthampton, May 18, 1947; 7, Mecox Bay, May 29, 1945. Stragglers are present in June and July, but no proof of summering is known (June 5, 9, 12, 15, 22, 28 and July 2, 4, 7, 9, 10), singles in different years in all instances. *Fall*—14, Moriches Inlet, July 14, 1957; 14, Easthampton, July 29, 1949; 53, Shinnecock and Mecox bays, Aug. 26, 1939; big flight autumn of 1944 at Idlewild (various observers); Sept. 8 (50), Sept. 18 (80), Sept. 23 (45), Oct. 7 (34); 5, Jamaica Bay Refuge, Oct. 18, 1958.

Extreme dates: Apr. 19 to Nov. 23. Rare after October.

Rare away from the outer coast. Casual inland—two specimens, subspecies not stated: Riverdale, Sept. 7, 1880 (Bicknell); Ossining, May 22, 1885 (Fisher).

Subspecies: The Willet is a Nearctic species of local distribution, with two widely separated populations: (*a*) coastal and primarily eastern (nominate race); (*b*) inland and western (race *inornatus*). The eastern race breeds in southern Nova Scotia, and on the south Atlantic coast north to southern New Jersey (as far as Beach Haven and Tuckerton). It formerly bred on the coast of Massachusetts; very rarely in southern Connecticut. No breeding evidence for Long Island, or for any place in our area. The western race, *inornatus*, breeds east to Manitoba, South Dakota, and Nebraska; formerly to Minnesota and Iowa.

Although the two subspecies may be differentiated in the field when side by side, and "typical" specimens may be picked out readily in a museum series, there is much overlap in size, markings, and color characters, both as to sex and age.

There are two spring specimens in the A.M.N.H. collection taken locally, both of the nominate race. This is not surprising, when it is considered that the only known breeding location north of us is in Nova Scotia and that is of relatively small extent. These two specimens were collected at Montauk Point, Apr. 29, 1890 and May 6, 1887.

In the same collection there are 25 fall specimens, all taken in August at various localities along the south shore of Long Island. With one, or possibly two exceptions, they are of the larger, paler, longer-billed, longer-legged, western subspecies.

GREATER YELLOWLEGS (*Totanus melanoleucus*)*

Range: Nearctic species, breeding south to southeastern Quebec and Newfoundland.

Status: Very common to abundant coastal migrant; regular in small numbers inland. Uncommon but regular in winter on the coast in recent years, formerly very rare; always a few present through the summer.

Migration: The Greater Yellowlegs is one of our most adaptable shorebirds insofar as environment is concerned. It is found in large numbers on coastal flats, marshes, and ponds, and is regular inland along streams, lakes, and also on flooded golf courses and fields after heavy rains.

Maxima: *Spring*—90, Easthampton, Apr. 29, 1932; big flight in late spring of 1927 (400, Easthampton, May 23; 250, Manasquan, N.J., May 28). *Fall*—300, Jones Beach, Aug. 12, 1931; 350, Idlewild, Aug. 27, 1950; 500, Easthampton, Sept. 22, 1922; 150, Jamaica Bay Refuge, Oct. 23, 1955. Usually rare before late March and after November.

Winter: This species winters north to South Carolina; more rarely to Long Island and Massachusetts. In our area there are no known winter specimens. First reported Feb. 21, 1935; regular since then.

Maxima: 10, Jamaica Bay area, Dec. 27, 1953; 10, Pelham Bay area, Dec. 23, 1961.

LESSER YELLOWLEGS (*Totanus flavipes*)*

Range: Nearctic species, breeding southeast to northern Ontario and west-central Quebec (James Bay). More western in its breeding distribution than the preceding species. Migrates in spring chiefly through the interior (Mississippi Valley, etc.).

Status: Common to abundant fall migrant on the coast, occasionally in very large numbers. Rare, but regular in spring. Very rare in winter. Rarer than the Greater Yellowlegs inland; and rarer on the coast in summer. Recorded every month of the year on the coast.

Migration: The Lesser Yellowlegs is partial to coastal ponds and to pools left by the receding tide on the salt marshes; it also frequents mud flats. As Griscom (1923) pointed out, this species has a shorter migration period in fall than the Greater Yellowlegs, but in favorable places along the coast, is often the more numerous of the two.

It also arrives earlier than that species, often as early as the last week in June or the first week in July. The Lesser Yellowlegs is most numerous from early July to about the middle of September, while the Greater Yellowlegs is most numerous in fall from early August to late October.

Maxima: 500, Newark Meadows, July 18, 1936; 5000, Easthampton to Montauk, Aug. 24, 1924 (Helmuth)—500, maximum flock; 600, Newark Meadows, Sept. 18, 1929. There is some evidence that this species has slightly decreased within the last 25 years. Recent maxima have been between 300 and 400. There are two spring specimens, both A.M.N.H.— May 10, 1873, and May 7, 1882. This species is regularly reported in spring, particularly in recent years, but almost always in very small numbers, rarely up to a half-dozen or so. Very unusual is a report of 25, Newark Meadows, May 12, 1934 (Urner). Rare before late April.

Winter: The Lesser Yellowlegs winters north to South Carolina; very rarely to Massachusetts (specimen). In our area, it is much rarer than the Greater Yellowlegs, with scarcely more than a dozen occurrences. There are no winter specimens taken locally. First reported Jan. 27, 1936. The maximum number reported is a group of four, Mecox Bay, Dec. 26, 1938, to Feb. 13, 1939 (many observers).

Remarks: There are a number of spring, winter, and inland sight reports made by inexperienced observers that are unsatisfactory. The beginner, who believes that the two yellowlegs are easy to identify in life, is greatly mistaken. Size, length of bill, and other characters are all relative and very deceptive, unless the two species are together for direct comparison. While their voices are different, caution is urged in using this method alone for identification.

KNOT *(Calidris canutus)**

Range: Holarctic species, the race *rufa* breeds south to Southampton Island. Winters north to South Carolina; rarely to Massachusetts (specimens).

Status: Very common to abundant coastal migrant; occasionally more numerous; stragglers throughout summer. Rare to fairly common in winter. Unreported inland.

Migration: The Knot is very much restricted to areas adjacent to the ocean and is ordinarily rare anywhere else, although occurring occasionally along the shores of Long Island Sound in small numbers—up to a dozen or so. It frequents bays and inlets along the outer coast, preferring mud and sand flats, and salt meadows.

Formerly (prior to 1890) reported to occur by the thousands, it decreased greatly, due to overshooting. Protected by 1913, it recovered markedly and since the 1930s is once more abundant, although not yet attaining its former numbers.

Maxima: *Spring*—one of the last shorebirds to arrive in numbers, the peak is reached during the final week of May—2500, Idlewild, May 30, 1945 (Bull and Eisenmann). *Fall*—maxima in late July, lesser flights in August, again in late September and October—1500, Meadow Island, near Jones Inlet, July 22, 1962 (Levine); 450, Idlewild, Aug. 10, 1944; 450, Moriches Inlet, Sept. 21, 1936; 400, Idlewild, Oct. 23, 1944. Generally arrives in mid-May; usually rare by late November.

Winter: Collected, Rockaway Beach, Jan. 20, 1875 (C. H. Eagle) A.M.N.H., previously unpublished. Next reported at this season in late December 1937.

Maxima: 26, Jones Beach, Dec. 24, 1939 (Elliott); 10, Raritan Bay, Dec. 29, 1953 (Brown, Eynon *et al.*); 6, Jamaica Bay Refuge, Jan. 27 to Feb. 22, 1955 (many observers); 18, Shinnecock Inlet, Dec. 26, 1956 (Wilcox).

PURPLE SANDPIPER (*Erolia maritima*)*

Range: A western Palearctic and eastern Nearctic species, breeding south to the east coast of Hudson Bay (Belcher Islands).

Status: Locally, a very common winter visitant on both outer and inner coasts.

Occurrence and maxima: The Purple Sandpiper, one of the tamest of shorebirds, frequents rock jetties on the coasts of Long Island and New Jersey; also similar situations and rocky islets in Long Island Sound. It has increased markedly with the continued construction of breakwaters. Now arrives earlier in fall and departs much later in spring than formerly— in fact it has been reported in every month. Very rarely found on the beaches except where directly adjacent to rocky areas.

It is estimated that the present total winter population on the many rock jetties from Atlantic Beach to the mile-long jetty at Short Beach contains at least 300 individuals.

Some maxima at various jetties: 85, Rockaway Point, Nov. 15, 1961; 100, Rye, N.Y., Dec. 1, 1940; 117, Short Beach, Jan. 13, 1962; 125, Long Beach, Apr. 15, 1950; 75, Atlantic Beach, May 19, 1951; 48, Long Beach, May 26, 1950.

The only local report away from salt water is that of a flock of 12 on the concrete abutment at Prospect Park Lake, Dec. 11, 1938 (Breslau), probably the result of a storm a few days previously.

Extreme dates: casual, Orient, Sept. 7, 1936 (Latham); Oct. 9 to June 2 and 6. Rare before late October. In recent years has lingered in numbers well into May.

Three summer records: specimen collected at Gardiner's Point, L.I., July 28, 1925 (Ellis), identification verified by Griscom; summer of 1961— one seen at Great Gull Island, July 31; and one at Short Beach, July 2 to Aug. 13 (various observers in both instances).

PECTORAL SANDPIPER *(Erolia melanotos)**

Range: Nearctic and eastern Palearctic species, breeding south to extreme northern Ontario.

Status: On the coast—common to locally abundant fall migrant; usually uncommon to fairly common, but regular spring migrant. Occasional inland, especially during periods of low water.

Occurrence and maxima: This species favors grassy pools and shores rather than exposed mud flats, and may be found on cut-over meadows on the coast after rainstorms; also in rain pools on golf courses and fields.

The Pectoral Sandpiper fluctuates markedly, in certain years appearing in very small numbers, in other years in sizable flocks. Inland it is ordinarily present only when the edges of ponds and reservoirs are exposed during dry years.

Maxima: *Fall*—55, Newark Meadows, July 25, 1936; unprecedented late August flight in 1924—700 on Aug. 24, 1200 on Aug. 25, Easthampton to Montauk (Helmuth); 350, Mecox Bay, Sept. 15, 1935; 80, same locality, Oct. 19, 1956. *Spring*—20, Newark Meadows, March 26, 1938 (Urner), exceptionally early; 20, Long Branch, Apr. 9, 1955 (Seeley); 40, Saga-ponack, May 31, 1929 (Helmuth). *Inland*—11, Titicus Reservoir, N.Y., Oct. 6, 1940; 6, Troy Meadows, Apr. 9, 1955 (Norse)—note coastal maxima, same date.

Extreme dates: *Fall*—July 6 to Dec. 11. *Spring*—March 18 to June 14 and 18. Specimens in the A.M.N.H. taken Nov. 5 and March 27. Rare after October and before April.

Unlike many other common shorebirds, *summering* nonbreeding stragglers of this species have not been reported in our area.

WHITE-RUMPED SANDPIPER *(Erolia fuscicollis)**

Range: Nearctic species, breeding south to Baffin and Southampton Islands.

Status: Fairly common to abundant fall migrant, uncommon to sometimes very common spring migrant on the coast, but numbers vary greatly from year to year. Very rare inland.

Occurrence and maxima: This species is often found among the large flocks of "peep" that throng the flats during migration, but prefers grassy pools and pond edges to the exposed flats. It is a notably late spring migrant, occurring chiefly the last week in May and the first half of June. In autumn, it is rare before late July, and the largest concentrations occur from late August to early October. However, groups of 2 to 12 are the rule and flocks of over 100 are few and far between. More rarely much larger concentrations have been reported. In spring the numbers are much smaller.

Maxima: *Fall*—1000, Easthampton to Shinnecock Bay, Aug. 23, 1930 (Helmuth); 400, Newark Meadows, Oct. 6, 1929 (Edwards and Urner). *Spring*—60, Easthampton, May 29, 1927; 75, Idlewild, June 5, 1949; 50, Mastic, June 10, 1934; 20, Jamaica Bay Refuge, June 19, 1959. Summer stragglers occur through late June and early July.

Extreme dates: Apr. 28 to Dec. 4. Rare before mid-May and after early November.

Remarks: Several species of shorebirds, notably the Pectoral, White-rumped, and Least Sandpipers that frequent short-grass areas have apparently decreased considerably within our area during the past 30 years or so. Formerly much salt hay was cut to provide forage for livestock. Nowadays the coastal meadows are no longer, or very rarely, mowed. The result is that these marsh-loving waders find conditions unsuitable, and the flocks are much smaller than in past years. Note that the maxima listed are greatest during the 1920s and 1930s for all three species—the period when salt-hay farming was at its height. It is suggested that in all probability large flocks pass over our region to more favorable areas elsewhere, and that the reduction in numbers of recent years is a local condition.

BAIRD'S SANDPIPER (*Erolia bairdii*)*

Range: Nearctic species, breeding south to southwestern Baffin Island. Migrates in spring chiefly through the Great Plains; very rare at this season east of the Mississippi River.

Status: Rare to uncommon, but regular fall migrant on the coast.

Occurrence and maxima: Baird's Sandpiper prefers wet grassy areas; pools and ponds along the bay side of the beach; and golf courses and fields, especially after rainstorms. It frequently associates with other "peep," but may be found alone.

Maxima: 5, Sagaponack, Aug. 9, 1938; 5, Baxter Creek, Bronx County, Aug. 14, 1955; 6, Mecox Bay, Aug. 22, 1923; 18, Easthampton, Sept. 16, 1933 (Helmuth)—14 together and 4 others nearby; a concentration such as this is exceptional in our area.

204

Casual inland: Amawalk Reservoir, N.Y., Sept. 13, 1941 (Breslau and Sedwitz), the only reliable report.

Extreme dates: July 16, Aug. 4, several other early August reports; Aug. 14 (specimen) to Oct. 30 (specimen), Nov. 2, 5, 7, and 15.

Remarks: In our area no spring specimens or other confirmation exist. Of 22 known specimens—all collected on Long Island—*none* was taken earlier than Aug. 14. Of 24 specimens collected in Massachusetts, *none* was taken in spring, nor do Griscom and Snyder (1955) accept any sight reports at that season. The same situation applies to other areas in the northeast. There are no spring records for Maine (Palmer, 1949), or for Maryland (Stewart and Robbins, 1958).

Reports of Baird's Sandpipers in our region in spring lack substantiating evidence and are here omitted. Griscom (1923) merely mentioned one spring "record," May 2, 1878, but gave no details. Despite Stone (1937) crediting Urner with a report of one seen on the New Jersey coast on May 30, 1929 (locality not stated), there is no adequate basis for this. Urner and Storer (1949) specifically stated, "no spring records." Cruickshank (1942) stated that it was accidental in spring, but at the same time said, "There are only 27 spring records . . ."(?) However, these "records" are all *sight reports* of birds ranging from Apr. 30 to June 14, plus an inland observation. All of the 27 spring "records" are from 1927 to 1939. It seems remarkable that there have been no confirmed spring reports either prior or subsequent to those years, despite a greatly increased number of observers since 1939. I have checked these reports, and not a single one has the slightest detail concerning identification. Two of the reports even had as many as six and nine individuals. While it is true that a number of these observations were made by experienced people, unusual reports should not be taken for granted, no matter how generally competent the observer. Moreover, Baird's Sandpiper, closely resembling other shorebirds, is one of the more difficult species to identify in the field.

Although the Golden Plover and Lesser Yellowlegs have a migration pattern similar to that of Baird's Sandpiper in spring, i.e., through central North America, nevertheless, Golden Plovers and Lesser Yellowlegs have been collected in spring in our area and are much more numerous in fall also. A spring specimen of Baird's Sandpiper is necessary before it is entitled to be called a spring migrant in the New York City region or, for that matter, anywhere in the coastal portions of the northeast.

LEAST SANDPIPER (*Erolia minutilla*)*

Range: Nearctic species, breeding south to Nova Scotia.

Status: Common to abundant coastal migrant; occasionally more numerous. Regular inland in small numbers. Very rare in winter.

Migration: The Least Sandpiper, like its more numerous associate the Semipalmated Sandpiper, frequents salt meadows, mud flats, and sand fill, preferring the more grassy areas to the open flats. It is more frequent inland than the Semipalmated Sandpiper and is found along the marshy edges of lakes and ponds.

Maxima: *Spring*—5000, Idlewild, May 19, 1939 (Mayer). *Fall*—1200, Oak Beach, July 18, 1948; 800, Sagaponack, Aug. 29, 1933; 1600, Moriches Inlet, Sept. 28, 1936, and 50, Mecox Bay, Oct. 25, 1936—a notably large and late flight that year. In more recent years groups of 20 to 50 are the rule (see White-rumped Sandpiper for explanation of supposed decrease).

Extreme dates: Apr. 3 to Nov. 18. Rare before late April and after early October. Summer stragglers are regular on the outer coast.

Winter: The Least Sandpiper winters north to North Carolina; rarely to Maryland and southern New Jersey (Cape May).

An individual seen at Sagaponack, March 10, 1946 (Fleisher, Jacobson, and Sedwitz), may have wintered, as the date appears to be much too early for a migrant. One was studied closely at Gravesend Bay, Brooklyn, Dec. 28, 1952 (Carleton). Most unusual were five carefully observed at Jamaica Bay, Jan. 2, 1955 (Mayer *et al.*). Another individual was well seen at Hewlett Bay, Dec. 30, 1961 (Berliner); it was with a group of 17 Semipalmated Sandpipers, an unusual occurrence in itself.

CURLEW SANDPIPER (*Erolia ferruginea*)*

Range: A northeastern Palearctic species, breeding in northern Siberia. Winters over a wide range from the British Isles (rarely) and the Mediterranean region south to South Africa and from tropical Asia south to Australia and New Zealand. In the western portion of its range, migrates along the Atlantic coasts of Europe and Africa. Wanders occasionally or regularly to eastern North America (New Brunswick, Maine, Massachusetts, Long Island, and New Jersey); recorded in the southern Lesser Antilles and in eastern Patagonia.

Status: Rare, occasionally uncommon, but apparently regular spring migrant along the south shore of Long Island; rarer in fall, but possibly overlooked.

Occurrence and maxima: This species has been reported at various localities on the south shore of Long Island from Jamaica Bay to Sagaponack and Georgica Pond; once on Fisher's Island. It was formerly observed frequently and more or less regularly on the Jones Beach strip (Tobay Pond to Gilgo and Oak Beach), particularly from 1937 to 1941, when this area was at optimum condition for shorebirds. It has been reported with great regularity in the Jamaica Bay area since 1947. The majority of occurrences on western Long Island are during May. Much rarer at the east end, but this may be due, in part, to less frequent coverage.

Curlew Sandpipers frequent mud flats, and to a lesser extent coastal ponds, associating most often with Dunlins, and occasionally with Knots. There are undoubtedly many more occurrences in spring than in fall because their dull plumage at the latter season may cause them to be overlooked.

Maxima: Pennsylvania Avenue flats, Jamaica Bay—4, May 14, 1949; 3, May 21, 1951 (numerous observers on both occasions).

Extreme dates: *Spring*—May 2, 4, and 10 to June 4 and 9 (specimen). *Fall*—one present at Tobay Pond, June 27 to Aug. 30, 1937 (various observers); July 8–10; July 16; and Aug. 7 to Oct. 15, Nov. 15, and 25. Casual on Dec. 19 (see Specimen data).

The July dates may represent summer vagrants, or possibly early fall arrivals (see Remarks).

Specimen data: Possibly as many as a dozen local specimens have been reported, but only six are extant. The early specimens are without data, some of these from Fulton Market may have come from Long Island. The existing specimens, all from Long Island, are: one in nearly full breeding plumage, Rockaway (date and collector unknown), A.M.N.H. No. 3406; another in partial breeding plumage, Good Ground (Hampton Bays), May 24, 1883 (Dutcher collection), A.M.N.H. No. 64973; one in full breeding plumage, labeled Long Island, June 9 1891, (Dutcher collection), A.M.N.H. No. 64974; Mecox Bay, Sept. 7, 1923 (Helmuth), in his collection; Fisher's Island, Dec. 19, 1923 (Fuertes), A.M.N.H. No. 752387, the only substantiated winter record; Jamaica Bay, Oct. 12, 1956 (Buckley), A.M.N.H. No. 707780, possibly the same individual present since Aug. 11.

Remarks: There are at least three theories why the Curlew Sandpiper, an Old World shorebird, occurs regularly on the Atlantic coast of the northeastern United States (Massachusetts, Long Island, New Jersey).

1. Nisbet (1959) is of the opinion that this species makes a direct east–west crossing from Europe to North America during migration.

2. Eisenmann (1960) suggests that this species (as well as the Ruff) may be carried across the tropical Atlantic by cyclonic storms while en route to Africa during the fall migration. He further suggests that their greater frequency in spring along our coast is the result of birds being carried by hurricanes to tropical America in preceding years, and then accompanying other shorebirds on the northward flight.

3. It is possible that a few individuals may migrate in fall from their Siberian nesting grounds east by way of Alaska and Canada to the Atlantic seaboard—a route used by certain shorebirds breeding in tundra country of northern Alaska, Yukon, and Mackenzie—i.e., Eskimo Curlew (formerly), Long-billed Dowitcher, Western Sandpiper, Buff-breasted Sandpiper. The Long-billed Dowitcher and other primarily American shorebirds also breed in northeastern Siberia.

207

Since writing the foregoing, a report from reliable sources states that the Curlew Sandpiper was discovered breeding on the coast of northern Alaska in the vicinity of Point Barrow during the summer of 1962.

DUNLIN (*Erolia alpina*)*

Range: Holarctic species, the race *pacifica* breeds south to northern Ontario (Hudson Bay).

Status: Common to locally abundant migrant and winter visitant on the coast. Summering stragglers are frequent. Very rare inland.

Migration: The Dunlin, or Red-backed Sandpiper, occurs on mud flats, coastal estuaries, and tidal pools on the salt marshes. It may be found in large flocks both spring and fall. In the former season it is seen chiefly in May, as it is a late migrant. In fall maximum numbers are present in October, for it arrives and departs late. Flocks seen in early April and again in late November and early December are birds which probably winter in or just south of our area.

Maxima: *Spring*—900, Far Rockaway, May 7, 1950. *Fall*—225, Idlewild, Sept. 9, 1944; 1800, Jones Inlet, Oct. 12, 1950 (Komorowski); 800, Idlewild, Oct. 26, 1952.

Very rare inland, but occasionally found on the tidal flats of the larger rivers: two specimens taken at Ossining, Oct. 3 and 24, 1881 (Fisher), M.C.Z. collection.

Change in winter status: Dunlins are found most numerously in winter on sand bars and flats at the inlets along the south shore of Long Island, where they often associate with Sanderlings. Cruickshank (1942) called this species, ". . . extremely rare in winter," but added, "there are now so many records for this season that it would be redundant to list them." The first winter report of a flock (55) was at Fire Island Inlet, Feb. 19. 1939. On Dec. 3 the same year, 475 were seen on the flats at Oak Beach. In contrast to former years Dunlins have been found in large concentrations through the winter months, since the mid-1940s.

Maxima: *Outer coast*—900, Idlewild, Dec. 22, 1950; 600, Jones Inlet, Jan. 16, 1960.

The recent wintering of this species in numbers along the Connecticut shore is an event that was unheard of formerly. On the Christmas counts of 1951, 1952, 1953, and 1955—10, 37, 100, and 110 were reported respectively in the area from Stamford to Westport. It will thus be seen that this species is sometimes locally common in that region in winter as compared to former years.

Remarks: No specimen of any other race of Dunlin in the New York City area is known, the 1892 report considered unsatisfactory by Griscom

208

(1937a). Recent sight reports are completely worthless because this species is extremely variable individually, as may be seen by an examination of a large series of study skins.

SHORT-BILLED DOWITCHER (*Limnodromus griseus*)*

Range: Nearctic species (for details, see Remarks).

Status: Common to very abundant coastal migrant. Summer vagrant in small numbers. Very rare in winter (species?).

Occurrence and maxima: This species is most numerous on broad, exposed mud flats such as those at Jamaica Bay and the areas adjacent to Jones Beach. Height of the spring migration—May; fall—July; lesser flights in August and September.

Maxima: *Spring*—4000, Far Rockaway, May 7, 1950; 8000, Idlewild, May 12, 1939. *Summer*—small numbers through June (up to 20). *Fall*— 400, Jamaica Bay Refuge, July 4, 1961; 850, Gilgo, July 14, 1940; 1200, Idlewild, July 30, 1950.

Extreme dates: March 24 and Apr. 11 to Nov. 19. Rare before May and after early October.

Winters north to South Carolina (species?). Very rare on Long Island at this season: 4, Jamaica Bay Refuge, Dec. 12, 1953 to Jan. 2, 1954 (many observers); 2 on latter date, Hempstead Reservoir (several observers); 1, Tobay Pond, Jan. 10. 1954 (many observers)—7 individuals at three localities. In no case was the species determined.

Very rare inland; 4, Overpeck Creek, N.J., Aug. 1, 1925 (Kassoy); 6, Greendell, N.J., Sept. 7, 1947 (Edwards and Eynon).

The early and late dates, winter and inland occurrences listed above are of sight reports without determination as to species. There are no known winter specimens, nor any from inland areas in our region of either species.

Remarks: As specimen identification of dowitchers is exceedingly critical, Pitelka's monograph (1950) is followed here. Unfortunately, he did not give full data on New York specimens in his work, nor did he initial the labels on the specimens in the A.M.N.H. collection. In nearly all instances, he neglected to cite year and museum catalog number. This necessitated an examination by the writer of the entire series of both species from the New York City area; measurements were taken and color variations of certain specimens were compared with the tables and text in Pitelka's paper. Based on specimens, Pitelka stated that the nominate race is the dominant form in the east. The breeding grounds are largely unknown, but suspected of being mainly in the interior of northern Quebec, possibly south to northern Ontario (see Hall and Clement, 1960). The subspecies *hendersoni* breeds in central Canada east to Hudson Bay, and regularly, but rarely, occurs during fall migration on the Atlantic coast north of Chesapeake Bay. There are several specimens in the A.M.N.H. collection taken on Long Island and designated as *L. g. hendersoni* by Pitelka. Many others erroneously identified as Long-billed Dowitchers, *L. scolopaceus*, were redetermined as *L. g. hendersoni*, or as intermediate between *L. g. griseus* and *L. g. hendersoni*. Four *L. g. hendersoni* collected on Long Island and identified by Pitelka as such, were taken on July 12, 19, Aug. 28, and September (years not stated). According to Pitelka, *L. g. griseus* outnumbers *L. scolopaceus* on the Atlantic coast by at least 10 to 1 on the basis of specimens, and it probably would be much higher, closer to 100 to 1, in our area.

Subspecific identification in the field is out of the question and many instances of large-appearing birds with long bills identified as *L. scolopaceus* are probably nothing more than *L. g. hendersoni*. This has been proved many times by specimens labeled as *L. scolopaceus* and redetermined by Pitelka as *L. g. hendersoni*. (See discussion under Long-billed Dowitcher.)

LONG-BILLED DOWITCHER (*Limnodromus scolopaceus*)*

Range: A northeastern Palearctic and northwestern Nearctic species, breeding east to northern Mackenzie.

Status: Regular fall migrant on the south shore of Long Island; rarely elsewhere.

Occurrence: The Long-billed Dowitcher prefers fresh-water pools and ponds along the coast where shores are exposed by low water. Frequently reported in late September and October when most individuals of the preceding species have departed. However, there are a number of occurrences from late July on.

Remarks: Pitelka (1950) listed a number of specimens of *L. scolopaceus* taken on Long Island, of which seven are in the A.M.N.H. collection, and a few in other museums, the extreme dates being July 23 to Oct. 10 (years not stated). Dutcher (1887–94) listed two specimens as this form, collected March 20, 1866, and Nov. 30 (year?), but apparently neither is extant.

The relationship of the dowitchers had long been misunderstood until Pitelka (*op. cit.*) did much to clarify it. They were formerly considered to be conspecific; some authorities still consider them so. Pitelka pointed out that they are morphologically and possibly ecologically distinct, but he did not discuss their vocalizations. Some authorities attribute different call notes to the two species.

Contrary to what is generally believed, *L. scolopaceus* can be indentified in the field under favorable circumstances. The flight note of this species is usually a single flat "keek" or "peet" (sometimes doubled) in contrast to the whistled double or triple "teu-teu" of *L. griseus*, the latter call not unlike the notes of the Lesser Yellowlegs. The old-time hunters and collectors "knew" these notes and more than one calling bird was collected years ago as *L. scolopaceus*, and subsequently proved correctly identified. In fact, a specimen still extant bears the notation on the label, "call note heard." This was shot at Rockaway Beach, Sept. 25, 1875 (N. T. Lawrence), A.M.N.H.

It is also true that under ordinary circumstances the two forms are often difficult to differentiate in the field, and sometimes in the skin. The non-breeding plumages are practically identical and bill lengths are often misleading, as the latter overlap. Even the call notes may not be fully diagnostic (see Bull, 1962, and Eisenmann, 1962). However, field work, with emphasis on sound recording, is now under way. Only when direct comparison is available and "extremes" picked out, may identification be certain, but *only* by experienced and competent observers familiar with plumage characters. Some very large, long-billed individuals, which called after being flushed, were surely this species. Rarely in late July or early August, individuals may be found in breeding plumage with underparts deep cinnamon or rufous, heavily barred on the flanks and under-tail coverts, of very large size, and extremely long bills. The writer saw such an individual at Lawrence, L.I., July 21, 1951 (Bull, 1953). Another in similar plumage was carefully observed on the Hackensack Meadows, July 21, 1962, by Jehl, who incidentally collected an adult male at this locality on Aug. 13 following, the specimen in the University of Michigan Museum collection, No. 157536; identification confirmed by Storer. Jehl states (*in litt.*), "The specimen is an adult male still retaining a good bit of the distinctive alternate [breeding] plumage."

It might be pertinent to emphasize a parallel situation where Semi-palmated and Western Sandpipers are differentiated in the field by plumage characters and bill length.

STILT SANDPIPER (*Micropalama himantopus*)*

Range: Nearctic species, breeding southeast to northern Ontario (Hudson Bay). Migrates in spring chiefly between the Mississippi River, and the Rockies; rare in the east. Migrates in fall over the spring route; also via the Great Lakes and particularly along the Atlantic coast south of Maine.

Status: Variously uncommon to locally common fall migrant on the coast, occasionally very common. Very rare in spring.

Occurrence and maxima: The Stilt Sandpiper is quite particular in its choice of habitat, favoring shallow pools and ponds (fresh and brackish) along the outer coast, especially where these areas have muddy shores with patches of grass; less often on tidal flats. It frequently associates with Lesser Yellowlegs and Dowitchers, thus affording a ready comparison.

It is exceedingly erratic in numbers, some years decidedly uncommon, in others locally numerous. The largest flights occurred in 1911, 1912, and 1948. In recent years there were also large numbers reported in 1933, 1938, and 1944. It occurs in maximum numbers from late July to early September.

Maxima: 45, Tobay Pond, July 23, 1949; 75, same locality, Aug. 1, 1933; 80, Oak Beach, Aug. 6, 1938; 57, Easthampton, Aug. 8, same year; 13 collected (A.M.N.H.) out of 200 seen, Mastic, Aug. 12, 1912 (W. Floyd and J. T. Nichols); 150, Idlewild, Aug. 14, 1948 (Mayer and Rose); 300, Mecox Bay to Napeague, Aug. 27, 1911 (Helmuth); 60, Newark Meadows, Sept. 2, 1933; 75, Easthampton, Sept. 16, 1944; 15, Jones Beach, Sept. 27, 1946.

Extreme dates: *Fall*—July 1 to Nov. 17 (specimens from July 15 to Sept. 14). Rare after early October. *Spring*—Apr. 13 and 26 to June 10 (specimen). The Stilt Sandpiper is very rare in spring. Altogether, there are 14 known occurrences at this season—three of them specimens. Never before published are three specimens secured by Latham (in his collection): Orient, May 25, 1925, and June 9, 1940; Shelter Island, June 10, 1942. These are in nearly full breeding plumage. They are the only local spring specimens that I am aware of.

This species is casual inland: Boonton Reservoir, Aug. 6, 1933 (Watson *et al.*); Titicus Reservoir, Aug. 10, 1939 (Pangburn); 2, Croton Reservoir. Sept. 2, 1956 (Nolan and Odell).

Specimen data: Many fall specimens have been shot in past years, but relatively few are extant. Eaton (1910) mentions that Dutcher knew of 150 or more taken on Long Island between 1882 and 1893, with many others seen in flocks up to 60. The American Museum has 41 local specimens, all from Long Island in fall, as follows: July (6), August (28), September (7).

SEMIPALMATED SANDPIPER (*Ereunetes pusillus*)*

Range: Nearctic species, breeding south to northern Ontario (Hudson Bay).

Status: Common to very abundant coastal migrant. Regular inland, but less numerous than the Least Sandpiper. Very rare in winter.

Migration: Our most abundant shorebird, often seen in flocks by the thousands in favorable places, such as the vast flats of the south shore (Long Island).

Maxima: *Spring*—25,000, Easthampton to Mecox Bay, May 19, 1924 (Helmuth). *Fall*—6000, Newark Meadows, Aug. 1, 1928; 6000, Idlewild, Aug. 24, 1951; 3000, Mecox Bay, Sept. 21, 1937. Summering, nonbreeding stragglers are regular and not uncommon.

212

Extreme dates: Apr. 3 to Dec. 7. Rare before late April and after October.

Winter: This species winters north to Maryland and southern New Jersey (rare); very rarely to Long Island (specimen) and Massachusetts (specimen). In our area, one collected at Brooklyn, January 1903 (collector unknown), A.M.N.H., previously unreported. The first recent winter report was of an individual seen at Easthampton, March 4, 1946 (Helmuth), which probably wintered. The species was reported again in 1949, 1953, 1954, and 1957, all in late December and into January. In fact, a total of ten individuals was reported on four Christmas counts, winter of 1953–54. Four birds were present all December 1953 at the Jamaica Bay Refuge, and at least two of these well into January 1954 (many observers); four, near Westport, Conn., Dec. 26, 1959 (P. C. Spofford); 17 were observed at Hewlett Bay, L.I., Dec. 30, 1961 (Berliner), a very unusual number for our area.

WESTERN SANDPIPER (*Ereunetes mauri*)*

Range: A northwestern Nearctic species, breeding so far as known only along the coast of Alaska, east to Point Barrow.

Status: Fairly common to locally abundant fall migrant on the coast. Rare to uncommon spring migrant. Very rare inland and in winter.

Migration: Very closely related to the Semipalmated Sandpiper and almost always found with that species. These are two of our more difficult birds to tell apart and only those experienced with plumage and bill characters are competent to identify the Western Sandpiper. Those who mistakenly believe that every individual is identifiable in the field should examine certain specimens in museum collections. More than one specimen has been misidentified by very able ornithologists. There is considerable variation in both plumage coloration and bill length.

Usually observed in groups up to 20, but occasionally large flocks are reported. Maxima: *Fall*—100, Oak Beach, Aug. 6, 1938; 200, Easthampton, Aug. 29, 1933; 500, Newark Meadows, Sept. 10, 1933 (Herbert and Hickey); 250, Mecox Bay, Sept. 18, 1944. *Spring*—8, Jones Beach, June 1, 1947 (Alperin and Sedwitz).

Extreme dates: *Fall*—July 2 to Nov. 25. Most numerous from early August to late September. *Spring*—Apr. 25 to June 18, but rare before the last week in May. No proof of summering nonbreeding individuals, as it is rarely reported in late June and early July.

Western Sandpipers have been reliably reported inland at Central Park, Grassy Sprain Reservoir (twice), and Croton Reservoir—all in September.

Specimen data: There are no known specimens from the New York City area collected in spring or winter, or from inland localities. At least 25

213

in the American Museum, all from Long Island, are distributed as follows: July (2), August (10), September (12), October (1). The dates of these specimens range from July 17 to Oct. 12.

Winter: This species winters north to South Carolina; more rarely to Maryland and southern New Jersey (Cape May).

In our area three individuals were present at the Jamaica Bay Refuge all December 1953 into early January 1954; they were seen with several Semipalmated Sandpipers by a number of observers. Another was observed in the same area, Dec. 13, 1959 (Norse).

BUFF-BREASTED SANDPIPER (*Tryngites subruficollis*)*

Range: A northwestern Nearctic species, breeding locally along the Arctic Ocean from northern Alaska east to King William Island (northern Keewatin). Migrates in spring chiefly through the Great Plains; in fall mostly over the spring route, but in small numbers to the Atlantic coast from Maine to New Jersey. Apparently very rare south of the latter state along the coast.

Status: Rare, but regular fall migrant on the coast; occasionally more numerous.

Occurrence and maxima: The Buff-breasted Sandpiper favors wet short-grass meadows and occasionally dry sandy fields along the coast, sometimes associating with Pectoral Sandpipers in the former habitat, and with Golden and Upland Plovers in the latter.

In the New York City area it has always been a rare species, although one or two are reported each fall. Rarely small groups are seen. Giraud (1844) reported a flock of 5 collected on the shore of Gowanus Bay (Brooklyn) in August 1841. In recent years, the maximum numbers reported are: 8, Hook Pond, Easthampton, Sept. 8, 1944 (Helmuth); there are several other observations of up to 5 individuals on the south shore of Long Island.

Extreme dates: Aug. 3 to Oct. 15.

Remarks: No spring or inland reports are properly confirmed or published in detail. Of 31 specimens taken in Massachusetts and 20 collected on Long Island, *all* are from coastal areas in fall. Moreover, there are no verified sight reports of this species in spring, either from New England or from New Jersey.

MARBLED GODWIT (*Limosa fedoa*)*

Range: A western Nearctic species, breeding east to southern Manitoba and western Minnesota; formerly to southern Wisconsin.

214

Status: Rare to uncommon, but regular fall migrant on the coast; occasionally more numerous. Very rare in spring.

Occurrence and maxima: The Marbled Godwit in our area is almost always found on broad mud flats, and often associates with Willets, both yellowlegs, and several species of smaller shorebirds.

Prior to 1890, a regular migrant in small numbers in May, August, and September; then very rare until the early 1930s, when it became regular in fall, and by the late 1930s and early 1940s reported occasionally in flocks up to ten, rarely more.

Maxima: 8, Idlewild, Aug. 14, 1951; 22, Manasquan Inlet, N.J., Aug. 31, 1954 (several observers); 10, Jones Beach, Sept. 6, 1944; 10, Moriches Inlet, Sept. 14, 1944.

Extreme dates: July 6, 15, and 21 (specimen) to Nov. 19. Rare before August and after September.

Very rare in spring, only five reliable reports in recent years: Moriches Inlet, March 27, 1950 (Fischer and Parkes); Jamaica Bay area—Apr. 8, 1962 (several observers), Apr. 12, 1953 (Cashman), May 3, 1958 (Jehl, Post, and Wolfarth—color photo), May 11, 1941 (Imhof).

Remarks: Winters north to South Carolina; casual in southern New Jersey and Long Island (specimen).

An individual present at Shinnecock Inlet all fall was collected Dec. 22, 1952 (Wilcox), specimen in A.M.N.H. Another was carefully observed at the Jamaica Bay Refuge, Dec. 30, 1961 (several observers).

No inland occurrence for our area.

BAR-TAILED GODWIT *(Limosa lapponica)**

Accidental: Palearctic species, also breeding in Alaska, but wintering exclusively in the Old World. Two specimens from Massachusetts (1907 and 1937) and two sight identifications from southern New Jersey are the only known reports from eastern North America other than the Long Island record below.

Adult of the nominate race collected on Moriches Bay, opposite Mastic, Nov. 15, 1946 (C. L. Muller), A.M.N.H. No. 308880 (Auk, 64: 326, 1947).

HUDSONIAN GODWIT *(Limosa haemastica)**

Range: Nearctic species, breeding south to northeastern Manitoba (Hudson Bay). Migration similar to that of the Golden Plover: in spring chiefly west of the Mississippi River; in fall chiefly over the Atlantic Ocean (offshore). Practically unreported on the coast south of New Jersey.

Status: Rare to uncommon, but regular fall migrant on the coast; occasionally more numerous after easterly gales. Very rare in spring.

Occurrence and maxima: The Hudsonian Godwit frequents mud flats. Formerly rare, but regular on Long Island. There were two large flights prior to 1925, both on Shinnecock Bay, the first in 1903, the second in 1922. In 1903 the flight occurred on Aug. 31, when gunners were reported to have killed a dozen or more apiece. In 1922 on Aug. 28—after a two-day northeaster—at least 26 birds were reported, including a flock of 16, two of which were collected.

Between 1922 and 1951 no large numbers were reported and Cruickshank (1941) stated that groups up to three were the maxima.

In the last decade (1953–62), the following maxima have been reported: 14, Moriches Inlet, July 31, 1955; 10, Jones Beach, Aug. 5, 1951, after two days of high northeast winds; 10, Moriches Inlet, Aug. 12, 1958; and at the same locality—9, Aug. 23, 1957, and 9, Sept. 9, 1961.

Extreme dates: July 3, 1925, Newark Bay (Urner), bird in breeding plumage; July 13 to Nov. 13 and 26. Rare after October.

Very rare in spring: no specimens, but at least six reliable sight reports, May 3–25. First reported in spring in 1925.

Remarks: Casual inland: Boonton Reservoir, Sept. 18 to Nov. 13, 1949; one to three individuals seen from time to time on the exposed flats—the reservoir was low, because of the very dry autumn; members of the Urner Club and other observers saw these birds. An individual carefully studied near Haverstraw, N.Y., Sept. 18, 1960 (Steffens), may have been the result of hurricane Donna of Sept. 12.

SANDERLING *(Crocethia alba)**

Range: Holarctic species, breeding south to the northwest coast of Hudson Bay (Keewatin).

Status: Common to abundant migrant on the outer coast. Much less numerous in winter, and as a summering nonbreeder. Usually an uncommon migrant on the inside coast, such as on Long Island Sound. Very rare inland.

Occurrence and maxima: The Sanderling is characteristic of the ocean beaches and is likely to be found there any day of the year. During its periods of maximum abundance in migration, it is seen in considerable numbers also on sand flats adjacent to bays and inlets and to a lesser extent on mud flats.

Maxima: *Spring*—1500, Easthampton, May 20, 1927; 800, Idlewild, June 6, 1946. *Fall*—1000, Idlewild, July 28, 1945; 1300, same locality, Aug. 9, 1947; 2000, Mecox Bay, Sept. 18, 1924. *Winter*—200, Plum Beach, Dec. 20, 1958; 300, Atlantic Beach to Point Lookout, all January 1952.

Many years ago, Fisher collected this species on the flats at the mouth of the Croton River: three specimens, all in the M.C.Z. collection, were taken on Sept. 24 and Oct. 3, 1881, and June 5, 1884. Today it is a rarity anywhere inland in our area.

RUFF (*Philomachus pugnax*)*

Range: Palearctic species—in the western portion of its range—breeding south to France, and wintering from the British Isles to South Africa. Highly migratory. Wanders occasionally to eastern North America (Canada to North Carolina); and to the Lesser Antilles.

Status: Very rare vagrant to the coast of Long Island, but of more frequent occurrence in recent years.

Change in status: The Ruff was considered accidental by both Griscom (1923) and Cruickshank (1942). The former knew of only three records (all specimens), the latter of two more (both sight reports).

Between 1942 and 1950 alone there were six occurrences and an additional dozen or so since 1950. I am at a loss to explain this apparent "sudden" increase, but there are far more observers today than in 1942. The males in breeding plumage are unmistakable, and even the females (Reeves) and immatures are not easily overlooked. Despite many more reports in recent years, the Ruff is not observed as regularly as that other Old World visitant, the Curlew Sandpiper, but is observed in small numbers on occasion. Within the decade 1952–62 the Ruff was unreported in our area in four of those years.

In addition to frequenting the shores of coastal ponds and grassy mud flats, the Ruff may be found in dry fields such as on the fill at Spring Creek (Jamaica Bay area) where a bird was seen in the company of Kill-deers during the spring of 1957.

The species has been observed on Long Island only along the south shore at Jamaica Bay, Jones Beach, Captree State Park, and Moriches Inlet; also once on Fisher's Island. Most observations were made at Jamaica Bay (10 individuals between 1951 and 1961), and Tobay Pond (5 times). Three different individuals were present at the Jamaica Bay Refuge during the spring of 1956 and were seen by numerous observers: an adult male appeared on April 21 and remained until May 6, when it was joined by another adult male; finally a female was seen on May 27.

Extreme dates: *Spring*—March 31 and April 12 to May 30 and June 9–12. *Summer stragglers*—June 23; July 4–20; July 22 to mid-August. *Fall*—Aug. 5 to Sept. 28 and October (specimen, see below).

Away from Long Island, there are only two reliable occurrences: adult male with black ruffs seen at Westport, Conn., May 25–30, 1946 (A. A. Saunders, Auk, 64: 137–138, 1947). This is the only known occurrence in Connecticut. Our only reliable inland report is that of a female seen with several Lesser Yellowlegs on the muddy shore of a small reservoir near Overpeck Creek, N.J., Apr. 13, 1947 (Eisenmann *et al.*).

Specimen data: Three of four known local specimens are extant: one collected on Long Island, October 1851, formerly in the Lawrence collection, is apparently not in existence; another specimen, an adult male in breeding plumage with chestnut and black ruffs, merely labeled Long Island (no date), is A.M.N.H. No. 3184; still another, labeled Long Island, May 18, 1868 (not May 15 as reported in the literature) is a female, A.M.N.H. No. 45502—both of these latter specimens in the Lawrence collection; immature male, taken near Freeport, Sept. 26, 1914 (Hendrickson), A.M.N.H. No. 11944.

Remarks: For hypotheses about why the Ruff is a relatively frequent visitor to the New World, see Remarks under Curlew Sandpiper.

AVOCETS, STILTS: RECURVIROSTRIDAE

AMERICAN AVOCET (*Recurvirostra americana*)*

Very rare fall visitant: A western Nearctic species, breeding east to southern Manitoba and western Minnesota (1959); formerly to eastern Wisconsin; also southern New Jersey where, according to Stone (1937), it was found nesting by Wilson in the salt marshes of Cape May County in 1810. According to Allen and Hickey (1940), it nested there until about 1829. Summering nonbreeding and fall birds have been regular in southern New Jersey since 1954. As many as 40 individuals were reported at Fortescue in 1954 and up to 18 at Brigantine in 1956 (Kunkle *et al.*, 1959).

In our area, the species is much rarer. Even in Giraud's time (1840s), it was "less frequent" than the Black-necked Stilt. Of three local specimens collected, two are extant. Both of these have little data attached, except that they were taken on Long Island: immature, received at Fulton Market, Oct. 29, 1831 (Lawrence collection), A.M.N.H. No. 45631; an adult secured prior to 1847 was collected by Bell, A.M.N.H. No. 3207.

Since that time, Griscom (1923) listed one report—Orient, Aug. 15–22, 1908 (Latham). It then went unreported until 1932 when Urner (1936) stated that hunters illegally killed 9 out of a flock of 12 (first reported Sept. 4) on the Newark Meadows. The three survivors remained until Oct. 4 and were seen by numerous observers. This represents the largest number ever reported in the New York City area. Since then it has been seen less frequently with never more than two at one locality.

Indeed, since Cruickshank (1942), it has been reported in only five years.

However, during 1960 four different individuals were noted on Long Island in August and September.

Extreme dates: Aug. 2 to Nov. 15.

The only recent spring occurrence in our area is that of an individual seen at Tobay Pond, June 9–16, 1962 (Buckley, Ward *et al.*).

BLACK-NECKED STILT (*Himantopus mexicanus*)*

Casual: An American species, breeding in the western United States north to southern Oregon and southern Idaho, but in the east only along the coast north to South Carolina. Nested in southern New Jersey up to 1810, where according to Wilson it was regular in Cape May County. Perhaps nesting there later, but definite evidence lacking (Stone, 1937). Last reported specimens taken in southern New Jersey in 1879 and 1894. Reported casually north to Newfoundland.

In our area seven specimens have been collected, all from Long Island, one of which may still be at the N.Y.S.M., Albany (Eaton, 1910). Five are in the A.M.N.H as follows: Nos. 3166, 3462, 3463, 436941, and 436942. Four of these specimens have little data attached, except that they were taken on Long Island. However, No. 436941 is an adult male, Great South Bay, 1843 (Pike). The following specimen record is published here for the first time: adult collected at Georgica, June 4, 1924 (Latham), in his collection.

Stilts were hatched successfully by Willets in southern New Jersey in 1952 from eggs secured in Florida (see Fables, 1955). The following report(s) might well be of birds derived from these eggs: two seen at Mecox Bay, May 23–31, 1953 (McKeever *et al.*) and possibly the same two on the coast of Massachusetts, June 5–26. A Stilt was also observed at Rumson, N.J., Apr. 18–26, 1961 and May 5, 1962 (Seeley *et al.*).

In Giraud's day (1840s) this species was considered much less rare than the Avocet. Today the Avocet is much more likely to occur.

Some authorities consider this species conspecific with the Old World *H. himantopus*, the Black-winged Stilt.

PHALAROPES: PHALAROPODIDAE

RED PHALAROPE (*Phalaropus fulicarius*)*

Range: Holarctic species of high latitudes, breeding south to the extreme northern portions of Quebec (Ungava) and Labrador.

Status: Regular pelagic migrant. Usually rare and irregular inshore, except after stormy weather, when sometimes abundant.

219

Occurrence and maxima: Phalaropes are adapted for an existence on the ocean where they feed to a great extent on various small marine organisms. They come to shore only when forced in by storms or during prolonged periods of fog. At such times they have been seen in the bays, inlets, and coastal ponds as well as on the ocean. This species occurs most numerously at the east end of Long Island, where the largest concentrations have been found in spring.

Maxima: Three big flights in 1937, 1939, and 1958. For interesting accounts of those in 1937 and 1958, see Wilcox (1938 and 1959a). A brief summary is presented here.

1500+, Shinnecock Bay, Apr. 28, 1937 (Wilcox), after a 60-mile-an-hour gale on Apr. 27. Many of the birds were seen feeding on a species of large red jellyfish. The phalaropes were in various stages of plumage and several were collected.

3000+, Easthampton region, May 16, 1939 (Helmuth). No details regarding this flight.

Nearly 4000, Westhampton Beach–Shinnecock Bay region, Apr. 28 to May 2, 1958 (Wilcox *et al.*), with a maximum of 3700 on Apr. 29. Nineteen were picked up dead that had struck wires or other obstructions. These birds were also in various stages of plumage.

On these flights, the "Reds" outnumbered the "Northerns" between 4 and 8 to 1. I have been unable to find comparable numbers for our area in fall. Perhaps this species keeps well offshore at that season.

Phalaropes have struck lighthouses on a number of occasions, either during periods of foggy weather, or perhaps at night while on migration. In the American Museum collection there are 19 specimens that hit the Montauk Point lighthouse on Apr. 30, 1898. These range from birds in nonbreeding plumage to full breeding plumage. Three were picked up dead at the base of this same lighthouse as late as Nov. 27, 1902.

Extreme dates: *Spring*—March 25 (specimen), March 29, 1962 (10 observed at close range, Montauk, by N. Smith), Apr. 7, and 19 (specimen) to June 12 (specimen). No summer specimens, but reported June 26 and July 30 (if correctly identified). *Fall*—late August and Sept. 8 (specimen) to Nov. 28 (specimen) and Dec. 12, 1937 (Helmuth); possibly later, but species not identified. Generally rare before April; and rare before September and after early November.

Very rare inland: Collected at Ossining, Oct. 14, 1919 (Brandreth), A.M.N.H.; several sight reports also.

NORTHERN PHALAROPE (*Lobipes lobatus*)*

Range: Holarctic species; of more southerly distribution than the preceding species, breeding south to islands in southern James Bay and along the Atlantic coast to southern Labrador.

Status: Similar to the preceding, but occurring more frequently inshore.

Occurrence and maxima: After storms or during foggy weather, this species may be seen swimming on coastal ponds or wading along the edges. If one is fortunate enough to be offshore on a calm day, Northern Phalaropes may be found resting on the ocean or flying by the boat. Like the Red Phalarope, this species occurs in greatest numbers at the east end of Long Island in *spring*, possibly indicating a more offshore migration in fall, much farther from land. It should be pointed out that both ocean-going phalaropes may not be found at all for long periods. Even the most active birdwatchers miss them some years, particularly if observations are limited to coastal areas.

Maxima: *Spring*—500+, Shinnecock Bay, Apr. 29, 1937 (Wilcox); 900+, Westhampton Beach to Shinnecock Inlet, Apr. 28 to May 2, 1958 (Wilcox); 500+, Easthampton, May 16, 1939 (Helmuth). All of these were accompanied by much larger numbers of Red Phalaropes (see discussion under that species). *Fall*—165, off Montauk Point, Sept. 13, 1916 (Helmuth).

Extreme dates: *Spring*—March 29 (specimen) and Apr. 2 to June 3 (specimen); summering stragglers—June 26 and 28 (from boats offshore); one collected at sea about seven miles off Easthampton, July 4, 1945 (Murphy), A.M.N.H., may represent either a summering straggler or an exceptionally early fall migrant. This species arrives much earlier in fall than the Red Phalarope: *Fall*—July 16, 19 (specimen), and July 28 to Nov. 15 (specimen) and Nov. 23, 1937 (Helmuth). Rare before mid-April and after mid-October.

Of great interest are eight specimens in the A.M.N.H. collection that struck the Montauk Point lighthouse, Aug. 26, 1892. This indicates that quite a few must come to grief hitting obstructions during migration.

Very rare inland: Collected at Ardsley, N.Y., May 24, 1894 (C. Travis), A.M.N.H. As far as I know, this is published here for the first time. There are several sight reports also. The report of a flock of 30 seen on an inland lake in New Jersey is without details and considered unsatisfactory.

WILSON'S PHALAROPE *(Steganopus tricolor)**

Range: A western Nearctic species, breeding east to northern Indiana, southern Michigan, and southeastern Ontario.

Status: Rare, but regular fall migrant on the coast. Very rare in spring.

Occurrence and maxima: In our area Wilson's Phalarope is seen most often along the shores of fresh and brackish ponds on the outer coast, frequenting such localities as Tobay Pond, Jamaica Bay Refuge, and other grassy ponds. It often accompanies Lesser Yellowlegs.

At most two or three individuals are observed during a season, but in 1934, quite a "flight" occurred: 4 each were observed at the following localities—Jones Beach, July 29 and Aug. 26; Newark Meadows, Aug. 8; and Orient, Sept. 4; finally a maximum of 6, Newark Meadows, Sept. 30.

Extreme dates: July 7 to Oct. 15 and Nov. 9. Casual on Fisher's Island, female collected, Nov. 20, 1960 (Ferguson), in his collection. Generally rare before late July and after September.

Very rare in spring, only about 20 occurrences ranging from May 8 to June 12, including three females in breeding plumage, Jamaica Bay Refuge, most of May 1958 (numerous observers). There are three local spring specimens: one, Moriches Bay, June 1, 1887 (N. T. Lawrence); two collected at Montauk by Latham, May 19, 1924 and June 1, 1931, both in his collection—not previously published.

It has been observed also on June 19, 26, and 28, but whether these represent migrants or summer stragglers is difficult to state.

Casual inland: Collected at Carmel, N.Y., in 1890 (W. A. Mead); one seen at Troy Meadows, May 18, 1932 (Griscom, Urner *et al.*).

Remarks: Wilson's Phalarope is placed here, following Hellmayr and Conover (1948). It seems to be a more natural arrangement than that of the A.O.U. *Check-list* (1957), where this species was placed between the Red and Northern Phalaropes. It differs from them in several respects: (*a*) It is confined to the Western Hemisphere; (*b*) it breeds far to the south of those two species in the interior of the country, around fresh-water lakes and in prairie sloughs; (*c*) in migration it occurs along the coast, as well as through the interior, but not on the ocean; (*d*) although it swims and spins around in pools, it often walks out on the mud flats; but the most important difference (*e*) is that the Red and Northern Phalaropes are structurally adapted for spending an existence on the high seas during the greater portion of the year—migration and winter—whereas the Wilson's Phalarope is utterly unsuited for such an existence. The first two species have the toes *lobed* and *webbed* at the basal half; Wilson's Phalarope, on the other hand, has the toes only *slightly emarginate* and *without webbing*. In sum, Red and Northern Phalaropes are—in the nonbreeding season—swimming birds; Wilson's Phalarope is a wader.

JAEGERS, SKUAS: STERCORARIIDAE

POMARINE JAEGER (*Stercorarius pomarinus*)*

Range: Holarctic species, breeding south to Baffin and Southampton Islands and northern Quebec.

Status: Regular, but uncommon pelagic migrant; occasionally more numerous. Usually rare inshore.

222

Occurrence and maxima: The presence or absence of jaegers is largely determined by the movements of fish. In good fishing years, jaegers may be found in numbers offshore; one can see them more readily from boats than from land. More trips offshore will be necessary to determine their exact relationships as to comparative abundance and seasonal movements, but we know more about them now than we did even 20 years ago.

This species is reported to be less common in our area than *S. parasiticus*, and this appears to be the case both as to the number of specimens taken and sight reports, at least in fall. It is, however, much less rare in spring than was formerly realized and is perhaps regular at that season. It is also likely, as Wynne-Edwards (1935) points out, that jaegers, at least occasionally, summer offshore in small numbers, and this is borne out by a number of observations at this season of both the commoner species.

Maxima: 40 or more "mostly" Pomarine, Easthampton, June 3, 1928 (Helmuth); 30 from five to 20 miles off Jones Beach, June 13, 1955 (Alperin, 1958); 5, about 20 miles off Easthampton, July 14, 1940; 8 off the beach, Mecox Bay, Aug. 29, 1936; 15, Montauk, Sept. 28, 1920.

Extreme dates: Apr. 13–20, 1958, Atlantic Beach (Levine, Penberthy, and Bull); May 6 to Nov. 12; Dec. 1, 1937, Easthampton (Helmuth).

Accidental inland: Immature male collected, Ossining, Oct. 18, 1877 (Fisher), M.C.Z.

Specimen data: Of eight local specimens in the American Museum, all are in the light phase and only one is adult. There are no spring specimens from our area.

Remarks: Winters principally at sea north to Bermuda, more rarely to North Carolina. The statement in the A.O.U. *Check-list* (1957), "Winters ... casually north to Massachusetts, New York, New Jersey," is not substantiated. There are no reliable reports for these areas later than the first week in December.

PARASITIC JAEGER (*Stercorarius parasiticus*)*

Range: Holarctic species, breeding south to the northern portions of Manitoba, Ontario, and Quebec.

Status: Similar to that of the preceding species, but apparently more numerous and more regular inshore.

Occurrence and maxima: The Parasitic Jaeger supposedly is the most numerous species in our waters, and this appears to be the case, based on specimens and observations. Frequent pelagic trips are necessary, however, to determine more exactly their relative numbers and seasonal movements than present knowledge permits.

Maxima: Good flight reported close inshore during 1936 when this species arrived early and departed late: 2—May 9, Jones Beach; 20—Aug. 31, Oak Beach (J. Mathews); 14—Sept. 2, Easthampton; 5—Oct. 25, Mecox Bay; 1—Dec. 5, Montauk (McKeever and Sedwitz), which represents the latest date. On Sept. 19, 1926, at Point Pleasant, Urner observed at least 70 jaegers, "the vast majority Parasitics." More recently 30 or more were seen off Moriches, Sept. 3, 1949 (Mayer and Rose), after an offshore hurricane on Aug. 29. Twelve were observed between five and 20 miles off Jones Beach, June 13, 1955 (Alperin, 1958).

That jaegers (nonbreeders) summer occasionally is deduced from a flock of six of this species seen in Gardiner's Bay, July 8, 1911 (Helmuth). An adult collected off Montauk, July 28, 1930 (Latham), may represent an early fall migrant.

Extreme dates: Apr. 28 and May 9 to Nov. 15 (specimen), Dec. 3 and 5.

Specimen data: Of 14 local specimens in the American Museum, all but one are in the light phase. Eight are immatures, six are adults. There are no spring specimens from our area.

Remarks: Winters mainly offshore north to the Carolinas, but the northern winter limits of all the jaegers are little known. The statement in the A.O.U. *Check-list* (1957), "Winters ... from Maine ... south ..." is erroneous. There are no known specimens or reliable sight reports of any jaegers anywhere in the northeast after the first week in December.

LONG-TAILED JAEGER (*Stercorarius longicaudus*)*

Very rare migrant: Holarctic species, breeding south to northern Quebec. The most pelagic of the jaegers, migrating well offshore both spring and fall, rarely coming close to land. Winters at sea, chiefly in the southern hemisphere. Reports of its wintering to latitude 40° N. (off the coast of central New Jersey) are unsubstantiated.

In our area it has occurred at least 13 times, with three specimens (all immatures) collected on Long Island: dark phase, Long Island (no date), Lawrence collection, A.M.N.H. No. 46094; light phase, Fire Island, Aug. 26, 1913 (Thurston), A.M.N.H. No. 358008; light phase, picked up dead in woodland near Mount Sinai, Sept. 26, 1963 (A. L. Walker), specimen too poor to save skin, but preserved as skeleton, A.M.N.H. collection. All of the fall sight reports and the latter specimens above occurred in August and September. Most of these were in the last week of August and the first week of September, as follows: adult seen with the other two jaegers off Sandy Hook, Sept. 7, 1918 (Murphy, who was unable to collect it); Long Beach, Aug. 28, 1923 (Watson); off Montauk Point, Aug. 25, 1935 (Breslau); off the beach at Georgica, Aug. 29, 1936 (Helmuth),

224

seen after a Florida hurricane; one harrying terns off Mecox Bay, Sept. 10, 1939 (Helmuth); one in the company of Laughing and Herring Gulls off Saltaire, Fire Island, Sept. 30, 1956 (Bull), the day after hurricane Flossie; two adults with both the other species, 30 miles off Jones Beach, Sept. 24, 1961 (Odell *et al.*). There are three spring reports: off Jones Beach, June 8, 1934 (J. Mathews); offshore opposite Amagansett, June 16, 1939 (Helmuth); one seen on a boat trip, at least five miles off Jones Beach, May 29, 1960 (numerous observers; see Bull, 1960).

The statement by Griscom and Snyder (1955) that "the total number of jaeger specimens in collections properly represent the proportionate number of records of the three species," applies to the New York City area as well. The dark-phased adult of the Long-tailed Jaeger is virtually unknown.

The adults with their long tails are readily identifiable in the field. However, immatures of this species and the Parasitic Jaeger are easily confused, direct size comparison being the only reliable method of distinguishing them in the field. The bluish or blue-gray tarsi often said to be restricted to *S. longicaudus*, are found in *all* immature jaegers, statements to the contrary notwithstanding. For correct soft-part colors see Witherby *et al.* (1941: 131, 137, 141). Specimen labels also confirm this. Thus it will be seen that leg color is *not* a criterion for separating immature jaegers.

SKUA (*Catharacta skua*)*

Accidental: An oceanic species occurring in two widely separated areas: the nominate race nests on islands in the eastern North Atlantic, west to Iceland; three other forms (possibly species) are found nearly throughout the southern oceans, south to Antarctica. The nominate race winters offshore mainly in the eastern Atlantic, but sparingly in the western Atlantic to Newfoundland and very rarely off Massachusetts; summering, nonbreeding birds are found rarely in those areas also. Wynne-Edwards (1935) considers this form essentially nonmigratory.

There are four local occurrences, all from eastern Long Island. Two of these are specimen records: one picked up dead on the beach at Amagansett, March 17, 1886 (Dutcher collection), A.M.N.H. No. 64633; another struck the lighthouse at Montauk Point, Aug. 10, 1896, but only the wing was saved (identified by A. K. Fisher), A.M.N.H. No. 67894. Previous A.O.U. *Check-lists* have included these records, but the 1957 edition unaccountably omits any reference to them. I have examined both specimens and there is not the slightest doubt as to their identity. Two sight reports are deemed worthy of consideration—both at Montauk Point in 1937—perhaps the same individual: one seen diving at Herring and Laughing Gulls, Nov. 11 (Arbib), and one observed on Dec. 14 (Helmuth). There are a few other sight reports, but they are considered unsatisfactory.

225

GULLS, TERNS: LARIDAE

GLAUCOUS GULL (*Larus hyperboreus*)*

Range: Holarctic species, the nominate race breeds south to central Labrador. Winters south to the coast of Long Island; more rarely farther south.

Status: Rare to uncommon, but regular winter visitant on or near the coast.

Occurrence and maxima: The Glaucous Gull almost invariably associates with Herring Gulls in our area. Like the Iceland Gull it frequents ocean beaches, but is especially partial to garbage dumps, where the largest numbers are seen. Unlike the Iceland Gull, however, it is rarely observed at sewer outlets. Consequently it is found most often wherever refuse is dumped, chiefly in the metropolitan area and near the larger cities.

It is very rare inland except in the vicinity of the Hudson River. The dump at Croton Point is a "good" locality for both "white-winged" species where a specimen of *L. hyperboreus* was taken on Jan. 19, 1889 (Fisher), M.C.Z. collection. Another was taken at Yonkers, five days earlier, Jan. 14, 1889 (Rowley), A.M.N.H. collection.

The adult is very rare in our area. Of ten local specimens in the A.M.N.H. collection, all are in various stages of immature plumage.

Formerly (prior to 1900), the Glaucous Gull was reported as more numerous than the Iceland Gull, but in recent years (since 1900), the latter species has been reported more frequently. However, numbers fluctuate from year to year.

Maxima: While some duplication is inevitable, the following yearly winter estimates are believed to be conservative and are useful for comparative purposes. Figures in parentheses represent yearly totals (December to February) based on all observations reported by credible observers in the region: 1926 (10), 1935 (9), 1937 (12), 1946 (5), 1960 (6). Note the decreased numbers reported since 1937, despite many more observers.

Maxima per locality: 5, Pelham Bay garbage dump, Feb. 17, 1935 (Kuerzi); 6, Montauk (village), Dec. 26, 1937 (Helmuth), at the wharf where fish were being cleaned (see next species for comparison).

"Extreme" dates: Usually present from November to April. Collected at Rockaway Beach, May 1, 1904 (Peavey), A.M.N.H. Reported every month of the year, but very rare in summer. An immature summered at Oakwood Beach, Staten Island, in 1932 (Wiegmann).

Remarks: That the Glaucous and Iceland Gulls may be confused at times in the field is indicated by the following: Griscom and Snyder (1955) stated, "As measurements . . . overlap, the two species are not always identifiable in life, and sight identifications are not entirely reliable." Salomonsen

226

(1950a), who has had much experience with both species in Greenland, remarked, "The striking similarity between these two species . . . makes identification in the field extremely difficult."

Perhaps the best character in separating them is bill size. Even when the two species "approach" each other in over-all length, the massive bill of *L. hyperboreus* (Glaucous Gull) is much heavier and relatively longer than the slender bill of *L. glaucoides* (Iceland Gull). For further comparison, the bill of the Herring Gull is somewhat intermediate, but many specimens of the latter show bill size near that of the Glaucous Gull.

ICELAND GULL *(Larus glaucoides)**

Range: Primarily a northeastern Nearctic species (see discussion under Subspecies).

Status: Variously rare to uncommon, but regular winter visitor on or near the coast. Has increased in recent years, now more numerous than the preceding species.

Occurrence and maxima: The Iceland Gull associates with the ever present Herring Gulls. Although found along the ocean beaches and inlets, it occurs most frequently and in largest numbers at garbage dumps, sewer outlets, and fish piers.

This species is very rare inland except in the vicinity of the Hudson River. It may be seen as far inland as the Croton Point dump, but even there it is irregular and relatively rare.

Adults are much rarer than the immature stages and the four local specimens in the A.M.N.H. collection are in the latter plumages. Formerly reported as much rarer than the Glaucous Gull. Prior to about 1900, only 4 local specimens of *L. glaucoides* were taken (2 extant) as compared to 12 of *L. hyperboreus* (10 extant). Numbers fluctuate, however, in both species.

Maxima: See discussion under Maxima of previous species regarding estimates and probable duplication. Figures in parentheses represent yearly totals (December to February): 1926 (16), 1934–35 (15), 1937 (17), 1956–57 (15). Maxima per locality: 8, Clason Point dump, Bronx County, Jan. 11, 1934 (Kuerzi *et al.*); 10, Montauk (village) fish pier, Dec. 26, 1937 (Helmuth)—see previous species for comparison; 5, Narrows (Brooklyn side) sewer outlet, Dec. 30, 1944 (many observers); 7, Central Park Reservoir, Feb. 7, 1957 (Messing; see Carleton, 1958).

"Extreme" dates: Usually present from November to March, but reported every month of the year. Very rare in summer.

Subspecies: A northeastern Nearctic species of limited breeding range. The official vernacular name is very inappropriate as it is actually quite rare in Iceland. Greenland Gull would be much more suitable although

227

apparently only the "white-winged" nominate race breeds on that island. The "gray-winged" race *kumlieni* breeds on southern Baffin Island and across Hudson Strait in extreme northern Quebec (Ungava). On the American side the species as a whole (both forms) winters along the North Atlantic coast south to Long Island; more rarely to southern New Jersey.

Gull taxonomy is notoriously complex and that of *L. glaucoides* is no exception. The larger species of the genus *Larus* have always been an exceedingly difficult group taxonomically, and authorities disagree on their exact relationship, even today. As to the *glaucoides–kumlieni–thayeri* complex, the interested reader is referred to the works of Dwight (1925), Taverner (1933), Rand (1942), Griscom (1944), Salomonsen (1950a), and Macpherson (1961). Neal Smith (unpublished data) has recently collected much valuable information on the breeding grounds of *L. g. kumlieni*.

The form *kumlieni* has been variously treated as: (*a*) a full species; (*b*) an eastern representative (subspecies) of the Pacific *L. glaucescens*, the Glaucous-winged Gull; (*c*) a hybrid of *L. glaucoides* and *L. argentatus*; (*d*) conspecific with *L. glaucoides* (A.O.U. *Check-list*, 1957: 218); and (*e*) by both Salomonsen (1950a) and Macpherson (1961) as an intermediate (morphologically, not geographically) but distinct subspecies between *glaucoides* and *thayeri*, the latter form regarded by them as *not* conspecific with *L. argentatus*.

There is even the possibility that the form *kumlieni* is partially a localized color variant or phase of *L. glaucoides*, somewhat analogous to that of the so-called "ringed" phase of the Common Murre (*Uria aalge*), or to the light and dark phases of the Gyrfalcon (*Falco rusticolus*). N. Smith's recent studies (unpublished) in eastern Baffin Island indicate that approximately 30 per cent of the breeding population of *L. g. kumlieni* in that area lack the gray pigment in the primaries, and appear morphologically identical to nominate *glaucoides* of Greenland. In other words, a "white-winged" phase in a predominantly "gray-winged" population in the area of sympatry.

Specimen data: Regardless of the taxonomic treatment accorded the form *kumlieni* and its relationship with nominate *glaucoides*, both forms have been collected in our area, notwithstanding place of origin of the specimens obtained. As mentioned above, four Iceland Gulls taken locally, have been examined in the A.M.N.H. collection. Three of the four specimens *appear* to be "*kumlieni* type" birds, one of them *definitely* so.

An immature collected at Rockaway Beach, March 9, 1898 (Peavey) *appears* to be this form and was independently determined by Braislin, Brewster, and Dwight to be *kumlieni*.

Another immature was captured alive at Jones Beach, Aug. 2, 1936 (Herbert, Hickey, Kassoy, and Kuerzi). This specimen was brought to the Bronx Zoo where it lived for nearly two years. When it died on May 2, 1938, it had attained a sub-adult plumage. The specimen is now A.M.N.H.

228

No. 448094. The gray primary pattern indicates it to be *kumlieni* (see Hickey, 1938a).

A third immature shot on a garbage dump at Rutherford, N.J., Feb. 2, 1958 (Jehl) is *apparently* this form.

However, the fourth bird, a more "advanced" sub-adult example with a partially gray mantle, collected at Kearny (near Rutherford) a short time later, on Feb. 28, 1958 (Buckley), is, in my opinion, referable to nominate *glaucoides*, having no gray color in the primaries. It matches comparable specimens of true *glaucoides* taken in Greenland.

Remarks: The relative abundance of *glaucoides* and *kumlieni* in the New York City region is not known. Sight reports of immatures allocated to one or the other forms are nothing more than unreliable guesses, and even specimens in the hand present difficulties. While it is easy enough to recognize adults at close range with the "maximum" amount of gray in the primaries as "probable" *kumlieni*, the extent of gray is variable and "gray-winged" individuals of *L. (argentatus?) thayeri* may even occur, although there are no known specimens of the latter form from our area—this form considered by some authorities to be a distinct species.

Further collecting of adults is desirable to determine the relative status of the various forms in our area, and this would have to be done over a period of years as the adult is greatly outnumbered by birds in various stages of immaturity. The assumption that *kumlieni* outnumbers *glaucoides* locally has been advanced by several recent observers, but this remains to be proved by more concrete evidence. The suggestion by Hickey (1954), of capturing immatures alive and studying their molts and plumage sequences, deserves trial.

GREAT BLACK-BACKED GULL (*Larus marinus*)*B

Range: A western Palearctic and eastern Nearctic species, essentially restricted in the breeding season to the North Atlantic region; on the American side breeds south to Long Island.

Status: Common to locally abundant visitant along the coast, most numerous on migration and in winter. Has greatly increased in recent years. Very local breeder on Long Island. Formerly rare and irregular inland; now regular in small numbers.

Change in status: Formerly (prior to 1920) a common migrant and winter visitant along the coast, rare inland, and casual in summer: then (1920–40) increasing as the species bred farther south along the New England coast, numerous summering, nonbreeding individuals appearing on the outer coast, and becoming regular, but still uncommon inland during the colder months. Now (1955–62) breeding in at least seven localities on Long Island, the southernmost nesting area in the Western Hemisphere.

1. Nonbreeding: The Great Black-backed Gull is essentially a coastal species, but regularly wanders up the larger rivers, and is occasional on the lakes and reservoirs of the interior.

Maxima: *Migration*—400, Jones Inlet, Sept. 7, 1947; 900, Owl's Head Park, Brooklyn, Sept. 20, 1961. *Winter*—1000, Fresh Kills, Staten Island, Jan 15, 1956; 1800, Narrows to Jamaica Bay (west of Cross Bay Boulevard), Dec. 22, 1958. *Summer* (nonbreeding)—15, Tobay Pond, June 8, 1947; 120, Atlantic Beach to Fire Island Inlet, July 31, 1959 (mostly immatures). *Inland*—70, Piermont, N.Y., Sept. 5, 1960.

2. Breeding: First nesting in Maine probably in 1928 (Palmer, 1949) and in Massachusetts in 1931 (Griscom and Snyder, 1955), in which places it is confined primarily to rocky islands. Cruickshank (1942) virtually predicted its breeding on Long Island. In that very year, the first breeding pair was, indeed, found in New York State, thus fulfilling his prediction.

This species breeds on Long Island in sandy areas with some scattered vegetation. These nests are placed invariably in or near Herring Gull colonies.

The following Table indicates this bird's increase as a breeder in our area (see map). The first year shown for each locality represents known initial nesting, other years known maxima. Numbers indicate actual pairs or nests:

LOCALITY	DATE	PAIRS OR NESTS
Cartwright Island	1942	1
Cartwright Island	1947	3
Cartwright Island	1955	10
Gardiner's Island	1948	3
Gardiner's Island	1951	7
Gardiner's Island	1957	35
Cartwright and Gardiner's Islands	1958	50+
Orient Point	1958	1
Shinnecock Bay	1954	1
Shinnecock Bay	1961	5
Captree State Park	1958	1
Captree State Park	1961	3
Fire Island State Park	1960	2
*Canarsie Pol, Jamaica Bay	1960	3

* This locality is the southernmost (westernmost) known to date.

Egg date: June 1.

230

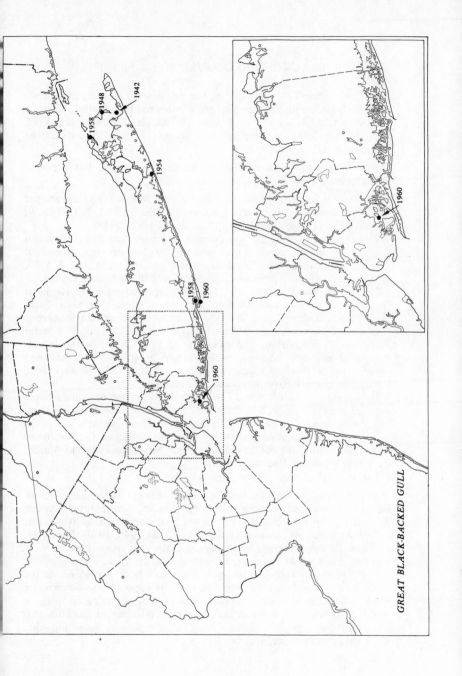

GREAT BLACK-BACKED GULL

LESSER BLACK-BACKED GULL (*Larus fuscus*)*

Range: A western Palearctic species, the race *graellsii* breeding in Iceland, the British Isles, and northern France. Winters south to central Africa.

Specimens collected in North America: Maryland (1948), New York State (Buffalo, 1949), and northern New Jersey (1958); all three specimens determined as *L. f. graellsii*.

Status: Very rare winter visitant on or near the coast, but reported annually since 1954.

Occurrence: Unreported prior to 1934. At least 30 observations *presumed* to be this species. Adult female collected at Rutherford, N.J., Feb. 9, 1958, A.M.N.H. No. 468815 (Jehl, Auk, 75: 349–350, 1958).

This species frequents garbage dumps; the above New Jersey specimen was shot at one. It occurs also at sewer outlets and on coastal beaches, tidal flats, and reservoirs. Roy Latham saw one at Orient, Jan. 8, 1959, on a plowed field with Herring Gulls and Great Black-backed Gulls.

The Lesser Black-backed Gull has been reported on Long Island at Orient, Shinnecock Inlet, Westhampton Beach, Heckscher State Park, Jones Beach (Tobay Pond), Atlantic Beach, and Hempstead Reservoir. Elsewhere in New York, from Westchester Creek (Bronx County), Central Park, New York harbor, and especially at Fresh Kills, Staten Island. This latter locality is adjacent to New Jersey, in which state it has been observed at Rutherford, Secaucus, Kearny, Jersey City, Newark Bay, Raritan Bay, Shark River Inlet, and Spring Lake.

During the winter of 1956–57, perhaps three or four individuals were believed to have been present in the New York–New Jersey area, but some duplication is possible because gulls move around considerably.

Like the Black-headed Gull, the Lesser Black-backed Gull is found most often during the colder months, chiefly from November to March. Only four reports before November.

Extreme dates: Aug. 30 and Sept. 8 to Apr. 14.

Remarks: No sight identifications of subspecies are considered satisfactory because of extent of variation within this species. Also hybrids between *L. marinus* and *L. argentatus* are known, and one probable hybrid *was collected* recently in our area (Jehl, Auk, 77: 343–345, 1960). Moreover, two west European subspecies of Herring Gulls with yellow legs and dark mantles could easily be confused with *L. fuscus*; *L. a. atlantis* of the Azores, Madeira, and the Canary Islands, and *L. a. michahellis* of the coasts of Spain and Portugal would be virtually impossible to differentiate from *L. fuscus* in the field. The possibility of their occurring on this side of the Atlantic cannot be ignored, and further collecting may well turn up some gull that appears to be *L. fuscus*, but proves to be something else. Such are the difficulties involved.

232

HERRING GULL (*Larus argentatus*)*B

Range: Holarctic species, the race *smithsonianus* breeds south to Long Island; locally on the coasts of New Jersey and Maryland; very rarely in Virginia.

Status: Very abundant resident, most numerous in winter. Locally common breeder on the coast.

Occurrence and maxima: The ubiquitous and extremely successful Herring Gull is one of our most numerous birds. Enormous numbers may be seen during the colder months when the local population is vastly augmented by arrivals from more northern areas. The largest concentrations are found about New York harbor, especially in the vicinity of sewer outlets and garbage dumps. Great throngs are to be seen also along the ocean, bays, Long Island Sound, and the numerous tidal estuaries and inlets. Lesser numbers frequent the larger inland lakes and reservoirs until the freeze-up. After heavy rains considerable numbers visit flooded fields, golf courses, and even empty parking lots.

Maxima, nonbreeding: It is impossible to give an adequate idea of how numerous this species really is. All that can be said is that winter estimates of between 30,000 and 40,000 are probably conservative for some localities. The total winter population for our area may run over 1,000,000, but this is merely a guess.

Maxima, breeding (see map p. 235): In our area, the Herring Gull nests on the ground among scattered vegetation. The early local history of the breeding of this species may be found in Cruickshank (1942), and McKeever (1940 and 1946a). However, the first known nesting was that of three pairs at Orient in 1931 (Latham), two years earlier than that on Fisher's Island (1933) as stated by Cruickshank. In 1933, R. P. Allen (Auk, 50. 433–434, 1933) found 21 nests on Wicopesset Island (one-half mile off Fisher's Island), and in 1939 on this same island, Poor reported at least 750 breeding pairs. By 1941, Cruickshank estimated over 1000 breeding pairs in six localities on Long Island, extending as far south (west) as Fire Island Inlet (see map).

Since then, it has spread widely and is now found in many new areas. Most numerous on eastern Long Island, decreasing westward. The following recent estimates (since 1948) of the largest colonies are based on nests and/or pairs:

LOCALITY	DATE	PAIRS OR NESTS
Fisher's Island and nearby islets	1961	800
Gardiner's Island	1948	800
Gardiner's Island	1951	2000

LOCALITY	DATE	PAIRS OR NESTS
Cartwright Island	1948	600
Cartwright Island	1951	750
Cartwright Island	1954	1500
Gardiner's and Cartwright Islands	1955	5000+
Captree State Park	1955	50
Captree State Park	1958	300
Captree State Park	1959	700
Captree State Park	1962	700
Canarsie Pol, Jamaica Bay	1953	200+
Canarsie Pol, Jamaica Bay	1960	50

The only known breeding in our section of Connecticut is that of a colony on the Sheep Rocks, off Norwalk where, in 1962, Clement found 50 nests with at least 85 young.

It would be interesting to determine the present population on Gardiner's and Cartwright Islands. The breeding density at Captree State Park has very likely reached the saturation point. The decrease on Canarsie Pol is possibly due to the island having grown up to scrub.

The steady increase within the past 20 years or so has been to the detriment of several colonies of terns, skimmers, and even Ospreys, and may have to be controlled, as has been done in other areas.

Egg dates: May 7 to June 22.

Remarks: The high Arctic form *thayeri* (considered a race of *L. argentatus* in the A.O.U. *Check-list* [1957], but variously treated as conspecific with *L. glaucoides* [Iceland Gull] by some authorities, and as a separate species by others), has not been taken within the New York City region to my knowledge, although reported as collected once each in Massachusetts and southern New Jersey.

Voous (1959) would make *smithsonianus* a synonym of *L. argentatus*, stating that the limits of variation are very similar within each form.

RING-BILLED GULL (*Larus delawarensis*)*

Range: Nearctic species, breeding south to Lakes Erie and Ontario, and Oneida Lake, N.Y.

Status: Common to abundant migrant and winter visitant, and locally common summer visitant along the coast. Has greatly increased in recent years. Relatively uncommon inland in our area.

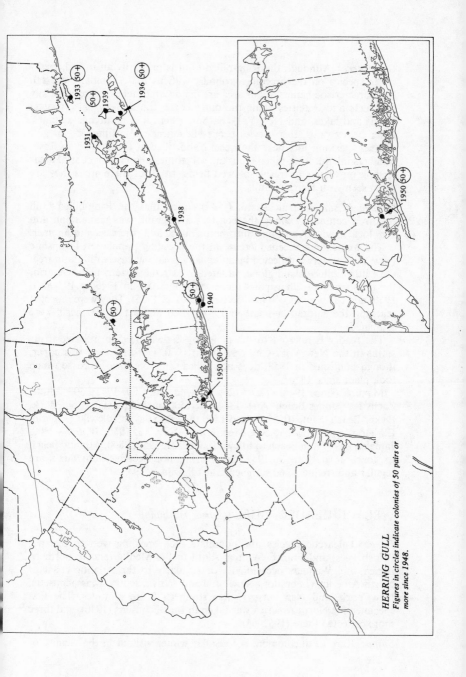

HERRING GULL
Figures in circles indicate colonies of 50 pairs or more since 1948.

Occurrence: Although the Ring-billed Gull is primarily an inland, fresh-water species on the breeding grounds, with us it is essentially coastal. Its characteristic haunts in our area are the ocean beaches, more especially the inlets and estuaries along the outer coast, the shallow bays, coastal ponds and lakes, and New York harbor, where it is numerous at times. After heavy rains, this species occurs in considerable numbers on golf courses, parking lots near the ocean, and filled-in areas; also in lesser numbers inland. Ring-billed Gulls are sometimes observed in coastal areas feeding on insects in freshly plowed fields. In all of these areas they are often seen with Herring Gulls.

Change in status: Cruickshank (1942) stated that the Ring-billed Gull occurred commonly along the coast as a migrant, was uncommon and very local in winter, and very uncommon but steadily increasing in summer.

The tremendous recent increase in the breeding population in upstate New York waters is reflected by an equally great increase within our area. On Little Galloo Island alone, situated in extreme eastern Lake Ontario, the number of breeding pairs increased from 1000 in 1946 to 19,000 in 1950, and to about 45,000 in 1955 (see Belknap, 1955). They were reported reaching the saturation point in 1961, when at least 63,000 nests were estimated.

The reader is referred to the paper by Sedwitz (1958b) relative to its status in the New York City area up to 1950. Unfortunately this paper, though published in 1958, does not indicate the big local increase which took place since 1950.

Maxima (since 1946): *Fall*—125, Idlewild, July 20, 1947; 500 adults, Zachs Bay, Jones Beach, Aug. 13, 1954; 1500, including 600 in one flock, Dyker Beach, Sept. 10, 1950, and 1500 the same day at Idlewild (Alperin, Carleton, and Sedwitz); 500, Mecox Bay, Nov. 15, 1958. *Winter*—2300, Jamaica Bay (Plum Beach to Idlewild), Dec. 27, 1952; 2800, Atlantic Beach to Jones Inlet, Jan. 3, 1953. Summering nonbreeding individuals are regular and frequent; 60 summered at Idlewild in 1949.

BLACK-HEADED GULL (*Larus ridibundus*)*

Range: Palearctic species, the nominate race breeding west to Iceland, British Isles, and France. Winters south to the Mediterranean, northern Africa, etc. Wanders occasionally or regularly to the Atlantic coast of North America (Labrador, Newfoundland, Nova Scotia, Massachusetts, New York, and New Jersey); also southern Lesser Antilles. The first specimen for North America was taken in Massachusetts (1930), and three more collected there (1952–53).

Status: Rare to uncommon, but regular winter visitant in the vicinity of

New York harbor. Very rare on the outer coast. Has greatly increased in recent years.

Change in status: First reported in 1937 at Montauk (two adults, Dec. 27, 1937 to Jan. 4, 1938, Helmuth). Occurring regularly in very small numbers from the winter of 1943–44 on. There is one local specimen (see below).

This species almost always associates with Bonaparte's Gulls, which it closely resembles, and is most likely to be found at sewer outlets where food is readily obtained. From the early 1940s to about 1954, the sewer outlet at the Narrows in Brooklyn was *the* place to see this species, as well as the Little Gull. However, installation of sewage disposal plants eliminated that "productive" locality, and the rarer gulls went to other sewer outlets on the Staten Island and New Jersey shores. They may be observed also at times from the Staten Island ferries.

This species has been reliably reported on Long Island from Montauk, Georgica Pond, Mecox Bay, Fire Island Inlet, Riis Park, and Prospect Park; in Central Park (chiefly the reservoir); Wolfe's Pond, Staten Island; and in New Jersey at Jersey City, Raritan Bay (South Amboy, etc.), Long Branch, Belmar, and Shark River Inlet which is at or near its most southerly known limits on the North American continent.

Maxima: 4, Narrows (Brooklyn side), winter of 1949–50 (numerous observers); 4 (2 adults, 2 immatures), Jersey City, March 9, 1958 (Wolfarth *et al.*); 6 (1 adult, 5 immatures), Shark River Inlet, March 19, 1961 (Grant); 9 (6 together), Upper Bay, Dec. 23, 1961 (Ryan *et al.*).

Unlike the Little Gull, the Black-headed Gull occurs most often during the colder months, while the former species is frequent in late spring and not rare in summer. In fact, the Black-headed Gull is most numerous from November to late March.

"Extreme" dates: casual, Aug. 18, 1956, adult, South Amboy (Black and Seeley); Oct. 11 to Apr. 16 (1961)—on the latter date, adult in full breeding plumage with the brown hood, Central Park (Carleton and Post); Mecox Bay, May 14, 1950 (Helmuth), also a fully adult bird. During late June 1963 a sub-adult was collected at South Amboy, N.J by R. Frohling.

As of 1963 several birds were reported summering in the vicinity of South Amboy, N.J., and one at the Jamaica Bay Refuge.

Remarks: Black-headed Gull is an unfortunate misnomer. The hood is chocolate-brown, not black. However, the name must stand, as there are other species of gulls called Brown-headed and Brown-hooded.

LAUGHING GULL (*Larus atricilla*)*B

Range: Nearctic and Caribbean species; of very local breeding distribution along the Atlantic coast, breeding north to southern New Jersey, north of which it is now known as a breeder only on Muskeget Island, Massachusetts;

rarely on the coast of Nova Scotia. It has greatly decreased as a breeder in recent years in the northern portions of its range.

Status: Common to locally abundant coastal migrant and summer visitant. Less numerous along the Hudson River and occasional on the larger inland lakes. Uncommon in winter, but increasing.

Occurrence and maxima: The Laughing Gull presents an anomaly. Despite its reduced nesting range within the past 30 years, it has increased greatly as a migrant and summering nonbreeder within the past 40 years. It is necessary to explain this erratic state of affairs with an account of its past and present distribution, as well as its habits.

1. Breeding: This species formerly nested on the south shore of Long Island, apparently confined to certain islands in Great South Bay, although according to Griscom (1923), it "formerly bred" at Orient Point also. It was reported by Dutcher (1887–94) as last nesting on Long Island in 1888. However, a set of three eggs in the A.M.N.H. collection was taken on Cedar Island, June 14, 1890 (Marshall). There has been no confirmed breeding anywhere in our area since that time.

Along the Atlantic coast the Laughing Gull nests in three distinct habitats: (*a*) salt marshes; (*b*) sand, either with much or little vegetation; (*c*) rocky islands with grassy areas. Habitats (*a*) and (*b*) are occupied in Florida and South Carolina. Habitat (*a*) is used "exclusively" in Virginia, Maryland, and New Jersey, habitat (*b*) in Massachusetts, and habitat (*c*) in Nova Scotia and Maine (formerly). The species nested in Maine until fairly recently on rocky offshore islands where there was a rank growth of grass and other vegetation, but disappeared prior to 1944 (Palmer, 1949), presumably because of depredations by Herring Gulls which have increased greatly in recent years. On Muskeget Island (off Nantucket) a thriving nesting colony was nearly wiped out by plume hunters during the height of the millinery trade. Protected in time, it greatly increased, only to become much reduced by an ever expanding population of Herring Gulls (Griscom and Folger, 1948). The Laughing Gulls nested on the sand, either under thickets of bayberry and poison ivy, or in clumps of beach grass. In southern New Jersey they nest "only" in salt marsh, either on the broad meadows adjacent to the mainland or on the coastal islands. The nests are placed in the drier areas, but are subject to flooding by high tides on occasion (Stone, 1937). There they have thus far escaped the ubiquitous Herring Gulls which now nest rarely as far south as Virginia. The northernmost breeding area of Laughing Gulls on the New Jersey coast is at Little Beach Island, just north of Brigantine. From there to Muskeget Island, Mass., there are no known nesting Laughing Gulls.

In view of the greatly increased numbers of summering birds in our area, it is surprising that nesting has been unreported anywhere on Long Island since 1890. The big mystery is where the Laughing Gulls go during the breeding season. The one small colony on Muskeget Island and the

238

rarity of the bird as a breeder in Nova Scotia do not account for the great numbers that migrate through our region. Griscom's statement (1923), "There is good reason to hope that it will be found nesting on Great South Bay in the near future," unfortunately has not come to pass.

Egg dates: June 14 to 28.

2. Migration: This species is most numerous around New York harbor and on Long Island Sound, and relatively uncommon along the ocean beaches or anywhere on the south shore, particularly at the east end, but it has increased on the bays at the west end in recent years. One of the features of the spring migration is their daily visitations to the reservoir in Central Park.

Maxima: *Spring*—800, Narrows, Apr. 28, 1949; 200, Centre Island, L.I., May 15, 1960. *Summer*—100, Piermont (Hudson River), June 25, 1933; 1000 (mostly immatures), Setauket, L.I., June 27, 1934. *Fall*—300, Idlewild, Aug. 24, 1951; 1000, Little Neck Bay, Aug. 27, 1946; 400, after hurricane, Easthampton region, Sept. 16, 1944; 1000, Little Neck Bay, Sept. 24, 1949; 300, Jamaica Bay Refuge, Sept. 27, 1959; 2000, Lower Bay, Oct. 28, 1951; 2000, coming into evening roost, Pelham Bay, Oct. 30, 1938; 250, Narrows, Nov. 16, 1945; 50, Hudson River near Chambers Street, lower Manhattan, Dec. 10, 1943; 75, Narrows, Dec. 14, 1947. Generally rare before late March and after mid-December. Now arrives earlier and departs later than formerly.

3. *Winter:* No known local winter specimens have been collected. Ordinarily only one to several individuals are seen each winter, but on occasion larger numbers have been observed.

Maxima: 14, New York harbor, Jan. 26, 1948; nearly 50, Connecticut-Westchester–Bronx–Manhattan–Brooklyn areas, Dec. 23, 1950.

FRANKLIN'S GULL (*Larus pipixcan*)

Accidental: A western Nearctic species, breeding east to the western portions of Minnesota and Iowa. Winters north in the Gulf of Mexico to Louisiana. Migrates rarely but regularly east to Lake Erie. Accidental or casual on the Atlantic coast from New Brunswick to Virginia. There are two specimens from Massachusetts (1885 and 1952), and six accepted sight reports from that state (see Griscom and Snyder, 1955).

Although this species has never been collected in our region there are two sight identifications on Long Island worthy of consideration and believed correct. The report listed in Cruickshank (1942) was later rescinded as being doubtful (*fide* Carleton). An adult in changing plumage was observed at Plum Beach, Nov. 7, 1948 (Alperin, Jacobson, and Sedwitz), with detailed description (Linnaean News-Letter, 2 [9]: Feb. 1949). Two birds, one in nonbreeding plumage, the other in partial breeding plumage, were seen at Shinnecock Inlet, Sept. 1, 1954 (W. Reid), full details submitted (*in litt.*). The observer, familiar with the species in the west, saw the birds in direct comparison with Laughing and Bonaparte's Gulls. Of interest was a Franklin's Gull reported the same week on Nantucket Island.

BONAPARTE'S GULL (*Larus philadelphia*)*

Range: A western Nearctic species, breeding southeast to west-central Ontario.

Status: Common to abundant migrant and winter visitant along the coast and in New York harbor; occasionally very abundant. Numbers fluctuate greatly. Occasional in summer. Rare on inland lakes and ponds.

Occurrence and maxima: Bonaparte's Gulls are most numerous in the waters around New York City, especially in and near the harbor. They may be observed there in greatest numbers in spring and fall. In winter they are numerous in the Montauk area also.

Maxima: *Fall*—2500, Lower Bay, Nov. 2, 1941. *Winter*—Montauk Point, 4500, Jan. 5, 1936, and 3500, Dec. 22, 1946; as many as 10,000, Gravesend Bay, early January 1962 (many observers). *Spring*—2500, Narrows, Apr. 12, 1947; 1000, Upper Bay, Apr. 26, 1931; 100, Jamaica Bay, May 25, 1957. Usually rare before October and after May.

Summer occurrences: Usually rare, but sometimes occurs in small numbers. Collected, Great Gull Island, July 8, 1889 (Chapman and Dutcher); 5, Long Beach, June and July, 1937; Raritan Bay, 20, June 27, 1954, and 30, July 28, 1923.

LITTLE GULL (*Larus minutus*)*

Range: Palearctic species, breeding west to Sweden, Denmark, and Germany. Winters from the British Isles south to the Mediterranean Sea. Wanders occasionally, perhaps regularly, to eastern North America (Maine, Massachusetts, New York, and New Jersey); and inland to Lakes Ontario and Erie, probably by way of the St. Lawrence River. Unreported on the Atlantic coast south of central New Jersey (Barnegat Inlet).

Status: Rare but possibly regular visitant to the coast, especially in and near New York harbor.

Occurrence and maxima: The first specimen taken in North America was an immature collected on Fire Island, Sept. 15, 1887 (R. Powell), A.M.N.H. No. 3156. The second record, also a specimen, was an immature taken at Rockaway Point, May 11, 1902 (Peavey), A.M.N.H. No. 437019.

Next reported in our area in 1929 when an adult was observed in Upper Bay on May 6 (Chapin, Auk., 46: 377–378, 1929). Cruickshank (1942) stated that from 1929 on, it was reported almost annually.

Its status since 1942 has not changed materially and while probably regular, definite proof is lacking. It has been unreported in six years within the last two decades, three of those years from 1950 to 1962, despite the fact that many more observers have been on the lookout for it. Since 1942, it has been a rarer bird than *L. ridibundus* (Black-headed Gull) —never more than *two* individuals seen together until 1962 (see below). Like *L. ridibundus*, the Little Gull in our area almost invariably associates with Bonaparte's Gulls and is found in the same places, i.e., sewer outlets in and around New York harbor. A more distinctive bird (both adult and immature) than *L. ridibundus*—the latter resembling the Bonaparte's Gull very closely in corresponding plumages—the Little Gull would be less likely to be overlooked.

The Little Gull is very rare away from the polluted waters of the metropolitan area, and aside from the Fire Island specimen listed above, it has been reported definitely from eastern Long Island only at Easthampton, Jan. 2–3, 1930 (Helmuth); also once at Jones Beach. Even on the New Jersey coast in our area, the only reports from "clean" waters are at Asbury Park, Shark River Inlet, and near Point Pleasant.

Maxima: Two each at the following localities—Narrows, Brooklyn, Jan. 2–19, 1944; same locality, all January 1948; Upper Bay, Dec. 26, 1954; Wolfe's Pond, Staten Island, Nov. 2–16, 1957; 4, South Amboy, early May to June 17, 1962 (many observers), on which latter date Frohling collected an immature female, the first specimen for New Jersey and the third taken locally.

Unlike the Black-headed Gull, the Little Gull has been seen the year around, having been reported in every month (but see Black-headed Gull).

"Extreme" dates: July 27 to June 17. Rarely reported before mid-August.

Remarks: One of the outstanding ornithological events in recent years was the discovery of Little Gulls breeding in North America. During the summer of 1962 three pairs nested in southeastern Ontario.

IVORY GULL *(Pagophila eburnea)**

Accidental: Holarctic species, breeding at high latitudes; south only to northern Baffin Island. Even in winter it is rare south of the drift ice, although reported occasionally south to Maine and more rarely to Massachusetts.

There are five coastal reports of this species in our area, including two specimens, apparently only one extant: adult collected on Great South Bay near Sayville, Jan. 5, 1893 (Goldswerth); immature picked up dead on the beach, Orient, Feb. 17, 1945 (Latham), in his collection. The following sight reports are probably reliable: one seen flying around Mount Sinai Harbor, "years ago" (Helme); adult, Orient Point, Feb. 21, 1934 (Latham); Manasquan Inlet, Jan. 28 to Feb 5, 1955 (several observers). No inland reports have been confirmed.

BLACK-LEGGED KITTIWAKE (*Rissa tridactyla*)*

Range: Holarctic species, the nominate race breeds south along the Atlantic coast to Newfoundland and islands in the Gulf of St. Lawrence. Winters mainly offshore south to eastern Long Island, more rarely to New Jersey; casual farther south.

Status: Variously uncommon to very common pelagic winter visitant—and off Montauk Point. Much rarer near land elsewhere, except after easterly storms.

Occurrence and maxima: The Kittiwake is confined almost exclusively to the ocean and is very rare anywhere else. Most often seen from November to February. It should be emphasized that Kittiwakes are seldom seen from land, and that the most active observers miss them on most field trips, even at Montauk.

Maxima: *Offshore* from fishing boats—40, ten miles off Long Beach (Cholera Banks), Dec. 19, 1913; 130 (approximately 70 adults and 60 immatures) from 15 to 25 miles off Long Branch, Dec. 31, 1904 (Wiegmann). From *land*—big flight in 1956–57: 110, Montauk, Nov. 10; 65, Jones Beach, Nov. 12 (after strong gale); 200+, Montauk, Jan. 26, 1957 (several observers).

Extreme dates: Sept. 20 and 23 to May 14 (specimen) and May 23. Immature found dead on beach, Georgica, May 14, 1949 (Helmuth), specimen in his collection. Rare before late October and after March. No summer reports confirmed.

Remarks: The Black-legged Kittiwake is one of the very few birds in which the immature is more readily identifiable in the field than the adult.

Griscom's statement (1923), "The adult should be identified with great caution . . ." is equally applicable today. At a distance it may be confused with the adult Ring-billed Gull, which is but slightly larger.

Although Kittiwakes may occur after gales in such places as Long Island Sound, it is the writer's opinion that most reports of this species listed on Christmas counts from that area are unreliable. Particularly suspicious are those counts that list this species but not Ring-billed Gulls, which are actually fairly common in those waters. There is one definite record of the Kittiwake for western Long Island Sound: an immature male collected near Stamford, Conn., Jan. 21, 1895 (Schaler), specimen in the Bruce Museum, Greenwich. The writer recently examined this specimen.

Accidental inland: Immature carefully identified after a storm at Boonton Reservoir, Dec. 21. 1957 (Wolfarth).

SABINE'S GULL (*Xema sabini*)*

Casual: Holarctic species, breeding south to Baffin and Southampton Islands. Winter range chiefly off Peru and in the South Atlantic Ocean. Pelagic in migration, occurring chiefly well offshore.

There are nine reports of this species in our area, three of them specimens, all from Long Island, as follows: One collected (not extant) at Raynor South (Freeport), July 1837 (*fide* Giraud); immature female taken on Gardiner's Bay, Oct. 6, 1899 (Worthington), in Latham's collection; immature, Dyker Beach, Oct. 14, 1926 (Johnston and Watson); adult female in nearly full breeding plumage taken at Oyster Pond, Montauk, Sept. 15, 1931 (Latham), in his collection—not previously published; adult seen after a southeast gale on Mecox Bay, Oct. 17–20, 1936 (Helmuth, who attempted to collect it); Easthampton, Oct. 10, 1938 (Helmuth); Moriches Inlet, Sept. 24, 1940 (J. Terry); two after hurricane, Easthampton, Sept. 16, 1944 (Helmuth); Jones Beach, Sept. 12, 1960 (Buckley and R. Fisher) immediately after hurricane Donna. No winter or early spring sight reports are accepted, as confusion with the immature Kittiwake is likely.

Extreme dates: July; Sept. 12 to Oct. 20.

GULL-BILLED TERN (*Gelochelidon nilotica*)*

Range: A nearly cosmopolitan species of local distribution, the race *aranea* breeding north along the Atlantic coast to southern Maryland; rarely to Delaware and very rarely to southern New Jersey (1958). Occurs as a vagrant north to Maine and New Brunswick.

Status: Very rare and irregular summer and fall visitant to the coast of Long Island; most records after hurricanes.

Occurrence: Although listed by Giraud (1844) as occurring on Long Island, he mentioned no specimens. The first definite report was that of a pair collected at South Oyster Bay (opposite Jones Beach), July 4, 1882 (Dutcher collection), A.M.N.H. Nos. 64666 and 64667. These appear to be the only local specimens extant. The species has also been taken at Shinnecock Bay (1884) and Point Lookout (1885). The two specimens reported by Cruickshank (1942) to have struck the Ellis Island light in 1913 were not seen by an ornithologist and are considered unsatisfactory.

Unreported again in our area for 50 years, when in 1934 one was seen at Oakwood Beach, Staten Island, Aug. 4 (Cruickshank), the only known local occurrence away from the south shore of Long Island. That same year several were seen after the Florida hurricane of Sept. 1, individuals observed at Jones Beach, Mecox Bay, and Sagaponack.

243

Since then the Gull-billed Tern has been reported intermittently; usually after tropical storms. A report of two adults feeding immatures able to fly at Moriches Inlet, July 26 to Aug. 4, 1956 (several observers), is not proof of breeding there. The birds may have come from one of the nearby southern nesting localities. Many terns still feed "young" after they have flown away from the nesting grounds.

The greatest incursion of this species into our area occurred after hurricane Donna, Sept. 12, 1960. The following day it was estimated that at least 28 were observed along the south shore of Long Island from Jones Inlet east to Sagaponack. In the Short Beach area alone, 16 or more were seen (Buckley, Levine, Norse, and Post).

Extreme dates: reported at Easthampton, May 14, 1950 (Helmuth); May 25 and June 6 (specimen) to Sept. 17. Casual at Mecox Bay, Nov. 29, 1954 (Boyajian, Penberthy, and Wilcox), full details submitted (1954 was a hurricane year). Hurricane vagrants are sometimes stranded and survive for long periods (see Black Skimmer).

FORSTER'S TERN (*Sterna forsteri*)*

Range: Nearctic species of local distribution with three widely separated breeding populations, one inland and two coastal: (*a*) chiefly fresh-water lakes south and east to southeastern Wisconsin and northwestern Indiana; (*b*) western Gulf coast east to Louisiana; (*c*) middle Atlantic coast of Virginia and southern Maryland, rarely north to southern New Jersey (1956 on), when it first nested at Brigantine (eight breeding pairs there in 1959).

Status: Variously uncommon to very common fall coastal migrant; has greatly increased in recent years. Occasional inland. Very rare in spring.

Occurrence and maxima: The Forster's Tern, now much more numerous than formerly, occurs regularly along the coast, frequenting the bays, inlets, salt marshes, coastal ponds, and ocean beaches. Its numbers, however, fluctuate from year to year. Our birds are probably derived from both the inland—western population (*a*) and the coastal population —(*c*) above. These latter individuals occur in the New York City region after hurricanes and/or as postbreeding wanderers like the "white" herons.

Prior to 1924 this species was merely a casual visitant to our area; in fact, Griscom (1923) placed it on the "extirpated" list. But in the fall of 1925 there was a large influx throughout the northeast. For an account of this flight in our region, see Griscom (1929).

Maxima: *Coastal*—25, Lake Como, N.J., Aug. 2, 1953; 75, Point Pleasant, Aug. 30, 1925; 700, Easthampton to Montauk, Sept. 15, 1944 (Helmuth), day after hurricane; the following after the 1928 hurricane— 200, Mecox Bay (Helmuth) and 230, Newark Bay (Urner), both on Sept. 23;

244

big late flight in 1936—100, Newark Bay, Oct. 12; 50, Rockaway Point, Nov. 6.

This species has been reliably reported *inland* on several occasions in fall. Maxima: 5, Annsville Creek, near Peekskill, Aug. 28, 1960 (Odell); 3, Boonton Reservoir, Sept. 23, 1951 (Thorsell); 5, Croton Point, Oct. 7, 1928 (Kuerzi).

Extreme dates: July 10 and 27 to Nov. 30. Rare before August and after early November.

Very rare in spring; no specimens, but at least five reliable sight reports on the coast, the few dates ranging from May 17 to June 9. Possibly overlooked among the other terns.

Remarks: Winters north to Virginia, rarely to Maryland. In recent years has been reported on several Christmas counts as far north as Cape May and Barnegat Bay, maximum of six at the former locality in 1954. One recently reported in winter on the Rhode Island coast (Baird, Wilson Bull., 73: 89, 1961).

Casual, Manhattan Beach, L.I., Dec. 26, 1925 (Hix and Nathan). Note that this was a flight year.

The report listed in Cruickshank (1942) of a bird seen on Apr. 6, 1940, if correctly identified as this species, is much too early for a spring migrant. Subsequent observations by numerous observers have failed to find any Forster's Terns prior to mid-May, as noted above (May 17). Perhaps it represents a bird that wintered just south of us.

COMMON TERN *(Sterna hirundo)**B

Range: Holarctic species, the nominate race is widespread but somewhat local, both on the coast and inland.

Status: Locally abundant breeder and migrant along the coast. Much less numerous on Long Island Sound and the lower Hudson River. Relatively rare inland.

Migration: Most numerous and widespread in fall. Maxima: *Outer coast—* 1500, Oak Beach, May 10, 1936; 5000, after a hurricane, Moriches Inlet, Sept. 3, 1949 (Mayer and Rose). *Inner coast—*150, Rye, Aug. 2, 1946; 500, Sunken Meadow Beach, L.I., Aug. 26, 1950 (Komorowski).

Extreme dates: Apr. 15 to Dec. 5. Rare before May and after mid-October.

Breeding: Variously rare to abundant. Nearly completely extirpated in the early 1900s during the height of the plume trade, until given full protection in 1913; recovered again by the 1920s.

The Common Tern breeds on the broad ocean beaches, on various islands in the bays along the south shore, on islands at the east end of Long Island, and very recently on islands along the Connecticut coast.

245

Relatively rare elsewhere. The nest is ordinarily placed on the sand where somewhat grassy. Maximum estimates are based on number of pairs or nests:

PERIOD	LOCALITY	DATE	PAIRS OR NESTS	REMARKS
Prior to 1900	Great Gull Island	1886	4000	
	Gardiner's Island	1899	2000	
Since 1920	Great Gull Island	1960	900	
	Great Gull Island	1961	400	Island more heavily vegetated
	Great Gull Island	1962	None	Vegetation "very lush and dense" (*fide* Cant)

The foregoing is an excellent example of ecological change—Great Gull Island becoming unsuitable for Common Terns but, at the same time, attractive to Roseate Terns (see Table under Roseate Tern).

Additional maxima for other localities:

LOCALITY	DATE	PAIRS OR NESTS	REMARKS
Orient Point	1930	6000	
Orient Point	1934	4000	Beaches
Orient Point	1941	500	developed
Shinnecock Bay	1950	1000	
Moriches Bay	1948	2000	
Moriches Bay	1961	5000+	
Fire Island State Park	1960	2000	
Cedar Beach	1950	750	
Cedar Beach	1961	1500	
Meadow Island and Short Beach	1959	1200	

The following is noteworthy for our section of the Connecticut coast: 200 pairs nested on Goose Island, off Norwalk, in 1962 (Clement); 21 nests with eggs on Little Tavern Island, also off Norwalk, in 1962 (Bradley and Spofford). These are the first *known* breeding records for our portion of Connecticut. Sage *et al.* (1913) did not record it as a nesting species there, nor did Spofford (*in litt.*) who states, "Going back to 1912 through my own records I can find nothing to show that terns ever nested along the southwest Connecticut shore prior to 1962." It would appear, however, that such a large colony described above on Goose Island probably had nesting Common Terns prior to 1962, but that this little frequented island was not visited regularly by field observers.

Egg dates: May 12 to Aug. 4.

Remarks: This species winters north to South Carolina. Casual in Massachusetts (two winter specimens). The following occurrence in our area probably represents wintering birds, as the date is nearly a month too early for spring arrivals: 6, Raritan Bay, March 20, 1938 (Cant and Eynon), and perhaps the same individuals seen off Staten Island on March 23 (Fables). In both instances they associated with Bonaparte's Gulls. One also seen with Bonaparte's Gulls off Montauk Point, Dec. 27, 1957 (Ryan).

ARCTIC TERN *(Sterna paradisaea)**

Accidental: Holarctic species, breeding south to Nantucket and Martha's Vineyard, Mass. After the nesting season apparently pelagic and little known in coastal waters, migrating offshore toward the European and African coasts. Other than one adult specimen in the United States National Museum, No. 58990, merely labeled New Jersey, June 1848, collected by Heermann (Duvall, Auk, 62: 627, 1945), there is no other evidence of occurrence south of Long Island.

Only two definite records in our area, both from Long Island: adult male in breeding plumage collected on Ram Island Shoals, L.I., July 18, 1884 (not July 1, as stated in the literature). This specimen was taken by Worthington and is A.M.N.H. No. 64696. The other, listed by Reilly and Parkes (1959), is an immature male taken on Long Island, Oct. 7, 1897 and is N.Y.S.M. No. 1707. The writer examined this specimen and took measurements. Dr. Reilly confirmed these measurements: exposed culmen —24.7 mm., and tarsus—14.6 mm., which are well within the range for this species.

Although there are a number of alleged sight reports for our area, including some published, field identification is extremely difficult. Some of these reports may be correct, but I cannot vouch for a single one. Most of these reports, if not all, were made in late summer or fall, when the bird is likely to be in nonbreeding plumage. At this time it is highly variable, both as to plumage characters and soft part colors. Even the voice is not wholly reliable and is considered variable also. As to relative tarsal length of Arctic Tern and Common Tern, overlap occurs, depending on age.

I can only quote from some leading authorities as to the difficulties involved. Forbush (1925), "The color of this tern varies so much with age and season that its various phases of plumage have been described from time to time and named as new species, as *S. pikei* Lawrence, *S. longipennes* Coues, and *S. portlandica* Ridgway." Peterson (1947), "Fall adults are not safely told either, as the red bill and feet become quite dusky. Moreover, some Common Terns lose the black bill-tip for a while in late summer, accounting for the sight records of Arctics south of New England. Sight records south of New England open to question." Griscom and Folger (1948), "With the approach of fall, it becomes impossible to distinguish the Arctic and Common Terns, consequently no definite fall status [Nantucket] has been established." Griscom and Snyder (1955), speaking of the Massachusetts coast, "In spite of every effort in the past twenty-five years, no evidence of any fall migration of transients down our coast has been found; all sight records are distrusted, and many birds believed to be Arctic Terns in winter plumage have been collected and proved to be Common Terns."

In connection with this last, it is of interest to note that as recently as May 29, 1960, a tern thought by some observers to be an Arctic Tern was collected several miles off Jones Beach and proved to be a Common Tern, and this individual was in *breeding* plumage. If specimens in museums are misidentified, as they most certainly have been, how can one be sure of identification in the field?

ROSEATE TERN (*Sterna dougallii*)*B

Range: A widespread Old World species, but of very local distribution in its American range (confined to the North Atlantic coast and the Caribbean Sea), breeding mainly on coastal islands and ocean beaches. Aside from the Dry Tortugas (Florida), in the breeding season it is confined to a very limited area of continental North America, occurring only from Nova Scotia to Virginia. Even within this range it is uncommon to rare as a breeder and migrant in southern New Jersey and Maryland, and local in many places elsewhere. The nominate race occurs in our area.

Status: A variously uncommon to locally abundant breeder and fall migrant at the east end of Long Island, west to Jones Beach; and on the Connecticut coast west to Norwalk. Rare and local elsewhere. Numbers fluctuate considerably from year to year.

Migration: South of Long Island, this species is reported as an uncommon to rare migrant. Even in our area it is ordinarily numerous only in the vicinity of Montauk, at the eastern extremity of Long Island Sound (Orient region), the Fire Island–Jones Beach area, and offshore. This suggests that during the nonbreeding season the Roseate Tern is primarily a pelagic or, at least, an offshore migrant, except to and from the Connecticut breeding colonies (see below).

248

Maxima: Usually seen in flocks up to 10 or 20, occasionally up to 75 or more, but in 1950 there was a very large flight on Aug. 21; at Montauk Point, Darrow and Helmuth estimated over 500 passing by in a few hours, and at least 2400 were observed on the shoals between the Point and Block Island in a four-hour period (N. P. Hill). Other maxima: *Fall*—800+, Jones Inlet to Sagaponack, Sept. 13, 1960—day after hurricane Donna; 25, Mecox Bay, Sept. 22, 1937, late for so many. *Spring*— 20, Rockaway Beach, May 19, 1956.

Extreme dates: May 2 to Oct. 9. Rare before mid-May and after September.

The Roseate Terns breeding on the Connecticut islands (see below), apparently arrive in spring from the east and depart in fall by the same route, as they are very rarely reported farther west along our section of Long Island Sound. Aside from a specimen secured at Stamford in 1881 (J. H. Miller), N.Y.S.M. collection, the species has been reliably reported on only two occasions at Rye; and once at Baxter Creek, Bronx County, Aug. 25, 1934 (Cruickshank). There is also one report from Newark Bay, Sept. 21, 1924 (Urner). The species is unknown inland in our area.

Breeding (see map p. 251): The Roseate Tern breeds in situations similar to those of the Common Tern, but the nests are generally placed in thicker vegetation. Locations in dense grass are preferred to open sandy areas with scattered grass.

One of the largest colonies outside our region is located on two islands off the coast of Connecticut near Guilford: Faulkner's Island, and especially the smaller Goose Island (not to be confused with Goose Island off Norwalk) have had Roseate Terns breeding for many years. During the height of the feather trade, as many as 500 pairs nested on these two islands in 1901 (*fide* Dutcher), one of the few areas that escaped the raids of the plume hunters. During the summer of 1941, at least 1600 pairs were found there (Heck, Hickey, and Peterson). They outnumbered the Common Terns by about 5 to 1. This colony is of importance as a probable source of migrants in the Orient–Montauk area as was discussed under migration.

The following Roseate Tern breeding localities in our area are listed from east to west. Estimates are based on the number of pairs or nests:

PERIOD	LOCALITY	DATE	PAIRS OR NESTS	REMARKS
Prior to 1900	Great Gull Island	1889	10	
Since 1900	Great Gull Island	1960	100	See comparative
	Great Gull Island	1961	600	figures under
	Great Gull Island	1962	1000	Common Tern

PERIOD	LOCALITY	DATE	PAIRS OR NESTS	REMARKS
Since 1900	Gardiner's Island	1914	30	
	Gardiner's Island	1937	35	
	Cartwright Island	1938	100	
	Cartwright Island	1944	"few pairs"	Reason for depletion not known
	Orient Point	1934	400	
	Orient Point	1943	3	Beaches developed
	Moriches Bay	1961	25	
	Fire Island State Park	1960	200	
	Cedar Beach	1958	15	
	Cedar Beach	1959	100	
	Cedar Beach	1960	150	
	Short Beach	1951	3	Westernmost colony known on Long Island

During the summer of 1962, R. C. Clement found 50 nesting pairs in a Common Tern colony on Goose Island, off Norwalk, for the first known breeding in our portion of Connecticut (see discussion of this locality under Common Tern).

Egg dates: May 28 to July 8.

SOOTY TERN (*Sterna fuscata*)*

Range: A pan-tropical species, the nominate race breeds north to the Bahama Islands; also on the Dry Tortugas (west of the Florida Keys). Ranges widely in the nonbreeding season over tropical and subtropical seas. Appearing most often after hurricanes, north to Nova Scotia.

Status: Very rare visitant occurring chiefly after tropical storms on the coast of Long Island; casual elsewhere.

Occurrence and maxima: The Sooty Tern is a highly pelagic species wandering far and wide over the oceans, except during the breeding season when it nests both on oceanic and continental islands. More than any other tropical species it has been recorded in our area most often after hurricanes.

Of more than 50 occurrences in the New York City region, 23 are specimens, most of them preserved, 7 of which are in the American Museum

250

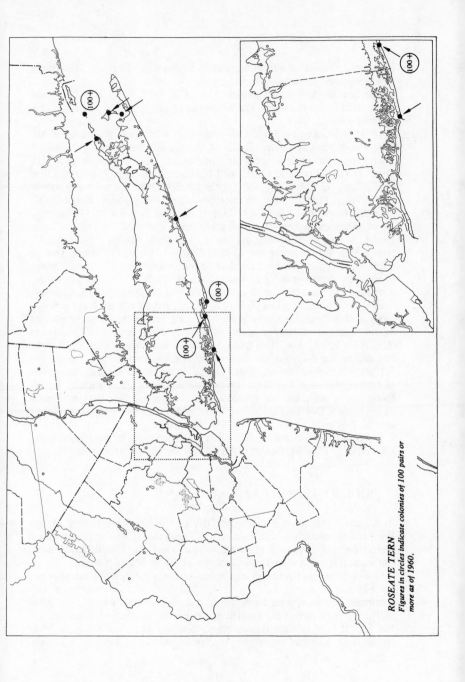

ROSEATE TERN
Figures in circles indicate colonies of 100 pairs or
more as of 1960.

of Natural History and 12 others chiefly in private collections. The species has been reported in 13 years since 1878.

The largest "invasions" occurred in 1878, 1928, 1955, and 1960, and are treated in detail below. The following are all specimen records unless otherwise noted.

1878: Hurricane on Sept. 12—numerous individuals picked up dead, others seen alive at various localities throughout the northeast—greatest inland flight on record—adult and immature, Lake Ronkonkoma, L.I., Sept. 13 (Dutcher collection), A.M.N.H.; adult female, Highland Falls, N.Y., Sept. 13 (Mearns), and another seen by him the following day at nearby West Point; immature male, Stamford, Conn., Sept. 16 (Porter).

1928: Hurricane on Sept. 19—biggest invasion in our area—16 records, 10 of them specimens: most of these birds occurred on eastern Long Island. Maxima—3 alive and 1 picked up dead, Mecox Bay, Sept. 23, (Helmuth), and another alive, but disabled, Georgica Pond, Oct. 1 (Helmuth); Wilcox found 2 dead at Moriches Bay, Sept. 21, and 2 more in a much decomposed condition, Shinnecock Bay, Dec. 24; 2 others were found in the latter condition that winter at Montauk and Sagaponack.

1955: Hurricane Connie, Aug. 12—10 occurrences, only 1 specimen— most of these were at the west end of Long Island, and 2 were seen at inland localities: Commonwealth Reservoir, N.J., Aug. 13 (Thorsell *et al.*); West Point, Aug. 14 (Treacy); 3 were seen flying over the Lower Bay and up the Narrows on Aug. 13 (several observers).

1960: Hurricane Donna, Sept. 12—12 Long Island occurrences, seven of these specimens. On Sept. 13 five were picked up at various south-shore points including an immature at Shinnecock Bay that had been banded on the Dry Tortugas two months earlier (*fide* Wilcox); one reported seen at Westport, Conn., Sept. 12 (M. Brown).

Extreme dates—based on live birds and specimens in fresh condition: July 17, 18, 21 (no hurricanes); Aug. 13 to Oct. 7 and 31.

BRIDLED TERN (*Sterna anaethetus*)*

Accidental: A pan-tropical species, the race *recognita* breeding in the West Indies, including the Bahamas. Ranges widely in the nonbreeding season over tropical and subtropical seas, rarely to Florida and South Carolina. Reported after tropical storms north to Massachusetts.

One definite occurrence in our area: An immature picked up alive on the beach at Quogue, L.I., Dec. 11, 1950 (Wilcox). The specimen was confirmed as this species by Amadon and is in Wilcox's collection. This individual may have been carried north by the severe tropical storm of Nov. 25. It is of interest that another specimen was secured on the New Jersey coast south of our region during the winter of 1950–51 and may also have been the result of the same storm. A detailed description of an adult well seen at Manasquan Inlet, N.J., Sept. 11, 1954 (Ryan), shortly after the passage of hurricane Edna, is probably correct. Although hurricane Donna of Sept. 12, 1960 brought Bridled Terns to Massachusetts, Rhode Island, and southern New Jersey, none was reported from Long Island.

LEAST TERN (*Sterna albifrons*)*B

Range: A nearly cosmopolitan species—widespread, but local—the race *antillarum* breeding on the Atlantic coast north to Massachusetts.

Status: Common to abundant migrant on the outer coast. Local breeder, occasionally numerous.

Migration: As the Least Tern breeds to the north of us only as far as Massachusetts, the following maxima may represent birds chiefly from nearby nesting grounds in our area, and postbreeding wanderers from more southern regions.

Maxima: *Spring*—300, Atlantic Beach, May 6, 1945. *Fall*—175, Moriches Inlet, Aug. 20, 1946; 500, same locality, Sept. 3, 1949 (Mayer and Rose), after a tropical storm.

Extreme dates: Apr. 20 to Oct. 9. Rare before May. No later fall dates confirmed. Departs very early, usually by late August or early September, and is rare by the middle of the latter month.

Breeding: The Least Tern, like the Piping Plover, nests on the open sand. It is found on the ocean beaches, and especially the sand flats where new fill has been dredged and pumped in the vicinity of bays and inlets.

Formerly common (prior to 1880), its numbers were severely depleted by the millinery hunters. With full protection in 1913, the species recovered strongly by the 1920s and is now once more numerous. Its future depends upon the preservation of beaches from being developed into bathing resorts.

Four nesting pairs at Long Beach, summer of 1926, was the first local breeding report since 1882. By 1942, Cruickshank reported six breeding colonies with a total of more than 300 pairs, all on the south shore of Long Island, west of Westhampton Beach.

Recent maxima: 75 pairs, Canarsie Pol, Jamaica Bay (1945); 50 pairs, Moriches Bay (1948); in June 1951, I estimated at least 200 pairs in the Short Beach area, nests being found back from the ocean beach, and on the new sand fill that had been dredged to deepen Jones Inlet. During the same summer, Komorowski discovered a small colony at Port Jefferson on the north shore, where Least Terns had previously been reported as very rare. He saw at least 20 pairs; five nests contained eggs. Perhaps it will be found elsewhere along the shore of Long Island Sound, although suitable areas are few.

253

The first known breeding for our portion of Connecticut occurred in 1960, when a pair was seen at its nest on Sherwood Island, off Westport (many observers). An increase to five pairs in 1961 and 1962 was reported there (Spofford).

Egg dates: May 10 to July 25.

Remarks: Although Sage *et al.* (1913) stated that, according to Hoyt, the Least Tern was formerly (1870s) "common" in Stamford harbor, the former did not list any more recent records (up to 1913) for the entire Connecticut shoreline. For .the Long Island Sound area, Cruickshank (1942) did not even mention this species as occurring along the shore in either Westchester or Bronx counties and stated, "and there are only a half dozen records west of Eaton's Neck" (north shore of Long Island).

Prior to hurricane Connie in mid-August 1955, the Least Tern was unreported inland. Immediately after this storm, a number of them were seen on the Hudson River as far as Cornwall, New York. Several observers noted as many as 13 at West Point and 6 more at Piermont, both on Aug. 14. Very unusual was a flock of 25 observed on the Hackensack River at North Arlington, July 27, 1958 (Wolfarth).

ROYAL TERN (*Thalasseus maximus*)*

Range: A species of very local and discontinuous breeding distribution: Pacific coast of Mexico; Gulf coast of Texas and Louisiana; Atlantic coast from Georgia to Maryland; West Indies; west coast of Africa. The nominate race breeds north to southeastern Maryland (Chincoteague Bay, since 1950). Wanders north to Massachusetts.

Status: Rare but now regular summer and fall visitant to the coast of Long Island. Sometimes numerous after tropical storms. Has greatly increased in recent years (since 1950).

Change in status: Formerly accidental and so considered by Griscom (1923) and Cruickshank (1942), both of whom listed only the old 1831 record. There are three Long Island specimens: Raynor South (now Freeport), Aug. 27, 1831 (Ward), A.M.N.H. No. 46008, possibly the oldest local specimen in existence; Gardiner's Bay, July 6, 1896 (Worthington), specimen in Latham's collection—never before published; Moriches Bay, Sept. 4, 1954 (Carleton and Grant), A.M.N.H. No. 648729, picked up dead after hurricane Carol of Aug. 31.

Reported at Point Pleasant, N.J., June 30, 1928 (Urner), adult with several Caspian Terns; another adult well seen after a tropical storm, Mecox Bay, Sept. 19, 1936 (Helmuth, diary), published here for the first time.

254

Regular on the south shore of Long Island since 1950 with the great increase of this species in the south; most often reported in the Moriches–Shinnecock area, usually but not always after hurricanes.

Maxima—no storm reported: Flock of 9, Shinnecock Inlet, Aug. 22, 1953 (Eisenmann and Grant).

Maxima—after hurricanes of 1944, 1954, and 1960:

1944: hurricane on Sept. 14—total of 16, Easthampton to Mecox, Sept. 16 (Helmuth), "many" Caspian Terns also.

1954: hurricanes Carol of Aug. 31 and Edna of Sept. 11—big flight—32, Moriches Inlet, Sept. 4 (Carleton and Grant); at least 60 on Sept. 12, Jones Inlet to Shinnecock Inlet (various observers).

1960: hurricane Donna of Sept. 12—"huge invasion"—65, Jones Inlet to Tobay, Sept. 13 (Buckley, Levine, Norse, and Post). An estimate of 300 was considered conservative along the south shore between Jones Inlet and Sagaponack on Sept. 13 and 14. With them were numerous Caspian Terns, and several Sandwich Terns. There were at least 14 Royal Terns on Flat Hummock Island (off Fisher's Island) as late as Oct. 9 (Ferguson).

Extreme dates: June 30 and July 6 (specimen) to Oct. 27 and Nov. 11; casual at Manasquan Inlet, Nov. 27, 1954 (Wolfarth)—note hurricane year.

Remarks: A report of an adult and one flying "young," at Moriches Bay, Aug. 15, 1959, is *not* proof of breeding at this locality. Terns are notorious wanderers and there are numerous instances of adults feeding juvenile birds at considerable distances from place of actual nesting.

Accidental inland: Adult male found dead near Lake DeForest, N.Y., June 18, 1960 (Mrs. Irving), is now in the collection of theTrailside Museum at Bear Mountain. The specimen was verified as this species by J. C. Orth (*in litt.*).

No other inland reports are accepted, as none is confirmed. Confusion with the Caspian Tern is likely.

SANDWICH TERN (*Thalasseus sandvicensis*)*

Casual: Chiefly a western Palearctic and Neotropical species. In the Old World breeds north to the British Isles and southern Sweden, but the New World race *acuflavidus* is very local, nesting in the Bahamas and on the South Atlantic coast only in North and South Carolina. Local breeder elsewhere in the Gulf of Mexico (coasts of Louisiana and Texas) and in the Caribbean Sea. Accidental north to southern Ontario.

In our area not definitely reported prior to 1957. The first reliable record for New York State is that of an adult female in nonbreeding plumage collected on Mecox Bay, June 30, 1957 (Buckley, 1959), A.M.N.H. No. 707775. Very likely the bird was carried northeast by hurricane Audrey of June 27, which lashed the Gulf coasts of Louisiana and Texas and then veered northeast toward the North Atlantic. During and after hurricane Donna of Sept. 12, 1960, there was an incursion of these birds in the northeast. On Long Island alone no less than 9 individuals were seen by numerous people from Sept. 13 through 16 and were reported at six different south-shore localities from Jones Beach east to Sagaponack.

CASPIAN TERN (*Hydroprogne caspia*)*

Range: A nearly cosmopolitan species, but absent in Central and South America. Breeds at widely scattered localities, being extremely local in eastern North America: (*a*) on *inland* lakes east to northern Michigan and southeastern Ontario, casually to northwestern Pennsylvania; (*b*) on the *coasts* of southern Labrador, Newfoundland, and southeastern Quebec; also Virginia (Cobb's Island) and islands off South Carolina.

Status: Regular fall coastal migrant, but generally uncommon; more numerous after hurricanes. Rare and irregular in spring, occasionally in small numbers. Very rare inland. Subject to marked fluctuations.

Occurrence and maxima: The Caspian Tern may be found along the ocean, on the beaches, and in the vicinity of bays, estuaries, and coastal ponds. It is very rare anywhere else in our region, having been reported but a few times on the Hudson River and on the larger inland lakes.

Maxima: *Fall*—most numerous after tropical storms; hurricane of Sept. 14, 1944—20, Jones Inlet to Oak Beach, Sept. 16 (Komorowski *et al.*), and 32 the same day, Easthampton to Mecox Bay (Helmuth); hurricane Donna of Sept. 12, 1960—"huge invasion" on Sept. 13—100+, Jones Inlet to Tobay (Buckley, Levine, Norse, and Post), and more than 400 estimated that day on the south shore between Jones Inlet and Sagaponack. *Spring*—9, Easthampton, May 6, 1932 (Helmuth); 19, Idlewild, May 16, 1953 (Mayer). *Inland*—4, Piermont, N.Y., Sept. 7, 1959 (Deed).

Extreme dates: *Spring*—Apr. 22 and 28 to June 4. *Summer* stragglers— June 22, 25, 30; an adult in breeding plumage, Fire Island Inlet, July 10, 1960 (Alperin), may belong in this last category or may represent an early fall arrival. *Fall*—July 20 and 21 (specimen) to Oct. 16 and 24; casual, Atlantic Beach, Nov. 23, 1952 (Bull). Rare after early October.

Remarks: The Caspian Tern winters north to South Carolina, casually to Maryland (1948) and southern New Jersey (Barnegat Bay and Cape May, one each, Dec. 29, 1946).

In our area one was seen from a fishing boat off Jones Beach, Dec. 28, 1958 (Ryan). Another was observed during a storm sitting on the ice on Prospect Park Lake, March 3, 1940 (Fleisher, Brennan, and Tengwall). This latter individual was probably a winter straggler, as the date is seven weeks earlier than the earliest spring date.

256

BLACK TERN (*Chlidonias niger*)*

Range: Holarctic species, the race *surinamensis* breeds *exclusively inland;* locally south to northwestern Pennsylvania, western and northern New York, northwestern Vermont, and the central portions of Maine and New Brunswick.

Status: Common to occasionally abundant fall migrant and usually uncommon spring migrant on the coast. In recent years a few nonbreeding individuals have summered along the outer coast. Rare inland.

Occurrence and maxima: The Black Tern, although nesting to the west and north of us on fresh-water ponds and marshes, is found chiefly in coastal waters in our region. Probably the majority of individuals migrate northward through the interior to their breeding grounds, as the species is relatively rare in spring on the Atlantic coast. On the other hand, in fall the great majority of birds migrate to the coast; in fact, numbers have been reported considerably offshore at this season. Most numerous in late August and September.

Maxima: *Fall*—30, Jones Beach, July 13, 1947; 1000, Easthampton, Aug. 25, 1933; 1500, Jamaica Bay, Sept. 6, 1955; 450 in one hour migrating off Jones Beach, Sept. 16, 1951; 2000, Napeague to Montauk, Sept. 22, 1922. *Spring*—50, Jones Inlet, June 9, 1946.

Extreme dates: Apr. 22, 1933, Boonton Reservoir (Edwards), and May 12; summer stragglers; to Oct. 15 and 27. Casual, Mecox Bay, Nov. 20, 1954 (Raynor), hurricane year. Rare before late May and after early October.

SKIMMERS: RYNCHOPIDAE

BLACK SKIMMER (*Rynchops nigra*)*B

Range: Widespread but local American species, the nominate race breeds on the Atlantic coast north to Long Island; rarely to Massachusetts.

Status: Locally common to abundant breeder on the south shore of Long Island. Usually a rare visitant elsewhere. Has greatly increased in recent years.

Change in status: Griscom (1923) called the Black Skimmer a casual visitant. Cruickshank (1942) stated that it was steadily increasing in the mid-1920s when it appeared regularly in very small numbers. In 1934 the first local breeding record was obtained.

Now (1962) abundant and widespread, most numerous after hurricanes. Since about 1950, it is not unusual to see Black Skimmers in groups up to a dozen flying over south-shore towns on their way to and from the ocean and bays. At dusk and well into the night, they may be seen or heard coming in from the seacoast up the inlets to feed in the smaller creeks.

1. Nonbreeding: The largest concentrations are reported after tropical storms, which is logical, such birds augmenting the local breeding population. After hurricanes a few have been seen also in such places as Long Island Sound, the Hudson River, and Newark Bay.

Maxima: (1934)—110, Jones Beach, Sept. 9. (1938)—200, Moriches Inlet, Sept. 27. (1944)—850, Easthampton to Mecox Bay, Sept. 16; 450, Plum Beach, Sept. 23; 300, Moriches Inlet, Oct. 15. (1954)—800, Mecox Bay to Shinnecock Bay, Sept. 9; 200, Jamaica Bay, Oct. 31. (1955)—600, Jones Inlet to Fire Island Inlet, Sept. 9; at least 1200 the same day, entire south shore. (1960)—1200+, Jones Inlet to Mecox Bay, Sept. 13.

Extreme dates: Apr. 26 to early November; later in hurricane years. Ordinarily rare before mid-May and after mid-October.

2. Breeding (see map): First found breeding in our area on Gilgo Island in Great South Bay in 1934 (Herholdt and Vogt). By 1942, it was also nesting on Oak Beach and near Moriches Inlet as well as on Gilgo Island—a total of about 40 pairs in three colonies. One pair nested in 1944 at Orient (Latham), for the only known breeding record away from the south shore.

This species prefers to breed in broad open sandy areas, such as occur along the south shore of Long Island. The nests are placed near the beach, and on new fill. They also nest in tern colonies in open expanses, but if the grass or other vegetation grows too dense, Black Skimmers eventually move to other areas. They nest along the causeways at Jones Beach, undisturbed by passing cars.

The following represent the largest known breeding colonies in our area —all since 1948. Maximum number of pairs in all cases.

LOCALITY	DATE	PAIRS
Moriches Bay area	1948	75
Moriches Bay area	1950	100
Moriches Bay area	1961	100
Jones Beach	1954	100+
*Jones Beach	1961	80
Short Beach	1951	30
Jamaica Bay Refuge	1953	75
Jamaica Bay Refuge	1962	120

* Includes Short Beach and Meadow Island.

Other smaller colonies occur at scattered south-shore points, especially on Fire Island—little visited by birdwatchers.

Egg dates: June 11 to Aug. 23.

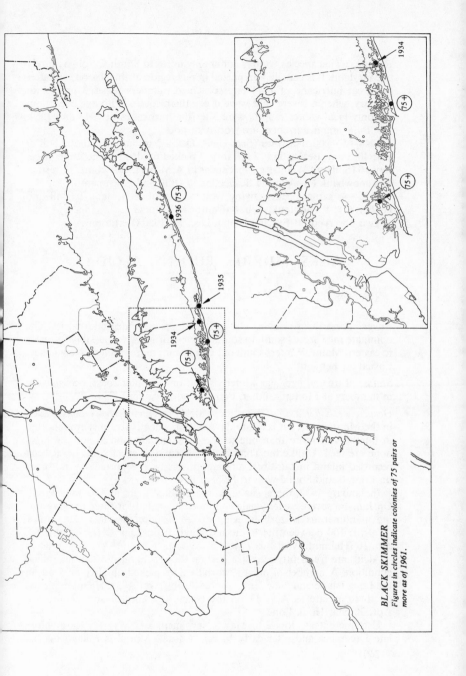

BLACK SKIMMER
Figures in circles indicate colonies of 75 pairs or more as of 1961.

Remarks: This species winters commonly north to South Carolina; rarely to Maryland. It is usually unreported in our region at this season, but after the great hurricane of 1944 unprecedented numbers lingered until mid-January, when a severe cold wave drove them south. With one exception, the only local winter reports were after the hurricanes of 1944 and 1954. The following occurrences are worthy of note:

1944–45—200, Narrows (Brooklyn), Dec. 22 to Jan. 4 (Elliott, Soll *et al.*); 40, Plum Beach, Jan. 7 (Grant); 3 picked up dead at the same place, Jan. 10 (Soll and Weinberg), specimens in A.M.N.H. collection; 11 resting in a snowbank (!), Atlantic Beach, Jan. 8 (Bull and Eisenmann).

1955—4, same locality, flying west off tip of jetty, Jan. 2 (Bull and Penberthy); 1, Montauk, Feb. 6 (Cantor and Norse).

Two observed off Fisher's Island, Dec. 17, 1950 (Ferguson).

AUKS, MURRES, PUFFINS: ALCIDAE

RAZORBILL *(Alca torda)**

Range: A northeastern Nearctic and northwestern Palearctic species. The nominate race breeds south to southern New Brunswick; possibly formerly to eastern Maine. Winters south to Long Island; more rarely to New Jersey. Casual farther south.

Status: Rare and irregular winter visitant on the outer coast, occasionally in numbers at Montauk Point. Perhaps more regular offshore.

Occurrence and maxima: Like most alcids, prefers a rocky coast. Even in the Montauk area it is a rare day, indeed, when Razorbills are reported in numbers of more than one to three individuals, and in some winters none are seen. Unlike the Thick-billed Murre, this species has never been recorded inland in our area, although it has been reported several times on Long Island Sound west to Pelham Bay.

In January 1932, there was an unprecedented flight at Montauk Point. On Jan. 1 a severe easterly gale continued unabated for three days, resulting in numerous Razorbills being driven inshore. Maxima: 80, Jan. 1 (Walsh); 100 between the Point and Ditch Plains, Jan. 3 (Helmuth); 50, Jan. 10 (Helmuth, Walsh *et al.*).

Alcids are frequently seen stranded on the beach, most often in an oiled condition. A number of oiled Razorbills were picked up alive or dead on the Long Island and New Jersey shores during April 1939. Helmuth picked up three as late as Apr. 17 on the beach at Georgica and another on Apr. 20 near Hook Pond.

Extreme dates: Nov. 2 to May 8 (specimen) and May 18. Rare before late December and after early March. Casual, Moriches Inlet, Aug. 25,

1939 (Helmuth), one picked up dead in fresh condition, but badly oiled. Another was found dead on the beach at the same locality, June 3, 1950 (Eisenmann and Grant).

COMMON MURRE *(Uria aalge)**

Casual: A species of the North Atlantic and North Pacific oceans, both in the Nearctic and Palearctic regions. The nominate race breeds south to southern Newfoundland and the Magdalen Islands; no proof of breeding in Nova Scotia. Winters mainly offshore south to Maine; more rarely to Massachusetts. Unreported south of New Jersey, except for evidence in the form of bones from Florida (Brodkorb, Auk, 77: 342, 1960).

This species was unrecorded in our area prior to 1936. Most individuals have been found oiled and either caught alive or picked up dead. Of ten reports, four are specimens—only one apparently preserved: one picked up dead, Moriches Inlet, March 31, 1936 (S. Raven); one caught alive and photographed, Oak Beach, Jan. 16, 1938 (Kimball, Bird-Lore, 40: 300, 1938); another caught alive, Long Beach, Feb. 21, 1940 (Arbib) and released Feb. 24; adult female, slightly oiled, found dead on the beach, Asbury Park, Feb. 3, 1946 (Van Deusen and Kunkle), A.M.N.H. No. 408896; one picked up dead, Fisher's Island, Feb. 12, 1951 (Ferguson). During the winter of 1951–52, three individuals were reported: Shark River Inlet, Dec. 8, 1951 (Q. Kramer *et al.*); one badly oiled, photographed, Jones Beach, Dec. 23, 1951 (Komorowski); one oiled, Montauk Point, March 9, 1952 (Arbib and Sloss). Also one in direct comparison with four Thick-billed Murres off Montauk, Dec. 27, 1958 (Ryan); and one found dead at Moriches Inlet, Apr. 4, 1961 (Guthrie).

As the two species of murres closely resemble each other, the above sight reports are restricted to experienced observers, several other reports being rejected as corroboration was lacking.

The vernacular name "Common" is a complete misnomer insofar as our area is concerned. The common species is the Thick-billed Murre. Tuck (1961) estimated that the total world population of Thick-billed Murres exceeds that of the so-called Common Murre by 3 to 1. In the western North Atlantic he estimated the ratio to be very much higher— nearly 10 to 1.

THICK-BILLED MURRE *(Uria lomvia)**

Range: Holarctic species, the nominate race breeds south to southern Newfoundland and Bird Rocks in the Gulf of St. Lawrence. Winters south to Long Island; more rarely to New Jersey, Delaware, and Maryland. Casual farther south. Occasional inland (Great Lakes and other fresh-water areas in the northeast).

261

Status: Rare and irregular winter visitant on the outer coast occasionally in some numbers. Perhaps more regular offshore. Rarely in numbers on the inner coast (Long Island Sound). Very rare inland.

Occurrence and maxima: In the New York City area, there have been six marked flights: 1883–84; 1890–91; December 1894; 1901–2; December 1926; December 1932.

The two largest incursions occurred during the winters of 1883–84 and 1890–91. In the former flight, 14 specimens were taken, nine of these in January on the south shore of Long Island, and "many" others reported seen, mostly at the east end. The latter flight took place off the Connecticut coast, at least 14 picked up in an exhausted condition near Stamford between Dec. 20 and Feb. 10.

That the Thick-billed Murre may winter offshore occasionally, or perhaps regularly, is deduced from a flock of ten seen ten miles off Sea Bright, N.J., Dec. 27, 1908 (Rogers).

Like other alcids, this species has been seen stranded on the beaches in an exhausted condition, either victims of storms or of crude oil discharged by tankers offshore.

Most of the aforementioned flights occurred along the coast, but in December 1894, a number of specimens were taken at inland localities including five from the lakes near Carmel, N.Y. (W. A. Mead) and another on the Hudson River at Ossining, Dec. 11 (Fisher), M.C.Z. collection. Other inland specimens are from Elmsford, N.Y., Dec. 20, 1890 (J. Rowley), A.M.N.H. collection and Orange Reservoir, N.J., Dec. 24, 1899 (Babson). It has also been seen on the Hudson River—at Riverdale, Feb. 12, 1928 (Cruickshank), Croton Point, Dec. 25, 1928 (Kuerzi), and Stony Point, Dec. 3, 1950 (several observers).

It is more than likely that most of these inland occurrences were due to the freezing up of the Great Lakes and other bodies of fresh water, rather than that the birds were blown in from off the ocean. First of all, this species is not rare on the Great Lakes and the St. Lawrence River at times; second, during the inland incursion of December 1894, a number of these birds were found frozen to death on various inland lakes and ponds throughout the northeast. That not all were dead is obvious as several were shot or picked up alive.

The Thick-billed Murre has been consistently rare in our area the past 30 years, nothing remotely resembling a flight having occurred since 1932. In fact, there have been several years when it was not reported at all, and in other years only one or two individuals.

Extreme dates: Nov. 13, 20, 22 (specimen) to March 24 (specimen) and Apr. 2. Most frequent from December through February.

Remarks: Great care must be taken in separating immature Razorbills from this species, as the former have relatively thin bills and are often mistaken for murres by inexperienced observers.

DOVEKIE *(Plautus alle)**

Range: Holarctic species of high latitudes, the nominate race breeding south only as far as west-central Greenland. Winters chiefly at sea, south to Long Island and less commonly to New Jersey.

Status: Rare but regular winter visitant on the outer coast. Occasionally great numbers are blown ashore after strong easterly gales. Essentially a pelagic species, most individuals seen in coastal waters are either oiled, exhausted, or emaciated.

Occurrence and maxima: The remarks of Wynne-Edwards (1935) regarding the habits and distribution of this species on the North Atlantic are so pertinent that his statement is quoted here: ". . . decidedly more pelagic than the other alcids in winter and at this season commonest in ice-laden waters, but south regularly to Long Island (offshore). It is alone among the Atlantic auks in being permanently satisfied with a planktonic diet, and is thus able to wander at large on the high seas."

For details regarding the 1932 flight, see Remarks.

Ordinarily only a few Dovekies are observed along our coast in winter, but on rare occasions large numbers have come to grief at the east end of Long Island. On Dec. 29, 1928, Wilcox saw more than 50 dead birds between Westhampton and Montauk, most of them oiled. Helmuth had the following experiences: from Easthampton to Montauk, Dec. 28, 1940, over 150, many alive but oiled, others dead, some emaciated; Easthampton, Jan. 4, 1945, 40 seen, 10 of which were dead, and from this date to late March over 40 picked up dead, many badly oil-soaked; same area, Dec. 31, 1949, 43 dead on the beach, many oiled. At Moriches Inlet, Dec. 27, 1957, Wilcox found 30 individuals, most of these dead and oil-soaked.

The Dovekie is most frequently reported from mid-November to early March, but has been reported every month of the year. One was collected at Montauk, Sept. 8, 1886 (Helme), and another at Jones Beach, May 30, 1911 (Griscom *et al.*).

During the summer of 1929 at Montauk Latham collected two individuals in full breeding plumage, one on June 28, the other on July 1, both in his collection. He saw as many as 12 in a single day and a few as late as the middle of July. Wilcox picked up a dead individual in breeding plumage at Speonk, June 15, 1957, specimen in his collection.

Prior to 1932 the only local inland occurrence was that of a specimen taken at Ossining, Dec. 5, 1898 (Fisher), M.C.Z. collection.

Remarks: On Nov. 19, 1932, a tremendous flight of Dovekies occurred off the Atlantic coast extending as far as southern Florida and Cuba. For graphic accounts of this historic flight, the reader should consult Murphy and Vogt (1933), and Nichols (1935).

263

Only a summary is presented here. On the aforementioned date, a raging northeast gale brought "thousands" of these birds close to our shores and numerous individuals were found stranded at localities as much as 100 miles inland.

Between Moriches and Shinnecock inlets, Wilcox estimated at least 3000, mostly flying birds, others swimming in the bays and inlets, and still others scattered about on the land. The great majority were seen between 11:00 A.M. and 4:00 P.M.

During the same day at Jones Beach, W. Drescher reported over 1000 flying over the breakers and some over land, with flocks up to 50. Most individuals were seen from 10:00 A.M. to 2:00 P.M.

Many of these birds—some dead, some alive—were picked up at various coastal points and inland localities. In the Peekskill area in northern Westchester County, nearly 50 miles from the ocean, three Dovekies were picked up dead on the day of the storm, and eight live ones were seen the following day.

BLACK GUILLEMOT (*Cepphus grylle*)*

Very rare winter visitant: Holarctic species, breeding south to eastern Maine. Winters chiefly in the breeding range south to Massachusetts and Rhode Island; very rarely to Long Island and casually to New Jersey.

Like the Harlequin Duck, this species frequents rocky shores and is casual along sandy beaches except in the vicinity of rock piles or breakwaters.

Of more than two dozen occurrences in our area, there are only three specimens, two of which are extant: an old specimen taken on Long Island (no date) formerly in the Lawrence collection; adult collected, Orient, Jan. 3, 1918 (Latham) in his collection, never before published; one taken at Quogue, Nov. 27, 1949 (B. Federico), A.M.N.H. No. 348699. Except for the old specimen, the Black Guillemot was unknown in our area before 1918. Since then, it has been reported several times each decade, with what might apologetically be called a flight during the winter of 1949–50 when four, including the above Quogue specimen, were noted along the south shore of Long Island. Half the reports are from Montauk Point and most of the remainder at the rock jetties on the south shore. Cruickshank (1942) listed sight reports from Rye and Newark Bay and there is also a 1958 report from the coast of New Jersey at Spring Lake. Most extraordinary is the inland observation at Boonton Reservoir, Nov. 26, 1939 (Cadbury and Hiatt), the former observer familiar with the species in Maine.

Extreme dates: Oct. 26 to April 2.

The relationship of the various subspecies is so complex and the race *atlantis* so poorly defined, that the species is treated here binomially. Storer (1952) treats *atlantis* as a synonym of *arcticus*, as does Parkes (1952).

Most breeding specimens along the east coast appear to be intermediate (wing and culmen measurements) and this applies to the 1949 Long Island specimen. Even the A.O.U. *Check-list* (1957: footnote, p. 249) admits to this intermediacy, although recognizing *atlantis*.

COMMON PUFFIN (*Fratercula arctica*)*

Casual: An eastern Nearctic and western Palearctic species, the nominate race breeding south along the coast to eastern Maine. Winters chiefly in the breeding range, rarely south to Massachusetts; casually to southern New Jersey.

This species prefers a rocky coast. According to Wynne-Edwards (1935) it is apparently the least migratory of the Atlantic alcids, spending the winter in the offshore zone not very far from the nesting grounds, and only occasionally wandering great distances to the south.

In the local area, all seven occurrences, including four specimens, are from Long Island: adult, ocean beach opposite Center Moriches, Dec. 15, 1882 (Foster), A.M.N.H. No. 64613; adult male picked up dead on the beach at Hither Plains, Montauk, March 30, 1902 (A. Miller), A.M.N.H. No. 359599; another too badly decomposed to save, may have been dead for some time, Montauk, Apr. 30, 1915 (Weber); adult male, Shelter Island, Apr. 15, 1941 (Latham), in his collection. The three sight reports are: Orient, Apr. 7, 1931 (Latham); two, Montauk Point, March 19, 1940 (Helmuth); adult, same place, Feb. 7, 1953 (Mayer and Rose).

Several published sight reports, including one from the north Jersey coast and another of four individuals at Montauk Point, are without details and not substantiated.

PIGEONS, DOVES: COLUMBIDAE

ROCK DOVE (*Columba livia*)*B

Introduced: A Palearctic species, widely introduced into various parts of the world.

The treatment here in using a binomial follows that of the A.O.U. *Check-list* (1957: 260), which states in part: "The mongrel wild stock found in our New World cities includes so many of the characters of . . . races and variants that it is listed only under the specific name *livia*."

Unlike other foreign species, its date of introduction into our area appears to be unknown.

The Rock Dove, or Domestic Pigeon, is found more or less wild throughout our cities and towns, nesting on buildings in the vicinity of parks and lawns, though mainly dependent on food provided by man. There is constant replacement by escapes from the countless dovecotes, so that it is hard to know how many should be considered truly feral. It also frequents farmyards and is seen even on the ocean beaches. It is resident wherever found and common to abundant in most places. Often a pest at feeding stations and a defiler of buildings and sidewalks.

Egg dates: Reported as breeding every month of the year.

WHITE-WINGED DOVE (*Zenaida asiatica*)*

Accidental: A Neotropical species, the nominate race breeding north to the Bahamas; occasionally reported in southern Florida. This species has been reported from Ontario and Maine, and one individual was recently (1961) captured and banded on Nantucket Island, Mass.

The only known record for New York State is that of a specimen collected at Water Mill, L.I., Nov. 14, 1929 (Wilcox), in his collection; identification verified by Chapin (Auk, 47: 265, 1930). This record was omitted from the A.O.U. *Check-list* (1957) despite the fact that it was included in the fourth edition (1931: 155).

MOURNING DOVE (*Zenaidura macroura*)*B

Range: Nearctic and northern Neotropical species, the race *carolinensis* occurring in our area.

Status: Common to locally abundant migrant, most numerous on the coastal plain. Regular in winter, greatly increased in recent years at this season. Common breeder.

Migration and winter: The Mourning Dove is highly migratory, as proved by banding. The writer has banded birds on Long Island which have been recovered as far south as Georgia and northern Florida. The largest concentrations occur on the coastal plain in early fall and again in winter.

Maxima: *Fall*—300, Idlewild, Aug. 24, 1946; 500, Mecox to Sagaponack, Sept. 2, 1924. *Winter*—340, Long Branch area, Dec. 28, 1952; 1700, all Christmas counts combined, late December 1953. Many of these winter individuals were at feeding stations. The enormous increase in feeders within the past ten years or so has resulted in a correspondingly large wintering population. Owing to numerous winter individuals present, it is difficult to supply arrival and departure dates, but migrant Mourning Doves are generally rare before mid-March and after mid-November.

Breeding: Nests most frequently in open country around agricultural areas, fields with second-growth thickets, and suburban districts and estates having both deciduous and coniferous trees.

Egg dates: March 20 to Aug. 25.

PASSENGER PIGEON (*Ectopistes migratorius*)*B

Extinct: Nearctic species, formerly bred south to the Berkshires, Catskills. and Poconos, and in the mountains to northern Georgia; rarely at lower elevations to northwestern Connecticut and southeastern New York. Wintered north to North Carolina, occasionally farther. Highly migratory.

The Passenger Pigeon is the best documented of the extinct species that occurred in the New York City area. The reasons for this are: (*a*) became extinct much later than the others; (*b*) far and away the most specimens in existence; (*c*) many more detailed observations. For a detailed history of this species, see the monograph by Schorger (1955).

In our region, this species was an abundant fall migrant, occurring in great flights principally in September. Flocks of "hundreds" were reported shot in a single day prior to the 1870s (*fide* Lawrence). It had become very rare by the 1880s. The last concentrations of any size were reported by Bicknell at Riverdale: 30 each on Sept. 16, 1878, and Oct. 6, 1877.

Of nearly 40 local specimens preserved with data, at least 24 are extant; 10 of these are in the American Museum of Natural History, the remaining 14 in six other museums. There may be others in private collections.

The last reported specimens taken in our area are as follows: 1889—Westchester County, Sept. 14; Rockland County, Sept. 18; Long Island, Oct. 13; 1893—a specimen shot out of a flock of ten birds at Morristown, N.J., Oct. 7 (A. B. Frost). Later reports proved to be Mourning Doves, including one shot at Englewood in 1896. The species became extinct around the early 1900s (except for one zoo specimen).

Extreme dates: *Fall*—Aug. 21 and 30, Sept. 6 (specimen) to Oct. 25 and Nov. 2 (specimen). *Winter*—no definite record. *Spring*—exceedingly rare, barely a dozen occurrences and only three specimens known; March 29 and Apr. 3 (specimen) to May 2 (specimen) and May 17. *Summer*—casual, collected at Oyster Bay, L.I., July 8, 1874 (T. Roosevelt), specimen in the United States National Museum (Paul Hahn, *in litt.*).

The only reported instance of breeding within the New York City area is the statement of Mearns (1878): "A few breed." He referred to its nesting in the Hudson Highlands between Cornwall and Highland Falls, Orange County.

Its apparent scarcity in spring in our region was probably due to its migrating inland, primarily through the Appalachians to its breeding grounds. The three known existing spring specimens were all taken west of the Hudson River in Orange County. Moreover, in many years of observation at Riverdale, Bicknell saw it only once in spring.

Its presence in fall was determined by an abundance of beech "mast" and acorns. Thus, it was most numerous in upland oak–beech forest, and relatively rare on the coastal plain.

Egg date: No data.

CUCKOOS: CUCULIDAE

YELLOW-BILLED CUCKOO (*Coccyzus americanus*)*B

Range: Nearctic and northern Neotropical species, the nominate race occurring in our area.

Status: Generally uncommon migrant and local breeder; some years more numerous. Numbers fluctuate from year to year.

Migration: The Yellow-billed Cuckoo is ordinarily quite secretive and is rarely seen in numbers of more than one or two.

Maxima: *Spring*—On May 13, 1952, Boyajian counted 34 individuals in a seven-mile stretch in the New Brunswick area. However, these birds may have represented, in part, some of the local breeding population rather than all of them migrants passing through. *Fall*—6, Montauk, Aug. 9, 1929; 6, Rockaway Beach, Oct. 5, 1956.

Extreme dates: Casual, Manhasset, Apr. 19, 1952 (J. Ricks), perhaps due to a southerly storm. Apr. 29 to Oct. 28 (specimen) and Nov. 2; collected at Oakdale, L.I., Nov. 11, 1950 (O. Thorne), specimen in Yale Peabody Museum. Usually rare before mid-May and after early October.

Breeding: Nests in thickets and scrubby fields, abandoned orchards and farmland advanced to the second-growth stage. This and the next species are more numerous in years of tent-caterpillar infestations. Both cuckoos are usually evenly distributed as breeding birds through most of our area, but this species is less common in the interior highlands, and along the immediate seacoast—at least on Long Island.

Egg dates: May 18 to Aug. 19.

Remarks: In late September and October 1954, there was a veritable flood of both cuckoos on eastern Long Island and on Sandy Hook. Many were picked up dead or alive on Fisher's Island (Ferguson), Orient (Latham), and Sandy Hook (G. Stout). It was estimated that altogether over 1000 of both species were passing through and that approximately two-thirds were Black-billed Cuckoos. A number were killed by cars, others hit obstructions, while many of those seen alive were in such a weakened condition that they were approached within a few feet. Not only were they observed in woodland, but also in open fields, salt marshes, and along the beaches. Many individuals were seen feeding on the ground. This remarkable flight was possibly the result of hurricane Edna of Sept. 11.

BLACK-BILLED CUCKOO (*Coccyzus erythropthalmus*)*B

Range: An eastern Nearctic species, breeding south to South Carolina.

Status: Similar to that of the preceding species.

Migration: In the exceptionally late fall of 1883, nine were picked up dead that had struck the Fire Island lighthouse, Sept. 30 (Dutcher).

Extreme dates: Casual, Bronx Park, Apr. 15, 1961 (Maguire and Hackett), perhaps due to a southerly storm. April 28 to Nov. 4 and Nov. 13 (Griscom, 1923). Rare before mid-May and after early October.

Breeding: While both cuckoos are fairly evenly distributed through most of the New York City region, this species is more numerous in the hills of the interior, which is what one would expect, being the more common of the two in the northern limits of the range. Consequently, it is somewhat surprising to find that it is also the commoner breeding cuckoo on the south shore of Long Island. Helmuth, in over 40 years of field experience, found that the Black-billed Cuckoo was the breeding species in the East-hampton area, and the writer found the same thing true on Fire Island and at Jones Beach.

Egg dates: May 21 to Aug. 3.

Remarks: See previous species.

BARN OWLS: TYTONIDAE

BARN OWL (*Tyto alba*)*B

Range: A nearly cosmopolitan species, but absent from the colder portions. The race *pratincola* occurs in our area.

Status: Uncommon, local resident on the coastal plain and in the lowlands of the interior; rare to absent in the mountains.

Occurrence and maxima: The Barn Owl is one of a number of "southern" species that has spread northward during the past half century or more. It was unknown to Giraud (1844). However, it is still a local species in our area and subject to mortality in severe winters. It is virtually non-migratory and has been reported as breeding every month of the year.

Unless one visits a breeding site or a winter roost, the Barn Owl is rarely observed in our area. Barn Owls are prevalent in the vicinity of garbage dumps, where they are attracted by numerous rats. Small concentrations are sometimes located in conifer groves during the winter months.

Maxima: 4, Pelham Bay Park, winters of 1953 and 1960; 4, Montauk, late December 1957.

Nesting places are found chiefly in urban and suburban areas and the vicinity of farms. The eggs are laid in barns, old buildings, steeples, abandoned water towers, and more rarely in hollow trees. A pair has nested in the Fire Island lighthouse for a number of years.

In 1939 at least 23 nesting pairs were reported in all sections of the New York City region. In 1940 it was found nesting in 22 localities, nearly half of these on Long Island. In the New Brunswick, N.J., area alone, four pairs bred in 1953.

No comparable breeding survey for the entire region has been undertaken in over 20 years, and it would be worthwhile, in order that its current status may be determined, as well as a comparison made with former years.

Egg dates: Reported every month except January; chiefly March to September.

OWLS: STRIGIDAE

SCREECH OWL (*Otus asio*)*B

Range: Nearctic species, the race *naevius* occurring in our area.

Status: Fairly common resident; most frequent in winter.

Occurrence and maxima: The Screech Owl, although essentially nonmigratory, is found in largest numbers during the winter months, indicating considerable dispersal at this season.

Maxima: 18, Queens and southern Nassau counties, Dec. 30, 1950; 11, Boonton Christmas count, Dec. 23, 1951.

This species breeds in orchards, farmland, village streets, and city parks. It still nests in such places as Central and Prospect Parks. The nest is situated in tree holes and bird boxes.

Egg dates: March 29 to May 18.

Remarks: As is well known, this species is dimorphic, having both a red and a gray phase. These color phases are not sex-linked. Not infrequently both color phases are found in the same nest. On the basis of 82 specimens in the American Museum taken in our area, the red phase apparently predominates. This is especially true on Long Island, where 31 out of 40 are in this phase. Elsewhere, there are 28 red and only 14 gray represented. A few specimens appear to be intermediate in color. A worthwhile cooperative project should be undertaken to study breeding pairs and their young to determine the present ratio of the color phases, as the great majority of the specimens examined were collected prior to 1900.

GREAT HORNED OWL (*Bubo virginianus*)*B

Range: A widespread American species, ranging from Alaska and Canada to extreme southern South America. The nominate race breeds in our area.

Status: Local resident, uncommon to fairly common in the wilder sections; virtually absent from western Long Island. Like all owls, most frequent in winter.

Occurrence and maxima: The Great Horned Owl, like the Pileated Woodpecker, has in recent years become more adapted to the metropolitan area, appearing on the outskirts of the larger towns and often seen in some of the larger city parks.

While this owl is usually found singly, flights occur on rare occasions in late fall and early winter, when large numbers have been shot at game farms, but no instances of this have been reported to me in recent years. Cruickshank (1942) stated that as many as 60 were killed at one game farm during a single winter, but he did not give the locality or date. It is possible that occurrences of individuals seen in such places as Central Park during the cold months take place in "flight" years.

Although breeding in the wilder sections of eastern Long Island and in the hills of the interior, it is very local, even in these areas. At the other extreme, nests have been found within the past few years in Bronx and Pelham Bay Parks. It breeds in the deserted nests of hawks, crows, and squirrels, occasionally in hollow trees, and very rarely on rock ledges such as those on the Palisades.

Egg dates: Late January to Apr. 20.

Subspecies: This species is also represented in our area by two records of the race *wapacuthu*, which breeds southeast to northern Ontario, and winters southeast to southern Ontario: casually to New York and southern New England. This pale subarctic form was collected in Bronx Park on Feb. 15, 1919 (*fide* Crandall), and is A.M.N.H. No. 144845. It is noteworthy that in the same collection are two more specimens of this race taken in southern Connecticut near New Haven in January of the same year. Another local specimen, previously unpublished, is one taken at Orient, Feb. 20, 1929 (Latham), in his collection, and recently examined by the writer.

SNOWY OWL (*Nyctea scandiaca*)*

Range: Holarctic species, breeding on the arctic tundra south to the northern portions of Manitoba, Quebec, and Labrador.

Status: Rare and irregular winter visitant, chiefly coastal, but one or two are reported on eastern Long Island nearly every year. At irregular intervals great flights take place. Very rare inland, except during flight years.

Occurrence and maxima: The Snowy Owl is most numerous along the seacoast, but also visits rat-infested garbage dumps along the larger tidal rivers. Late November and December are the principal periods of occurrence in our area, when the greatest numbers are reported.

Since Cruickshank (1942), only three major flights have occurred: 1945–46, 1949–50, and 1960–61.

By far the greatest irruptions occurred during the years 1890–91 and 1926–27. During the former flight at least 20 where shot at Montauk alone in a two-week period prior to Dec. 6, and over 70 were shot on eastern Long Island between Nov. 24 and Dec. 12 and mounted by the taxidermist Knoess of Riverhead. The only record for Central Park was in mid-December of 1890. In the great fall flight of 1926, 40 were killed on Fisher's Island alone in November and December, and a single taxidermist received 36 additional birds just from eastern Long Island. At Long Beach, eight were shot on the morning of Dec. 5, and at least 75 more were shot elsewhere in the New York City region. Many others were seen through January 1927.

Present-day observers who see from one to six in a day's trip on Long Island and call it a "big" flight should bear in mind that their counts are insignificant when compared with the two aforementioned flights. Maxima of four to six birds were reported at coastal localities during the winters of 1937–38 and 1941–42, and up to four in 1960–61.

Extreme dates: Oct. 12 to May 4. Rare before November and after March.

Remarks: Presumably due to an absence or scarcity of lemmings, arctic hares, and ptarmigan, upon which they feed, Snowy Owls must migrate southward or starve. At *irregular intervals* they wander as far as New England, New York, and New Jersey; occasionally farther south. I emphasize irregular intervals because it has often been stated that these flights are supposed to occur every four years. Such is definitely not the case in our area, with certain exceptions. From 1937 to 1949, there were four four-year intervals, but there were two ten-year intervals—one between 1926 and 1937, the other between 1949 and 1960—when very few were reported. Griscom and Snyder (1955) point out that in Massachusetts there have been as many as 16 years without a marked flight, and in our area there was no major incursion between 1905–6 and 1926–27, a span of 21 years.

HAWK OWL (*Surnia ulula*)*

Accidental: Holarctic species, the race *caparoch* breeds south to southern Quebec and New Brunswick. Winters south to the Adirondacks and northern New England; irregularly to Massachusetts.

In our area there are five occurrences, three of them specimens: one collected, Bay Ridge, Brooklyn, about 1863, A.M.N.H. No. 437332; "one seen at a distance of twenty feet," Stamford, Conn., winter of 1879 (Hoyt), according to Sage *et al.* (1913); one taken, Orient, L.I., Dec. 28, 1900 (Latham), but specimen lost; one shot in Essex County, N.J., winter

272

of 1904 (Dickinson collection), examined by L. K. Holmes; one seen, New Brunswick, N.J., Dec. 19, 1926 (S. C. Brooks, Auk, 44: 251-252, 1927).

One or two recent sight reports, while possibly correct, were not corroborated.

BARRED OWL *(Strix varia)**B

Range: Nearctic species, the nominate race occurs in our area.

Status: Uncommon to fairly common resident on the mainland, but very rare on Long Island.

Occurrence and maxima: Although essentially a resident species, the Barred Owl is reported most frequently in winter, as is true of all our local owls. At this season small groups roost in conifer groves.

Maxima: 5, Bronx Park, late December 1943.

The Barred Owl is partial to low rich woods and wooded swamps. It breeds in the deserted nests of hawks, crows, and squirrels, and occasionally in hollow trees. Searching for and finding owl nests requires lots of patience and hard work, so that the following breeding densities are noteworthy. In 1908, Chapin and Cleaves located 11 nests on Staten Island. Both in 1941 and 1948 Stearns found five nesting pairs in the Great Swamp area of New Jersey.

Egg dates: March 4 to May 8.

Remarks: One of the mysteries of bird distribution is that of the Barred Owl on Long Island and in coastal Massachusetts. Although this species is common enough on the coastal plain from Florida to New Jersey, it has "always" been a very rare bird on Long Island, and is "lacking on the coastal plain" of Massachusetts (see Griscom and Snyder, 1955).

Of the many specimens in the American Museum collection taken locally, only one is from Long Island: adult female, Brooklyn, Nov. 28, 1899 (Braislin), which incidentally had its stomach filled with House Sparrows. Within a 50-year period in the Orient region, Latham called it a very rare winter visitant. He collected one specimen there Oct. 15, 1932. The Fergusons (father and son), with nearly 50 years' experience on Fisher's Island, also called it very rare, collecting one on Apr. 8, 1922. In over 40 years' field experience at Easthampton, Helmuth could find the Barred Owl on only five occasions, and no breeding evidence.

Indeed, this species has been reported to nest on Long Island at only five locations, the first in Nassau County, the balance in Suffolk County: Meadowbrook (near Jericho), Hecksher State Park, East Patchogue, Sag Harbor, and Shelter Island. The Sag Harbor record is based on a nest containing two eggs taken on March 26, 1924 (Latham), in his collection. No breeding has been reported on Long Island for over 20 years.

GREAT GRAY OWL (*Strix nebulosa*)*

Accidental: Holarctic species, the nominate race breeds southeast to Ontario. Winters south to the Adirondacks; very rarely to Massachusetts. The record cited by the A.O.U. *Check-list* (1957: 286) from Mendham, N.J., is considered unsatisfactory (see Griscom, 1923). The *Check-list* also omits two old specimen records from Connecticut: Stratford, 1843, and North Haven, 1893 (see Sage *et al.*, 1913). The latter specimen is in the Yale Peabody Museum collection, New Haven.

In our area there are two Long Island records. One shot at Mount Sinai (date not stated) by Helme; the whereabouts of this specimen is unknown. Another collected at Orient, Dec. 29, 1902 (*fide* Latham), but specimen not preserved; this latter record is published here for the first time.

Several sight reports are unconfirmed. Inexperienced observers are likely to confuse this species with Barred Owls and possibly immature Great Horned Owls.

LONG-EARED OWL (*Asio otus*)*B

Range: Holarctic species, the race *wilsonianus* breeds south to Virginia.

Status: Uncommon to locally fairly common winter visitant. Rare and local breeder, perhaps overlooked.

Nonbreeding: The Long-eared owl is our most gregarious woodland owl, roosting in conifer plantings in late fall and winter. Usually only one to three or four are encountered, but on occasion much higher numbers are found. Pelham Bay Park has long been a favorite locality for these owls, as may be seen by the following high counts:

Maxima: 15 each—winters of 1943 and 1945; 37, Jan. 2, 1961 (several observers), a remarkable concentration. These roosts are occupied principally from late October to early April.

Breeding: This species may be less rare as a nesting bird in our region than is realized, but finding the nest entails patient searching and hard work. It breeds usually in conifers, occasionally in deciduous woods in abandoned crow nests; more rarely in hollow trees, or even on cliffs.

The breeding of the Long-eared Owl in our area is of sufficient interest that a detailed inventory of localities by section is given as completely as possible.

New York State (mainland): In the late 1870s and 1880s A. K. Fisher considered this species as common as the Screech Owl in the Ossining area (Westchester County), but only after diligent effort was he able to locate several nests in a dense stand of hemlock and white pine. He collected a

274

female and five eggs, May 2, 1879, and another set of five eggs, March 31, 1880. A pair nested and raised young on Constitution Island, Hudson River (Putnam County) in 1880 (Mearns).

New Jersey: A set of five eggs was taken at Morristown (Morris County) on Apr. 5, 1886 by M. Green, A.M.N.H. collection. A bird was seen incubating at Caldwell (Essex County) on March 18, 1935, by Rusling, and Cant found a nest near the Raritan River (Middlesex County) on Apr. 25, 1937.

Long Island: Nestlings collected in the pine barrens of eastern Long Island at Lake Grove and Selden (Suffolk County), both on May 30, 1889, by Howell, are in the American Museum collection. Also in Suffolk County, Latham collected a nest with four eggs at Orient, Apr. 18, 1931, and observed two pairs breeding in old crow nests near Orient in the spring of 1944. In Nassau County, Allen and Cruickshank discovered a pair at their nest with eggs in a red cedar near Massapequa on Apr. 18, 1937, and a nest and four downy young were found by Smigel at Lattingtown on May 18, 1939.

Cruickshank (1942) stated, "In the last twenty years at least twelve nesting sites have been found in the New York City region, half of these on Long Island." Unfortunately he did not give localities or years.

No new breeding data in our area have been added during the past 18 years (since 1944).

Egg dates: March 18 to May 3.

SHORT-EARED OWL (*Asio flammeus*)*B

Range: Holarctic region; South America (chiefly temperate); Greater Antilles (local). The nominate race occurs in our area, but is a rare and local breeder south of central New Jersey.

Status: Generally uncommon migrant and winter visitant on the coast and on the tidal river marshes; occasionally fairly common; locally numerous. Local breeder, greatly decreased in recent years.

Occurrence and maxima: 1. Nonbreeding—the Short-eared Owl is quite erratic in its visitations to our area, but is reported most often between October and April. It may be seen along the coastal beaches and marshes, and in the vicinity of our larger river marshes, but is most prevalent near refuse dumps which have a large rodent population. Like all our owls, it is most frequent during the winter; and like the Long-eared Owl is often gregarious.

Maxima: Winter of 1934–35—16, Pelham Bay area; 18, Newark Meadows; 24, Newark Meadows, Jan. 12, 1947 (Urner Club). During the early winter of 1959, Herbert Johnson estimated not less than 40 on Canarsie Pol, Jamaica Bay; the owls were attracted by large numbers of rats and mice and disappeared after the rodents had been cleaned out.

It should be pointed out that the above concentrations are few and far between and that in many seasons the species is scarce and hard to find.

Of great interest is the record of an individual captured, banded, and released on a trawler ten miles off Shinnecock Inlet, Oct. 13, 1961 (Wilcox).

2. Breeding—this species nests on the ground in marshes and meadows. As a breeder it is now quite rare and local, formerly not uncommon at this season.

Maxima: 5 nests, Elizabeth (N.J.) marshes in 1923 (Urner).

Egg dates: Apr. 24 to June 23.

BOREAL OWL (*Aegolius funereus*)*

Accidental: Holarctic species, the race *richardsoni* breeding south to Ontario, Quebec, and New Brunswick. Winters south to the northern portions of New York (Adirondacks) and New England; more rarely to Massachusetts. Two old specimens from northern Connecticut; one recent specimen from New Jersey.

One definite record for our area: A bird found alive after having struck a building at the Raritan Arsenal, near Bonhamtown, Middlesex County, N.J., Nov. 1, 1962, is now a specimen in the Newark Museum. This specimen was submitted to the American Museum of Natural History, where it was verified as this species by several ornithologists. A brief report on this bird is of sufficient interest to mention here, and is taken from a letter to me received from Irving H. Black, Curator at the Newark Museum: "It was taken to the home of a boy, Joseph Mish (about 15), . . . and kept alive for about a week. After death it was buried carefully in a cloth. Before death there evidently had been no feeling that the bird was anything of interest, but later the boy kept pointing to illustrations of the Boreal Owl and insisted that that was what his bird was. Because of this the bird was dug up in early February and brought to the Newark Museum. It was in surprisingly good condition for a bird that had been dead three months."

Two sight reports are considered unsatisfactory. The 1929 report listed by Cruickshank (1942) is doubtful as the observer told me that, although he believed it to be this species, he had not seen a Saw-whet Owl up to that time. Another report of one seen at Croton Point, N.Y., in 1951 is also unsatisfactory; unfortunately no one else was informed about it until too late and thus no confirmation was possible.

SAW-WHET OWL (*Aegolius acadicus*)*B

Range: Nearctic species, the nominate race breeds south to the coastal plain on Cape Cod, inland to southern Connecticut and in the mountains to Maryland; once on Long Island.

Status: Rare to uncommon, but regular winter visitant. One breeding record.

Occurrence and maxima: Like other woodland owls, the Saw-whet Owl is most often found in conifers during winter. It is usually remarkably tame; some individuals may be caught by hand. I have seen birds taken in this manner, banded, and replaced on the same branch from which they had been removed. Ordinarily only one individual is seen at a locality, but on occasion more are found.

Maxima: 4, Central Park, nearly all March 1958; at least 8, Jones Beach area, winter of 1959–60 (many observers in both instances).

Extreme dates: Oct. 10 (earliest specimen, Oct. 13) to Apr. 17 (specimen), Apr. 22 (banded), Apr. 28, and 30. Usually rare before November and after March. Casual: Sept. 22, 1961, Peekskill (J. Given)—mist-netted and banded; May 9, 1962, Belle Mead, N.J.—just out of our area (Frohling); May 13, 1947, Rye (Cruickshank); early June 1842, one shot in St. Paul's Churchyard, New York City (*fide* Giraud); June 21, 1947, Poundridge Reservation (Bull, Darrow, and Wheeler)—one seen at dusk and heard calling, but no breeding evidence obtained.

Remarks: One known breeding record for our area—nest with five eggs, Miller Place, L.I., 1879 (Helme). It is of interest to note that this breeding occurred following a great flight during the winter of 1878–79. Stone (1937) stated that at a roost located in a cedar grove near Princeton, N.J. (outside our area), ten were shot on Dec. 10, 1878, and seven more the following day.

It is quite possible that this species has bred elsewhere in our area, but definite evidence is lacking. Nest sites are probably overlooked.

NIGHTJARS: CAPRIMULGIDAE

CHUCK-WILL'S-WIDOW (*Caprimulgus carolinensis*)*

Accidental: A southeastern Nearctic species breeding north to southern New Jersey. Reported regularly in lower Cape May County from 1930 on, and found nesting in 1952. During June 1954, possibly as many as 20 different individuals were heard calling. It is now well established there.

This species is accidental north to Ontario, New Brunswick, and Nova Scotia. Specimens were taken in eastern Massachusetts in 1884 and 1915, and at New Haven, Conn., in 1889.

In our region there is one definite record, published here for the first time: Adult female collected at Riverhead, L.I., May 2, 1933 (Latham), specimen in his collection and examined recently by the writer. This represents the first known specimen for New York State.

Observers familiar with this species have heard individuals calling in our area on three occasions in New Jersey and once on Long Island. While very likely correct, all were made by single observers and in no instance was a bird actually seen. In the case of such a rare species, it is thought best to omit details of these reports since they lack corroborative evidence.

WHIP-POOR-WILL (*Caprimulgus vociferus*)*B

Range: Nearctic species, the nominate race occurs in our area.

Status: Fairly common to uncommon, but local breeder; more numerous on the coastal plain. Rare, but regular migrant.

Migration: This species is recorded annually by the active birdwatcher in such localities as the city parks, where individual Whip-poor-wills may be seen perched lengthwise on some tree limb, or flushed from the ground. It is a rare occasion, however, when more than one individual is seen in any one locality, as they are nocturnal in habits.

Extreme dates: Apr. 2, 1961, Prospect Park (J. Doll); Apr. 8 and 13 to Oct. 20; casual, Nov. 6, 1945, Northport, L.I. (Elliott), bird flushed. Rare before late April and after early October.

Breeding: This species prefers dry woodland, where it nests on the ground. It is locally numerous in the pine barrens of eastern Long Island and Monmouth County, N.J., and to a lesser extent in deciduous woodland elsewhere.

To give an idea of its occasional abundance on Long Island, Helmuth (diary) estimated 50 calling birds on May 9, 1942, between Mecox Bay and Montauk, most of these "on territory." Much farther west in the Seaford–Massapequa area, Elliott ("Long Island Bird Notes," weekly newspaper column in *Nassau Daily Review-Star*) heard 30 or more in mid-May 1945, and he had found the nest as far west as Bellmore, but these birds have now almost entirely disappeared as breeders—their haunts having been destroyed by building developments. On Staten Island, Cleaves (Auk, 62: 304–305, 1945) stated that it was regular and locally numerous, nesting in a half dozen or more localities, including the vicinity of Pleasant Plains, where it was chiefly second-growth woodland. However, many of these areas have been or are being rapidly ruined and the Whip-poor-will has vanished as a breeding species from many a former haunt.

Egg dates: May 12 to June 25.

278

COMMON NIGHTHAWK (*Chordeiles minor*)*B

Range: Nearctic and northern Neotropical species, the nominate race occurring in our area.

Status: Common to abundant fall migrant inland, but relatively uncommon along the outer coast. Local breeder, much less numerous than formerly.

Migration: The height of the fall migration is during late August and early September, rarely later. Maxima: 1000, Port Chester, N.Y., Aug. 23, 1949, and Sept. 4, 1936; 1000, Somers, N.Y., Aug. 26, 1951; 900, Grassy Sprain Reservoir, N.Y., Sept. 2, 1950; 500, Elizabeth, N.J., Sept. 22, 1936; 400, Westport, Conn., Sept. 30, 1961, unusually late for so many.

Extreme dates: Apr. 12 to Oct. 6, 11 (specimen), and Oct. 19; casual, Idlewild, Nov. 8, 1958 (Mayer), and Wolfe's Pond, Staten Island, Nov. 11, 1954 (Lincoln and Wolfarth), possibly a cripple. Rare before mid-May and after September.

Breeding: In our area the Common Nighthawk breeds in two distinct types of habitat: (*a*) on the ground in open areas; (*b*) on flat rooftops in cities and towns.

The latter locations are thought to be relatively recent and the birds have increased in some places. However, Zerega (Forest and Stream, 18: 467, 1882) stated that a pair nested on a Manhattan rooftop on 71st Street as far back as 1882. Braislin (1907) first noted it nesting in Brooklyn on roofs with a covering of tar and pebbles. The Nighthawk now rarely nests in New York City, but does so regularly in New Jersey, as at Newark, Passaic, New Brunswick, and many smaller towns. It still nests occasionally on rooftops in Westchester County, at White Plains, Port Chester, New Rochelle and Mount Vernon.

As a ground nester, however, it has greatly decreased. Formerly nesting in open pine barrens, pastures, and sterile fields, it has abandoned most of these locations. Latham (1946) has given an interesting history of its breeding status on eastern Long Island: Last nesting on gravel beaches at Orient Point and Shelter Island, 1920; Napeague, 1926; Southold, 1928; on sand dunes at Riverhead, 1938; nesting on Gardiner's Island as late as 1944 on low flat rocks in pastures and on the beaches, and may still nest there. He found it still nesting (1954) at Riverhead in pine barrens. Elsewhere, it has abandoned many of its former ground nest sites. One or two pairs were found nesting on slate outcrops in pasture land in the vicinity of Blooming Grove, Orange County, during the late 1950s (M. Earl).

Egg dates: May 24 to June 28.

SWIFTS: APODIDAE

CHIMNEY SWIFT (*Chaetura pelagica*)*B

Range: An eastern Nearctic species, breeding from southern Canada to Texas and Florida.

Status: Common to occasionally abundant fall migrant inland, relatively uncommon along the outer coast. Locally common breeder.

Migration: Like the Nighthawk, this species is at maximum numbers during late August and early September: 200 descending into chimney for the night, Eastport, L.I., Aug. 21, 1951; 1500, Fort Tryon Park, Manhattan, Aug. 30, 1947 (B. Gilbert); 3000, Montclair, Sept. 2, 1940 (Wolfarth), a very unusual number.

Extreme dates: Apr. 3, 5, and 12 to Oct. 28 and Nov. 4. Rare before late April and after early October.

Breeding: This species nests commonly throughout the region in unused chimneys. There is no recent evidence of nesting in hollow trees in our area.

Maxima: 100 pairs, Buchanan, Westchester County, summer 1954 (Nolan).

Egg dates: May 24 to July 3.

HUMMINGBIRDS: TROCHILIDAE

RUBY-THROATED HUMMINGBIRD (*Archilochus colubris*)*B

Range: Primarily an eastern Nearctic species, breeding from southern Canada to Texas and Florida.

Status: Uncommon to occasionally fairly common fall migrant. Local breeder.

Migration: The Ruby-throated Hummingbird is greatly attracted to flowers, especially red ones like trumpet creeper, jewel weed, bee balm, salvia, and others, and during late fall to petunias. Ordinarily only one or two are observed around a flowerbed, but on occasion many more are reported.

Maxima: 18, Bayside, L.I., Sept. 8, 1941 (Fischer), an unusual concentration for our area; 6, Jones Beach, Sept. 12, 1948.

Extreme dates: Apr. 14, 19, and 24 to Nov. 1, 9, and 11. Rare before May and after mid-October.

280

Breeding: This species prefers rural areas, nesting in a variety of situations, such as gardens, orchards, roadside thickets and trees, and woodland clearings, often near streams.

Egg dates: May 14 to July 25.

Remarks: A female hummingbird was observed at Riis Park from Nov. 26 to Dec. 13, 1961. It was observed on the first date by F. Enders and on the last date by H. Steck. It was seen also on Dec. 3 (Carleton). The weather during this period was relatively mild. According to Carleton the bird was observed catching insects in the air after leaving its perch on a bare twig. At no time was it seen to visit the flowers of a certain unidentified shrub still bearing white blossoms at this late date.

KINGFISHERS: ALCEDINIDAE

BELTED KINGFISHER (*Megaceryle alcyon*)*B

Range: Nearctic species, the nominate race occurring in our area.

Status: Fairly common migrant. Regular in winter in small numbers, on or near the coast. Local breeder.

Migration and winter: Usually from two to six a day are found during the spring and fall migration, and perhaps from one to three in winter, chiefly along the coast.

Maxima: 37, Mecox Bay to Montauk, Sept. 18, 1930 (Helmuth), an exceptional number. Ordinarily arrives in mid-March and departs by late November.

Breeding: Kingfishers are dependent upon suitable banks for nesting, along streams, lakes, and coastal estuaries, and may be found in these situations, both inland and coastal.

Egg dates: May 1 to June 16.

WOODPECKERS: PICIDAE

YELLOW-SHAFTED FLICKER (*Colaptes auratus*)*B

Range: Primarily an eastern Nearctic species, the race *luteus* breeding in our area.

Status: Abundant fall migrant on the coast. Common breeder. Rare to uncommon, but regular in winter.

Migration: The Yellow-shafted Flicker is our most numerous woodpecker, inhabiting chiefly open and semi-open country. It is quite terrestrial in

281

habits, often feeding on the ground on ants in such places as lawns in city parks and suburbs. Usually arrives in early March and departs in late November.

Maxima: *Spring*—150, Atlantic Beach, Apr. 6, 1947; 65, Prospect Park, Apr. 12, and 65, Jones Beach, Apr. 18, both in 1953. *Fall*—spectacular mass migration on the outer beaches, chiefly the last week of September—800, Far Rockaway, Sept. 24, 1949 (within two hours); 2000, Saltaire, Fire Island, Sept. 29, 1953 (morning flight); 1000, Short Beach, Sept. 30, 1951 (in less than an hour).

Winter: Maxima—Ordinarily only one or two birds are seen in winter, but occasionally more are noted: 40, Easthampton area, Dec. 31, 1949. Rare and local inland at this season.

Breeding: This widespread species nests wherever there are trees, sometimes in poles, generally in open country, also in woodland clearings, and regularly in city parks and suburban yards.

Urban and suburban nest sites are often taken over by Starlings.

Egg dates: Apr. 23 to June 28.

Remarks: Reports of "hybrid" flickers in our area are not supported by specimens. In fact, Dr. Lester Short tells me that he knows of none taken anywhere in the northeast, although he has examined specimens approaching "hybrid type." Short (ms.) would treat this species as conspecific with *C. cafer* (Red-shafted Flicker) and *C. chrysoïdes* (Gilded Flicker), stating that there is much gene flow between the forms where they occur together.

PILEATED WOODPECKER (*Dryocopus pileatus*)*B

Range: Nearctic species, the race *abieticola* occurs in our area.

Status: Fairly common, but local resident in the wilder areas. Has greatly increased in recent years. Virtually absent from the coastal plain.

Change in status: The Pileated Woodpecker was formerly almost exclusively an inhabitant of heavy forest in the wildest sections of the interior, and it still is most prevalent in such areas today. Since the 1920s, however, it has become more tolerant of "civilized" conditions, has adapted itself to large trees near habitations, and since Cruickshank (1942), it has further increased to the extent that it breeds occasionally on the outskirts of metropolitan New York close to large towns, and occasionally visits feeding stations where it was unheard of formerly.

The species has even been seen in the following New York City parks: Bronx Park, Apr. 20, 1939 (Komorowski); Fort Tryon Park, Apr. 12 1959 (Gilbert); Inwood Hill Park, Apr. 23, 1961 (Kallman and Norse); Van Cortlandt Park, Apr. 9, 1962 (McGuire and Van Wert). Note that all four occurrences were in April.

Woodpeckers: Picidae

Some idea of its recent status may be seen by the following: In 1955 at least 12 breeding pairs were reported in Rockland County and a number of other individuals seen; on all local Christmas counts combined (1953–54), a total of 34 was reported, some of these at suburban feeders, eight in the Bear Mountain region alone.

Egg dates: "The few local egg dates are all in May" (Cruickshank, 1942).

Remarks: Casual on Long Island. The bird was unknown to Giraud (1844), although Akhurst took two specimens, neither apparently extant: one at East New York (Brooklyn) in 1842 or 1843; the other near Jamaica in 1879. Most remarkable, and previously unpublished, is an adult female collected at Quogue, Suffolk County (south shore), Nov. 12, 1891 (L. B. Woodruff), A.M.N.H. No. 229497. The only other reliable occurrence is that of an adult male seen in dense swampy woods near Barcelona Point, Sag Harbor, June 22, 1947 (Helmuth).

RED-BELLIED WOODPECKER (*Centurus carolinus*)*

Range: A resident Nearctic species of the southeastern United States, but breeding locally north to southeastern Pennsylvania, western New York, and extreme southern Ontario; in recent years to southern New Jersey.

Status: Formerly accidental or casual; since 1955 a rare to uncommon visitant on or near the coast. Reported every month of the year—least often in summer. No proof of breeding.

Past history: There appears to be a wrong impression of the former status of the Red-bellied Woodpecker in the New York City region from the time of Giraud (1844). That writer merely stated, ". . . not very abundant with us," which is about as vague as one can be. Not a few of his statements are ambiguous, indeed it is difficult in this instance to be certain whether he was referring to Long Island or anywhere else in the eastern United States. Moreover, the Red-bellied Woodpecker was unknown on the adjacent mainland (Connecticut, New York, New Jersey), except as an accidental straggler. Thus we have the anomalous situation of this species being the *only* one of *many* southern birds occurring in "numbers" on Long Island, but of extreme rarity elsewhere along the eastern seaboard until the latitude of southern Pennsylvania and Maryland is reached.

Nor can I find anything to substantiate the statement by Eaton (1914) that "in New York State it *evidently* was common . . . in the lower Hudson valley fifty years ago" (about 1864); italics mine.

Sage *et al.* (1913) listed only two dated records for the entire state of Connecticut—1842 and 1874, and another without date.

Stone (1937) stated the following: "In New Jersey it seems to be nowhere more than an accidental straggler." He listed only five records for the

283

southern part of the state—including one specimen—between 1903 and 1935.

In view of the foregoing, I conclude that prior to 1955 it was nothing more than a vagrant in our area.

Specimen data: Of eight old specimens collected locally only three appear to be extant—adult male, merely labeled Long Island, no date (Lawrence collection), A.M.N.H. No. 44179, may have been one of those reported as taken on Long Island in 1867, 1870, or 1895; adult male, Keyport, N.J., Nov. 23, 1887 (L. S. Foster), A.M.N.H. No. 98148; adult male, Orient, July 21, 1921 (Latham), in his collection. The latter two specimens are published here, apparently for the first time.

Change in status: 1. *Prior to 1955.*

(*a*) Griscom (1923) called it an "accidental visitant," and knew of only a *single* occurrence between 1895 and 1923.

(*b*) Cruickshank (1942) also spoke of it as an "accidental visitor," but listed *eight* additional occurrences.

(*c*) Fables (1955) stated that for northern New Jersey since 1942, there was only *one* individual, during the winter of 1953–54.

(*d*) Carleton (1958) could find but *two* reports since 1942 in Central and Prospect Parks, one in the former locality in 1948, one in the latter in 1951.

2. *Since 1955.* That there has been a northward extension of range, together with a great increase in recent years, cannot be doubted. From 1956 to 1960, one to four individuals per year were reported in our area. During the winter of 1960–61 there were *five different* individuals at New Jersey feeding stations in the counties of Bergen, Sussex, Hunterdon, Somerset, and Monmouth. In mid-May 1961, *six* were observed on western Long Island alone: Prospect Park, Forest Park (2), South Ozone Park, Port Washington, Jones Beach (1 dead, but not preserved). During the fall of 1961 no less than *eight* were reported: two inland in Westchester County, where the species had not been reported previously; and six along the coast, five of these on the south shore of Long Island, and one on the coast of New Jersey.

A much larger incursion took place during the spring of 1962: most of the New York City parks had one or more present with a probable total of over *thirty* individuals for the entire region.

Remarks: According to Fables (1955) it has nested in "recent" years in southwestern New Jersey in the vicinity of the Delaware Valley in Salem and Cumberland Counties.

Although vaguely reported as breeding in the New Brunswick, N.J. area in the "late 1950s," there is nothing mentioned in the *Supplement* (Kunkle *et al.*, 1959) concerning this.

284

Moreover, Black (*in litt.*) states that there is no definite evidence of nesting anywhere in northern New Jersey. The nearest known breeding locality is just south of our area at Princeton, where it nested for the first time in 1962 (Rogers). Judging from its northward spread and increase locally, breeding can be expected in the near future.

Subspecies: The species is treated here binomially in the northern portion of its range—the race *zebra* not recognized. The A.O.U. *Check-list* (1957: 316, footnote) states, "The definite boundary between the two subspecies *zebra* and *carolinus* remains to be determined." Parkes (1952) would make *zebra* a synonym of *carolinus*. He points out that the so-called morphological differences are not correlated on geographical grounds, the supposed differences occurring at both ends of the range.

RED-HEADED WOODPECKER (*Melanerpes erythrocephalus*)*B

Range: Primarily an eastern Nearctic species, the nominate race occurring in our area.

Status: Rare to uncommon, but regular migrant; very erratic in its movements. Occasional in winter. Local breeder. Has greatly decreased for many years; formerly more numerous and widespread.

Past history: The Red-headed Woodpecker was at one time (prior to 1890) a common bird throughout much of the northeast, although rare in northern New England. In former years it occurred in great flights in fall, often accompanying Yellow-shafted Flickers. Berier (Bull. Nuttall Ornith. Club, 6: 11–13, 1881) stated that at Fort Hamilton, Brooklyn on Sept. 20, 1877, "great numbers" were passing through, outnumbering the Flicker on this date. He remarked that a friend "collected" over 100 specimens at Tarrytown, N.Y., that autumn. Helme (Ornith. and Ool., 7: 107, 1882) speaks of a very large fall flight at Miller Place, L.I., in 1881. He saw the first individual on Sept. 10, three more on Sept. 12, and on Sept. 24 before 10 A.M.—"several hundred," principally immatures—securing several specimens. He saw his last one of the season on Oct. 10, except for a straggler on Nov. 23. Sage *et al.* (1913) stated that it formerly occurred with the big Flicker flights in fall along the Connecticut coast. Nothing remotely resembling these fall flights has been reported in the northeast since the early 1880s.

With the advent of the automobile and the Starling around 1890, and particularly after 1900, the Red-headed Woodpecker became markedly reduced in numbers. While this sounds like circumstantial evidence, nevertheless a number of ornithologists of that period attributed its decrease to these two factors: (*a*) The Red-headed Woodpecker's habit of flycatching during the warm months and darting down on the road after insects made it a victim of passing cars. Quite a number are still picked up dead along the highways, particularly in the Midwest. Stone (1937), referring to Pennsylvania and New Jersey, stated that it "has been a victim of the automobile." (b) Starlings appropriated the nest holes, particularly in towns and around farming country. Urner (1930) remarked that in northern New Jersey, "Starlings very destructive to eggs."

Be that as it may, the Red-headed Woodpecker has retired from most of its northeastern range and for the past half-century has been rare and local east of the Hudson River, and local east of the Delaware River.

A further reduction took place around 1930 and it is now scarce everywhere in our area except in the watershed of the upper Passaic River—especially in the Hatfield Swamp–Troy Meadows region—where several pairs still nest somewhat regularly. From time to time it is fairly common in parts of Sussex County.

Migration: In localities such as Central and Prospect Parks and along the coastal beaches, where this species neither breeds nor winters, it is easy to determine arrival and departure dates, and "peak" numbers during migration. These cannot be determined with certainty in areas where it does breed and winter. In spring it is reported chiefly in May; in fall primarily in September and October, but most often and in largest numbers during September. The spring migration is most pronounced inland, while the fall flight is essentially coastal. Ordinarily only one to three individuals are reported each season, but during the fall of 1956 a "big" flight occurred, at least ten were observed on the coast, with the following maxima: 3, Jones Beach, Sept. 23; 4, Riis Park, Sept. 28.

"Extreme" dates: *Spring*—March 24 to May 28. *Fall*—Aug. 25 to Nov. 17. Dates based on "proved" migrants.

Winter: This species is dependent upon a supply of acorns and beechnuts which form its staple winter diet. Formerly much less scarce at this season; in recent years a few have been reported at feeding stations. Most numerous in New Jersey; rare elsewhere.

Maxima: *Prior to 1930*—21, Passaic and Dead River valleys, Feb. 16, 1913 (Miller and Rogers); 26, Essex County Christmas census, Dec. 23, 1928 (Edwards, Urner *et al.*). *Since 1930*—10, Hatfield Swamp, Jan. 23, 1944 (Lang).

Breeding: This species breeds in two distinct habitats. (a) in river bottoms and open wooded swamps, the nests often situated in dead trees standing in water; (b) more widely in open parklike upland woods, or on golf courses and along roadsides with large scattered trees, telephone poles, and fence posts.

Maxima: 12 nest sites in Sussex County, N.J., 1958 (Cherepy); total of 15 breeding pairs in Sussex County, 1960—8 pairs in the vicinity of Hamburg alone (J. Zamos).

286

It thus appears that in our area, Red-headed Woodpeckers nest regularly in numbers only in parts of northern New Jersey.

Egg dates: May 13 to June 20.

LEWIS' WOODPECKER *(Asyndesmus lewis)*

Accidental: A western Nearctic species, breeding east to southwestern South Dakota. Casual farther east and accidental east of the Mississippi River. One specimen collected in Rhode Island in November 1928.

An individual of this unmistakable bird was observed at Ossining, N.Y., from Oct. 27 to Nov. 6, 1954. It was first discovered by Gerard Swope at his feeding station and seen by such experienced people as Grierson, Kieran, Nolan, and Walsh.

YELLOW-BELLIED SAPSUCKER *(Sphyrapicus varius)**B

Range: Nearctic species, the nominate race breeds south to the Poconos, Catskills, and Berkshires, more rarely to the Litchfield Hills in north-western Connecticut; also farther south in the Appalachians at higher elevations. Winters north to Maryland and southern New Jersey; more rarely to New York and Massachusetts.

Status: Uncommon spring migrant inland, but rare on the coast; common fall migrant, especially on the coast, but numbers vary from year to year. Rare, but usually reported each winter. One breeding record.

Migration: This species fluctuates in numbers, especially in spring. It is almost entirely silent on migration. Usually arrives in early April and departs in early November.

Maxima: *Fall*—28, Saltaire, Fire Island, Sept. 30, 1956; 24, Bronx Park, Oct. 4, 1925. *Spring*—usually uncommon inland, but a big flight occurred during the spring of 1927—20, Central Park, Apr. 13; 15, Englewood, Apr. 15. Almost always rare on the coast at this season, a count of 8 at Lawrence, L.I., Apr. 15, 1961 (several observers), is very unusual.

Extreme dates: Aug. 23 and 28 to May 28 and June 3. Rare before mid-September and after mid-May. In view of this, it is hard to understand the following statements: Cruickshank (1942), "Spring flight . . . is concluded by the fourth week in May." Fables (1955), ". . . frequently recorded on migration as late as the last week in May." Actually this species is very rare after the middle of this month and the data at hand indicate only five occurrences after May 20, including the two extreme dates given above.

Winter: Unlike most birds, but like the Bluebird, the Yellow-bellied Sapsucker is less rare in winter inland and much rarer at this season on the coast. Four of the five winter specimens taken locally are from inland localities, and the great majority of sight reports are inland. On all Christmas counts in late December 1951, there were 12 reported; ten of these were inland in Connecticut and New Jersey, most of them in the vicinity of feeding stations.

Remarks: Casual in summer—collected at Brooklyn, Aug. 1, 1892 (E. F. Carson), A.M.N.H.; 1909, Central Park, July 1 (Crolius), and Prospect Park, July 14 (Vietor); one found dead on Dunderberg Mountain, Rockland County, July 2, 1949 (J. Kenney), specimen in the Bear Mountain Museum—this last is probably the basis for the erroneous statement, "... possible summer resident," in the *Birds of Rockland County* (1959).

Most unusual is a report of breeding in our area: pair at nest in hemlock gorge of the Byram River, near Wooley Pond, Conn. (near the New York State line), summer of 1929 and apparently also in 1930 (P. C. Spofford); this information published here for the first time.

HAIRY WOODPECKER (*Dendrocopos villosus*)*B

Range: A widespread Nearctic species; also in the mountains to western Panama; Bahamas. The nominate race occurs in our area.

Status: Fairly common resident, except over most of Long Island, where relatively rare to uncommon. Occasional fall migrant.

Nonbreeding: While the Hairy Woodpecker is essentially a resident species of deep woods, it does appear in more open country during winter, also coming into city parks and visiting feeding stations. On rare occasions, it occurs in flights during fall, when it may be seen even on the outer coast with often nothing more to perch on than bushes and telephone poles. At Easthampton on Oct. 5, 1928, Helmuth saw five along the beach. In 1954, there was a large widespread flight (see Griscom and Snyder, 1955). On Oct. 23 of that year, while watching a hawk flight at Anthony's Nose, N.Y., several observers counted at least 35 moving southward along the ridge, a very unusual number.

Breeding: This species prefers to nest in extensive mature woodland with plenty of large trees, dead stubs, and fallen logs. In such places it will be found in rich upland areas, and in river bottoms and wooded swamps
Egg dates: Apr. 20 to May 27.

DOWNY WOODPECKER (*Dendrocopos pubescens*)*B

Range: Nearctic species, the race *medianus* occurring in our area.

Status: Common resident. Occasional fall migrant.

Nonbreeding: Like the Hairy Woodpecker, this species is subject to occasional flights, chiefly in fall. That it is not a rare bird on the outer

288

beaches, as has been stated, is proved by banding: 6, Jones Beach, Nov. 8, 1958 (Buckley and Carleton). During the fall of 1960, there was a marked flight—at Tiana Beach near Westhampton, Wilcox and W. Terry banded 18 between Sept. 29 and Oct. 31, with a maximum of 4 on Oct. 11; just south of our area at Island Beach, N.J., 19 people banded a total of 94 from Aug. 27 through Oct. 1, with a maximum of 12 on Sept. 3. *Spring—* 28, Prospect Park, March 25, 1945 (Soll), an exceptional number at any season.

Breeding: The Downy Woodpecker nests in open woodland, orchards, suburbs, and city parks.

Egg dates: May 10 to June 23.

RED-COCKADED WOODPECKER (*Dendrocopos borealis*)*

Accidental: A resident Nearctic species of the southeastern United States, breeding north to southern Maryland. It occurs almost exclusively in pine land. Accidental in Pennsylvania and New Jersey (specimens).

An adult male of the nominate race was collected at Hoboken, N.J., sometime prior to 1866 by C. Galbraith, A.M.N.H. No. 44035 (see Lawrence, 1866). This record was queried because of some doubt as to the correctness of the locality. However, there appears to be no reason to question that it was actually taken in New Jersey.

BLACK-BACKED THREE-TOED WOODPECKER (*Picoïdes arcticus*)*

Very rare winter visitant: Nearctic species, breeding south to northern New York and northern New England. Mainly resident, but very rarely winter irruptions occur south to Long Island and northern New Jersey.

In the New York City region there have been four winter incursions, two of these lasting only two to three years (1886–87 and 1935–37) in what might be called minor flights in view of its rarity, as the former period produced only two birds and the latter but three. The other two incursions were of major proportions lasting from five to six years (1923–27 and 1956–61), with at least 12 individuals reported in the former period and 16 or more in the latter.

Some individuals were found frequenting a relatively small area for months at a time and seen by numerous observers, such as the Bronx Botanical Gardens bird that remained from Nov. 14, 1926, to Jan. 31, 1927, and the Oradell Reservoir bird that spent the winter of 1956–57; also a male and female at the latter locality from early December 1958 to mid-March 1959.

Three of the four local specimens taken in the first three flight periods are extant, all adult males in the American Museum: Sag Harbor, fall of 1887 (Dutcher collection), No. 65239; Englewood, Nov. 29, 1923 (Griscom and Weber), No. 181127; Easthampton, Oct. 13, 1936 (Helmuth), No. 423621.

Cruickshank (1942) gave details of the incursion of 1923–27. The period from 1956–61 established record arrival and departure dates: Sept. 28 to April 21. Casual at Greenwich, May 13, 1961 (R. C. Clement).

These woodpeckers are fond of feeding on beetles that attack dead and dying trees. The trees may be either evergreen or deciduous. In the former category hemlock and pine seem to be the favorite, Helmuth's 1936 specimen having been shot while feeding in pitch pines. In the deciduous category, gray birch and elm have been reported as frequented by these woodpeckers. The Sept. 28, 1958, individual was color-photographed in Central Park as it fed on a diseased elm (J. Bloom). Strips of bark on the ground beneath infested trees are often an indication of this wood-pecker's presence. The Black-backed Three-toed Woodpecker is usually exceedingly tame and often may be approached at very close range.

TYRANT FLYCATCHERS: TYRANNIDAE

EASTERN KINGBIRD (*Tyrannus tyrannus*)*B

Range: A widespread Nearctic species, breeding from Canada to north-eastern California and southern Florida.

Status: Common to occasionally abundant fall migrant. Fairly common breeder, widely distributed.

Migration: This species is numerous at times in fall, particularly on the coast.

Maxima: 110, Easthampton, Aug. 16, 1923; 300, Mastic, Aug. 24, 1912 (J. T. Nichols); 125, Easthampton, Sept. 3, 1930; 75, Sayville, L.I., Sept. 16, 1958.

Extreme dates: Apr. 15 and 22 to Oct. 21 (specimen) and Oct. 24. Usually rare before May and after mid-September. Casual: Eastport, L.I., Apr. 4, 1931 (Wilcox), after a strong southerly storm; Riis Park, Nov. 7–11, 1954 (numerous observers), one with four Western Kingbirds.

Breeding: The Eastern Kingbird breeds along roadsides in rural areas, in open woodland, orchards, farmland, and generally in open country along lake and river shores.

Egg dates: May 24 to July 12.

GRAY KINGBIRD (*Tyrannus dominicensis*)*

Accidental: Neotropical species, the nominate race breeds north to southern Florida; very rarely to South Carolina. Casually wandering north or driven by tropical storms to the coasts of Massachusetts, New York, and New Jersey.

At least six occurrences of this species have been reported in our region, all along the coast. One specimen taken at Setauket, L.I., in 1874 is apparently not extant, but an adult female taken at Orient, Apr. 29, 1921 (Latham), is in his collection. Four sight reports made by experienced observers are probably correct: Jones Beach, June 7, 1930 (Hix); Dyker Beach, L.I., Aug. 22, 1930 (Johnston); Point Pleasant, N.J., Sept. 18, 1946 (Edwards and Clausen); Westhampton Beach, Sept. 18, 1960 (Dunning, Yeaton *et al.*) and again the next day (Wilcox), was very likely the result of hurricane Donna of Sept. 12.

WESTERN KINGBIRD (*Tyrannus verticalis*)*

Range: A western Nearctic species, breeding east to western Minnesota; rarely to southern Ontario, southern Michigan, and northwestern Ohio. Winters chiefly from Mexico to Nicaragua, but regularly in small numbers in southern Florida, and occasionally north to coastal South Carolina.

Status: Rare to uncommon, but regular fall migrant on the outer coast. Very rare in winter; also inland.

Occurrence and maxima: Like many other western species, the Western Kingbird has extended its breeding range farther east in recent years and there are many more local records than formerly.

Griscom (1923) called it casual. There are only two specimens taken locally as far as I am aware, both collected away from the outer coast curiously enough: Riverdale, N.Y., Oct. 19, 1875 (Bicknell), the first record for New York State; Miller Place, Sept. 6, 1912 (Helme), first record for Long Island. I have seen neither of these specimens and do not know of their present whereabouts.

While on migration in our region, this species is pretty much confined to ocean-front areas, and is rare anywhere else. It is often seen perched on telephone wires, fence posts, and bushes. It is not often seen with Eastern Kingbirds as the two species have somewhat different migration periods. The latter species is commonest in August and early September, while *T. verticalis* occurs principally later on.

In some years, only one to four are seen, but in others a dozen or more individuals are reported. There are more reports since Cruickshank (1942),

291

but there are also many more observers who visit the coast than formerly. However, larger numbers per day are noted, indicating that they are definitely more numerous now than prior to 1942.

Maxima: 3, Fire Island, opposite Mastic, Sept. 10, 1955; 4, Riis Park Nov. 13, 1954; 4, Montauk, Dec. 8, 1956. Maximum total reported per year: 23 (1954); 13 (1956). The principal months of occurrence appear to be September, October, and November.

Extreme dates: Aug. 14 and 19 to Jan. 14. Rare before September and after early December. First winter report for our area was at Montauk Point, Jan. 1, 1921 (Crosby, Griscom, and Janvrin)—the only one for many years. Not reported again in winter until 1946, next in 1952, after which several were seen, including three different individuals in late December 1956, at Riis Park, Jones Beach, and Montauk; the Riis Park individual remained until Jan. 14, 1957 (numerous observers).

What happens to these winter birds is not known. They may not survive the season, or perhaps they may withdraw to more southern localities. At this season they have been observed feeding on *Eleagnus* (Russian olive) berries.

Reported by reliable observers as far inland as Scarborough, N.Y., Oct. 15, 1938 (Slaker); Bear Mountain, Dec. 6–26, 1953 (Orth and Kenney).

Purely casual in spring: One well observed at Easthampton, June 3, 1950 (Helmuth); another at Pleasant Plains, Staten Island, June 16, 1958 (Cleaves), full details submitted.

SCISSOR-TAILED FLYCATCHER (*Muscivora forficata*)*

Casual: A Nearctic species of the south-central United States, breeding north to southern Nebraska and east to western Missouri. Winters chiefly in Middle America, but regularly in small numbers in southern Florida. Recorded widely but sporadically during the spring and fall migration in various places in the United States and Canada as far north and east as Quebec and New Brunswick.

One specimen has been taken in our area: Adult male, Sag Harbor, L.I., June 11, 1939 (Latham), in his collection, published here for the first time. There are seven satisfactory sight reports: Gilgo Beach, Nov. 23, 1940 (Mr. and Mrs. F. Austin); Rye, N.Y., May 7, 1945 (Mrs. Cruickshank); Easthampton, June 12, 1947 (F. E. Eldredge), reported in detail to Helmuth; Dunellen, N.J., June 29, 1958 (Buckley, Jubon, Murray *et al.*), color-photographed by the two latter observers; the same or another, Carteret, N.J., Sept. 8, 1958 (Ryan); Prospect Park, May 20, 1959 (O. Raymond); one present at Atlantic Beach from Oct. 30 to Nov. 7, 1960 (Buckley, Cashman, Isleib, and many others). The last individual was studied at leisure and many color photographs were taken. It was actively engaged in flycatching and was observed feeding on dragonflies and grasshoppers, supplementing this diet with the fruit of *Eleagnus* (Russian olive), and bayberries.

GREAT CRESTED FLYCATCHER (*Myiarchus crinitus*)*B

Range: An eastern Nearctic species, breeding from southern Canada to Texas and Florida. The race *boreus* occurs in our area.

Status: Uncommon to fairly common migrant, subject to marked fluctuations. Widespread breeder.

Migration: The Great Crested Flycatcher is most numerous as a migrant during May, late August, and early September. Maxima: *Spring*—18, Easthampton, May 18, 1929. *Fall*—9, Far Rockaway, Sept. 8, 1956.

Extreme dates: Casual at Orient, Apr. 17, 1919 (Latham), perhaps the result of an early southerly storm; Apr. 25 to Oct. 25, Nov. 3 and 8. Rare before May and after September.

Breeding: This species is primarily a woodland bird, but breeds also in orchards and in large deciduous trees in cultivated areas. Our only local hole-nesting flycatcher, it occupies bird houses and posts as well as tree cavities.

Egg dates: May 18 to June 29.

Remarks: This species winters in small numbers regularly north to southern Florida. Reports of individuals in winter in our area are unsubstantiated. Confusion with Western Kingbirds by inexperienced observers is likely. However, Fleisher, an experienced observer, claims to have seen one at Riis Park, Dec. 8, 1955. Moreover, he saw two Western Kingbirds there the same day. Nevertheless, another possibility remains.

Myiarchus cinerascens, the Ash-throated Flycatcher, a species of western North America, breeds east to Colorado and Texas, and is casual in Louisiana and Florida. There are two specimens in the U.S.N.M. collection taken in Maryland: Nov. 25, 1911, and Nov. 30, 1957 (see Stewart and Robbins, 1958). J. Baird mist-netted and collected an immature female on Block Island (about 12 miles east of Montauk Point) on Sept. 15, 1960, perhaps the result of hurricane Donna of Sept. 12. The identity of this specimen was confirmed by Lanyon (see Baird, Auk, 79: 272, 1962).

Smaller pale-looking *Myiarchus*, and especially late fall and winter individuals of this genus should be collected to determine definitely the species involved. There is enough similarity between these species so that skins of the two are often confused. Field identification is a guess at best.

EASTERN PHOEBE (*Sayornis phoebe*)*B

Range: Primarily an eastern Nearctic species, breeding from southern Canada south—in the east to the mountains of northern Georgia.

Status: Fairly common to very common migrant. Widely distributed breeder, but local on the coastal plain. Rare in winter, but regular in recent years.

Migration: The Eastern Phoebe is, at times, quite numerous on migration.

Maxima: *Spring*—35, Atlantic Beach, March 27, 1949; 15, Central Park, Apr. 15, 1943. *Fall*—65, Idlewild, Sept. 25, 1949; big coastal flight in 1957—40, Far Rockaway, Sept. 25; 60, Fire Island, Sept. 28.

"Extreme" dates: March 10 to late November or early December. Usually arrives in mid-March and departs by early November.

Breeding: This species is exceedingly adaptable in its nesting habits and breeds in a great variety of situations. Nests have been found in such diverse locations as under bridges, eaves of barns, overhanging edges of banks, upturned tree roots, on ledges of country houses, and on rock ledges and cliffs. Mearns (1878), speaking of the Hudson Highlands, stated that, "a pair for several years built their nest in a shaft of an iron mine, in a dark and extremely humid situation." Howes (1928), referring to the Stamford, Conn., area stated, "Nests also in wells and commonly in caves."

Egg dates: Apr. 14 to July 8.

Winter: This species winters north to Maryland; more rarely farther north. In our area, there are apparently no winter specimens. It has been reported more frequently at this season since 1942. Whether this is due to many more observers covering more areas, or perhaps an increase in the number of milder winters, or both, is difficult to say. Nearly all occurrences at this season are along the coast, where these birds have been reported to feed on fruiting shrubs.

In 1945 there was a total of four reported. On all local Christmas counts combined in 1952 six were reported, and in 1953 no fewer than nine. Prior to 1942 the maximum number reported per winter was only two and the species was not seen every winter.

YELLOW-BELLIED FLYCATCHER (*Empidonax flaviventris*)*

Range: Primarily an eastern Nearctic species, breeding south to the northern portions of New York and New England; rarely to the Pocono and Catskill Mountains.

Status: Regular, but uncommon migrant; occasionally fairly common.

294

Occurrence and maxima: The Yellow-bellied Flycatcher may be found during the last week in May and the first week in June, and again in August and early September. It is not rare at these times, if one makes a special search for it in second-growth woodland or thickets, in either moist or dry areas.

Maxima: *Spring*—5, Far Rockaway, May 27, 1954; 8, Central Park, May 30, 1953. *Fall*—8, Long Beach, Sept. 2, 1920.

Extreme dates: *Spring*—May 13 and 17 (specimen) to June 10, 17, and 19 (specimen). *Fall*—July 29 and Aug. 4 (specimen) to Sept. 28 and Oct. 6 (specimen). There are several sight reports between May 5 and 10, but the species is doubtful. Rare before late May and after mid-September.

Of great interest is a specimen taken on the Atlantic Ocean, about 25 miles SSE of Freeport, L.I., June 7, 1958 (Jehl); label data indicates "landed on boat, 1:30 P.M., no fat—died of exhaustion," specimen in A.M.N.H. collection.

Remarks: It should be pointed out that the Yellow-bellied Flycatcher, except when singing, is not *always* easy to identify in the field. This species can be confused with the Acadian Flycatcher at times, especially during fall when some individuals of the latter are quite yellowish in appearance (see Mengel, 1952). A specimen in the A.M.N.H. taken at West Orange, N.J., Sept. 10, 1898 (Dwight collection) and identified and published as *E. virescens*, was reidentified as *E. flaviventris* (A. R. Phillips, *in litt.*).

ACADIAN FLYCATCHER *(Empidonax virescens)**B

Range: A southeastern Nearctic species, formerly breeding northeast to Long Island, southwestern Connecticut, and southeastern New York (mainland); casually farther north. In recent years breeding north to central New Jersey.

Status: Since about 1900 has greatly decreased in the New York City area; now very rare except south of the Raritan River, N.J., where extremely local. Formerly a local breeder throughout at lower elevations, but absent on the coastal plain of Long Island.

Migration: The following dates are based exclusively on specimens and reliable reports of singing birds by competent observers familiar with the song. Many other observations without details are completely worthless and are rejected.

Extreme dates: May 8 (singing bird) and May 10 (specimen) to Sept. 19 and 30 (specimens). Rare before late May. That this species still occurs rarely as a migrant, or perhaps as a vagrant in places where it does not breed, is indicated by the following two specimens examined and measured by the writer: Orient, May 30, 1932 (Latham), in his collection; one hit by a car at Jones Beach, May 29, 1954 (D. Guthrie), in Tackapausha Museum, Seaford, L.I. The fall specimen listed above under Extreme dates was an individual picked up dead at Jones Beach, Sept. 30, 1938 (Elliott), identified by Zimmer, but present whereabouts of specimen not known.

Breeding: The Acadian Flycatcher nests in deep, shady, moist, deciduous forest, in wooded ravines, and along stream bottoms. Often reported frequenting rich beech and chestnut woods.

"Since 1900 the Acadian Flycatcher is definitely known to have abandoned the greater part of its northeastern breeding range" (Griscom, 1933).

1. Status, prior to 1900:

On Long Island, this species formerly bred on the north shore from Flushing and Jamaica to Miller Place; reported also on Gardiner's Island. Nest and three eggs collected, Northport, June 17, 1888 (Marshall), A.M.N.H., identity confirmed by Bendire. According to Eaton (1914), two nests with eggs were taken at Miller Place (dates not stated) by Helme. Eaton also stated that it was fairly common at Oyster Bay (T. Roosevelt), and at Woodhaven, Queens County, and at Northport (Howell).

Nest and eggs, West Brighton, Staten Island, June 13, 1887 (J. Richardson), A.M.N.H. collection.

Central Park, bred as late as 1892 (*fide* Chapman).

In Westchester County, it was most common in the Hudson valley: nest and eggs, Dobbs Ferry, June 2, 1896 (in Bruce Museum, Greenwich, Conn.). Bicknell (1878), speaking of the Riverdale region (then located in Westchester County) gave a good account of its former status. He stated that there were perhaps six breeding pairs in the mid-1870s, but never more than a single pair in any one locality. He secured two nests. It usually arrived the last week in May and it frequented "cool shaded glens or unspoiled woodland usually near a running stream." He later called it a "still common summer resident in the 1880s," but by the late "nineties," it had become scarce. Common summer resident at Ossining from 1870 to about 1896 (*fide* A. K. Fisher).

In Connecticut, according to Sage *et al.* (1913), it was "most common west of Stamford." Forbush (1927) called it a rare local summer resident, chiefly near the coast, but it had become quite rare there by 1906. "Numerous" nests and eggs collected between Stamford and Greenwich from 1875 to 1896, with several pairs up to 1906.

Eaton (1914) stated that, according to Brownell, it was fairly common in summer at Nyack, Rockland County, but we have little information of its past history on the west side of the Hudson River, north of New Jersey.

In northern New Jersey, Griscom (1923) listed it as breeding formerly at Plainfield, West Englewood, along the Palisades, and locally inland to at least Newton, Sussex County, but it had greatly decreased by the early 1900s.

2. Status: 1900–50:

Kuerzi (1927) stated that "several" pairs were still nesting at Grassy

Sprain, Westchester County, as recently as 1925, and Cruickshank (1942) said that two or three pairs were nesting irregularly in southern Westchester County and a few occasionally in Monmouth County, N.J.

3. Status: 1951–62:

Since 1950, it has not been reported as a breeding bird in our area away from New Jersey, except for one pair at a finished nest, Lake DeForest, Rockland County, May 24, 1957 (Deed *et al.*); the nest later destroyed by a rainstorm.

In New Jersey, Fables (1955) says, ". . . found along Swimming River, Monmouth County" (near Red Bank). In the same general area, Ryan found two pairs nesting in a "river bottom" near Lincroft, summer of 1955. Two pairs were found nesting along a stream northeast of Frenchtown, Hunterdon County, "for the first time in 1960" (Abraitys). I know of no other recent breeding reports.

The reasons for its disappearance are not clear but, like certain other species on the periphery of their ranges, the Acadian Flycatcher has withdrawn from its northeastern limits. Similar to that other southern species, the Kentucky Warbler, it is today not found regularly or in any numbers until one reaches the lower Delaware valley, particularly on the Pennsylvania side.

Egg dates: May 30 to June 27.

TRAILL'S FLYCATCHER (*Empidonax traillii*)*B

Range: Nearctic species, the nominate race breeding south to Rhode Island (1956), the south shore of Long Island (1958), and at higher elevations to northern Georgia (1958). Reported breeding on the Delaware coast (1962). Now breeding much farther south and east (coastal plain) than in former years.

Status: Fairly common fall migrant, as proved by banding. Uncommon to fairly common, but local breeder.

Migration: This species, like most others of the genus *Empidonax*, may be identified in the field only when singing, which happens on rare occasions in spring. The following data are based on singing birds, banding records, and collected specimens.

Thanks to modern methods of capturing *Empidonax* flycatchers by the use of mist nets, and by checking wing formulae in the hand, we have more detailed information on relative abundance and "peak" dates than was formerly possible. At the Kalbfleisch Research Station near Huntington, L.I., in 1961, *sixteen* individuals of this species were banded and carefully measured between Aug. 23 and Sept. 9 by Lanyon and his assistants. *Twelve* of these were captured between Aug. 28 and Sept. 1 with a maximum of *five* (four banded, one collected) on Aug. 30.

297

Extreme dates: May 11 (singing bird) to Sept. 16 (specimen), Sept. 20 (banded), and Sept. 26 (specimen). Rare before late May and after early September. A specimen taken at Huntington, July 25, 1962 (Lanyon and Gill), indicates that some individuals migrate early in fall—the species is not known to breed at this locality.

Change in breeding status: The Alder Flycatcher, as it was formerly called, nests in alder swamps, wet bushy meadows, and moist thickets composed of various shrubs. It is generally, although somewhat locally, distributed north of the coastal plain. In our area it is most numerous and widespread in New Jersey wherever extensive swampy thickets occur, such as those in the contiguous Great Swamp–Hatfield Swamp–Troy Meadows area. At the latter locality in June 1947, members of the Urner Club estimated at least 32 nesting pairs. During the summer of 1952, eight to ten pairs were found along the Raritan River between Bound Brook and New Brunswick (Boyajian), a region where they were formerly rare.

This species has bred within New York City proper in at least two localities: Van Cortlandt Park, Bronx County; Flushing, Queens County. At the former locality it has nested more or less since the time of Bicknell. He found as many as four pairs breeding in that vicinity in 1888 and 1893. The species was not reported as breeding there by either Griscom (1923) or Cruickshank (1942), but possibly because of ecological changes in the swamp during the latter year, it resumed nesting shortly thereafter. At any rate reports indicate that up to six pairs bred in 1946. It nested there as recently as the early 1950s and at least two pairs through the 1950s. In 1962, J. Zupan (*in litt.*) reported "four pairs . . . all with the 'fitz-bew' song. Ten young from three nests, the fourth nest destroyed." In the Flushing area Fischer found it nesting at Kissena Park in 1939—the first breeding record for Long Island. This locality was later destroyed, but in June 1949 he found five singing males at nearby Flushing Meadow Park where they probably nested. Fischer (1950) reported these birds to sing "fitz-bew."

Prior to the mid-1950s Traill's Flycatcher was not reported as breeding along the outer coast in our area. In 1956 and 1957 a nesting pair was present at West Long Branch, Monmouth County (Seeley). During the summer of 1958 this species bred on the south shore of Long Island at two localities. The writer discovered a pair feeding young on July 13 in a swampy thicket at the west end of Tobay Pond, Nassau County; as many as three pairs nested there during 1962 and 1963 (several observers). At least two pairs, one with occupied nest, were seen at East Moriches, Suffolk County in 1958 (Puleston, Raynor, and Wilcox), and at least one pair bred there in 1959 and 1960. At Idlewild, Queens County, singing birds were found by Mayer and Rose, both in 1959 and 1960; in 1961 they located two pairs with young.

Egg dates: June 12 to July 9.

298

Remarks: Much has been written about the voice of this species, and space limitations preclude detailed discussion here. Stein (1958) has summarized nearly all of the literature relative to taxonomy, ecology, and ethology, as well as voice.

Readers who are interested in these various aspects should consult also the papers of Aldrich (1951 and 1953), McCabe (1951), Parkes (1954a), and especially Snyder (1953). Articles by Fischer (1941 and 1950) and Eisenmann (1953) contain information concerning our own area.

Stein (*op cit.*) suggests that two morphologically very similar populations (siblings) of *E. traillii*, based on song types, represent distinct species. His studies were mainly carried out in western New York in the Ithaca region and later in British Columbia—both areas in which he observed and collected examples of the two song types. His assumption that two discrete populations occur together is strengthened by the following:

1. Song: Birds singing both song types are sympatric over a relatively broad range; the "fee-bee-o" song of *E. t. traillii*, primarily a northern and eastern bird, is recognizably different from the "fitz-bew" song of *E.t. "campestris"* (not recognized by the A.O.U. *Check-list* committee, 1957), primarily a western bird. Stein stated that ". . . recordings . . . showed the contrast between the two patterns of song, and suggested a constancy of each pattern over a large geophraphical range"; response by playbacks to opposite patterns of song were negative in 82 out of 85 cases, thus tending to indicate that song was probably *the* reproductive isolating mechanism.

2. Nest: Stein found that the "fitz-bew" type builds a neat, compact nest like a Yellow Warbler or Goldfinch nest, while that of the "fee-bee-o" type is a coarse, loose, and "untidy" nest like a Song Sparrow or Indigo Bunting nest. He further stated, "Aside from 2 'fitz-bew' nests, . . . all 'fitz-bew' nests (38) were higher above the ground than all those (17) of the 'fee-bee-os'."

Morphologically the two forms are very close, which is not at all surprising in the genus *Empidonax*. Stein found that while certain slight differences in color characters and measurements were relatively stable within a series, nevertheless overlap does occur. More work is needed before morphological characters can be correlated with (1) and (2) above.

It is the opinion of a number of field workers that the more "aggressive" "fitz-bew" type has spread eastward and northward into the range of the "fee-bee-o" type within the last 50 years or so, and that in certain areas "fitz-bews" have largely replaced "fee-bee-os."

Insofar as the New York City area is concerned, both song types have been reported. The relative status of the two in this region is unknown as no local specimens have been taken with the known song type recorded, although local observers maintain that the "fitz-bew" is the prevailing form. It should be emphasized, however, that the differences in the two songs are not always so dissimilar—both have a certain "buzzy" quality.

Indeed two experienced field ornithologists of long standing maintain that the song of the Acadian Flycatcher resembles that of *E. traillii*. W. W. H. Gunn (in Snyder, 1953) is of this opinion, as is also A. R. Phillips, who states (*in litt.*), "I might also remark that the sight records based on song are by no means certain, because the song of Acadian [Flycatcher] resembles to some extent the song of the western type ['fitz-bew'] of Alder Flycatcher. . . ."

Observers should visit breeding localities, make notes on the song types heard and, most important, record nest construction, height of nest, and any differences in habitat.

Since the above was written, I have read Stein's latest monograph (1963) containing a great deal of additional information since his 1958 paper, which he believes further strengthens his concept of *two* species. He would call the "fee-bee-o" type, *E. traillii*, and the "fitz-bew" type, *E. brewsteri*.

Stein further suggests (1963: 48) that (*a*) "The song types are more distinct in sympatric areas of the west than of the east. A longer period of contact between western populations is suggested as the probable explanation." (*b*) "The general habitat of the song types is *somewhat* different. 'Fee-bee-os' occur along streams and lake edges in *wooded* areas, 'Fitz-bews' along streams and lake edges in *grassland* areas." (Italics mine.)

In connection with (*b*), it is likely that in our area the "fitz-bew"-type habitat is occupied locally throughout our lowland areas, where suitable, and that in a few of the more wooded sections of the interior highlands with bogs, ponds, and streams, a small population of "fee-bee-os" does actually exist. Such localities as the more remote "boreal" type areas of Bear Mountain Park and the wilder regions of Putnam County still possess some of these latter habitats. It is important that such places be visited to determine if, in fact, "fee-bee-o" type Traill's Flycatchers do breed there today. I suspect that they do—if only a few.

LEAST FLYCATCHER (*Empidonax minimus*)*B

Range: Nearctic species, breeding south and east to the edge of the coastal plain in southeastern New York (Long Island) and central New Jersey; farther south at higher elevations to northern Georgia.

Status: Common migrant throughout. Common breeder inland, but rare on Long Island.

Migration: This species is at maximum abundance during the second and third weeks of May, and again during late August and early September. As many as 20 to 30 may be seen in a day at these times, but some individuals of other species of this genus are undoubtedly present.

Extreme dates: Apr. 20 to Oct. 4 (specimen). Rare before May. There are sight reports to the end of October, but the species is in doubt.

Breeding: The Least Flycatcher nests in rural areas, preferring shade trees, orchards, and woodland edges. It is near its southern limits in our region, widely distributed inland, but breeding rarely on the north shore of Long Island and to the edge of the coastal plain in Middlesex County, New Jersey. There is no definite nesting evidence for Staten Island.

Egg dates: May 27 to June 24.

Remarks: An *Empidonax* flycatcher was observed at New Rochelle, N.Y., Dec. 21 and 25, 1940 (Bull and Friedle). Attempts to collect it on the latter date were unsuccessful.

EASTERN WOOD PEWEE (*Contopus virens*)*B

Range: An eastern Nearctic species, breeding from southern Canada to Texas and Florida.

Status: Fairly common migrant. Widely distributed breeder.

Migration: This species is found throughout our area, even along the outer coast, wherever there are trees.

Maxima: *Spring*—12, Prospect Park, June 3, 1945. *Fall*—15, Far Rockaway, Sept. 21, 1952.

Extreme dates: May 2 to Oct. 30 (specimen). Rare before mid-May and after early October. April sight reports are very dubious, as confusion with the Least Flycatcher is likely.

Breeding: The Eastern Wood Pewee breeds in both heavy forest and open woodland, also nesting in large shade trees along village streets and in parks. Common in the pine barrens of eastern Long Island.

Egg dates: June 6 to July 13.

Remarks: The published report (Griscom, 1923, and Cruickshank, 1942) of a Wood Pewee supposedly collected at New Rochelle, N.Y., Dec. 13, 1900, is unsatisfactory, and apparently was only an observation (see Bird-Lore, 3: 33, 1901). There is no specimen in the American Museum collection taken at this locality and date to substantiate such a remarkable occurrence. More than likely the observer saw a Phoebe with a trace of wing-bars.

Some authorities would make this species and the Western Wood Pewee (*C. sordidulus*) conspecific.

Note: A juvenal male specimen taken at Morristown, N.J., Aug. 30, 1887 (Thurber), A.M.N.H. No. 49277, has been identified as *C. sordidulus* by A. R. Phillips. If correctly determined, it represents the only known specimen for eastern North America. The separation of *C. virens* and *C. sordidulus* is critical indeed, the alleged differences based on slight color and mensural characters.

OLIVE-SIDED FLYCATCHER (*Nuttallornis borealis*)*

Range: Nearctic species, breeding south in the mountains to Pennsylvania, New York, and Massachusetts; farther south at higher elevations to North Carolina and Tennessee.

Status: Regular, but uncommon migrant.

Occurrence and maxima: The Olive-sided Flycatcher, one of our latest spring migrants, prefers the dead upper branches of tall trees and may be found in such situations in open woodland and city parks. Apparently more widespread in fall than in spring, judging from the following maxima:

5, Prospect Park, Aug. 19, 1944; 4, Englewood, Aug. 30, 1925; 3, Lawrence, Sept. 8, 1953; 3, Ossining, Sept. 15, 1879 (specimens). During the last year listed, A. K. Fisher at Ossining collected a total of nine, including six between Aug. 19 and 31, and the three aforementioned individuals on Sept. 15—all in M.C.Z. collection. In most years the active observer is likely to see only one or two in a season.

Extreme dates: *Spring*—May 8 to June 12. *Fall*—July 27 and Aug. 3 to Sept. 25 and 26 (specimens) and Oct. 2. No later fall dates confirmed. Rare before late May and after mid-September.

Remarks: Just north of our area in Algonquin Park, near Newburgh, Orange County, a pair feeding young in the nest was observed on July 24, 1954 (*fide* Treacy).

LARKS: ALAUDIDAE

SKYLARK (*Alauda arvensis*)*B

Introduced: A Palearctic species, the nominate race introduced in 1887 in the Flatbush and Flatlands sections of Brooklyn. The Skylark—a bird of open grassland—seemed well established by 1898 and was present continually until at least 1907. According to Braislin (1907), its song could be heard from March to October. With rapid development of open land, it had disappeared completely by 1913.

The following three specimens, all from Flatbush, are in the American Museum: adult female, Feb. 22, 1888 (Marshall), No. 68249; immature, June 13, 1887 (Marshall), No. 68248; immature, July 1, 1887 (Dutcher collection), No. 65319. There was also a report of adults, nest, and eggs on July 28, 1895 (Proctor).

302

HORNED LARK (*Eremophila alpestris*)*B

Range: Holarctic species (for details, see below).

Status: Very common to abundant migrant and winter visitant along the coast. Relatively rare and local inland, occasionally more numerous. Locally common breeder on the south shore of Long Island; uncommon to rare elsewhere.

In the New York City region three subspecies occur: (1) the nominate race, (2) *hoyti*, and (3) *praticola*. The first two are essentially winter visitants; the third is the local breeding population, although present every month of the year.

Migration and winter: 1. The nominate race breeds south to east-central Ontario, southeastern Quebec, and islands in the Gulf of St. Lawrence. It is the most numerous form in our area during the colder months. Large flocks may be seen along the beaches, salt marshes, and in open country on bare ground or short grassy fields. Inland it is much scarcer, but may be found in similar situations particularly after winter storms.

Maxima: 1000, Montauk, Nov. 7, 1924; 1500, Orient, Dec. 27, 1934; 800, Jones Beach, March 11, 1956. Most numerous from November to March.

Extreme dates: Sept. 21 and Oct. 2 (specimen) to May 1 (specimen) and May 3. Rare before mid-October and after early April.

2. The race *hoyti* breeds southeast to extreme northwestern Ontario. Winters south to Long Island and northern New Jersey; occasionally farther. In our area it has been collected at least 12 times. Ten specimens are extant, all of which I have examined. Worthington took a series of seven on Shelter Island between 1887 and 1901, dates ranging from Dec. 20 to March 7, and one as late as Apr. 26. These were all determined by Dwight and six of them are in the A.M.N.H. collection. In Latham's collection are two taken by him at Orient, March 4, 1924, and March 9, 1927. Sage *et al.* (1913) report a specimen from Stamford, Conn., Feb. 17, 1894 (Porter). Recently two were shot at Dover, N.J., Feb. 2, 1952 (Baird and Thorsell), specimens in A.M.N.H. collection. No sight reports accepted as the identification of this subspecies is extremely critical. Some of the specimens in museums labeled as *E. a. hoyti*, are nothing more than intermediates with the subspecies *praticola*.

Breeding: 3. The race *praticola*, or as it is generally known, "Prairie" Horned Lark, has spread eastward and southward and now breeds from Nova Scotia to North Carolina. It has increased greatly within the past 30 years or so, and in our region is reported as nesting in nearly every county (1962).

Horned Larks are most numerous and widely distributed along the outer coast and to a lesser extent in suitable areas back from the coast, but inland they are rare and local due to lack of proper habitat. Any barren, sterile area in open country is home to this adaptable bird, the nest being found on bare ground, or surrounded by short grass or other sparse vegetation. It has been known to nest on airports, golf courses, abandoned agricultural fields, upland pastures, sandy areas near the ocean, filled-in marshland, gravel strips along parkways, and even in waste lots of large cities.

McKeever (1941 and 1946c) gave accounts of its status up to those times and remarked that the areas of Jamaica Bay and Jones Beach were the best places to see Horned Larks in numbers. In 1941 as many as 34 pairs were found in the former region and 15 pairs in the latter. Today (1962) the breeding population has more than tripled in those places.

Other recent breeding maxima: Numbers represent pairs and/or nests. New Jersey—12, Newark and Hackensack Meadows (1955); 15, New Brunswick area (1950). Long Island—6, Sagaponack to Easthampton (1947). Bronx County—5, Baxter Creek (1955).

This species is unique among local passerines for length of the breeding season; eggs have been found as early as the last week in February with snow still on the ground and as late as mid-July. The species has at least two broods locally.

Egg dates: Feb. 28 to July 18.

SWALLOWS: HIRUNDINIDAE

TREE SWALLOW (*Iridoprocne bicolor*)*B

Range: Nearctic species, breeding along the coast south to Virginia; more local inland. Winters north to Long Island; more rarely to Cape Cod.

Status: Common to very abundant migrant, particularly in fall along the outer coast. Rare in winter, chiefly on the coast, but occasionally small flocks are reported. Local breeder.

Migration: The first swallow to arrive in spring—regularly by late March, sometimes earlier. The first and last to depart in fall, one of the first birds to move south, regularly by the first week in July; the fall migration is of long duration—into early November, or even later. On the coast it is regular into December.

Occurs in truly extraordinary numbers in fall on the outer coast; perhaps one of the most abundant birds in our area. At times it literally swarms by the thousands, certainly one of the most spectacular events of the fall migration. The height of this movement is from late August to the middle of September. On the south shore of Long Island, estimates of 50,000 to

100,000 or more are frequently noted. Inland, flocks from 5000 to 10,000 have been reported.

Winter: Reported every month of the year. In winter Tree Swallows feed extensively on bayberries, and are rare to absent when this plant has "off" years.

Maxima: 45, Point Lookout, Jan. 4, 1947; 60, Gilgo Beach, Jan. 20, 1952; 66, Raritan Bay, Dec. 29, 1953; 100 or more wintered, Oak Beach, 1950–51. Most unusual: "13 collected from a flock of 'hundreds,' Englewood, Dec. 31, 1882" (Chapman).

Breeding: Although distributed widely throughout our area, the Tree Swallow is local and the number of breeding pairs in any one locality is seldom numerous. Breeds in wooded swamps, nesting in tree holes; also in bird boxes; in dock pilings on Fisher's Island (Ferguson).

The largest concentration of breeding Tree Swallows reported in our area was approximately 50 nesting pairs in dead trees in a wooded swamp along the Pocantico River, Westchester County, in 1950 (Walsh).

Egg dates: Apr. 28 to June 19.

BANK SWALLOW (*Riparia riparia*)*B

Range: Holarctic species, the nominate race occurring in our area, and breeding south along the coast to Virginia; inland locally farther south.

Status: Common to occasionally abundant migrant, but subject to marked fluctuations, scarce some years. Local breeder, occasionally numerous.

Migration: This species is ordinarily seen in small numbers—up to a dozen or so—but on occasion large flocks are reported.

Maxima: *Spring*—300, Boonton Reservoir, May 14, 1952. *Fall*—400, Jones Beach, Aug. 28, 1953. These concentrations are exceptionally high, however, and groups up to 20 or 30 are more usual.

Extreme dates: Apr. 2 and 9 to Oct. 1 (specimen), Oct. 4, and 11. Rare before late April and after mid-September.

Breeding: The Bank Swallow is a colonial nester, breeding in sandy banks, usually near water, both on the coast and inland. These colonies appear and disappear, as new banks are formed, or old ones deteriorate or are destroyed. An idea of the location and size of some of these colonies appears from the following, with numbers indicating nesting pairs or nest holes—50, Montauk Point, 1936; 170, Nixon, Middlesex County, 1946; 100, Annsville Creek, near Peekskill, Westchester County, 1950, but reduced to 30 pairs by 1954; 120, Andover, Sussex County, 1956.

Egg dates: May 22 to June 26.

ROUGH-WINGED SWALLOW (*Stelgidopteryx ruficollis*)*B

Range: This widespread American species breeds from Argentina to southern Canada in the west, but only to the central portions of New York and New England in the eastern part of its range. The race *serripennis* occurs in our area.

Status: Fairly common, but local migrant and breeder, much rarer on the coastal plain.

Migration: The Rough-winged Swallow is surprisingly scarce where it does not nest, as along the south shore of Long Island. Maximum numbers reported appear to be about 30 individuals at several inland localities, usually in late April or early May.

Extreme dates: March 24 and 31 to Sept. 10. Rare before mid-April. This species and the Orchard Oriole are among our earliest birds to depart in fall—usually immediately after the nesting season in late July or early August. The Rough-winged Swallow is rare after mid-August. Reports of it occurring into early October are probably misidentifications of brownish immature Tree Swallows with dusky throats.

Breeding: This species, unlike our other swallows, is not a colonial breeder, but nests singly, or at the most up to a dozen scattered pairs. Nests are built usually in the vicinity of water, in such diverse situations as under bridges, culverts, in holes of retaining walls, pipes, and sometimes in banks and bluffs.

Prior to 1923, it was much more uncommon, but in recent years it has spread northward, principally up the river valleys, and to a lesser extent along the inner coast. It is most numerous along the Delaware and Hudson rivers and around the interior lakes and ponds. It is still rare on Long Island, except at the extreme east end of the north shore. It is generally rare and local anywhere on the coastal plain.

Egg dates: May 4 to July 4.

BARN SWALLOW (*Hirundo rustica*)*B

Range: Holarctic species, the race *erythrogaster* occurring in our area.

Status: Common to abundant migrant, occasionally very abundant. Common and widespread breeder.

Migration: This species is most numerous in May and August. Maxima: *Spring*—250, Easthampton, May 7, 1929; 3000, Boonton Reservoir, May 14, 1952; 250, Long Beach, May 30, 1917. *Fall*—800, Long Beach, Aug. 8, 1920; 1000, Easthampton, Aug. 31, 1929.

On Aug. 23, 1958, at Jones Beach, Buckley, Nisbet, Scheider *et al.* observed a tremendous migration of Barn Swallows. They estimated over

306

25,000 passing along the coast, with a peak between 10 : 00 A.M. and 2 : 00 P.M. when approximately 5000 per hour were flying by (see Nisbet, Kingbird, 8: 111, 1959).

Extreme dates: March 15 and 21 to Nov. 28, 1953, when they were noted at several places on the south shore of Long Island between Jones Beach and Rockaway Point; one, Nov. 29, same year, Fisher's Island (Ferguson); also one found dying on Dec. 1, same year, Purdys, N.Y., specimen preserved (Grierson); casual, Jones Beach, Dec. 19, 1937 (Cruickshank). Rare before mid-April and after October.

Breeding: The Barn Swallow breeds in open country, nesting in barns, sheds, or old buildings; also under bridges.

Egg dates: May 12 to July 7.

CLIFF SWALLOW (*Petrochelidon pyrrhonota*)*B

Range: Nearctic species, widely distributed in the west, breeding from Alaska to central Mexico; very local in the east, breeding from southern Canada to the mountains of North Carolina and near the coast to New Jersey, but absent on the coastal plain. The nominate race occurs in our area.

Status: Rare to uncommon migrant, at infrequent intervals occurring in large numbers. Now a rare and local breeder, formerly much more numerous and widespread.

Migration: This species is scarce where it does not breed, particularly along the coast. Flocks ranging from a few individuals to about ten are the rule, but on rare occasions big flights take place, all at inland localities.

Maxima: *Spring*—500, Boonton Reservoir, May 14, 1952 (Baird); 500, Annsville Creek, near Peekskill, May 22, 1948 (Walsh). *Fall*—200, New Brunswick, Aug. 18, 1952 (Boyajian). These concentrations are, however, very unusual.

Extreme dates: Apr. 7 to Oct. 11. Rare before late April and after early September.

Breeding: The decline of the Cliff Swallow over much of the northeast, since about 1890, is due, in part, to fewer unpainted barns now (today's barn wall with its smooth surface is difficult for the birds to attach their mud nests to) and to persecution by the House Sparrow. In the New York City area Cliff Swallows nest almost exclusively under the eaves of barns and farmhouses. I know of only one relatively recent nesting on cliffs, that of six pairs found on a small cliff near Cornwall, Orange County, June 20, 1932 (Helmuth). According to Mearns (1878), it "formerly nested in large colonies upon the stone buildings of the West Point Military Academy."

Whereas in former years colonies of up to several hundred pairs bred in this area, since the 1930s colonies of over 20 pairs are a rarity, and even

307

these are confined mainly to northern New Jersey. It has always been most numerous in the highlands of the interior and very scarce near the coastal plain; this applies to migration as well as to breeding. Indeed, as a breeder it is primarily montane in the east and lacking everywhere on the entire coastal plain.

That it was formerly locally numerous on eastern Long Island is evidenced by the following: Braislin (1907) quoted Worthington: "I can remember when about 50 pairs nested under the eaves of our barn [Shelter Island] but now [about 1904] it is rare to see more than two or three nests together." Cruickshank (1942) stated that "the Cliff Swallow has not been known to nest on Long Island since 1904." However, Latham (*in litt.*) states that he found three pairs nesting on a barn at Cutchogue during the summer of 1924, the last known nesting on Long Island. Note that neither of these localities is on the coastal plain.

Deed's statement in *Birds of Rockland County* (1959), "Rather rare transient," implies that it does not breed. In a recent letter to me, he stated, "I have never known of their nesting in Rockland County." This is difficult to understand. Rockland County, with considerable rural country left, is no different from adjacent areas to the north and south where the species does breed. No doubt it has been overlooked; as long ago as 1844, Giraud stated, "Mr. Bell has informed me that he found its nest near his residence in Rockland County...."

The following summary, based largely upon data from northern New Jersey, emphasizes the continued decline of the Cliff Swallow. In 1960, a breeding survey was conducted to determine its status in our area: last bred in the Long Branch (Monmouth County) area in 1934 (*fide* Seeley); has generally declined since 1955, five nesting sites having disappeared in the Sussex–Franklin (Sussex County) area (*fide* Zamos); four to six pairs nesting at Sandyston Township, Sussex County in 1958 and 1959, but deserted when the buildings were painted (*fide* Kientzler); 18 nests on unpainted barn, Augusta, Sussex County, 1954, none since then, as barn was painted (*fide* Barber); six nests in 1952 and ten pairs in 1953, Ringwood, Passaic County, but half the nests were seized by House Sparrows (*fide* Waldron); six nests in 1958, Penwell, Hunterdon County, but none in 1960, "Barn and farmyard infested with English Sparrows and Starlings" (*fide* Abraitys); 40 nests, Newfoundland, Passaic County, 1947 (Eynon), but only 15 there by 1955 (M. Ferguson); a more unusual location was a dam at Wanaque Reservoir, Passaic County, where 20+ pairs nested in 1954 (Boyajian); only three pairs there in 1960 (Ryan).

Reports of nesting birds in recent years away from New Jersey are very few. According to L. Bradley, "none" was breeding in 1960 in southwestern Fairfield County, Conn. In New York State in Westchester County, a small colony of 14 pairs nesting in 1947 on an unpainted barn in the Poundridge Reservation was reduced to a single pair by 1951 when the barn was painted (*fide* Wheeler). In Orange County, Treacy (*in litt.*) stated that this species has become rare since 1954. He knew of only three pairs near Blooming Grove and one pair at Chester, both in 1962. It is almost certain that this species breeds, or has bred, in the rural areas of Putnam County, where observers should check its status.

Egg dates: May 16 to June 29.

PURPLE MARTIN (*Progne subis*)*B

Range: Nearctic species, the nominate race occurs in our area.

Status: Usually a rare migrant away from breeding localities. Very infrequently large flocks are reported in fall. Very local breeder, generally decreased in recent years. Formerly more numerous and widespread.

Migration: Most numerous in late August and early September, but ordinarily this species is rare any time away from nesting areas.

Maxima: 300, Northport, L.I., Sept. 2, 1954 (Mudge); by far the largest concentration ever reported in our area was 2000+, Lake Ronkonkoma, L.I., Aug. 30, 1952 (Darrow and Herbert). This unusual gathering was observed during an early morning fog which may have grounded the birds, most of which were seen perched on telephone wires.

Extreme dates: Casual at Easthampton, March 12, 1941 (Helmuth), one picked up dead, specimen in his collection; March 27 to Oct. 6. Rare before mid-April and after mid-September. Reports of flocks seen in late September and early October by inexperienced observers are probably Tree Swallows.

Breeding: This colonial-breeding swallow nests in multichambered bird houses, preferably near water. Although reported as nesting in suspended gourds and in hollow trees, it rarely does so in this region. In former years colonies were more widely distributed, but after the introduction of those two Old World pests, the House Sparrow and Starling, Purple Martins decreased rapidly. Feeding exclusively on flying insects, this species is also decimated by long cold rains in May and early June. Nevertheless, there are certain colonies thriving in a few areas, particularly when encouraged and protected.

Today (1962) this species breeds locally on Long Island, chiefly at the east end. It is found also in a number of localities in New Jersey, but there, too, it is local. In the rest of the area, it is rare, with very few colonies reported.

Of special interest is the following history of two long-studied colonies, one of which is within New York City limits:

1. Rye, Westchester County (Oboiko *et al.*):
    1913–colony established, "several" nesting pairs, no further information until 1932, when active records were kept

309

1932–colony at maximum size, 140 pairs in seven houses
1937–colony greatly reduced, only 40 pairs, reason not stated
1939–slight increase, 50 pairs
1940–drastic reduction, only 8 pairs; heavy mortality in the south
      due to cold March rains, plus a cold wet spring at Rye
1941–slight recovery, 14 pairs
2. Princess Bay, Staten Island (Cleaves):
    1917– 1 pair, no further nesting until 1951
    1951– 2 pairs
    1953– 6 pairs
    1954–14 pairs
    1955–21 pairs in two houses
    1956–30 pairs
    1958–46 pairs
    1959–64 pairs in four or five houses
    1960–54 pairs
    1961–50 pairs

The largest colony reported for the New York City area comprised approximately 200 pairs in six houses at Whitehouse, Hunterdon County, in 1956 (Drinkwater). A worthwhile project would be a survey to ascertain "all" breeding colonies in our area.

Egg dates: May 18 to June 14.

CROWS, JAYS, MAGPIES: CORVIDAE

BLUE JAY (*Cyanocitta cristata*)*B

Range: An eastern Nearctic species, the race *bromia* occurring in our area.

Status: Common to abundant migrant, but resident as a species. Widespread breeder.

Migration: The Blue Jay is highly migratory, both inland and along the coast, appearing in loose flocks spring and fall.

Maxima: *Spring*—700, Wood-Ridge, N.J., Apr. 29, 1960; 1000, Bear Mountain, May 12, 1947; 1000, Orient, May 14, 1944; 1200, Wood-Ridge, May 17, 1958. *Fall*—1200, Oakland, N.J., Sept. 24, 1961; 3000, Riis Park, Sept. 27, 1957 (several observers), an unusual number; 500, Montauk Point, Oct. 14, 1950.

Breeding: This species shows a strong preference for areas where oaks are numerous, and nests most commonly in such areas, even in city parks and the suburbs. Although quite omnivorous in habits, the staple food in the wild during winter is acorns, varied with a diet of sunflower seeds and corn

310

at feeding stations. During the autumn of 1961 there was an almost complete lack of acorns in our area—and a corresponding scarcity of Blue Jays that year.

Egg dates: Apr. 10 to June 22.

BLACK-BILLED MAGPIE *(Pica pica)**

Very rare visitant: A Palearctic and western Nearctic species, the race *hudsonia* breeding (mainly resident) east to central Manitoba and the western portions of the Dakotas, Nebraska, etc. Wanders east to western Quebec and the Mississippi Valley; more rarely or casually to the Atlantic seaboard from Massachusetts to Virginia.

In the New York City area Magpies have been reported most often on or near the coast, principally from October to May, with more than 30 occurrences; first reported locally in 1927. There are three local specimens, all extant: Adult male caught in a mink trap, Iona Island, Hudson River, Nov. 14, 1935 (Carr), A.M.N.H. No. 300598; two in Latham's collection—female, Orient, Dec. 20, 1927 (not published before); female, Islip, March 28, 1951; also one shot by a duck hunter, East Moriches, Nov. 1, 1953, specimen not preserved (*fide* Raynor). All three specimens are in *fresh unworn* plumage suggesting wild uncaged birds.

There are at least 27 sight reports, 24 of single birds and three others of two individuals together. The majority are from 1951 to 1961 inclusive—22 in all. During early 1956 possibly five different individuals were seen on the coast of Long Island: East Islip, Jan. 20; Hampton Bays, Feb. 22; Tobay Beach, March 3; Orient, March 30; Montauk, Apr. 5.

Magpies are very fond of meat. Two individuals fed on meat scraps and bones at the Meyer feeder, near Bedford Village, N.Y. These birds remained in the vicinity during most of the autumn of 1947 and into January 1948 and were seen by numerous observers. Another Magpie at Montauk, observed at intervals between Oct. 28, 1956, and January 1957, fed along the highway on carcasses of rabbits and other animals killed by passing cars (Darrow *et al.*).

Remarks: More than any other species occurring in the New York City region, the Magpie's status is difficult to evaluate with any degree of certainty. This is due to the fact that this species has always been a popular pet and cage bird. The natural inclination to treat individuals seen in a wild state as escapes from captivity cannot be overlooked and in some instances may be justified. A few birds—probably escapes—have even been reported within the past few years as becoming established and breeding in West Virginia and the vicinity of Pittsburgh. Several others were "known" to have escaped in northern New Jersey: Cranford, fall of 1952; Pequannock, fall of 1957 (*fide* C. K. Nichols).

However, I do not believe for one moment that nearly three dozen occurrences of Magpies in our area were *all* escapes. Deciding which were wild and which escapes is, of course, out of the question, and it would be presumptuous to attempt it. That Magpies do wander great distances on occasion cannot be denied. Linsdale, in Bent (1946) states, "Nonmigratory, but given to erratic wanderings. . . . fall and winter movements are noted regularly within the general range of the bird, and in some years well-defined migrations occur outside that range."

In our area at least four birds were observed in sustained flight—as if traveling some distance: Cruickshank saw one flying over Rye, Dec. 21, 1935, the same year an individual appeared at Van Cortlandt Park on Oct. 31, remaining until Dec. 22; a third individual was collected on Nov. 14 (see above specimen); and a fourth observed between Alpine and Englewood on Feb. 12, 1936. Boyajian, Penberthy, and the writer saw a lone Magpie flying in a westerly direction high above Woodmere Woods on May 6, 1955, and the next day Alperin and Carleton independently observed Magpies—also flying westward—in the Jamaica Bay region, two near the Belt Parkway in the vicinity of Spring Creek, and one at Plum Beach. Moreover, others have been noted at coastal points along the outer beaches during times when this species would most likely be on the move—in late fall, winter, and spring. One such individual was observed at Short Beach, May 13 and 14, 1951 (Bull, Eisenmann *et al.*). The species has also been observed at other coastal localities, such as Sandy Hook, Jones Beach, Fire Island, Montauk, and Orient. Latham has collected it once (see specimen data) and observed it three times at the last-named locality.

COMMON RAVEN (*Corvus corax*)*

Range: Holarctic species, the race *principalis* is rare and local in the eastern United States, breeding south to the coast of southeastern Maine, also in the Appalachian Mountains from western Pennsylvania to northern Georgia. Formerly nested along the coast of Virginia north to southern New Jersey, but no definite evidence in the latter state since 1889.

Status: Very rare to rare vagrant, but possibly a regular fall migrant along the ridges of northern New Jersey and southeastern New York. Casual elsewhere. No proof of breeding in the New York City area.

Occurrence: This species has been observed during the fall hawk flights, chiefly at "Raccoon Ridge" in the Kittatinny Mountains, much more rarely at Bear Mountain, and at one or two other inland localities. Despite these migratory movements, the Common Raven is mainly a resident species where it breeds in the few remote places in the east. Two individuals seen, one of which was collected at Culver's Gap, N.J., Sept. 21, 1918 (Von Lengerke), may have represented wandering birds, as the date

312

Crows, Jays, Magpies: Corvidae

appears early for migrants and the species covers a wide territory. Both at "Raccoon Ridge" and Hawk Mountain it has been observed chiefly during the second half of October and the first half of November. The maxima seen in our area are—4, "Raccoon Ridge," Oct. 22, 1944 (Urner Club), and 2, Bear Mountain, Nov. 10, 1946 (Komorowski).

Ravens have been collected locally on at least five occasions, including the above New Jersey specimen. It was reported collected also in that state at Morristown in 1881. On Long Island individuals were reported taken at Commack Hills in 1836 and near Prospect Park in 1848. Only one local specimen is apparently extant, possibly one of the early specimens listed above: Long Island, no date, (N. Pike), A.M.N.H. No. 438996. Another specimen, not preserved, was shot on Fisher's Island, Oct. 23, 1914 (Ferguson).

As to sight reports away from the ridges, there are at least eight observations between December and early May made by competent and experienced people. A number of other sight reports are considered very doubtful and are without substantiating details. These latter reports were made by beginners—believing that Ravens are easily differentiated from Crows. Such a belief is definitely wrong. Size is deceptive, unless direct comparison is obtained. The voice of the Common Raven is diagnostic, but is seldom heard in these parts.

COMMON CROW (*Corvus brachyrhynchos*)*B

Range: Nearctic species, the nominate race occurring in our area.

Status: Common resident, abundant migrant inland, and locally very abundant in winter roosts. Widespread breeder.

Migration: Although found every day of the year in most places, the Common Crow, like the Blue Jay, is highly migratory. Large numbers pass through every spring and fall. These flights are most noticeable and occur in largest numbers along the inland ridges, where usually anywhere from 100 to "several thousand" may be seen in a single day. Most numerous in March and again in October and November.

Winter roosts: Now much less numerous than formerly. In earlier days the roosts were broken up and "many" thousands were shot annually. In recent years increased pressure from advancing civilization has been the dominant factor, long-established roosting sites having been replaced by building developments. Emlen (1938) listed two large roosts in southern New York in the winter of 1932–33: 20,000 at Kensico Reservoir and 15,000 at Jamesport, eastern Suffolk County. He did not mention what must have been one of the largest roosts in our area—Melville, western Suffolk County. During the winter of 1938–39, it was estimated to contain a minimum of 50,000 birds. The following winter it had decreased to

313

30,000, and in 1942–43 diminished to 20,000. This roost, if still in existence, has not been investigated within recent years. At present, it is not certain how many roosts exist or what size they are. At Boonton, N.J., there were 6000 in 1951–52 and 9000 in 1953–54.

Breeding: Nests in woodland adjacent to agricultural areas, and in wooded clearings in wilder country; more rarely in suburban areas.

Egg dates: March 3 to June 12.

Remarks: Some authorities treat this species as conspecific with the Palearctic *C. corone*, the Carrion Crow, and *C. cornix*, the Hooded Crow, these latter two forms themselves often considered as one species.

FISH CROW (*Corvus ossifragus*)*B

Range: A southeastern Nearctic species, breeding north to the coasts of Connecticut and Rhode Island. Partially migratory in the northern portion of its range.

Status: Uncommon to locally common migrant, and usually rare or uncommon in winter, but occasionally more numerous at both seasons. Local breeder.

Migration: Arrives regularly in mid-March and departs early, usually by late August, except, of course, the relatively small winter population.

Maxima: 175, Easthampton, March 31, 1914; 200, same area, Aug. 30, 1922; 100, Shark River, Nov. 20, 1957.

Winter: Erratic at this season—40 wintered at Baxter Creek, Bronx County, 1935; 60, Staten Island, Dec. 26, 1959; 150, Sandy Hook, Dec. 26, 1914 (Rogers and Wiegmann).

Breeding: The Fish Crow is almost exclusively confined to tidewater areas and is very rare and irregular anywhere else. It was unknown to Giraud (1844), but had increased and spread northward along the coast and inland through the larger river valleys by the 1870s.

It is fairly common in the vicinity of Long Island Sound, the bays around New York City, and up the larger river valleys, especially the Hudson. However, it is local and relatively uncommon in the nesting season on the south side of Long Island. It is locally numerous on Staten Island and along the north Jersey coast.

Egg dates: Apr. 27 to June 5.

Remarks: Specimen collected, Stag Lake, N.J., Apr. 16, 1922 (Von Lengerke), for a proved inland occurrence. Many other inland reports away from water are probably misidentified young Common Crows, a frequent mistake of inexperienced observers confusing the calls of the two, which are exceedingly similar. Size is not a dependable field mark either, unless both species are together.

TITMICE: PARIDAE

BLACK-CAPPED CHICKADEE (*Parus atricapillus*)*B

Range: Nearctic species, the nominate race breeds south to central New Jersey.

Status: Widespread resident, but most numerous in fall and winter; occasionally abundant in fall flights. Fairly common breeder.

Migration and winter: During the winter months, especially, the Black-capped Chickadee is one of the tamest and most confiding of birds, a frequent visitor at the feeding station, and sometimes taking food from the hand.

At long and irregular intervals, this species irrupts southward in great numbers in fall and early winter, and at such times is abundant. During these irruptions individuals may be found in small patches of shrubbery in the midst of large cities and have been observed flying into open windows of Manhattan skyscrapers.

One of the largest flights in recent years took place in the autumn of 1941. Commencing in late September, it reached a peak (no actual numbers or estimates at hand) during the latter half of October with numbers diminishing in early December. However, they were still numerous at the time of the Christmas counts in late December, when these migrants from farther north undoubtedly augmented the local population. That the flight was mainly inland is indicated by the numbers reported on the Christmas counts: 640, Bronx–Westchester, N.Y.; 540, Essex County, N.J.; maximum on Long Island only 128, southern Nassau County (see also Poor, 1946).

Breeding: The Black-capped Chickadee breeds in open woodland and near habitations, sometimes in city parks. The nest is situated in tree holes and cavities; often in bird boxes.

Egg dates: Apr. 21 to June 27.

CAROLINA CHICKADEE (*Parus carolinensis*)*B

Range: A southeastern Nearctic species, the race *extimus* breeding north to southern Pennsylvania and central New Jersey.

Status: Reaches its northern limits in our area in central New Jersey, but exact status not certain. Resident.

Breeding: Similar to the preceding species, nesting in tree holes and cavities, and to a lesser extent, in bird boxes.

Egg dates: No data.

Remarks: The Carolina and Black-capped Chickadees are very closely related species (siblings), their appearance being exceedingly similar and their vocalizations and behavior often not dissimilar. Some authorities consider the two forms conspecific.

In our area (central New Jersey) the exact breeding distribution of these two forms is not well known and awaits further investigation. Although the Black-capped Chickadee is migratory, the Carolina Chickadee is essentially sedentary, the former being found well within the range of the latter during the winter months.

In the New York City area the Carolina Chickadee has been reported definitely only from New Jersey. The A.O.U. *Check-list* (1957) defined the northern limits as ". . . central New Jersey (Princeton, Point Pleasant) . . ." which is more or less correct. At the former locality, just south of our region, this species is the breeding form, with numerous specimens collected (*fide* C. H. Rogers).

I have not seen breeding specimens from Point Pleasant, but in the American Museum collection there is none taken at this season north of Lakehurst (south of our region), with one exception noted below.

It has been thought that the vicinity of the Raritan River was the "dividing line" between the two forms, but the meager evidence available indicates that *P. atricapillus* breeds considerably to the south of that area. All local specimens taken in the breeding season that I have examined from north of the Raritan River are *P. atricapillus* and several to the south are the same. On May 12, 1907, W. de W. Miller and J. P. Chapin collected a mated pair at Old Bridge, Middlesex County, about four miles south of the Raritan River. These two specimens are A.M.N.H. Nos. 307891 and 307892. The former is a male *P. atricapillus* (measurements: tail, 62 mm., wing [chord], 69 mm.); the latter a female *P. carolinensis* (tail, 55 mm., wing [chord], 62 mm.). These measurements are well within the extremes given by Tanner (1952). A specimen taken at Helmetta, Middlesex County, July 31, 1959, is stated to be an immature *P. carolinensis* by the collector (B. Murray).

Tanner (*op. cit.*) emphasized amount of overlap in these two forms, both as to mensural and color characters, due, in part, to molt. It is therefore almost impossible to determine which form is represented by certain specimens.

Lunk (1952) also stressed size disparity in chickadees, as well as great individual and seasonal variation. He particularly emphasized the difficulty of working with study skins, noting the "marked effects of poor preparation, dirty plumage, wear, fading, and foxing, and discoloration of some older specimens."

Exact breeding limits of these two forms outside our region, as well, is imperfectly known, more work needing to be done. Their range of supposed sympatry is admittedly very slight, as evidenced by the following

316

data. Tanner (1952) found them to be allopatric altitudinally, in the southern Appalachians, *P. atricapillus* occurring at higher elevations and *P. carolinensis* lower down. Todd (1940), however, reported them breeding "together" along the Ohio River in Beaver County, western Pennsylvania, but with an area of overlap of undetermined width. Stewart and Robbins (1958) stated that a similar situation existed in Allegany County, western Maryland, although *P. carolinensis* was considered less common. Brewer (1961) found them "slightly" sympatric in Illinois, with a "large proportion of the birds" possible hybrids.

In view of the foregoing discussion, the statements of Cruickshank (1942) and Fables (1955) concerning the apparently "reliable" sight identifications of alleged *P. carolinensis* for Essex, Union, Middlesex, and Somerset counties are very doubtful and *all* sight reports from those areas are discarded here, although the southern portions of the last two counties may lie within the breeding range of *P. carolinensis*.

Much careful field work remains to be done in order to determine the status of these two forms at the southern extremity of our region. Observations by competent persons thoroughly familiar with both species (voice and morphology), supplemented by discriminate collecting of *known* breeding populations is essential. It is a difficult problem at best, but one well worthwhile.

BOREAL CHICKADEE *(Parus hudsonicus)**

Very rare winter visitant: Nearctic species, breeding south to northern New York and northern New England. Mainly resident, but winter irruptions occur very rarely south to Long Island and northern New Jersey.

In our area there have been five major incursions as follows: 1916–17, 1951–52, 1954–55, 1959–60, 1961–62. Lesser flights occurred in 1913–14 and 1941–42. In nearly all of these flights, heavy irruptions of Black-capped Chickadees occurred, preceding the arrival of Boreal or Brown-capped Chickadees by more than a month.

Four of the five known local specimens are extant and are in the American Museum collection. The first known record for the New York City region was that of one taken at Ramsey, N.J., Nov. 1, 1913 (C. R. Sleight), No. 448048. Three specimens were obtained during the flight of 1916–17: Plainfield, N.J., Dec. 31, 1916 (Miller), specimen apparently not extant; one shot out of a flock of five, New Dorp, Staten Island, Jan. 14, 1917 (Griscom), No. 757122—flock remaining from Dec. 2 to early February and among the largest number reported; one, Chappaqua, N.Y., March 24, 1917 (J. M. Valentine), No. 240959, this record not previously published. The fifth specimen was secured during the big flight of 1961–62 at Newfoundland, N.J., Dec. 23 (Jehl), No. 781085.

The flight of 1961–62 was by far the most extensive, and was widespread in small numbers throughout the region—from inland areas to Montauk. Most reports came from northern New Jersey with a probable total there of 22 individuals in late December. As many as four each were seen at Newfoundland and East Orange, N.J. Between 35 and 40 were estimated for the entire New York City region. Some of the birds were present at feeding stations, others were seen in pine groves and, in a number of instances, were associated with Black-capped Chickadees.

Extreme dates: Oct. 29 to Apr. 18.

This species is treated binomially here, the poorly marked form *littoralis* being doubtfully distinct. Color and mensural differences appear to be of average quality, with considerable overlap in wing length and the upper parts only "slightly browner." Moreover, there is much individual variation depending upon age and season. Fresh specimens are not comparable with old material—the latter being noticeably "foxed" (browner).

TUFTED TITMOUSE (*Parus bicolor*)*B

Range: A southeastern Nearctic species, breeding (resident) north to central and southeastern New York and southwestern Connecticut; casual breeder on Long Island (1960), and once in eastern Massachusetts (1958). Spreading northward in recent years.

Status: Common to locally abundant resident west of the Hudson River, decreasing northward; much less numerous east of the Hudson, but has greatly increased in recent years. Absent in the mountains. Very rare and irregular on Long Island.

Change in status: The Tufted Titmouse is generally not as tame and confiding as the Black-capped Chickadee, keeping mostly to the woodlands except in winter, when it visits feeding stations. Unlike the latter species, which occasionally migrates, the Tufted Titmouse is virtually a resident species remaining with us throughout the year, although more numerous in winter concentrations, especially in the vicinity of feeders.

Prior to the early 1950s this species was rare and local to absent, except in New Jersey where it has "always" been numerous, this latter area being at or near the northern limits of its range. Griscom (1923) stated that it was "purely accidental" east of the Hudson River as well as on Long Island. However, it was apparently less rare at one time on Long Island as Giraud (1844) says, ". . . not so abundant as the former [Black-capped Chickadee] . . ."—thus implying that the Tufted Titmouse was common. At any rate it is now scarce there. Cruickshank (1942) called it "extremely uncommon east of the Hudson" and even in New Jersey he considered 12 in a day about maximum. He expressed surprise at the "remarkable total" of 89 on the Essex County Christmas census in 1938. On Staten Island,

318

Cleaves (*in litt.*) stated that it was "very rare in the 1930s and 1940s and had slightly increased since about 1950. Has nested very recently at Eltingville."

1. *Winter:* An enormous increase took place in 1954, when the species became quite numerous in northern New Jersey, spreading north to Rockland County, N.Y., and east to Fairfield County, Conn. The cause of this population "explosion" is not clear, but it is now (1962) numerous everywhere except Staten and Long Islands, and, of course, New York City proper. A trend toward milder winters in recent years is partly responsible. Eaton (1959) suggested ecological changes in western New York as a possible factor in its increase there, although this seems not to be the case in our area. Some allowance should be made for a vast increase in the number of feeding stations in recent years.

The following numbers on Christmas counts listing two areas—one on each side of the Hudson River, as examples—emphasizes this increase. Allowance for an increase in the number of observers should be taken into account, but the figures are useful for comparative purposes and indicate the rising trend:

GREAT SWAMP, WATCHUNG, N.J.		WESTPORT, CONN.	
1954	190	1954	24
1955	205	1955	73
1956	177	1956	90
1957	230	1957	95
1958	370	1958	190
1959	440	*1959	260
1960	416	1960	280

* About half at feeders.

The 1960 figures for various Christmas counts indicate extension of range and comparative abundance of this species: (*a*) West of the Hudson —380, Hackensack–Ridgewood; 300, Ramsey; 220, Rockland County. (*b*) East of the Hudson—180, Bronx–Westchester; 130, Greenwich–Stamford; 280, Westport; 100, northern Westchester; 70, Putnam County. Twenty years before, Tufted Titmice were virtually unreported from Putnam County and Connecticut.

2. *Breeding* (see map p. 321): The Tufted Titmouse is found most often in low rich woodland, wooded swamps, and more rarely in suburban areas, where plenty of large trees are available. It nests in tree holes and less often in bird houses.

The following is a brief summary indicating expansion of range north and east of New Jersey. (*a*) West of the Hudson—Rockland and Orange counties—Deed *et al.* (1959) stated that it became established around 1930; in 1949 it was found north to Jones Point, and by 1959 north to Newburgh (just outside our area). Treacy (*in litt.*), speaking of Orange County, stated that it was "accidental" prior to 1954, but "quite common now" (1962). (*b*) East of the Hudson—first breeding in Bronx County at Pelham Bay Park in 1935 (Hickey *et al.*), and in Westchester County at New Rochelle in 1936 (Bull); Grierson (*in litt.*) stated that there has been a steady increase in northern Westchester County since 1949, becoming "well established" by 1952, and present in most localities by 1959; at least 12 nesting pairs present in the Tarrytown area in 1960 (Walsh). In northern Putnam County one pair each nested at Carmel and Fahnestock State Park in 1957 (Odell). First reported breeding in Connecticut at Weston in 1949 (Long) and second nesting at Westport in 1953 (Brown); steadily increasing since. The first definite breeding reported on Long Island in more than a century occurred in 1960: pair feeding young at Oyster Bay, Nassau County (Cahalane *et al.*); another pair feeding young at Brentwood, Suffolk County (Mayer and Rose). It is still a very rare bird on Long Island.

Egg dates: May 4 to June 17.

Remarks: Very rare in Central Park. Aside from five reports of single birds, the only other occurrence there was a group of six seen Oct. 2–10, 1957 (Bloom and Carleton). First reported in recent times in Prospect Park during the winter of 1961–62, when a pair was observed (*fide* Carleton).

Two specimens taken by Latham at Three Mile Harbor in extreme eastern Suffolk County, Oct. 16, 1928, and Apr. 2, 1931, are unique, as the species is virtually unknown on the east end of Long Island. Helmuth's only record at Easthampton was that of two seen Dec. 6–10, 1928, the same year Latham collected his first specimen.

NUTHATCHES: SITTIDAE

WHITE-BREASTED NUTHATCH (*Sitta carolinensis*)*B

Range: Nearctic species, the race *cookei* occurring in our area.

Status: Fairly common resident, but local breeder on the coastal plain. More widespread during migration; most numerous in winter.

Migration and winter: The migration of the White-breasted Nuthatch—both a migratory and resident species in our area—can be ascertained with certainty in a locality such as Central Park where it does not breed and where it is usually rare in winter. Here we find (*a*) that it is definitely migratory; (*b*) that height of the migration or peak periods can be established; and (*c*) that fall arrival and spring departure can be determined. It would be virtually impossible to collect such data in the surrounding countryside, where it breeds and winters.

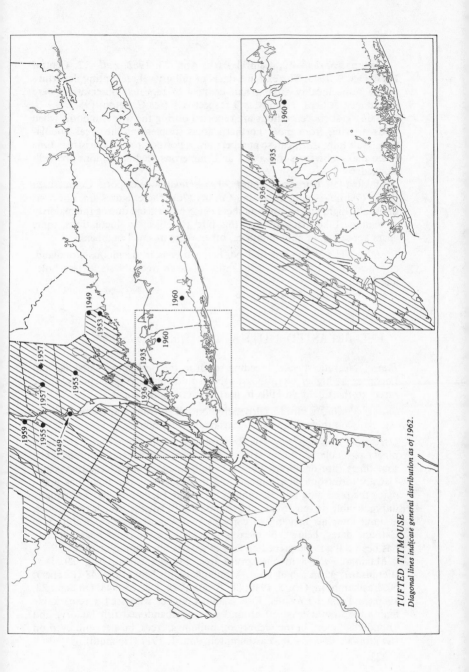

TUFTED TITMOUSE
Diagonal lines indicate general distribution as of 1962.

Maxima: *Spring*—10, Central Park, Apr. 23, 1962. *Fall*—12, Central Park, Oct. 9, 1943. The extreme dates of fall arrival and spring departure in the same locality after a half century of repeated observation were determined as Sept. 7 and May 9 respectively (see Carleton, 1958).

The largest concentrations are reported during the winter months when birds arriving from more northern areas supplement the local population. Naturally the greatest numbers are reported around Christmas time when many observers are afield and numerous feeding stations are well-stocked.

Maxima on Christmas counts, 1954: *Inland*—Westport, Conn., area (325). *Coastal*—southern Nassau County (76). These figures are, however, unusually high, much lower numbers being more usual during the majority of winters. Like many species, this bird is subject to fluctuations, some years appearing in large numbers, other years in small numbers.

Breeding: The White-breasted Nuthatch breeds in deciduous woodland, and near habitations with a quantity of large trees. Nests in tree holes and bird boxes.

Egg dates: Apr. 15 to May 26.

RED-BREASTED NUTHATCH (*Sitta canadensis*)*

Range: Nearctic species, breeding south to the Berkshires, Catskills, and Poconos; at higher elevations farther south in the Appalachians; more rarely to the Litchfield Hills in northwestern Connecticut.

Status: Variously rare to fairly common fall migrant and winter visitant, especially on the coast, where occasionally common.

Occurrence and maxima: The Red-breasted Nuthatch is found chiefly in pines, particularly during winter. It is very erratic and unpredictable, sometimes rare or almost absent in fall, in other years very numerous. Usually rare (sometimes unreported) in spring, unless a flight has taken place the preceding fall. Its time of arrival and length of stay are equally unpredictable, in most years not common until late September or October, at long intervals arriving as early as mid-August or even in July (see Extreme dates, below). Numerous in winter on the outer coast, if there has been a flight the preceding fall, otherwise uncommon or rare.

Maxima: *Fall*—8 in one spruce tree, Fisher's Island, Aug. 29, 1937 (Ferguson); 45 in a half hour, Montauk Point, Sept. 18, 1948 (Fischer); 50, Easthampton, Oct. 5, 1946; 30, Bronx Park, Oct. 5, 1943. On Sept. 22, 1906, at Point o' Woods, Fire Island, Dutcher witnessed a remarkable flight. He saw at least 50 around a large abandoned fish factory, and "hundreds" more in the vicinity on buildings, trees, bushes, and even on the ground. *Winter*—36, Easthampton, Jan. 1, 1917 (Helmuth).

"Extreme" dates: Bicknell (see Griscom, 1927) at Riverdale reported the following: In 1878 arrived on July 10, and became "abundant" by Aug. 12; in 1886 present from July 1 to 5, but very rare later on in fall; in 1889 arrived July 18, and then observed from Aug. 8 on. Helmuth at East-hampton saw five on Aug. 18, 1909, of which he collected two. He reported its arrival in 1929 on Aug. 7. In recent years it has arrived as early as the first week in August (1951) at various coastal points. In 1961 it was present from early July, and was common by late August.

In spring, it has been noted as late as June 4 and 10. In 1892, Chapman reported the species in Central Park through *June* and into *July*.

Usually, however, this species arrives in flight years by early September, is most numerous later on in that month and in October, is locally common throughout the winter, and reported in spring chiefly in May, when it may found late into that month.

Remarks: On June 15, 1921, at Orient, Latham collected a female with enlarged ovaries and saw another individual nearby. In my opinion, this does not constitute a breeding record. The sex of the other individual was unknown and, from what has been indicated above of this bird's erratic behavior, it is included here as a nonbreeding summer occurrence.

CREEPERS: CERTHIIDAE

BROWN CREEPER (*Certhia familiaris*)*B

Range: Holarctic species, in the east breeding south in the mountains to Tennessee and North Carolina; rarely at low elevations to Long Island and central New Jersey. The race *americana* occurs in our area.

Status: Fairly common to common migrant, occasionally very common in fall. Uncommon in winter inland, but usually rare on the coast. Very rare and local breeder.

Migration: Usually one to a dozen Brown Creepers are observed in a day during migration, but occasionally more are seen.

Maxima: *Spring*—35, Far Rockaway, May 6, 1950, a notably late season. *Fall*—75, Easthampton, Oct. 5, 1946 (Helmuth).

Extreme dates: Aug. 28 and 31 to May 21 and June 5, 1953, Central Park (Carleton *et al.*). Rare before mid-September and after mid-May. Usually arrives in early April and departs in mid-November.

Winter: A few Brown Creepers are usually seen with a mixed flock of kinglets, chickadees, and woodpeckers—all searching for food.

Maxima: Total of 85 on three inland Christmas counts, late December 1951. Uncommon to rare at this season on the coast.

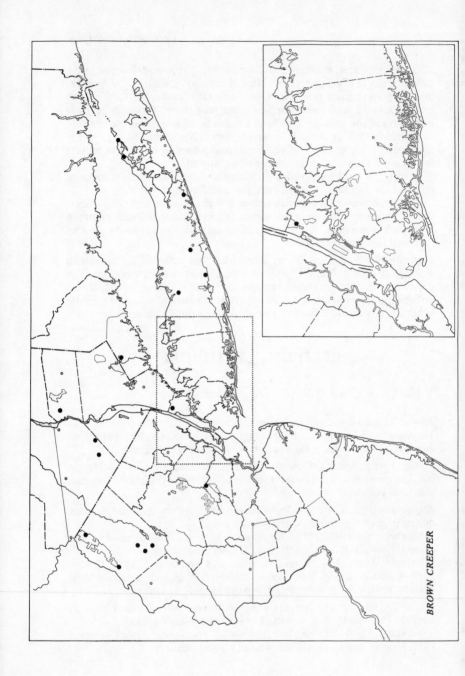

BROWN CREEPER

Breeding (see map): The Brown Creeper breeds locally in highland swamps of the interior; more rarely at lower elevations along the coast, where it is at its southern limits. The nest is placed behind strips of bark and occasionally in a tree cavity. The following are actual nesting records by region:

1. New Jersey. Griscom (1923) stated, "a rare, but regular breeder in an elm swamp near Andover, Sussex County (P. B. Philipp)." Cruickshank (1942) mentioned this information, but gave the locality as "near Springdale." Neither writer was specific as to years but apparently the nestings took place from 1906 to 1908. Actually, Andover and Springdale are only two or three miles apart. There must have been several breeding records in this area during this period, because I find a report of a nest with six young in a dead stub near Newton, May 19, 1907 (R. H. Southard, Proc. Linnaean Soc., N.Y., 20–23: 5, 1913). In the American Museum collection there is a set of five eggs also taken at Newton on May 3, 1913 (Philipp). Newton is two or three miles north of Springdale and about five miles north of Andover. How many breeding locations are involved is hard to say. Cruickshank also mentioned two adults with five young seen near Summit, Union County, July 23, 1905 (H. Hans). Much more recently a female was observed feeding young in a swamp on Kittatinny Mountain near Crater Lake, Sussex County, summer of 1954 (Fables and Kennedy). In 1962 two pairs were observed breeding in High Point State Park, Sussex County: one pair in a cedar swamp (Abraitys); the other in "Beaver Swamp" (G. Johnson).

2. New York State (mainland). Deed (*in litt.*) stated that this species is a "regular" but "sparse" breeder in highland swamps at elevations of 1000 feet or more at Island Pond and Pine Swamp, both in Harriman Park, Orange County. Kuerzi (1931) stated that "several" pairs bred in swamps east of Cold Spring, Putnam County. Cruickshank found a nest with young at Van Cortlandt Park, Bronx County, May 27, 1926.

3. Connecticut. A pair nested at the Audubon Nature Center, Round Hill, Fairfield County, during the summer of 1961 (Clement and H. S. Peters), the nest collected later.

4. Long Island. Reported only in Suffolk County, as follows: pair summered at East Marion in 1923, possibly bred, but no nest or young found (Latham); in 1947 this species was discovered breeding at two localities—pair at nest, Orient (Latham), and two broods, nests of five eggs each, Smithtown (D. G. Nichols), May 15 and June 13, situated behind loose bark in locust trees. This latter nesting was located in unconventional "dry upland." (For complete account, see Auk, 65: 612–613, 1948.) During the summer of 1950 Wilcox found a pair feeding young in swampy woods at East Quogue. A nest with eggs behind loose bark was found in swampy woodland near Yaphank, summer of 1963 (Raynor);

also a pair seen carrying food to a nest at Sayville the same year (Puleston)·
The East Quogue and Sayville records are the only known breeding
reports in our area located on the coastal plain.

Egg dates: May 3 to June 13.

WRENS: TROGLODYTIDAE

HOUSE WREN (*Troglodytes aedon*)*B

Range: Nearctic species, the nominate race breeding in our area.

Status: Fairly common migrant. Widespread breeder.

Migration: Though found throughout our area in migration, the House
Wren is not reported in large numbers, ordinarily only a few individuals
being seen at any one locality. The maximum reported appears to be 12,
Easthampton, Sept. 26, 1927.

Extreme dates: Apr. 12 to Nov. 3 (specimen); a number of later November dates and several into early December. Rare before late April and
after mid-October.

Breeding: The House Wren breeds in rural and suburban areas in gardens,
orchards, and estates, also in dense thickets and swampy woodland. It is a
very adaptable species in nesting habits. The nest is placed in a variety of
situations such as tree cavities, upturned tree roots, stone walls, bird
houses, tin cans, coat pockets, iron pipes, mailboxes, etc.

A high breeding density was noted in New Jersey on the Cardinali farm
at Jamesburg, Middlesex County, summer of 1960: 18 pairs, all in nest
boxes, bred on the 34-acre farm—approximately one pair per two acres.

Egg dates: May 4 to July 19.

Winter: This species winters north to North Carolina, more rarely to
Maryland. There is one definite local winter record: One collected at
West Orange, N.J., Jan. 13, 1894 (Van Rensselaer), A.M.N.H. No. 374424,
never before published. Cruickshank (1942) lists one January sight report.
There are also a number of other observations in March, and several on
Christmas counts, some of which may be correct, but others are very
dubious, probably nothing more than misidentified Winter Wrens.

Subspecies: According to Kunkle *et al.* (1959), a specimen of the poorly
marked race *baldwini*, breeding just to the west of the nominate race, was
taken near New Brunswick, N.J., Dec. 4, 1954 (Baird). I have not seen this
specimen. However, three others in the A.M.N.H. collection from the New
York City area, determined by Oberholser as *baldwini*, do not appear to
differ from nominate *aedon*.

Remarks: Some authorities would make this species and the Neotropical
T. musculus conspecific.

WINTER WREN (*Troglodytes troglodytes*)*B

Range: Holarctic species, breeding south to the Berkshires, Catskills, and Poconos; rarely to northwestern Connecticut; also higher mountains to northern Georgia. The race *hiemalis* occurs in our area.

Status: Usually uncommon to fairly common migrant and winter visitant, but numbers fluctuate; occasionally more numerous on migration. Casual breeder (1962).

Migration and winter: During migrations and in winter this secretive species frequents brush piles and dense thickets, but may be "squeaked" out of hiding, and thus more easily observed. Ordinarily only one to three Winter Wrens are observed, but sometimes more are seen.

Maxima: *Fall*—6, Prospect Park, Oct. 3, 1944; 10, Atlantic Highlands, Nov. 8, 1946. *Winter*—12, Port Chester Christmas count, Jan. 2, 1954. *Spring*—22, Stokes State Forest, Apr. 22, 1944.

Extreme dates: Sept. 11 to May 21. Rare before late September and after early May.

There are at least a dozen reports of singing individuals in late May, June, and July in the interior highlands, but in none of these instances was breeding proved, although this was possible, or even probable. To my knowledge, there has been no definite evidence of nesting anywhere in our area prior to 1962.

Breeding: The Winter Wren was definitely established as a breeding species in the New York City region during the summer of 1962 at *two* localities:

1. New York: A pair and four fledglings—the latter "barely able to fly"—were located on Aug. 16 in "hurricane blowdown" in an area of "second-growth deciduous forest" at the Westmoreland Sanctuary (elevation about 700 feet) between Mount Kisco and Bedford Village, Westchester County. These birds were found by S. Dearolf, the resident naturalist, and were also seen by Grierson.

2. New Jersey: An adult was observed feeding three young in early June at Lake Girard, Sussex County, by Cherepy, and seen again on June 14 (Edwards and Lang).

BEWICK'S WREN (*Thryomanes bewickii*)

Accidental: A primarily southern Nearctic species, widely distributed, but absent from the Atlantic coastal plain. The race *altus* breeds northeast to Fulton County, Pa., is mainly resident, and apparently becomes scarce as the House Wren increases.

All six local reports have been of singing individuals seen under ideal conditions, in some cases by numerous observers: Central Park, Apr. 10 to May 8, 1928 (Miss Capen and many others), an individual well studied by amateurs and professionals; Hohokus, N.J., May 24, 1935 (Helmuth); Prospect Park, May 13, 1946 (Soll and Whelen); same locality, Apr. 15–23, 1952 (Carleton, Grant, and many others); Croton Point, May 8, 1952 (Walsh); Sunrise Mountain, N.J., Apr. 20, 1958 (Crowell, Wolfarth, *et al.*).

A specimen is desirable to establish definitely its occurrence in our area.

CAROLINA WREN (*Thryothorus ludovicianus*)*B

Range: An eastern Nearctic species. The nominate race is near the northern limits of its range in our area, although occurring rarely north to the central portions of New York and New England.

Status: Locally, a fairly common resident at lower elevations, but rare in many other places that appear suitable, its distribution being very uneven and erratic. Absent in the mountains. Subject to marked fluctuations.

Occurrence and maxima: The Carolina Wren is a very adaptable species, occurring in such diverse terrain as thickets in sand dunes in the Sunken Forest on Fire Island, and cliff ledges on the Palisades. Elsewhere, it is found in wooded ravines, dense tangles near streams and swamps, and often places its nest in an assortment of locations such as bird boxes, stone walls, hollow tree stumps, tin cans, old hats, outhouses, etc. And yet away from known breeding areas the Carolina Wren is rare and irregular.

This species is very sensitive to severe winters—being decimated by ice storms, heavy snows, and long periods of sub-zero weather. With a succession of mild winters, the species recovers and re-establishes itself.

It is most numerous though local on eastern Long Island, along the Palisades, and generally in the southern limits of our area in central New Jersey. Note that the following maxima are all from these areas, with the exception of one from Connecticut.

Maxima: *Early period*—10 within a distance of one mile, Englewood area, July 3, 1892; 20 on the Palisades, Fort Lee to Englewood, Dec. 24, 1911; 15, Gardiner's Island, Dec. 25, 1908. *Recent period*—12 nesting pairs, Easthampton to Montauk, summer of 1932; 26 singing birds, Gardiner's Island, June 1939; 6 pairs, Orient to Southold, summer of 1956; 6 pairs in eight miles, Raritan River, June 1952; 1957–58 Christmas counts —18, Rockland County, mostly along the Hudson River; 16, Westport, Connecticut area, where it was formerly rare. A number of these winter individuals were present at feeding stations.

Egg dates: Apr. 27 to July 25.

LONG-BILLED MARSH WREN (*Telmatodytes palustris*)*B

Range: A widespread Nearctic species, breeding from southern Canada to northern Mexico and Florida.

328

Status: Locally common to abundant breeder. Rare but regular in winter on the coastal marshes, occasional in mild winters in inland marshes. Very rare as a migrant.

Migration and winter: As it occurs both summer and winter, migration dates are difficult to determine; but this species usually arrives on the breeding grounds by early May and departs in October. Being a night migrant and very secretive during the day, it is rarely reported away from the breeding grounds.

The following winter maxima are based on Christmas counts: Dec. 26, 1949—6, Troy Meadows; 8, Hackensack Meadows; total of 22, Queens—southern Nassau Christmas counts, late December to early January 1953–54.

Breeding: The Long-billed Marsh Wren breeds colonially in cattails inland and along the larger tidal rivers, and to a lesser extent in *Phragmites* and other grasses in both brackish and salt marshes on the coast. Naturally the number of pairs depends upon the size of the marsh.

Maxima: Newark—Elizabeth Meadows, 100+ pairs, 1898 (marsh very wet), only 20 pairs, 1932 (marsh much dried out, *fide* Urner); in respect to its former abundance in that area, Stone (1937) stated that one collector obtained between 400 and 500 eggs within a single day; Van Cortlandt Park, 1938, 47 nests, but some of these may have represented "dummy" nests, a well-known characteristic of this species; Croton Point, 1942, 100 nesting pairs; Troy Meadows, 1947, 160 nesting pairs.

Egg dates: May 22 to July 26.

Subspecies: A highly polytypic species, of which two subspecies occur in the New York City area. The nominate race breeds in coastal and tidal river marshes from Virginia north to Long Island, Connecticut, and Rhode Island. The race *dissaëptus* breeds in inland marshes south and east to western Pennsylvania, central New York, and eastern Massachusetts.

In our area specimens taken in the breeding season from brackish estuarine marshes, as along the lower Hudson River, Hackensack River, and from Newark Bay are referable to nominate *palustris*. To which subspecies breeding birds from Troy Meadows as well as other inland freshwater marshes in our area belong is not known, as no breeding material from those localities is available for examination, and the A.O.U. *Check-list* (1957: 418) does not define the eastern breeding limits of *T. p. dissaëptus* south of central New York and Massachusetts.

Undoubtedly many individuals of *T. p. dissaëptus* pass through our region during migration, as it occupies a wide range to the north and west of nominate *palustris*. In fact, several spring and fall specimens from our area in the A.M.N.H. collection examined by me are referable to the inland breeding form *dissaëptus*.

329

SHORT-BILLED MARSH WREN (*Cistothorus platensis*)*B

Range: A widespread American species, ranging from southern Canada to southern South America, but very local throughout; absent from western North America and the West Indies. The race *stellaris* breeds south to Virginia.

Status: Uncommon to rare and very local breeder. Rare or very rare and little known migrant. Very rare in winter.

Migration and winter: The Short-billed Marsh Wren is exceptionally secretive and about as easy to study as a mouse. Rare and little known as a migrant, it is very difficult to state accurately its arrival and departure dates. This species is extremely rare away from breeding localities. Indeed, Carleton (1958) lists only three occurrences for Central Park and one for Prospect Park. It has been reported as arriving on the breeding grounds at Mastic, L.I., as early as April 18 (J. T. Nichols). In fall, it is rarely reported after October, and from the evidence before me it is seen less rarely in October than at any other time. In nearly 30 years in the Ossining area, A. K. Fisher recorded the species only three times during migration, and these were birds collected in October in different years.

This species winters north to Maryland; much more rarely to New Jersey and Long Island. Collected at Jones Beach, Dec. 28, 1913 (Griscom), A.M.N.H. No. 142895. Otherwise reported very rarely and irregularly at this season in coastal salt marshes. A number of unconfirmed sight reports by inexperienced observers are probably misidentified Long-billed Marsh Wrens.

Breeding: This species, unlike the Long-billed Marsh Wren, shuns cattail marshes, being found inland in damp grassy or sedgy meadows and bogs, and along the coast in short *Spartina* grass on salt and brackish meadows, where it is not too wet. As Cruickshank (1942) stated, regarding inland localities, it disappears as a breeder if its nesting site ". . . becomes too dry through draining or too wet through flooding." It is also sensitive to ecological change, moving out of an area when the meadow grows up to scrub. In the past 15 years the Short-billed Marsh Wren has decreased in our region. A number of its former haunts have been obliterated by building developments, chiefly on Long Island, where also burning of brackish coastal meadows has driven these birds out.

This wren nests occasionally in small "colonies," but ordinarily only one or two pairs are present. The largest "colony" reported in recent years in our area was one of eight pairs at Troy Meadows during the summer of 1947 (Urner Club). However, "none" was found there in 1962 (*fide* Jehl). Four pairs were reported breeding in brackish meadows at Idlewild in 1960 (Mayer), although "none" was reported from Long Island in 1962 (*fide* Elliott).

Egg dates: May 19 to Aug. 20.

330

MOCKINGBIRDS, THRASHERS: MIMIDAE

MOCKINGBIRD (*Mimus polyglottos*)*B

Range: A southern Nearctic and northern Neotropical species, the nominate race breeding north to central New Jersey; more rarely and irregularly
along the coast to Long Island and Massachusetts; casually to southern
Maine.

Status: Locally common resident in north-central New Jersey (great
increase since 1955); rare to uncommon and local elsewhere. Regular fall
migrant along the outer coast. Increasing in winter in recent years. Absent
in the mountains.

Change in status: Few species have increased in our region as markedly as
the Mockingbird. In fact there has been such a pronounced change in
status that it is worth quoting Cruickshank (1942): "At present the bird
is seldom seen anywhere in the New York City region but on the other
hand occurs annually and is a rare possibility at any time of the year in
any locality."

In our area the Mockingbird has apparently always been rare and
erratic north of central New Jersey. Stone (1908) mentioned that colonies
existed in northern Monmouth County as far as Keyport and Sandy Hook
until at least 1892, but had suffered severely during the famous blizzard of
1888. It has been rare in our area since then until its recent comeback in
the mid-1950s. About the only thing regular is its occurrence on the coast
each fall in small numbers.

Migration: If it were not for such places as Central and Prospect Parks,
one would think of the Mockingbird as being resident and not migratory
at all, but since it does not breed in either locality (however, bred in Central
Park, 1963) it is easy to determine migrants passing through during spring
and fall. Carleton (1958) stated that although it is rare and irregular there,
it has occurred nearly every spring in recent years, chiefly in April and May.
It is rare there in fall, as the migration is chiefly coastal.

Along the outer beaches this species arrives regularly in mid-August,
(has arrived as early as July 27), is most likely to be observed in September,
when as many as four per day per locality have been seen. Numbers taper
off in late October and November (to Nov. 26). As many as nine were
observed during the autumn of 1946, five of these in September; also nine
during the fall of 1954.

Winter: Prior to the early 1950s a few individuals were found each year,
but with the great increase since 1957 birds have lingered into winter, some
remaining and surviving the season at feeding stations or subsisting on
fruiting shrubs. The following maxima taken from Christmas counts

331

indicate how numerous this species has become in our area, especially in central New Jersey: 1957—27 on all counts, 20 in New Jersey alone; 1958—37 on all counts, 29 in New Jersey alone; 1959—86 on all counts, 72 in New Jersey alone, 48 in Somerset and Hunterdon counties; 1960—120 on all counts, 95 in New Jersey alone, nearly 70 in the four counties of Hunterdon, Somerset, Middlesex, and Monmouth.

Breeding (see map): The Mockingbird breeds most frequently in agricultural country and residential districts especially in New Jersey, nesting in thickets and hedgerows. On Long Island most nests have been found in thickets or shrubbery (once in a low pine), often near the seashore. Two other nests, including one on Staten Island, were situated in vines.

The following summary indicates recent breeding, section by section:

1. New Jersey. Large breeding population in *Monmouth, Middlesex, Somerset*, and *Hunterdon counties*, especially since 1955. The following maxima in these areas were taken from a 1960 survey: *Monmouth County*—13 pairs between Keyport and Eatontown (Ryan); 8 pairs between Oceanport and Wreck Pond (Seeley). *Middlesex and Somerset counties*—Murray (*in litt.*) stated that there was a great increase since 1955, common in the farm country around Bound Brook and New Brunswick, less common in the towns, at least 40 pairs!; northern *Hunterdon County*—Abraitys (*in litt.*) mentioned a "stable" breeding population of about 15 to 20 nesting pairs found around dooryards and thickets, especially where *Rosa multiflora* is prevalent. The species decreases farther north in New Jersey, breeding sparingly to the New York State line.

2. New York State—except Long Island—and Connecticut (dates represent first reported nesting): *Staten Island*—reported nesting only at New Dorp (1961). *New York County*—Central Park, pair raised two young (1963). *Rockland County*—New City (1957); Suffern, Lake DeForest, and near Hook Mountain (1960); New Hempstead (1962). *Orange County*—first reported in 1962, single pairs, except as noted: Blooming Grove (2); Washingtonville; Hamptonburgh. *Westchester County*—reported nesting only at Tarrytown (1960). *Putnam County*—one pair at Patterson (1959). *Fairfield County, Conn.*—Westport and Weston (1958).

3. Long Island, nesting chiefly along the south shore (dates represent first reported nesting): *Queens County*—Roxbury, Rockaway peninsula (1956); Riis Park (1958); Jamaica Bay Refuge (1959). *Nassau County*—Hewlett, Oceanside, and Levittown (1962). *Suffolk County*—Mecox Bay (1956); Orient, two pairs (1956); Manorville (1959), two nests (1962); Napeague (1961); Pinelawn, two nests (1962); Babylon and Fort Salonga (1962).

The 1956 records are the first definite instances of breeding known on Long Island in nearly a half century.

Egg dates: June 3 to July 3.

332

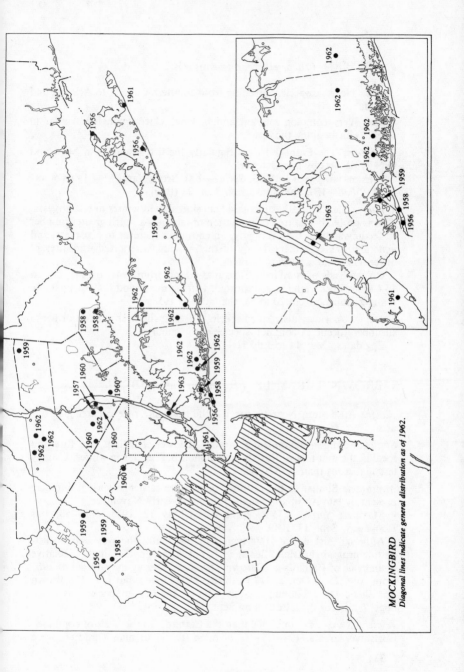

MOCKINGBIRD

Diagonal lines indicate general distribution as of 1962.

CATBIRD (*Dumetella carolinensis*)*B

Range: Nearctic species, breeding from southern Canada to Arizona and Florida.

Status: Very common migrant and breeder. Uncommon but regular in winter, chiefly along the coast.

Migration: The Catbird arrives regularly the first few days in May, and usually departs by late October.

Maxima: Big year in 1953. *Spring*—100, Bronx Park, May 14 (Komorowski). *Fall*—150, Far Rockaway, Sept. 23 (Bull).

Winter: The Catbird has increased considerably in winter in recent years. This is probably due to a combination of factors—a much greater number of feeding stations than formerly, an enormous increase in observers, and generally milder winters. Many of the individuals reported were present at feeders, some wintering through.

On the basis of combined Christmas counts from 1941 to 1948, one to 15 Catbirds per winter were reported. During the period 1949 to 1960, the numbers ranged from 20 to 58, the latter in 1958.

Breeding: A widely distributed species, nesting wherever thickets or dense shrubbery occur. A common species in the suburbs.

Egg dates: May 14 to July 31.

BROWN THRASHER (*Toxostoma rufum*)*B ˙

Range: An eastern Nearctic species, the nominate race occurring in our area.

Status: Common migrant and breeder at lower elevations, but rare and local in the mountains. Rare to uncommon but regular in winter. Usually less numerous than the Catbird.

Migration: Similar to the Catbird, but arrives earlier in spring, numbers present by late April, and usually remains to early November.

Maxima: *Spring*—23, Prospect Park, May 12, 1945. *Fall*—50, Far Rockaway, Sept. 17, 1949.

Although just outside our region to the south, the very active mist-netting program at Island Beach, N.J., provides a good example of relative abundance of Catbirds and Brown Thrashers. During the autumn of 1960 from Aug. 25 to Oct. 2, 717 Catbirds were banded, but only 136 Brown Thrashers. The maximum one-day total for the former species was 72 on Sept. 7, and for the latter, 34 on Sept. 24.

Winter: Much less numerous than the Catbird. On the basis of combined Christmas counts (1941–52), from none (twice) to nine Thrashers were reported. From 1953 to 1960, the numbers greatly increased, but this may have been due to the same reasons listed under the Catbird; namely many more observers and more feeding stations, as well as a trend toward milder winters. In only four years did the figures for Brown Thrasher exceed 20, but in 1960 not less than 42 were reported as against only 24 Catbirds, the only time in 20 years when the Catbird was outnumbered. The total estimate for the 20 years is as follows: Catbird—455; Brown Thrasher—194.

Breeding: Brown Thrashers prefer to breed in dry open country. Nests in thickets and scrubby fields, particularly numerous on the coastal plain. While they also nest around dwellings in suburban areas, they are much less familiar than the previous species.

Egg dates: May 8 to June 25.

SAGE THRASHER (*Oreoscoptes montanus*)

Accidental: A western Nearctic species, breeding east to southeastern Wyoming. Casual east to the Great Plains. Accidental in New York State, specimen collected in Monroe County in 1942.

In our area one was caught in a mist net, banded, color-photographed, and released, Shinnecock Inlet near the Tiana Coast Guard station, Oct. 18, 1958 (Wilcox and W. Terry); identification verified at the American Museum of Natural History by Eisenmann and the writer.

THRUSHES: TURDIDAE

ROBIN (*Turdus migratorius*)*B

Range: A widespread Nearctic species, the nominate race breeding in our area.

Status: Very abundant migrant and abundant breeder. Usually rare to uncommon in winter; locally numerous some years.

Migration and winter: The Robin is one of our most numerous and widely distributed birds; flocks ranging up to 3000 have been observed in evening roosts in late summer and early fall (August and early September), and almost as many in October, particularly along the coast. In spring the migration is more protracted and concentrations from 50 to 300 are the rule, chiefly in March and early April. There are always some present throughout the winter in areas where fruit is available, and the winter of 1956 was notable for the numbers present. Flocks up to 900 were reported in inland New Jersey. It is difficult to ascertain, however, whether Robins present in flocks in late January, and particularly in February, are birds that over-wintered, or represent newly arrived individuals from more southern areas. Usually arrives by late February or early March and departs in late November.

Breeding: This species is very adaptable and may be found breeding almost everywhere. It may even nest in woodland clearings or in treeless areas provided lawns with shrubs are available. Robins often build their nests under the eaves of houses and on window sills.

Egg dates: Apr. 6 to July 24.

Subspecies: This Nearctic species is represented in our area by two subspecies, the nominate race whose status is described above, and the northeastern race *nigrideus*, which breeds from northern Quebec and Labrador south to Newfoundland. The latter, a well-marked form, is probably a regular spring and fall migrant, as well as wintering in the New York City region. There are at least four local specimens of *T. m. nigrideus* in the American Museum collection determined by Aldrich as this subspecies, all adult males: Manhattanville, New York City, January 1846 (Lawrence collection); Morristown, March 6, 1886 (Thurber); Rockaway Point, Nov. 1, 1903 (Peavey); Shelter Island, Dec. 15, 1903 (Worthington). Aldrich and Nutt (1939) also listed another Shelter Island specimen taken on March 28 (year not stated). I have not seen this specimen. A specimen in the United States National Museum was collected at Highland Falls, Jan. 18, 1882 (Mearns), also a male, and examined by Parkes. Two males recently collected in New Jersey at Blairstown on Apr. 4, 1959 (Jehl), were examined by me, and appear to be this race. They are also in the A.M.N.H. collection.

The writer agrees with Parkes (Auk, 66: 366, 1949) that adult males are identifiable in the field, although it is true that only cautious and discriminating students, familiar with the critical characters, are competent to identify them in the field.

VARIED THRUSH (*Ixoreus naevius*)*

Casual: A northwestern Nearctic species, breeding southeast to northwestern Montana. Winters chiefly south of the breeding range. Stragglers recorded east to the Atlantic coast from Massachusetts to New Jersey.

In our area, there are at least eight occurrences. Four of these are specimens, only one apparently extant, not examined by me. It is, therefore, not known whether the subspecies involved is nominate *naevius* of the Pacific coast or the more eastern *meruloides* (perhaps the more likely race).

The specimens reported are as follows: Hoboken, December 1851 (Lawrence collection); Islip, fall of 1874 (Lawrence collection); adult male caught in a rabbit trap, Port Jefferson, Dec. 20, 1889 (Helme), in collection of Harold H. Bailey; Miller Place, Nov. 19, 1905 (Helme).

336

The following four sight reports are: Ossining, Nov. 10, 1928 (Miss M. Sheridan), reported in detail to Griscom; one with a flock of Robins feeding on persimmons in the garden of Mrs. J. Boesch, Port Richmond, Staten Island, Nov. 24 to Dec. 6, 1936, also seen and photographed by Davis and Wiegmann (Auk, 54: 394–395, 1937); one seen at a feeder about three miles northwest of Ridgefield, Conn., just outside our area, but close to the Westchester County line, February and March, 1960 (numerous observers); one at the Williams feeder, Bellport, L.I., Dec. 16–31, 1963 (many observers, color photo taken). Note that all local occurrences have been in late fall or winter, as was an immature female taken outside our region at Watertown, N.Y., Dec. 9, 1958 (N.Y.S.M.).

WOOD THRUSH (*Hylocichla mustelina*)*B

Range: An eastern Nearctic species, breeding from extreme southern Canada and southern Maine to Florida; spreading northward.

Status: Fairly common to occasionally common spring migrant. Common breeder inland; less common near the coast, but increasing. Casual in winter.

Migration: Unlike other species of the genus *Hylocichla*, which breed farther north and consequently pass through in large numbers, the Wood Thrush is usually seen in small scattered groups up to a dozen. However, there is evidence that during the last 15 or 20 years it has spread northward into northern New England and New York and is more numerous on migration than formerly. During the spring of 1950, a big flight occurred: May 5, Central Park (40); Prospect Park (35); May 6, Bronx Park (35). In such places as city parks, where the species is absent or very rare as a breeding bird, it can be safely established that most individuals are migrants. On the coastal strip, where it is also a rare breeder, I saw at least 40 at Far Rockaway, May 8, 1961. In fall, migration is much more protracted, the local breeding population departs relatively early and consequently few individuals are observed on any one day.

Extreme dates: April 20 (specimen) to Oct. 27, Nov. 12, and 25. Rare before May and after mid-October.

Breeding: Nests in moist open woodland, but increasing in suburban areas where there are numerous shade trees and shrubbery. Formerly scarce on the coastal plain, it has increased there in recent years. Fables (1955) stated that Seeley reported a "tremendous" increase in Monmouth County since about 1945. On Long Island at Mastic, J. T. Nichols (*in litt.*) states, "It has greatly increased since 1910 as the Hermit Thrush decreased. One nesting pair [Wood Thrush] in 1910, now [1955] there are at least ten pairs probably due to cutting of the pitch pines and planting of deciduous trees."

Egg dates: May 16 to July 18.

Remarks: This species winters from southern Texas to Panama. It is very rare at this season in Florida and has been collected once in North Carolina.

Consequently it is very surprising to find seven apparently reliable sight reports by experienced observers in winter in the New York City area, at least three of these at feeding stations: Plainfield, Dec. 19–25, 1909 (W. de W. Miller); two at the Irving feeder, West Nyack—one, Dec. 19, 1944, to Jan. 15, 1945, the other, Jan. 26 to late March 1950 (several observers); Flushing, Dec. 22, 1947, to Feb. 24, 1948 (Reid and many others)—this last individual remained at a feeder following the big snowstorm of Dec. 27; one at the edge of a swamp, Eastport, L.I., Dec. 26, 1959 (Evans and Puleston); most remarkable were two different individuals observed the same day—Dec. 26, 1961—one at Eastport, the other near Mastic, these localities about six miles apart (6 observers).

HERMIT THRUSH (*Hylocichla guttata*)*B

Range: Nearctic species, the race *faxoni* breeds south to the higher mountains of western Maryland, Pennsylvania, northern New Jersey, southeastern New York, northwestern Connecticut, and Massachusetts, and locally on the coastal plain—in the pine barrens of eastern Massachusetts, including Cape Cod (formerly on Martha's Vineyard), and Long Island. Winters north to southern Maryland; more rarely from Cape May to Cape Cod.

Status: Common to occasionally abundant migrant. Rare, but regular in winter. Fairly common, but local breeder on eastern Long Island; rare breeder in the interior highlands.

Migration: The Hermit Thrush is most numerous in October and again in April.

Maxima: *Fall*—300, Orient, Oct. 12, 1952; 350, Prospect Park, Oct. 15, 1950; big coastal flight, Oct. 28, 1944—75 Orient; 120, Jones Beach; 170, Prospect Park; 55, Long Branch; on Nov. 16, 1957, 30 were picked up dead, having hit telephone wires during a heavy morning fog at Sea Bright, N.J. *Spring*—250, Far Rockaway to Woodmere Woods, May 6, 1950, a notably late spring. Usually most numerous in late April during the latter season.

Extreme dates (nonbreeders): Casual, Aug. 11, 1926, Riverdale (Griscom); Aug. 25, 26 (specimens) and early September to late May; casual, June 6, 1928, Central Park (Capen and Watson). Rare before late September and after mid-May. Cruickshank's statement (1942) that ". . . all migration is normally terminated by the end of this month" (May), and "Stragglers are rarely recorded up to the third week in June," must refer to breeding birds as migrants are rare after mid-May. There are *no* late

338

May or June migrant specimens in the A.M.N.H. collection. Usually arrives in early April and departs by late November.

Winter: This species frequents scattered stands of red cedars and dogwoods, feeding on the berries; also occurs at feeding stations at this season. There are several local winter specimens in the A.M.N.H. collection.

Maxima: 12 wintered at Plainfield, 1909–10 (Miller); 5 wintered at New Rochelle, 1939–40.

Breeding: The Hermit Thrush breeds in two totally different habitats in two widely separated areas.

1. It is a rare, local breeder inland at higher elevations in mixed coniferous-deciduous forest, particularly where hemlock or spruce is prevalent —in Rockland and Orange counties, N.Y., in the Palisades Interstate Park, and in northern New Jersey. In the latter state, Fables (1955) reported that it is " a local breeding bird in the Kittatinnies and in the highlands." He mentioned a nest found near Sunfish Pond, Warren County in 1951 (Kunkle and Thorsell), and ten singing males in the Stokes State Forest and High Point State Park, both in Sussex County in 1954. Deed *et al.* (1959) stated, "Rare summer resident in highlands of Bear Mountain Park." Kuerzi (1931) stated that it probably bred in Putnam County, N.Y., although no definite evidence was found other than adult birds seen and heard. Singing birds were also heard from 1955 to 1960, and a pair was seen in the summer of 1959 at the Audubon Nature Center, Round Hill, Conn., but no evidence of nesting was obtained (*fide* Spofford).

2. On Long Island, it is found mainly in pine barren areas of the eastern half, although it has nested in mixed deciduous woodland, both second-growth and heavy forest. Its distribution there is, however, discontinuous, particularly in recent years, much of the woodland having been destroyed. Breeding has been reported as far east as Hither Hills on the Montauk peninsula and as far west as Lake Ronkonkoma, Suffolk County. McKeever (1941) gave a detailed summary of the bird's breeding status up to that time. He found an isolated group of "several" pairs nesting as far west as Huntington in 1938. His 1941 total for all of Long Island was estimated at "somewhat under 100 pairs." The breeding range on Long Island has shrunk considerably since then because of much clearing of pine land. On July 24, 1953, Elliott heard at least eight singing birds near Speonk.

Egg dates: May 14 to June 22.

Subspecies: The poorly marked race *crymophila*, breeding in Newfoundland, and reported collected several times in our area, is but a slight variant of *H. g. faxoni* and is not recognized here. Some breeding specimens from Newfoundland almost match those taken at the same season from the adjacent mainland. The alleged color differences do not hold in a large series. Moreover, Griscom and Snyder (1955) state, "It is now well known that all *Hylocichla* thrushes collected three or four decades ago are subject to post-mortem color changes. As a result, no information can be given about ... *crymophila*. . . , barely identifiable in fresh condition. Breeding series from Newfoundland are inseparable from New England series; nor can transients be picked out."

SWAINSON'S THRUSH (*Hylocichla ustulata*)*

Range: Nearctic species, the race *swainsoni* breeds south to the Berkshires, Catskills, and Poconos; farther south in higher mountains to West Virginia; formerly in Maryland.

Status: Common to very common migrant; occasionally reported as an abundant nocturnal migrant, especially in fall.

Occurrence and maxima: Swainson's Thrush, or Olive-backed Thrush as it was formerly called, is perhaps the most numerous member of the genus in our area.

Maxima: *Spring*—200, Central Park, May 11, 1914 (Helmuth), very early for so many; 90, Far Rockaway, May 23, 1957. *Fall*—abundant nocturnal migrant—2000, Far Rockaway, Sept. 7, 1953, hardly any seen the following morning; 1000, same locality, Sept. 20, 1952, about 150 observed the next day (Bull). The foregoing estimates of these nocturnal migrants were based on calling birds flying overhead—chiefly between 8:00 and 11:00 P.M.

Extreme dates: *Spring*—Apr. 27 to June 11; casual to June 21, 1951, singing bird, Roselle Park, N.J. (Fables). There are *no* local April specimens in the large A.M.N.H. series. *Fall*—casual, Central Park, Aug. 5, 1957 (Carleton, Messing, and Post); Aug. 22 (specimen) to Nov. 6 (specimen) and Nov. 10 (possibly later). Rare before mid-May and after early June, and before mid-September and after October.

Remarks: This species winters from southern Mexico to northern Argentina, and no winter specimens, to my knowledge, have been reported from the southern United States. Since 1950, there have been about a half-dozen sight reports of this species in December and early January from the New York City region, nearly all by reliable and experienced observers and, in several instances, by three or more people. While some, or all, of these observations may be correct, in the absence of a specimen so far north of its winter range, it seems advisable to reject them. In so difficult a group, a specimen is needed to establish a winter record.

Subspecies: The poorly marked race *clarescens*, breeding in Newfoundland and Nova Scotia, is of doubtful valid status. I am unable to find any significant differences, sufficient for recognition of this form either by measurements or color characters. Godfrey (1959) does not recognize

340

clarescens, stating that much individual variation occurs. According to Burleigh and Peters (1948), this race is paler than the wide-ranging *swainsoni*, which is the opposite of what one would expect in a humid area, where nearly all Newfoundland subspecies are darker than their mainland representatives.

GRAY-CHEEKED THRUSH (*Hylocichla minima*)*

Range: Nearctic and northeastern Palearctic species, the nominate race breeding south to eastern Quebec and Newfoundland; the race *bicknelli* breeding south to the summits of Mount Greylock in the Berkshires and Slide Mountain in the Catskills.

Status: Fairly common to common migrant; more numerous in fall, when reported as a nocturnal migrant in larger numbers.

Occurrence and maxima: The Gray-cheeked Thrush is much less numerous than the preceding species in our area.

Maxima: *Spring*—50, Central Park, May 20, 1924. *Fall*—300, Far Rockaway, Sept. 20, 1952 (nocturnal migration), only 20 or so observed the following morning (Bull); see discussion under Swainson's Thrush.

Extreme dates: *Spring*—May 1 to June 7 and 12. *Fall*—Aug. 25 and 31 to Nov. 8. Collected, Ossining, Nov. 21, 1922 (Brandreth), A.M.N.H.; one picked up dead at Far Rockaway, Nov. 28, 1961 (Bull), A.M.N.H. Rare before mid-May, and before mid-September and after October. Casual at the Brooklyn Botanic Garden, Dec. 16, 1910 (collector unknown), A.M.N.H., previously unpublished. All of these specimens are of the nominate race. Sight reports in April, before late August, and several in winter remain unconfirmed and are considered unsatisfactory; see discussion under previous species. Sight reports of *H. m. bicknelli* are also unsatisfactory.

Subspecies: Many specimens collected and banded locally prove that nominate *minima* is more numerous. Beals and Nichols (1940), worked out the relative abundance of the two subspecies in our area. During an eight-year period (1932–39) at Elmhurst, L.I., a total of 378 individuals of this species were banded and identified subspecifically. A number of others (intermediates) could not be identified because of overlap in measurements. This survey indicated that the race *bicknelli* was considerably less numerous than nominate *minima*. This is logical when it is realized that the breeding range of *H. m. bicknelli* is much more restricted than that of nominate *minima*.

The following Table, adapted from Beals and Nichols (*op. cit.*), indicates comparative abundance and extent of migration of the two forms.

341

	H. m. minima		*H. m. bicknelli*	
	NO.	DATE	NO.	DATE
Total banded	237		141	
Total banded (spring)	76		24	
Total banded (fall)	161		117	
Max. per day (spring)	11	May 21	5	May 27
Max. per day (fall)	29	Sept. 29	9	Oct. 3
Extreme dates (spring)		May 7 to May 31		May 11 to May 27
Extreme dates (fall)		Sept. 10 to Oct. 19		Sept. 7 to Oct. 14

One *bicknelli* was banded as late as Nov. 8, 1936

The Table indicates that both races were more numerous during the fall migration; that nominate *minima* was more numerous at both seasons; and that the extent of the migration period was approximately the same for each subspecies.

Wallace (1939), in his extensive monograph on *H. m. bicknelli*, indicates that, on the basis of collected specimens taken locally, the extreme dates for *bicknelli* agree pretty much with the extreme dates listed above under the banding summary. Wallace identified specimens ranging from May 12 to 22, and Sept. 17 to Oct. 15, all taken in the New York City area.

He also found that both subspecies exhibit post-mortem color differences (as is true with other species of this genus) and that two color phases are present in each race.

VEERY (*Hylocichla fuscescens*)*B

Range: Nearctic species, the nominate race breeding south to the coastal plain of central New Jersey and Long Island, and in the mountains to northern Georgia.

Status: Common to very common migrant; occasionally abundant nocturnal migrant in fall. Widespread breeder, but very local on the coastal plain.

Migration: The Veery fluctuates in numbers—some years only a few are seen, in others considerable numbers.

Maxima: *Spring*—25, Central Park, May 5, 1950. *Fall*—occasional, or perhaps a regular abundant nocturnal migrant—as Cruickshank (1942) rightly said, "Singularly, the species is seldom recorded in any numbers at this season during the day." This is illustrated by the following: Far Rockaway—150, Sept. 1, 1953; 500, Sept. 3, 1949; 700, Sept. 10, 1946 (on all occasions, flying over at night; very few seen the following day, Bull); 75, Sheepshead Bay, Sept. 22, 1953 (heard flying over between 6:00 and

7 : 00 A.M., "only one remained later," Alperin); 29 struck the Fire Island lighthouse, Sept. 30, 1883 (*fide* Dutcher), a notably late fall.

Extreme dates: Apr. 20 to Oct. 3 (specimen), Oct. 11, and 16. Rare before May and after September. There are no April specimens from our area in the American Museum series. Earlier spring and later fall dates than those listed above are not substantiated by specimens and are considered unsatisfactory.

Breeding: The Veery nests on or near the ground in moist rich woodland. It is especially plentiful on the mainland—11 pairs nested on a 40-acre tract at Grassy Sprain, Westchester County, summer of 1941 (Hickey). Rare and local on the south shore of Long Island, but breeds east to Massapequa, at least, and in the center of the island between Yaphank and Manorville (since 1958). Raynor (1959) stated, however, that Veeries have been regular but local breeders in swampy woodland along the south shore near Oakdale and Carman's River since the mid-1950s, and a nest was found at Calverton on the Peconic River in 1958. He attributed their spread to an increase in shrubs and trees along the borders of formerly open marshes and ponds, thus altering the habitat to become favorable for breeding. According to Fables (1955), it breeds on the coast of New Jersey, "as far south as Turkey Swamp, Monmouth County" (*fide* Black).

Egg dates: May 19 to July 6.

Subspecies: Nominate *fuscescens* has been discussed above. The races *fuliginosa* and *salicicola* have probably occurred in our area, as the former (breeding in southern Quebec and Newfoundland) has been taken in Massachusetts, Maryland, and Virginia, and the latter (breeding south and east to southern Ontario and northern Ohio) has been collected in New Jersey (outside our area). Fresh material is necessary from both the breeding grounds, as well as migrants, of all three subspecies for critical color determination, as older specimens have faded and/or "foxed" considerably. Only random collecting will prove the undoubted occurrence of *H. f. fuliginosa* and *H. f. salicicola* in our region.

Godfrey (1959) considers *fuliginosa* a very poor race with much variation occurring. He states that there are two color phases—(*a*) "tawny," (*b*) "darker reddish brown." "Identification of migrants . . . should be attempted with extreme caution." But Griscom and Snyder (1955) would recognize *fuliginosa* as a "good" race.

EASTERN BLUEBIRD (*Sialia sialis*)*B

Range: Primarily an eastern Nearctic species, but ranging in the mountains to Nicaragua. The nominate race occurs in our area.

Status: Uncommon spring migrant; common to very common, occasionally abundant fall migrant. Regular and fairly common to locally common in winter, chiefly inland. Local and generally uncommon to rare breeder.

Migration: Depending on weather conditions, this species arrives from late February to mid-March; in fall it usually departs by late November. The Eastern Bluebird is usually uncommon to rare on the coast, and ordinarily much more numerous inland. However, there was a big flight on Long Island during the autumn of 1944: 500, Long Beach, Oct. 26 (Komorowski); 400, Orient, Nov. 5 (Latham); 50, Prospect Park, Nov. 12. These numbers are exceptional, however, as this species is ordinarily quite rare on western Long Island at any time of year.

Winter: This species is subject to winter killing, both in the south and locally after heavy snow and ice storms. However, there have been severe winters in the past and Bluebirds have survived and recovered after a series of mild winters. Winter flocks subsist largely on the fruits of various berry-bearing shrubs and vines. Notable winter concentrations: 50 each at Oyster Bay, Jan. 2, 1921, Easthampton, Jan. 1, 1946, and Orient, Jan. 4, 1947; 200, Rye, Feb. 12, 1934 (Drescher).

Breeding: The Eastern Bluebird was formerly more numerous as a breeding species over much of its range, but because of depredations by Starlings and House Sparrows it has greatly decreased in recent years. Removal of dead trees and stubs has also been a serious factor in its decline. It breeds most frequently around farms and orchards, also in and near open woodland. It is our only hole-nesting thrush, building in tree cavities, and is very fond of bird boxes, chiefly in rural areas.

The following recent high-breeding density, quite unusual in our area and especially so nowadays, is due to the intensive efforts and foresight of Stiles Thomas, who erected many boxes in 1960 within the northwestern portion of Bergen County, N.J. In a north–south direction between Mahwah and Waldwick (distance about six miles) and in an east–west direction between Saddle River and Franklin Lakes (also about six miles), he reported that out of 42 boxes used by Bluebirds, 28 had successful nestings.

Egg dates: March 29 to July 18.

WHEATEAR (*Oenanthe oenanthe*)*

Casual: Holarctic species, the race *leucorhoa* breeds south to northern Quebec and Labrador. Migrates across the Atlantic Ocean to Europe and then south through western Europe. Winters in tropical western Africa. Recorded casually or accidentally along the Atlantic coast from New Brunswick to Long Island and New Jersey; also Bermuda and Cuba.

In our area there are seven or eight occurrences, all from Long Island, except one. There are three specimens—all in the A.M.N.H. collection:

Adult female taken on Long Island, fall of 1863 (Elliot collection), No. 1236; two adult females collected at Jamaica in 1885 (Akhurst), Nos. 439561 and 439562. The five sight reports are: one with a flock of 50 Snow Buntings, Montauk, Dec. 27, 1936 (Breslau); one in breeding plumage, Moriches Inlet, June 3, 1941 (Wilcox); one on the New York Central railroad embankment, Peekskill, N.Y., Nov. 15, 1947 (Cruickshank); one at Glen Oaks Village, Queens County, Sept. 9–16, 1951 (G. Scheffel and many other observers); one at Orient, May 13, 1956 (Latham). The 1951 individual was observed on the ground, on large boulders, and even on rooftops.

This interesting bird is the only one of a large group of Old World thrushes that has colonized arctic North America, breeding from Alaska to Greenland, but retracing its ancestral route to its winter quarters in tropical Africa, migrating with the western Palearctic population.

TOWNSEND'S SOLITAIRE (*Myadestes townsendi*)*

Accidental: A western Nearctic species, the nominate race breeds east to southwestern South Dakota and western Nebraska. Winters east to western Kansas. Casual east to Ontario, Michigan, and Ohio; accidental in southeastern New York and New Brunswick.

One local record: Adult male collected at Kings Park, L.I., Nov. 25, 1905 (J. A. Weber), A.M.N.H. No. 377452.

Just north of our area, a specimen was collected at Amenia, Dutchess County, N.Y., March 16, 1953, A.M.N.H. No. 707718.

GNATCATCHERS, KINGLETS: SYLVIIDAE

BLUE-GRAY GNATCATCHER (*Poplioptila caerulea*)*B

Range: Southern Nearctic and northern Neotropical species, the nominate race breeding northeast to west-central New York and northern New Jersey; rarely to southeastern New York (mainland) and southwestern Connecticut; casually to Rhode Island and Massachusetts (1961), and Long Island (1963).

Status: Uncommon, but regular migrant chiefly in spring, occasionally fairly common. Usually rare in fall. Numbers fluctuate markedly from year to year. Has greatly increased since 1947. Local breeder in New Jersey, rare elsewhere.

Change in status: 1. *Migration*—Griscom (1923) considered the Blue-gray Gnatcatcher a generally rare migrant. Cruickshank (1942) stated

"... three to twelve birds are recorded every year, and on one occasion as many as three were seen in one day in Bronx County." Usually only one to three are seen in a day by one observer, except during flight years.

During the spring of 1947, there occurred the greatest flight of Gnatcatchers on record in our area. It is estimated that at least 150 individuals were reported, observers in Prospect Park alone estimating 55 birds in April and May. Other exceptional years were 1954 and 1956, with at least 80 reported in the former year and about 60 in the latter.

Daily maxima: *Spring* (1947)—9 Bronx Park, Apr. 18; 8, Prospect Park, Apr. 26. *Fall*—5, Central Park, Aug. 24, 1953; 6, Montauk Point, Sept. 18, 1948.

Extreme dates: *Spring*—Apr. 3 (Apr. 18, earliest specimen) to late May. *Summer*—vagrants through June and July. *Fall*—early August (Oct. 25, latest specimen) to Nov. 27 (at least 8 November reports); Dec. 5, 1910, Stamford (Howes). Rare before mid-April and after mid-October.

2. *Breeding:* (see map)—This species prefers to nest in second-growth areas in and near wet woods, often along streams and rivers.

Cruickshank (1942) knew of only one breeding record, that of a nesting pair at Swartswood Lake, Sussex County, in 1928. No further breeding was reported until 1946, when adults were seen feeding young near Red Bank, Monmouth County, June 16 (Black, Seeley *et al.*).

During the year of the great spring flight of 1947, this species bred in northern New Jersey in Essex and Somerset counties (at least four nests). From that year until 1954, another four nests were found, including two in Morris County. By the next big flight year of 1954, this bird had spread northward and eastward to New York State and Connecticut, with one nest reported from Rockland County, and one from Fairfield County. Altogether, seven breeding sites were located in 1954. From that time on, breeding Gnatcatchers have been found regularly, but locally in central New Jersey, most often in parts of Somerset and Hunterdon counties, in the latter section along the larger streams (especially the Musconetcong River) of northern Hunterdon County (Abraitys, *in litt.*), with an estimate there of ten breeding pairs in 1960.

Summary of breeding: A minimum of 45 breeding localities has been reported since 1947, the great majority in New Jersey. Increased numbers of breeding pairs were reported after the big spring flights of 1947 and 1954. The center of concentration appears to be in the vicinity of the Delaware and Musconetcong rivers and their tributaries, and in the drainage of the Raritan and Passaic rivers. To date (1962), the species has been reported as definitely nesting in all the northern New Jersey counties, except Passaic, Bergen*, and Hudson (see map), and probably has bred in the first two. In southern New York, it is unreported as a breeding species from Westchester and Bronx counties, and on Staten Island. To

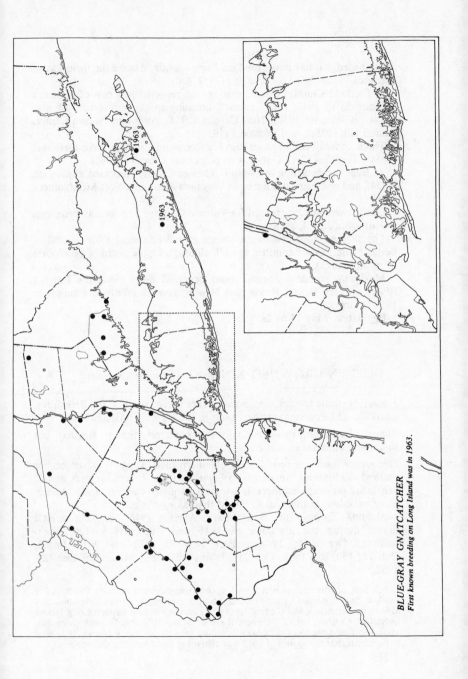

BLUE-GRAY GNATCATCHER
First known breeding on Long Island was in 1963.

my knowledge it has never bred on Long Island*, despite the inclusion of that area in the A.O.U. *Check-list* (1957:450).

In Fairfield County, Conn., nesting was reported just east of our area at Fairfield in 1947. First reported breeding inside our section of that county at Weston (1950), New Canaan (1954), Audubon Nature Center, Round Hill (1958), and Westport (1959).

Three known breeding localities for Rockland County: Lake DeForest (1954); Tomkins Cove (1960); two pairs near Congers (1962).

At least two breeding localities in Orange County: reported at Goshen (1954), and one pair built a nest at Weyant's Pond near Fort Montgomery (1962).

One known breeding record for Putnam County: pair feeding fledglings at Patterson, July 4, 1958.

The species should be found breeding in Westchester County, and in Bergen* and Passaic counties as well, although I have heard of no reports from those areas.

Maximum breeding density: Four occupied nests along the Raritan River, between Bound Brook and New Brunswick (about five miles) in 1954 (Murray).

Egg dates: May 15 to 28.

GOLDEN-CROWNED KINGLET (*Regulus satrapa*)*

Range: Nearctic species, the nominate race breeds south to the Berkshires, Catskills, and Poconos; farther south in the higher Appalachians.

Status: Uncommon to occasionally very common migrant. Regular, but in varying numbers in winter.

Occurrence and maxima: The Golden-crowned Kinglet is subject to marked fluctuations, appearing in great numbers in certain years and in very small numbers in others. In winter it frequents conifers, and is usually more prevalent at this season inland than along the coast.

Maxima: *Spring*—100, Bronx Park, Apr. 3, 1946. *Fall*—big coastal flights during the autumns of 1946 and 1950 (1946—150, East-hampton, Oct. 5; 100, Prospect Park, Nov. 10; 1950—100, Jones Beach, Oct. 15; 150, Riis Park, Oct. 21). *Winter*—85, Bear Mountain, Dec. 27, 1952.

* A nest of this species was found at the Greenbrook Sanctuary in 1963, for the first known Bergen County record. Most interesting, and indicating consider-able range extension, was the finding of two nests in 1963 on eastern Long Island in Suffolk County, both by Gilbert Raynor: Manorville and Noyack (near Sag Harbor). These are the first *known* breeding records for Long Island. It is well to point out that the spring of 1963 was also a big flight year for this species.

348

Extreme dates: Sept. 8 to May 19. Casual, Little Neck, L.I., Aug. 15, 1953 (J. Terres). Rare before late September and after April.

Remarks: By some authorities, considered conspecific with the Palearctic *R. regulus*, the Goldcrest.

RUBY-CROWNED KINGLET (*Regulus calendula*)*

Range: Nearctic species, the nominate race breeds south to the northern portions of New York (very rarely) and Maine. Winters north to Maryland; more rarely to New Jersey, New York, and New England.

Status: Fairly common to very common migrant. Rare in winter.

Occurrence and maxima: The Ruby-crowned Kinglet arrives earlier in fall and departs later in spring than the Golden-crowned Kinglet. Its numbers are more stable than the latter and less subject to wide fluctuations.

Maxima: *Spring*—100, Bronx Park, Apr. 17, 1944; big flight during the late spring of 1950 (50, Mill Neck, Apr. 30; 60, Prospect Park, May 5; 50, Woodmere Woods, May 6). *Fall*—100, Sandy Hook, Oct. 10, 1953; 100, same area, Nov. 11, 1952. *Winter*—rare, but regular, usually frequenting conifer groves or dense thickets near the coast. Ordinarily only one to three individuals are reported in winter, but with more feeding stations in recent years, this species has become less rare. For example, on eight Christmas counts during the winter of 1953–54, not less than 19 were reported, mostly at feeders—eight of these in the Port Chester area.

Extreme dates: Aug. 22, 25, and 29 to May 27 and 30. Rare before mid-September and after early May. Arrives in early April and departs by late November.

WAGTAILS, PIPITS: MOTACILLIDAE

WATER PIPIT (*Anthus spinoletta*)*

Range: Holarctic species, the race *rubescens* breeds south to Newfoundland; rarely to southern Quebec (Gaspé peninsula); probably on the summit of Mount Katahdin, Maine. Winters chiefly along the coast north to Maryland; rarely and irregularly to New Jersey and Long Island.

Status: Variously uncommon to fairly common spring migrant, common to occasionally abundant fall migrant; usually rare and irregular in winter, rarely in flocks. Erratic and unpredictable, numbers fluctuating widely, although of regular occurrence in fall along the coast.

349

Occurrence and maxima: The Water Pipit inhabits open country, where it frequents plowed fields, burned-over meadows, beaches, short-grass lake and river shores, and waste areas (fill). Regular and most numerous during October and the first half of November; otherwise erratic in its occurrence. Usually arrives in mid-March and departs in late November.

Maxima: *Fall*—500, Hicksville, Oct. 16, 1935; 600, Orient, Oct. 29, 1944; 500, Idlewild, Nov. 2, 1946. *Spring*—rarely to 50 a day, usually in very small numbers. *Winter*—125, Idlewild, Dec. 25, 1934 (Sedwitz); 50, Croton Point, Jan. 22, 1949 (Darrow). These winter numbers are, however, very unusual—particularly the latter.

Extreme dates: Aug. 13, 16, 19, and various later August dates (Sept. 9, earliest specimen) to May 18, 23, 29, and 30. Rare before late September and after mid-April.

WAXWINGS: BOMBYCILLIDAE

BOHEMIAN WAXWING *(Bombycilla garrulus)**

Very rare winter visitant: Palearctic and western Nearctic species, the race *pallidiceps* breeding southeast to northern Manitoba. Winters south and east to southern Ontario, Quebec, and Nova Scotia; very rarely or casually to Ohio, Pennsylvania, New York, Massachusetts, and Connecticut.

Of nine specimens reported taken in our area only four are extant: two collected in Rockland County (year not stated) by J. G. Bell, A.M.N.H. Nos. 36641 and 36642; according to Giraud (1844), "several" were shot on Long Island in 1830 and 1832; one taken at "Crow Hill," Brooklyn, in 1851 (*fide* Eaton); one, Cold Spring, Putnam County, winter of 1870 (Mearns); adult, North Haven, Suffolk County, April 18, 1889 (W. Lucas), A.M.N.H. No. 66001; previously unpublished—a male collected on Fisher's Island, Feb. 17, 1918 (Latham), in his collection; one, Westchester County, February 1924 (*fide* Chapman).

The following sight reports from Westchester County were made by competent and experienced observers and are probably correct: Mount Kisco, Nov. 23, 1924 (Janvrin, Tucker *et al.*); Chappaqua, March 14, 1936 (Pangburn); two in a flock of Cedar Waxwings, Rye, Jan. 5, 1942 (Oboiko); six in a flock of at least 350 Cedar Waxwings (big flight year for the latter species), Pleasantville, Apr. 18, 1947 (Helmuth). Individuals seen at Cos Cob, Conn., March 14, 1962 (Roesler) and Flemington Junction, N.J., Apr. 10–22, 1962 (Abraitys *et al.*) were also with Cedar Waxwings, providing direct comparison. That year (1962) was a notable flight year for Bohemian Waxwings in eastern Canada and in northern New

York and New England. The last two reports are the only reliable ones from our section of Connecticut and New Jersey.

Other sight reports in recent years were either unconfirmed or unreliable —inexperienced observers believing that any waxwing having a "lot" of white in the wings "must" be a Bohemian.

Extreme dates: Nov. 23 to Apr. 18 (specimen) and Apr. 22.

CEDAR WAXWING (*Bombycilla cedrorum*)*B

Range: Nearctic species, in the east breeding south in the mountains to northern Georgia, but along the coastal plain only to Virginia, rarely to North Carolina.

Status: Regular, common to abundant early fall migrant (chiefly August and September), especially along the coast, occasionally in large numbers. At times erratic and unpredictable, sometimes rare or absent in winter, at other times in large flocks. Usually uncommon in early spring, but regular in late May and even early June. Common breeder in rural country, chiefly inland, but relatively uncommon on Long Island, and rare breeder on the coastal plain.

Migration and winter: The Cedar Waxwing is one of those species whose movements and numbers are erratic and variable. Most numerous and regular in early fall. Large fall coastal migration in 1953, at least 1000, Far Rockaway, Sept. 8, many birds flying overhead. Big flight, winter and early spring of 1946–47, as follows: 225, Smithtown, Dec. 23; 300, Easthampton, Dec. 28; 1000, Ramsey, all February; 350, Pleasantville, April 18; 100, Mattituck, April 20; also 50, Bronx Park, May 14, 1927. Notably late spring migrant, usually arriving in mid-May.

Breeding: This species and the American Goldfinch are among our latest breeding birds, occasionally nesting well into August or even September. The Cedar Waxwing nests either in coniferous or deciduous trees in open, usually second-growth, woodland, also in the vicinity of orchards and often near water. It is generally rare and local as a breeder over much of the coastal plain.

Egg dates: June 12 to Sept. 15.

SHRIKES: LANIIDAE

NORTHERN SHRIKE (*Lanius excubitor*)*

Range: Holarctic species, the race *borealis* breeding south to northern Ontario, northern Quebec, and central Labrador.

Status: Rare to uncommon, irregular winter visitant, chiefly on the coast. Least rare at Montauk, where seen nearly every winter.

Occurrence and maxima: This species, while most often observed along the outer coast perched on telephone wires, fences, and exposed branches of trees and bushes, is also seen in similar situations at inland localities in open fields and pastures, and in agricultural areas. Occasional individuals visit feeding stations, particularly during flight years.

As with many other boreal birds, the Northern Shrike occurs in marked southward incursions in late fall and winter. These incursions, coming at irregular intervals, presumably are due to a scarcity of food within the bird's "normal" winter range farther north.

Three of the biggest flights in recent years took place during the winters of 1926–27, 1930–31, and 1949–50. A total of 20, 26, and 18 individuals, respectively, were reported during those years on the Christmas counts within the New York City area. On Dec. 11, 1949, Darrow observed eight in the Montauk area, and on Jan. 1, 1950, Helmuth saw at least 12 between Easthampton and Montauk Point. The barred, brownish immatures outnumber the adults in our region.

Extreme dates: Oct. 21 (specimen) to Apr. 28 (specimens), the latter date representing two immatures collected at Orient Point in 1927 by Roy Latham. Note that 1927 was a flight year. While it is possible that sight reports on earlier fall and later spring dates than those listed above may be correct, the chance of confusion with the Loggerhead Shrike is likely (see discussion under that species). Rare before November and after March.

LOGGERHEAD SHRIKE (*Lanius ludovicianus*)*B

Range: See under Remarks.

Status: Rare to uncommon, but regular fall coastal migrant. Occasional winter visitant. Very rare and irregular in spring. Rare inland, even in fall. One old breeding record and one very recently.

Occurrence and maxima: The Loggerhead Shrike inhabits open country and is seen most often on telephone wires, fence posts, and exposed perches of bushes and small trees. Observers visiting the outer coast from late August to early October have the best chance to see this species, as the majority of fall occurrences are primarily coastal.

Maxima: Usually from two to six individuals are reported each fall, but occasionally more are seen; 1936 (11) and 1954 (14). The largest number reported in one day per locality is four, several times in late August and September, the principal months of occurrence.

"Extreme" fall dates: Aug. 2, 4, 9, and 13 to Nov. 28. Rare before late August and after early November.

Winter: This species winters north to Maryland; rare farther north. Six winter specimens taken locally, of which three are extant—Ossining, Jan. 23, 1884 (Fisher), M.C.Z.; Baldwin, Jan. 12, 1910 (A. O. Heinrich), A.M.N.H.; Orient, Jan. 10, 1952 (Latham), A.M.N.H. The published report of one collected Jan. 26, 1930, at Queen's Village, L.I., was actually a Northern Shrike (see Nichols, Auk, 59: 593, 1942). There are a number of winter sight reports for our area, particularly in recent years.

Spring: Only one known local specimen—Passaic, March 31, 1928 (G. S. Yerbury), A.M.N.H. Because of its wintering occasionally, spring arrival dates are difficult to determine. Most spring observations are during late March and early April. There are about two dozen apparently reliable April reports, but the species is casual in May, apparently only four local occurrences: May 3, 10, 26, and 28.

Many winter and early spring observations are undoubtedly correct, but there are others that are highly questionable. Confusion with the Northern Shrike is most likely in March and early April, when both species may be present, the adults then resembling each other very closely. Beginners are cautioned about the difficulty in identification of shrikes at this time (see Zimmerman, 1955).

Remarks: Nearctic species. According to the A.O.U. *Check-list* (1957: 463), the race *migrans* breeds from the southern portions of Ontario, Quebec, and New Brunswick south to Virginia and Maryland. Actually it is extremely rare and local, or even absent as a breeder over much of its northeastern range. Except for Miller's brief statement (1931), "The race [*migrans*] is of irregular and local distribution in ... the north Atlantic states, New England, ..." its rarity as a breeder here has not been emphasized, and may account for its local rarity as a migrant. Although fairly common in western and central New York (Eaton, 1914), and northwestern Pennsylvania (Todd, 1940), it is uncommon in New Hampshire and Vermont (Forbush, 1929), uncommon and local but regular in Maine (Palmer, 1949), and uncommon to rare and local in Maryland (Stewart and Robbins, 1958). Griscom and Snyder (1955) list four old breeding records and two recent ones for Massachusetts. In Connecticut, Sage *et al.* (1913) give only one old nesting record. It is unreported as a breeder in Rhode Island and New Jersey.

In our area there are two known breeding records: A fledgling collected at Ossining, Westchester County, June 16, 1877 (Fisher). And see below.

An explanation for its rare and very local breeding distribution over a large portion of the northeast is probably an *ecological* one. The Loggerhead Shrike breeds regularly and not uncommonly in portions of western and central New York, northwestern Pennsylvania, and Ohio—nesting most often in open areas where trees and bushes with *thorns* are prevalent. Numerous instances of this habitat preference may be found in Eaton (1914), Forbush (1929), Todd (1940), and Trautman (1940). These authorities state that the Loggerhead Shrike frequents agricultural areas and open fields. The preferred nesting sites are situated in dense bushes and trees of the genus *Crataegus* (hawthorns) and in osage oranges—the latter often planted in hedgerows. Both of these plants are equipped with *thorns*. upon which shrikes impale their prey as well as on barbed-wire fences.

It may be significant that the plant growths named above are scarce in our area, and in much of the eastern portions of the region outlined above and, as a result, shrikes are correspondingly scarce as breeders.

A letter received from Mrs. Martha Earl states the following: "On June 6, 1963 at Blooming Grove [Orange County], I found a pair of Loggerhead Shrikes at their nest, the latter containing 5 young birds. The nest was situated in a *thorn* bush in an old pasture—well populated with *thorn* bushes and other growth." (Italics mine.) This is further proof of the species' preference for *thorn* vegetation during the breeding season.

It is suggested that the great majority of our fall migrants along the coast are birds arriving chiefly from the west or northwest. Their rarity in spring in our area is probably accounted for by the very few breeding birds to the north and east of us. Most of the spring migrants quite likely travel west of the Appalachians.

STARLINGS: STURNIDAE

STARLING (*Sturnus vulgaris*)*B

Introduced: Palearctic species, widely introduced and established in various parts of the world. The nominate race occurs in our area.

First introduced into Central Park in 1890, the Starling spread north and northeast, "arriving" at Ossining, N.Y., in 1899 and Stamford, Conn., in 1900. During the latter year it also spread south to Plainfield, N.J. By 1907, it had pushed west into New Jersey as far as Morristown, and east on Long Island all the way to Orient. It was first reported on Gardiner's Island in 1908, but not until 1911 at Easthampton. By 1912 the Starling was firmly established and abundant "around" New York City (Griscom, 1923).

By the early 1930s this species was reported in enormous winter roosts, often associating with native icterids, as at the famous "blackbird" roost in the Raritan River marshes; or chiefly by themselves as in Manhattan at the 125th street viaduct near the Hudson River. Estimates of up to 150,000 Starlings were reported from each of these areas coming into roost on winter evenings during the 1940s and 1950s. It is now one of our most numerous birds.

354

Unfortunately, like those other two introduced pests—the Rock Dove and House Sparrow—this species is here to stay and, among other things, has the obnoxious habit of driving off desirable native birds, such as Flickers and Bluebirds, ganging up on them and usurping their nesting holes. It is a nuisance around buildings and in the suburbs, being both dirty and noisy.

That the Starling is partially migratory is proved by banding. It was found that certain individuals were resident, while others moved about more in some years and less in other years (see Kessel, 1953, and Davis, 1960).

Egg dates: March 18 to Aug. 20.

VIREOS: VIREONIDAE

WHITE-EYED VIREO (*Vireo griseus*)*B

Range: Primarily a southeastern Nearctic species, the race *noveboracensis* breeds north to southeastern New York, southern Connecticut, and Rhode Island.

Status: Rare migrant. Local and uncommon breeder at lower elevations; rare to absent elsewhere.

Migration: This species is rare on migration. Usually only one or two a season are seen by an active observer away from breeding areas. This is not surprising as the White-eyed Vireo is near its northern limits in our area. It has also decreased considerably since before 1900 over much of the northeast, and has not shown any signs of increasing.

On Sept. 30, 1883—a very late fall—20 individuals struck the Fire Island lighthouse (Dutcher, Auk, 1: 174, 1884). Nothing remotely resembling this number has been reported in our area before or since.

Extreme dates: Apr. 15 and 17 to Oct. 13 and 17. Rare before May and after September.

Breeding: The White-eyed Vireo breeds in lowland areas, nesting in thickets in and near swamps; more rarely in thickets in drier country as on hillsides and along rural roads.

Egg dates: May 17 to July 5.

BELL'S VIREO (*Vireo bellii*)

Accidental: Primarily a southwestern Nearctic species, the nominate race breeding east to central Indiana. Wanders eastward in migration to New Hampshire (specimen), New York, and New Jersey (specimen).

There is one definite record of Bell's Vireo for our area: an individual mist-netted, banded, and color-photographed, at Tiana Beach, near Shinnecock Inlet, Sept. 25, 1959 (Wilcox). The identification from the photograph was confirmed as this species by Eisenmann and the writer with direct comparison of skins.

During the same fall another individual, a female, was mist-netted and collected at Island Beach, N.J. (just south of our area) on Sept. 15, A.M.N.H. No. 708118 (see Jehl, Wilson Bull., 72: 404, 1960). This is the only definite record for New Jersey.

Although sight reports for our area have been published (Cruickshank 1942: 364, and Carleton, 1958: 38), there is an element of doubt concerning the correctness of these observations. Four spring observations within six years in Central and Prospect Parks—all in May—are very surprising for a western species. While the song of Bell's Vireo is very different from that of the White-eyed Vireo, as far as I know *none* of the individuals seen was heard singing. These two species do, however, resemble each other in appearance. Immature Solitary Vireos are somewhat similar also, which is borne out by comparing museum specimens. In fact, one very detailed description of a supposed Bell's Vireo mentions a resemblance to a pale washed-out Solitary Vireo, except for its smaller size. Observers should bear in mind that the Bell's Vireo has a *pale* bill; the Solitary Vireo, a *dark* bill. In addition, both White-eyed and Solitary Vireos possess *conspicuous* eye-rings; Bell's Vireo does not, merely a trace. It would be most desirable to procure a spring specimen in order to establish actual occurrence at that season. I know of no confirmed spring records in the eastern United States along the Atlantic coast.

YELLOW-THROATED VIREO (*Vireo flavifrons*)*B

Range: An eastern species, breeding from Maine to Florida.

Status: Rare to uncommon migrant. Fairly common breeder north of the coastal plain, but rare on Long Island.

Migration: This species is rare as a migrant, seldom reported away from nesting areas, although regular in spring in Central and Prospect Parks. Ordinarily only one or two are reported at a locality in a day—6, Central Park, May 11, 1913 (Helmuth), appears to be the maximum.

Extreme dates: Apr. 25 to Oct. 5 (specimen), Oct. 9 and 12. Rare before May and after September. Unconfirmed reports of birds seen during the first three weeks of April are probably Pine Warblers.

Breeding: The Yellow-throated Vireo breeds in rich open woods and swampy woodland, less frequently in large shade trees in rural areas. Like the White-eyed and Warbling Vireos, it too has decreased considerably since about 1900, although more widespread than those species in suitable habitat.

Egg dates: May 21 to June 23.

SOLITARY VIREO (*Vireo solitarius*)*B

Range: Nearctic species, breeding from central Canada—in the west through the higher mountains south to Honduras and El Salvador; in the east to the mountains of South Carolina and Georgia, and casually at lower elevations to eastern Massachusetts and southern Connecticut. The nominate race breeds in our area.

Status: Uncommon to fairly common migrant, but numbers fluctuate from time to time. Very rare and local breeder.

Migration: The Solitary Vireo, or Blue-headed Vireo as it was formerly called is, after the Red-eyed Vireo, our most common member of the genus during migration, although not occurring in anywhere near the large numbers of that species. It is quite variable in numbers—some seasons only a few are observed. It is the earliest vireo to arrive in spring and the last to depart in fall.

Maxima: *Spring*—12, Prospect Park, May 6, 1950. *Fall*—20, Prospect Park, Oct. 15, 1947 (Alperin and Jacobson).

Extreme dates: *Spring*—Apr. 8 to June 2. *Fall*—Sept. 1 to Nov. 26 and Dec. 1. Rare before late April, after mid-May, before late September, and after October.

Breeding: Solitary Vireos nest in mixed coniferous-deciduous woodland at higher elevations. This species has been definitely reported as breeding in our area on only three occasions. In northern New Jersey a nest under construction was observed near the Delaware Water Gap, Warren County, summer of 1930 (Urner), and another nest being built near Wawayanda Mountain, Sussex County, summer of 1946 (Wolfarth). The Solitary Vireo probably breeds elsewhere in the highlands of northern New Jersey, as well as at higher elevations in Orange, Rockland, and Putnam counties in New York—all in places where birds either have been heard singing or have been seen during the nesting season, but positive breeding evidence from these areas is lacking. Breeding pairs have been found just outside our area at Bethel, Conn. (southeast of Danbury); at three localities in Dutchess County, N.Y.; and in the Pocono Mountains, Penn.

Most unusual is the following breeding record only a short distance from Long Island Sound: Nest and three eggs taken on a hillside containing mountain laurel and mixed deciduous growth near Stamford, Fairfield County, Conn., June 8, 1897 (C. L. Howes), the nest and eggs in the Bruce Museum, Greenwich (see Howes, 1928); nest and eggs were recently verified as of this species at the American Museum. (See also Black-throated Blue Warbler.)

Egg date: June 8.

Remarks: The Solitary Vireo winters north to central North Carolina. There are two reports at this season in our area: singing bird carefully studied, Eatontown, N.J., Feb. 16, 1954 (Ryan); adult of the nominate race picked up dead near Great Neck, L.I., Dec. 27, 1958 (Heck and Yeaton), specimen, A.M.N.H. No. 763822. This individual may have been present for some time, as it was found in a frozen condition. There had been a severe cold wave the previous week.

RED-EYED VIREO (*Vireo olivaceus*)*B

Range: Nearctic species (absent in the southwest), breeding from central Canada to Florida and Texas.

Status: Common to very common migrant. Common and widely distributed breeder.

Migration: In our area the Red-eyed Vireo easily outnumbers all the other species of this genus combined.

Maxima: *Spring*—50, Prospect Park, May 17, 1945. *Fall*—91 hit the Fire Island light, Sept. 23, 1887 (*fide* Dutcher); 39 struck the tower at the Westhampton Air Force Base, Oct. 5, 1954.

Extreme dates: Casual on Apr. 18, 19, 22, and 24 (most of these storm-driven); May 1 to Nov. 10 and 14. Rare before mid-May and after mid-October.

Breeding: This species breeds in deciduous woodland and in large shade trees in city parks and suburban areas. Some idea of its abundance at this season may be gained by the following: 11 nesting pairs, Inwood Hill Park, Manhattan, summer of 1937 (Karsch); 18 nesting pairs on a 40-acre tract, Grassy Sprain, Westchester County, summer of 1941 (Hickey).

Egg dates: May 24 to July 27.

PHILADELPHIA VIREO (*Vireo philadelphicus*)*

Range: Nearctic species, breeding south to the southern portions of Ontario and Quebec, northern New Hampshire, and central Maine, but uncommon and local in the eastern section of its range. Migrates in spring chiefly through the Mississippi Valley; in fall also east of the Appalachians.

Status: Rare to uncommon but regular fall migrant; very rare in spring.

Occurrence and maxima: The Philadelphia Vireo is seldom seen locally except by the more active and experienced observers. September is the

358

principal month of occurrence, but it is unusual to see more than one or two in a day. Ten of the 12 fall specimens from our area were collected in that month, the others in October. Three of these were taken at East-hampton in 1914 by Helmuth within two days—two, Sept. 9, the other, Sept. 10.

Maxima: 5, Easthampton area, Sept. 20, 1940; 5, Gilgo Beach to Point Lookout, Sept. 20, 1958. Maximum total per year—9 (1940); 8 (1958).

Just to the south of us at Island Beach, N.J., an intensive mist-netting operation in 1960 captured nine individuals each on Sept. 11 and 21, and a total of 36 from Aug. 29 to Sept. 28. This is another instance where more individuals of a species are trapped in a day in one locality than would be observed by most active birdwatchers during a season.

Extreme dates: *Fall*—Aug. 20 (several later), Sept. 4 (earliest specimen) to Oct. 20 (specimen) and Oct. 23. *Spring*—May 11 to June 1. Rare before September, after early October, and before late May.

This species is very rare in spring. Griscom (1923) listed one spring specimen (May 21), but gave neither the year, locality, nor the whereabouts of the specimen. Griscom (1929) reported that during the spring of 1927, no fewer than six were observed, three of these in Central Park. Since that year only 17 reliable spring reports are at hand, never more than two per spring.

Most spring dates are late in May. It has appeared as early as the eleventh (three different years).

Remarks: Early May and early August sight reports are rejected due to possible confusion with yellowish Warbling Vireos and Tennessee Warblers. The Philadelphia Vireo is very rare in August and these early dates have not been substantiated in recent years despite many more observers.

WARBLING VIREO (*Vireo gilvus*)*B

Range: Nearctic species, widespread and fairly numerous in the west, but local and rare to uncommon in the east. The nominate race breeds in our area.

Status: Rare and little-known migrant. Local and uncommon breeder, but rare to absent on the coastal plain. Formerly more numerous.

Migration: Dull colored and generally unobtrusive in habits, the Warbling Vireo is easily overlooked in the tops of tall shade trees or hidden amongst their dense foliage, unless heard singing. Away from breeding areas this species is rarely reported, although one or two are observed each season, especially in spring. The maxima appear to be only three, Prospect Park, May 12, 1943.

Extreme dates: Apr. 28 to Oct. 15. Regular the first week in May; rare after September.

359

Breeding: The Warbling Vireo breeds chiefly in rural areas in parks, villages, and along streams and lakes in open country. The nest is placed in tall shade trees, preferably elms; also locusts, willows, sycamores, and maples. This is another of the vireos that has decreased considerably since about 1900. It has probably suffered more than the others and decreased further because of widespread spraying of diseased elms. Many of the elms, now dead or dying, formerly supported nesting pairs.

Probably the best place to see Warbling Vireos locally is at Van Cortlandt Park, where they have bred for decades. Here three or more pairs nest in the vicinity of the swamp. In 1962 six pairs were reported breeding in this general vicinity (Heath and Zupan).

The Warbling Vireo is a very local breeder on the south shore of Long Island, where it has been reported as definitely nesting only at Idlewild, Queens County and Easthampton, Suffolk County. The species is rare over the entire coastal plain and may go unreported for several years at a time even during migration.

Egg dates: May 18 to June 17.

WOOD WARBLERS: PARULIDAE

BLACK AND WHITE WARBLER (*Mniotilta varia*)*B

Range: Primarily an eastern Nearctic species, breeding south to central Georgia.

Status: Common to very common migrant, especially in spring. Uncommon to fairly common breeder.

Migration: The Black and White Warbler is one of our more numerous warblers during migration.

Maxima: *Spring*—150, Englewood, May 3, 1924; 100, Woodmere Woods, May 6, 1950. *Fall*—one of the first warblers to move south, regularly by the first week in August—25, Far Rockaway, Aug. 14, 1954.

Extreme dates: Apr. 10 to Nov. 14. Rare before late April and after mid-October.

Breeding: Nests on the ground chiefly in deciduous woodland, but rare and local on the coastal plain. Like most of our breeding warblers, it is most prevalent in rich woods on the mainland.

Egg dates: May 11 to June 28.

Remarks: This species winters north to central Florida; casually to coastal South Carolina. Accidental at this season in Massachusetts and on Long Island.

One was seen in swampy woods at Baldwin, L.I., Jan. 2, 1950 (Pettit).

360

PROTHONOTARY WARBLER (*Protonotaria citrea*)*B

Range: Southeastern Nearctic species, breeds north to southern Ontario (rarely), central New York (locally), and northern New Jersey (locally); once in southwestern Connecticut (1946).

Status: Rare but regular spring migrant; very rare in fall. Local breeder in New Jersey.

Migration: This species is restricted to wet areas even during migration and may be looked for along wooded ponds and streams, and particularly in swamps. Most reports are during the last week in April and in May. There are four spring specimens for our area.

Ordinarily only one or two individuals are observed each spring, but in recent years more have been reported, indicating a slight increase since 1942: 6 (1944) from Apr. 30 to May 14, with 2 on May 4; 7 (1954) from Apr. 19 to May 23. A specimen was collected at Morristown, N.J., June 14, 1888 (L. P. Scherrer), adult male, U.S.N.M. collection.

It is very rare in fall, scarcely over a dozen reports. An adult male hit the Montauk Point lighthouse, Aug. 27, 1886 (Dutcher collection), A.M.N.H.

Extreme dates: Apr. 19 and 24 to Sept. 12 and 22. On the last date, one was reported in 1933 at Bayside, L.I. (McBride). Levine saw two on the coast in 1960 on Sept. 22, one at Jones Beach, the other at Gilgo Beach, perhaps the result of hurricane Donna on Sept. 12.

Breeding (see map p. 363): The Prothonotary Warbler is the only member of this family within our area that is a hole-nester. It is an inhabitant of swampy woods or streams, often nesting in dead trees or stumps standing in water.

In our area this species has been reported breeding only in northern New Jersey, on seven occasions: In 1924, 1925, and 1928 possibly the same pair nested in Morris County along the Passaic River, in the vicinity of Pine Brook; in 1925 the birds were discovered building a nest in an old tin can on May 9 (Van Deusen). No further breeding reported in our area for twenty years.

Since 1942 this species has been reported breeding in four "new" localities: A pair bred in the Great Swamp, Morris County, summer of 1948 (Wolfarth); one pair was found nesting in Sussex County along the Wallkill River near Franklin, summer of 1952 (Jehl); on July 9, 1954, a pair was observed feeding young in Bergen County on the Hackensack River at River Vale (Armitt); another pair nested in Somerset County along the Raritan River in the vicinity of Bound Brook in 1955 (Boyajian).

Increased reports in recent years of singing males in "suitable" localities during June are not proof of breeding.

Egg dates: No data.

Remarks: Just outside our area a nest was found in a dead stub in a small swamp near Fairfield, Conn., during the summer of 1946 (Burdsall and Spofford). This is the first known breeding record for Connecticut, in fact the first east of the Hudson River.

SWAINSON'S WARBLER (*Limnothlypis swainsonii*)

Accidental: A southeastern Nearctic species, breeding north to western West Virginia and southeastern Maryland.

A sight report of this well-marked warbler was made at Prospect Park, May 5, 1950 (Carleton and Helmuth), and the next day (Alperin and Grant). This observation by four experienced people is probably correct (see Alperin, Wilson Bull., 64: 109–110, 1952).

WORM-EATING WARBLER (*Helmitheros vermivorus*)*B

Range: A southeastern Nearctic species, breeding north to central New York, northern Connecticut, and western Massachusetts (rarely).

Status: Usually a rare migrant; at long intervals uncommon to fairly common. Locally common breeder north of the coastal plain, but very rare on Long Island.

Migration: The Worm-eating Warbler, generally a rare bird away from breeding areas, is especially scarce on the south shore of Long Island. Even in spring one to three are the usual number seen in a day, even by the active observer.

Maxima: *Spring*—5, Central Park, Apr. 27, 1925 (Griscom *et al.*), early for so many; big flight, spring of 1950 (12, Prospect Park, May 5; 5, Forest Park and 10, Van Cortlandt Park, May 6). Much rarer in *Fall*—5 struck the Fire Island lighthouse, Aug. 28, 1898 (*fide* Dutcher).

Extreme dates: April 10, 1949, Far Rockaway (Bull) and Apr. 14 to Oct. 11 and Oct. 17, 1954, Prospect Park (Carleton). Rare before late April and after mid-September.

Breeding: This species nests on the ground among dense undergrowth on heavily wooded hillsides, chiefly along river valleys. In such country it often breeds with Hooded Warblers. At least ten pairs were present on a 40-acre tract at Grassy Sprain, Westchester County, in the summer of 1941 (Hickey).

Egg dates: May 21 to June 22.

GOLDEN-WINGED WARBLER (*Vermivora chrysoptera*)*B

Range: An eastern Nearctic species, having a fairly wide east-west breeding range (southeastern Manitoba and the eastern portions of Minnesota

362

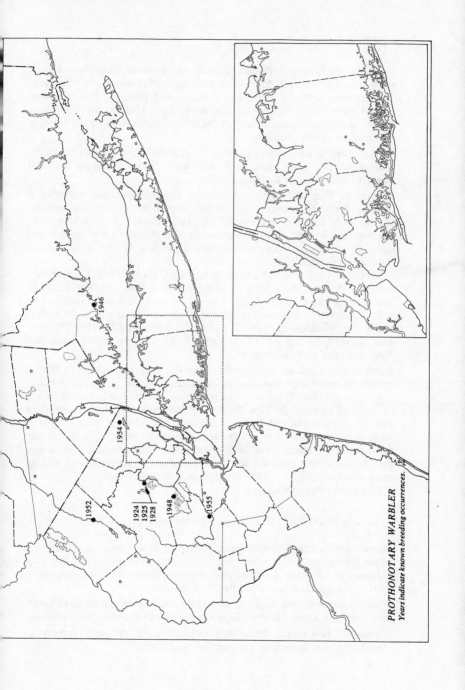

PROTHONOTARY WARBLER
Years indicate known breeding occurrences.

and Iowa to Massachusetts and Connecticut), but with a relatively narrow north–south breeding distribution (in the west from Wisconsin, Michigan, and southern Ontario to Illinois, Indiana, and Ohio; in the east from central New York and Massachusetts to Pennsylvania, northern New Jersey, and Connecticut; locally at higher elevations to northern Georgia and western South Carolina).

Status: Rare to uncommon but regular migrant, especially scarce on the coastal plain of Long Island and New Jersey. Fairly common but local breeder in the interior highlands.

Migration: The Golden-winged Warbler is a rare migrant wherever it does not breed, except on occasion when large flights of warblers are passing through, and even then more than two individuals are seldom seen together. It is rare any time on the coastal plain, though a few are reported annually in August. Most often reported the first half of May and the latter half of August.

Maxima: 12, Bronx to Van Cortlandt Parks, May 8, 1943 (Komorowski *et al.*); 7, Prospect Park, May 10, 1946 (Jacobson, Soll, and Whelan), both very unusual numbers; 2 appear to be the maxima per locality in fall.

Extreme dates: *Spring*—Apr. 26 and 30 (specimen), several sight reports between these dates, to May 30; casual, Idlewild, June 11, 1938 (Mayer). *Fall*—July 12, 17, and 22 to Oct. 6 and 10. Rare before May, in June and July, and after early September.

Breeding: This species is generally more northern and occurs at higher elevations than the Blue-winged Warbler, but the habitat is similar. Consequently, during the breeding season, it is restricted to the highlands of northern and western New Jersey, and Rockland, Orange, and Putnam counties in New York. But even in some of these areas, it is quite local in its distribution. Elsewhere, it has been reported breeding only in extreme northwestern Westchester County, where it is rare; one pair observed in the vicinity of Anthony's Nose, summer of 1928 (Kuerzi); and nesting once near Ossining in 1885 (Fisher), female feeding young.

Egg dates: May 18 to June 27.

BLUE-WINGED WARBLER (*Vermivora pinus*)*B

Range: An eastern Nearctic species, breeding distribution similar to that of the Golden-winged Warbler, but not ranging as far north and breeding at lower elevations including the coastal plain south to Delaware. Generally more numerous and less local than that species.

Status: Uncommon to fairly common migrant; occasionally more numerous. Common breeder in lowland areas, but rare to absent in the highlands.

Migration: This species fluctuates in numbers and is variously common to uncommon, but sometimes rare on the coastal plain.

Maxima: *Spring*—25, Prospect Park, May 4, 1953. *Fall*—10, Bronx Park, Aug. 18, 1946.

Extreme dates: Apr. 15, 19, 22, and 25 to Oct. 6 and 12. Casual, Central Park, Oct. 30, 1950 (Cobb). A male was caught by a cat near Cross River, N.Y., Nov. 29, 1958 (Grierson), specimen preserved. Rare before May and after early September.

Breeding: The Blue-winged Warbler nests on the ground in scrubby overgrown fields, second-growth woodland in clearings and at the edge, and particularly where brier thickets occur, usually in the drier portions, but occasionally in moist areas. It has increased and spread eastward and northward into Golden-winged Warbler range throughout the northeast within the past 40 years or so.

Egg dates: May 11 to June 24.

Remarks: This species winters in Middle America. Accidental at this season in New York: one picked up dead, in fresh condition, Bronx Botanical Garden, Jan. 6, 1900 (Britton). Specimen examined by Chapman, but apparently not in the American Museum collection. This bird was originally seen on Dec. 10, 1899, and again several days later.

HYBRID WARBLERS (*Vermivora chrysoptera x pinus*)

"BREWSTER'S" WARBLER (*V. "leucobronchialis"*)*

"LAWRENCE'S" WARBLER (*V. "lawrencei"*)*

The New York City area is excellent for the study of these hybrid warblers. Wherever the two parental species, the Golden-winged and Blue-winged Warblers, breed commonly "together," as in portions of northern New Jersey, southeastern New York, and southwestern Connecticut, the hybrid forms may be expected to occur in limited numbers. "Lawrence's" Warbler, believed to express the action of recessive genes, is much rarer than the hybrid form known as "Brewster's" Warbler. For the serious student interested in the intricate relationship of these forms the article by Parkes (1951) is recommended (see also Berger, 1958). Recent studies by Short (1962) indicate a very complex situation with more work to be done.

Very briefly, and at the risk of oversimplification, one type of "Brewster's" Warbler *may* result from a first-generation (F_1) cross between a "pure" Golden-wing and Blue-wing mating. "Lawrence's" Warbler, however, *may* result either from a second-generation (F_2) cross, or a back-cross from a subsequent generation. It should be emphasized here that the word "may" is important. As a result of back-crosses with the progeny of the parental species, many birds are not definitely determinable as "typical" hybrid forms. There are some specimens that cannot with certainty be assigned to either hybrid "type." Variation in color of the underparts, upperparts, and wing-bars, and extent of throat patch and eye stripe are considerable, and should be noted by observers whenever possible.

Migration: Both hybrid forms are very rare in migration, particularly "Lawrence's" Warbler. Many experienced observers have never seen "Lawrence's" even in our area. As it is almost impossible to distinguish "genuine" migrants from breeding birds throughout most of our region the following data are restricted to the New York City parks and the coastal plain where they either do not nest or do so very rarely. In a 36-year period (1927-62), "Brewster's" outnumbered "Lawrence's" by more than three to one, 39 of the former and only 12 of the latter being reported. All but two of the 12 "Lawrence's" Warblers occurred in spring, and only seven of the 39 "Brewster's" Warblers occurred in fall.

Extreme dates: "Brewster's" Warbler—Apr. 28 to Sept. 29. "Lawrence's" Warbler—May 1 to Sept. 10.

Breeding: In order to understand the relative status of the hybrid forms, it is necessary to ascertain the extent of their breeding ranges and compare distribution with the parental species.

"Brewster's" Warbler is the hybrid form in predominantly Golden-wing country, the latter being the prevalent species north of the main breeding range of the Blue-wing, as in parts of central New York State and Massachusetts, although the Blue-winged Warbler has penetrated into Golden-winged Warbler areas since the late 1940s, especially in the vicinity of Ithaca, N.Y., and very likely elsewhere; "Brewster's" Warbler occurs also at higher elevations farther south, as in the Litchfield Hills of northwestern Connecticut, the foothills of the Poconos (Pennsylvania), Catskills and Shawangunks (New York), and in our area in the highlands of northern New Jersey, and the highlands of Orange, Rockland, and Putnam counties, N.Y.

"Lawrence's" Warbler is the hybrid form in predominantly Blue-wing country, just south of Golden-wing range, and at lower elevations adjacent to the latter. Its breeding range is much more localized than that of "Brewster's" Warbler, being restricted "almost entirely" in and near the New York City area, which explains why nearly all known *breeding* "Lawrence's" Warblers have been found in this area (see below).

The accompanying map indicates *known* breeding localities for both hybrid forms, most of which have been published. There are undoubtedly others, especially in those counties that are "blank" on the map, i.e. Warren, Orange, and Putnam. The "heart" of the hybrid country appears to be in the contiguous counties of Passaic, Bergen, Rockland, and Westchester, where the most varied terrain and elevation render it "suitable" for all four forms to occur.

The following definite matings have been reported (see map and legend for symbols): 1—Welch Lake and West Nyack (Rockland County), and

366

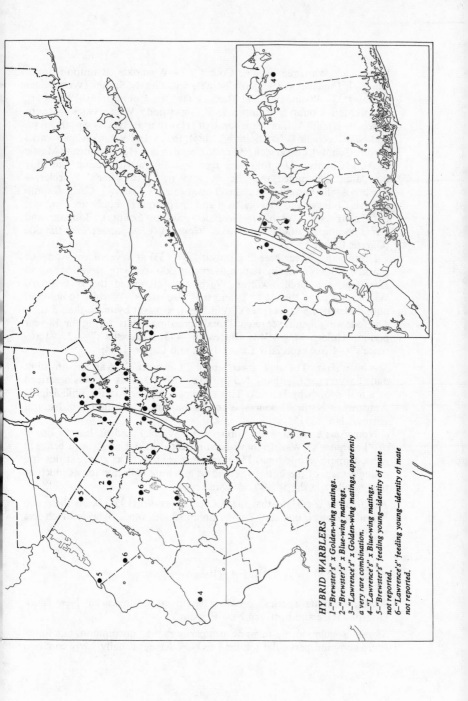

HYBRID WARBLERS

1—"Brewster's" x Golden-wing matings.
2—"Brewster's" x Blue-wing matings.
3—"Lawrence's" x Golden-wing matings, apparently
a very rare combination.
4—"Lawrence's" x Blue-wing matings.
5—"Brewster's" feeding young—identity of mate
not reported.
6—"Lawrence's" feeding young—identity of mate
not reported.

Wyanokie=Wanaque (Passaic County); 2—Wyanokie; Boonton (Morris County), Englewood (Bergen County), and Grassy Sprain (Westchester County); 3—Wyanokie; and Ramsey (Bergen County); 4—Pattenburg (Hunterdon County), Ramsey and Englewood; West Nyack; Mount Kisco, Briarcliff Manor, Scarborough, Hawthorne, Grassy Sprain, Rye, and New Rochelle (Westchester County), Bronx and Van Cortlandt Parks (Bronx County), Greenwich (Fairfield County), and Huntington and Mastic (Suffolk County). The following represent adults with young, but only one parent determined, the other not known; 5 ("Brewster's" Warbler)—Flatbrookville and Wawayanda Plateau (Sussex County), Great Swamp (Morris County), and Croton River and Chappaqua (Westchester County); 6 ("Lawrence's" Warbler)—Greendell (Sussex County), Boonton and Great Swamp; Little Falls (Passaic County), Chappaqua; and Bayside (Queens County).

During an 18-year breeding census (1916–33) at Wyanokie=Wanaque (Passaic County), a hilly region averaging 500 feet with elevations up to 1200 feet, the Golden-winged Warbler outnumbered the Blue-winged Warbler by more than 2 to 1, and the "Brewster's" Warbler (dominant) outnumbered the "Lawrence's" Warbler (recessive) by more than 3 to 1. The following figures represent "total" breeding adults during the 18-year period: Golden-wing—948; Blue-wing—445; "Brewster's"—13; "Lawrence's"—4 (see especially Eaton, 1934, and Carter, 1944).

Specimen data: The type specimen of "Lawrence's" Warbler, an adult male, taken near Chatham, N.J., in May 1874 (Dickinson), was described as a new species by Herrick. This specimen, formerly in the Philadelphia Academy of Natural Sciences, is now in the American Museum of Natural History, No. 325755.

Numerous specimens of "Brewster's" Warbler and at least a dozen of "Lawrence's" Warbler have been collected in our area, both being in great demand at one time. They were eagerly sought as great rarities and a single male of the latter was sold to a private collector for as much as thirty dollars in the 1880s (*fide* Dutcher).

Remarks: It is curious that the A.O.U. *Check-list* (1957) ómits these two hybrid warblers, but at the same time includes other hybrids much less known.

TENNESSEE WARBLER (*Vermivora peregrina*)*

Range: Nearctic species, breeding south to northeastern New York (Adirondacks) and northern New England.

Status: Regular spring migrant, ordinarily rare to uncommon, but sometimes common particularly inland in New Jersey; usually fairly common to common fall migrant. Numbers fluctuate yearly at both seasons. Formerly (prior to 1900) very rare.

Occurrence and maxima: The Tennessee Warbler, although much more numerous since about 1900, is still variable in numbers, especially in spring. During some years very few are reported, in others considerable numbers are observed.

Maxima: *Spring*—35, Morristown, May 14, 1956; 30, Inwood Hill Park, May 16, 1960; 9, Northport, May 17, 1957. *Fall*—12, Prospect Park, Aug. 19, 1944; 30, including 12 in one tree, Far Rockaway, Sept. 7, 1949 (Bull); 35, Central Park, Sept. 20, 1958; on the rainy night of Sept. 22, 1953, 42 struck the Empire State Building; 15, Idlewild, Oct. 8, 1949.

Extreme dates: *Spring*—Apr. 29 to June 3 and 9. *Fall*—Aug. 9 to Oct. 25 and 29. Rare before mid-May and after early October.

Remarks: This species winters from southern Mexico to northern South America. Accidental at this season in Tennessee (specimen) and New York (specimen).

An adult present at the feeding station of Mrs. B. D. Wood, Ossining, N.Y., Jan. 12, 1955, was picked up dead there on Jan. 30 and presented to the American Museum, No. 788901 (see Bull, Auk, 78: 263–264, 1961).

ORANGE-CROWNED WARBLER (*Vermivora celata*)*

Range: Primarily a western Nearctic species, the nominate race breeds east to Hudson Bay (rarely in northwestern Quebec), and south to central Ontario. Winters (in the east) along the south Atlantic coast north to South Carolina; very rarely to Massachusetts (two specimens). Migrates in spring through the Mississippi Valley; in fall mainly over the spring route, but regularly in small numbers along the Atlantic coast.

Status: Rare but regular fall migrant; very rare spring migrant. Usually rare winter visitant, but occasionally uncommon at this season.

Occurrence: The Orange-crowned Warbler, although unobtrusive, inconspicuous, and occasionally difficult to identify, is nevertheless not as scarce as some observers believe. In October, when more are seen than at any other time (except on three occasions in winter), they are less arboreal in habits and often are found low down in scrub growth, especially in old, overgrown, weedy fields adjacent to woodland. In spring, when they are much rarer, they are more often observed in the taller trees, but usually only during the biggest warbler waves. The species occasionally sings at this time. Even in fall, it is rare enough that I have seen reports of no more than two or three individuals at any one time.

There are no known local winter specimens, but a number of sight reports at this season exist, including three individuals at Tod's Neck,

Conn., Jan. 6, 1935 (Cruickshank), one of which was singing. Three other individuals remained throughout the winter: New Dorp, Staten Island, Dec. 25, 1923, to March 8, 1924 (several observers); one at the Ritchie feeder, Baldwin, L.I., Jan. 1 to March 3, 1947 (numerous observers), which fed mostly on suet; one at the Conn feeder, Bound Brook, N.J., Nov. 26, 1947, to end of February 1948 (many observers), feeding on both suet and bayberries.

Most unusual was a group of six, plus two more in the Shark River area, N.J., Jan. 2, 1955 (Jehl, Kunklè et al.). They were with Myrtle Warblers. The same week 11 were observed on the Cape May Christmas count—evidently a flight to the coast.

On Long Island, three spent the entire month of January 1955 at a Babylon feeder (M. A. Nichols), one of these wintering through. Total for our area during the winter of 1955—at least 11—the biggest number on record!

Extreme dates: Sept. 7 and 10 (earliest specimen—Sept. 28) to May 13 (specimen), several later dates, and May 22. Rare before October. Fall departure and spring arrival are difficult to determine because of wintering birds.

Specimen data: There are at least 11 specimens taken locally, three of these in spring: Hoboken, N.J., May 1865 (Galbraith); adult male, Highland Falls, N.Y., May 13, 1875 (Mearns); adult male, West Orange, N.J., Apr. 14, 1898 (Van Rensselaer), A.M.N.H. collection.

Remarks: August reports are considered unsatisfactory and have been rejected because of confusion with dull or immature Yellow Warblers and Tennessee Warblers. Several years ago, a warbler thought to be an Orange-crowned was picked up dead in late August and brought to a Linnaean Society meeting for identification. It was variously identified by those present as: Orange-crowned, Nashville, Tennessee, Yellow, and female Wilson's Warblers. Upon examination of skins, it was correctly identified as an immature Yellow Warbler.

NASHVILLE WARBLER (*Vermivora ruficapilla*)*B

Range: Nearctic species, the nominate race breeds south to the mountains of Maryland; rarely to the lowlands of southern Connecticut and Rhode Island.

Status: Uncommon to fairly common migrant. Local breeder in the highlands of New Jersey; probably elsewhere.

Migration: As with certain other species, the Nashville Warbler fluctuates in numbers from time to time, is uncommon some years, fairly common in others.

370

Maxima: 5, Central Park, Apr. 28, 1924; 9, Far Rockaway, May 3, 1953; 12, Far Rockaway, May 13, 1956. A report of over 100 in one spring day at one locality in recent years was not confirmed. No fall maxima available.

Extreme dates: *Spring*—Apr. 20 to June 6, 13, and 16 (specimens on two latter dates). *Fall*—3, Inwood Hill Park, July 24, 1953 (Carleton); July 31 and Aug. 7 to Nov. 30 and Dec. 4. Usually arrives in late April. Rare after May, before late August, and after mid-October.

Breeding: The Nashville Warbler nests on the ground in two distinct habitats—in moist boggy areas, and in dry second-growth clearings—often in stands of gray birch. Despite statements to the contrary, I have heard of no positive proof of breeding in our area, except locally in the higher portions of northern New Jersey (but not at Englewood, as stated in the A.O.U. *Check-list*, 1957: 484). Probably breeds in similar country in Rockland, Orange, and Putnam counties, N.Y., but there is no definite evidence concerning those areas. Although reported breeding at Bridgeport (Sage *et al.*, 1913), there is no nesting evidence for our portion of Connecticut. In Westchester County, a pair was observed at Poundridge Reservation, summer of 1947 (Wheeler), but no nest or young was found. A current detailed breeding survey would be most desirable.

Egg dates: May 18 to June 17.

Remarks: The Nashville Warbler winters from southern Texas to Guatemala; rarely in southern Florida. Casual north to Massachusetts (specimen).

Two sight reports of winter individuals in the New York City region are believed correct: Van Cortlandt Park, Dec. 16, 1917 to Jan. 9, 1918 (Chubb and Miller); near Short Hills, N.J., Dec. 27, 1953 (Chalif).

PARULA WARBLER (*Parula americana*)*B

Range: An eastern Nearctic species, breeding from southern Canada to Texas and Florida.

Status: Common to very common migrant, especially in spring. Very rare breeder.

Migration: This species is one of our most numerous spring warblers.

Maxima: *Spring*—200, Prospect Park, May 14, 1950; 150, Morristown, N.J., May 17, 1958. *Fall*—34 hit the tower at the Westhampton Air Force Base, Oct. 5, 1954.

Extreme dates: Casual, Huntington, L.I., Apr. 1, 1944 (McKeever); Apr. 9, 13, and various other dates during this month; summer vagrants; mid-August to Nov. 10, 18, and 26. Casual, Rye, Dec. 9, 1951 (Cruickshank). Rare before late April; before late August, and after early October.

Breeding: In the northeast, at least, the Parula Warbler is primarily a coastal species, always more numerous on or near the coast. It has greatly decreased in the New York City area since the early 1930s with the almost total disappearance of its nesting material, the *Usnea* lichen or "beard moss." Formerly locally common on eastern Long Island, it bred where this plant was prevalent, as in swampy areas of the pine barrens, and to a lesser extent in moist or even dry deciduous woodland. Cruickshank (1942) stated that there were six pairs on Gardiner's Island in 1924, but none since 1932; 20 pairs on Shelter Island in 1925, none since 1934. The last breeding on Long Island that he noted was at Hither Hills in 1938.

Inland it has always been rare and local. According to Sage *et al.* (1913), it disappeared along with the *Usnea* in southern Connecticut as far back as the early 1900s, and has "entirely" left that area. In New Jersey it formerly bred in the interior bogs of the highlands in the northern and western sections, but there are no recent instances of nesting reported. That it did not nest exclusively among *Usnea* at inland localities, however, is indicated by the fact that several nests were made of grasses, mosses, and shredded bark. Elsewhere inland in New York, it is unreported as a breeding species in Westchester, Putnam, Rockland, and Orange counties.

Since 1942, Parula Warblers have been found definitely breeding only twice, both times on Long Island in Suffolk County: pair feeding four young, Oakdale, July 4, 1946 (Elliott); two nests in swampy woods, Greenport, summer of 1951 (Latham). A pair seen in June 1955, at North Sea, Suffolk County (Latham), may have nested also.

Egg dates: May 17 to June 13.

Remarks: The question that naturally arises is: Why did the *Usnea* lichen disappear? As far as can be ascertained, the reason(s) seem to be unknown. Whether it was due to possible climatic change, disease, or other cause, is uncertain.

YELLOW WARBLER (*Dendroica petechia*)*B

Range: A widespread American species, the race *aestiva* breeding in our area.

Status: Fairly common to common migrant and breeder.

Migration: This species is widespread in migration, occurring from the interior woodlands to the coastal beaches.

Maxima: *Spring*—25, Central Park, May 23, 1954. *Fall*—8, Far Rockaway, Aug. 21, 1955.

Extreme dates: Apr. 19 and 20 (specimen) to Sept. 30 (specimen), Oct. 5 and 11 (specimen). No later sight reports accepted, due to likely confusion with Orange-crowned Warblers (see discussion under that species). Rare before late April and after mid-September.

Breeding: The Yellow Warbler is quite adaptable in its breeding locations. It nests in shrubbery in rural and suburban gardens; in bushes and trees, often in willows along streams, lakes, swamps, and marshes; also in dense thickets of poison ivy and bayberry on coastal sand dunes.

The Urner Club estimated at least 50 breeding pairs at Troy Meadows, June 1, 1947.

Egg dates: May 10 to June 24.

Subspecies: The local breeding race *aestiva* has been discussed. The race *amnicola* breeds from central Alaska southeast to central Ontario, southeastern Quebec, and Newfoundland. It has been taken along the coast from Maine to Virginia and is probably a regular migrant in our area. Parkes (1952) examined nine specimens in the American Museum collection which he referred to this race, five in spring and four in fall, dates ranging from May 16 to 22 and Aug. 21 to Sept. 14. In addition, a specimen determined by A. R. Phillips as *amnicola* was taken at Bedloe's Island, Sept. 30, 1889, also A.M.N.H.

Further collecting may well turn up the Pacific coast race *rubiginosa*, which breeds in Alaska and British Columbia, as this subspecies has been taken in Massachusetts. *D. p. rubiginosa* closely resembles *D. p. amnicola*, and is barely separable from it; if these two forms are "lumped," *rubiginosa* will have to be used, as it is the prior name.

MAGNOLIA WARBLER (*Dendroica magnolia*)*B

Range: Nearctic species, breeding south to the Berkshires, Catskills, and Poconos, and in the higher mountains to Virginia; rarely at high elevations in New Jersey.

Status: Common to very common migrant, especially in spring; occasionally more numerous. Rare, local breeder in northwestern New Jersey.

Migration: The Magnolia Warbler is, at times, one of our most numerous members of this family.

Maxima: *Spring*—70, Prospect Park, May 10, 1948; 45, Englewood, May 18, 1913; a report of 250, Central Park, May 23, 1954 (several observers), is most unusual and undoubtedly involves some duplication. *Fall*—32 struck the Empire State building, Sept. 22, 1953.

Extreme dates: *Spring*—Apr. 27 to June 11; casual, June 23, 1953, Central Park (Skelton). *Fall*—Aug. 4 to Oct. 23, Nov. 2, 6 (specimen), Nov. 11, 20, and 30. Rare before mid-May, after early June, before late August, and after early October.

Breeding: The Magnolia Warbler is confined in the breeding season to the highest portions of the Kittatinny Mountains in northwestern New Jersey. There is no conclusive proof of breeding elsewhere. It breeds in mixed coniferous-deciduous areas in open woodland, where the nest is usually situated in young hemlock or spruce, surrounded by deciduous growth: an adult was observed feeding young on July 4, 1925, at Flatbrookville, Sussex County (J. Kessler); on June 8, 1947, between that locality and near the Delaware Water Gap, Warren County, three singing males and one female were found, but no nests were located; one mated pair was present in a hemlock grove in the Stokes State Forest, Sussex County, June 19, 1955, although no nest or young was observed. It probably nests in this general region occasionally, if not regularly.

Egg dates: No data.

Remarks: This species winters in Middle America and in the Greater Antilles; very rarely in southern Florida; accidental in Virginia (specimen, 1947).

In our area, an individual was carefully studied at Smithtown, L.I., Dec. 28, 1940 (Fischer).

CAPE MAY WARBLER (*Dendroica tigrina*)*

Range: Nearctic species, breeding south to northeastern New York (Adirondacks) and northern New England.

Status: Uncommon to fairly common spring migrant; fairly common fall migrant, often common along the coast. Numbers vary considerably, however, and during some years it may even be rare. Formerly (prior to 1900) very rare.

Occurrence and maxima: The Cape May Warbler is notable for its fluctuations. Some seasons it is fairly numerous, in others it is quite scarce.

Maxima: *Spring*—12, Highland Falls, N.Y., May 6, 1959; 15 (14 males), Far Rockaway, May 16, 1954; during May 1956, Mrs. Dater banded 46 at Ramsey, N.J. *Fall*—on Sept. 3, 1944, 10, Central Park and 12, Seaford, L.I.; 45, Easthampton, Sept. 15, 1946 (Helmuth).

Extreme dates: *Spring*—Apr. 23, 25, and 29 to June 5. *Fall*—Aug. 10 to Nov. 5. Casual, Hewlett, L.I., Dec. 5, 1916 (Bicknell). Rare before mid-May and after this month; rare before late August and after mid-October.

Remarks: This species winters chiefly in the West Indies north to the Bahamas; rare in southern Florida. Accidental at this season in New York (specimen, Dutchess County, 1946).

In our area, a male was well observed at Point Lookout, L.I., Dec. 30, 1956 (Bull and Eisenmann).

BLACK-THROATED BLUE WARBLER (*Dendroica caerulescens*)*B

Range: An eastern Nearctic species, breeding south to northern New Jersey, southeastern New York (mainland), and Connecticut; and at high

374

elevations to the mountains of Georgia and South Carolina. The nominate race occurs in our area.

Status: Variously uncommon to common migrant. Local breeder in the mountains and highlands of the interior.

Migration: As with many other warblers, the numbers of this species fluctuate from time to time and in certain years the Black-throated Blue Warbler is decidedly uncommon.

Maxima: *Spring*—50, Bronx Park, May 6, 1953; 30, Prospect Park, May 10, 1946; during the spring of 1954, there was a big flight—30, Far Rockaway, May 16 (only 1 female); 40, Central Park, May 23. *Fall*—48 struck the Fire Island lighthouse, Oct. 12, 1883, an exceptionally late fall.

Extreme dates: *Spring*—casual, Tobay Pond, Apr. 11, 1955 (Buckley and Post); Apr. 24 to June 12 and 14. *Fall*—Aug. 7 and 11 (specimen) to Nov. 10 (specimen), Nov. 14, and 21; adult male present from Nov. 27 to Dec. 9 (specimen, A.M.N.H.); also Dec. 10 and 11. Rare before and after May, and before late August and after mid-October.

Breeding: The Black-throated Blue Warbler is locally distributed at higher elevations during the breeding season, nesting in mixed deciduous-coniferous woodland, often on hillsides among mountain laurel thickets.

In northern New Jersey it has been found breeding in the Kittatinny Mountains of Sussex and Warren Counties, and in several localities on the Wawayanda Plateau, Sussex County. In 1940 one pair nested at Bowling Green (near Green Pond), Morris County, and two or three pairs at Bloomingdale, Passaic County (see McKeever, 1941). It has also been found in the breeding season in the Wyanokie (= Wanaque) area, Passaic County.

Although Deed *et al.* (1959) do not mention breeding for Rockland County, N.Y., Cruickshank (1942) stated that "in our portion of New York state it is confined as a breeder to the highest sections of northern Rockland County where it is decidedly scarce." Moreover, McKeever (*op. cit.*) listed "six pairs in the Ramapo Mountains" during a breeding survey in 1940, although he did not specify whether they were located in Rockland County or in adjacent Bergen and Passaic counties, N.J.

This species probably nests in Orange County, N.Y., but of this we do not have definite information. However, across the Hudson River in Putnam County, N.Y., Kuerzi (1931) stated, "Black-throated Blue Warblers . . . breed commonly in the higher swamps east of Cold Spring and west of Carmel."

The only other breeding record for our area that I am aware of is in Connecticut—in a very unusual locality: a nest with three eggs was collected near Stamford, Fairfield County, June 8, 1897 (C. L. Howes), in the Bruce Museum, Greenwich. Most extraordinary, the nest and eggs of a Solitary Vireo were taken on the same day in the same general area. Identification of the nest and eggs of both these species was verified at

375

the American Museum. Both of these records were published by Howes (1928).

Egg date: June 8.

Remarks: This species winters in the West Indies. It is accidental at this season in Maryland and Massachusetts (midwinter sight reports).

In our area, an adult male was present at a feeder, Northport, L.I., Dec. 1–31, 1954 (Mudge).

MYRTLE WARBLER (*Dendroica coronata*)*

Range: Nearctic species, the nominate race breeding south to the Poconos, Catskills, and Berkshires; very rarely to the Shawangunk Mountains (1952), just north of our area.

Status: Common to abundant migrant. Variously rare to very common in winter along the coast, depending upon the absence or presence of bayberries; usually much rarer inland at this season.

Migration: The Myrtle Warbler is our most numerous member of the family, on certain days outnumbering all other warblers combined.

Maxima: *Spring*—325, Prospect Park, Apr. 30, 1953; 650, Bronx Park, May 5, 1949. *Fall*—big flight on Oct. 15, 1950: 800, Bronx Park; 1000, Prospect Park.

Extreme dates: Aug. 4, 9, 12, 13, and 19 to June 9, 12, 17, and 22. Rare before September and after mid-May. Inland it usually arrives in mid-April and departs in mid-November.

Winter: The Myrtle Warbler, insectivorous during the warmer months, is able to survive bitter cold weather and snow, provided there is a good winter crop of bayberries.

Maxima: More than 800, Easthampton to Montauk, January and February 1924. Inland this species is ordinarily very rare at this season, but occurs locally wherever bayberry and red cedar are found. Very unusual is a total of 280 reported on the 1952 Rockland County Christmas count.

Remarks: Often considered conspecific with *D. auduboni*, Audubon's Warbler of western North America.

TOWNSEND'S WARBLER (*Dendroica townsendi*)

Accidental: A northwestern Nearctic species, breeding east to northwestern Wyoming. Casual farther east. Accidental in Pennsylvania (specimen).

376

In our area an adult male was found in Prospect Park, May 8, 1947 (Alperin, Carleton, Jacobson, and Sedwitz), and was seen through May 10 (Levine, Whelen, and others). This observation is probably correct (see Jacobson, Auk, 65: 459, 1948).

A 1934 fall report (of a female?) is considered unsatisfactory. The chances of confusion of this species in nonbreeding plumage with those of the Blackburnian and Black-throated Green Warblers in similar plumage are too great. Note also statement of the observer (Proc. Linnaean Soc., N.Y., 47: 128, 1935).

BLACK-THROATED GREEN WARBLER (*Dendroica virens*)*B

Range: An eastern Nearctic species, breeding south to the New York City region, and in the mountains to Georgia; a local race breeds along the coast from Virginia to South Carolina. The nominate race occurs in our area.

Status: Fairly common to very common migrant. Locally common breeder in coniferous woodland inland, but rare to uncommon on the coastal plain.

Migration: The Black-throated Green Warbler is widespread throughout our area and is one of the more numerous warblers on migration.

Maxima: *Spring*—50, Bronx Park, May 6, 1953; 75, Prospect Park, May 10, 1946. *Fall*—22, Easthampton, Oct. 6, 1946; 17, Pelham Bay Park, Oct. 20, 1927, an unusually late fall.

Extreme dates: Casual, Hempstead, March 30, 1935 (Mayer); Apr. 4 and 9 to late November, Dec. 1, 3, 7, and 9. Rare before late April and after October.

Breeding: Inland this species breeds primarily in hemlock groves, among stands of Scotch pines where planted extensively around reservoirs, and occasionally in white pines. On Long Island, it is scattered through the pine barrens, wherever pitch pines grow to large size, but has decreased there in recent years because of much cutting and burning. It is somewhat surprising to find it also nesting in deciduous woodland in western Suffolk County where, in the West Hills area in 1946, Elliott found "several" nesting pairs in oak-hickory woodland. It has also been observed recently at this season in similar situations nearby.

Egg dates: May 12 to June 21.

Remarks: This species winters north to southern Florida. It is accidental at this season in New York, where an individual was found chiefly in a pine grove at Van Cortlandt Park from Nov. 8, 1943, to Jan. 1, 1944 (Komorowski *et al.*). It was observed feeding on pine aphid eggs much of the time.

CERULEAN WARBLER (*Dendroica cerulea*)*B

Range: A southeastern Nearctic species, breeding northeast to extreme southern Ontario, west-central New York, eastern Pennsylvania, northern New Jersey (since 1947), western and northern Maryland, and western Delaware, with an isolated population in southeastern New York (Dutchess County). The species is essentially inland in distribution, generally avoiding the Atlantic coastal plain, even in migration, and is extremely local throughout the easternmost portions of its range.

Status: Very rare to rare spring migrant. Casual or very rare in fall. Rare and local breeder in New Jersey, but increasing in recent years.

Migration: The Cerulean Warbler is one of the rarest warblers that occurs with any degree of regularity within our region. Away from its breeding grounds the most active observer is fortunate if he sees one or two in ten years. Carleton (1958) listed only three reports each of spring migrants within the previous 20 years for Central and Prospect Parks, the two best watched and most thoroughly worked areas anywhere. Only since 1951 have migrants been reported annually and then but a single individual in four of those years. The maximum reported was during 1955, when *six* were seen from May 5 to 15.

May is the principal month of occurrence with about 50 reports. In fall, there are but 13, eight of these in September.

Extreme dates: *Spring*—Apr. 27, 28, 29, and May 5 to May 30 and June 5. *Fall*—July 24 and Aug. 3 to Sept. 25 (specimen), several later dates, and Oct. 5. Rare before mid-May.

Specimen data: There are six known local specimens: Brooklyn, "many years ago" (see Griscom, 1923); Highland Falls, N.Y., May 17, 1875 (Mearns); Boonton, N.J., Sept. 1, 1887 (Judd); Palisades Park, N.J., Sept. 25, 1909 (Weber); adult male, Orient, L.I., May 16, 1942 (Latham), specimen in his collection; another adult male, Mount Sinai, L.I., May 17, 1947 (Murphy), specimen in A.M.N.H. collection.

Change in breeding status (see map): In 1922 the Cerulean Warbler was discovered breeding immediately north of our limits in Dutchess County, chiefly along wooded streams flowing into the Hudson River. Three or more "colonies" were subsequently found near Poughkeepsie, Hyde Park Rhinebeck, and Tivoli, the last near the Columbia County line (see Griscom, 1933, for details). This isolated population, situated along the east bank of the Hudson, is separated from the "main" breeding population in Pennsylvania by at least 100 miles. These Dutchess County "colonies" are still flourishing, according to reports. It is possible that these breeding birds originated not from the south, but from the west, perhaps by way of the Delaware and Susquehanna valleys, and were derived from breeding stock located in western New York and/or Pennsylvania.

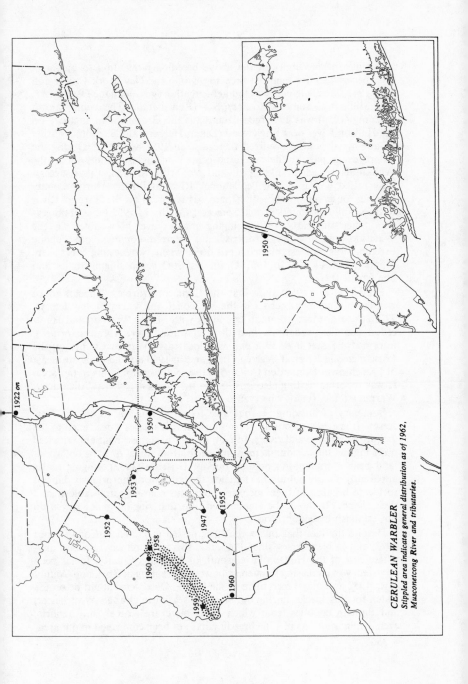

CERULEAN WARBLER
Stippled area indicates general distribution as of 1962,
Musconetcong River and tributaries.

Despite the proximity of the above breeding population to our area, this species was not reported breeding within the New York City region until 1947, when a female was found incubating eggs along the Dead River, near Millington, Somerset County, N.J. (Rebell et al.). The second known breeding (1950) was in Bergen County, at the Greenbrook Sanctuary on the Hudson River near Englewood (Dater, Herbert, and Skelton). Nesting or attempted nesting occurred there also in 1951 and 1952. During the latter year a pair at the nest was located in Sussex County along the Wallkill River near Franklin (Jehl and Wolfarth). In 1953, a pair successfully raised young on the Pequannock River at Butler, Morris County (various observers). A breeding pair was reported on the Raritan River in the vicinity of Bound Brook, Somerset County in 1955 (several observers). Since the early 1950s, singing males have been noted in the Waterloo area in Sussex, Morris, and Warren counties, but definite breeding was not established until 1958 when two nesting pairs were found (Black et al.). In 1961 Grant reported seven singing males and one female there.

Kunkle et al. (1959) state that the Cerulean Warbler "appears to be well established as a breeder in the Musconetcong Valley" (New Jersey). This stream forms a common boundary with Morris, Warren, and Hunterdon counties, and flows into the Delaware River. Abraitys (in litt.), informed me that in 1959 a pair was located in Warren County on the Musconetcong River at Warren Glen, and in 1960 another pair northeast of Frenchtown, Hunterdon County, at the southwestern limits of our area. It was reported nesting also in 1960 on the Pequest River at Allamuchy, Warren County (many observers).

Summary of breeding: In our area found at this season only in New Jersey. It is evident from the foregoing that this species is restricted to the vicinity of streams and rivers. In fact, its nest is almost invariably situated quite high in tall deciduous trees in river-bottom forest or in heavy woodland near a stream. As pointed out by Griscom (1933), singing males apparently greatly outnumber females, the latter being notoriously difficult to locate because of their inconspicuous and relatively drab colors, and their silence. It should be emphasized also that singing males per se do not establish breeding records.

Despite the fact that this species has nested in Dutchess County since 1922, and in New Jersey since 1947, it is still an extremely rare bird anywhere east of the Hudson River south of Dutchess County. It has been reported with increasing frequency, however, in spring in Rockland County since 1952 and may breed there in the future. Observers should be on the watch for this species during the breeding season in Orange, Westchester, and Putnam counties from which areas there are scarcely any reports, even in migration. As of 1963 breeding has not been confirmed in our area, except in New Jersey; one or two birds on eastern Long Island in 1962 and 1963 merely summered, but did not breed.

Egg dates: June 3 to 27.

BLACKBURNIAN WARBLER (*Dendroica fusca*)*B

Range: An eastern Nearctic species, breeding south to northern New Jersey and southeastern New York; in the mountains to northern Georgia.

Status: Uncommon to fairly common migrant. Local breeder at high elevations, but very rare in our area east of the Hudson River.

Migration: The Blackburnian Warbler, though widely distributed, is never numerous in our area.

Maxima: *Spring*—15, Bronx Park, May 6, 1953 (Komorowski), unusually early for so many; 15, Woodmere Woods, May 23, 1954. *Fall*—6, Far Rockaway, Aug. 14, 1954; 6 hit the Fire Island light, Sept. 23, 1887.

Extreme dates: *Spring*—Apr. 19, 23, and 25 to June 9 and 13. *Fall*—Aug. 3 to Oct. 20. Usually rare before mid-May and rare after September.

Breeding: The Blackburnian Warbler, though found in mixed coniferous-deciduous woodland, breeds chiefly in dense stands of hemlock. In northern New Jersey, it is most widely distributed, but is nowhere common. During the summer of 1956 in Sussex County, as many as four nesting pairs were found in the High Point area (Urner Club). According to Deed *et al.* (1959), it "breeds regularly in hemlock woods between Lake Tiorati and Island Pond," in the Orange County section of the Palisades Interstate Park. East of the Hudson River, it is apparently much rarer. In Putnam County, Kuerzi found a pair present during June 1929 in a hemlock swamp east of Cold Spring, which probably bred. In the same county on June 1, 1949, Scofield found a pair at their nest in Fahnestock State Park. Although the A.O.U. *Check-list* (1957: 497) lists Harmon-on-Hudson (Westchester County) as a breeding locality, I am unaware of the source of this information. However, it is conceivable that it may nest nearby in the hemlock gorge of the Croton River. It should also be looked for during the breeding season in the Mianus Gorge area—containing numerous large hemlocks.

Egg dates: May 28 to June 9.

YELLOW-THROATED WARBLER (*Dendroica dominica*)*

Range: A southeastern Nearctic species (for details, see Subspecies).

Status: Very rare to rare but regular (1951 on) spring migrant, chiefly coastal. Casual in fall.

Occurrence: The Yellow-throated Warbler is one of our rarest warblers, although it has increased slightly within the last dozen years. This may be due, in part, to the enormous increase in observers in recent years.

The principal periods of occurrence are late April and May. There are at least 20 reports in the former month and nearly 35 in the latter. Since 1951, from two to four individuals per year have been the usual number reported, but seven each were noted in 1956 (Apr. 24 to May 12) and 1959 (May 9 to 24).

Extreme dates: Apr. 15 and 17 (specimen) to June 6; casual twice in early July (specimens); only four fall records—Sept. 2, 16, 26 (specimen), and Oct. 6, all coastal.

Subspecies: The nominate race breeds chiefly on the coastal plain north to the central portions of Maryland and Delaware, possibly to extreme southern New Jersey (Cape May County). Stone (1937) stated that although there were a number of summer occurrences, ". . . no nest has yet been found, nor young seen." However, Fables (1955) stated, "T. E. McMullen found a nest in a small pine tree at the latter locality [Cape May point] on May 21, 1922. The nest contained 4 young."

The inland race *albilora* breeds northeast to southern Ohio, with an isolated population along the Delaware River in west-central New Jersey. It was discovered breeding in 1954 just south of our area in lower Hunterdon County on the New Jersey side of the Delaware River at Raven Rock by Vincent Abraitys (see Drinkwater, 1955). According to Abraitys (*in litt.*), it has nested at this locality every year since then, at least one pair each year. They were reported nesting in "riverside woods," mostly in sycamores, appropriately enough, as this is the vernacular name used for this race. Baird (1958) gives a good account of its habits there.

Although the A.O.U. *Check-list* (1957: 498) includes the Delaware River area under nominate *dominica*, Baird collected specimens in 1955 (one at Stockton on June 20, and another at Raven Rock on June 22), and submitted them to Sutton, who identified them as *D. d. albilora*. Both these specimens are now in the University of Oklahoma collection.

In the New York City area, six specimens have been collected, five from Long Island. Of the six, four belong to the nominate race: adult male, "Crow Hill," Brooklyn, "mid 1800s" (Akhurst), A.M.N.H. No. 440264; adult male, Oyster Bay, July 8, 1907, first seen July 4 (T. Roosevelt), A.M.N.H. No. 99697; Sag Harbor, July 15, 1933, first seen July 4 (Wilcox), specimen in his collection; adult male, Orient, May 11, 1927 (Latham), specimen in his collection, published here for the first time. The two local specimens of *D. d. albilora* are: adult female, Central Park, Apr. 18, 1919, first seen Apr. 17 (J. M. Valentine), A.M.N.H. No. 240958; adult male, Garden City, Sept. 26, 1953 (P. McAllister), specimen in the collection of the Tackapausha Museum at Seaford, L.I. I have examined all these specimens except the one from Sag Harbor.

Subspecific identification is limited to specimen records and no sight reports are accepted. For the difficulties involved, see Parkes (1953).

382

CHESTNUT-SIDED WARBLER (*Dendroica pensylvanica*)*B

Range: An eastern Nearctic species, breeding south to central New Jersey, Long Island, and Connecticut, but rare on the coastal plain; in the mountains to northern Georgia.

Status: Fairly common to common migrant, especially in spring. Common breeder north of the coastal plain.

Migration: The Chestnut-sided Warbler is one of a number of warblers that is more numerous in spring than in fall.

Maxima: *Spring*—30, Prospect Park, May 10, 1946; 20, Far Rockaway, May 16, 1954; 45, Central Park, May 23, 1954, a notably late spring. No comparable numbers in fall, but like many other species the fall migration is greatly protracted over a two-month period (first week in August through first week in October), while the bulk of the spring migrants pass through during the first three weeks in May. *Fall*—8 struck the Empire State building, Sept. 11, 1948; 5 hit the Montauk Point lighthouse, Oct. 7, 1950 (Helmuth), late for so many.

Extreme dates: Apr. 25 to Oct. 16. Casual, Central Park, Nov. 13, 1958 (Messing), full details submitted. Rare before May and after early October.

Breeding: This species breeds south to the edge of the coastal plain in our area, but is very local on it. Like most of our breeding warblers, it is most numerous on the mainland. Very rare prior to about 1840, it greatly benefited by the cutting of the forests, and became common wherever clearings were made. It nests in second-growth deciduous woodland and thickets adjacent to woodland. During the summer of 1941, at least eight pairs nested on a 40-acre tract at Grassy Sprain, Westchester County (Hickey).

Egg dates: May 14 to July 12.

BAY-BREASTED WARBLER (*Dendroica castanea*)*

Range: An eastern Nearctic species, breeding south to northeastern New York (Adirondacks) and northern New England.

Status: Fairly common to common spring and fall migrant, but rare some years, numerous in others. Subject to yearly fluctuations.

Occurrence and maxima: The Bay-breasted Warbler is notable for its variable numbers, fluctuating markedly in certain years. During some seasons only a few are observed in a day; at other times it is quite numerous.

Maxima: *Spring*—20, Forest Park, L.I., May 17, 1951; 22, Englewood, May 19, 1920; 42, Grassy Sprain, May 19, 1948 (Small); 13 in one tree, Tuckahoe, N.Y., May 22, 1947 (Darrow). *Fall*—18, Easthampton, Sept. 7, 1924. On the rainy night of Sept. 22, 1953, 63 hit the Empire State building.

Extreme dates: *Spring*—May 1 to June 9 (specimen) and June 11; adult male, collected, Far Rockaway, June 23, 1870 (N. T. Lawrence). *Fall*—July 26 and Aug. 4 (latest specimen, Oct. 13) to Nov. 2. Casual, Riis Park, Nov. 25 to Dec. 1, 1956 (Mayer, Carleton, Harrison *et al.*), a bright male with rufous flanks, well seen. Rare before mid-May, after early June, before mid-August, and after early October.

Remarks: Caution is urged on the identification of dull-plumaged Bay-breasted and Blackpoll Warblers insofar as leg color is concerned. While the Bay-breasted Warbler has dark legs and the Blackpoll Warbler *usually* has pale legs, some individuals of the latter species possess dark-colored legs (see Young, Kentucky Warbler, 21: 1–3, 1945). This important point was corrected in the latest Peterson *Field Guide* (1961).

BLACKPOLL WARBLER (*Dendroica striata*)*

Range: Nearctic species, breeding south to northern New York and northern New England; rarely to the summits of Slide Mountain (Catskills) and Mount Greylock (Berkshires).

Status: Common to very common spring migrant, often abundant in fall.

Occurrence and maxima: The Blackpoll Warbler is one of our most numerous warblers at times, on certain days in autumn outnumbering all other warblers, excepting only the Myrtle Warbler.

Maxima: *Spring*—100, Woodmere Woods, May 16, 1953; 130, Prospect Park, May 17, 1945. *Fall*—The following data are taken from Dutcher (1888) of birds that had struck the Fire Island lighthouse: out of a total of 595 birds picked up dead on Sept. 23, 1887, 356 (about 60 per cent) were Blackpoll Warblers; on Sept. 30, 1883, a very late fall, 230 individuals of this species were collected at the base of the light. On Oct. 5, 1954, Wilcox counted 114 that had hit the tower at the Westhampton Air Force Base.

Extreme dates: *Spring*—Apr. 28, 29, 30; and May 1, 1944, an exceptionally early spring, when this species arrived at various localities in our area; regularly to mid-June. *Summer*—June 18, 20, 22, and 26; casual in July—July 5 and 11; adult male, Central Park, all June and July 1953 (Carleton and Messing). *Fall*—Aug. 23, 29, and 30 (specimen), but very rare in August; to Nov. 20 (specimen), Dec. 2 (specimen), and Dec. 3. Rare before mid-May and after mid-October.

Remarks: This species winters in South America. Casual at Montauk Point, March 30, 1941 (Helmuth), adult male in breeding plumage, picked up dead at base of the lighthouse. Whether this represents a wintering bird or an abnormally early arrival is difficult to say. The date is almost a month earlier than the earliest listed above.

384

PINE WARBLER (*Dendroica pinus*)*B

Range: An eastern Nearctic species, breeding from southern Canada to Texas and Florida—principally along the coast; rare and local inland. The nominate race occurs in our area.

Status: Variously rare to fairly common migrant. Very rare in winter. Local breeder in pine woods of the coastal plain, but very rare inland. Formerly more numerous.

Migration: In recent years, at least, this species has become quite rare. Its numbers fluctuate markedly and on migration it is very erratic, some years fairly common in spring, but for some reason has almost always been rare in fall. It is our earliest spring warbler, arriving regularly the first week in April.

Maxima: *Spring*—8, Van Cortlandt Park, Apr. 8, 1950; 20, Fort Lee, N.J., Apr. 20, 1915; 15, Bronx Park, Apr. 23, 1955. *Fall*—20, Easthampton to Montauk, Oct. 8, 1932 (Helmuth). No other fall reports before me have anywhere near this number.

"Extreme" dates: Because it winters occasionally, fall departure dates are difficult to determine, but it is usually rare by early November; however, there are at least a dozen late-December reports which possibly represent winter birds. The earliest spring arrival appears to be March 18. Rare before April.

Winter: This species winters north to the coast of Maryland, rarely to Massachusetts. Although there are no local winter specimens in the American Museum collection, there are at least a dozen reliable midwinter sight reports, chiefly along the south shore of Long Island.

Breeding: The Pine Warbler is restricted to the pine barrens where mature stands of pitch pines occur and avoids the scrub areas where the Prairie Warbler breeds. It breeds most numerously in extensive stands of pine land on eastern Long Island and in Monmouth County, N.J. In recent years, however, particularly on Long Island, much of the pine has been cut and burned over and, consequently, this species has decreased markedly within the past 10 or 15 years.

Inland, it is exceedingly rare and local, nesting wherever pitch pines occur and more rarely in white-pine groves. It has been found sporadically in northern New Jersey: in Sussex County—on the Wawayanda Plateau and along the Kittatinny ridge. The only other reported nesting in the interior was that of a breeding pair found in a pitch-pine grove near Bedford Center, Westchester County, spring and summer of 1940 (Wheeler).

Egg dates: May 4 to June 12.

PRAIRIE WARBLER (*Dendroica discolor*)*B

Range: A southeastern Nearctic species, the nominate race breeding north to the central portions of New York and New England; rarely farther. Has spread northward in recent years.

Status: Fairly common to common migrant, particularly on the coast; rare to absent in the mountains. Widespread breeder on the coastal plain in suitable habitat; fairly common, but local inland.

Migration: The Prairie Warbler is one of the very few members of this family that is more numerous on Long Island and coastal New Jersey than on the mainland.

Maxima: 30, Prospect Park, May 5, 1946; 30, Woodmere Woods, May 6, 1950. I have seen no maximum numbers listed for fall.

Extreme dates: Apr. 16 to Nov. 11 and 18; rarely to Nov. 29, 1958, Jones Beach (several observers). Rare before late April and after mid-October.

Breeding: This species is particularly numerous in the scrub oak and pine barrens of Long Island, and in Monmouth County, N.J. Speaking of Long Island, Elliott (1951) stated, "Scrub fires appear to be beneficial in making up the habitat. When scrub oaks and pines become high and dense, this species usually vacates." Inland it nests in open scrubby fields and on hillsides with a scattering of cedars and brier tangles. It has greatly increased in the past 40 or 50 years in these latter environments.

Egg dates: May 18 to June 22.

PALM WARBLER (*Dendroica palmarum*)*

Range: Nearctic species, the nominate western race breeds southeast to east-central Ontario and central Michigan; the eastern race *hypochrysea* breeds south to central Maine and east-central New Hampshire. Nominate *palmarum* migrates *southeastward* in fall toward the Atlantic coast and winters chiefly in Florida and the West Indies, rarely north along the coast to Massachusetts; in spring migrates chiefly west of the Appalachians, rare in the east. The race *hypochrysea* migrates *southwestward* in fall toward the Gulf coast, its chief wintering grounds; rarely north to the middle Atlantic states; in spring migrates *northeastward* along the Atlantic coast, rare farther west. In other words the two subspecies essentially "cross" each other's migration routes both spring and fall.

Status: The race *palmarum* is a common to very common fall coastal migrant; rare but regular in spring. Rare in winter along the coast. The race *hypochrysea* is a fairly common to occasionally abundant spring

386

migrant, but is subject to marked fluctuations; relatively uncommon in fall. Rarer in winter than nominate *palmarum*.

Occurrence and maxima: The Palm Warbler (collectively), excepting the Pine Warbler, is our earliest spring warbler—arriving regularly by early April.

1. *D. p. palmarum*—80, Easthampton, Sept. 15, 1946; 30, Montauk Point, Oct. 14, 1950. In fall, arrives earlier and departs later than *D. p. hypochrysea*. The "Western" Palm Warbler is essentially coastal with us at all seasons.

Extreme dates: Aug. 26 and 28 (earliest specimen, Sept. 8) to May 23. Three spring specimens—Apr. 6, 29, and May 5. Regular in small numbers into early December and specimen collected at Orient, Jan. 14, 1932 (Latham). This subspecies is much less rare in winter in our area, at least on the basis of sight reports. Rare before mid-September and generally after November.

2. The bird known as the "Yellow" Palm Warbler, *D. p. hypochrysea*, is sometimes abundant in *Spring*—200, Central Park, Apr. 21, 1929; a big late flight in 1950 as follows: 300, Van Cortlandt Park, May 1; 80, Woodmere Woods, May 6. *Fall*—34, Easthampton, Oct. 8, 1932.

Extreme dates: Sept. 11 to May 27 (notably late spring of 1917). No winter specimens, but a very small number of sight reports. Rare before April, after early May, before October, and after early November.

The following winter maxima taken from Christmas counts include both subspecies: 12, Brooklyn to Atlantic Beach, late December 1952; total of 19 on five coastal counts, 1953–54; also 4, Hempstead, Jan. 4, 1947.

Remarks: It must not be inferred that the above data, especially those dealing with relative abundance and seasonal status, are entirely correct as to separation of the two forms in the field—the human element of error is definitely a factor here. The student should realize that separating the two subspecies in the field during fall and winter is often difficult and unreliable; intermediates occur, as revealed by careful examination of large museum series.

OVENBIRD (*Seiurus aurocapillus*)*B

Range: Essentially an eastern Nearctic species, the nominate race breeds from central Canada south to Oklahoma in the west, and Georgia and South Carolina in the east.

Status: Common to very common migrant, especially in spring. Widespread breeder.

Migration: The Ovenbird is one of our best-known warblers, as well as one of the most numerous. It is also subject to high mortality, frequently hitting obstructions, as may be seen by the maxima listed below.

Maxima: *Spring*—big flight in early May 1950—May 5, Prospect Park (160); May 6, Bronx Park (70) and Woodmere Woods (100); another large flight on May 11, 1914—200 each in Central Park and Englewood; 200, Madison Square Park, May 15, 1921 (Chapin), after a heavy fog and rain the previous night; 42, Fire Island light, May 19, 1891. *Fall*—78, Empire State building, Sept. 11, 1948; 39, Shinnecock light, Sept. 17, 1890; 22, tower at Westhampton Air Force Base, Oct. 5, 1954, late for so many. These fall totals represent birds that hit obstructions.

Extreme dates: Apr. 10, 15, and 19 to Nov. 24. Rare before May and after early October.

Breeding: The Ovenbird nests on the ground chiefly in deciduous woods, less commonly in coniferous areas (pine barrens). There were 23 nesting pairs on a 40-acre tract at Grassy Sprain, Westchester County, summer of 1941 (Hickey).

Egg dates: May 14 to July 4.

Remarks: The Ovenbird winters regularly north to Florida, rarely to coastal South Carolina. Accidental at this season in Massachusetts (specimen).

In our area there are three sight reports: one at Inwood Hill Park, Dec. 21, 1935 (Karsch and Norse); one at a feeding station, Baldwin, up to Dec. 31, 1955 (Mrs. Teale and many observers); and one at Poundridge (village), Dec. 21–30, 1961 (Grierson *et al.*).

Subspecies: The race *furvior* breeds in Newfoundland. It has been reported in migration from Massachusetts to Georgia, and probably has occurred within our area, although I have not seen any "typical" specimens—only a few that appear to approach *S. a. furvior*.

NORTHERN WATERTHRUSH (*Seiurus noveboracensis*)*B

Range: Nearctic species, breeding south to the northern portions of the New York City region; farther south in the mountains to West Virginia and Maryland; and very rarely and locally to the edge of the coastal plain in southeastern Massachusetts and Rhode Island.

Status: Fairly common to common migrant. Local breeder at higher elevations.

Migration: The Northern Waterthrush is widespread during migration, occurring from inland bogs, swamps, lake and river shores, as well as in woodland, to coastal ponds, salt creeks, and even thickets along the outer beaches.

Maxima: *Spring*—12, Central Park, May 6, 1950. *Fall*—10 struck the Fire Island lighthouse, Aug. 19, 1888; 23, Prospect Park, Aug. 29, 1944; 28 hit the Shinnecock light, Sept. 17, 1890; 38 hit the Westhampton Air Force Base tower, Oct. 5, 1954.

Extreme dates: *Spring*—Apr. 14, 15, and 20 to June 7; one of the first warblers to move south in *Fall*—July 12 and 19 to Oct. 30 and Nov. 2; casual, Prospect Park, Nov. 30, 1908 (Vietor). Rare before May; and before August and after mid-October.

Breeding: In our area this species is a local breeder in the interior highlands. It nests on or very near the ground in woodland swamps. Most breeding reports are from northern New Jersey, especially Sussex County and the adjacent portion of Passaic County. Three nesting pairs were located in a hemlock-rhododendron swamp at High Point State Park (Sussex County), summer of 1951 (Fables). It has been found south to the Great Swamp, Morris County, "where it nested in 1951 and 1952" (Fables, 1955). It should be found breeding also in the higher portions of Warren County.

Elsewhere in our area I know of only three definite breeding records, all in New York State: adult feeding young, east of Cold Spring, Putnam County, late June 1929 (Kuerzi); nest with four eggs in a swamp at Lake Waccabuc, Westchester County, June 9, 1947 (P. C. Spofford); pair nested at Sterling Forest, Orange County, summer of 1962 (Treacy). It should be searched for in the breeding season in the many wooded swamps of Rockland County, especially in and near the Bear Mountain section.

Reports of its breeding at low elevations along the coast in our area have not been corroborated. However, this species apparently has been extending its nesting range slightly during recent years, having been found in coastal red maple-white cedar swamps in southeastern Massachusetts (see Anderson and Maxfield, Wilson Bull., 74: 381–385, 1962).

Egg dates: May 28 to June 19.

Subspecies: The poorly defined race *notabilis* is not recognized here. Eaton (1957) in a discussion of the Northern Waterthrush concluded, ". . . in view of the clinal and rather slight nature of the variation, it is suggested that the species be regarded as monotypic." He found that both color characters and measurements were subject to individual variation, and could not be correlated on a geographical basis.

LOUISIANA WATERTHRUSH *(Seiurus motacilla)**B

Range: A southeastern Nearctic species, breeding north to the central portions of New York and New England, but rare and local on the coastal plain from New Jersey to Massachusetts.

Status: Uncommon to rare migrant inland; very rare along the coast. Fairly common but local breeder north of the coastal plain; rare on the north shore of Long Island.

Migration: Even in such excellent warbler localities as Central and Prospect Parks, the Louisiana Waterthrush, though regular in spring, is an uncommon species. The maximum appears to be three to four per day in late April.

Extreme dates: March 25 and 28 (Apr. 4, earliest specimen) to Oct. 4 and 12. Rare before mid-April and after mid-September. The published report of an individual at Central Park, Nov. 24, 1910, is an error; it should be Apr. 2, 1916 (see Hix, Copeia, 30: 31, 1916).

The extreme rarity of this species on the south shore of Long Island has never been emphasized. While this may be surprising in view of its fairly widespread distribution as a breeding bird on the mainland, it is nevertheless a fact. Although numerous migrant waterthrush specimens from Long Island are in the American Museum collection, *not one* is of this species. Of more than 80 individuals that struck the Fire Island and Shinnecock lighthouses within a three-year period (1888–90), *none* was *S. motacilla.* Just outside our area, of 93 waterthrushes banded at Island Beach, N.J., during the fall of 1960 (Aug. 25 to Oct. 2), only *one* was a Louisiana Waterthrush. During 15 years of intensive observation at Far Rockaway, both spring and fall, I noted only *five* individuals (2 in spring, 3 in fall). J. T. Nichols' earlier experience at Far Rockaway was similar. He saw *none* between 1891 and 1900. In over 40 years at Garden City, Nichols *never* recorded this species, and during the same period only *twice* at Mastic. Helmuth, during the period from 1908 to 1950 in the Easthampton region, observed it *twice* in spring and only *four* times in fall. Bicknell at Long Beach saw only *one* in fall within 10 years of steady observation. At Manorville, Raynor has seen it only *twice* in nearly 30 years. It will thus be seen that the Louisiana Waterthrush is one of the rarest warblers on the coastal plain. It is most likely that migration is chiefly by way of the interior river valleys, especially in spring.

Breeding: This species is near the northern limits of its range in our area. It nests on or very near the ground in banks and in overturned tree roots along rapid streams in wooded highlands and along slow streams in moist bottomland forest. It is distributed throughout the mainland in this habitat, but is very local on the north shore of Long Island between Mill Neck (Nassau County) and Miller Place (Suffolk County); rare breeder also at Greenport, eastern Suffolk County.

Egg dates: May 1 to June 24.

Remarks: Many birds identified in the field as migrant Louisiana Waterthrushes are pale Northern Waterthrushes with whitish superciliaries, especially those individuals seen in late spring (after the middle of May) and in fall as well. As Carleton remarked in an earlier paper on the "Birds of Central Park" (1947), "Pale looking Northern Waterthrushes, or birds that are not satisfactorily determinable, are constantly being reported as Louisianas" (see also similar comments in Griscom and Snyder, 1955: 206).

390

KENTUCKY WARBLER (*Oporornis formosus*)*B

Range: A southeastern Nearctic species, breeding northeast to northern New Jersey and southeastern New York (mainland); formerly to southwestern Connecticut.

Status: Now a very rare migrant and breeder. Formerly fairly common, but local on the mainland.

Migration: This species is now one of our rarest warblers. During the past 37 years (1926–62) the Kentucky Warbler has been unreported as a migrant during 11 of those years, and has been "missed" 15 spring seasons —total of 44 spring migrants—all in May. It is much rarer in fall, reported only 17 times, chiefly late August and the first half of September, most reports from coastal points.

There was an unprecedented flight (at least in recent years) of this species in May 1947, when six were observed in three days, three of these in one day: May 11—Eltingville, Staten Island; May 12—Bronx and Central Parks, and Haverstraw, N.Y.; May 13—Prospect Park and Woodmere Woods. Even more unusual were three supposedly different singing males carefully observed in swampy woods near Freeport, May 22, 1960 (Dignan and Ward).

Extreme dates: *Spring*—May 1, 2 (specimen), and May 6 to May 28; *Fall*—Aug. 19 (specimen) to Sept. 23, 29, and Oct. 2. This latter date, Oct. 2, 1948, represents a male well observed at Belmont Lake State Park (Elliott). The early fall specimen referred to is of interest as it was picked up dead at the base of the Fire Island lighthouse, Aug. 19, 1888 (Dutcher), the same day and place a dead Mourning Warbler was found, the latter quite notable in itself.

Rare before mid-May and after mid-September.

Breeding: Like the Acadian Flycatcher, this species is at its northern limits here, has greatly decreased since about 1900 in our area, and has withdrawn over much of its former northeastern nesting range, for reasons apparently unknown. The likelihood of its being overlooked as a breeder is slight, as it is a loud and persistent singer, the song similar to that of the Carolina Wren.

Its favored haunts are rich, moist, usually hilly woodlands, especially those having ravines with stream bottoms and an understory of dense, luxuriant vegetation. There are still many areas with these habitats.

To find this species in numbers, one must travel outside our area to the lower Delaware Valley, especially on the Pennsylvania side, where it becomes progressively more common southward as one nears Philadelphia.

The local history of the Kentucky Warbler is best illustrated by summarizing its past and present occurrence in three time-periods.

1. 1870 to 1900: Apparently most numerous near the Hudson River. In New York State, Fisher (Bull. Nuttall Ornith. Club, 3: 191, 1878) stated that near Ossining, Westchester County, between May 21 and July 5, 1875, he saw 16 individuals, nine of which were collected. He located four nests in a "deeply wooded ravine about three miles long, with a stream running through." Bicknell (1878) found it a "not uncommon breeder in the Riverdale area [then chiefly in Westchester County] in woodland up to 250 feet, usually among low swampy growth." He also found it breeding in the same general vicinity near Hillview Reservoir until 1898. The only definite nesting record for Connecticut was that of a female seen feeding a well-fledged nestling in swampy woods near Greenwich, Fairfield County, July 10, 1892 (C. G. Voorhees); the male was secured later that day. As to Bergen County, N.J., Chapman (1889) stated *"Formerly* nested locally from Englewood to Fort Lee." (Italics mine.) One would infer from Chapman's statement that the bird had disappeared by 1889 or earlier. This seems to be at variance with the following.

2. 1900 to 1942: Griscom (1923) stated, *"Formerly* a fairly common summer resident on the west slope of the Palisades south of Englewood, last nesting in 1914." Cruickshank (1942) remarked, "A few pairs *still* nest along the Palisades." (Italics mine.) It would appear that this species has bred there more or less continuously despite the conflicting statements.

During the mid-1920s until 1942, possibly the best-known and most frequently worked area for this species was in the region along the Saw Mill River valley in southern Westchester County. As many as six breeding pairs were found in 1928 between Elmsford and Grassy Sprain, west to Irvington, although it had disappeared as a breeder at Grassy Sprain by 1939. As recently as 1942, Robert Hines located two nests at Worthington (south of Elmsford) and banded the young. The present nesting status in that area is not known because little field work has been done in recent years.

3. 1942 to 1962: The only definite information to my knowledge concerning breeding is from the southern portion of our area in New Jersey. Aside from a nesting pair at East Millstone, Somerset County, 1956 to 1958 (Swinebroad), the only other section with breeding birds reported is from adjacent Hunterdon County where Abraitys (*in litt.*), stated that there has been a "slight increase since 1954 in the Delaware River drainage. Two or three pairs are regular on the lower Musconetcong Mountain at Spring Mills and West Portal which represent an extension from the Piedmont region to the highlands of New Jersey."

Singing males have been reported in Rockland, Orange, and Putnam counties, N.Y., as well as on Long Island on the Orient peninsula, but in no case has nesting been proved, although it is quite possible. The two old reports of breeding on the south shore at Bellport and Sayville, Suffolk County, are without details—the localities highly unlikely.

Egg dates: May 31 to June 12.

CONNECTICUT WARBLER (*Oporornis agilis*)*

Range: Nearctic species, breeding east to eastern Ontario and extreme western Quebec, south to northern Michigan. Migrates in spring through the Mississippi Valley, in fall mainly along the Atlantic coast.

Status: Uncommon to rare, but regular fall migrant, chiefly on or near the coast. Formerly much more numerous. Casual in spring.

Occurrence and maxima: The Connecticut Warbler occurs most often during the latter half of September and the first two weeks of October. At this time, the active observer, if alert and cautious, will see this species regularly in the proper places.

Relatively rare inland, it frequents moist, young woodland thickets where swamp maple, shadbush, and *Clethra* (white alder) tower above a rank growth of jewel weed and other herbs; in drier localities where wooded edges adjoin overgrown weedy fields and pastures; and occasionally in groves of gray birch.

Along the coast it is partial to dense tangles of ragweed, sunflowers, and asters, especially in waste areas; and on the outer coast among almost impenetrable thickets of *Smilax* (catbrier), poison ivy, and bayberry, as confirmed recently by mist-net operations.

There is abundant evidence to show that the Connecticut Warbler was much more numerous formerly (prior to 1910) and that it has not as yet regained this former abundance. It was eagerly sought by collectors who took many specimens in the late nineteenth century.

Of more than 180 specimens taken in the New York City area, at least 44 are in the American Museum collection, and *many* others have been recorded in the literature. About 130 of these were collected between 1880 and 1910, only 30 since then, as there has been much less collecting in recent years.

Maxima, early period (prior to 1910): the following were reported by Dutcher in his field notes as having struck the Fire Island lighthouse—57, Sept. 23, 1877; 1883—16, Sept. 30, and 18, Oct. 12; a notably late migration that fall. During the last few days of September 1900, Cherrie collected 10 just south of Jamaica and reported that he had seen "many" others. The number reported above on Sept. 23, 1877, is unique. Most present-day observers would not see that many in 10 years.

Maxima, recent period (since 1910): 10 hit the Empire State building, Sept. 11, 1948 (*fide* Aronoff); on Oct. 5, 1954, Wilcox picked up 13 dead individuals that had struck the Westhampton Air Force Base tower.

The average observer today is lucky to see from one to four during an entire fall, and then only if he is actively afield. Rarely have as many as six individuals per locality been found in one day. At Idlewild on Sept. 30, 1951, Mayer saw five, including one that he banded.

Extreme dates: Aug. 17 (earliest specimen, Aug. 26) to Oct. 30 (specimen); four times in November—2, 6, 17, and Nov. 26, 1938, Easthampton (Helmuth). Rare before September and after mid-October.

Griscom's remarks (1923), ". . . rare on the south shore," and Cruickshank's statement (1942), ". . . irregularly lingers into October," have proved otherwise.

Remarks: Casual in spring, one specimen record: adult male collected at Fort Lee, N.J., May 25, 1917 (Weber), U.S.N.M. collection.

The number of recent sight reports of spring birds, almost all of them not adequately substantiated, are out of proportion to the number collected and seen prior to 1910, when the species occurred much more frequently in fall. Moreover, within the past two decades, I have been able to find only two reliable spring sight identifications by experienced observers, despite a vastly increased number of "birders" today. The total number of reliable reports at this season probably does not exceed a dozen, and many an observer who has had thirty or more years' field experience has never seen this species in spring.

Extreme dates: May 13 to 29. This latter date represents an adult male banded at Astoria, L.I., May 29, 1941 (Hines), identification confirmed by Frank Watson.

MOURNING WARBLER (*Oporornis philadelphia*)*

Range: Essentially an eastern Nearctic species, breeding south to the Berkshires, Catskills, and Poconos; in the higher mountains to Virginia and West Virginia.

Status: Rare to uncommon but regular spring migrant, apparently rarer in fall; occurs chiefly north of the coastal plain.

Occurrence and maxima: The best times and places to look for this species are during the last ten days of May and the first week in June, in city parks wherever plantings of thick shrubbery occur, usually near ponds and swampy situations. Elsewhere inland the Mourning Warbler may be found in low, wet woods where extensive growths of skunk cabbage, nettle, and jewel-weed abound. While it is particularly retiring and secretive in such places, individuals may be heard singing, sometimes for long periods. Its song, similar to that of the Kentucky Warbler, has certain notes and phrases not unlike the Yellowthroat, and on several occasions I have traced an "off" Yellowthroat song to discover that it was actually a Mourning Warbler.

This species is exceedingly difficult to observe in autumn because of the heavy vegetation at that season and because the bird does not sing then. Nevertheless, nine fall specimens have been collected, only six in spring.

394

The Mourning Warbler is very rare on the south shore of Long Island even in fall and particularly so at the east end. Helmuth, in over 40 years of field work in the Easthampton area, reported it but once, May 20, 1947. During approximately the same period of time in the Westhampton region, Wilcox recorded only a single individual, a bird that he mist-netted and banded at Tiana Beach, Sept. 5, 1959. Although numerous dead Connecticut Warblers have been picked up at the Fire Island lighthouse, only one Mourning Warbler has been recorded there—Aug. 19, 1888 (Dutcher).

Maxima: *Spring*—4, Central Park, June 2, 1930 (Watson); 5, Van Cortlandt Park, but date not given (Cruickshank). *Fall*—what might almost be called a flight occurred in Central Park in 1923, when eight supposedly different individuals were reported from Aug. 14 to 29 (Griscom *et al.*).

Extreme dates: *Spring*—May 8 to June 10 (several times), including two adult males taken at Orient, June 10, 1951 (Latham), in his collection. *Fall*—Aug. 5, 6, and 11 (specimen) to Sept. 30 (specimen), Oct. 7 and 12. Rare before late May and after mid-September. Several sight reports during the first few days in May are unconfirmed; the Mourning Warbler is a notably late spring migrant.

YELLOWTHROAT (*Geothlypis trichas*)*B

Range: Nearctic and northern Neotropical species, breeding from Alaska and Canada to southern Mexico. The nominate race occurs in our area.

Status: Common to abundant migrant. Common, widespread breeder. Rare but regular in winter near the coast.

Migration: The Yellowthroat is one of our best known, most numerous and widely distributed warblers.

Maxima: *Spring*—250, Central Park, May 11, 1914 (Helmuth); 150, Prospect Park, May 14, 1950; 133 hit the Fire Island light, May 19, 1891; 40, Central Park, May 23, 1954; 25, Central Park, May 30, 1950 (very late for so many). *Fall*—100, Far Rockaway to Riis Park, Sept. 2, 1958; 63 hit the Westhampton Air Force Base tower, Oct. 5, 1954.

"Extreme" dates: Apr. 7 (specimen) to late October; numerous November and early December dates. Rare before May and after October.

Breeding: The Yellowthroat nests commonly throughout the area in wet places, but also breeds wherever there are dense thickets and tangles away from water. Maxima: 46 pairs, Troy Meadows, June 1, 1947 (Urner Club).

Egg dates: May 14 to July 9.

Winter: This species winters north to South Carolina; rarely to New York and Massachusetts (two specimens in the latter state). In our area Griscom (1923) listed only one winter occurrence and Cruickshank (1942) seven more. Since 1950 at least one or two have been found in winter each year and during 1953–54, six spent all or part of the winter, mostly at feeding stations. This increase may represent, in part, a much greater number of observers, more feeders in operation, milder winters, or a combination of all three. No local winter specimens are in the large A.M.N.H. series.

Subspecies: Insofar as our area is concerned, this species is treated here as monotypic. In the northeastern portion of its range, *G. trichas* is currently divided into two races, the nominate subspecies and *G. t. brachidactylus.* These two races allegedly meet and intergrade in central New Jersey. However, Todd (1940) and Parkes (1952 and 1954b) contend that the two forms are inseparable, in that much overlapping exists in both coloration and measurements. There is also much individual variation.

YELLOW-BREASTED CHAT (*Icteria virens*)*B

Range: Nearctic species, the nominate race breeding north to central New York and the southern portions of Vermont and New Hampshire.

Status: Rare to uncommon migrant. Local breeder at lower elevations. Rare but regular in winter (since 1950).

Breeding: The Yellow-breasted Chat is a widely distributed species in the lowlands of our region but it is erratic and local in its occurrence, in some areas tending to breed in small, loose "colonies," in other areas only single pairs. Similar localities elsewhere, however, will be untenanted. Perhaps, nearing its northern breeding limits, there are not enough pairs to "go around." At any rate, this species shows a strong preference for open country, nesting in brushy fields, and in dense, often impenetrable thickets, especially blackberry, catbrier, sumac, etc.

While reputed to be commoner on the mainland than on Long Island, it is by no means rare in the latter area, as may be seen in the following breeding survey undertaken in 1940: Long Island—22 pairs in 10 localities; Westchester and Rockland Counties—30 pairs in 11 localities; northern New Jersey—55 pairs in 13 localities. In more limited areas, it was found that during the summer of 1937 no fewer than 12 pairs nested between Chappaqua and Mount Kisco (Westchester County) in approximately four miles of suitable territory.

More recently Mudge (*in litt.*) found a "colony" of five to eight pairs nesting on an abandoned, overgrown golf course of about 125 acres near Northport (Suffolk County) in 1961. Ferguson (*in litt.*) estimated over a dozen breeding pairs on Fisher's Island in the late 1950s.

Egg dates: May 19 to July 6.

Change in nonbreeding status: 1. *Migration*—Cruickshank (1942) stated, "Wherever the bird does not nest it is an astonishingly uncommon to rare transient visitant in spring and ... even rarer ... in fall," and "by the middle of September the species is a decided rarity."

While it is still true that the Yellow-breasted Chat is secretive and relatively few are seen by even active observers, it is much less rare nowadays in fall, and is even regular in October (see below). It should be pointed out, however, that these maximum numbers represent dead birds picked up after hitting obstructions, and birds that were mist-netted. The observer will rarely see more than one or two in a day per locality.

Maxima: 5, Empire State building, Sept. 11, 1948; 6, Mitchel Air Force Base tower, Sept. 19, 1950; 3, Westhampton Air Force Base tower, Oct. 5, 1954; 4, Montauk Point lighthouse, Oct. 7, 1950; Wilcox and W. Terry mist-netted and banded a total of 17 at Tiaña Beach, L.I., from Sept. 5 to Oct. 25, 1960, with a maximum of 3 on Sept. 26.

Extreme dates: Apr. 26 to Oct. 31. Rare before mid-May and after October.

2. *Winter:* This species normally winters from Mexico to Panama, but since 1950 individuals have wintered regularly north to Massachusetts (specimens). Casual in our area at this season prior to 1950. Griscom (1923) knew of no winter occurrences, and Cruickshank (1942) listed only two, including one that spent the winter of 1932–33 at a feeding station in Forest Hills, L.I. (many observers). However, as far back as 1911, one was seen at South Norwalk, Conn. from Dec. 24, 1911, to Jan. 1, 1912 (W. F. Smith). A bird was present at New Dorp, Staten Island, from Dec. 28, 1943, through January 1944 (Cleaves).

It was not until 1950 that this species was again reported in winter. The first and only known local winter specimen was collected at Orient, Feb. 7, 1950 (Latham). Since that year one or more Chats have been reported each winter.

Maxima: On all local Christmas counts combined (1952), 6 were reported; during the winter of 1956–57, no fewer than 11 were seen, some of which were present at feeding stations.

Remarks: Why a species that has not increased appreciably as a breeding bird is reported oftener in winter and migration, particularly in fall, is a mystery, as relatively few individuals occur north of us. There are many more observers now than in 1942, but this does not entirely account for the increase. Possibly these fall individuals are derived from the west, as is the case with several other species that migrate toward the east coast in fall. Baird *et al.* (1959) suggest that fall coastal Chats come from more southern regions, as evidenced by their appearance after southwest winds "within tropical warm sectors."

HOODED WARBLER (*Wilsonia citrina*)*B

Range: A southeastern Nearctic species, breeding north to central and southeastern New York, central Connecticut, and Rhode Island.

Status: Rare to uncommon migrant. Locally common breeder north of the coastal plain, but absent from Long Island; local breeder along the coast of Monmouth County, N.J.

Migration: The Hooded Warbler is a scarce migrant away from breeding areas considering that it is rather common as a breeding species in nearby country, but in this respect it is similar to the Worm-eating and Golden-winged Warblers.

Maxima: 4, Woodmere Woods, May 6, 1950; 5, Prospect Park, May 12, 1945.

Extreme dates: Apr. 18 and 20 to Oct. 9. Casual: Englewood, Nov. 8, 1903 (Rogers); adult male color-photographed, Northport, L.I., Dec. 3–7, 1954 (Mudge). Rare before May and after mid-September.

Breeding: This species is near the northern limits of its range in our region. Inland it nests in the undergrowth of moist, rich woodland, chiefly on hillsides, often among mountain laurel thickets. An entirely different habitat is occupied on the coast of New Jersey, where it frequents white cedar swamps in and near the pine barrens. No definite evidence of breeding on Long Island.

During the summer of 1947, six nesting pairs were observed at Pound-ridge Reservation, Westchester County (Bull and Darrow). Here they were breeding with Canada Warblers on wooded slopes covered with a growth of mountain laurel. This is an interesting example of a "southern" and "northern" species nesting side by side.

Egg dates: May 18 to July 4.

WILSON'S WARBLER (*Wilsonia pusilla*)*

Range: Nearctic species, the nominate race breeds south to the southern portions of Ontario and Quebec, and northern New England.

Status: Uncommon to fairly common spring migrant; rare to uncommon fall migrant. Numbers fluctuate from year to year.

Occurrence and maxima: Like certain other warblers, Wilson's Warbler occurs in varying numbers, usually uncommon, occasionally more numerous.

Maxima: 8, Prospect Park, May 14, 1950; 43, Westchester County, late May (year not stated), "in a vigorous day of birding" (Cruickshank). There is a report (Carleton, 1958: 48) of 100 seen in one day in Central Park. If correct, this number is unprecedented, but there is probability of much duplication. No fall maxima available.

Extreme dates: *Spring*—Apr. 29 (1914 and 1950) to June 7. *Fall*—July 26 and 31 to Oct. 31. Casual, Nov. 22, 25, 27, and 30; exceptionally to

Dec. 19, 1961, Stony Point, N.Y. (Kennedy). Rare before mid-May, before mid-August, and after September.

Remarks: Winters from Mexico to Panama. Accidental at this season in Maryland (specimen, 1947) and New York. An adult male was present at a feeding station, Katonah, N.Y., from Nov. 30 to Dec. 25, 1936 (Wheeler).

CANADA WARBLER (*Wilsonia canadensis*)*B

Range: An eastern Nearctic species, breeding south to northern New Jersey and southeastern New York, and in the higher mountains to northern Georgia; rarely to the coasts of Massachusetts, Rhode Island, and Connecticut.

Status: Common to very common migrant. Fairly common breeder in the highlands.

Migration: The Canada Warbler is one of our more numerous members of this family, appearing in largest numbers during late May and again in August.

Maxima: *Spring*—50, Mill Neck, May 20, 1956; 75, Central Park, May 23, 1954. *Fall*—25, Prospect Park, Aug. 12, 1953; 35, Far Rockaway, Aug. 23, 1958.

Extreme dates: *Spring*—Apr. 23, 28, 30, and May 2 to June 7 and 12. *Fall*—casual July 1, 1892, Central Park (Chapman) and July 6, 1948, Wantagh, L.I. (Elliott); July 26 to Oct. 29; casual Nov. 13, 1935, Inwood Hill Park (L. N. Nichols). Rare before mid-May; before mid-August, and after mid-September.

Breeding: The Canada Warbler is generally, though somewhat locally, distributed in suitable habitat in the interior highlands of northern New Jersey and in New York in the counties of Orange, Rockland, Putnam, and Westchester. It nests in rich, moist woodland on hilly slopes covered with mountain laurel, and in woodland swamps with a hemlock-rhododendron growth. In mid-June 1960 at least 20 singing males were heard in the vicinity of the Delaware Water Gap, Warren County, N.J. In that state it breeds south to the Great Swamp, Morris County (Fables, 1955). East of the Hudson River it breeds fairly commonly south to Poundridge Reservation, Westchester County and probably locally in the Mianus River Gorge area of New York and adjacent Fairfield County. In the last-named, it was reported as breeding at Round Hill, Conn. in 1955—pair with young (several observers).

Egg dates: May 29 to June 16.

AMERICAN REDSTART (*Setophaga ruticilla*)*B

Range: Nearctic species, breeding south to Georgia, but very local along the coast.

Status: Common to very common migrant, especially in fall. Locally common breeder north of the coastal plain, but rare to absent on it.

Migration: The American Redstart is one of our most numerous warblers, at times outnumbering all others during late August and early September, especially on the coast.

Maxima: *Spring*—60, Central Park, May 23, 1954. *Fall*—30, Far Rockaway, Aug. 14, 1954; 180, Far Rockaway to Riis Park, Sept. 2, 1958; 150, Far Rockaway, Sept. 4, 1952; 100, Prospect Park, Sept. 13, 1950; 25 hit the tower at the Westhampton Air Force Base, Oct. 5, 1954.

Extreme dates: Apr. 22 to late October; at least five November reports to Nov. 23. Rare before May and after mid-October.

Breeding: This species inhabits low moist woodland and the drier uplands, in which places it breeds mainly in deciduous second-growth. Although widely distributed on the mainland, even there it is somewhat spotty and is rare to absent in seemingly suitable habitat. For example, in southern Westchester County it is a rare breeder in the Nature Study Woods, New Rochelle, but common at Grassy Sprain where, during the summer of 1941, Hickey found 21 nesting pairs on a 40-acre tract. On the north shore of Long Island it is locally distributed, fairly common in some sections, rare or absent in others.

Ferguson (*in litt.*) stated that on Fisher's Island it is "one of the commonest summer residents, nesting in all the maple swamps in abundance." Along the south shore of Long Island according to Cruickshank (1942) it is ". . . an uncommon local summer resident . . . from Mastic to Montauk," thus implying that it does not breed along the south shore west of Mastic, which is true for the most part. Nevertheless, Darrow and the writer found three or four nesting pairs during the summer of 1950 in the Sunken Forest on Fire Island.

Egg dates: May 18 to July 6.

Remarks: The American Redstart winters from Mexico and the West Indies to northern South America; rare at this season in southern Florida.

Accidental in winter in our area: adult male seen, Inwood Hill Park, Manhattan, Dec. 10–27, 1931 (O. Meyers and Cruickshank).

Subspecies: Although the A.O.U. *Check-list* (1957: 519) recognizes the more northern breeding race *tricolora*, it is regarded as unsatisfactory by many authorities and is so treated here. It is a poorly marked form at best. Adult males are inseparable and the alleged color differences in females and immatures are of average quality only, with considerable individual variation present.

400

WEAVER FINCHES: PLOCEIDAE

HOUSE SPARROW (*Passer domesticus*)*B

Introduced: Palearctic species, widely introduced and established in various parts of the world. The nominate race occurs in our area.

First introduced into Brooklyn in 1850, where the House Sparrow soon did well and multiplied. First reported in New Jersey at Chatham in 1868, Caldwell in 1870, and East Orange in 1874. According to Sage *et al.* (1913) it was abundant in Connecticut in all the larger towns by 1877. First reported at Riverdale, N.Y., in 1879 (Bicknell).

By the 1890s it was probably at its peak of abundance. During the summer of 1892 Chapman estimated 4000 bathing in one little pool in Central Park.

Supposedly because of the passing of the horse, arrival of the automobile, and competition with the Starling, the House Sparrow rapidly declined after 1913, especially in the large cities. It is still widespread and all too numerous in city parks, suburbs, and agricultural areas, in fact wherever man dwells. It is often a pest at feeding stations, sheer numbers keeping desirable species away, and a particular scourge during the breeding season, like the Starling utilizing the vast majority of nest sites, particularly in suburban and farming areas.

The House Sparrow is a resident species. It breeds in tree and building cavities, bird houses, and rarely builds bulky domed nests in trees.

Egg dates: March 23 to Aug. 18.

BLACKBIRDS: ICTERIDAE

BOBOLINK (*Dolichonyx oryzivorus*)*B

Range: Nearctic species, breeding south to the mountains of Maryland and West Virginia, rarely to North Carolina (1959); and to the edge of the coastal plain in southern New Jersey.

Status: Common to abundant fall migrant, especially along the coast, occasionally even very abundant; much less numerous in spring. Uncommon local breeder; formerly more numerous.

Migration: The Bobolink is both a diurnal and a nocturnal migrant. In our area during the autumnal southward flight, many Bobolinks are seen flying overhead, comparatively few alighting—on their way to the wild-rice marshes of the southern states.

Maxima: *Spring*—200 males, Milltown, N.J., May 16, 1934 (P. L. Collins); this is exceptional, however, the numbers usually seen in spring are much fewer; also 60, Brookhaven, L.I., May 16, 1960. *Fall*—migrates both night and day as evidenced by the following: 8000, Mastic, Aug. 24, 1912—mostly between 4:00 and 8:00 A.M. (J. T. Nichols); 5000, Far Rockaway, Sept. 8, 1953—between 7:00 and 10:00 A.M. (Bull); 3000, same locality, Sept. 16, 1947—flying over at night between 9:00 P.M. and midnight (Bull). The flight note of this species is one of the familiar night sounds.

It should be stressed that ordinarily groups of only a few individuals are observed, although flocks containing 20 to 30 occasionally alight in a weedy field or in the vicinity of marshes. Rarely larger flocks are seen feeding.

Extreme dates: Casual, Van Cortlandt Park, Apr. 19, 1909 (E. G. and L. N. Nichols); Apr. 28 to Nov. 2; casual, male collected, Fresh Kills, Staten Island, Nov. 26, 1960 (Jehl), specimen A.M.N.H. No. 766748.

Rare before May and after early October.

Breeding: The Bobolink is now a greatly decreased breeder, due to the decline in agriculture and the elimination of much open country for building purposes. Even in favorable areas, it is local and erratic, appearing and disappearing from time to time for reasons not readily apparent, occupying certain areas, absent in others that are similar in appearance. It nests on the ground in grassy fields and meadows.

It occasionally nests in colonies, depending on the size of an area. In 1935, 93 pairs bred on the Newark Meadows (Urner), but numbers rapidly thinned out because of the spread of the giant reed (*Phragmites*). A breeding survey of our area in 1940 revealed a total of more than 250 nesting pairs in 45 localities. McKeever (1941), in his detailed account of this breeding survey, found that Bobolinks bred in four types of habitat: (*a*) natural prairie—the former Hempstead Plains, now all but obliterated; (*b*) upper brackish marshes—the drier portions of the coastal salt meadows, where ditched and diked; (*c*) fallow fields—along the coast in farming areas; (*d*) lush upland fields—chiefly in inland regions, both on Long Island and on the mainland.

The natural prairie is, or was, the "only" permanent habitat, as it consisted of a climax vegetative type composed mainly of beard grass (*Andropogon*). On the other hand, the remaining habitats are of a temporary nature, the meadows and fields being cut for hay, plowed for cultivation, or, if allowed to remain fallow, eventually growing up to weeds and scrub, causing them to become unsuitable for breeding Bobolinks. Today, habitat (*d*) is most often occupied in our area.

Egg dates: May 26 to June 29.

EASTERN MEADOWLARK *(Sturnella magna)**B

Range: A fairly widespread American species, the nominate race occurring in our area.

Status: Fairly common to very common migrant, most numerous on the coast in fall. Uncommon but regular in winter along the coast; formerly much more numerous at this season. Locally common breeder.

Migration and winter: The Eastern Meadowlark is most numerous on and near the coast, where it is prevalent in salt marshes and fields. It has decreased greatly since the 1920s.

Maxima: *Fall*—150, Easthampton, Oct. 15, 1933 (Helmuth). *Winter*—375, Orient region, Dec. 25, 1911 (Latham). Present-day numbers are much smaller at both seasons.

Usually arrives in early March and departs in late October.

Breeding: This species nests on the ground in grassy fields and meadows. Now much more local than in former years, due to the decline of agriculture and development of open areas.

Egg dates: May 3 to July 22.

WESTERN MEADOWLARK *(Sturnella neglecta)*

Accidental: A western Nearctic species, breeding east to southeastern Ontario, southern Michigan, and central Ohio. Lanyon (1957) has indicated a marked extension of breeding range eastward since 1900 and a further spread since 1950. A specimen was collected at Rochester, N.Y., on Apr. 18, 1948 (Klonick, Auk, 68: 107, 1951). Near the same locality in the summer of 1957, an adult was observed feeding young out of the nest (Miller, Kingbird, 7: 115, 1958).

In our area there are no specimens, but four reports of singing birds, all in New Jersey, made by experienced observers, are believed correct: South Plainfield, Apr. 28, 1940 (Hunn); Troy Meadows, May 2–9, 1953 (at least eight observers); Bound Brook, May 15, 1954 (Boyajian, Harrison, and Stearns); same area, Apr. 10, 1956 (Conn). It would be desirable to collect a specimen to establish definitely its occurrence in our area.

For an account of why the two meadowlarks are considered distinct species, see Lanyon *(op. cit.)*.

Of great interest is a singing male Western Meadowlark found just north of our area near Poughkeepsie, N.Y., during June 1962 (Dutchess County Bird Club and Carleton). Lanyon later found it mated with a female Eastern Meadowlark; he caught the female on the nest along with three young, and the male was captured in a mist net. Lanyon (oral comm.) states that the entire family are now (1963) in captivity at the Kalbfleisch

Research Station where three young are being raised; these three birds are hybrids—one male and two females.

YELLOW-HEADED BLACKBIRD (*Xanthocephalus xanthocephalus*)*

Very rare visitant: A western Nearctic species, breeding east to northwestern Indiana and locally in northwestern Ohio. Reported east to the Atlantic coast from Maine to Florida.

There are at least 14 reports of the Yellow-headed Blackbird for our area, of which three are specimens: One taken at Westbury, L.I., date unknown (J. Hicks, *fide* John F. Mathews)—whereabouts of specimen unknown; adult female, Stamford, Conn., Aug. 13, 1888—not July as stated in the literature (E. K. Colbron), A.M.N.H. No. 71952; adult female, Orient, Sept. 9, 1943 (Latham), in his collection.

There are the following acceptable sight reports: Flushing, March 29 to May 7, 1932 (Walker, Watson, Berliner *et al.*); adult male, Jones Beach, Sept. 1, 1932 (Lunt); adult male with Common Grackles at roost, New Hyde Park, L.I., Aug. 5, 1934 (Cruickshank and Sedwitz); Orient, Oct. 4, 1940 (Latham); adult male at feeding station with flock of Red-winged Blackbirds, Blue Point, L.I., Apr. 17, 1947 (S. T. Miller); Easthampton, Oct. 30, 1948 (Helmuth); adult male, and female or immature male, present at Baxter Creek, Bronx County, from Sept. 18 to Oct. 12, 1954 (H. and V. Bauer and numerous observers)—these were also seen with Red-winged Blackbirds; female or immature male, Mecox Bay, Sept. 19, 1956 (Fry, Ingersoll, and Walter); adult male, color-photographed at feeder, Saddle River, N.J., Apr. 2–16, 1961 (Komorowski); female banded, Flushing, May 2, 1961 (Astle).

Extreme fall dates: Aug. 5 to Oct. 30.

This species winters north to southern Louisiana.

A female observed with a mixed flock of "blackbirds" at the Sloss feeder, Hewlett, L.I., Jan. 13, 1962, and on Jan. 16 (Berliner), is the first reported winter occurrence in the northeast.

RED-WINGED BLACKBIRD (*Agelaius phoeniceus*)*B

Range: A widespread American species, the nominate race breeding in our area.

Status: Very common to very abundant fall migrant. Uncommon to very common in winter; locally very abundant at winter roosts. Common to abundant breeder.

Migration and winter: The Red-winged Blackbird is one of our most

404

numerous birds, at times swarming by the thousands at coastal winter roosts. Often a common visitor at feeding stations, and frequently becomes quite tame around such places as Jones Beach—picking up food scraps left by picnickers.

Maxima: *Fall*—2000, Easthampton, Sept. 26, 1930; 50,000, Iona Island, Hudson River, Nov. 5, 1954 (Orth). *Winter*—Raritan River roost, Christmas counts—200,000, Dec. 23, 1939; 125,000. Dec. 23, 1952.

Usually arrives by late February or early March, the males always preceding the females by as much as two to three weeks; usually departs by mid-November.

Breeding: Red-winged Blackbirds breed in marshes, open swamps, wet meadows, and occasionally in upland grassy fields. The nest is placed in a low bush or in marsh vegetation, more rarely on the ground.

Maxima: 180 nesting pairs, Troy Meadows, June 1947 (Urner Club).

Egg dates: May 7 to July 4.

ORCHARD ORIOLE (*Icterus spurius*)*B

Range: A southeastern Nearctic species, breeding north to central New York and Massachusetts.

Status: Rare to uncommon spring migrant. Rare to uncommon breeder over most of area; fairly common, but local in New Jersey.

Migration: The Orchard Oriole is recorded regularly as a spring migrant only by the most active observers, and even then only one or two individuals are observed on any one day. Occasionally more are seen.

Maxima: 10, Riis Park to Jones Beach—5 of these in one tree at Point Lookout—May 4, 1958 (Carleton, Eisenmann, and Grant); 6, Easthampton, May 14, 1950 (Helmuth). One of the first birds to depart in fall, rarely seen after mid-July. No fall flight apparent; very rare after August, no local specimens in the American Museum collection later than Aug. 15.

Extreme dates: Apr. 25 and 28 to Sept. 22 and 27. Rare before May.

Breeding: This species nests in orchards, shade trees in farming country, nurseries, estates, and in scattered trees near ponds and streams. Formerly (*ca.* 1900) more numerous and widespread; considerable decrease within the past half-century. Concerning its presence on Long Island, Giraud (1844) stated, "This species, more abundant than the Baltimore, is found in all our orchards." When J. T. Nichols resided at Far Rockaway, Queens County, from 1891 to 1900, he said of this species (*in litt.*), "tolerably common summer resident, more numerous than the Baltimore Oriole," with a maximum of five nesting pairs per year. The Orchard Oriole has not bred there for many years, and is now only a rare spring migrant.

Elsewhere it has decreased as agriculture declined and orchards became scarce, although it breeds locally in nurseries and gardens. McKeever

(1941) gave a detailed summary for our area up to that time. As late as the latter part of the 1940s, as many as a dozen pairs nested on the Long Island Sound shore in the Port Chester, N.Y., area east to Greenwich, Conn. (*fide* Cook).

Today the only portion of our region where it is fairly common, although local, is in the lowlands of New Jersey, particularly in parts of Monmouth, Middlesex, Somerset, and Hunterdon counties; locally along the Delaware River. A current breeding survey would be most desirable.

Egg dates: May 24 to June 23.

Remarks: The statement in the *Birds of Rockland County* (1959: 35), "occasional in winter," is unsatisfactory. This species winters in the tropics from southern Mexico to northern South America, without a proved winter occurrence even in Florida; in fact the Orchard Oriole is scarce there by October. No winter records have been substantiated anywhere in the northeast. The two supposed winter sight reports for Rockland County were based on "a battered male" and "a brightly colored male," and are uncorroborated. The "battered male" was in all probability a dull-plumaged Baltimore Oriole. As for the "brightly colored male," even adult males are olive in winter.

BALTIMORE ORIOLE (*Icterus galbula*)*B

Range: An essentially eastern Nearctic species, breeding from southern Canada to northern Georgia, but rare and local on the coastal plain.

Status: Fairly common to common migrant. Widespread breeder, except on the coastal plain where uncommon and local. Very rare to rare in winter, but regular in recent years.

Migration: The Baltimore Oriole regularly arrives during the first week of May.

Maxima: *Spring*—22, Central Park, May 12, 1933; 38, Easthampton, May 14, 1950. *Fall*—30, Far Rockaway, Sept. 4, 1952. Just south of our area at Island Beach, N.J., 72 were banded on Sept. 3, 1960.

"Extreme" dates: Apr. 14, 16, and several other mid-April dates (some after southerly storms) to early November; adult male collected, Elmsford, N.Y., Dec. 1, 1892 (J. Rowley), A.M.N.H., previously unpublished. Rare before May and after mid-October.

Breeding: The Baltimore Oriole prefers to nest in elms, but will occasionally choose other trees such as maples. During a survey conducted by the Urner Club in northern New Jersey, Frohling (1950) reported that of more than 500 nests examined during the winter of 1948-49, approximately 300 (60 per cent) were located in elms, about 150 (30 per cent) were located in maples, and the remaining 50 (10 per cent) in other types. Of these 500 nests, about 75 per cent were situated in trees over or near roads, and about

406

25 per cent in trees over fields, both cultivated and uncultivated. Without exception, *all* nests were in relatively open situations, *none* being found in woodland.

Egg dates: May 16 to July 7.

Change in winter status: This species winters from Mexico to Colombia and Venezuela. Rare at this season in southern Florida; more rarely to South Carolina; in recent years north to Massachusetts.

In the New York City area, Griscom (1923) called it accidental in winter, listing two occurrences for Central Park and one at Hackensack, N.J. Cruickshank (1942) stated that he knew of four reports in January and three in February, and an individual that overwintered at Huntington, L.I., 1935–36.

Since the winter of 1946–47, the Baltimore Oriole has been reported every year, with at least one each winter.

Maxima: Seven each, winters of 1954–55 and 1959–60. The great majority of winter occurrences are at feeding stations. During late December 1957, there were at least eight reported, including three at Montauk Point; one of the latter, thought to have been a Bullock's Oriole, and collected on Dec. 28, proved to be a female Baltimore Oriole, specimen in A.M.N.H. collection. Three immatures or females present at a feeder at Easthampton, L.I., throughout January 1959 (Latham), are very exceptional.

RUSTY BLACKBIRD *(Euphagus carolinus)**

Range: Nearctic species, the nominate race breeding south to northeastern New York (Adirondacks), the northern portions of Vermont and New Hampshire, and central Maine.

Status: Fairly common migrant, except on Long Island where rare to uncommon. Locally common to abundant in New Jersey. Rare and local in winter elsewhere.

Occurrence and maxima: The Rusty Blackbird is generally found in wooded swamps, occasionally in other wet habitats. It occurs in insignificant numbers, compared to the other "blackbirds," and is "lost" among the hordes of those species, when associating with them.

Maxima: *Spring*—300, Troy Meadows, March 21, 1943. *Winter*—150, Troy Meadows, Dec. 21, 1952; Raritan River roost—250, Feb. 5, 1939, and 400, Dec. 23, 1939. These numbers are, however, exceptional, ordinarily only a few individuals or small flocks seen in most places.

Extreme dates: Sept. 9, 12, and 18 to May 16, 22, and 26. Rare before October and after early May. Sight reports on earlier fall and later spring dates by inexperienced observers are unacceptable as confusion with immature Common Grackles is likely. Migrants usually arrive during late

February or early March, and ordinarily depart before December.

Subspecies: The poorly defined race *nigrans*, breeding south to Nova Scotia, is of doubtful validity and barely separable; apparently only distinguishable in fall males. Parkes (1952) lists a specimen, A.M.N.H. No. 440946, taken at Brooklyn, November 1861, as this form. In a later paper (1954b), he "reluctantly" admits the validity of this subspecies. Godfrey (1959) likewise considers *nigrans* a poor race.

COMMON GRACKLE (*Quiscalus quiscula*)*B

Range: Nearctic species (for details, see Subspecies).

Status: Collectively this species is a common to very abundant migrant, particularly inland. Locally common to very abundant in winter roosts. Common widespread breeder.

Migration: While this species is numerous both spring and fall, it is especially so during the latter season, particularly in October and November along the inland ridges and river valleys where the spectacular flights take place, thousands and thousands flying overhead each fall. Less numbers occur along the coast, although Latham estimated a flock to contain 10,000 at Orient, Sept. 29, 1951—very unusual indeed.

Common Crackles are ubiquitous, occurring from the wooded interior highlands to the coastal beaches—in the latter area often observed picking up scraps of food from the refuse baskets at beach clubs.

Arrives in late February or early March and departs by late November.

Winter: In coastal areas Common Grackles congregate during the winter months and they are locally numerous at this season, notably in enormous roosts of mixed "blackbirds." On Long Island there was, and possibly still is, a very large roost at Hecksher State Park where, on Feb. 14, 1938, at least 15,000 were estimated (Cruickshank and Hickey). The most notable winter roost is situated along the Raritan River, N.J., where during the Christmas counts of 1946 and 1952, more than 70,000 Common Grackles were estimated during each of those years. However, in most areas it is usually much rarer than either the Red-winged Blackbird or the Brownheaded Cowbird—particularly at feeding stations.

Breeding: Common Grackles nest singly or in small colonies, preferably wherever tall ornamental conifers occur, especially spruce and pine. Thus they are most numerous in the suburbs, parks, golf courses, estates, nurseries, and around farms, or as Cruickshank (1942) so appropriately stated, in "disturbance communities."

Egg dates: Apr. 25 to June 30.

Subspecies: The races *stonei* and *versicolor*, formerly known as the "Purple" and "Bronzed" Grackles, respectively, occur in the New York City area. We are in the zone of intergradation, although "pure" *stonei*

408

breeds at least in that portion of New Jersey at the southern bounds of our region, as in Monmouth, Middlesex, Somerset, and Hunterdon counties. The subspecies *versicolor* breeds mainly north and west of our area—Massachusetts, Rhode Island, most of Connecticut, upstate New York, and the more western portions of Pennsylvania. The statement in the A.O.U. *Check-list* (1957: 540), "Hybridizes [intergrades] . . . along the line of junction from southern Louisiana to Massachusetts," is misleading. Actually the "hybrid" zone is quite broad, at least in the northeastern portions (this population formerly known as "*ridgwayi*").

In other words, we are at the northern limits of *Q. q. stonei.* Nearly all winter specimens taken locally are *Q. q. versicolor,* and undoubtedly it is this race that occurs so numerously during migration.

BROWN-HEADED COWBIRD (*Molothrus ater*)*B

Range: Nearctic species, the nominate race breeding in our area.

Status: Common to abundant migrant. Uncommon to very common in winter; locally very abundant at winter roosts. Common widespread breeder.

Migration and winter: The Brown-headed Cowbird is one of our most familiar and, at times, very numerous species in open country, especially along the coast, where it is often seen in flocks feeding in short-grass fields and on lawns along the highways.

Maxima: *Fall*—1100, Water Mill, Oct. 13, 1936; 425, Central Park, Oct. 31, 1957. *Winter*—35,000, Raritan River roost, Dec. 23, 1946. Flocks up to 1000 have been seen elsewhere in winter, though this is unusual. Often a visitor at feeding stations, and becomes very tame at the beaches around picnic grounds and even in the refreshment areas, picking up scraps at the very feet of the patrons.

Usually arrives in mid-March and departs in late November.

Breeding: This species is unique among our local birds in that it parasitizes other species, laying its eggs in other birds' nests. During this season it frequently deserts its usual open-country haunts and the female seeks out nests of many woodland species as well as those around farms and suburban areas.

Egg dates: Apr. 26 to July 4.

TANAGERS: THRAUPIDAE

WESTERN TANAGER (*Piranga ludoviciana*)*

Casual: A western Nearctic species, breeding east to central Saskatchewan and western Nebraska. Winters chiefly from southern Mexico to Costa

Rica. Stragglers recorded east to the Atlantic coast from Maine to New Jersey, particularly in recent years.

In our area there are at least 12 acceptable reports (chiefly October–January), one a specimen: immature male, taken at Highland Falls, N.Y., Dec. 21, 1881 (Mearns), U.S.N.M. No. 235651 (*fide* Wetmore); adult male observed in a small patch of oak woods, Wainscott, L.I., May 20, 1934 (Helmuth); female or immature, Jones Beach, Nov. 16, 1952 (Sedwitz and Bull) to Jan. 16, 1953 (many observers); one, feeding chiefly on grapes, color-photographed at the Cherepy feeder, Franklin, N.J., Jan. 2 to April 1, 1953 (over 200 observers); Riis Park, L.I., Dec. 19, 1953 (Messing and Post) to early January 1954 (many observers), also color-photographed; two, same locality, Oct. 31 to Nov. 11, 1954 (many observers); adult male with trace of red on head, Far Rockaway, Oct. 1–3, 1955 (Bull); no fewer than three different reports during the fall of 1956—immature or female banded at Montclair, N.J., Nov. 10 (F. Frazier); Riis Park, one, Dec. 1, and two, Dec. 8 (Carleton, Mayer *et al.*); Jones Beach, Dec. 31 (several observers)—Riis Park, Oct. 9, 1960 (Arbib); female found dead at Rye, N.Y., May 12, 1961, sent to the Audubon Nature Center, Greenwich (H. S. Peters, R. C. Clement, and P. C. Spofford), the specimen unfortunately not preserved. The coastal individuals were observed feeding principally on the berries of *Eleagnus* (Russian olive).

SCARLET TANAGER (*Piranga olivacea*)*B

Range: An eastern Nearctic species, breeding from extreme southern Canada to Oklahoma and Georgia, but local over much of the coastal plain.

Status: Fairly common to common migrant. Common and widely distributed breeder in deciduous woodland north of the coastal plain.

Migration: Scarlet Tanagers are usually observed in small groups up to three or four, but occasionally larger numbers are reported.

Maxima: *Spring*—16 males in two white oaks, Far Rockaway, L.I., May 9, 1951; 25, same locality, May 13, 1956 (males outnumbering females 2 to 1); most exceptional were 60 within a half-mile, Ramsey, N.J., May 15, 1947 (C. K. Nichols and others), approximately 50 per cent each of both sexes—a particularly cold late spring, many of the birds feeding on the ground. *Fall*—during the very late migration of 1883, 7 struck the Fire Island light, Sept. 30, and 7 more on Oct. 12 (*fide* Dutcher); 24 hit the tower at the Westhampton Air Force Base, Oct. 5, 1954 (Wilcox), a late date for so many.

Extreme dates: Casual, adult male picked up dead, Amityville, Apr. 8, 1957 (Elliott), specimen in Tackapausha Museum, Seaford, L.I.; Apr. 12,

17, 19, and 26 (some of these storm driven) to Oct. 22 and Nov. 7; casual, Van Cortlandt Park, Nov. 21, 1927 (L. N. Nichols).

Rare before May and after mid-October.

Breeding: The Scarlet Tanager shows a decided preference for oak woods and is especially widespread on the mainland. It is rare and local over much of the sandy coastal plain, even where oaks predominate.

Egg dates: May 18 to July 20.

Remarks: No winter reports are accepted, due to confusion with other tanagers in obscure plumage. An individual seen at Short Beach, L.I., during late December 1960 by a number of observers was "identified" as three different species of this genus (Western, Scarlet, and Summer Tanagers). Unfortunately it was not collected.

SUMMER TANAGER (*Piranga rubra*)*

Range: A southern Nearctic species, the nominate race breeding north to Maryland and central Delaware; formerly to southern New Jersey. Wanders north to New Brunswick and Nova Scotia.

Status: Rare but regular spring migrant; very rare in fall. Occurs chiefly near the coast.

Occurrence: At least 17 specimens of the Summer Tanager have been taken in our area, of which seven are in the American Museum collection and four in private collections. I have seen all of these. The whereabouts of the remaining six are not known, and some of them may not be extant. Of these 17 specimens, 16 were collected in spring (7 in April, 9 in May).

This species, although still rare, has been reported more frequently during recent years perhaps due, in part, to a greatly increased number of observers. It has been reported each spring since 1947. The greatest number of individuals observed in one year was five each in 1955 and 1959, dates ranging from May 2 to 13 and May 12 to 29, respectively, but usually only one to three birds a spring are noted over the entire region.

Occurrence by month: *Spring*—April (20); May (50); June (1). *Fall*—September (10); October (5); curiously there are no August reports.

Extreme dates: *Spring*—Apr. 6, 7, and 8 (latter two, specimens) to May 29 and June 12; reported July 6, 1940, Central Park (Wiegmann), and July 29, 1938, Clifton, N.J. (Mangels). *Fall*—Sept. 3 (specimen) to Oct. 3 and 6; reported Oct. 19, 1947, Point Lookout, L.I. (Ryan and Sutton), adult male in changing plumage—sketch and detailed description submitted.

Although this species arrives far ahead of the Scarlet Tanager in the south, the spring arrival of the early April individuals listed above were due to southerly storms. At least two April specimens were picked up dead the day after a storm, and one observer reported that he saw a Summer Tanager during a "violent downpour."

However, not all of the 20 April occurrences were the result of tropical storms. The Summer Tanager arrives along the Gulf coast and in southern Florida as early as mid-March, often by the latter half of that month, so it is not surprising that 10 April reports in our area were recorded before Apr. 15.

Remarks: Prior to 1870, this species nested in southern New Jersey, outside our region. Fables (1955) stated, "It may return in the future as a breeding species, and should be searched for in open pine woods in the southern part of the state. . . ." That very same year in southern New Jersey, it "bred at Springtown, Cumberland Co., June, 1955 (H. H. Mills)," *fide* Kunkle *et al.* (1959). No reports of nesting in New Jersey since then.

FINCHES, GROSBEAKS, BUNTINGS, SPARROWS:

FRINGILLIDAE

CARDINAL (*Richmondena cardinalis*)*B

Range: A southern Nearctic and northern Neotropical species, the nominate race breeding (resident) north to central New York and Connecticut; casually to Massachusetts (1958 on). Steadily spreading northward since about 1930.

Status: Fairly common to locally abundant resident throughout lowland areas in suitable habitat, but local and uncommon over much of the sandy coastal plain. Rare to absent in the mountains, and along the ocean beaches.

Change in status: The increase and spread of the Cardinal in the New York City region, as well as throughout much of the northeast, particularly since the mid-1940s, and more especially in the 1950s, has been positively phenomenal. Few, if any, species have made such gains.

412

Griscom (1923) stated, "The rapid advance of the suburbs and the consequent clearing of woods and thickets has either destroyed the bird's haunts or rendered them uninhabitable. As a result it is now extirpated in practically all sections." This opinion is scarcely tenable in view of the further deterioration of much of this same area in the nearly 40 years since 1923, and at the same time the undeniable increase of the Cardinal in our area is a fact. The Cardinal's withdrawal from the northern limits of its range (New York City area) by the first quarter of the century cannot be denied. By 1920 it was rare in our area nearly everywhere north of the Plainfield, N.J. region. However, causes other than those advanced by Griscom must have been in effect as this species had multiplied tremendously in recent years in spite of suburban advance and habitat reduction. A cycle of milder winters may have been a major cause of the recent increase. There may be other biologic factors involved as well. However, at present, population overflow into "new" territory is continuing unabated.

Cruickshank (1942) remarked that "in recent years the species has been slowly but steadily re-establishing itself northward. Like all permanent residents which reach the northern limits of their range here the Cardinal is subject to severe winter killing." However, it usually survives the severest winters at feeding stations.

Winter: I cannot help but believe that the vast increase in the number of feeding stations within the past 20 years has been of the utmost importance in maintaining a very large number of Cardinals in winter when they are more concentrated than at any other season. This is substantiated by figures listed below. As many as 17 Cardinals have been reported at a single New Jersey feeding station in one winter, as proved by banding; also 12 at a Connecticut feeder and 7 at a Long Island feeder. These were birds present during the winters of 1958 and 1959.

The following Table of figures based on Christmas counts indicates the abundance of this species everywhere except on eastern Long Island, where it is still relatively rare, although increasing. As may be seen in this table, the area west of the Hudson River has the greatest number of Cardinals, where they have "always" been most numerous. While there are several variables present, including size differences of the areas, number of counts taken, and number of participants, with some inevitable duplication in counting, nevertheless the estimates are considered useful in comparing relative abundance within the following four subdivisions of the New York City area: (*A*) entire area *west* of the Hudson River including Staten Island; (*B*) mainland area *east* of the Hudson River; (*C*) western Long Island (east to Port Jefferson and Patchogue); (*D*) eastern Long Island. The left-hand figures in the lettered columns indicate total number of individuals observed, the figures in parentheses indicate number of counts taken.

413

	A		B		C		D	
1954	614	(11)	132	(6)	37	(5)	none	(3)
1955	610	(9)	201	(6)	44	(4)	none	(3)
1956	636	(11)	231	(6)	59	(4)	none	(4)
1957	853	(11)	253	(6)	62	(4)	10	(4)
1958	928	(12)	411	(6)	69	(4)	8	(4)
1959	1304	(12)	691	(6)	116	(4)	22	(4)
1960	1922	(12)	1050	(6)	190	(4)	17	(4)

The small numbers for Long Island which include very few Christmas counts represent only a portion of the large territory involved, but it is believed that there would not be an appreciable difference in numbers if several more counts had been taken at the east end of Long Island.

Breeding (see map): The Cardinal is quite adaptable, frequenting low, rich, but open woodland, brushy swamps, woodland borders, thickets and—in recent years—has become common in suburban yards and even city parks, provided dense shrubbery is available. The nest is most often placed in bushes, hedges, and vines.

At the time Cruickshank wrote (1942), the Cardinal was slowly but steadily increasing in northern New Jersey, breeding regularly though sparsely on Staten Island and in the southern portions of Rockland and Westchester counties, and was casual "elsewhere," the last undoubtedly referring to Long Island. Cruickshank probably secured his information chiefly from McKeever's detailed account (1941). At that time it was just becoming established east of the Hudson River.

Within a year after publication of Cruickshank's book, the Cardinal really started to "go places" as evidenced by the following. Not only did it push northward in numbers into Rockland and Orange counties, but by the mid-1940s it had also greatly increased and become well established in southern Westchester County. In fact, as early as 1942, this species nested in Connecticut as far east as Riverside, Fairfield County.

In the meantime, the Cardinal increased once more on Staten Island, and re-established itself on Long Island, nesting in Prospect Park in 1943, the first definite report of breeding on Long Island in over 40 years. While its increase in numbers on Long Island was not as rapid as on the mainland, it nevertheless spread eastward as indicated by the following reports of first nestings (see map); 1944—Manhasset (north shore) and Seaford (south shore), Nassau County; 1946—near Kings Park, western Suffolk County (north shore); 1947—near Patchogue, western Suffolk County (south shore); 1949—Greenport, extreme eastern Suffolk County (north shore); 1952—Southampton, eastern Suffolk County (south shore); 1958—Fisher's Island (just off the southwest tip of the Rhode Island coast) where, by 1961, Ferguson (*in litt.*) reported six breeding pairs.

414

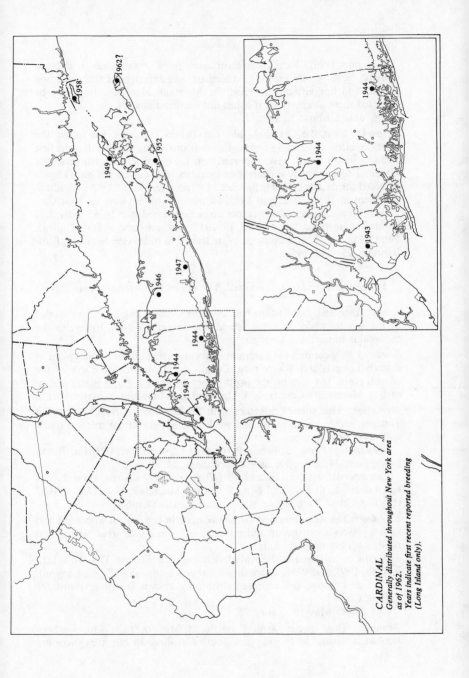

CARDINAL
Generally distributed throughout New York area as of 1962.
Years indicate first recent reported breeding (Long Island only).

It is now (1962) locally common and "fully" established in Putnam County, N.Y., southwestern Connecticut, and throughout western Long Island, and has virtually reached the Montauk area. Breeding may be expected there at any time, if it has not occurred already.

Egg dates: May 5 to July 11.

Remarks: That the Cardinal—like the Tufted Titmouse, but unlike the Mockingbird—is virtually nonmigratory is proved by the fact that the first two species are almost never reported from the outer beaches. However, the Cardinal does wander, appearing at localities where it has not been known to breed for decades. This is indicated by specimens taken by Roy Latham at Orient in 1930, 1932, and 1938, all three in his collection. That Cardinals travel considerable distances on occasion is shown by an individual banded at Hartford, Conn., Dec. 13, 1957, and recovered at State College, Penn., May 2, 1958, a distance of at least 270 miles (see Bordner, Bird-Banding, 29: 244, 1958).

ROSE-BREASTED GROSBEAK (*Pheucticus ludovicianus*)*B

Range: Essentially an eastern Nearctic species, breeding south to the edge of the coastal plain on Long Island and in central New Jersey; in the mountains to northern Georgia.

Status: Fairly common to common migrant, except on the coastal plain of eastern Long Island, where rare. Locally common breeder north of the coastal plain, but rare on the north shore of western Long Island and in eastern Monmouth County, N.J. Unreported as breeding on Staten Island.

Migration: This species, together with the Baltimore Oriole and Scarlet Tanager, arrive regularly the first week in May and lend a tropical touch with their bright colors.

Maxima: *Spring*—35, Bronx Park, May 12, 1950. *Fall*—25, Far Rockaway, Sept. 24, 1949; 30, Bronx Park, Sept. 24, 1955.

Extreme dates: Apr. 16 and 20 (after southerly storms; several later April dates) to Oct. 23 and Nov. 5. Casual, Montclair, N.J., Dec. 4, 1932 (Fry)—species? Rare before May and after early October.

Breeding: The Rose-breasted Grosbeak nests in rich, moist woodland and swampy woods on the uplands; occasionally in shade trees along rural roads with extensive thickets.

A pair or two bred at the Kalbfleisch Research Station, Dix Hills, L.I., in 1958, 1960, and 1961, where they inhabited a "dry slope" (*fide* Lanyon). As far as I know, this represents the only known breeding record for Suffolk County.

Egg dates: May 18 to June 28.

Remarks: This species winters north to Mexico, rarely to southern Louisiana; casual in Florida and South Carolina. In our area there are

416

several reports at unusually late dates, two of which may have been escapes, the third almost certainly one: adult male captured in Central Park, Dec. 16, 1909, and turned over to the zoo; another adult male, Bronx Park, Dec. 27, 1959 (several observers); adult female, collected in the same locality, Jan. 3, 1907, A.M.N.H., very likely a cage bird as it is a "runt" and has feathers missing at the base of the bill—almost a sure sign; immature male at feeder, Rutherford, N.J., Jan. 26 to Feb. 13, 1908 (Brown). From what we know now, this latter individual as well as the bird reported from Montclair (sex not stated) might have been Black-headed Grosbeaks, a species not recognized in the field locally until 1945 (see discussion under Black-headed Grosbeak).

BLACK-HEADED GROSBEAK (*Pheucticus melanocephalus*)

Casual: A western Nearctic species, breeding east to central Nebraska. Winters chiefly in Mexico; occasionally north and east to Louisiana (since about 1950). Casual in migration or winter east to the Atlantic coast from Massachusetts (color photo, 1954) to Virginia (specimen, 1960) and South Carolina (specimen, 1957).

In our area it has been reported at least nine times, having occurred in Connecticut, New York, and New Jersey. Although never collected in the New York City region, there is at least one color photograph to substantiate its occurrence here. Nearly all individuals were reported at feeding stations.

The occurrences are as follows: Adult male in "changing" plumage, Woodmere Woods, L.I., Sept. 28, 1945 (Bull); female, Idlewild, L.I., Dec. 27, 1953, to Apr. 24, 1954 (Mayer, Carleton *et al.*); immature male, Bristow feeder, New Canaan, Conn., Feb. 20 to Apr. 19, 1954 (Grierson, Poor *et al.*); male, Grierson feeder, Katonah, N.Y., Feb. 26 to Apr. 23, 1954 (numerous observers); adult male, Boyajian feeder, Englewood, N.J., Jan. 24 to end of February 1955 (many observers); "nearly" adult male, Stansbury feeder, Palisades (village), N.Y., Apr. 23–30, 1955 (several observers); male, Strout feeder, Allendale, N.J., Jan. 21 to Feb. 3, 1957 (Dater *et al.*); "sub-adult" male, feeder, Old Greenwich, Conn., Apr. 24 to May 3, 1957 (color photograph by Mrs. L. Chamberlain—photo examined by Bull, Eisenmann, and P. C. Spofford, all of whom concurred in identification); female, R. Chamberlain feeder, Maplewood, N.J., Feb. 4 to Apr. 9, 1960 (Eisenmann, Grant *et al.*).

Several other reports have not been confirmed. One was originally reported as a female Rose-breasted Grosbeak and subsequently "identified" as *P. melanocephalus*. It is highly desirable that a specimen be collected to further establish the occurrence of the Black-headed Grosbeak in the New York City area. It is possible that one or more of the above birds were of hybrid stock, for these two species are known to interbreed freely where their ranges overlap in the region from Saskatchewan to

417

Kansas, particularly in Nebraska (see Short, Nebraska Bird Rev., 29: 19–20, 1961; and West, 1962).

BLUE GROSBEAK (*Guiraca caerulea*)*B

Range: A southern Nearctic and northern Neotropical species, the nominate race breeding north to Maryland and Delaware, rarely to southeastern Pennsylvania and southern New Jersey; casually in northern New Jersey (since 1958). Wanders north to southern Canada.

Status: Rare but regular spring and fall migrant on the coast. Very rare inland, where it has bred recently at two localities in New Jersey.

Change in status: 1. *Migration*—As recently as 1942, Cruickshank considered the Blue Grosbeak an "accidental visitant," listing only six "unquestionable" records. From that year until 1947, I could find only four additional reports.

Beginning in 1948, however, this species has been reported regularly, from two to four individuals observed each year through 1956. It has further increased since 1957—six fall reports that year; and in 1958— three spring, four fall reports. During the spring of 1961, as many as seven individuals were reported from Apr. 27 to May 13, six of these on the south shore of Long Island between Riis Park and Moriches. Wilcox banded a male at Center Moriches on Apr. 27, and Walter Terry banded three individuals (all males) at Patchogue, Apr. 27, May 1, and May 13, and color-photographed one.

The Blue Grosbeak may now be seen annually in spring and fall along the outer coast by the active observer, where it may be found in thickets and hedgerows. In fall it is reported chiefly during September and October; in spring during late April and May.

Extreme dates: *Fall*—July 27, 30, and Aug. 8 to Oct. 23, 29, and Nov. 11; casual, Riis Park, Nov. 25, 1961 (Mayer and Rose). *Spring*—casual, Roselle, N.J., March 31 to Apr. 15, 1958 (Fables); Apr. 20, 26, 28 (two latter, specimens) to May 21. Rare before September, after mid-October; and before late April.

2. *Specimen data*—Five specimens (3 extant) have been taken locally— two listed by Griscom (1923): Manhattan Island, May 15, 1838; Canarsie, May 1843. Cruickshank (1942) listed an additional specimen: immature male, Moriches Inlet, Sept. 20, 1934 (Wilcox), in his collection. An adult male collected at Orient, Apr. 26, 1929 (Latham), not previously published; immature male taken at Montauk, Apr. 28, 1944 (Latham), both in his collection.

3. *Breeding*—This species has bred in our region in New Jersey at two localities. "A pair nested and fledged one young at Middlebush, Somerset County, in August 1958 (T. Butler)," *fide* Kunkle *et al.* (1959). They

418

nested there again in 1959 and 1960, adults and young banded in the latter year (Murray). A breeding pair was found near Metuchen, Middlesex County, in 1962 (Grant). These reports represent considerable breeding range extension, heretofore reported north only to southern New Jersey.

Egg dates: No data.

Remarks: Beginners are cautioned to identify this species with care. Inexperienced observers continually misidentify male Indigo Buntings in changing plumage, believing that individuals of the latter species having patches of brown in the wing and "looking big," must be Blue Grosbeaks. Careful study of color plates and museum skins will readily indicate differences between the two in any plumage. A seldom-mentioned field character of the Blue Grosbeak is the vigorous twitching of the tail from side to side. The Indigo Bunting sometimes does this, but not with such vigor.

INDIGO BUNTING (*Passerina cyanea*)*B

Range: An eastern Nearctic species, breeding from extreme southern Canada to Texas and Florida.

Status: Uncommon to fairly common migrant, numbers fluctuating yearly. Somewhat local breeder, fairly common on the mainland, but rare to uncommon on Long Island.

Migration: This species, though usually seen singly or in groups of two or three, sometimes occurs in larger numbers. In May and October it may be seen on lawns with scattered shrubs, particularly in city parks, and in the same environment on the coast just back of the beaches.

Maxima: *Spring*—18, Van Cortlandt Park area, May 19, 1946. *Fall*— 6 hit the Fire Island Light, Sept. 23, 1887; 15, Jones Beach, Sept. 30, 1951; 8, Prospect Park, Oct. 10, 1947. Cruickshank (1942) called this species casual in October, but it is now regular during that month, especially along the coast. Of late years, it has even lingered into November.

Extreme dates: Casual, two at Orient, Apr. 10, 1959 (Latham); over two dozen April reports from the fifteenth to the thirtieth (earliest specimen, Apr. 19), some probably due to southerly storms; to Nov. 1 (specimen), Nov. 5, 8, 11, and 13; casual, Astoria, L.I., Dec. 7, 1944 (Hines), male banded. Rare before mid-May and after mid-October.

Breeding: The Indigo Bunting nests in bushy fields, abandoned overgrown farmland, second-growth clearings and woodland edge, and thickets along country roads. Local on Long Island and the coastal plain generally.

Egg dates: May 27 to July 12.

Remarks: The Indigo Bunting winters north to Florida. Accidental at this season in Maryland (specimen), New Jersey, Long Island, and Massachusetts.

In our area, there are two winter occurrences: one at a feeding station, Riverhead, L.I., throughout December 1957 (Latham); male with some blue patches, Schneider feeder, Verona, N.J., nearly all January 1960 (numerous observers, color photo taken).

PAINTED BUNTING (*Passerina ciris*)*

Accidental: A southeastern Nearctic species, the nominate race breeds north to southeastern North Carolina. Accidental north to Massachusetts.

All old records were assumed to be escaped cage birds and two specimens, one extant, probably were: adult male in somewhat worn plumage, Riverdale, N.Y., July 13, 1875 (Bicknell); adult male in good condition, Long Island, June 10, 1899 (Leutloff), A.M.N.H. No. 72045.

The following five recent occurrences, including a specimen, are possibly wild birds, as it has been illegal to cage these birds since 1913. However, one or two dealers in the metropolitan area were found to be in possession of Painted Buntings imported from Mexico. It is conceivable that reports of birds seen in the city parks, at least, were escapes from these sources.

Adult male, Central Park, Sept. 9–23, 1927 (Miss Samek and many others); adult female, Van Cortlandt Park, Sept. 29, 1937 (E. Petersen); adult male, Easthampton, May 13, 1947 (Helmuth); adult female, Central Park, Oct. 19, 1949 (Helmuth); adult male in good condition, found dead on road, East Hempstead, L.I., May 28, 1952 (R. Holmes), A.M.N.H. No. 748473.

Other reports by inexperienced observers lack confirmation.

DICKCISSEL (*Spiza americana*)*B

Range: Primarily a central Nearctic species, breeding sporadically north and east to southern Ontario, west-central New York, Ohio, Maryland, and once in southern New Jersey (Burlington County, 1939, *fide* Potter). No confirmed breeding record for Massachusetts in recent years, despite inclusion by A.O.U. *Check-list* (1957: 555).

Winters from southern Mexico to northern South America; rarely north to the Gulf states. In recent years in winter at feeding stations north to Massachusetts (specimen, 1946), and Long Island (specimen, 1961).

Status: Rare to uncommon but regular fall migrant, chiefly along the outer coast. Occasional in winter and spring at feeding stations, chiefly inland.

Change in status: The Dickcissel has had a unique and remarkable history, perhaps best illustrated by division into three time periods:

420

1. Early period (prior to 1880). This species formerly ranged widely in the breeding season over the Atlantic states from Massachusetts to South Carolina, being found in open country. It was restricted mainly to lowland areas where it nested on or near the ground in lush grassy fields and meadows grown up to alfalfa, clover, daisies, timothy, etc., avoiding the drier sections. On migration, however, then as now it frequented dry grassy fields, and lawns with hedgerows or thickets. There is no exact information as to how numerous it was in the early and middle nineteenth century, except that the early writers stated that it was "common" or "abundant." Nor do we know why or exactly when it disappeared from much of this region. It had apparently become very rare by the 1860s or 1870s in the New York City area. For an excellent account of its past history in the northeast, see Rhoads (1903).

2. Middle period (1880–1945). Between 1880 and 1900, there were scarcely any local records; two specimens collected on Long Island in 1888 and 1890, both in fall.

From 1900 to 1937, there were apparently only four additional occurrences. W. de W. Miller discovered a nesting pair in New Jersey at Plainfield, Union County, on July 4, 1904, and collected a juvenile female—specimen in A.M.N.H. collection; this represents our only known breeding record since the mid-nineteenth century. Three fall migrants, including a specimen at Speonk, L.I., Oct. 16, 1929 (Wilcox), in his collection.

In 1938 Helmuth saw two at Mecox Bay, L.I., Oct. 22 and 25, and took a specimen on the latter date, in his collection. By this time, it was becoming less rare and within the next seven years six more were reported, including an immature picked up dead at Scarsdale, N.Y., Oct. 14, 1941 (G. Dock) specimen in A.M.N.H. collection. The first spring individual reported since the "old" days was a singing male at Easthampton, L.I., May 18, 1944 (Helmuth).

3. Recent period (1946–62). (a) *Migration:* From 1946 to 1950, a regular autumn migrant—anywhere from two to six individuals reported each year. Big coastal flights from 1951 on—most numerous in late September and October. During 1954 at least 19 were reported in fall, as many as four in a day per locality, and one hit the Westhampton Air Force Base tower on Oct. 5 (Wilcox), specimen in his collection.

During the fall of 1963 flocks containing from five to over a dozen were observed on the coast of Long Island; maxima—14, Montauk, Sept. 28 (Yeaton *et al.*).

Most interesting is a Dickcissel banded at Middletown, R.I., Oct. 28, 1957, and recovered (trapped and released) at Rockaway, Morris County, N.J., Dec. 5, 1957. This bird remained in the latter locality until March 11, 1958 (see Baird and Cannon, Bird-Banding, 29: 183, 1958).

"Extreme" dates: Aug. 18 and 25 (specimen) to Nov. 30 (Oct. 25, latest specimen), possibly later—coastal migrants.

No evidence of a return spring migration prior to 1962, as the few spring individuals reported had overwintered at feeding stations. As of 1962, however, spring migrants were observed at such coastal localities as Short Beach and Mecox Bay.

(b) *Winter:* First winter occurrence was one at a feeder, Ramsey, N.J., all January and February, 1947 (Runk), color-photographed, and seen by numerous observers; another at the Schultz feeder, Hewlett, L.I., Feb. 19–24, 1949 (many observers). Numerous reports at feeding stations from 1952 on, as many as four or five at a single feeder (as proved by banding); 1952–53, at least 14 at inland feeders, distributed as follows: Connecticut (5), New Jersey (5), New York, mainland (3), Long Island (1). Most of these survived the winter, some remaining until mid-April, and one even stayed at a New Brunswick feeder until "early summer." The first winter specimen for our area was a female collected on Fisher's Island, Jan. 22, 1961 (Ferguson), in his collection. It was at his feeder in company with House Sparrows.

These wintering Dickcissels are in a category similar to the Yellow-breasted Chat and Baltimore Oriole; all three species winter in the tropics, but certain individuals remain far north of their usual range, generally at feeding stations.

(c) *Summer vagrants:* Singing males, Easthampton, June 10, 1949 (Helmuth), and Lawrence, July 30, 1960 (Bull), both on the south shore of Long Island.

Remarks: This species frequently associates with House Sparrows in migration and at feeders in winter. In fact female and immature Dickcissels are quite similar in appearance to female House Sparrows.

The Dickcissel should be looked for carefully during the breeding season, as it is possible that it may be found nesting again in our area in the near future. It has been reported as being very erratic in distribution and numbers, even in its midwestern breeding range, fluctuating from year to year. For an account of its recent status in the northeast, see Gross (1956).

EVENING GROSBEAK (*Hesperiphona vespertina*)*B

Range: Nearctic species, the nominate race has greatly extended its breeding range eastward in recent years; prior to 1950, east to Ontario and Michigan; since 1950, east and south to Quebec, northeastern New York (Adirondacks); Maine (1959); virtually reaching the Atlantic seaboard by 1960 (New Brunswick); south to western Massachusetts (1957); by 1962 breeding in central and southeastern New York, southern Connecticut, and northern New Jersey.

The most notable range extension occurred in 1962. Evening Grosbeaks were found breeding south of their boreal range for the first time in the east: in New York State at Rochester, Ithaca, Schenectady, and Stissing

Finches, Grosbeaks, Buntings, Sparrows: Fringillidae

(Dutchess County); Wallingford, Conn.; and in our area in northern New Jersey, the most southerly penetration to date (see under breeding).

Status: Now (1962) a regular and locally common to occasionally abundant winter visitant inland, arriving much earlier and departing much later than 20 years ago. Irregular and relatively rare on Long Island and anywhere on the coastal plain, except in flight years when locally very common.

Change in status: The Evening Grosbeak was unknown in our area prior to 1890, only one occurrence in northern New Jersey; not reported again for 20 years; first specimen taken in 1911 at Plainfield, N.J., Feb. 12 (Miller), A.M.N.H.; and reported for the first time the same year in New York State (Port Chester) and on Long Island (Forest Hills), both on Jan. 8; adult male collected on Fisher's Island, March 10, 1920 (Ferguson). Prior to 1925 not arriving before mid-November and departing by late April.

Cruickshank (1942) spoke of it as still a "rare and irregular winter visitant," almost every year a few reaching the northern sections, and he knew of only 73 "records."

Since about 1945, and especially 1947, it has enormously increased, regular and locally numerous, thus coinciding with its gradual but steady spread eastward and southward as a breeder; large flocks, especially at inland feeding stations.

Since 1950, several "huge" irruptions, particularly 1951–52 and 1954–55; "hundreds" reported at feeding stations, as proved by banding; also regular and in flocks each fall along the "hawk" ridges. Now arriving much earlier and departing much later (see extreme dates).

This species is especially fond of the fruit of the box elder or ash-leaved maple (*Acer negundo*), also choke cherry and *Eleagnus* (the so-called Russian olive). It is best known, however, as an enormous consumer of sunflower seeds, as anyone knows who is fortunate enough to have these birds at the feeding station. Most numerous from late January to early March.

Maxima: Flocks up to 50, early October 1959 and early May 1958; winter concentrations of 150 to over 300 (banded) at certain inland feeders, particularly in northern New Jersey. During the 1951 invasion, there was a conservative estimate of 6000 Evening Grosbeaks at all feeders combined in the New York City area. Big coastal flight, winter of 1945–46: 45, Massapequa, Dec. 30; 80; Baldwin, March 8 (both at feeding stations).

Extreme dates: Sept. 21 to June 7. Usually rare before late October and after April.

Breeding: This species has now (1962) been found breeding within our area. During July of that year breeding evidence was obtained at two localities in northern New Jersey: young being fed at Smoke Rise, Morris County (H. Smith and N. Wade), and a male feeding sunflower seeds to a young bird at Branchville, Sussex County (P. Truex).

Egg dates: No data.

PURPLE FINCH (*Carpodacus purpureus*)*B

Range: Nearctic species, the nominate race breeding south to northern Pennsylvania, northern New Jersey, southeastern New York (including Long Island), and southern Connecticut; in the mountains to Maryland and West Virginia.

Status: Erratic and unpredictable migrant and winter visitant; usually common, occasionally abundant in fall, less numerous in spring, and often rare in winter, but on several occasions even abundant. Uncommon to rare, local breeder especially rare on the coastal plain.

Migration and winter: The Purple Finch is somewhat irregular in its movements and length of stay, and exceedingly variable in numbers. During some seasons it is common to abundant, or again may be rare or absent for long periods.

Maxima: *Fall*—big inland flight in 1943—200, Bronx Park, Oct. 5; 400, New Rochelle, Oct. 24. Heavy coastal flight in 1952—400, Far Rockaway, Oct. 25. *Winter*—100, Van Cortlandt Park, Jan. 19, 1928; 1953 Christmas counts—250, Smithtown, L.I.; 120, Westport, Conn., but in both these latter instances some may have been House Finches. *Spring*—big flight in 1939—70, Central Park, March 14; 330, Easthampton, March 22. During this flight the following were banded at Boonton, N.J. (Swart): March 1–15 (160); March 16–31 (352); April 1–15 (325); April 16–30 (222); May 1–6 (37); total for the period was 1096. For details of this flight, see Weaver (1940). Also reported—30, Prospect Park, May 10, 1946.

"Extreme" dates: Aug. 18 to May 26, possibly later. Rare before mid-September.

Breeding (see map): This species is near its southern breeding limits in the New York City region and it has always been rare to uncommon, irregular, and extremely local as a nesting bird. With the introduction of the House Finch in the early 1940s, the situation has become quite confused, and a great deal of misunderstanding has arisen. The two species were and still are mistaken for one another (see discussion under House Finch). As a result, some of the recent reports of Purple Finches nesting in this area are extremely doubtful and open to question.

Nevertheless those who persist in the mistaken notion that the Purple Finch does not and never did breed on the coastal plain of Long Island and in the lowlands of the mainland are grossly misinformed. The Purple Finch bred here long before the House Finch was introduced in the east.

It is deemed best to summarize here its distribution and breeding status in order to clarify the situation. First of all, *C. purpureus*, unlike *C. mexicanus*, is more restricted in its choice of nesting sites, and its habitat is almost exclusively confined to coniferous growth. However, like *C. mexicanus*, *C. purpureus* will and does nest in ornamental evergreens about

424

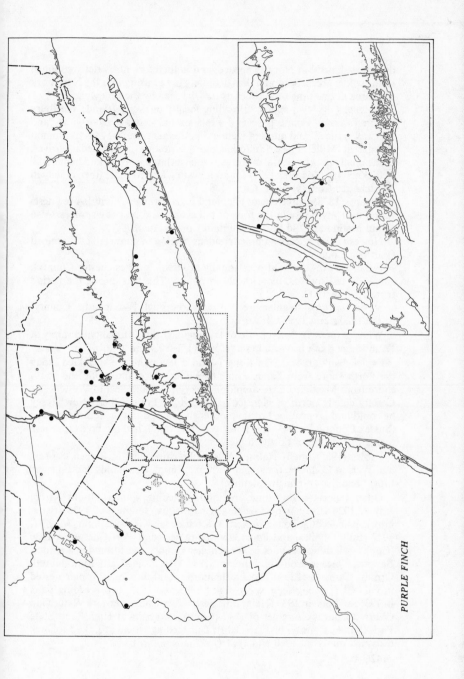

PURPLE FINCH

dwellings, chiefly in Norway spruce, and is therefore not strictly confined to the wilder areas. Second, it has definitely bred throughout the New York City area at one time or another as may be seen by the following:

Dutcher (1887–94) states, "Breeding locally on Long Island; Westbury region [Nassau County], several nests in red cedars, arbor-vitae, and Norway spruce," and quoting Helme, ". . . regular, but not very common breeder at Miller Place [Suffolk County], nesting in red cedar groves, occasionally in ornamental evergreens such as larch, spruce, and hemlock."

Bicknell (in Griscom, 1927) found it nesting at Riverdale (then chiefly in Westchester County) in 1876 and 1881.

Mearns (1878), "Breeds near Highland Falls [Orange County]. A few nests found near my house in the tops of tall cedars and Norway spruces. Also found nesting at Cold Spring [Putnam County] in 1874."

Howes (1928), "Rare summer resident nesting in conifers" at Stamford (Fairfield County).

Fisher (in litt.), "nested occasionally at Ossining [Westchester County], chiefly in tall spruces, more rarely in pines." This was during the period from 1870 to 1900.

Slaker (in litt.), "regular breeder at Scarborough [Westchester County] in the 1920's and 1930's."

Wheeler (in litt.), "bred more or less regularly at Katonah, and rarely at Poundridge [both in Westchester County], 1930's and 1940's."

Cruickshank (1942), "On Long Island a few pairs are sprinkled along the north shore from Sands Point to Miller Place and along the south shore from Mastic to Easthampton. A very few pairs nest in Westchester County chiefly north of Kensico" (Reservoir). For northern New Jersey he could find no positive breeding other than a nest in the High Point area (Sussex County) in 1941. It is hard to believe that it had not bred elsewhere in the vast region of northern New Jersey.

Fables (1955) briefly states, "A local breeding bird in Bergen, Sussex, and Warren Counties, occurring both in swampy woodlands and on ridge tops," but gives no further details.

Other reports of breeding are: adults feeding young, Mount Kisco, July 5, 1926 (Baker); pair nesting, Chappaqua, summer of 1936 (Pangburn); pair feeding young in nest in a red cedar, Grassy Sprain, May 31, 1942 (Bull, Oboiko, and Poor); two pairs nested at Port Chester in 1926 (Cook)—all these localities in Westchester County. Nest found in a spruce, Bayside, Queens County, June 15, 1878 (R. F. Pearsall, Bull. Nuttall Ornith. Club, 4: 122, 1879); Easthampton (Suffolk County), pair nested in red cedar, young seen, summers of 1933 and 1934, two breeding pairs in 1936, and one in 1939 (Helmuth); nest across from Delaware Water Gap (Warren County), summer of 1947 (Conn); two pairs at High Point State Park (Sussex County) in 1956 (Jehl); pair feeding young at Lake Mohawk (Sussex County) in 1960 and 1961 (J. Zamos, in litt.).

Except in the mountains, other recent nestings (particularly since 1942) on Long Island, Connecticut, Westchester and Rockland counties, New York, and New Jersey are open to question, since confusion with the House Finch is possible. Nevertheless, Raynor (oral comm.) states that in recent years he has found Purple Finches definitely breeding in eastern Suffolk County, L.I. at least twice; on the north shore at East Marion, and on the south shore in the vicinity of Southampton.

Egg dates: May 10 to June 23.

Subspecies: The poorly defined race *nesophilus*, described from Newfoundland and included by the A.O.U. *Check-list* (1957: 559), is rejected here. The color characters and measurements differ only on an average basis and there is much overlap. Moreover, certain breeding specimens from New England and New York almost exactly match breeding material from Newfoundland. Parkes (1952), Blake (1955), Griscom and Snyder (1955), and Godfrey (1959) do not consider it a valid subspecies either.

HOUSE FINCH (*Carpodacus mexicanus*)*B

Introduced: A western Nearctic species, the race *frontalis* breeding (mainly resident) from southern British Columbia to the highlands of southern Mexico, east to western Nebraska and central Texas.

Status: Locally common to very common resident on Long Island and along the coast of Connecticut (Fairfield County) and New York (Westchester County); fairly common to rare elsewhere in the New York City region, but increasing and spreading to adjacent areas.

Origin and early status: The first reported occurrence of a House Finch in our area was that of an adult male observed around the bathing pavilions at Jones Beach, Apr. 11, 1941 (Fischer and Hines) and seen up to Apr. 20 by numerous observers. This observation is unique because, to the best of my knowledge, the species has been reported only casually from that vicinity since then—two, October 1961 (Dignan and Ward). Cruickshank (1942) naturally did not list House Finch, as the 1941 observation was assumed to be just another escaped cage bird and there were no further reports until after his book was published. Little did anyone realize what had happened or what was about to take place.

As early as 1940 a number of dealers in Brooklyn, and perhaps elsewhere in the metropolitan area, had in their possession illegally caged House Finches from California. When informed that the species was protected, the dealers presumably released the captives somewhere on Long Island and possibly elsewhere. For details, see Fleisher (1947) and especially Elliott and Arbib (1953).

The species was first reported in the wild state in a nursery at Babylon during the spring of 1942 by Elliott, and the following year at that locality he discovered the first nest with young on May 28 in a small Austrian pine. Within the next few years House Finches were noted at Westbury, Hewlett, and Lawrence (all in Nassau County) where they soon became established. By 1950 the species had been reported west to Neponsit and Riis Park (Queens County), north to Roslyn (Nassau County), and east to Wyandanch and East Islip (Suffolk County). As early as 1948 a pair had been observed on the mainland in Westchester County at Tarrytown, and by 1951 as far north as Armonk and Bedford, and east into Connecticut at Riverside. The first report in New Jersey was at Ridgewood, Bergen County, in 1949, but it was not until 1954 that they were reported elsewhere in that state. For a detailed report of status and relative abundance up to 1953, the reader is referred to the account by Elliott and Arbib (*op. cit.*).

Status since 1953: The following data indicate the extent of spread into the outlying districts, including those outside the New York City area— north to Poundridge Reservation, N.Y. (1954); east to Fairfield, Conn., and Brookhaven, L.I. (1957), and Montauk, L.I. (1958); west to Rockaway, N.J. (1956); south to Long Branch, N.J. (1956); southwest to Somerville, N.J. (1958) and Princeton, N.J. (1959); northwest to New City, N.Y. (1960). As of 1962 House Finches have been reliably reported south to Baltimore, Md., and Washington, D.C.

The House Finch in the New York City area is mainly a bird of suburban localities and is less common in rural districts. It is almost entirely absent from the centers of large cities and is unreported from Central and Prospect Parks (Carleton, 1958), and has very rarely been reported from Bronx County (late 1960 on). As of 1960 this species was unreported on the Orient peninsula (Latham) and on Staten Island (Cleaves), nor am I aware of any published occurrences for the more distant portions of our region as in Putnam, Orange, Sussex, and Warren Counties. As of 1962, House Finches have been seen by competent observers in Putnam County (1961) and Staten Island (1962). For the most recent paper on this species, see Cant (1962). Fables (1955) did not list it for New Jersey, although it had been reliably reported there as far back as 1949. However, as far distant as the Philadelphia-Camden area, House Finches were reliably reported as early as the winter of 1955–56 (see section under Banding, below). As of 1963 one pair each bred in two Manhattan parks: Inwood Hill Park and Fort Tryon Park.

Maxima: Because of its mostly sedentary habits the only large concentrations are in winter at an ever increasing number of feeding stations. The Christmas count figures are meaningless, at least on Long Island, because the areas covered take in much less than half the House Finch range there. As many as 150 have been present at a single Long Island feeder during one winter, as proved by banding. Flocks up to 40 have been counted.

Finches, Grosbeaks, Buntings, Sparrows: Fringillidae

Breeding: The House Finch frequents nurseries, estates, and suburban residential areas, where it is an extremely adaptable species breeding in a great variety of situations. Its nesting sites may be classified in two main categories: (*a*) evergreen trees, rarely deciduous growth; (*b*) man-made structures. In the former category occupied nests were situated in Austrian and white pine, red cedar, arbor-vitae, and, especially on Long Island, in ornamental spruce; also in hedges and a clematis vine. In the latter category nest sites have been found in such varied situations as: ivy on walls of houses, barns, and other buildings; rose trellis on side of building; potted *Euonymus* on porch rail; on ledge under eave of house; in folding porch screen; behind shutters; at junction of leader pipe and stonework of house; and perhaps most unusual of all—in a vacated Barn Swallow's nest!

It was stated by Elliott and Arbib (1953: 37) that "thus far, its breeding grounds are not contiguous with those of the Purple Finch, . . .", but the two species not only are contiguous, they are sympatric (see comments on breeding distribution under Purple Finch).

Egg dates: Apr. 12 to July 20 (*fide* W. E. Lanyon).

Banding: While primarily a resident species in the west, the House Finch does migrate in the more northerly portions of its range. In our area it is mainly sedentary, but banding has proved that certain individuals have traveled as much as 150 miles (see Cant and Geis, 1961). The following data are taken chiefly from their paper. Although their banding stations at Mamaroneck, N.Y., and Riverside, Conn., are only nine miles apart, neither bander has taken each other's birds in the course of banding over 300 individuals apiece. Furthermore, birds banded by Cant and Geis in summer or early fall have been recovered in Ardmore, Penn. (suburb of Philadelphia) the following winter and then retaken at the home station the next spring or summer:

MAMARONECK-RIVERSIDE	ARDMORE	MAMARONECK-RIVERSIDE
Date banded	*Date recovered*	*Date retaken*
July 6, 1959	Feb. 18, 1960	Apr. 15, 1960
Sept. 4, 1959	Dec. 19, 1959	June 20, 1960

This represents a distance of between 115 and 125 miles.

An immature banded at Riverside, July 24, 1956, was recovered at Huntington, L.I. (north shore), Feb. 14, 1959, about 14 miles in a southeast direction across Long Island Sound. An adult female also banded at Riverside, Dec. 6, 1956, was recovered at East Islip, L.I. (south shore), Apr. 18, 1958, approximately 30 miles in a southeast direction. It is noteworthy that, so far, no House Finches banded on Long Island have been taken in Connecticut or Westchester County. Two individuals banded at Ardmore, Penn., on Feb. 28, 1960, and March 5, 1960, were captured at

Blue Point and Speonk, L.I. (both on the south shore) on Apr. 14, 1960, and Apr. 28, 1960, respectively. The last locality is fully 150 miles from place of banding.

Specimen data: The following local specimens have been collected: Hewlett, L.I., adult male, Jan. 17, 1948, and a pair, Apr. 22, 1951 (Arbib), all in A.M.N.H.; adult female, Westbury, L.I., March 20, 1949 (D. G. Nichols), A.M.N.H.; adult male, Amityville, L.I., Apr. 18, 1956 (M. Nilka), Tackapausha Museum; adult male, Bound Brook, N.J., Dec. 31, 1959 (Murray), Rutgers University Museum. All of these specimens are of the widespread subspecies *frontalis.*

The comments by Elliott and Arbib (1953: 34–35), concerning "sooting" of specimens, are of interest and their summary (p. 37) of this aspect is repeated here: "The Long Island birds appear in the field to be extremely dark and dusky." With this there is no disagreement. They further state, "But this appearance is caused by sooting, and washed specimens are identical with specimens . . . from California."

My own feeling in this matter is that sooting, while possible in a few isolated cases and proved in two or three specimens, is overemphasized. The dusky coloration of some House Finches throughout Long Island, Connecticut, and elsewhere in the northeast is possibly due to humidity, perhaps the result of environmental adaptation. As stated above, in our area this is a species of suburban residential areas, rural estates, nurseries, etc., and *not* an inhabitant of large industrialized cities where sooting would be a factor. Some sooting may occur in those individuals that breed in such places as ivy-covered walls, where dirt might adhere to feathers, but this would not apply to other populations nesting in "clean" surroundings. Moreover, some specimens taken locally match favorably with those specimens from various humid Pacific coast localities. Why should House Finches differ from any other species in this respect? The interested reader is referred to the paper by Salt (1952) who discusses in detail the aspects of climate and its effects on the *Carpodacus* finches. Salt stresses that "high air moisture" (humidity) is an important factor in dark populations. It should be stressed that House Finches are also variable *individually* as to color, regardless of sex and age. Further studies are necessary before color and environment are correlated, as several factors appear to be involved.

Field identification: Many an eastern observer and bird bander has been confused by his first meeting with the House Finch in the field and this confusion is not limited, by any means, to the beginner. Pointing out morphological and voice differences between the two species may be helpful. Only adults are considered here, as immatures somewhat resemble each other. Certain immature individuals of *C. purpureus* are quite as dark as *C. mexicanus,* judging from examination of museum skins.

430

MORPHOLOGY

C. purpureus

1. Form—robust
2. Adult male—wing-bars pinkish
3. Adult male—belly and flanks unstreaked
4. Adult male—pinkish color quite uniform on dorsal surface, no contrast with head and rump
5. Adult female— prominent superciliary especially behind eye; often with a noticeable malar streak
6. Adult female—marked resemblance to female Rose-breasted Grosbeak in miniature; distinct heavy streaking on whitish background
7. Bill—culmen straight
8. Tail—slightly forked or notched

C. mexicanus

1. Form—slender
2. Adult male—wing-bars white or whitish
3. Adult male—belly and flanks conspicuously streaked with dusky
4. Adult male—crown and rump red, in striking contrast to dull gray-brown back
5. Adult female—no superciliary, or barely perceptible; no malar streak
6. Adult female—over-all dingy and dusky coloration; streaking tends to coalesce, imparting a uniformly dark appearance
7. Bill—culmen convex (variable)
8. Tail—"square" or slightly rounded

Characteristics (7) and (8) are useful for banders, but it should be pointed out that the tail difference, so much emphasized in the banding literature, is subject to variation when birds are in molt. Purple Finches with worn rectrices have a square-tailed appearance, so that this character is not infallible. The bill character is least reliable, contrary statements to this effect appearing in banding literature, notwithstanding. The culmens of certain specimens of *C. mexicanus* appear quite straight, and examination of a large series of study skins indicated that bill shape is quite variable. The difference in (1) above is relative, but when the two species are together for direct comparison, that difference is "obvious."

Characteristics (2) through (6) are, to this writer, the most easily recognizable characters in the field, and (2) and (3) are "absolutely" diagnostic, as may be readily determined by an examination of a large series of museum skins.

VOICE

C. purpureus

1. Song—more or less continuous warble *without* emphatic ending

C. mexicanus

1. Song—more or less disjointed, ending (usually) in a two-noted "chit-chur" with rasping quality

C. purpureus	C. mexicanus
2. Call note—single dull metallic "pit" or "tic"	2. Call note—single or double "chur" or "churp," somewhat like that of House Sparrow, but with a sweet quality, often with a rising inflection

Remarks: The House Finch, an attractive addition to our avifauna, is a melodious, tame, and very adaptable species. It is definitely established here, and perhaps best of all, competes successfully with House Sparrows at the feeding station and so far, apparently, for nesting sites.

PINE GROSBEAK (*Pinicola enucleator*)*

Range: Holarctic species (for details, see Subspecies).

Status: Very rare, irregular winter visitant; at long intervals locally common during flight years. More numerous inland than near the coast.

Occurrence and maxima: The Pine Grosbeak is the rarest of the "winter" finches, both in numbers and in occurrence. Flocks up to 40 are the maximum recorded and these are exceptional, groups of a half dozen to 20 being more usual. Moreover, within the past 80 years, there have been only five "major" flights, of which the first four were at least 20 years apart: 1883–84; 1903–4; 1929–30; 1951–52; 1961–62.

Maxima in each of the flight years:

1883–84: Fisher at Ossining, N.Y., collected a total of 48 specimens, including 25 from Jan. 21 to Feb. 1, of which 16 were adult males; most of these are in the M.C.Z. collection.

1903–4: Of 27 specimens in the A.M.N.H. collection, 21 were taken during this flight; 10 at Plainfield, N.J., Jan. 3 and 4 (Miller), and 8 at Miller Place, L.I., Dec. 4 (Helme).

1929–30: Flocks to 40, Cold Spring, N.Y. (L. N. Nichols), and Watchung Reservation, N.J. (Urner), both on Dec. 26.

1951–52: Widespread flight, arriving in late October, principally early November, with flocks up to 33 seen at inland localities, including the "hawk" ridges, to lesser groups at coastal points, chiefly in Prospect Park. At least 90 were reported on five inland Christmas counts. Most individuals left by mid-March.

1961–62: Chiefly an inland flight; according to Carleton (Audubon Field Notes, 16 [1]; 14, 1962), "150 birds were seen in a half day at Katonah, N.Y., Nov. 23 (W. C. R[ussell])." These probably represented several flocks over a relatively wide area. As many as 56 were observed on the Sussex County, N.J., Christmas count.

432

Extreme dates: Oct. 25 (earliest specimen, Nov. 6) to Apr. 20. Rare before mid-November and after mid-March.

Pine Grosbeaks are greatly attracted to the fruit of sumac, ash, and mountain ash, and are very fond of apple seeds. They have also been reported to feed on the fruits and seeds of various other deciduous and coniferous plants. Unlike Evening Grosbeaks, the present species in our area rarely visits feeding stations.

Subspecies: Two subspecies occur within the New York City region: the race *eschatosus*, breeding south to northern New Hampshire and central Maine, is much the commoner of the two in our area, the great majority of specimens belonging to this smaller, southeastern population. According to Fables (1955), specimens collected at Vernon, N.J., Feb. 12, 1952 (Baird and Eynon), belong to this race. The larger, more northerly race *leucura*, breeds south to the central portions of Ontario, Quebec, and Newfoundland. There are only a few specimens of "typical" *leucura* from our area, the following two in the A.M.N.H. series: Garrison, N.Y., Dec. 12, 1874 (C. H. Eagle); Montauk Point, Jan. 26, 1914 (Dwight collection). A specimen taken at Newfoundland, N.J., Dec. 23, 1961 (Jehl), A.M.N.H., appears to be this race also. These specimens were examined by the writer. See Griscom (1934) for subspecific distinctions.

Remarks: The inclusion in the A.O.U. *Check-list* (1957: 563) under breeding, "once in Connecticut (Wilton)," should be deleted. Wilton, in southwestern Fairfield County, is at most 100 feet above sea level, and is mainly in the deciduous woodland belt. The Pine Grosbeak breeds chiefly in spruce forest in Canada and northern New England and is unreported as a nesting bird even in the Adirondacks.

The alleged breeding occurrence appeared in the Auk, 50: 442–443, 1933. This account is so completely vague that one wonders why it was ever published, much less accepted by the *Check-list* committee. More than likely the Purple Finch was the species involved.

EUROPEAN GOLDFINCH (*Carduelis carduelis*)*B

Introduced: Palearctic species, introduced in various parts of the United States; becoming temporarily established, but now extirpated (since the late 1950s).

The first known record of the European Goldfinch in the New York City region was that of a specimen collected at Hoboken, N.J., March 2, 1878. This species was introduced the following year into Central Park, where it increased for some time, but had disappeared by 1907, except for stragglers. It became temporarily established about Englewood, N.J., and Massapequa, L.I., around 1910, but was last reported at the former locality in 1915.

433

In the Massapequa area, however, it increased and spread to surrounding country—north to Garden City and rarely Westbury, west to Baldwin, and east to Amityville, rarely as far as Babylon. By the mid-1940s as many as 17 were found in the Seaford–Massapequa sector, but as the real-estate boom progressed after World War II, the species faded out. Elliott (1956b) stated that fewer than six birds existed in 1955, and with expansion of building developments, the birds did not survive much later.

According to Witherby *et al.* (1938a: 58) its preferred breeding habitat in the British Isles is ". . . chiefly gardens, orchards, and open cultivated land with sprinkling of trees. . . ." A similar environment was frequented by the small colony on Long Island. Unlike the European population, which is partially migratory, the Massapequa birds were reported to spend the winter months in nearby weedy fields and around farms, but apparently did not visit feeding stations.

A dead fledgling taken from a nest containing four young at Massapequa, June 10, 1944 (Elliott), is A.M.N.H. No. 325836. The nest was situated in an arbor-vitae tree. Five other nests in the same area were located in Norway maples (see Elliott, *op. cit.*).

Egg dates: Apr. 26 to July 5.

The European Goldfinch is common in captivity and is frequently caged. Numerous recent observations of single individuals at various times of the year, particularly in and near New York City, are probably escaped cage birds.

Remarks: The A.O.U. *Check-list* (1957: 567) includes all North American records under the race *britannica*, and Hellmayr (1938: 264) states that "a single adult from Long Island is unequivocally the British form." I do not know the present whereabouts of this specimen. However, the Hoboken specimen referred to above (A.M.N.H. No. 41858) appears to be nominate *carduelis* of continental Europe. Three specimens shot by Hendrickson at Long Island City during the winter of 1889 are apparently not extant, and another—an adult male taken at Hastings, N.Y., Apr. 15, 1895 (Rowley), A.M.N.H. No. 11379—I have not seen.

Vaurie (Amer. Mus. Novit., 1775: 13, 1956) states that *C. c. britannica* "is very near nominate *carduelis* in characters." The characters are chiefly those of degree rather than of kind (average differences). Very likely examples of both races were imported into North America.

HOARY REDPOLL (*Acanthis hornemanni*)*

Accidental: Holarctic species, the race *exilipes* breeds south to the northern portions of Manitoba, Quebec, and Labrador. Winters south to Massachusetts, casually farther.

There are two certain records for our region: Immature male collected at Tuckahoe, N.Y. (not Van Cortlandt Park as stated in the literature),

March 24, 1888 (Dwight), A.M.N.H. No. 366587; identification confirmed by H. Johansen. The other specimen, also an immature male, was taken at West Englewood, N.J., April 1, 1960 (F. B. Gill); determined by Tordoff and now in the University of Michigan collection, No. 155143 (Wilson Bull., 73: 388–389, 1961). Both of these specimens were with Common Redpolls, the 1960 individual at a feeder. As is the case in Massachusetts, where this species is less rare, the occurrence of Hoary Redpolls takes place almost invariably when there are great irruptions of the commoner species.

The identification in life of the two redpolls is a difficult matter at best. While several observations may be correct, none is convincing and no proper corroboration was made. Size is deceptive in the field even when direct comparison is possible. Coloration and amount of streaking in these birds are so variable that individual specimens in large museum series have been determined as different forms from time to time by competent taxonomists. In view of this, what chance does the observer have of positive identification in the field?

Some authorities consider the Hoary Redpoll conspecific with the Common Redpoll (*A. flammea*).

COMMON REDPOLL (*Acanthis flammea*)*

Range: Holarctic species (for details, see Subspecies).

Status: Irregular winter visitant, absent or very rare some years, common to occasionally very abundant in others.

Occurrence and maxima: This species frequents alders and birches, weedy fields, and to some extent conifers. Relatively uncommon at feeding stations, except during the late winter of 1960. Often associates with Pine Siskins and Goldfinches. Ordinarily small flocks of five to 20 are seen, but during flight years much larger numbers are reported.

The Common Redpoll is at maximum abundance during January, February, and March. In recent years, great flights have taken place during late winter in 1936, 1947, 1953, 1956, and 1960. In 1947 and 1953, large flocks up to 2000 were reported in inland areas of northern New Jersey during February and early March. In late January 1960, over 2000 were estimated on Long Island from Short Beach to Zachs Bay. During March 1960, concentrations of over 5000 were reported in Rockland and Bergen counties, where two banders trapped over 1400 birds each.

Extreme dates: Oct. 18 and 30 (earliest specimen, Nov. 9) to Apr. 8, 21, 29, and May 4 (specimens on the last two dates). Usually rare before December and after March.

Subspecies: Two races of this species occur in our area. Nominate *flammea*, breeding south to southeastern Quebec and Newfoundland, the form most often recorded, has been discussed above. The much rarer race *rostrata*, breeding on Baffin Island, Greenland, and Iceland, has been collected locally at least three times: female, Shelter Island, Feb. 11, 1879 (Worthington), formerly in A.M.N.H. collection, but apparently not extant; two, Ossining, Feb. 12 and 13, 1883 (Fisher), M.C.Z. Nos. 305783 and 305784. It is possible that *A. f. rostrata* occurs in our area less rarely than realized, particularly during flight years. Only careful collecting will determine this point. No sight reports of this subspecies are accepted. The remarks pertaining to the Hoary Redpoll concerning field identification apply even more to *A. f. rostrata.*

Although the A.O.U. *Check-list* (1957: 569) includes the race *holboellii*, a footnote qualifies this treatment with the remarks: "The validity of this race is uncertain from present information; possibly it is not separable from *A. f. flammea.*" The writer follows Vaurie (1959), who does not recognize *A. f. holboellii*, considering it merely an individual variant of nominate *flammea* (see also his discussion, Amer. Mus. Novit., 1775: 23, 1956). In view of this, the published record (Griscom, 1923: 266 and Cruickshank, 1942: 442) of a specimen of *A. f. holboellii* from Long Island is disregarded here.

PINE SISKIN (*Spinus pinus*)*B

Range: Nearctic species, the nominate race breeds south to the mountains of northern New York and New England; rarely and irregularly to the Berkshires, Catskills, and Poconos; casually at lower elevations.

Status: Regular fall migrant and irregular winter visitant, numbers varying greatly, rare some years, common to occasionally very abundant in others. Present in numbers in spring provided a flight occurred the preceding fall, otherwise rare to absent. Two breeding records.

Migration and winter: This species frequents conifers, birches, and alders, also weedy fields, and is fond of the fruit of sweet gum (*Liquidambar*).

Maxima: *Fall*—large coastal flights—1500 in two hours, Jones Beach, Nov. 9, 1946; 1500, Riis Park, Nov. 9, 1951; 2000, Orient, Oct. 27, and 1500, Jones Beach, Nov. 9, both in 1952. *Winter*—1000, Jones Beach to Brooklyn, late December 1952; 1500, near Rockland Lake, N.Y., Jan. 24, 1958. *Spring*—100, Alley Pond Park, L.I., Apr. 23, 1946.

Extreme dates: 6, Fire Island, Sept. 5, 1906 (Dutcher); Sept. 28 to late May, June 6, and 10. Rare before October and after early May

Breeding: Like the Red Crossbill, the Pine Siskin is very erratic and unpredictable, though more regular in occurrence and, like that species, has nested twice in the New York City region, following large flights the preceding autumn. On May 25, 1883 (the same year it bred in eastern Massachusetts), at Ossining, Westchester County, A. K. Fisher collected a nest with four eggs in a red cedar. J. A. Allen also collected a nest with four eggs in a Norway pine, as well as both adults, at Cornwall, Orange County, May 12, 1887. This latter collection formed the basis of a habitat group in the American Museum of Natural History (see Allen, Auk, 4: 284–286, 1887).

Egg dates: May 12 to 25.

AMERICAN GOLDFINCH (*Spinus tristis*)*B

Range: A widespread Nearctic species, the nominate race occurring in our area.

Status: Resident in varying numbers; subject to marked fluctuations during migration and winter. Common breeder.

Migration and winter: The American Goldfinch, although regular in spring in small numbers, is notably erratic in fall and winter, common to occasionally very abundant some years, rare in others. Its presence in winter is largely dependent upon the available food supply, chiefly weed seeds, and the fruit of birch, alder, pine, etc.

Maxima: *Fall*—big flight in 1946, both coastal and inland—550, Van Cortlandt Park, Nov. 7; over 2000, Atlantic Beach, Nov. 10; 1200, Fire Island Inlet, Nov. 13, 1955. *Winter*—500, Warwick, N.Y., Jan. 13, 1934. *Spring*—100, Prospect Park, May 14, 1946.

Usually arrives in late March and departs by November.

Breeding: This species nests in open country, often in agricultural areas—in overgrown fields, hedgerows, and orchards. One of our latest nesting birds, sometimes not breeding until August.

Egg dates: June 26 to Aug. 24.

RED CROSSBILL (*Loxia curvirostra*)*B

Range: Holarctic species (for details, see Subspecies).

Status: The most erratic and irregular of local birds. Chiefly a migrant and winter visitant, but recorded every month of the year; variously rare to locally very common. Has bred twice.

Occurrence and maxima: The Red Crossbill occurs most often from late November to March; sometimes present in flocks during late spring. This species occasionally associates with White-winged Crossbills in big flight years, but ordinarily will be found in pure flocks, feeding on seeds extracted from the cones of hemlock and various pines. These flights are believed to be due to failure of the cone crop in the north, especially that of spruce.

The unpredictable nature of the Red Crossbill is best illustrated in Griscom's monograph (1937b), portions of which are extracted and summarized here. Note particularly the great irregularity as to time of year; also the apparent gap between 1904 and 1952, during which period relatively few birds were reported:

"1874–1875, abundant throughout, south to southern New York from late October to mid-May; breeds casually at Riverdale; great flight of White-winged Crossbills also. . . .

"1877, a few vagrant flocks to southern New York in early May. . . .

"1878, a few birds in southern New York, June 13–July 20. . . .

"1882–1883, marked flight from Nov. 22 to mid-May; breeds casually at Miller Place. . . .

"1884, present near New York City from Apr. 1–May 18. . . .

"1888, scattered records from January to June 13, southern New York and New Jersey, but great flight of [L. c.] sitkensis. . . .

"1899–1900, White-winged Crossbills common in southern New York and New Jersey from late October on, and great flight of Red Crossbills also, many specimens taken [mostly L. c. minor]. . . .

"1903, one flock, northern New Jersey, July 19. . . .

"1904, common all winter south to the New York City region until early March."

No marked flights reported for nearly 50 years. During the early winter of 1952, and again from late November 1952 to February 1953, there was a great irruption of both crossbills, especially near the coast. Flocks of Red Crossbills from 40 to over 100 were seen on the south shore of western Long Island at Riis Park, Jones Beach, and along the Wantagh Causeway by numerous observers. Some individuals were very tame, feeding on the ground as well as in the pines, others appeared to be sick or starving and could be picked up from the ground. A number were found dead or dying, but few specimens were preserved.

Breeding: Like the Pine Siskin, this species has nested twice in the New York City region after heavy flights the preceding fall. The two occurrences are: (*a*) Riverdale (then in Westchester County), 1875 (Bicknell). On Apr. 22, a female was observed finishing a nest, which contained three eggs on Apr. 30. It was situated in a red cedar adjacent to ornamental larches and spruces on an estate. (*b*) Miller Place, Suffolk County, 1883 (Helme). Nest and eggs were secured on Apr. 10.

Reports of birds breeding in recent years are not satisfactory. Singing males in May and June, and streaked young in late August are not conclusive proof of nesting in the area. As mentioned above, Red Crossbills are exceedingly erratic and are notorious wanderers.

Egg dates: Apr. 10 to 30.

Subspecies: Three subspecies occur in our area:

1. *L. c. minor* breeds over a wide area extending from Minnesota east to Nova Scotia and is the race found nesting in the spruce forests of the Adirondacks and northern New England. Breeds rarely and irregularly

438

south to Massachusetts, southeastern New York (two local breeding records above), central and southern New Jersey, and in the highest mountains to Tennessee and North Carolina. Numerous specimens collected in our area, including 13 at Ossining, N.Y., in the spring of 1884 (Fisher), all in M.C.Z. collection; two adult males taken at Cold Spring, N.Y., July 6, 1913 (Blaschke), specimens in N.Y.S.M. at Albany.

2. *L. c. pusilla* breeds in Newfoundland. Wanders in winter sporadically south to Maryland and northern Virginia. It is distinguished by its large bill and by darker coloration of the males. At least four specimens were taken locally: adult male, Highland Falls, N.Y., March 10, 1875 (Mearns), A.M.N.H.; adult male, Hartsdale, N.Y., Apr. 22, 1890, Dwight collection, A.M.N.H.; two, Riverhead, L.I., Apr. 20, 1932 (Wilcox), in his collection.

3. *L. c. sitkensis* breeds and is mainly resident along the Pacific coast from southern Alaska to northern California. Wanders in winter sporadically east and south to Ontario and Quebec and along the Atlantic coast from Massachusetts to South Carolina. This race is distinguishable by its small size, short stumpy bill, and brick-red, rather than scarlet, plumage of the males. Numerous specimens were taken along the Atlantic seaboard during the great flight of 1888. Four adult males in the A.M.N.H. collection were taken in January and February of that year at Hicksville, Setauket, and Hither Plains (Montauk), L.I., and at Morristown, N.J. Another male (A.M.N.H.) was collected at Hastings, N.Y., Apr. 10, 1893 (Rowley); also adult female, Garrison, N.Y., Dec. 27, 1874 (see Parkes, 1952). There are other females and immatures taken locally (see Griscom 1937b).

Sight reports of subspecies are not accepted.

Note: An adult female Red Crossbill, picked up dead at Jones Beach on Dec. 29, 1963, by S. R. Leffler, was identified by him as *L. c. benti*. According to Leffler (*in litt.*), "identification has been verified by Dr. Richard F. Johnston and Mr. Max C. Thompson." The specimen is now in the University of Kansas collection. I have recently examined this specimen and having compared it with the series of Red Crossbills in the American Museum, I would say that it appears to match comparable specimens of *L. c. benti*. This subspecies breeds south and east to the Black Hills of South Dakota; wanders in winter east to northern Michigan. There appears to be no published record of a specimen of *L. c. benti* taken east of Michigan and this is the first known specimen of this race collected on the Atlantic seaboard.

WHITE-WINGED CROSSBILL (*Loxia leucoptera*)*

Range: Holarctic species, the nominate race breeds south to the southern portions of Ontario, Quebec, New Brunswick, and Nova Scotia; more rarely or casually to the northern parts of New York and New England.

Status: Rare and irregular winter visitant, occasionally locally common in flight years. Much less frequent than the Red Crossbill, though occasionally outnumbering that species when they occur together.

Occurrence and maxima: The White-winged Crossbill prefers the cones (seeds) of hemlocks in inland areas, while on the coast it is greatly attracted to pitch and black pines, the latter an introduced tree planted extensively along the sand dunes and state parks of the seashore.

Griscom (1923) mentioned but did not list "fourteen marked flights" up to that time, the last in 1899–1900, when it "occurred in great numbers." Cruickshank (1942) knew of no additional flights; in fact he was aware of only 27 "scattered records of small flocks" between 1900 and 1942.

It was not until 1953, more than a half century later, that a flight of major proportions occurred.

Maxima (1899–1900): Arrived in early November with peak of the flight on Nov. 20. On this date, Helme at Mount Sinai, L.I., collected 16 out of several flocks totaling at least 150 birds.

Maxima (1953): Arrived in early February, the maximum reported on Feb. 8. On this date, the species was widespread inland and along the coast. Flocks up to 50 in New Jersey were reported at Summit, Montclair, Verona, and Caldwell, with a number present at feeding stations. On the south shore of Long Island several flocks totaling over 200 were seen in the Jones Beach area, with smaller flocks at Riis Park. These birds were excessively tame; many were weak and starved, and could be picked up from the ground. A few dead ones were found in a very emaciated condition.

There was a smaller coastal flight in November 1954. On Nov. 13 as many as 80 were reported in the Montauk area, and lesser numbers at Jones Beach and Riis Park. A few individuals remained through the winter and a flock of 35 was present at Oak Beach as late as March 8, 1955. This flight was practically confined to the coast.

It should be emphasized that during most winters this species is not observed at all and that in others only a few vagrants are reported.

Extreme dates: Oct. 6 and 18 to Apr. 19; more rarely to May 10 and 16. Casual at Scarborough, N.Y., May 29, 1900 (Fuertes and Thayer), a big flight year. Rare before November and after March.

GREEN-TAILED TOWHEE (*Chlorura chlorura*)

Accidental: A western Nearctic species, breeding east to southeastern Wyoming, migrating east to western Kansas, and wintering north and east to southern Texas. Accidental in Massachusetts, New Jersey, Virginia, and South Carolina.

Finches, Grosbeaks, Buntings, Sparrows: Fringillidae

In our area there are two reports from New Jersey: one seen near Overpeck Creek, Dec. 23, 1939, and Jan. 30, 1940 (Cantor and Norse, Proc. Linnaean Soc., 52, 53: 140–141, 1941); another arrived, after a heavy snowstorm, at the Johnson feeder, Newton, Jan. 21, 1961, and remained until April 27. This latter individual was color-photographed, and seen by over 100 observers.

RUFOUS-SIDED TOWHEE *(Pipilo erythrophthalmus)**B

Range: A widespread Nearctic species, the nominate race breeding in our area.

Status: Very common migrant; rare to uncommon but regular in winter —more numerous in recent years at feeding stations. Common breeder at lower elevations, especially on the coastal plain.

Migration: The Rufous-sided Towhee is particularly numerous in spring.

Maxima: 110, Central Park, Apr. 30, 1947; 200, Far Rockaway to Woodmere, May 6, 1950; 50, Madison Square Park, N.Y.C., May 15, 1921. No fall maxima available, but the migration is much more protracted at that season, extending from mid-September well into November.

Usually arrives in early April and departs by mid-November.

Change in winter status: Towhees were formerly rare though regular during the winter months. With the great increase in feeding stations in recent years considerable numbers of these birds are now present. A trend toward milder winters has probably been a factor also.

During late December 1949 there were at least 40 reported on the various Christmas counts in our area. During the same period in 1951 more than 80 were reported.

An unprecedented number was present in late December 1958—on all local Christmas counts combined nearly 200 were observed, the vast majority at feeders; the regional breakdown as follows: Connecticut coast between Greenwich and Westport, 140; New York (mainland), 22; New Jersey, 20; Long Island, 13.

Maxima: January 1962—8, Orient feeder; 7 males, Brookhaven feeder (both on eastern Long Island).

Breeding: This species nests on or near the ground in dry open woodland, dense thickets, and is particularly numerous in scrub-oak and pitch-pine areas of the sandy coastal plain.

Egg dates: May 8 to June 25.

Subspecies: Nominate *erythrophthalmus*, the breeding race, discussed above.

The western race *arcticus*, formerly considered a separate species, *P. maculatus* ("Spotted" Towhee), breeds east to the Dakotas and Nebraska, and winters north and east to Kansas.

Three specimens, all females, of *P. e. arcticus* have been collected in our area: (*a*) Metuchen, N.J., Dec. 24, 1952 (Baird), originally thought to be of the race *montanus*, was redetermined as *P. e. arcticus* by Sibley; specimen in U.S. Fish and Wildlife Service collection, No. 421001 (see Baird, Condor, 59: 401–402, 1957). (*b*) One discovered at Jones Beach, Dec. 28, 1956 (Grant), subsequently observed by many people, was collected Feb. 16, 1957 (Buckley), specimen in N.Y.S.M. collection, No. 19019; identification confirmed by Sibley. (*c*) One found at Bronx Park, Nov. 30, 1958 (T. Peszell *et al.*), subsequently seen by numerous observers, was taken Dec. 23, 1958 (Buckley), A.M.N.H. No. 707778; identification confirmed by Eisenmann. For details on all three occurrences, see Buckley (1959).

These specimens are the first known records of *P. e. arcticus* for the Atlantic seaboard.

LARK BUNTING (*Calamospiza melanocorys*)*

Accidental: A central Nearctic species of the Great Plains, breeding east to southwestern Minnesota. Wanders east to the Atlantic coast from New Brunswick to Georgia.

In our area, there are five occurrences (three specimens), all from Long Island: specimen collected at Montauk Point, Sept. 4, 1888 (Evans), A.M.N.H. No. 65941; another collected, Miller Place, Sept. 11, 1896 (Helme), specimen in collection of Harold H. Bailey; one observed on the ground and in flight with Horned Larks and Lapland Longspurs, Wainscott, Nov. 27, 1937 (Helmuth); one collected, Easthampton, Aug. 31, 1939 (Helmuth), in his collection, neither of these latter two previously published; adult female, Jamaica Bay Refuge, June 6, 1959 (Carleton, Harrison, Mayer, and Bull).

IPSWICH SPARROW (*Passerculus princeps*)*

Range: Confined in the breeding season to Sable Island, off Nova Scotia. Winters on the Atlantic coast from Massachusetts (rarely) and Long Island to Georgia.

Status: Regular, but rare to uncommon, occasionally fairly common migrant and winter visitant along the outer coast. Very rare elsewhere. Formerly more numerous.

Occurrence and maxima: The Ipswich Sparrow is almost exclusively confined to the sand dunes and beaches, and is most likely to be seen where beach grass (*Ammophila*) grows. It occurs much more rarely along the

442

shores of Long Island Sound, chiefly the Connecticut coast and the north fluke of extreme eastern Long Island (Orient peninsula).

There is evidence to indicate that this bird was more common a half century ago. Its reduction in numbers might possibly be explained by the erosion of its limited breeding grounds on Sable Island.

The Ipswich Sparrow was shot in great numbers by collectors during the 1870s and 1880s to provide choice specimens for exchange or sale to museums and private collections. There are 330 specimens in three Massachusetts museums taken in that state alone, of which 265 are in the Museum of Comparative Zoology, Cambridge (see Griscom and Snyder, 1955).

In the American Museum of Natural History there are 127 specimens and at least another 100 in other public and private collections, all from Long Island. The writer recently came across a specimen in a small institution with the notation on the label, "purchased for $1.50"; this specimen was collected at Rockaway Beach in 1899. Over 50 of the 127 specimens were taken during the winter of 1885 alone, and 55 were secured in February (the principal month) in various years.

On a two-mile stretch of Rockaway Beach, Dutcher and Fisher collected 11 on Feb. 7, 1885, collected 13 more and saw an additional 13 on Feb. 23 (same year) at the same locality, making a total of at least 37 in two days. One of Dutcher's collectors on Fire Island took 29 individuals between Dec. 17 and 29, 1883.

Sage *et al.* (1913) listed about 20 specimens collected on the south shore of Connecticut (outside our region) chiefly in the New Haven area, between 1875 and 1911, but stated that it was always a rare migrant and a very rare winter visitant "in the beach grass of the seashore." The only specimen that I know of from either the Westchester County or Connecticut shore in our area is of one taken at Norwalk, Conn., Jan. 20, 1917 (L. H. Porter). A specimen taken at Oyster Bay, L.I., Dec. 28, 1878 (T. Roosevelt), in the U.S.N.M. collection, is perhaps the only specimen from the north shore of western Long Island.

In recent years we have the following maxima: 10, Gilgo Beach, Nov. 11, 1950; 7, Orient, Dec. 26, 1927; 14, Long Beach, Feb. 12, 1926; 12, Jones Beach, March 20, 1942; 9, Moriches area, March 24, 1951. Cruickshank (1942) stated that he saw as many as 27 in a day during November along the entire Jones Beach strip (17 miles). Today (1962) one or more individuals are reported annually along the west impoundment at the Jamaica Bay Refuge.

Because of destruction or development of beach areas on western Long Island Sound, this species is very rarely reported there in recent years.

Extreme dates: Sept. 20 and 28 (specimen) to Apr. 8 (specimen), and various other dates to Apr. 25. Sight reports during early September and

May, although possibly correct, are rejected because of probable confusion with the Savannah Sparrow. Rare before late October and after March. For detailed accounts of this species, see Elliott (1955 and 1956a).

Remarks: This large, pale relative of the Savannah Sparrow (*P. sandwichensis*) is considered by many authorities to be conspecific with it.

SAVANNAH SPARROW *(Passerculus sandwichensis)**B

Range: Nearctic species (for details, see Subspecies).

Status: Common to very abundant fall migrant along the coast; much less numerous inland. Uncommon to occasionally very common in winter on the coast. Locally numerous breeder on the coast, but rare to uncommon inland.

Migration and winter: Although Savannah Sparrows are ordinarily encountered in small numbers ranging from a few to a dozen, there are times when large concentrations occur along the outer coast during October.

Maxima: *Fall*—1200, Easthampton, Oct. 2, 1930 (Helmuth); 2000, Orient, Oct. 12, 1955 (Latham). *Winter*—120, Brooklyn Christmas count, Dec. 24, 1950; 210, Jamaica Bay area, Dec. 20, 1952.

Usually arrives in late March and departs by mid-November.

Breeding: A rare and local bird inland, nesting in grassy fields and pastures. The only exception to this was on the Hempstead Plains where Giraud (1844) stated that it was "very plentiful." Before that area was destroyed in the mid-1940s, this species was a locally common breeder there.

Although it nests locally along the coast on sand dunes, especially where beach grass (*Ammophila*) is prevalent, the Savannah Sparrow is most numerous on filled-in grassy areas adjacent to bays and inlets. During the summer of 1932, when the Newark Meadows were being filled, Urner found 44 nesting pairs. By 1935, much of the salt marsh had been filled and had become very dry, and the population had increased to about 125 nesting pairs. In the Jamaica Bay area in 1953, Mayer estimated at least 100 breeding pairs from Idlewild to Canarsie, including the bay islands. The birds were nesting chiefly on sand fill that had grown up to grass and weeds.

Egg dates: May 5 to June 28.

Subspecies: This species is widespread in the west, breeding from Alaska to Guatemala; whereas in the east it is restricted in range, breeding only from Labrador and Quebec to Maryland and West Virginia. Three races occur in our area:

1. *P. s. savanna* breeds south to Maryland and West Virginia at higher elevations but is local on the coastal plain south of Long Island. Discussed in detail above.

2. *P. s. labradorius* breeds south to Newfoundland and islands in the Gulf of St. Lawrence. It has been collected on a number of occasions in our area, chiefly along the south shore of Long Island—dates ranging from Oct. 6 to May 1. It has also been taken inland in New Jersey at Morristown and near New Brunswick. Further collecting may prove it to be regular during migration and winter, at least on the coast. Because of great individual variation, no sight reports are accepted.

3. *P. s. oblitus* breeds southeast to south-central Quebec. Although Peters and Griscom (1938) did not list this race for the New York City area, it has been taken in Virginia and North Carolina. There is one local specimen: adult collected at Hadley Airport, N.J., Dec. 23, 1952 (J. Baird), Rutgers University collection.

Remarks: Fables (1955) listed a northern New Jersey specimen of the "race" *mediogriseus*, but this form is not recognized by the A.O.U. *Check-list* committee. It appears to represent nothing more than a cline or intermediate population between the races *savanna* and *oblitus*.

GRASSHOPPER SPARROW (*Ammodramus savannarum*)*B

Range: A widespread though local American species, breeding from southern Canada to Ecuador; Greater Antilles (except Cuba), and on the islands of Curacao and Bonaire. The race *pratensis* occurs in our area.

Status: Rare, occasionally uncommon migrant. Fairly common but local breeder; formerly more numerous and widespread. Three winter occurrences.

Migration: The Grasshopper Sparrow is rarely reported during migration, except by those who visit the outer coast in October. Even there, however, it is unusual to find more than one or two in a day at any given locality. On rare occasions, "flights" are reported.

Maxima: *Spring*—8, Madison Square Park, N.Y.C., May 15, 1921 (Chapin). This remarkable number was seen after a heavy fog and rain the previous night. That same day many dead birds of various species were picked up at the base of the Metropolitan Life Insurance building nearby. Unfortunately, most of them were thrown away so that we have no idea how many Grasshopper Sparrows might have been present. *Fall*—8, Oct. 1; 6, Oct. 14, 1933, Easthampton (Helmuth); 4 banded, Tiana Beach, L.I., Oct. 25, 1961 (Wilcox and W. Terry).

Extreme dates: March 20 (specimen), Apr. 1 and 7 to Oct. 25 and 27 (specimens); several early November dates to Nov. 19 and 23. Rare before late April and after October.

In view of the above October maxima, Cruickshank's statement (1942), "After this month [September] the species is purely fortuitous," is not applicable; it is regular in October.

Breeding: Nests on the ground in dry grassy fields and pastures. This species has suffered severely within the past two decades, many of its former haunts destroyed for industrial and housing developments. Once a very common breeder on the extensive Hempstead Plains, this unique prairie-type habitat was nearly completely obliterated after World War II (see Upland Plover for extent of this area). J. T. Nichols told me that he conservatively estimated 100 nesting pairs on the Hempstead Plains in the late 1920s. As recently as 1940 he had found at least 20 breeding pairs in the Garden City area alone.

After the Newark Meadows had become ditched and diked in the early 1930s, Urner estimated 19 breeding pairs there in 1935.

During recent years we have the following breeding maxima for Long Island: On the abandoned Curtis Wright airport at Valley Stream, I counted eight or more pairs in 1954, but this locality was destroyed several years later for a shopping center; in the same year Latham reported seven pairs on Shelter Island; in 1955 Elliott found at least 17 pairs in the Montauk region, chiefly concentrated in pastures where cattle were grazing; in 1961 Ferguson reported over a dozen pairs nesting on Fisher's Island.

I have no recent breeding densities for the rest of our area with the exception of 11 pairs in the Poundridge Reservation, Westchester County, during the summer of 1959 (W. Russell).

The species is reported as holding its own fairly well in the agricultural districts of western New Jersey, and in Orange County, N.Y.

Egg dates: May 12 to July 4.

Remarks: This species winters north to North Carolina; very rarely to Maryland, Pennsylvania, New York, and Massachusetts (all specimens).

In our area it has been reported in winter on three occasions: one seen, Hampton Bays, L.I., Dec. 24, 1949 (Wilcox); one found dead, Mount Kisco, N.Y., Dec. 17, 1950 (Grierson), specimen preserved; an apparently injured bird observed, Grassy Point, N.Y., Dec. 27, 1952 (Orth and Kenney).

BAIRD'S SPARROW *(Ammodramus bairdii)**

Accidental: A central Nearctic species of the Great Plains, breeding east to southern Manitoba and western Minnesota. Casual anywhere east of the plains and accidental in New York.

One positive record: specimen taken at Montauk, Nov. 13, 1899 (Helme), identification confirmed by Dwight, specimen in collection of Harold H. Bailey.

Two sight reports, made by experienced and competent observers, are believed correct: one on the lawn south of the Belvedere in Central Park,

Oct. 24, 1949 (Helmuth), full details submitted; the other a week later, Short Beach, L.I., Oct. 31, 1949 (Alperin, Jacobson, and Sedwitz, Linnaean News-Letter, 3[8]: Jan. 1950). One or two additional reports are not satisfactory.

HENSLOW'S SPARROW (*Passerherbulus henslowii*)*B

Range: An eastern Nearctic species of local distribution, the race *susurrans* breeding in our area.

Status: Rare and little-known migrant. Rare to uncommon and very local breeder; occasionally more numerous.

Migration: The Henslow's Sparrow is very rarely reported as a migrant away from breeding areas, principally because of its secretive nature. I am unaware of more than one individual being reported at any given locality at one time. In the Ossining area A. K. Fisher collected a total of only five migrants within a period of more than 30 years—all in October between the fifth and ninth of that month in different years—these specimens in the M.C.Z. collection. Carleton (1958) listed only four sight reports—two each in spring and fall—for Prospect Park, and none for Central Park.

Extreme dates: Apr. 4 to Nov. 20 (specimen) and Nov. 27. Rare before late April and after mid-October.

Breeding: The Henslow's Sparrow breeds on the ground in grassy fields and meadows with scattered bushes and herbaceous plants, both in wet and dry situations. In such places the species' presence may be determined by its insect-like song; otherwise it is usually overlooked. However, the species is decidedly local and unpredictable; many areas which appear to be ideal for it are untenanted, and other localities are deserted after one or more years. Usually only one or two pairs are found breeding at a single locality, but in a few places small "colonies" have been reported. Some indication of maximum numbers and distribution are illustrated by the following:

Long Island: Elliott (1941) stated that on the south shore the species was distributed locally, with the center of occurrence extending from Massapequa east to Babylon. In 1941, the largest "colony" had six or seven pairs at Lindenhurst, and a total of less than a dozen pairs in three separate "colonies" in the Massapequa area. Most of the birds were located where upland meets the salt or rather brackish portions of the meadows, the nesting having taken place chiefly in the drier sections. The following year grass fires destroyed the habitat and the birds deserted both localities. However, they apparently reappeared there around 1944. In a later article, Elliott (1954) stated, "A rather abrupt decrease came

447

about seven or eight years ago [about 1946] and there were no reports of this bird nesting in 1953 although the nesting grounds remained practically unaltered."

Westchester County: Breeding chiefly in the northern portion at widely scattered localities, both in dry fields and damp meadows. During the summer of 1950, several observers reported 21 nesting pairs at eight localities —all from Kensico Reservoir to the Putnam County line—including a "colony" of at least 10 breeding pairs in the Cross River area (Wheeler), but the following year he was unable to find any at that locality. The reason for their disappearance was unknown, the conditions "apparently similar" during both years.

New Jersey: Widely, but locally distributed in "suitable" localities. In 1952 near New Brunswick, Boyajian reported six pairs nesting in wet meadows.

Many former breeding sites in our area have been obliterated due to housing developments.

Egg dates: May 21 to June 24.

SHARP-TAILED SPARROW (*Ammospiza caudacuta*)*B

Range: Nearctic species (for details, see Subspecies)

Status: Common to locally abundant coastal migrant, particularly in fall. Regular but rare to uncommon in winter; occasionally more numerous. Common to locally abundant breeder in coastal salt marshes.

Migration and winter: For various subspecies, see below. In our area the Sharp-tailed Sparrow (collectively) is very rarely reported away from its saline environment. Carleton (1958) listed only three observations from Central Park and one from Prospect Park, all in May.

Maxima: *Fall*—Sharp-tailed Sparrows may be seen by the hundreds in the coastal marshes, especially during fall. For several days after the hurricane of Sept. 21, 1938, Latham saw at least 1000 in the Orient region, most of them dead, presumably drowned by abnormally high tides and buffeted by 150-mile-per-hour winds (see Proc. Linnaean Soc. N.Y., 50–51: 68–69, 1940). *Winter*—More frequent at this season than the Seaside Sparrow; 32, Jones Beach area, winter of 1940–41 (Elliott).

Usually arrives in late April and departs by late October.

Breeding: The Sharp-tailed Sparrow breeds in the drier portions of the salt meadows, preferring the higher sections where there is a growth of the shorter grasses, such as *Spartina patens* and *Distichlis spicata*. Detailed accounts of its nesting habits, ecology, and distribution are found in papers by Montagna (1942), Elliott (1953), and Woolfenden (1956).

It is more generally distributed than the Seaside Sparrow, breeding farther east on Long Island as far as Gardiner's Bay and on the Montauk peninsula to Napeague Bay; also locally common on both shores of Long Island Sound. It still nests regularly (1962) in the few remaining salt marshes in the Westport, Conn., area (M. Brown). It is becoming less numerous on Staten Island, Hackensack Meadows, Newark Bay, and along the north Jersey coast, where the tidal marshes are gradually being filled.

Maxima: Over 200 pairs on the north side of Jamaica Bay from Idlewild to Spring Creek (Queens County), up until the mid-1940s, when most of the area was filled for Idlewild airport (Mayer); 57 pairs, including 16 occupied nests, Baldwin–Oceanside (Nassau County) marshes, summer of 1947 (Morgan); at least 120 pairs, Pelham Bay area (Bronx County), 1955 (Young *et al.*).

Formerly bred in the Harlem River marshes, last reported in 1882 (*fide* Bicknell). According to Deed *et al.* (1959), it was "considered by Brownell in 1908 to have been a fairly common summer resident . . . at Piermont [Hudson River, Rockland County]." Careful search may reveal its presence there now during the breeding season.

Egg dates: May 9 to Aug. 4.

Subspecies: Four subspecies or races occur in the New York City area as follows: (*a*) nominate *caudacuta*; (*b*) *subvirgata*; (*c*) *altera*; (*d*) *nelsoni*.

a) The nominate race, breeding exclusively in salt marshes of the Atlantic coast, ranges from extreme southwestern Maine south to southern New Jersey (near Tuckerton).

Five fall specimens of this race in the A.M.N.H. collection were taken inland on the Hudson River at Piermont in 1888; two, Oct. 10, and three, Oct. 19 (all Dwight collection).

The only local winter specimens in the large series of the A.M.N.H. collection are *all* of the nominate race, taken on the south shore of Long Island: Far Rockaway, Feb. 23, 1885 (Foster); Amityville, Feb. 23, 1891 (Dutcher); Bellport, Feb. 24, 1894 (Van Rensselaer).

Nominate *caudacuta*, the breeding form in our coastal salt marshes, has been discussed under Breeding.

b) The race *subvirgata* breeds locally in salt and brackish marshes in southern Quebec (south shore of the lower St. Lawrence River); and from Nova Scotia and New Brunswick south to southwestern Maine (intergrading with nominate *caudacuta*). Common migrant along the coast, both spring and fall. Winters on the south Atlantic coast; the statement in the A.O.U. *Check-list* (1957: 594) concerning wintering—"casually north to New York (Long Island)" is not substantiated by specimens, insofar as Long Island is concerned.

On the basis of specimens, the extreme dates are: *Fall*—Sept. 29 to Oct. 19; two collected at Moriches Inlet, Nov. 24, 1951 (Fischer), Cornell University Museum collection (see Parkes, 1952). Notably late *Spring* migrant—May 26 to June 8, specimens in all instances.

449

No sight reports accepted, although this is the prevailing form (other than nominate *caudacuta*) in spring based on specimens, *altera* and *nelsoni* having been collected in our area only in fall.

Collected inland as follows: Three taken in the marshes at the mouth of the Croton River; Oct. 1, 1880, Oct. 7, 1885, and Sept. 29, 1886 (all by A. K. Fisher), specimens, M.C.Z. collection; this is not too surprising as this form breeds in the lower St. Lawrence Valley and a few probably migrate south by way of the Champlain–Hudson Valley.

c) The race *altera* breeds in brackish and salt marshes of James Bay in northeastern Ontario and west-central Quebec. Fall migrant inland and along the Atlantic coast. Winters on the coast of the south Atlantic states; the statement in the A.O.U. *Check-list* (1957: 595) about wintering—"casually north to New York (Long Island)"—is inapplicable. There are no known winter specimens from Long Island.

Based on specimens, the extreme fall dates are: Sept. 30 to Oct. 19; also a specimen collected at "Island Hall," Westchester County, Nov. 15, 1879 (Zerega), A.M.N.H. collection.

In addition to the above 1879 specimen, this race was collected inland in the marshes at the mouth of the Croton River by Fisher on three occasions: Sept. 30, 1880; Oct. 17, 1885; Oct. 4, 1888, specimens in M.C.Z. collection; also one taken at Highland Falls, N.Y., Oct. 16, 1874 (Mearns), A.M.N.H. collection. There are no known local spring specimens.

No sight reports accepted.

d) The race *nelsoni* breeds inland in fresh-water prairie marshes east to central Manitoba and northwestern Minnesota. Winters along the Gulf and south Atlantic coasts. Probably a regular fall migrant along the Atlantic coast, recorded from Maine to Florida. No known spring specimens from the New York City region.

Based on specimens, the extreme fall dates are: Sept. 28 to Oct. 27; one collected at Moriches Inlet, Nov. 24, 1951 (Fischer), Cornell University Museum collection (see Parkes, 1952).

At least nine specimens have been taken in the marshes of the Hudson River, seven at the mouth of the Croton River (Fisher); one at Piermont (Dwight collection) A.M.N.H.; one as far inland as Highland Falls (Mearns).

No sight reports accepted.

Remarks: Further collecting in our area is desirable to determine (*a*) which subspecies occur in winter and (*b*) which subspecies occur during migration in inland fresh-water marshes; I have seen no specimens from such areas as Troy Meadows, where Sharp-tailed Sparrows undoubtedly occur occasionally.

I cannot emphasize strongly enough the extreme difficulties involved in determining specimens of the various subspecies. While it is relatively easy to separate nominate *caudacuta* from the others, trying to differentiate

450

subvirgata, altera, and *nelsoni* from each other is an entirely different matter. After examining large series in several museums and after consulting the reviews of Peters (1942), Todd (1942), and Montagna (1942), as well as the more recent paper by Parkes (1952), I find the whole problem exceedingly complex, Elliott's remarks (1962: 120–121) concerning taxonomy notwithstanding.

Todd (1942), who described *altera* in 1938, stated, "*A. c. altera* is intermediate between the plainly colored race, *subvirgata,* . . . and the richly colored form, *nelsoni,* . . ."

Montagna (1942) speaking of *subvirgata* said, ". . . a gradual transition from birds inhabiting salt-water marshes in western Maine to those in fresh-water habitat . . . on the St. Lawrence. There is little doubt that *subvirgata* represents the closest eastern relative of the James Bay birds (*altera*) . . ."

Peters (1942), in his thorough review of the problem, critically examined numerous specimens of *subvirgata, altera,* and *nelsoni,* and stated in part: "There are several points that must be constantly borne in mind when dealing with *Ammospiza caudacuta.* . . . the plumage abrades very rapidly and the more the birds become worn the more the races resemble one another; . . . there is much variation in comparable series from any given locality, chiefly observable in a greater or lesser amount of streaking beneath, the depth of the buff markings on the sides of the head, and the shade of reddish-brown on the wing coverts."

"To understand the relationships of *altera* it is also necessary to have a clear idea of the variation of *subvirgata,* . . ."

Concerning the first winter and adult winter plumage of *altera,* Peters stated, "Exceedingly close to the corresponding plumage of *subvirgata,* in fact I can find no characters that will definitely separate the more rufescent specimens of *subvirgata* from the less rufescent specimens of *altera;* . . ."

Concerning *nelsoni* in the fall and winter plumage, Peters remarked, "Less readily distinguishable from *altera* than in the preceding (nuptial) plumage, but averaging browner in series, . . ."

In the American Museum of Natural History, there is a specimen collected on Staten Island, May 30, 1908, with the following notations: originally labeled *nelsoni,* reidentified as *subvirgata.* and on the reverse side of the label determined as "nearer" *altera.*

Does anyone care to identify subspecifically Sharp-tailed Sparrows in the field?

SEASIDE SPARROW (*Ammospiza maritima*)*B

Range: A southeastern Nearctic species of the coastal salt marshes, the nominate race breeding north to Massachusetts; local north of Long Island.

Status: Locally common to very common breeder along the coast, but rare and local at the extreme east end of Long Island, and on Long Island Sound. Regular but rare to uncommon in winter; occasionally more numerous.

Migration and winter: The Seaside Sparrow is casual away from its saline environment. Cruickshank (1942) knew of a single observation at Van Cortlandt Park in late April, and Carleton (1958) listed only three sight reports from Central Park and one from Prospect Park, all in May. These reports are probably reliable, as they were made by observers familiar with the species. Fisher collected one at the mouth of the Croton River, N.Y., Oct. 2, 1885, specimen in M.C.Z. collection, the farthest inland report known for our area.

Less frequent in winter than the Sharp-tailed Sparrow. Maxima: 12, Long Beach, Dec. 12, 1920 (Janvrin); 11, Jones Beach, winter of 1940-41 (Elliott). Reported annually on the south shore of Long Island during winter.

Usually arrives by late April and departs in late October.

Breeding: The Seaside Sparrow occurs exclusively on the salt meadows and is casual anywhere else. It nests in the wetter portions almost invariably, according to Elliott (1953) and Woolfenden (1956), the former stating that it "occupies the wetter areas of taller, coarser grasses, . . ." such as *Spartina alterniflora.* However, it occasionally breeds in dry sandy areas among beach grass very close to the salt marsh, as at the Jamaica Bay Refuge.

Its numerous occurrences in the extensive marshes on the south shore of Long Island may be seen from the following: In the Baldwin–Oceanside area (Nassau County), Morgan found at least 50 pairs breeding, including 21 occupied nests in 1946, and in 1947 he estimated 70 pairs including 27 nests actually found.

East of Shinnecock Bay, this species is rare and local, as suitable salt marshes are few. Helmuth never actually found it nesting in the Easthampton area, although he suspected that it might. However, he did locate one nesting pair at Sag Harbor in 1947. Latham found it breeding formerly, though rarely, in the Orient region, but not in recent years.

It breeds commonly on the north Jersey coast in suitable areas, but is disappearing elsewhere as the marshes are drained or filled. Howes (1928) stated that it was "common" in the Stamford, Conn., area, but few suitable places remain along Long Island Sound. This species nested in the Harlem River marshes up to 1881 (*fide* Bicknell). Young found four pairs breeding in the Pelham Bay area (Bronx County) in 1955.

That it has nested up the Hudson River is proved by several specimens taken, the following in the American Museum collection: adult female (seen with young), collected at Piermont marsh (Rockland County), June 6, 1892 (Rowley); adult and three immatures taken at the same locality, Aug. 24, 1888 (Chapman). Hellmayr (1938) also listed specimens for this locality, six (dates not stated) in the collection of the Chicago Natural History Museum. This species was omitted from *Birds of Rockland County* (1959). It should be searched for in the breeding season at Piermont to see if it is still present.

Egg dates: May 23 to July 2.

VESPER SPARROW (*Pooecetes gramineus*)*B

Range: Nearctic species, the nominate race breeding in our area.

Status: Uncommon to fairly common migrant, occasionally common on the coast in fall. Rare to uncommon but regular in winter on the coast; occasionally more numerous. Now an uncommon, local breeder; formerly more numerous.

Migration and winter: The Vesper Sparrow occurs regularly during migration in relatively small numbers of two to six birds in short-grass country both inland and along the coast; occasionally small flocks are observed in autumn. Generally rare in winter. The following counts are all from Long Island, except one.

Maxima: *Spring*—25, Easthampton, Apr. 25, 1927. *Fall*—37, Easthampton, Oct. 24, 1939; 50, Idlewild, Nov. 15, 1952. *Winter*—several midwinter specimens, including four collected at Jamaica Bay, Feb. 7, 1905 (Weber); the following maxima are exceptional—30, Bayside, Feb. 1, 1930 (Yeaton); 35, farm fields back of Woodmere Woods, Dec. 29, 1946 (Berliner, Bull, and Eisenmann); 35, plowed fields near Greenwich, Conn., Dec. 27, 1959 (numerous observers).

Usually arrives in late March and departs by late November.

Breeding: Of all the breeding birds that have suffered because of a rapid decline in agriculture in our area, the Vesper Sparrow has decreased the most, as it is more dependent on farming than the other open-country species are. With the disappearance of one farm after another, this species has virtually retired as a breeding bird to the remotest areas of western New Jersey, Orange County, N.Y., and extreme eastern Long Island where the few remaining farms exist. Even in these places Vesper Sparrows are local. The once vast Hempstead Plains were favored breeding grounds also.

The Vesper Sparrow nests on or near the ground in dry fields and pastures.

Egg dates: May 2 to July 14.

LARK SPARROW (*Chondestes grammacus*)*

Range: Nearctic species, the nominate race breeding east to southern Ontario, Michigan, and Ohio; very rarely to western New York, central Pennsylvania, and northern Virginia; formerly in western Maryland.

Status: Rare but regular fall migrant on the coast; very rare in spring.

Occurrence: Like several other western species, the Lark Sparrow has spread eastward with the clearing of the forests. This species prefers dry sandy fields and in our area is most often found in such places along the outer coast during fall migration. Rare inland.

The principal months of occurrence are August, September, and October. This species is scarce in July and November, only three reports in the former month, 10 in the latter. Usually from one to three individuals are seen each fall, but occasionally more are noted: seven each in 1952, 1953, and 1954.

The maximum per day is three, Jones Beach, Sept. 13, 1958 (Buckley, Levine, and Restivo); one of these was collected, but the specimen was not preserved.

Extreme dates: *Fall*—casual, Shelter Island, July 7, 1924 (Latham); July 25 and 28 to Nov. 27 (specimen). Rare before mid-August and after mid-October.

In spring there are 10 known occurrences; two in April, six in May, and two in June.

Extreme dates: *Spring*—Apr. 11, 1939, Riverdale, N.Y. (Griscom), a singing male; Apr. 30 to June 1 and 12.

Specimen data: There are at least seven specimens taken locally, all in fall, but none are in the American Museum collection. The only specimen from our area seen by me was an immature male taken at Easthampton, Aug. 17, 1934 (Helmuth), in the Cornell University Museum collection.

Remarks: The statement in the A.O.U. *Check-list* (1957: 599), "Winters . . .; occasionally north along Atlantic coast to northern New Jersey (Bergen County)" is misleading, if not erroneous. The species winters from Louisiana and Texas south to El Salvador. It is *accidental* at this season north of southern Florida (where very rare). Sprunt (1949) lists it as accidental in South Carolina (one October record), and Stewart and Robbins (1958) mention *no* winter occurrence for Maryland.

The foregoing statement in the *Check-list* may be based on the report of an individual banded by Mrs. McEntee at Ridgewood, Bergen County. This bird appeared on Jan. 14, 1953, when it was banded, and returned to the traps at irregular intervals until Feb. 4. Another Lark Sparrow was carefully observed at Bound Brook, N.J., Jan. 4, 1959 (B. Murray; see Kunkle *et al.*, 1959).

BACHMAN'S SPARROW (*Aimophila aestivalis*)*

Accidental: A southeastern Nearctic species, the race *bachmani* breeds north to southwestern Pennsylvania and central Maryland. Stragglers have occurred north to southern Ontario.

In our area there is one specimen record, a singing male taken at Fort Lee, N.J., May 9, 1918 (Weber), specimen in U.S.N.M., No. 442569 (*fide* Wetmore). This record was overlooked by Stone (1937). One sight report of a singing bird made by experienced observers is probably correct; Prospect Park, April 21, 1948 (Carleton), and the following day (Jacobson, Sedwitz, and Whelen; see Carleton, Kingbird, 2: 82, 1952). One or two other recent reports were not confirmed.

BLACK-THROATED SPARROW (*Amphispiza bilineata*)

Accidental: A southwestern Nearctic species, breeding north to south-western Wyoming, east to southeastern Colorado, and the western portions of Oklahoma and Texas. Winters in the southern parts of its breeding range, south into Mexico. Accidental in Wisconsin, Illinois, Ohio, Massachusetts, and New Jersey, all within four years (1959–62).

In our area one appeared at the MacKenzie feeder near New Brunswick, N.J., Oct. 30, 1961, and remained for nearly six months, until Apr. 23, 1962. It was seen by numerous observers and photographed in color.

In absence of a specimen, the subspecies is undeterminable.

SLATE-COLORED JUNCO (*Junco hyemalis*)*B

Range: Nearctic species, the nominate race breeding south to the Poconos, Catskills, and Berkshires; rarely to Connecticut and Dutchess County, New York (both outside the New York City area). Parkes (1954b) says that this latter breeding population is intermediate between nominate *hyemalis* and the more southern race *carolinensis.*

Status: Common to abundant migrant; less numerous in winter. Two breeding records.

Migration and winter: The Slate-colored Junco is especially numerous in fall along the coast, great flocks appearing at times. It is regular in much smaller numbers in winter at feeding stations.

Maxima: *Fall*—800, Prospect Park, Oct. 15, 1950; 1000, Riis Park, Oct. 25, 1953; 850, Easthampton, Nov. 2, 1930. Usually present from mid-September to early May. Vagrants reported twice each in June, July, and August on Long Island and in Westchester County.

Breeding: Although the nest of this species has not been found in our area, evidence in the form of midsummer dates and young birds indicates breeding in northern New Jersey: pair and three young (able to fly), Stokes State Forest, Sussex County, July 2, 1949 (Fables); an adult with one young in the streaked juvenal plumage, Ramapo Mountains near Wanaque Reservoir, Passaic County, July 26, 1953 (Eynon and Laubinger).

Egg dates: No data.

Subspecies: The race *cismontanus* breeds east to western Alberta and winters east to Wisconsin. Casual east to Massachusetts, New York, and Virginia. A specimen of this race was taken at Hastings, N.Y., date and collector not stated (see Miller, 1941). No observations are accepted because of the difficulties involved. There is much variation in *J. hyemalis* and *J. oreganus*. The form *cismontanus* was formerly considered to be a hybrid population by Dwight until A. H. Miller (1941: 329–345 and 402–404) treated it as a subspecies, this treatment followed by the A.O.U. *Check-list* (1957).

OREGON JUNCO (*Junco oreganus*)*

Very rare visitant: A western Nearctic species, breeding east to south-western Saskatchewan. Winters east to South Dakota and Nebraska. Wandering in migration and winter east to the Atlantic coast from Massachusetts to Maryland.

Of three specimens taken locally, two were determined by A. H. Miller to be the race *montanus*, and are in the American Museum collection: adult male trapped at Poundridge, N.Y., Dec. 2, 1946 (F. C. Scott), No. 344035; adult male at the Wachenfeld feeding station, Orange, N.J., first seen Jan. 24, 1958, collected Feb. 23 (Buckley), No. 707870. Miller (*in litt.*) stated, "I have examined both juncos and would place them in the race *montanus*. The Poundridge specimen being quite typical, the other somewhat atypical, although clearly within this group." (See also Buckley, 1959.)

The writer was informed by Ferguson (*in litt.*) that a male collected by him at his feeding station on Fisher's Island, Jan. 2, 1961, was identified as this species at the Yale Peabody Museum, New Haven; specimen in Ferguson's collection—also determined as the race *montanus* (George Watson, oral comm.).

There are at least 13 credible sight reports of Oregon Juncos in our area observed either in fall migration or in winter at feeding stations. In all cases, adult males were reported; observations of females and so-called "Pink-sided" Juncos are rejected, as confusion with Slate-colored Juncos is likely, and hybrids are possible.

Two reports were listed by Cruickshank (1942): Easthampton, Oct. 8, 1932 (Helmuth); Bernardsville, N.J., November 1938 (Chalif). There are the following reports since then: Easthampton, Oct. 18, 1943 (Helmuth); Far Rockaway, Oct. 10, 1945 (Bull); same locality, at Bull feeder, Jan. 3–4, 1948 (many observers), following the heavy snowstorm of Dec. 27, 1947; Lemmon feeder, Wilton, Conn., Jan. 7–16, 1951 (Heck and others); Jones Beach, Oct. 26, 1953 (Bull); Cherepy feeder, Franklin, N.J., mid-December 1953 to mid-March 1954 (many observers); two, Irving feeder, West Nyack, N.Y., March 21, 1956 (several observers), after a heavy

456

snowstorm; Boyajian feeder, Englewood, Dec. 24, 1959, to late February 1960 (several observers); Nye feeder, Bayard Cutting Arboretum, Great River, L.I., January through March 1961 (numerous observers), also after a heavy snowstorm; one banded and color-photographed, Ramsey, N.J., March 2–27, 1961 (Dater and others); Mather feeder, Centerville, Hunterdon County, N.J., late December 1961 through March 1962 (numerous observers).

Extreme dates: October 8 to April 1.

Remarks: Some authorities consider *J. hyemalis* (Slate-colored Junco) and *J. oreganus* (Oregon Junco) conspecific. There is considerable interbreeding between the two and hybrids are frequent.

TREE SPARROW (*Spizella arborea*)*

Range: Nearctic species, the nominate race breeding south to northern Ontario, northern Quebec, and Labrador.

Status: Common to occasionally abundant winter visitant.

Occurrence and maxima: The Tree Sparrow is sometimes found in great numbers during severe winters, and much less commonly in mild seasons. It occurs in open country and is particularly fond of weedy and brushy fields, but is a frequent visitor at feeding stations.

Maxima: 280, Orient, Dec. 25, 1909; 1500 on two Christmas counts, eastern Morris County, N.J., Dec. 31, 1944.

Extreme dates: Oct. 10 (specimen) to May 8 and 12. Rare before November and after early April. Earlier fall dates than that listed have not been confirmed and need substantiation—preferably by a specimen.

CHIPPING SPARROW (*Spizella passerina*)*B

Range: A widespread Nearctic species, the nominate race occurring in our area.

Status: Common to very common, occasionally abundant migrant. Rare but regular in winter. Locally common breeder.

Migration: Chipping Sparrows are very fond of lawns and short-grass fields with areas of bare ground. During migration they are often found in such places, feeding with other sparrows.

Maxima: *Spring*—200, Prospect Park, May 2, 1945. *Fall*—125, Easthampton, Oct. 11, 1937; 250, Bronx Park, Oct. 15, 1950. Usually rare before April and after early November.

Winter: This species winters north to southeastern Maryland; rarely north to Massachusetts (specimens). In the large series at the A.M.N.H.

from the New York City area, however, there is none taken in winter. Nevertheless, it is reported each year and on at least two occasions more than one were observed at a single locality: 3 at a feeder with Tree Sparrows, Westport, Conn., Dec. 26, 1953 (several observers); 4 banded at Freeport, L.I. (Penberthy and Arbib)—1, Jan. 19, 1957, and 3 more, Feb. 3. It should be borne in mind, however, that the Chipping Sparrow is rare at this season, and a number of sight reports are extremely doubtful and not properly corroborated. There are too many Tree Sparrows misidentified by inexperienced observers on Christmas counts, especially in recent years.

Breeding: The Chipping Sparrow breeds around farms, gardens, suburban yards, city parks, estates, and in much of the settled rural country. Its nest is placed in trees, bushes, vines, and often in low ornamental conifers.

Egg dates: May 10 to July 26.

CLAY-COLORED SPARROW (*Spizella pallida*)*

Range: A western Nearctic species, breeding east to central Ontario and Michigan; east to southeastern Ontario (1950 on). In fall migration, rarely but regularly east to the Atlantic coast of Massachusetts, Long Island, New Jersey (all specimens); south to South Carolina and Florida.

Status: Rare but regular fall migrant on the coast.

Occurrence: Prior to 1950, when it first bred east as far as Toronto, the Clay-colored Sparrow was reported only five times in the New York City region. But from 1950 on, it has been reliably reported annually in fall along the outer coast by active observers. Of more than 35 *acceptable* reports, the great majority occur during September and October, with the maximum number reported in the latter month (4 each in 1955 and 1960). Usually only one individual is observed per *day* per *locality*, but on occasion two or three have been seen.

The only known local specimen is that of an immature collected near Riis Park, L.I., Oct. 12, 1956 (Buckley), A.M.N.H. No. 707782. There are also several specimens from the coast of New Jersey south of our region (see Buckley, 1959).

Extreme fall dates: Sept. 7 to Nov. 19.

There are only two reliable spring reports for our area: adult, Far Rockaway, May 14, 1950 (Bull); singing bird, South Ozone Park, L.I., Apr. 16, 1954 (Carleton and Mayer). No inland observations have been adequately confirmed.

Locally Clay-colored Sparrows frequent sandy areas with short grass, particularly near the ocean. They have been reported most often on the south shore of Long Island at Riis Park, Zachs Bay, and Gilgo Beach, but the species has been seen as far east as the lighthouse at Montauk

Point. They sometimes associate with migrant Chipping Sparrows, affording an opportunity for comparison.

It should be stressed that only those observers thoroughly familiar with the different plumages of the genus *Spizella* are competent to identify this pale western species. An examination of museum specimens will reveal some of the subtle differences in immature fall examples of *S. pallida* and *S. passerina*, differences not found in color plates.

BREWER'S SPARROW (*Spizella breweri*)

Accidental: A western Nearctic species, the nominate race breeds east to the western portions of the Dakotas and Nebraska. In migration east to western Kansas. Accidental in Massachusetts (specimen, 1873).

In our area it has been reported twice on Long Island by experienced observers: Gilgo Beach, Oct. 26, 1947 (Alperin, Carleton, Jacobson, and Sedwitz); Montauk Point, Oct. 14, 1950 (Eisenmann, Grant *et al.*). These observations are believed correct. For details, see Linnaean News-Letter, 1 (6): Nov. 1947, and 4 (7): Dec. 1950.

What has been said of the Clay-colored Sparrow as to field identification applies to Brewer's Sparrow as well, except that the latter is very much rarer in the east. It is desirable to collect a specimen in order to establish definitely its occurrence in our area.

FIELD SPARROW (*Spizella pusilla*)*B

Range: An eastern Nearctic species, the nominate race breeding in our area.

Status: Common to very common migrant. Rare to occasionally common in winter. Locally common, but widespread breeder.

Migration and winter: Field Sparrows are common migrants both inland and along the coast, often associating with other sparrows. On rare occasions in winter small flocks are noted in swampy thickets.

Maxima: *Migration*—55, Easthampton, Nov. 2, 1930. *Winter*—105, Bronx–Westchester Christmas count, Dec. 26, 1949; 115, Queens County Christmas count, Dec. 20, 1952. Arrives in late March and departs in mid-November.

Breeding: The Field Sparrow nests in open country on or near the ground in brushy fields and thickets.

Egg dates: May 6 to July 13.

Subspecies: The race *arenacea* breeds east to the Dakotas, Nebraska, etc., and winters east to Mississippi. Casual in migration to western Tennessee. Accidental in New Jersey (specimen).

459

An example of this well-marked subspecies was collected near New Brunswick, N.J., Dec. 30, 1953 (Baird), A.M.N.H. No. 708124.

HARRIS' SPARROW (*Zonotrichia querula*)

Accidental: A western Nearctic species, breeding southeast to northern Manitoba. Winters east to Tennessee and Louisiana. Casual farther east and accidental in Massachusetts (specimen, 1929).

This well-marked bird has not been collected in our area, but has been adequately observed on three occasions: Troy Meadows, May 7, 1935 (E. Eliot, Janvrin, and Tucker); City Hall Park, Manhattan, May 23, 1956 (Walsh); adult with some black patches still present, near the Fire Island lighthouse, Sept. 30, 1956 (Bull).

WHITE-CROWNED SPARROW (*Zonotrichia leucophrys*)*

Range: Nearctic species, the nominate race breeds south to central Ontario, southeastern Quebec, and northern Newfoundland. Winters north to Maryland; much more rarely to southern New Jersey and New York; casually to Massachusetts (specimen).

Status: Uncommon to very common migrant, numbers greatly fluctuating; usually more numerous in fall, especially on the coast. Very rare in winter, but reported more frequently in recent years (since about 1947); formerly accidental at this season.

Migration: This species is particularly fond of lawns with hedges and thickets, but may also be found in open fields in agricultural districts.

Maxima: *Spring*—big flight in 1956—Central Park, May 10 (80), May 14 (25); very large coastal flight at Jones Beach, May 9, 1961, "several hundred," including a flock of 67 (Levine and Ward). This unusual concentration was attributed to a dense early-morning fog. *Fall*—70, Jones Beach, Oct. 10, 1956; big flight in 1939—Mecox Bay to Montauk (Helmuth), Oct. 21 (118), Oct. 24 (146); 60, Riis Park, Oct. 22, 1955.

Extreme dates: *Fall*—Sept. 23 to Nov. 10, irregularly into December. *Spring*—Apr. 10 (specimen) and Apr. 17 to May 30 (specimen) and May 31; casual, Elmsford, N.Y., June 14, 1933 (Fry), and Greenbrook Sanctuary, N.J., June 27, 1962 (*fide* D. Roser), adults in both instances. Generally rare before mid-May.

Winter: As with a number of other species in our area, formerly very rare to unknown in winter; more and more feeding stations, plus a trend toward milder winters, have attracted birds such as the White-crowned Sparrow in recent years. No local specimens of this species in the large series at the American Museum have been taken during this season, nor

460

did Griscom (1923) list any winter occurrences. Even Cruickshank (1942) called it very rare, listing only two overwintering individuals, both at feeders. Since about 1947, this species has been reported almost every winter, usually at feeders, a few remaining into April. There were as many as three individuals present at a New Canaan, Conn., feeder with White-throated Sparrows on Dec. 29, 1951, and into January 1952, seen by numerous observers.

Subspecies: The more western race *gambelii*, breeding east to northern Manitoba, has been collected on the Atlantic coast from Massachusetts to Virginia, as well as inland in New York and Pennsylvania but, as far as known, it has not been taken in our area. This well-marked subspecies should be looked for and collected if possible. No local sight reports have been adequately confirmed.

GOLDEN-CROWNED SPARROW (*Zonotrichia atricapilla*)

Accidental: A western Nearctic species, breeding east to southwestern Alberta. Winters east to eastern Colorado. Accidental in Massachusetts (specimen, 1928) and Pennsylvania (banded, 1952—verified by Griscom, Wetmore *et al.*).

Reported once in our area: Immature at Jones Beach—first seen Jan. 31, 1954 (Carleton)—remained until Apr. 24 and studied by hundreds of observers.

WHITE-THROATED SPARROW (*Zonotrichia albicollis*)*

Range: Nearctic species, breeding south to the Poconos, Catskills, and Berkshires; rarely to northwestern Connecticut (Litchfield Hills).

Status: Common to abundant migrant, especially in fall. Locally common in winter near the coast; less numerous inland.

Migration and winter: This species and the Slate-colored Junco are the most numerous sparrows in fall, flooding the country and easily outnumbering all the others combined. Occasionally thousands may be seen in a day in fall along the outer coast.

Maxima: *Spring*—700, Central Park, Apr. 30, 1947. *Fall*—1000, Prospect Park, Oct. 15, 1950. In winter it is one of the commonest species at feeding stations and numbers up to 30 are not rare.

"Extreme" dates: Early September to late May, but there are a number of August dates and several June dates. In fact, the species has been reported every month of the year with no less than *seven* July occurrences, some of these singing birds. No evidence of breeding in our area. Rare

461

before mid-September and after mid-May. Usually arrives in early April and departs in early November.

Remarks: An intergeneric hybrid, a male *Zonotrichia albicollis* × *Junco hyemalis* (White-throated Sparrow × Slate-colored Junco), was collected at the Kalbfleisch Research Station near Huntington, L.I., Oct. 14, 1959 (Lanyon), A.M.N.H. No. 775741.

FOX SPARROW (*Passerella iliaca*)*

Range: Nearctic species, the nominate race breeding south to north-central Ontario, southeastern Quebec, and southern Newfoundland.

Status: A migrant in varying numbers, some years uncommon, in others common to occasionally abundant. Regular but usually uncommon in winter.

Migration and winter: This species frequents thickets, undergrowth in woodland, shrubbery and hedgerows, and in winter is not rare at feeding stations near the coast. The Fox Sparrow is noted for its rapid spring migration, often remaining in an area for only a day or two.

Maxima: *Spring*—big flight in 1933—700, Franklin Lake area, N.J., Mar. 25; 100, Central Park, Mar. 31. *Fall*—200, Hohokus, N.J., Nov. 18, 1934. *Winter*—300, Nassau and Queens counties, late December 1952 Christmas counts.

Extreme dates: Sept. 30 and Oct. 2 to May 9 and 11. Rare before late October and after early April. Casual, Central Park, Aug. 9, 1913 (Griscom). Usually arrives in early March and departs in late November.

LINCOLN'S SPARROW (*Melospiza lincolnii*)*

Range: Nearctic species, the nominate race breeding south to northern New York (Adirondacks) and central Maine.

Status: Rare to uncommon but regular migrant.

Occurrence and maxima: The Lincoln's Sparrow, a shy and usually secretive species, favors thickets, hedgerows, and brush bordering wet areas. However, it is often found on lawns adjacent to shrubbery.

Maxima: *Spring*—3 hit the Fire Island light, May 9, 1882; in 1956 there was quite a flight in Central Park, several observers noted 4 on May 10 and 7 on May 14; 5, Riis Park, May 8, 1961. *Fall*—3, Easthampton, Sept. 24, 1944; 6, Fisher's Island, Oct. 13, 1955.

Extreme dates: *Spring*—Apr. 29 (specimen) to May 30, June 3 and 7. *Fall*—Sept. 2 (specimen) and Sept. 9 to Nov. 10, 27 (specimen), Nov. 29, and Dec. 4. Usually rare before mid-May; and before late September and after October.

462

Earlier April reports, summer reports including those in August, and most winter observations have not been corroborated, nor are there any specimens taken at these seasons in the A.M.N.H. collection. Misidentification of immature Swamp and Song Sparrows is likely.

Remarks: This species winters north to Georgia; casually to Pennsylvania and Massachusetts (specimen). One acceptable winter record for our area: adult at the Klein feeder, Little Neck, L.I., March 5, 1960, after a heavy snowstorm, to March 13 (several observers, including Sam Yeaton and the writer; also photographed). Several other winter observations have not been adequately confirmed. Most unfortunate is an article published in Ebba News, 24: 137, 1961, concerning a local bander's claim to have trapped and banded individuals of this species in northern New Jersey in December 1947, January 1948, June 1948, and even more improbable, June 27, 1961, and July 1956—all without substantiating evidence. This is an excellent example of erroneous data appearing in print and becoming perpetuated. Immature Swamp and Song Sparrows are often called Lincoln's Sparrows.

SWAMP SPARROW (*Melospiza georgiana*)*B

Range: Nearctic species, the nominate race breeding in our area.

Status: Common to very common migrant, particularly in fall. Usually rare to uncommon in winter, but locally very common along the coast, occasionally inland in mild winters. Locally common breeder inland, but rare on the coastal plain of Long Island and local on the north shore.

Migration and winter: Swamp Sparrows are commonly found on lawns, in parks, and to a lesser extent in weedy fields with other sparrows during migration but, true to their name, they retire to swampy places in winter. Maxima: *Spring*—40, Central Park, May 14, 1933. *Fall*—46 hit the tower at the Westhampton Air Force Base, Oct. 5, 1954; 175, Easthampton to Montauk, Oct. 14, 1929. *Winter*—65, Easthampton, Dec. 31, 1949 (Helmuth); 55, Troy Meadows, Dec. 23, 1950 (Urner Club). Usually arrives in early April and departs in early November.

Breeding: The Swamp Sparrow breeds in fresh-water marshes, swamps, and along wooded streams and ponds; more rarely in coastal brackish meadows. Ordinarily only a few pairs are found nesting at a given locality, but on occasion it nests semicolonially: 120 pairs, Troy Meadows, summer of 1947 (Urner Club); 20 pairs, Idlewild, summers of 1946 and 1949 (Mayer), is very unusual for the coastal plain—this locality now destroyed.

Egg dates: May 6 to June 28.

Subspecies: The northern race *ericrypta*, breeding south to central Ontario and southern Quebec, has been collected in Massachusetts. One specimen of this well-marked subspecies was taken at New Brunswick, N.J., Oct. 11, 1952 (Baird), A.M.N.H. No. 708125.

SONG SPARROW (*Melospiza melodia*)*B

Range: A widespread Nearctic species (for details, see Subspecies).

Status: Common to abundant migrant. Rare to locally common in winter, especially near the coast. Common and widespread breeder.

Migration and winter: Although rarely occurring in such large flocks as do the Slate-colored Junco and White-throated Sparrow, nevertheless the Song Sparrow is one of our more numerous species on migration. It winters regularly in small numbers at feeders.

Maximum abundance for the entire year is attained in March and October: *Spring*—125, Flushing Meadow Park, March 30, 1940. *Fall*—75, Central Park, Oct. 13, 1953; 400, Easthampton to Montauk, Oct. 14, 1929. *Winter*—185, Orient region, Dec. 22, 1918. Usually arrives in early March and departs in late November.

Breeding: The Song Sparrow, one of our most numerous birds, is ubiquitous, breeding in a great variety of habitats from the interior highlands to the coastal beaches. It nests in woodland clearings, thickets and hedgerows in farming country, brushy fields, at the edge of marshes, swamps, streams, and lakes, in city parks and suburban yards with plenty of shrubs, and in thickets on coastal sand dunes.

Egg dates: Apr. 20 to Aug. 14.

Subspecies: A highly polytypic species, the nominate race breeding throughout our area except on the barrier beaches and along the outer coastal salt meadows. Two additional races are alleged to occur within the limits of the New York City area, but the situation is not clear-cut.

1. The race *atlantica*, as the name implies, is a coastal population breeding from North Carolina north to at least southern New Jersey, although stated by the A.O.U. *Check-list* (1957: 631) to extend as far as eastern Long Island (Shelter Island). Stone (1937) stated that *M. m. atlantica* nests on the coast islands of extreme southern New Jersey, and he took specimens as far north as Atlantic City. Fables (1955) listed it as "the breeding race of the coastal barrier islands" (which extend as far north as the upper end of Barnegat Bay), but he did not say how far north it occurred. Cruickshank (1942) did not include this subspecies.

This well-marked race described by Todd (Auk, 41: 147, 1924) from Smith's Island, Virginia, is characterized by him as "strikingly different from *M. m. melodia*, much grayer above, the black streaking more distinct, and the reddish-brown feather edging reduced to a minimum." The "much heavier bill," mentioned by Stone (*op. cit.*), is not a constant character as many nominate *melodia* specimens have just as "heavy" bills. Parkes (1952) stated that "the breeding Song Sparrows of Long Island and Staten Island are, by and large, referable to *atlantica*, but they are more variable than Virginia . . . birds, and more rufescent individuals appear in the population. Definite cline in this race." He admitted having insufficient breeding material, however, and stated that "perhaps Long Island is in the zone of intermediacy, or at least with some *melodia* blood present."

J. T. Nichols (*in litt.*) stated, "I have never seen a typical *atlantica* from Long Island, but have seen specimens which I would call intermediates." Although I have not seen any breeding material from the coast of Staten Island, I have examined more than 20 Long Island specimens from the south shore collected in June and July and am in complete agreement with Nichols. Even specimens taken during the breeding season on Fire Island and as far west as Rockaway Beach appear to be intermediate. In view of this, the range of *M. m. atlantica* should be revised to exclude, at least, Long Island.

Further collecting of breeding material on the coast of northern and central New Jersey is desirable to determine the status of those birds.

2. The less well-marked inland race *euphonia*, breeding east to southern Ontario, western New York, western Pennsylvania, western Maryland, etc., is likewise stated by Parkes (*op. cit.*) to have been collected in our area—three specimens taken in Westchester County: one found dead, Scarsdale, March 21, 1946 (Fischer), examined by Parkes, who called it "typical"; two taken by Parkes at the Westchester County airport (near Purchase), date not stated, were determined by Wetmore as *M. m. euphonia*. I have not seen these specimens, but Parkes further states, "The two races (*melodia* and *euphonia*) are not strikingly different."

It would appear that *M. m. euphonia* is a clinal population between the eastern *M. m. melodia* and the still more western *M. m. juddi*.

LAPLAND LONGSPUR (*Calcarius lapponicus*)*

Range: Holarctic species, the nominate race breeding south to the northern portions of Ontario, Quebec, and Labrador.

Status: Variously rare to locally very common winter visitant on the coast; numbers subject to marked fluctuations.

Occurrence and maxima: The Lapland Longspur often associates with Horned Larks and sometimes with Snow Buntings. It frequents short-grass fields, airports, filled-in areas near inlets and bays, the drier portions of salt marshes, and beaches. Usually very rare inland where it occasionally may be found on plowed fields and on fill. Ordinarily only one to three birds are seen, but occasionally large flocks are reported on the coast.

465

Maxima: 75, Idlewild, Nov. 11, 1951; 125 in several flocks, Jamaica Bay area, Dec. 20, 1952; 4 collected and 25 seen, Long Island City, Feb. 28, 1885; 75, Newark Meadows, Apr. 6, 1935.

Extreme dates: Oct. 3, 4 (banded), Oct. 8, and 18 (specimen) to Apr. 18 (specimen), several later dates, and May 9. Rare before late October and after mid-April.

Collected inland at Croton Point, Feb. 20, 1885 (Fisher), M.C.Z. collection.

Remarks: The often-published report of a specimen taken at Shinnecock Bay, Aug. 12, 1881 (Dutcher), may be an error, as the date is nearly two months earlier than that given above (Oct. 3). The whereabouts of this specimen is unknown. Furthermore, Dutcher himself (1889: 137) states that a specimen secured Oct. 18, 1888, is "... the earliest date of which I have any record." (See above specimen under Extreme dates.)

CHESTNUT-COLLARED LONGSPUR (*Calcarius ornatus*)*

Accidental: A central Nearctic species of the Great Plains, breeding east to southwestern Minnesota. Winters east to Louisiana. Stragglers recorded east to the Atlantic coast from New Brunswick to Maryland.

In our region recorded only from Long Island, three specimens and a sight report as follows: adult male with a flock of Lapland Longspurs, taken at Long Island City, Feb. 16, 1889 (Hendrickson), A.M.N.H. No. 65626; one collected, Miller Place, Sept. 14, 1891 (Helme), in collection of H. H. Bailey; adult male in nearly full breeding plumage, Orient, first seen April 21, 1923 (Latham), and collected on April 27, specimen in his collection; adult male in breeding plumage, well seen at Dyker Beach, Apr. 29, 1944 (Grant *et al.*, see Auk, 62: 463, 1945).

SNOW BUNTING (*Plectrophenax nivalis*)*

Range: Holarctic species of high latitudes, the nominate race breeding south to the northern portions of Quebec and Labrador.

Status: Winter visitant in varying numbers, common to abundant some years, rare to uncommon in others. Most numerous on the outer coast. Usually rare inland, exceptionally in flocks after severe snowstorms.

Occurrence and maxima: Snow Buntings are seen most frequently on ocean beaches, sand dunes, plowed fields, and open grassy and filled-in areas around bays and inlets. They often associate with Horned Larks, but sometimes occur in pure flocks. Inland they are found in open fields with a sparse cover of grass.

466

Maxima: *Coastal*—400, Fire Island Inlet, Nov. 12, 1956; 1000, Long Beach, Dec. 27, 1919; 1500, Orient region, Feb. 10, 1956. *Inland*—200, Yonkers, N.Y., Jan. 24, 1881; 150, Boonton, N.J., Jan. 26, 1930.

Extreme dates: Oct. 3, 4, and 8 to Apr. 14, 20 (specimens) and Apr. 21. Casual, Oak Beach, L.I., May 9, 1948 (Elliott).

Rare before November and after March.

Escapes

One of the most perplexing problems in compiling a list of birds is the treatment of possible escapes. At least eight species (see below) reported from the New York City region are of questionable standing insofar as origin is concerned. Birds of these species are always suspect when seen in our area because they are, with few exceptions, frequently kept in confinement. They are popular as captives because of their bright plumage, attractive song, ability to breed readily in captivity, or because of their desirability as pets.

Whether, in fact, an individual of a given species has occurred within the area as a *bona fide* wanderer, has escaped from confinement, or has been transported under artificial circumstances is, in most instances, difficult if not impossible to prove. The fact that an individual bird is in "perfect" plumage and in apparent good health is not in itself proof that the bird was not an escape. All things being equal, if the individual in question is an escape and should survive the rigors of wild conditions, it will eventually molt into fresh plumage and, as such, be indistinguishable from a wild bird. On the other hand, a battered or frayed individual, while not certainly an escape, is likely to be a bird of captive origin.

Birds may gain their freedom either by (1) deliberate or by (2) accidental release. The first category includes those species that are transported from one place to another and then liberated, such as game birds and waterfowl for stocking purposes. Introduction into North America of these and many other types of birds has been made (see especially Phillips, 1928). The second category comprises those species that manage to escape from confinement. Sources of escaped stock are zoos, aviaries, game farms, pet shops, and private homes. The origin of a few "suspicious" birds seen in the field has sometimes been traced successfully to these sources, but that of many others has not. The mere fact that "all local zoos have been checked," proves little. It does not mean that other possible sources of escape have been eliminated.

Among the most difficult birds to evaluate are those from overseas. Even during migration, birds have taken advantage of free passage on ships between the continents. There is good evidence of an American passerine observed during the fall migration about 50 miles off the east coast and obviously "lost." This bird flew aboard an ocean liner offshore and remained during the entire trip to England. It was fed scraps of food and took water. According to the testimony of the eyewitness (by chance an ornithologist) as the ship approached the English coast at dawn, the bird left the ship and reached land. An unsuspecting birdwatcher, unaware of what had actually happened, subsequently reported the accidental visitant as another instance of genuine wandering. This is merely an example of how birds may be assisted in their travels. For specific instances of assisted passage aboard ship the reader is referred to the following articles in *British Birds*—50: 209–210, 1957; 51: 358, 1958; 52: 237–238, 1959; 53: 39–41, 1960; 54: 253–254, 1961; 54: 439–440, 1961. See articles by Alexander and Fitter (1955) and Goodwin (1956). See also *Canadian Field-Naturalist*—47: 139–140, 1933; 49: 119–120, 1935, and *Audubon Magazine*, 62: 276, 1960. All of these references pertain to American species in Europe.

I have been able to find only two published references to Old World passerine species that have crossed the Atlantic on board ship and "reached" North America: (1) involved four Greenfinches (*Chloris chloris*) that flew aboard ship out of Southampton, England on October 9, 1927. The birds were fed and watered. Three remained aboard ship until the Newfoundland coast was sighted, when they "apparently" flew ashore (see *British Birds*, 21: 282, 1928). (2) involved a Pied or White Wagtail (*Motacilla alba*) seen on board a ship that traveled between Liverpool and Montreal. The bird was observed flying aboard ship at Belfast, Ireland, on August 19, 1939. It was fed bread crumbs and was seen every day until the ship entered the Straits of Belle Isle (between Labrador and Newfoundland). The date the bird was last seen is not stated (see *Canadian*

Field-Naturalist, 53: 121, 1939). The point to be emphasized here is that if Greenfinches and a Pied Wagtail crossed the Atlantic by assisted passage, so might the Redwing, Fieldfare, and Brambling, all of which have occurred once in our region.

An unassisted transoceanic east–west migration by a passerine bird is much less likely to be successful than the reverse, as a Palearctic species has to contend with adverse winds, namely the prevailing westerlies.

Importation of birds into the United States for zoos, private dealers, and the like, is big business today. Many thousands of birds are shipped annually by plane, as well as by boat, and occasionally somewhere along the line birds are lost in transit between place of landing and point of delivery. Often seed-eating birds attracted to grain shipments on trains and ships are transported great distances before escaping.

The following birds reported from our area are open to question because in nearly all cases proof of their being either "wild" or escaped is lacking. Each species is commented on in the annotated list and will not be discussed here. Note the high proportion of the family Anatidae, the members of which are commonly kept in aviaries: American Flamingo, Cinnamon Teal, Tufted Duck, Caracara, Burrowing Owl, Redwing, Fieldfare, and Brambling. None of these has been recorded locally more than twice, and most of them only once. They are included in the "escape" list. The Barnacle Goose, Eurasian Teal, Black-billed Magpie, Painted Bunting, and European Goldfinch are all commonly kept in captivity, but with the exception of the goose (4 times) and bunting (5 times), the others have been recorded so often in our area that it is impossible to believe that all individuals were escapes. These five species, therefore, are placed in the regular category.

This list is by no means complete, as certain individuals of other species normally considered "wild" may have escaped from captivity also. Nor is it to be inferred that all individuals listed above were escapes. The important point to be emphasized is that in most instances we just do not know which individuals are genuine wild vagrants and which ones are not.

At the other extreme is the long list of exotics that frequently escape. In 1962 a pair of one of the South American cardinals was reported nesting at West Sayville, L.I. The escaped pair not only had built a nest, but had also succeeded in raising young! One might just as well include on a faunal list the numerous parrots, parakeets, bulbuls, mynahs, canaries, waxbills, and various exotic finches and buntings that are so commonly imported for cage purposes and which are occasionally seen flying about freely in the "wild." Just recently several honeycreepers of the genus *Cyanerpes*, imported from tropical America, escaped from Idlewild airport—at least one individual was observed around bushes in the vicinity (see comments under Redwing, *Turdus iliacus*).

470

FLAMINGOS: PHOENICOPTERIDAE

AMERICAN FLAMINGO *(Phoenicopterus ruber)**

A Neotropical species, breeding north to Cuba and the Bahamas. Non-breeding birds present in recent years in Florida Bay, many of which are believed by Allen (1956) to be escapes from the Hialeah race track near Miami. Casual north to North Carolina and Bermuda. Accidental on Long Island.

Two specimens from Long Island: one shot by duck hunters at Speonk, about 1915, mounted specimen still in Westhampton; adult taken on Shinnecock Bay, Oct. 3, 1931 (Wilcox), in his collection. According to Wilcox (oral comm.), the latter specimen is somewhat faded and presumably escaped from captivity. The Westhampton individual, examined by Wilcox, was stated by him to be in bright plumage and possibly wandered north or was hurricane borne, but of this we cannot be certain. Flamingos are commonly kept in captivity.

Some authorities would make two other forms conspecific with *P. ruber: P. roseus*, the Greater Flamingo of the Old World, and *P. chilensis*, the Chilean Flamingo of southern South America.

SWANS, GEESE, DUCKS: ANATIDAE

CINNAMON TEAL *(Anas cyanoptera)*

A western Nearctic and Neotropical species, the race *septentrionalium* breeding east to western Nebraska. Winters north to southern Texas. Casual east to Minnesota and in winter in the southeastern states from Florida to North Carolina. Accidental in western New York (Seneca Lake, mid-April 1886, specimen).

An adult male was present on a pond in the Massapequa State Park, L.I., from Jan. 12 to Feb. 10, 1957 (M. A. Nichols and many other observers). Although able to fly, this individual was very tame and had a few primaries missing. Whether, in fact, it was an escape from some game farm or aviary, or a wild bird, is impossible to ascertain. This species is not uncommon in captivity according to Delacour (1956).

TUFTED DUCK *(Aythya fuligula)*

A Palearctic species, breeding west to Iceland. Great increase in Europe in recent years, extending its breeding range. Winters commonly from the

471

British Isles southward. Casual in Greenland. Accidental in Massachusetts in the early winter of 1954, but at least one of two birds reported was suspected of being an escape from a nearby game farm (see Griscom and Snyder, 1955).

A supposed female was seen on the Harlem River near Spuyten Duyvil from Dec. 26, 1955, to Feb. 1, 1956 (numerous observers), photographed in color by E. T. Gilliard. Possibly a wild bird, but the chance of its having escaped cannot be overlooked. The species is commonly raised in captivity (see Delacour, 1959). In fact, T. D. Carter of Boonton, N.J., had lost two specimens from his aviary. He told me that an adult female had escaped in late August 1954 and a male a month later. Despite a lapse of nearly 16 months between the escape of the female and the field observation, there is a possibility that this was the same individual.

An adult male was observed on Jerome Reservoir, Bronx County, March 15, 1962 (Sedwitz). It was with Ring-necked Ducks, Lesser Scaup, and Canvasbacks. Full details on file.

CARACARAS, FALCONS: FALCONIDAE

CARACARA (*Caracara cheriway*)

A resident Neotropical species, the race *audubonii* breeding north to central Florida. One collected in Ontario, July 18, 1892.

On Sept. 28, 1946, at Alley Pond Park, L.I., J. H. Flavin identified an individual, later confirmed by Eisenmann as an immature Caracara (Auk, 64:470, 1947); observed by Elliott and Astle to Oct. 5. Local zoos reported no missing Caracaras. However, an individual kept as a pet at Malverne, L.I., in 1945 was reported to have escaped "some time later" (*fide* A. Dignan). The possibility exists that the captive bird and the "wild" individual were the same.

C. cheriway is probably conspecific with *C. plancus* of eastern and southern South America, as some authorities assert.

OWLS: STRIGIDAE

BURROWING OWL (*Speotyto cunicularia*)*

An American species, the race *hypugaea* breeds east to Minnesota. Accidental in Ontario, Indiana, Michigan, New Hampshire, Massachusetts, New York, and Virginia (all specimens).

472

An individual caught alive in New York City, Aug. 8, 1875, was suspected of having been an escaped cage bird. A specimen shot at Westhampton, L.I., Oct. 27, 1950 (A. Cooley), was possibly a genuine wanderer, but there is, of course, no proof. The specimen was determined by Zimmer as the western race, *hypugaea;* now in the collection of LeRoy Wilcox.

THRUSHES: TURDIDAE

REDWING (*Turdus iliacus*)

A Palearctic species, the nominate race breeding on the continent (Europe), the race *coburni* breeding in Iceland. Both subspecies recorded from Greenland.

An individual of this species was seen at the Jamaica Bay Refuge, Feb. 20–24, 1959, and is the first reported occurrence for continental North America. It was discovered by Herbert Johnson, the Refuge manager, and identified by Charles Young (Wilson Bull., 71:382–383, 1959). It was seen subsequently by over 400 observers, some of whom came from as far as Boston, Buffalo, and Pittsburgh. Collecting it was out of the question, but several satisfactory color photos were secured. This individual appeared to be in good condition. It flew well and was shy when approached too closely. There is, however, the chance it had escaped from captivity. Nearby Idlewild airport has a very large receiving area for almost daily shipments of birds from all over the world and, on several occasions, birds have been reported as missing.

The specific name *musicus* is currently recognized by the A.O.U. *Check-list* (1957: 430). For use of the name *iliacus*, see Mayr (Ibis, 94: 532–534, 1952). The latter name is also employed by Vaurie (1959).

FIELDFARE (*Turdus pilaris*)*

A Palearctic species. Established as a resident in southern Greenland since about 1937 (see Salomonsen, 1950b). Accidental in the Baffin Island region.

One local record: Specimen collected at Stamford, Conn., April 1878 (Schaler), now in Yale Peabody Museum, New Haven. Forbush (1929) and the A.O.U. *Check-list* (1957) do not list this record. Sage *et al.* (1913) include it in their hypothetical list, but remarked that the condition of plumage and feet indicated that it certainly had "not been recently in captivity." The collector, Schaler, stated "that its actions were those of a wild bird." Whether, in fact, it was a wild bird or an escape is impossible to state.

FINCHES, GROSBEAKS, BUNTINGS, SPARROWS:

FRINGILLIDAE

BRAMBLING (*Fringilla montifringilla*)*

A northern Palearctic species; winters in the western portion from Scotland south to Portugal.

Never before recorded in eastern North America, an adult male was collected at Stanton, Hunterdon County, N.J., Dec. 17, 1958 (Drinkwater, Abraitys, and Barlow), specimen in the Princeton University collection. According to C. H. Rogers, the plumage and feet were in good condition. While this in itself is not conclusive that the specimen was a wild bird, the record is presented for whatever it may be worth.

Two Bramblings captured in western Massachusetts in March 1962 were suspected of being escapes. This species, like many others of the family Fringillidae, is commonly kept in captivity.

Hypothetical List

The following five species marked ** are believed to be correctly identified, but lack the required *three* observers per *observation*.

The remaining 14 species are, for one reason or another, considered unsatisfactory. Reasons for their inclusion here rather than in the main list are discussed under each species.

HERONS, BITTERNS: ARDEIDAE

GREAT WHITE HERON (*Ardea occidentalis*)**

A Neotropical species, the nominate race breeds on the Florida Keys north to Cape Sable. Wanders casually to northern Florida. Accidental north to North Carolina and Pennsylvania; collected, Pymatuning Lake, May 14, 1938, specimen in Carnegie Museum (see Todd, 1940).

On Sept. 3, 1949, shortly after the Florida hurricane of Aug. 29, a large white heron with yellowish bill and legs appeared at Tobay Pond, Jones Beach (Bull). It was seen in direct comparison with Great Blue Herons and Great Egrets. The same, or another individual, was observed later at Mecox Bay, and noted several times from Sept. 17 to Oct. 15 (Helmuth and McKeever).

Perhaps a color phase of *A. herodias*, as some authorities suggest.

TYRANT FLYCATCHERS: TYRANNIDAE

FORK-TAILED FLYCATCHER (*Muscivora tyrannus*)**

A Neotropical species widely distributed through South and Central America, breeding north to southern Mexico. The southernmost races are highly migratory and winter north to Trinidad and the southern Lesser Antilles. A number of individuals have wandered, or been carried by tropical storms, much farther north and specimens have been collected in Maine, Pennsylvania, and southern New Jersey (three in the latter state).

In our area two observations are probably correct. On the day of the great hurricane of Sept. 14, 1944, one was observed at East Quogue, L.I., by Mrs. H. Walter and Mrs. H. Ward, who gave a detailed description to Mrs. Fry. This bird was watched perching on bayberry bushes and in flight. The other report was of one seen on telephone wires and also in flight at Heckscher State Park, L.I., Sept. 23, 1947 (Eckelberry).

SAY'S PHOEBE (*Sayornis saya*)**

A western Nearctic species, the nominate race breeds east to Manitoba and Nebraska. Accidental in the northeast, including two specimens from eastern Massachusetts (1889 and 1920) and one from Gaylordsville, Conn. (outside our area) in 1916.

No confirmed reports from our area, but two sight identifications are probably correct: one seen at Dyker Beach, L.I., Sept. 25–28, 1926 (W. Eaton and Nathan); the other at Gilgo Beach, Sept. 16, 1958 (Buckley and Restivo). Attempts to collect this latter individual failed.

WOOD WARBLERS: PARULIDAE

BLACK-THROATED GRAY WARBLER (*Dendroica nigrescens*)**

A western Nearctic species, breeding east to central Colorado. Accidental east to Ontario, Ohio, New York (specimen, Ithaca, 1936), and Massachusetts (specimen, Lenox, 1923).

In the New York City area the only report is that of an immature male or female observed at Jones Beach, Sept. 22, 1961 (G. Tudor and M. Kleinbaum). These observers submitted an extremely detailed report.

On Sept. 30, the same year, another individual, described as an adult male, was seen outside our region at Cape May, N.J.

476

BLACKBIRDS: ICTERIDAE

BOAT-TAILED GRACKLE (*Cassidix mexicanus*)**

Primarily a Neotropical species, although the race *torreyi* breeds along the Atlantic coast north to southern New Jersey.

In the northern parts of its range, Boat-tailed Grackles are restricted to salt marsh. Formerly very rare in southern New Jersey and unknown there prior to 1892 when a specimen was collected in Cape May County. In 1933 four pairs were found nesting across from Cape May in Delaware. First reported breeding in New Jersey in 1952 with fifteen nests in three colonies near Fortescue on Delaware Bay. By 1958, possibly as many as 75 pairs nested along Delaware Bay.

In our area there are two reports by experienced observers familiar with the species. These occurrences were probably due to hurricane Carol of Aug. 31, 1954: adult male on salt marsh, Cliffwood, N.J., Aug. 31 (Ryan); adult female, Brookhaven, L.I., Sept. 1 (Puleston).

If the contention of Selander and Giller (1961) is accepted, that the southwestern and Neotropical *C. mexicanus* and the more northern *C. major* are distinct species, then the form ranging from New Jersey to Georgia would be called *C. major torreyi*.

SWANS, GEESE, DUCKS: ANATIDAE

WHITE-FACED TREE DUCK (*Dendrocygna viduata*)*

An African and South American species with no known records in continental North America north of Costa Rica; accidental in the West Indies.

The record of one killed on the Hackensack Marshes, N.J., early October 1912, was almost certainly that of an escape. Moreover, the bird was very tame and allowed a close approach (see Griscom, 1923). Delacour (1954) says that this species is common in captivity.

RED-CRESTED POCHARD (*Netta rufina*)*

A southern Palearctic species, local in western Europe.

An immature male purchased in Fulton Market in February 1872 was supposedly taken on Long Island Sound, but this was never proved. Many game birds in this market were known to have come from distant areas, including Europe. The specimen is no longer in existence. This species, like many other members of the Anatidae, is commonly kept in captivity (see Delacour, 1959) and the possibility exists that this individual either originated in some preserve or, as stated above, was part of a shipment from abroad.

Formerly known as the Rufous-crested Duck.

MASKED DUCK (*Oxyura dominica*)

A Neotropical species, breeding north to northeastern Mexico (Tamaulipas) and Cuba. Accidental in the northeastern states: Massachusetts (Aug. 27, 1889, specimen) and Maryland (Sept. 8, 1905, specimen). The record cited in the A.O.U. *Check-list* (1957) from Vermont should be expunged, as the specimen had one wing clipped and was presumably an escape (see Forbush, 1925).

An unconfirmed report of a flock of seven on the north Jersey coast shortly after hurricane Donna of Sept. 12, 1960, is not satisfactory. No one competent to substantiate the report was notified until too late.

CRANES: GRUIDAE

WHOOPING CRANE (*Grus americana*)

This western Nearctic species formerly bred east to Minnesota and Iowa and wintered east to Florida. Many old accounts of its occurrence during migration in the northeastern states are very indefinite, including unsubstantiated reports in New York, Pennsylvania, and New Jersey (see A.O.U. *Check-list*, 1957: 150).

As far as our area is concerned, there is no proof that it ever occurred. No specimen or other evidence exists. The often-quoted remarks of De Vries mentioning "White Cranes" occurring on the coast of New York Bay in the 1600s could have been white herons (egrets) which many people called, and still call, "cranes." Moreover, De Vries was an explorer and historian, not an ornithologist. Allen (1952), likewise considered this report of no value.

GULLS, TERNS: LARIDAE

MEW GULL (*Larus canus*)

A Palearctic and western Nearctic species, the nominate race breeding west to the Faeroes and the British Isles. Winters south to the Mediterranean Sea. Casual in western Greenland. Accidental in Massachusetts (specimens, 1908 and 1951). The race *brachyrhynchus*, formerly called Short-billed Gull, breeds southeast to northern Saskatchewan. Winters on the Pacific coast from Alaska to California. Accidental in Wyoming.

478

This latter race was erroneously reported in the A.O.U. *Check-list* (1957: 225) as occurring accidentally in Massachusetts. This record was that of nominate *canus* (see Griscom and Snyder, 1955). In addition to the above specimen records from Massachusetts, there are four accepted sight reports of adults from that state (Griscom and Snyder, *op cit.*).

In our area there is a published sight report of a "sub-adult" in Jersey City in the fall of 1955 (Kunkle *et al.*, 1959). While adults of the Mew Gull and Ring-billed Gull are readily distinguishable in the field, immatures are practically identical, both as to plumage and soft-part colors. Separating them in the field would be virtually impossible, field guides to the contrary notwithstanding.

TRUDEAU'S TERN (*Sterna trudeauii*)

A species of southern South America, breeding near the Pacific coast of northern Chile and near the Atlantic coast of central Argentina. Winters and migrates to southern Chile and from southern Argentina to southeastern Brazil (Rio de Janeiro). The likelihood of its occurrence in the northern hemisphere is extremely remote.

Supposedly accidental on the coast of southern New Jersey where the type specimen was reported taken at Great Egg Harbor. The type, formerly at Vassar College, is now in the collection of the American Museum of Natural History, No. 156650. That there is doubt as to the correct type locality is indicated by the statement of Stone (1937), "The original specimen ... which was supposed to have come from Great Egg Harbor seems to have been obtained in Chile."

Its "occurrence" on Long Island, based on old sight reports, is unsatisfactory (see Griscom, 1923).

This species resembles very closely the nonbreeding plumage of Forster's Tern.

AUKS, MURRES, PUFFINS: ALCIDAE

GREAT AUK (*Pinguinus impennis*)

This extinct species of the North Atlantic Ocean formerly bred south to Bird Rocks, Gulf of St. Lawrence; also Funk Island, Newfoundland. Wintered south to the coast of Massachusetts as far as Martha's Vineyard, possibly farther, but evidence is lacking. Accidental in Florida, bones from archaeological sites (Brodkorb, Auk, 77: 342, 1960).

No proof of occurrence in the New York City area exists for the Great Auk. There are no specimens reported. The only information is based on an account (1803) by one Singleton Mitchill, an old-time writer—not an ornithologist—who merely mentioned "Penguins." Griscom (1923) does not place too much reliance on this "record." On the other hand, Murphy (1962) believes that the name "Penguin," supposedly used in colonial days for the Great Auk, applied to that species. However, "Penguin" could have also referred to Razorbills or Thick-billed Murres (neither mentioned by Mitchill), both of which have occurred in western Long Island Sound, the area where the "Penguins" were supposed to have been seen. It seems to me that the evidence presented is too inconclusive to warrant placing the Great Auk on the regular list.

PIGEONS, DOVES: COLUMBIDAE

GROUND DOVE (*Columbigallina passerina*)

A Neotropical and southern Nearctic species, the nominate race breeding north to South Carolina. Casual north to Maryland (two specimens), Pennsylvania, and southern New Jersey (specimen).

The supposed record of a Ground Dove shot "many years ago" on Manhattan island is unsatisfactory. The specimen was not preserved and no competent ornithologist ever saw it (see Griscom, 1923).

PARROTS: PSITTACIDAE

CAROLINA PARAKEET (*Conuropsis carolinensis*)

This extinct eastern Nearctic species formerly ranged north to southern Virginia and wandered casually to Maryland and Pennsylvania. Reports of its occurrence farther north are very indefinite.

In our area the only intimation of its "occurrence" was in New Jersey in the 1850s (see Cruickshank, 1942). However, the evidence is inconclusive. The observer was not an ornithologist, and no specimens were taken.

WOODPECKERS: PICIDAE

NORTHERN THREE-TOED WOODPECKER (*Picoïdes tridactylus*)

Holarctic species, breeding in coniferous forest. The race *bacatus* occurs south to the Adirondacks and northern New England. Resident throughout its range. Unlike *P. arcticus*, which is given to wandering, *P. tridactylus* is mainly sedentary. There is no confirmed data even for Massachusetts (see Griscom and Snyder, 1955). I can find no basis for the inclusion of Long Island as stated in the A.O.U. *Check-list* (1957: 331).

Its supposed occurrence in our area rests on the report of a single observer. While the observation may have been correct, no corroboration was made (see Griscom, 1923). As some individual Hairy Woodpeckers possess yellowish crowns, several recent sight reports of *P. tridactylus* made by inexperienced observers are considered unsatisfactory.

THRUSHES: TURDIDAE

MOUNTAIN BLUEBIRD (*Sialia currucoides*)

A western Nearctic species, breeding east to northeastern North Dakota, Casual in Minnesota. No definite record in eastern North America.

Two recent local sight reports were not confirmed; no specimen or other evidence exists.

BLACKBIRDS: ICTERIDAE

BULLOCK'S ORIOLE (*Icterus bullockii*)

A western Nearctic species, breeding east to the western portions of the Dakotas, Nebraska, and Kansas. Winters chiefly in Middle America, rarely north and east to southern Louisiana and southern Florida. Accidental in the northeast, specimens reported taken in New York (Onondaga County, May 17, 1885) and Maine (Nov. 15, 1889). Recently, color photographs were taken of adult males at feeders on the coast of Massachusetts during the winters of 1952–53 and 1953–54; these birds remained into April (see Griscom and Snyder, 1955).

In our area there have been several recent unconfirmed sight reports, but the chance of confusion with Baltimore Orioles is very great. While adult males and "typical" females of *I. bullockii* are identifiable in the field, interbreeding with *I. galbula* is frequent, and hybrids are as likely as "pure" *I. bullockii*. For discussions on this subject, see Sutton (1938) and Short (Nebraska Bird Rev., 29: 18–19, 1961). Sibley and Short (in press) maintain that the two forms are conspecific.

Until a specimen or at least a satisfactory color photograph is produced, Bullock's Oriole remains on the hypothetical list.

Note: The following information was received too late to incorporate into the main list; the Bullock's Oriole should, therefore, be removed from the Hypothetical list. On Dec. 12, 1963 an immature male of this species appeared at a feeding station in Eastport, L.I., where it was identified by LeRoy Wilcox. It was still present at the close of 1963 and was studied at leisure by hundreds of observers. Wilcox trapped and banded the bird on Dec. 20 and took several color photographs. These photographs were submitted to the American Museum and compared with skins of various orioles. Examination indicates that the bird in question is a Bullock's Oriole. It would be most desirable, however, to collect any "strange-looking" orioles in the future, to further establish its occurrence in our area. As stated previously, hybrids are as likely to occur as *I. bullockii*.

BREWER'S BLACKBIRD (*Euphagus cyanocephalus*)

A western Nearctic species, breeding east to south-central Ontario, eastern Michigan, and northwestern Indiana. Winters north and east to the Carolinas (specimens). In migration east to Ohio (specimens).

In recent years (1946–62), there have been numerous sight reports of birds alleged to be this species, in late fall, winter, and early spring in Maryland, Delaware, southern New Jersey, and southeastern Pennsylvania, including flocks on Christmas counts. However, no specimen exists for those areas and the A.O.U. *Check-list* (1957) does not include any of those states in the range.

The statement by Walkinshaw and Zimmerman (1961), "In migration and winter it now appears on the Atlantic seaboard from New York to . . . Florida" is based, in part, on an unconfirmed sight report made in nearby Sullivan County, N.Y., in 1953.

As iridescent male Rusty Blackbirds in fall are frequently misidentified as Brewer's Blackbirds, unconfirmed reports of the latter species in the New York City region are not acceptable. Although adult females of the two species may be told apart in the field on the basis of eye color, immatures of both forms have dark eyes and thus would be indistinguishable from females. While it is possible, or even probable, that Brewer's Blackbird will be recorded eventually in our area, there is no reliable report. Until a specimen is secured to prove actual occurrence, Brewer's Blackbird remains on the hypothetical list.

FINCHES, GROSBEAKS, BUNTINGS, SPARROWS:

FRINGILLIDAE

McCOWN'S LONGSPUR (*Rhynchophanes mccownii*)

A central Nearctic species of the Great Plains, breeding east to southwestern Manitoba and north-central North Dakota; formerly east to southwestern Minnesota. Winters east to the Gulf coast of Texas. Casual east to Illinois.

An alleged Christmas count sight report of two birds in New Jersey (Audubon Field Notes, 15: 136, 1961), without details, is considered unsatisfactory in absence of a specimen or other confirmation. Moreover, there are no known specimens anywhere east of Illinois.

Fossil Birds

Very few remains of fossil birds have been reported from the New York City region. This is not surprising as bird bones are very fragile, few having been found in a well-preserved condition. Of the four local species known, all were discovered in Monmouth County, N.J. Three were located in Pleistocene deposits, the fourth in Eocene.

The following are listed in Wetmore (1956)—two extinct species of turkeys, and one of Diatryma.

Meleagris celer—Pleistocene, Monmouth County (locality not stated).

Meleagris superba—Pleistocene, Manalapan, Monmouth County.

An extinct group known as the Diatrymas is represented by a single species: *Barornis regens*—Eocene, Squankum, Monmouth County. This was a giant flightless creature, superficially resembling ostrichlike birds, but believed related to the cariamas or cranes.

The above specimens are in the Peabody Museum, Yale University.

The following is listed in Wetmore (1958)—one modern species of crane: *Grus canadensis* (Sandhill Crane)—Pleistocene, Monmouth County (locality not stated). This specimen is in the Princeton University Museum. It was originally described as an extinct species, until re-examined by Wetmore (1958) and determined by him to be a Sandhill Crane.

Appendixes

Glossary

ABBREVIATIONS

A.M.N.H.–American Museum of Natural History, New York, N.Y.
M.C.Z.–Museum of Comparative Zoology, Cambridge, Mass.
N.Y.S.M.–New York State Museum, Albany, N.Y.
U.S.N.M.–United States National Museum, Washington, D.C.

Terms

ZOOGEOGRAPHIC REGIONS

Nearctic. Arctic and temperate North America (including Greenland) north of tropical Mexico. **Palearctic.** Europe, northern Africa (including the Sahara), and arctic and temperate Asia. **Holarctic.** The Nearctic and Palearctic regions combined (*q.v.*). **Neotropical.** West Indies, Middle America, and South America. **Cosmopolitan.** Worldwide, or nearly so.

BIOLOGICAL AND TAXONOMIC

Sympatric. Species ranges overlap in breeding season.
Allopatric. Species ranges do not overlap in breeding season.
Polytypic. A species divided into two or more subspecies.
Monotypic. A species not divided into subspecies.
Polymorphic. A species with two or more color or size variants (phases).
Nominate. The first-named subspecies of a polytypic species.

Bibliography

The bibliography includes material through December 1962, with the exception of one important monograph published early in 1963.

ALDRICH, JOHN W.
1951. A review of the races of the Traill's Flycatcher. Wilson Bull., 63: 192–197.
1953. Habits and habitat differences in two races of Traill's Flycatcher. Wilson Bull., 65: 8–11.

ALDRICH, JOHN W. and HERBERT FRIEDMANN
1943. A revision of the Ruffed Grouse. Condor, 45: 85–103.

ALDRICH, JOHN W. and DAVID C. NUTT
1939. Birds of eastern Newfoundland. Sci. Publ. Cleveland Mus. Nat. Hist., 4: 13–42.

ALEXANDER, W. B. and R. S. R. FITTER
1955. American land birds in western Europe. British Birds, 48: 1–14.

ALLEN, JOEL A.
1880. Destruction of birds by lighthouses. Bull. Nuttall Ornith. Club, 5: 131–138.

ALLEN, ROBERT P.
1938a. Black-crowned Night Heron colonies on Long Island. Proc. Linnaean Soc. N.Y., 49: 43–53.
1938b. Report of the Field Work Committee, 1937–38. Proc. Linnaean Soc. N.Y., 49: 84–92.
1952. The Whooping Crane. Natl. Audubon Soc. Res. Rep., no. 3.
1956. The flamingos: their life history and survival. Natl. Audubon Soc. Res. Rep., no. 5.

ALLEN, ROBERT P. and JOSEPH J. HICKEY
1940. Report of the Field Work Committee, 1938–1939. Proc. Linnaean Soc. N.Y., 50–51: 73–75.

ALPERIN, IRWIN M.
1958. Spring jaegers—1955. Proc. Linnaean Soc. N.Y., 66–70: 87–89.

ALPERIN, IRWIN M. and EUGENE EISENMANN
1951. Brewer's Sparrow on Long Island. Proc. Linnaean Soc. N.Y., 58–62: 74–75.

AMADON, DEAN
1949. The seventy-five per cent rule for subspecies. Condor, 51: 250–258.

A.O.U. CHECK-LIST COMMITTEE
1957. Check-list of North American birds (5th ed.). Amer. Ornith. Union.

ARBIB, ROBERT S., JR.
1940. Report of the Field Work Committee, 1939–1940. Proc. Linnaean Soc. N.Y., 50–51: 76–78.

1950. The importance of field notes. Linnaean News-Letter, 3 (8): Jan.

BAGG, AARON M.
1955. Airborne from gulf to gulf. Bull. Mass. Aud. Soc., 39: 106–110; 159–168.

BAIRD, JAMES
1958. Yellow-throated Warblers collected in sycamores along the Delaware River in New Jersey. Urner Field Observer, Jan.

BAIRD, JAMES, CHANDLER S. ROBBINS, AARON M. BAGG, and JOHN V. DENNIS
1958. "Operation Recovery"—the Atlantic coastal netting project. Bird-Banding, 29: 137–168.

BAIRD, JAMES, AARON M. BAGG, IAN C. T. NISBET, and CHANDLER S. ROBBINS
1959. Operation recovery—report on mist-netting along the Atlantic coast in 1958. Bird-Banding, 30: 143–171.

BAIRD, JAMES and IAN C. T. NISBET
1960. Northward fall migration on the Atlantic coast and its relation to offshore drift. Auk, 77: 119–149.

BEALS, MARIE V. and JOHN T. NICHOLS
1940. Data from a bird-banding station at Elmhurst, Long Island. Birds of Long Island, 3: 57–76.

BELKNAP, JOHN B.
1955. The expanding range of the Ring-billed Gull. Kingbird, 5: 63–64.

BENT, ARTHUR C.
1946. Life histories of North American jays, crows, and titmice. U.S. Natl. Mus. Bull., no. 191.

BERGER, ANDREW J.
1958. The Golden-winged–Blue-winged Warbler complex in Michigan and the Great Lakes area. Jack-Pine Warbler, 36: 37–73.

BICKNELL, EUGENE P.
1878. Evidence of the Carolinian fauna in the lower Hudson valley. Bull. Nuttall Ornith. Club, 3: 128–132.

BLAKE, CHARLES H.
1955. Notes on the Eastern Purple Finch. Bird-Banding, 26: 89-116.
BOCK, WALTER J.
1959. The status of the Semipalmated Plover. Auk, 76: 98-100.
BOYAJIAN, NED
1955. The 1954 fall migration. Linnaean News-Letter, 8 (8): Jan.
BRAISLIN, WILLIAM C.
1902 Notes concerning certain birds of Long Island. Auk, 19: 145-149.
1907 A list of the birds of Long Island, New York.
      Abstr. Proc. Linnaean Soc. N.Y., 17-19: 31-123.
BREWER, RICHARD
1961. Comparative notes on the life history of the Carolina Chickadee.
      Wilson Bull., 73: 348-373.
BROUN, MAURICE
1935. The hawk migration during the fall of 1934 along the Kittatinny
      ridge in Pennsylvania. Auk, 52: 233-248.
1948. Hawks aloft. Dodd, Mead, New York.
BROWN, CLARENCE D.
1939. Historical sketch of the Kingsland (New Jersey) roost (black-
      birds). Urner Ornith. Club Bull., 1: 6-7.
1947. King Rail at Troy [Meadows]. Urner Field Observer, 2:
      3-4.
BUCKLEY, PAUL A.
1959. Recent specimens from southern New York and New Jersey
      affecting A.O.U. Check-list status. Auk. 76: 517-520.
1960. Hurricane! Linnaean News-Letter, 14 (6): Nov.
1961. The 1960 fall migration in the New York City region. Linnaean
      News-Letter, 14 (8): Jan.
BULL, JOHN L.
1946. The ornithological year 1944 in the New York City region. Proc.
      Linnaean Soc. N.Y., 54-57: 28-35.
1948. An unusual winter in the Atlantic Beach-Lawrence area. Linn-
      aean News-Letter, 2 (1): March.
1953. Shorebirds in breeding plumage on the southbound flight.
      Linnaean News-Letter, 6 (9): Feb.
1958. Birds of the New York City area. Amer. Mus. Nat. Hist., New
      York.
1960. Pelagic bonanza. Linnaean News-Letter, 14 (4): June.
1962. Further comments on field identification of the Long-billed
      Dowitcher with especial reference to voice. Linnaean News-
      Letter, 15 (8): Jan.
BURLEIGH, THOMAS D. and HAROLD S. PETERS
1948. Geographic variation in Newfoundland birds. Proc. Biol. Soc.
      Wash., 61: 111-124.

490

CANT, GILBERT B.
1941. Wilson's Plover again nesting in New Jersey. Proc. Linnaean Soc. N.Y., 52–53: 130–131.
1962. The House Finch in New York State. Kingbird, 12: 68–72.

CANT, GILBERT B. and HOPE P. GEIS
1961. The House Finch: a new east coast migrant? Ebba News, 24: 102–107.

CARLETON, GEOFFREY
1958. The birds of Central and Prospect Parks. Proc. Linnaean Soc. N.Y., 66–70: 1–60.

CARTER, T. DONALD
1944. Six years with a Brewster's Warbler. Auk, 61: 48–61.

CHAPMAN, FRANK M.
1889. Notes on birds observed in the vicinity of Englewood, New Jersey. Auk, 6: 302–305.
1906. Birds of the vicinity of New York City. Amer. Mus. Journ., 6: 81–102.
1908. The Fish Hawks of Gardiner's Island. Bird Lore, 10: 153–159.
1940. Handbook of birds of eastern North America (2nd rev. ed.). Appleton-Century, New York.

COOCH, GRAHAM
1961. Ecological aspects of the Blue–Snow Goose complex. Auk, 78: 72–89.

CRUICKSHANK, ALLAN D.
1942. Birds around New York City. Amer. Mus. Nat. Hist., New York.

DAVIS, DAVID E.
1960. Comments on the migration of Starlings in eastern United States. Bird-Banding, 31: 216–219.

DEED, ROBERT F.
1951. Notes on the northward movement of certain species of birds into the lower Hudson Valley. Proc. Linnaean Soc. N.Y., 58–62: 63–66.

DEED, ROBERT F. *et al.*
1959. Birds of Rockland County and the Hudson Highlands. Rockland Audubon Soc.

DELACOUR, JEAN
1951. Preliminary note on the taxonomy of Canada Geese, *Branta canadensis*. Amer. Mus. Novit., no. 1537.
1954. The waterfowl of the world. vol. 1, Country Life, London.
1956. *Ibid.* vol. 2.
1959. *Ibid.* vol. 3.

DELACOUR, JEAN and ERNST MAYR
1945. The family Anatidae. Wilson Bull., 57: 3–55.

DELACOUR, JEAN and JOHN T. ZIMMER
  1952.   The identity of *Anser nigricans* Lawrence 1846. Auk, 69: 82–84.
DONKER, J. K.
  1959.   Migration and distribution of the Widgeon, *Anas penelope* L. in Europe, based on ringing results. Ardea, 47: 1–27.
DRINKWATER, HOWARD
  1955.   Yellow-throated Warbler breeding along the Delaware River, Hunterdon County, New Jersey. Wilson Bull., 67: 65.
DRURY, WILLIAM H. and J. A. KEITH
  1962.   Radar studies of songbird migration in coastal New England. Ibis, 104: 449–489.
DUNN, GORDON E. and BENNER I. MILLER
  1960.   Atlantic hurricanes. Louisiana State Univ. Press, Baton Rouge.
DUTCHER, BASIL H.
  1889.   Bird notes from Little Gull Island, Suffolk Co., N.Y. Auk, 6: 124–131.
DUTCHER, WILLIAM
  1884.   Bird notes from Long Island. Auk, 1: 174–179.
  1888.   *Ibid.* Auk, 5: 169–183.
  1889.   *Ibid.* Auk, 6: 131–139.
  1887–   Long Island notes. vol. 1—water birds; vol. 2—land birds (hand-
  1894   written account). In library of the American Museum of Natural History.
  1891.   The Labrador Duck; a revised list of the extant specimens in North America, with some historical notes. Auk, 8: 201–216.
  1893.   Notes on some rare birds in the collection of the Long Island Historical Society. Auk, 10: 267–277.
  1894.   The Labrador Duck; another specimen, with additional data respecting extant specimens. Auk, 11: 4–12.
DWIGHT, JONATHAN
  1900.   The sequence of plumages and moults of the passerine birds of New York. Annals N.Y. Acad. Sci., 13: 73–360.
  1925.   The Gulls (Laridae) of the world; their plumages, moults, variations, relationships, and distribution. Bull. Amer. Mus. Nat. Hist., 52: 63–408.
EATON, ELON H.
  1910.   Birds of New York. vol. 1, Univ. State of New York, Albany.
  1914.   *Ibid.* vol. 2.
EATON, STEPHEN W.
  1957.   Variation in *Seiurus noveboracensis*. Auk, 74: 229–239.
  1959.   The Tufted Titmouse invades New York. Kingbird, 9: 59–62.
EATON, WARREN F.
  1934.   Eighteen years of Wyanokie (1916–1933). Abstr. Proc. Linnaean Soc. N.Y., 43, 44: 14–26.

1936. A list of the birds of Essex Co. and of Hudson Co., N.J., with especial reference to city growth and bird population. Proc. Linnaean Soc. N.Y., 47: 1–76.

EDWARDS, JAMES L.
1939. General observations on hawk migration in New Jersey. Urner Ornith. Club Bull., 1: 8–11.

EISENMANN, EUGENE
1950. An autumn day at Montauk Point, with comments on the field identification of certain sparrows. Linnaean News-Letter, 4 (7): Dec.

1951. What to do with specimens of rare birds. Linnaean News-Letter, 5 (6): Nov.

1953. Notes on the voice of the Alder or Traill's Flycatcher. Linnaean News-Letter, 7 (5): Oct.

1955. The species of Middle American birds. Trans. Linnaean Soc. N.Y., vol. 7.

1956. Opportunities for studies from birds killed in striking obstacles on migration. Linnaean News-Letter, 10 (6): Nov.

1960. Palearctic waders in eastern North America. British Birds, 53: 136–140.

1962. The voices of dowitchers. Linnaean News-Letter, 15 (9): Feb.

ELLIOTT, JOHN J.
1941. The Henslow's Sparrow on Long Island. Proc. Linnaean Soc. N.Y., 52, 53: 142–144.

1951. The Prairie Warbler on Long Island. Proc. Linnaean Soc. N.Y., 58–62: 72–73.

1953. The nesting sparrows of Long Island. 1. Sparrows of the marshes. Long Island Naturalist, 2: 15–24.

1954. *Ibid.* 2. Sparrows of the uplands. Long Island Naturalist, 3: 10–18.

1955. The Ipswich Sparrow on the northeastern seaboard. Part 1. Kingbird, 4: 91–96.

1956a. *Ibid.* Part 2. Kingbird, 6: 3–10.

1956b. British Goldfinch on Long Island. Long Island Naturalist, 5: 3–13.

1959. Ways of the "Sea Gulls." Kingbird, 9: 116–120; 142–148.

1960. Falcon flights on Long Island. Kingbird, 10: 155–157.

1961. Recent history of the Barrow's Goldeneye in New York. Kingbird, 11: 131–136.

1962. Sharp-tailed and Seaside Sparrows on Long Island, New York. Kingbird, 12: 115–123.

ELLIOTT, JOHN J. and ROBERT S. ARBIB, JR.
1953. Origin and status of the House Finch in the eastern United States. Auk, 70: 31–37.

EMLEN, JOHN T., JR.
1938. Midwinter distribution of the American Crow in New York State. Ecology, 19: 264–275.

EYNON, ALFRED E.
1941. Hawk migration routes in the New York City region. Proc. Linnaean Soc. N.Y., 52–53: 113–116.

EYNON, ALFRED E. and GILBERT B. CANT
1939. Preliminary report on blackbird roosts (N.J.). Urner Ornith. Club Bull., 1: 2–5.

FABLES, DAVID JR.
1955. Annotated list of New Jersey birds. Urner Ornith. Club.

FISCHER, RICHARD B.
1941. Alder Flycatcher breeding on Long Island. Proc. Linnaean Soc. N.Y., 52–53: 144–147.
1950. Notes on the Alder Flycatcher. Linnaean News-Letter, 4 (3): May.

FISHER, JAMES
1952. The Fulmar. Collins, London.

FLEISHER, EDWARD
1947. Further notes on the Long Island House Finches. Linnaean News-Letter, 1 (4): June.

FOLEY, DONALD D.
1960. Recent changes in waterfowl populations in New York. Kingbird, 10: 82–89.

FORBUSH, EDWARD H.
1925. Birds of Massachusetts and other New England States. vol. 1. Mass. Dept. Agric., Boston.
1927. *Ibid.* vol. 2.
1929. *Ibid.* vol. 3.

FRIEDMANN, HERBERT
1950. The birds of North and Middle America. Smithsonian Inst. Bull., 50 (11)

FROHLING, ROBERT C.
1950. Studies on Baltimore Oriole nest locations in New Jersey. Urner Ornith. Club Bull., 2: 1–18.

GIRAUD, JACOB P.
1844. Birds of Long Island. Wiley and Putnam, New York.

GODFREY, W. EARL
1959. Notes on Newfoundland birds. Natl. Mus. Canada Bull., 172: 98–111.

GOODWIN, DEREK
1956. The problem of birds escaping from captivity. British Birds, 49: 339–349.

GORDON, MALCOM S.
1955. Summer ecology of oceanic birds off southern New England. Auk, 72: 138–147.

GREENWAY, JAMES C., JR.
1958. Extinct and vanishing birds of the world. Amer. Comm. Internatl. Wildlife Protection, New York.

GRISCOM, LUDLOW
1923. Birds of the New York City region. Amer. Mus. Nat. Hist., N.Y.
1927. The observations of the late Eugene P. Bicknell at Riverdale, New York City, fifty years ago. Abstr. Proc. Linnaean Soc. N.Y., 37, 38: 73–87.
1929. Changes in the status of certain birds in the New York City region. Auk, 46: 45–57.
1933. Birds of Dutchess County, New York. Trans. Linnaean Soc. N.Y., vol. 3.
1934. The Pine Grosbeaks of eastern North America. Proc. New England Zool. Club, 14: 5–12.
1937a. European Dunlins in North America. Auk, 54: 70–72.
1937b. A monographic study of the Red Crossbill. Proc. Boston Soc. Nat. Hist., 41: 77–209.
1939. The Ring-necked Duck as a transient in the northeastern states. Auk, 56: 134–137.
1943. Notes on the Pacific Loon. Bull. Mass. Aud. Soc., 27: 106–109.
1944. Difficulties with Massachusetts Gulls. Bull. Mass. Aud. Soc., 28: 181–191.
1945. Modern bird study. Harvard Univ. Press.
1949. Birds of Concord. Harvard Univ. Press.

GRISCOM, LUDLOW and EDITH V. FOLGER
1948. Birds of Nantucket. Harvard Univ. Press.

GRISCOM, LUDLOW and DOROTHY E. SNYDER
1955. Birds of Massachusetts. Peabody Mus., Salem, Mass.

GRISCOM, LUDLOW, ALEXANDER SPRUNT JR. *et al.*
1957. The warblers of America. Devin-Adair, New York.

GROSS, ALFRED O.
1935. The life history cycle of Leach's Petrel on the outer sea islands of the Bay of Fundy. Auk, 52: 382–399.
1944. The present status of the Double-crested Cormorant on the coast of Maine. Auk, 61: 513–537.
1956. The recent reappearance of the Dickcissel in eastern North America. Auk, 73: 66–70.

HAARTMAN, LARS VON
1958. The decrease of the Corncrake (*Crex crex*). Soc. Scient. Fennica. Comment. Biol., 18: 1–29.

495

HAILMAN, JACK P.
   1959.   Consolidation of northward extension of the Glossy Ibis's breeding range. Bird-Banding, 30: 231–232.
HALL, HENRY M. and ROLAND C. CLEMENT
   1960.   A gathering of shorebirds. Devin-Adair, New York.
HASBROUCK, EDWIN M.
   1944.   Apparent status of the European Widgeon in North America. Auk, 61: 93–104.
HELLMAYR, CHARLES E.
   1938.   Catalogue of birds of the Americas and the adjacent islands. Field Mus. Nat. Hist. Zool. Series, 13 (11).
HELLMAYR, CHARLES E. and BOARDMAN CONOVER
   1948.   *Ibid* vol. 13 (1), (2).
   1949.   *Ibid.* vol. 13 (1), (4).
HELMUTH, WILLIAM T.
   1930.   Notes from eastern Long Island, New York. Auk, 47: 528–532.
   1954.   The hurricane of 1938—in retrospect. Birds of Long Island, 8: 225–241.
HICKEY, JOSEPH J.
   1938a. Notes on a captive Kumlien's Gull (*Larus kumlieni*). Proc. Linnaean Soc. N.Y., 49: 63–66.
   1938b. Report of the Field Work Committee, 1936–37. Proc. Linnaean Soc. N.Y., 49: 73–83.
   1942.   Eastern population of the Duck Hawk. Auk, 59: 176–204.
   1943.   A guide to bird watching. Oxford Univ. Press, New York.
   1951.   Occurrence of European Teal on Long Island. Proc. Linnaean Soc. N.Y., 58–62: 70–71.
   1954.   First year plumage of Kumlien's Gull. Linnaean News-Letter 8 (7): Dec.
HOWES, PAUL G.
   1926.   A Turkey Vulture's nest in the state of New York. Bird Lore, 28: 175–180.
   1928.   Notes on the birds of Stamford, Connecticut and vicinity. Oölogist, 45: 70–96.
HUMPHREY, PHILIP S. and KENNETH C. PARKES
   1959.   An approach to the study of molts and plumages. Auk, 76: 1–31
JEHL, JOSEPH R. JR.
   1961.   Remarks on the Great Cormorant in New Jersey. Urner Field Observer, 9: 1–14.
JOHNSON, JULIUS M.
   1941.   Report on the Wyanokie bird census 1934 to 1940 inclusive. Proc. Linnaean Soc. N.Y., 52, 53: 120–123.
KELLOGG, PETER P.
   1962.   Vocalizations of the Black Rail and the Yellow Rail. Auk, 79: 698–701.

KENDEIGH, S. CHARLES
 1944. Measurement of bird populations. Ecol. Monogr., 14: 67–106.
KESSEL, BRINA
 1953. Distribution and migration of the European Starling in North America. Condor, 55: 49–68.
KIERAN, JOHN
 1959. A natural history of New York City. Houghton, Mifflin, Boston.
KORTRIGHT, FRANCIS H.
 1942. The ducks, geese, and swans of North America. Amer. Wildlife Inst., Washington.
KUERZI, JOHN F.
 1927. A detailed report on the bird life of the greater Bronx region. Abstr. Proc. Linnaean Soc. N.Y., 37, 38: 88–111.
 1931. Summer birds of Putnam County, New York. Abstr. Proc. Linnaean Soc. N.Y., 41, 42: 57–60.
KUNKLE, DONALD E. *et al.*
 1959. First supplement to the annotated list of New Jersey birds. Urner Ornith. Club.
LACK, DAVID
 1959. Migration across the sea. Ibis, 101: 374–399.
LANYON, WESLEY E.
 1957. The comparative biology of the meadowlarks (*Sturnella*) in Wisconsin. Publ. Nuttall Ornith. Club, Cambridge, Mass.
 1961. The vertebrates of the Kalbfleisch field research station. Amer. Mus. Nat. Hist., N.Y.
LATHAM, ROY
 1946. Eastern Long Island records of the Nighthawk. Proc. Linnaean Soc. N.Y., 54–57: 50–51.
 1954. Nature notes from Orient (L.I.). Long Island Naturalist, 3: 3–9.
 1957. Breeding hawks on eastern Long Island. Kingbird, 7: 77–79.
LAWRENCE, GEORGE N.
 1866. Catalogue of birds observed on New York, Long, and Staten Islands, and the adjacent parts of New Jersey. Ann. Lyceum Nat. Hist. N.Y., 8: 279–300.
LINSDALE, JEAN M.
 1937. The natural history of magpies. Pacific Coast Avifauna, 25.
LOWERY, GEORGE H., JR.
 1955. Louisiana birds. Louisiana State Univ. Press, Baton Rouge.
LUNK, WILLIAM A.
 1952. Notes on variation in the Carolina Chickadee. Wilson Bull., 64: 7–21.
MACKAY, GEORGE H.
 1929. Shooting journal (1865–1922). Cosmos Press, New York.

497

MACPHERSON, A. H.
  1961. Observations on Canadian Arctic *Larus* gulls, and on the taxonomy of *L. thayeri* Brooks. Arctic Inst. North Amer., 7.

MANNING, THOMAS H.
  1942. Blue and Lesser Snow Geese on Southampton and Baffin Islands. Auk, 59: 158–175.

MANNING, THOMAS H., E. O. HÖHN, and A. H. MACPHERSON
  1956. The birds of Banks Island. Bull. Natl. Mus. Canada, 143.

MAYR, ERNST
  1942. Systematics and the origin of species. Columbia Univ. Press.

MAYR, ERNST, E. GORTON LINSLEY, and ROBERT L. USINGER
  1953. Methods and principles of systematic zoology. McGraw-Hill, N.Y.

MCCABE, ROBERT A.
  1951. The song and song-flight of the Alder Flycatcher. Wilson Bull., 63: 89–98.

MCKEEVER, CHRISTOPHER K.
  1940. The breeding of the Herring Gull on Long Island in 1939. Proc. Linnaean Soc. N.Y., 50–51: 32–33.
  1941. Distribution and habitat selection of some local birds. Proc. Linnaean Soc. N.Y., 52–53: 84–112.
  1946a. Data on some of the seabird colonies of eastern Long Island. Proc. Linnaean Soc. N.Y., 54–57: 44–46.
  1946b. New York City seabird colonies. Proc. Linnaean Soc. N.Y., 54–57: 46–47
  1946c. Further spread of the Prairie Horned Lark on Long Island. Proc. Linnaean Soc. N.Y., 54–57: 52–53.

MEANLEY, BROOKE
  1957. Notes on the courtship behavior of the King Rail. Auk, 74: 433–440.

MEANLEY, BROOKE and DAVID K. WETHERBEE
  1962. Ecological notes on mixed populations of King Rails and Clapper Rails in Delaware Bay marshes. Auk, 79: 453–457.

MEARNS, EDGAR A.
  1878. A list of the birds of the Hudson highlands. Bull. Essex Inst. (issued in 7 parts up to 1881).

MENDALL, HOWARD L.
  1958. The Ring-necked Duck in the northeast. Univ. Maine Press.

MENGEL, ROBERT M.
  1952. Certain molts and plumages of Acadian and Yellow-bellied Flycatchers. Auk, 69: 273–283.

MEYERRIECKS, ANDREW J.
  1960. Comparative breeding behavior of four species of North American herons. Publ. Nuttall Ornith. Club, 2.

498

MILLER, ALDEN H.
1931. Systematic revision and natural history of the American shrikes (*Lanius*). Univ. Calif. Publ. Zool., 38: 11–242.
1941. Speciation in the avian genus *Junco*. Univ. Calif. Publ. Zool., 44: 173–434.

MONTAGNA, WILLIAM
1942. The Sharp-tailed Sparrows of the Atlantic coast. Wilson Bull., 54: 107–120.

MURPHY, ROBERT C.
1936. Oceanic birds of South America (2 vols.). Macmillan-Amer. Mus. Nat. Hist.
1962. Mitchill's "Birds of Plandome", Long Island. Proc. Amer. Phil. Soc., 106: 48–52.

MURPHY, ROBERT C. and WILLIAM VOGT
1933. The Dovekie influx of 1932. Auk, 50: 325–349.

NICHOLS, JOHN T.
1920. Limicoline voices. Auk, 37: 519–540.
1935. The Dovekie incursion of 1932. Auk, 52: 448–449.

NISBET, IAN C. T.
1959. Wader migration in North America and its relation to trans-atlantic crossings. British Birds, 52: 205–215.

NORRIS, C. A.
1947. Report on the distribution and status of the Corn Crake. Part 2— a consideration of the causes of the decrease. British Birds, 40: 226–244.

OBERHOLSER, HARRY C.
1937. A revision of the Clapper Rails (*Rallus longirostris*). Proc. U.S. Natl. Mus., 84: 313–354.

ORTH, JOHN C.
1960. Vertebrates of the Bear Mountain and Harriman State Parks. Palisades Interstate Park Comm. (mimeographed).

PALMER, RALPH S.
1949. Maine birds. Bull. Mus. Comp. Zool., 102.
1962. Handbook of North American birds—loons to flamingos (ed. by R. S. Palmer), vol. 1. Yale Univ. Press.

PARKES, KENNETH C.
1951. The genetics of the Golden-winged x Blue-winged Warbler complex. Wilson Bull., 63: 5–15.
1952. The birds of New York State and their taxonomy. Part 1—Non-passerines: 1–302. Part 2—Passerines: 303–612. Cornell Univ., unpublished PH.D. thesis.
1953. The Yellow-throated Warbler in New York. Kingbird, 3: 4–6.
1954a. Traill's Flycatcher in New York. Wilson Bull., 66: 89–92.
1954b. Notes on some birds of the Adirondack and Catskill Mountains, New York. Annals Carnegie Mus., 33: 149–178.

1954c. Notes on gull relationships. Linnaean News-Letter, 8 (5): Oct.

1955. Critically needed bird specimens from New York. Kingbird, 4: 96–99.

1958. Systematic notes on North American birds: the waterfowl (Anatidae). Annals Carnegie Mus., 35: 117–125.

PETERS, JAMES L.
1942. The Canadian forms of the Sharp-tailed Sparrow, *Ammospiza caudacuta*. Annals Carnegie Mus., 29: 201–210.

PETERS, JAMES L. and LUDLOW GRISCOM
1938. Geographical variation in the Savannah Sparrow Bull. Mus. Comp. Zool., 80: 447–478.

PETERSON, ROGER T.
1947. A field guide to the birds (2nd rev. ed.). Houghton, Mifflin, Boston.

1961. A field guide to western birds (2nd ed.). Houghton, Mifflin, Boston.

PETERSON, ROGER T., GUY MOUNTFORT, and P. A. D. HOLLOM
1954. A field guide to the birds of Britain and Europe. Collins, London.

PETTINGILL, OLIN S., JR.
1951. A guide to bird finding east of the Mississippi. Oxford Univ. Press.

PHILLIPS, JOHN C.
1928. Wild birds introduced or transplanted in North America. U.S. Dept. Agric. Tech. Bull., 61.

PITELKA, FRANK A.
1950. Geographic variation and the species problem in the shorebird genus *Limnodromus*. Univ. Calif. Publ. Zool., 50: 1–170.

POOR, HUSTACE H.
1946. The Chickadee flight of 1941–42. Proc. Linnaean Soc. N.Y., 54–57: 16–27.

POST, PETER W.
1961a. Range extensions of herons in the northeastern United States. Wilson Bull., 73: 390–393.

1961b. The American Oystercatcher in New York. Kingbird, 11: 3–6.

1962. Glossy Ibis breeding in New York. Auk, 79: 120–121.

POTTER, JULIAN K.
1926. The calls of the King and Virginia Rails. Auk, 43: 540–541.

POUGH, RICHARD H.
1946. Audubon bird guide—eastern land birds. Doubleday, New York.

1951. Audubon water bird guide. Doubleday, New York.

1957. Audubon western bird guide. Doubleday, New York.

RAND, AUSTIN L.
1942. *Larus kumlieni* and its allies. Canadian Field-Naturalist, 56: 123–126.

1948. Probability in subspecific identification of single specimens. Auk, 65: 416–432.

RAND, AUSTIN L. and MELVIN A. TRAYLOR

1950. The amount of overlap allowable for subspecies. Auk, 67: 169–183.

RAPP, WILLIAM F., JR.

1944. The Swallow-tailed Kite in the northeastern states. Bird-Banding, 15: 156–160.

RAYNOR, GILBERT S.

1959. Recent range extension of the Veery on Long Island. Kingbird, 9: 68–69.

RHOADS, SAMUEL N.

1903. Exit the Dickcissel—remarkable case of local extinction. Cassinia, 7: 17–28.

SAGE, JOHN H., LOUIS B. BISHOP, and WALTER P. BLISS

1913. The birds of Connecticut. State Geol. and Nat. Hist. Surv. Bull., 20, Hartford.

SALOMONSEN, FINN

1950a. Birds of Greenland. Munksgaard, Copenhagen.

1950b. The immigration and breeding of the Fieldfare (*Turdus pilaris* L.) in Greenland. Proc. Xth Internatl. Ornith. Congr. Uppsala: 515–526.

1958. The present status of the Brent Goose (*Branta bernicla* L.) in western Europe. Internatl. Wildfowl Res. Bur., 4: 43–80.

SALT, GEORGE W.

1952. The relation of metabolism to climate and distribution in three finches of the genus *Carpodacus*. Ecol. Monogr., 22: 121–152.

SAUNDERS, ARETAS A.

1950. Changes in status of Connecticut birds. Auk, 253–255.

1951. A guide to bird songs. Doubleday, New York.

SCHOLANDER, SUSAN I.

1955. Land birds over the western north Atlantic. Auk, 72: 225–239.

SCHORGER, ARLIE W.

1955. The Passenger Pigeon; its natural history and extinction. Univ. Wisconsin Press.

SEDWITZ, WALTER

1936. The half hardy birds that wintered through 1933–1934 in the New York City region. Proc. Linnaean Soc. N.Y., 47: 90–97.

1951. A numerical study of shorebirds on Long Island in 1947. Proc. Linnaean Soc. N.Y., 58–62: 49–54.

1958a. Six years (1947–1952) nesting of Gadwall on Jones Beach, Long Island, N.Y. Proc. Linnaean Soc. N.Y., 66–70: 61–70.

1958b. Five year count of the Ring-billed Gull on eastern Long Island. Proc. Linnaean Soc. N.Y., 66–70: 71–76.

SEDWITZ, WALTER, IRWIN ALPERIN, and MALCOLM JACOBSON

1948. Gadwall breeding on Long Island, New York. Auk, 65: 610–612.

1951. Gadwall nest found on southwestern Long Island. Proc. Linnaean Soc. N.Y., 58–62: 68–70.

SELANDER, ROBERT K. and DONALD R. GILLER

1961. Analysis of sympatry of Great-tailed and Boat-tailed Grackles. Condor, 63: 29–86.

SHORT, LESTER L., JR.

1962. The Blue-winged Warbler and Golden-winged Warbler in central New York State. Kingbird, 12: 59–67.

SNYDER, L. L.

1953. On eastern Empidonaces with particular reference to variation in *E. traillii*. Contr. Royal Ontario Mus. Zool. and Paleont., 35.

1957. Arctic birds of Canada. Univ. Toronto Press.

SOPER, J. DEWEY

1946. Ornithological results of the Baffin Island expeditions of 1928–1929 and 1930–1931, together with more recent records. Auk, 63: 1–24.

SPRUNT, ALEXANDER, JR.

1949. South Carolina bird life. Univ. South Carolina Press.

STEIN, ROBERT C.

1958. The behavioral, ecological, and morphological characteristics of two populations of the Alder Flycatcher. New York State Mus. Bull., 371.

1963. Isolating mechanisms between populations of Traill's Flycatchers. Proc. Amer. Phil. Soc., 107: 21–50.

STEWART, ROBERT E. and CHANDLER S. ROBBINS

1958. Birds of Maryland and the District of Columbia. U.S. Dept. Interior, Fish and Wildlife Serv., Washington.

STONE, WITMER

1908. Birds of New Jersey. Ann. Rep. N.J. State Mus., Trenton.

1937. Bird studies at old Cape May (2 vols.). Delaware Valley Ornith. Club.

STORER, ROBERT W.

1952. A comparison of variation, behavior, and evolution in the sea bird genera *Uria* and *Cepphus*. Univ. Calif. Publ. Zool., 52: 121–222.

STREET, PHILLIPS B.

1956. Birds of the Pocono Mountains. Delaware Valley Ornith. Club.

SUTTON, GEORGE M.

1931. The Blue Goose and Lesser Snow Goose on Southampton Island, Hudson Bay. Auk, 48: 335–364.

1938. Oddly plumaged orioles from western Oklahoma. Auk, 55: 1–6.

502

TANNER, JAMES T.

1952. Black-capped and Carolina Chickadees in the southern Appalachian Mountains. Auk, 69: 407–424.

TAVERNER, PERCY A.

1933. A study of Kumlien's Gull (*Larus kumlieni* Brewster). Canadian Field-Naturalist, 47: 88–90.

TODD, W. E. CLYDE

1940. Birds of western Pennsylvania. Univ. Pittsburgh Press.

1942. Critical remarks on the races of the Sharp-tailed Sparrow. Annals Carnegie Mus., 29: 197–199.

TRAUTMAN, MILTON B.

1940. Birds of Buckeye Lake, Ohio. Univ. of Michigan Press.

TUCK, LESLIE M.

1961. The murres. Canadian Wildlife Service, Ottawa.

TUCKER, BERNARD W.

1949. Subspecies and field ornithology. British Birds, 42: 200–205.

URNER, CHARLES A.

1929. The southward shorebird flight on the New Jersey coast in 1928. Auk, 46: 311–325.

1930. Birds of Union County, N.J., and its immediate vicinity—a statistical study. Abstr. Proc. Linnaean Soc. N.Y., 39–40: 44–98.

1934a. The eel grass blight on the New Jersey coast. Abstr. Proc. Linnaean Soc. N.Y., 43–44: 37–39.

1934b. What ditching and diking did to a salt marsh. Abstr. Proc. Linnaean Soc. N.Y., 43–44: 40–42.

1936. Shorebirds on the north and central New Jersey coast. Proc. Linnaean Soc. N.Y., 47: 77–89.

URNER, CHARLES A. and ROBERT W. STORER

1949. The distribution and abundance of shorebirds on the north and central New Jersey coast, 1928–1938. Auk, 66: 177–194.

VAN TYNE, JOSSELYN

1956. What constitute scientific data for the study of bird distribution? Wilson Bull., 68: 63–67.

VAURIE, CHARLES A.

1959. Birds of the Palearctic fauna (Passeriformes). Witherby, London.

VOGT, WILLIAM

1935. A preliminary list of the birds of Jones Beach, Long Island, N.Y. Proc. Linnaean Soc. N.Y., 45–46: 39–58.

VOOUS, K. H.

1959. Geographical variation of the Herring Gull, *Larus argentatus*, in Europe and North America. Ardea, 47: 176–187.

WALKINSHAW, LAWRENCE H. and DALE A. ZIMMERMAN

1961. Range expansion of the Brewer Blackbird in eastern North America. Condor, 63: 162–177.

WALLACE, GEORGE J.
1939. Bicknell's Thrush, its taxonomy, distribution, and life history. Proc. Boston Soc. Nat. Hist., 41: 211–402.
WEAVER, RICHARD L.
1940. The Purple Finch invasion of northeastern United States and the maritime provinces in 1939. Bird-Banding, 11: 79–105.
WEST, DAVID A.
1962. Hybridization in grosbeaks (*Pheucticus*) of the great plains. Auk, 79: 399–424.
WETMORE, ALEXANDER
1956. Check list of the fossil and prehistoric birds of North America and the West Indies. Smithsonian Misc. Coll., 131 (5).
1958. Miscellaneous notes on fossil birds. Smithsonian Misc. Coll., 135 (8).
WILCOX, LEROY
1938. A flight of Red Phalaropes (*Phalaropus fulicarius*) on Long Island, N.Y. Proc. Linnaean Soc. N.Y., 49: 60–63.
1959a. Large flights of Red Phalaropes on Long Island. Kingbird, 9: 24–25.
1959b. A twenty-year banding study of the Piping Plover. Auk, 76: 129–152.
WITHERBY, H. F., F. C. R. JOURDAIN, N. F. TICEHURST, and B. W. TUCKER
1938a. Handbook of British birds. vol. 1. Witherby, London.
1938b. *Ibid*. vol. 2.
1939. *Ibid*. vol. 3.
1940. *Ibid*. vol. 4.
1941. *Ibid*. vol. 5.
1943, 1944 (rev. eds.).
WOOLFENDEN, GLEN E.
1956. Comparative breeding behavior of *Ammospiza caudacuta* and *A. maritima*. Univ. Kansas Publ., 10: 45–75.
1957. Specimens of three birds uncommon in New Jersey. Wilson Bull., 69: 181–182.
WYNNE-EDWARDS, V. C.
1935. On the habits and distribution of birds on the North Atlantic. Proc. Boston Soc. Nat. Hist., 40: 233–346.
ZIMMERMAN, DALE A.
1955. Notes on field identification and comparative behavior of shrikes in winter. Wilson Bull., 67: 200–208.

Gazetteer

The numbered names in the following list will be found on the map on pages 506 and 507. The unnumbered cities and towns are not located on the map in this book, but will be found on road maps. Only localities mentioned in this volume are included. The four major divisions of the New York City region are: Long Island; New York; New Jersey; Connecticut.

PLACE	COUNTY	REGION	
Acabonack	Suffolk	L.I.	
Allamuchy	Warren	N.J.	
Allendale	Bergen	N.J.	
Alley Pond Park	Queens	L.I.	1
Alpine	Bergen	N.J.	
Amagansett	Suffolk	L.I.	
Amawalk Reservoir	Westchester	N.Y.	
Ambrose lightship			
Amityville	Suffolk	L.I.	
Andover	Sussex	N.J.	
Annsville Creek	Westchester	N.Y.	
Anthony's Nose	Westchester	N.Y.	2
Ardsley	Westchester	N.Y.	
Armonk	Westchester	N.Y.	
Arverne	Queens	L.I.	
Asbury Park	Monmouth	N.J.	
Astoria	Queens	L.I.	
Atlantic Beach	Nassau	L.I.	3

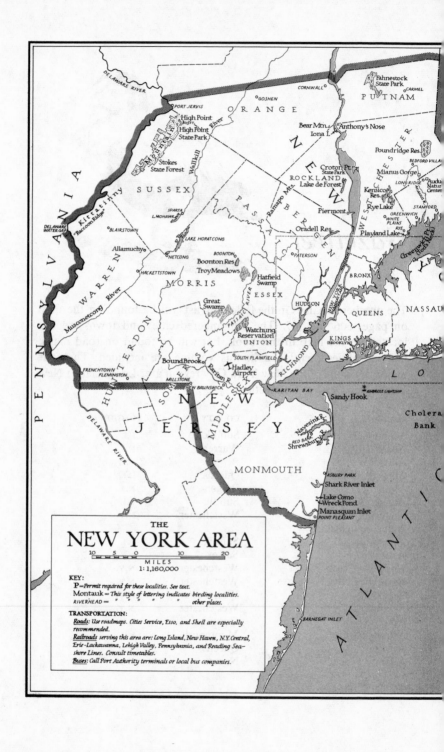

THE
NEW YORK AREA

10   5   0   10   20
MILES
1:1,160,000

KEY:
P=*Permit required for these localities. See text.*
Montauk = *This style of lettering indicates birding localities.*
RIVERHEAD =   "   "   "   "   *other places.*

TRANSPORTATION:
Roads: Use roadmaps. Cities Service, Esso, and Shell are especially recommended.
Railroads serving this area are: Long Island, New Haven, N.Y. Central, Erie-Lackawanna, Lehigh Valley, Pennsylvania, and Reading Seashore Lines. Consult timetables.
Buses: Call Port Authority terminals or local bus companies.

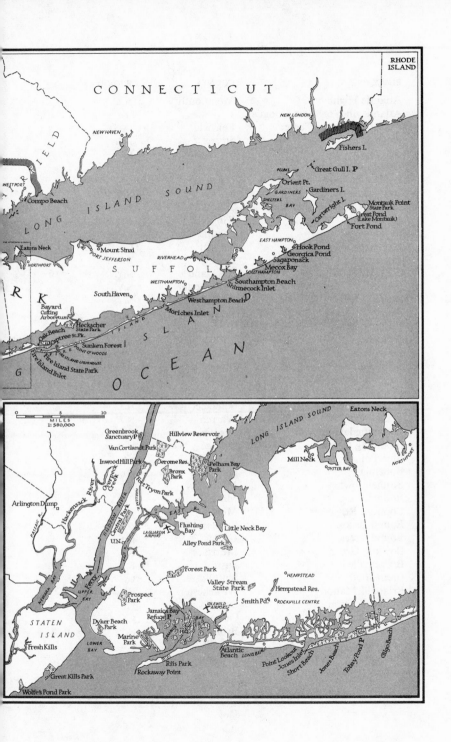

PLACE	COUNTY	REGION	
Atlantic Highlands	Monmouth	N.J.	
Atlanticville (*see* East Quogue)			
Audubon Nature Center	Fairfield	CONN.	4
Augusta	Sussex	N.J.	
Babylon	Suffolk	L.I.	
Baisley Pond Park	Queens	L.I.	
Baldwin	Nassau	L.I.	
Baxter Creek	Bronx	N.Y.	
Bayard Cutting Arboretum	Suffolk	L.I.	5
Bay Ridge	Kings	L.I.	
Bayside	Queens	L.I.	
Bayville	Nassau	L.I.	
Bearfort Mountain	Passaic	N.J.	
Bear Mountain	Rockland	N.Y.	6
Bedford Center	Westchester	N.Y.	
Bedford Hills	Westchester	N.Y.	
Bedford Village	Westchester	N.Y.	
Bedloe's Island			
Bellmore	Nassau	L.I.	
Bellport	Suffolk	L.I.	
Belmar	Monmouth	N.J.	
Belmont Lake State Park	Suffolk	L.I.	
Bergen Beach	Kings	L.I.	
Bernardsville	Somerset	N.J.	
Blairstown	Warren	N.J.	
Bloomingdale	Passaic	N.J.	
Blooming Grove	Orange	N.Y.	
Blue Point	Suffolk	L.I.	
Bohemia	Suffolk	L.I.	
Bonhamtown	Middlesex	N.J.	
Boonton	Morris	N.J.	
Boonton Reservoir	Morris	N.J.	7
Bound Brook	Somerset	N.J.	
Bound Creek	Union	N.J.	
Bowling Green	Morris	N.J.	
Branchville	Sussex	N.J.	
Brentwood	Suffolk	L.I.	
Briarcliff Manor	Westchester	N.Y.	
Bridgehampton	Suffolk	L.I.	
Broad Channel	Queens	L.I.	
Bronx Park	Bronx	N.Y.	8
Brookhaven	Suffolk	L.I.	
Brooklyn	Kings	L.I.	

PLACE	COUNTY	REGION	
Buchanan	Westchester	N.Y.	
Butler	Morris	N.J.	
Byram River	Fairfield	CONN.	
Caldwell	Essex	N.J.	
Calverton	Suffolk	L.I.	
Canarsie	Kings	L.I.	
Canarsie Pol	Kings	L.I.	
Captree State Park	Suffolk	L.I.	9
Carman's River	Suffolk	L.I.	
Carmel	Putnam	N.Y.	
Carteret	Middlesex	N.J.	
Cartwright Island	Suffolk	L.I.	10
Cedar Beach	Suffolk	L.I.	
Cedar Island	Suffolk	L.I.	
Center Moriches	Suffolk	L.I.	
Centerville	Hunterdon	N.J.	
Central Park	New York	N.Y.	11
Centre Island	Nassau	L.I.	
Chappaqua	Westchester	N.Y.	
Chatham	Morris	N.J.	
Chester	Orange	N.Y.	
City Hall Park	New York	N.Y.	
Clason Point	Bronx	N.Y.	
Cliffwood	Monmouth	N.J.	
Clifton	Passaic	N.J.	
Cold Spring	Putnam	N.Y.	
Cold Spring Harbor	Suffolk	L.I.	
Commack Hills	Suffolk	L.I.	
Commonwealth Reservoir	Essex	N.J.	
Compo Beach	Fairfield	CONN.	12
Coney Island	Kings	L.I.	
Congers	Rockland	N.Y.	
Constitution Island	Putnam	N.Y.	
Cornwall	Orange	N.Y.	
Cos Cob	Fairfield	CONN.	
Cranford	Union	N.J.	
Crater Lake	Sussex	N.J.	
Cross River	Westchester	N.Y.	
Cross River Reservoir	Westchester	N.Y.	
Croton Point	Westchester	N.Y.	13
Croton Reservoir	Westchester	N.Y.	
Croton River	Westchester	N.Y.	
Crow Hill	Kings	L.I.	

510

PLACE	COUNTY	REGION	
Fisher's Island	Suffolk	L.I.	19
Flatbrookville	Sussex	N.J.	
Flatbush	Kings	L.I.	
Flat Hummock Island	Suffolk	L.I.	
Flatlands	Kings	L.I.	
Flemington Junction	Hunterdon	N.J.	
Floral Park	Nassau	L.I.	
Flushing	Queens	L.I.	
Flushing Bay	Queens	L.I.	20
Flushing Meadow Park	Queens	L.I.	
Fords	Middlesex	N.J.	
Forest Hills	Queens	L.I.	
Forest Lake	Westchester	N.Y.	
Forest Park	Queens	L.I.	21
Fort Hamilton	Kings	L.I.	
Fort Lee	Bergen	N.J.	
Fort Montgomery	Orange	N.Y.	
Fort Pond	Suffolk	L.I.	22
Fort Salonga	Suffolk	L.I.	
Fort Tryon Park	New York	N.Y.	23
Franklin	Sussex	N.J.	
Franklin Lake	Bergen	N.J.	
Franklin Lakes	Bergen	N.J.	
Freeport	Nassau	L.I.	
Frenchtown	Hunterdon	N.J.	
Fresh Kills	Richmond (Staten Island)	N.Y.	24
Garden City	Nassau	L.I.	
Gardiner's Bay	Suffolk	L.I.	
Gardiner's Island	Suffolk	L.I.	25
Gardiner's Point	Suffolk	L.I.	
Garrison	Putnam	N.Y.	
Georgica	Suffolk	L.I.	
Georgica Pond	Suffolk	L.I.	26
Germonds	Rockland	N.Y.	
Gilgo Beach	Suffolk	L.I.	27
Gilgo Island	Suffolk	L.I.	
Glenbrook	Fairfield	CONN.	
Glen Cove	Nassau	L.I.	
Glen Oaks Village	Queens	L.I.	
Good Ground (*see* Hampton Bays)			
Goose Island	Fairfield	CONN.	
Goshen	Orange	N.Y.	

PLACE	COUNTY	REGION	
Gowanus Bay	Kings	L.I.	
Grassy Point	Rockland	N.Y.	
Grassy Sprain Reservoir	Westchester	N.Y.	
Gravesend Bay	Kings	L.I.	
Great Gull Island	Suffolk	L.I.	28
Great Kills	Richmond		
	(Staten Island)	N.Y.	29
Great Neck	Nassau	L.I.	
Great Pond (now Lake Montauk)	Suffolk	L.I.	30
Great River	Suffolk	L.I.	
Great South Bay	Suffolk	L.I.	
Great South Beach	Suffolk	L.I.	
Great Swamp	Morris	N.J.	31
Greenbrook Sanctuary	Bergen	N.J.	32
Greendell	Sussex	N.J.	
Green Pond	Morris	N.J.	
Greenport	Suffolk	L.I.	
Greenwich	Fairfield	CONN.	
Greenwood Lake		N.J.-N.Y.	
Hackensack	Bergen	N.J.	
Hackensack Meadows		N.J.	33
Hackensack River		N.J.	
Hadley Airport	Middlesex	N.J.	34
Hamburg	Sussex	N.J.	
Hampton Bays	Suffolk	L.I.	
Hamptonburgh	Orange	N.Y.	
Harlem River		N.Y.	
Harmon	Westchester	N.Y.	
Harriman Park		N.Y.	
Hartsdale	Westchester	N.Y.	
Hastings	Westchester	N.Y.	
Hatfield Swamp		N.J.	35
Haverstraw	Rockland	N.Y.	
Hawthorne	Westchester	N.Y.	
Heckscher State Park	Suffolk	L.I.	36
Helmetta	Middlesex	N.J.	
Hempstead	Nassau	L.I.	
Hempstead Plains		L.I.	
Hempstead Reservoir	Nassau	L.I.	37
Hewlett	Nassau	L.I.	
Hewlett Bay	Nassau	L.I.	
Hicksville	Nassau	L.I.	
Highland Falls	Orange	N.Y.	

PLACE	COUNTY	REGION	
High Point	Sussex	N.J.	38
High Point State Park	Sussex	N.J.	39
Hillview Reservoir	Westchester	N.Y.	40
Hither Hills State Park	Suffolk	L.I.	
Hither Plains	Suffolk	L.I.	
Hither Woods	Suffolk	L.I.	
Hoboken	Hudson	N.J.	
Hohokus	Bergen	N.J.	
Hook Mountain	Rockland	N.Y.	
Hook Pond	Suffolk	L.I.	41
Hudson Highlands			
Hudson River			
Huntington	Suffolk	L.I.	
Hunt's Point	Bronx	N.Y.	
Idlewild	Queens	L.I.	
Inwood Hill Park	New York	N.Y.	42
Iona Island	Rockland	N.Y.	43
Irvington	Westchester	N.Y.	
Island Pond	Orange	N.Y.	
Islip	Suffolk	L.I.	
Jamaica	Queens	L.I.	
Jamaica Bay		L.I.	
Jamaica Bay Refuge		L.I.	44
Jamesburg	Middlesex	N.J.	
Jamesport	Suffolk	L.I.	
Jericho	Nassau	L.I.	
Jerome Reservoir	Bronx	N.Y.	45
Jersey City	Hudson	N.J.	
Jones Beach		L.I.	46
Jones Inlet	Nassau	L.I.	47
Jones Point	Rockland	N.Y.	
Katonah	Westchester	N.Y.	
Keansburg	Monmouth	N.J.	
Kearny	Hudson	N.J.	
Kensico Reservoir	Westchester	N.Y.	48
Keyport	Monmouth	N.J.	
Kings Park	Suffolk	L.I.	
Kissena Park	Queens	L.I.	
Kittatinny Mountain	Sussex	N.J.	
Kittatinny Mountains	Sussex	N.J.	
Lafayette	Sussex	N.J.	
Lake Agawam	Suffolk	L.I.	
Lake Como	Monmouth	N.J.	49

PLACE	COUNTY	REGION	
Lake DeForest	Rockland	N.Y.	50
Lake Girard	Sussex	N.J.	
Lake Grove	Suffolk	L.I.	
Lake Mohawk	Sussex	N.J.	
Lake Parsippany	Morris	N.J.	
Lake Ronkonkoma	Suffolk	L.I.	
Lake Success	Nassau	L.I.	
Lake Tiorati	Orange	N.Y.	
Lake Waccabuc	Westchester	N.Y.	
Lamington	Somerset	N.J.	
Larchmont	Westchester	N.Y.	
Lattingtown	Nassau	L.I.	
Lawrence	Nassau	L.I.	
Leonardo	Monmouth	N.J.	
Levittown	Nassau	L.I.	
Lewisboro	Westchester	N.Y.	
Lido Beach	Nassau	L.I.	
Lincroft	Monmouth	N.J.	
Lindenhurst	Suffolk	L.I.	
Little Captain Island	Fairfield	CONN.	
Little Falls	Passaic	N.J.	
Little Gull Island	Suffolk	L.I.	
Little Neck	Queens	L.I.	
Little Neck Bay	Queens	L.I.	51
Little Reed Pond	Suffolk	L.I.	
Little Tavern Island	Fairfield	CONN.	
Long Beach	Nassau	L.I.	
Long Branch	Monmouth	N.J.	
Long Island City	Queens	L.I.	
Long Island Sound			
Loop Causeway	Nassau	L.I.	
Lower Bay			
Madison	Morris	N.J.	
Madison Square Park	New York	N.Y.	
Mahwah	Bergen	N.J.	
Malverne	Nassau	L.I.	
Mamaroneck	Westchester	N.Y.	
Manalapan	Monmouth	N.J.	
Manasquan	Monmouth	N.J.	
Manasquan Inlet		N.J.	52
Manhasset	Nassau	L.I.	
Manhattan Beach	Kings	L.I.	
Manorville	Suffolk	L.I.	

514

PLACE	COUNTY	REGION	
Maplewood	Essex	N.J.	
Marine Park	Kings	L.I.	53
Massapequa	Nassau	L.I.	
Massapequa State Park	Nassau	L.I.	
Mastic	Suffolk	L.I.	
Matawan	Monmouth	N.J.	
Mattituck	Suffolk	L.I.	
Meadowbrook	Nassau	L.I.	
Meadowbrook Causeway	Nassau	L.I.	
Meadow Island	Nassau	L.I.	
Mecox Bay	Suffolk	L.I.	54
Melville	Suffolk	L.I.	
Mendham	Morris	N.J.	
Merrick	Nassau	L.I.	
Merrick Bay	Nassau	L.I.	
Metuchen	Middlesex	N.J.	
Mianus Gorge			55
Middlebush	Somerset	N.J.	
Middle Island	Suffolk	L.I.	
Millbrook	Warren	N.J.	
Miller Place	Suffolk	L.I.	
Millington	Somerset	N.J.	
Mill Neck	Nassau	L.I.	56
Milltown	Middlesex	N.J.	
Mitchel Air Force Base (Mitchel Field)	Nassau	L.I.	
Mohansic Lake	Westchester	N.Y.	
Money Island	Suffolk	L.I.	
Montauk	Suffolk	L.I.	
Montauk Point	Suffolk	L.I.	57
Montclair	Essex	N.J.	
Moriches Bay	Suffolk	L.I.	
Moriches Inlet	Suffolk	L.I.	58
Morris River		N.J.	
Morristown	Morris	N.J.	
Mount Kisco	Westchester	N.Y.	
Mount Sinai	Suffolk	L.I.	59
Mount Vernon	Westchester	N.Y.	
Musconetcong Mountain	Hunterdon	N.J.	
Musconetcong River		N.J.	60
Muscoot Reservoir	Westchester	N.Y.	
Napeague Bay	Suffolk	L.I.	
Narrows			

PLACE	COUNTY	REGION	
Neponsit	Queens	L.I.	
Newark	Essex	N.J.	
Newark Bay		N.J.	
Newark Meadows		N.J.	
New Brunswick	Middlesex	N.J.	
New Canaan	Fairfield	CONN.	
New City	Rockland	N.Y.	
New Dorp	Richmond (Staten Island)	N.Y.	
Newfoundland	Passaic	N.J.	
New Hempstead	Rockland	N.Y.	
New Hyde Park	Nassau	L.I.	
New Rochelle	Westchester	N.Y.	
Newton	Sussex	N.J.	
Nixon	Middlesex	N.J.	
North Arlington	Essex	N.J.	
North Haven	Suffolk	L.I.	
Northport	Suffolk	L.I.	
North Sea	Suffolk	L.I.	
Northwest Woods	Suffolk	L.I.	
North White Plains	Westchester	N.Y.	
Norwalk	Fairfield	CONN.	
Noyack	Suffolk	L.I.	
Nyack	Rockland	N.Y.	
Oak Beach	Suffolk	L.I.	61
Oakdale	Suffolk	L.I.	
Oakland	Bergen	N.J.	
Oakwood Beach	Richmond (Staten Island)	N.Y.	
Ocean Beach	Suffolk	L.I.	
Oceanport	Monmouth	N.J.	
Oceanside	Nassau	L.I.	
Old Bridge	Middlesex	N.J.	
Old Greenwich	Fairfield	CONN.	
Oradell	Bergen	N.J.	
Oradell Reservoir	Bergen	N.J.	62
Orange	Essex	N.J.	
Orange Reservoir	Essex	N.J.	
Orient	Suffolk	L.I.	
Orient Point	Suffolk	L.I.	63
Ossining	Westchester	N.Y.	
Overpeck Creek	Bergen	N.J.	64
Owl's Head Park	Kings	L.I.	

PLACE	COUNTY	REGION	
Oyster Bay	Nassau	L.I.	
Oyster Pond	Suffolk	L.I.	
Palisades	Rockland	N.Y.	
Palisades, the			
Palisades Park	Bergen	N.J.	
Parkville	Kings	L.I.	
Passaic	Passaic	N.J.	
Passaic River			
Patchogue	Suffolk	L.I.	
Paterson	Passaic	N.J.	
Pattenburg	Hunterdon	N.J.	
Patterson	Putnam	N.Y.	
Peach Lake		N.Y.	
Peconic Bay	Suffolk	L.I.	
Peconic River	Suffolk	L.I.	
Peekskill	Westchester	N.Y.	
Pelham Bay	Bronx	N.Y.	
Pelham Bay Park	Bronx	N.Y.	65
Penwell	Hunterdon	N.J.	
Pequannock	Morris	N.J.	
Pequannock River		N.J.	
Pequest River	Warren	N.J.	
Phillipsburg	Warren	N.J.	
Piermont	Rockland	N.Y.	66
Pine Brook	Morris	N.J.	
Pinelawn	Suffolk	L.I.	
Pine Swamp	Orange	N.Y.	
Plainfield	Union	N.J.	
Playland Lake	Westchester	N.Y.	67
Pleasant Plains	Richmond (Staten Island)	N.Y.	
Pleasantville	Westchester	N.Y.	
Plum Beach	Kings	L.I.	
Plum Island	Suffolk	L.I.	
Pocantico River	Westchester	N.Y.	
Point Lookout	Nassau	L.I.	68
Point Pleasant		N.J.	
Point o' Woods	Suffolk	L.I.	
Pompton Lakes	Passaic	N.J.	
Ponquogue (*see* Quogue)			
Port Chester	Westchester	N.Y.	
Port Jefferson	Suffolk	L.I.	
Port Jervis	Orange	N.Y.	

PLACE	COUNTY	REGION	
Port Monmouth	Monmouth	N.J.	
Port Richmond	Richmond (Staten Island)	N.Y.	
Port Washington	Nassau	L.I.	
Poundridge	Westchester	N.Y.	
Poundridge Reservation	Westchester	N.Y.	69
Poxabogue	Suffolk	L.I.	
Princess Bay	Richmond (Staten Island)	N.Y.	
Prospect Park	Kings	L.I.	70
Purchase	Westchester	N.Y.	
Purdys	Westchester	N.Y.	
Queens Village	Queens	L.I.	
Quogue	Suffolk	L.I.	
"Raccoon Ridge"	Warren	N.J.	71
Ramapo Mountains			
Ram Island	Fairfield	CONN.	
Ram Island	Suffolk	L.I.	
Ramsey	Bergen	N.J.	
Raritan	Middlesex	N.J.	
Raritan Bay		N.J.	
Raritan River		N.J.	
Raynor South (*see* Freeport)			
Red Bank	Monmouth	N.J.	
Reed Pond	Suffolk	L.I.	
Remsenburg	Suffolk	L.I.	
Reynold's Channel	Nassau	L.I.	
Ridgewood	Bergen	N.J.	
Riis Park	Queens	L.I.	72
Ringwood	Passaic	N.J.	
Riverdale	Bronx	N.Y.	
Riverhead	Suffolk	L.I.	
Riverside	Fairfield	CONN.	
River Vale	Bergen	N.J.	
Rockaway	Morris	N.J.	
Rockaway Beach	Queens	L.I.	
Rockaway Point	Queens	L.I.	73
Rockland Lake	Rockland	N.Y.	
Rockville Centre	Nassau	L.I.	
Roselle	Union	N.J.	
Roselle Park	Union	N.J.	
Roslyn	Nassau	L.I.	
Round Hill	Fairfield	CONN.	

518

Gazetteer

PLACE	COUNTY	REGION	
Roxbury	Queens	L.I.	
Rumson	Monmouth	N.J.	
Rutherford	Bergen	N.J.	
Rye	Westchester	N.Y.	
Rye Lake	Westchester	N.Y.	74
Saddle River	Bergen	N.J.	
Sagaponack	Suffolk	L.I.	75
Sag Harbor	Suffolk	L.I.	
Saltaire	Suffolk	L.I.	
Sands Point	Nassau	L.I.	
Sandy Hook	Monmouth	N.J.	76
Sandy Hook Bay	Monmouth	N.J.	
Sandy Hook State Park	Monmouth	N.J.	
Sandyston Township	Sussex	N.J.	
Saw Mill River	Westchester	N.Y.	
Sayville	Suffolk	L.I.	
Scarborough	Westchester	N.Y.	
Scarsdale	Westchester	N.Y.	
Schooley's Mountain	Morris	N.J.	
Sea Bright	Monmouth	N.J.	
Seaford	Nassau	L.I.	
Secaucus	Hudson	N.J.	
Selden	Suffolk	L.I.	
Setauket	Suffolk	L.I.	
Sexton Island	Suffolk	L.I.	
Shark River	Monmouth	N.J.	
Shark River Inlet	Monmouth	N.J.	77
Sheep Rocks	Fairfield	CONN.	
Sheepshead Bay	Kings	L.I.	
Sheffield Island	Fairfield	CONN.	
Shelter Island	Suffolk	L.I.	
Sherwood Island	Fairfield	CONN.	
Shinnecock Bay	Suffolk	L.I.	
Shinnecock Hills	Suffolk	L.I.	
Shinnecock Inlet	Suffolk	L.I.	78
Short Beach	Nassau	L.I.	79
Short Hills	Essex	N.J.	
Shrewsbury	Monmouth	N.J.	
Shrewsbury River	Monmouth	N.J.	
Sing Sing (see Ossining)			
Smith's Pond	Nassau	L.I.	
Smithtown	Suffolk	L.I.	
Smoke Rise	Morris	N.J.	

519

PLACE	COUNTY	REGION	
Somers	Westchester	N.Y.	
Somerville	Somerset	N.J.	
South Amboy	Middlesex	N.J.	
Southampton	Suffolk	L.I.	
South Haven	Suffolk	L.I.	80
South Norwalk	Fairfield	CONN.	
Southold	Suffolk	L.I.	
South Oyster Bay	Nassau	L.I.	
South Ozone Park	Queens	L.I.	
South Plainfield	Middlesex	N.J.	
Speonk	Suffolk	L.I.	
Splitrock Pond	Warren	N.J.	
Spring Creek	Queens	L.I.	
Springdale	Sussex	N.J.	
Spring Lake	Monmouth	N.J.	
Spring Mills	Hunterdon	N.J.	
Springs	Suffolk	L.I.	
Spuyten Duyvil		N.Y.	
Squankum	Monmouth	N.J.	
Stag Lake	Sussex	N.J.	
Stamford	Fairfield	CONN.	
Stanton	Hunterdon	N.J.	
Sterling Forest	Orange	N.Y.	
Stokes State Forest	Sussex	N.J.	81
Stony Brook	Suffolk	L.I.	
Stony Point	Rockland	N.Y.	
Suffern	Rockland	N.Y.	
Summit	Union	N.J.	
Sunfish Pond	Warren	N.J.	
Sunken Forest	Suffolk	L.I.	82
Sunken Meadow Beach	Suffolk	L.I.	
Sunrise Mountain	Sussex	N.J.	
Sussex	Sussex	N.J.	
Swartswood Lake	Sussex	N.J.	
Swimming River	Monmouth	N.J.	
Syosset	Nassau	L.I.	
Tarrytown	Westchester	N.Y.	
Three Mile Harbor	Suffolk	L.I.	
Tiana Beach	Suffolk	L.I.	
Titicus Reservoir	Westchester	N.Y.	
Tobay Beach	Nassau	L.I.	
Tobay Pond	Nassau	L.I.	83
Tod's Neck	Fairfield	CONN.	84

520

PLACE	COUNTY	REGION	
Tomkins Cove	Rockland	N.Y.	
Tottenville	Richmond (Staten Island)	N.Y.	
Troy Meadows	Morris	N.J.	85
Tuckahoe	Westchester	N.Y.	
Turkey Swamp	Monmouth	N.J.	
University Heights	Bronx	N.Y.	
Upper Bay			
Valley Stream	Nassau	L.I.	
Valley Stream State Park	Nassau	L.I.	86
Van Cortlandt Park	Bronx	N.Y.	87
Vernon	Sussex	N.J.	
Verona	Essex	N.J.	
Wading River	Suffolk	L.I.	
Wainscott	Suffolk	L.I.	
Waldwick	Bergen	N.J.	
Wallkill River			
Wallpack	Sussex	N.J.	
Wanaque Reservoir	Passaic	N.J.	
Wantagh	Nassau	L.I.	
Warren Glen	Warren	N.J.	
Warwick	Orange	N.Y.	
Washingtonville	Orange	N.Y.	
Watchung Reservation	Union	N.J.	88
Waterloo	Morris	N.J.	
Water Mill	Suffolk	L.I.	89
Wawayanda Mountain	Sussex	N.J.	
Welch Lake	Rockland	N.Y.	
West Brighton	Richmond (Staten Island)	N.Y.	
Westbury	Nassau	L.I.	
Westchester Creek	Bronx	N.Y.	
West Englewood	Bergen	N.J.	
Westhampton	Suffolk	L.I.	
Westhampton Beach	Suffolk	L.I.	90
West Hills	Suffolk	L.I.	
West Islip	Suffolk	L.I.	
West Long Branch	Monmouth	N.J.	
West Nyack	Rockland	N.Y.	
Weston	Fairfield	CONN.	
West Orange	Essex	N.J.	
West Point	Orange	N.Y.	
Westport	Fairfield	CONN.	

Index

Index

A CATALOGUE OF SELECTED DOVER BOOKS
IN ALL FIELDS OF INTEREST

A CATALOGUE OF SELECTED DOVER BOOKS
IN ALL FIELDS OF INTEREST

AMERICA'S OLD MASTERS, James T. Flexner. Four men emerged unexpectedly from provincial 18th century America to leadership in European art: Benjamin West, J. S. Copley, C. R. Peale, Gilbert Stuart. Brilliant coverage of lives and contributions. Revised, 1967 edition. 69 plates. 365pp. of text.

21806-6 Paperbound $3.00

FIRST FLOWERS OF OUR WILDERNESS: AMERICAN PAINTING, THE COLONIAL PERIOD, James T. Flexner. Painters, and regional painting traditions from earliest Colonial times up to the emergence of Copley, West and Peale Sr., Foster, Gustavus Hesselius, Feke, John Smibert and many anonymous painters in the primitive manner. Engaging presentation, with 162 illustrations. xxii + 368pp.

22180-6 Paperbound $3.50

THE LIGHT OF DISTANT SKIES: AMERICAN PAINTING, 1760-1835, James T. Flexner. The great generation of early American painters goes to Europe to learn and to teach: West, Copley, Gilbert Stuart and others. Allston, Trumbull, Morse; also contemporary American painters—primitives, derivatives, academics—who remained in America. 102 illustrations. xiii + 306pp.

22179-2 Paperbound $3.50

A HISTORY OF THE RISE AND PROGRESS OF THE ARTS OF DESIGN IN THE UNITED STATES, William Dunlap. Much the richest mine of information on early American painters, sculptors, architects, engravers, miniaturists, etc. The only source of information for scores of artists, the major primary source for many others. Unabridged reprint of rare original 1834 edition, with new introduction by James T. Flexner, and 394 new illustrations. Edited by Rita Weiss. 6⅝ x 9⅝.

21695-0, 21696-9, 21697-7 Three volumes, Paperbound $15.00

EPOCHS OF CHINESE AND JAPANESE ART, Ernest F. Fenollosa. From primitive Chinese art to the 20th century, thorough history, explanation of every important art period and form, including Japanese woodcuts; main stress on China and Japan, but Tibet, Korea also included. Still unexcelled for its detailed, rich coverage of cultural background, aesthetic elements, diffusion studies, particularly of the historical period. 2nd, 1913 edition. 242 illustrations. lii + 439pp. of text.

20364-6, 20365-4 Two volumes, Paperbound $6.00

THE GENTLE ART OF MAKING ENEMIES, James A. M. Whistler. Greatest wit of his day deflates Oscar Wilde, Ruskin, Swinburne; strikes back at inane critics, exhibitions, art journalism; aesthetics of impressionist revolution in most striking form. Highly readable classic by great painter. Reproduction of edition designed by Whistler. Introduction by Alfred Werner. xxxvi + 334pp.

21875-9 Paperbound $3.00

THE RED FAIRY BOOK, Andrew Lang. Lang's color fairy books have long been children's favorites. This volume includes Rapunzel, Jack and the Bean-stalk and 35 other stories, familiar and unfamiliar. 4 plates, 93 illustrations x + 367pp.

21673-X Paperbound $2.50

THE BLUE FAIRY BOOK, Andrew Lang. Lang's tales come from all countries and all times. Here are 37 tales from Grimm, the Arabian Nights, Greek Mythology, and other fascinating sources. 8 plates, 130 illustrations. xi + 390pp.

21437-0 Paperbound $2.75

HOUSEHOLD STORIES BY THE BROTHERS GRIMM. Classic English-language edition of the well-known tales — Rumpelstiltskin, Snow White, Hansel and Gretel, The Twelve Brothers, Faithful John, Rapunzel, Tom Thumb (52 stories in all). Translated into simple, straightforward English by Lucy Crane. Ornamented with head-pieces, vignettes, elaborate decorative initials and a dozen full-page illustrations by Walter Crane. x + 269pp. 21080-4 Paperbound **$2.00**

THE MERRY ADVENTURES OF ROBIN HOOD, Howard Pyle. The finest modern versions of the traditional ballads and tales about the great English outlaw. Howard Pyle's complete prose version, with every word, every illustration of the first edition. Do not confuse this facsimile of the original (1883) with modern editions that change text or illustrations. 23 plates plus many page decorations. xxii + 296pp.

22043-5 Paperbound $2.75

THE STORY OF KING ARTHUR AND HIS KNIGHTS, Howard Pyle. The finest children's version of the life of King Arthur; brilliantly retold by Pyle, with 48 of his most imaginative illustrations. xviii + 313pp. 6⅛ x 9¼.

21445-1 Paperbound $2.50

THE WONDERFUL WIZARD OF OZ, L. Frank Baum. America's finest children's book in facsimile of first edition with all Denslow illustrations in full color. The edition a child should have. Introduction by Martin Gardner. 23 color plates, scores of drawings. iv + 267pp. 20691-2 Paperbound **$3.50**

THE MARVELOUS LAND OF OZ, L. Frank Baum. The second Oz book, every bit as imaginative as the Wizard. The hero is a boy named Tip, but the Scarecrow and the Tin Woodman are back, as is the Oz magic. 16 color plates, 120 drawings by John R. Neill. 287pp. 20692-0 Paperbound $2.50

THE MAGICAL MONARCH OF MO, L. Frank Baum. Remarkable adventures in a land even stranger than Oz. The best of Baum's books not in the Oz series. 15 color plates and dozens of drawings by Frank Verbeck. xviii + 237pp.

21892-9 Paperbound $2.25

THE BAD CHILD'S BOOK OF BEASTS, MORE BEASTS FOR WORSE CHILDREN, A MORAL ALPHABET, Hilaire Belloc. Three complete humor classics in one volume. Be kind to the frog, and do not call him names . . . and 28 other whimsical animals. Familiar favorites and some not so well known. Illustrated by Basil Blackwell. 156pp. (USO) 20749-8 Paperbound $1.50

THE ARCHITECTURE OF COUNTRY HOUSES, Andrew J. Downing. Together with Vaux's *Villas and Cottages* this is the basic book for Hudson River Gothic architecture of the middle Victorian period. Full, sound discussions of general aspects of housing, architecture, style, decoration, furnishing, together with scores of detailed house plans, illustrations of specific buildings, accompanied by full text. Perhaps the most influential single American architectural book. 1850 edition. Introduction by J. Stewart Johnson. 321 figures, 34 architectural designs. xvi + 560pp.
22003-6 Paperbound $5.00

LOST EXAMPLES OF COLONIAL ARCHITECTURE, John Mead Howells. Full-page photographs of buildings that have disappeared or been so altered as to be denatured, including many designed by major early American architects. 245 plates. xvii + 248pp. 7⅞ x 10¾.
21143-6 Paperbound $3.50

DOMESTIC ARCHITECTURE OF THE AMERICAN COLONIES AND OF THE EARLY REPUBLIC, Fiske Kimball. Foremost architect and restorer of Williamsburg and Monticello covers nearly 200 homes between 1620-1825. Architectural details, construction, style features, special fixtures, floor plans, etc. Generally considered finest work in its area. 219 illustrations of houses, doorways, windows, capital mantels. xx + 314pp. 7⅞ x 10¾.
21743-4 Paperbound $4.00

EARLY AMERICAN ROOMS: 1650-1858, edited by Russell Hawes Kettell. Tour of 12 rooms, each representative of a different era in American history and each furnished, decorated, designed and occupied in the style of the era. 72 plans and elevations, 8-page color section, etc., show fabrics, wall papers, arrangements, etc. Full descriptive text. xvii + 200pp. of text. 8⅜ x 11¼.
21633-0 Paperbound $5.00

THE FITZWILLIAM VIRGINAL BOOK, edited by J. Fuller Maitland and W. B. Squire. Full modern printing of famous early 17th-century ms. volume of 300 works by Morley, Byrd, Bull, Gibbons, etc. For piano or other modern keyboard instrument; easy to read format. xxxvi + 938pp. 8⅜ x 11.
21068-5, 21069-3 Two volumes, Paperbound $12.00

KEYBOARD MUSIC, Johann Sebastian Bach. Bach Gesellschaft edition. A rich selection of Bach's masterpieces for the harpsichord: the six English Suites, six French Suites, the six Partitas (Clavierübung part I), the Goldberg Variations (Clavierübung part IV), the fifteen Two-Part Inventions and the fifteen Three-Part Sinfonias. Clearly reproduced on large sheets with ample margins; eminently playable. vi + 312pp. 8⅛ x 11.
22360-4 Paperbound $5.00

THE MUSIC OF BACH: AN INTRODUCTION, Charles Sanford Terry. A fine, nontechnical introduction to Bach's music, both instrumental and vocal. Covers organ music, chamber music, passion music, other types. Analyzes themes, developments, innovations. x + 114pp.
21075-8 Paperbound $1.95

BEETHOVEN AND HIS NINE SYMPHONIES, Sir George Grove. Noted British musicologist provides best history, analysis, commentary on symphonies. Very thorough, rigorously accurate; necessary to both advanced student and amateur music lover. 436 musical passages. vii + 407 pp.
20334-4 Paperbound $4.00

"ESSENTIAL GRAMMAR" SERIES

All you really need to know about modern, colloquial grammar. Many educational shortcuts help you learn faster, understand better. Detailed cognate lists teach you to recognize similarities between English and foreign words and roots—make learning vocabulary easy and interesting. Excellent for independent study or as a supplement to record courses.

ESSENTIAL FRENCH GRAMMAR, Seymour Resnick. 2500-item cognate list. 159pp.
(EBE) 20419-7 Paperbound $1.50

ESSENTIAL GERMAN GRAMMAR, Guy Stern and Everett F. Bleiler. Unusual short-cuts on noun declension, word order, compound verbs. 124pp.
(EBE) 20422-7 Paperbound $1.25

ESSENTIAL ITALIAN GRAMMAR, Olga Ragusa. 111pp.
(EBE) 20779-X Paperbound $1.25

ESSENTIAL JAPANESE GRAMMAR, Everett F. Bleiler. In Romaji transcription; no characters needed. Japanese grammar is regular and simple. 156pp.
21027-8 Paperbound $1.50

ESSENTIAL PORTUGUESE GRAMMAR, Alexander da R. Prista. vi + 114pp.
21650-0 Paperbound $1.35

ESSENTIAL SPANISH GRAMMAR, Seymour Resnick. 2500 word cognate list. 115pp.
(EBE) 20780-3 Paperbound $1.25

ESSENTIAL ENGLISH GRAMMAR, Philip Gucker. Combines best features of modern, functional and traditional approaches. For refresher, class use, home study. x + 177pp.
21649-7 Paperbound $1.75

A PHRASE AND SENTENCE DICTIONARY OF SPOKEN SPANISH. Prepared for U. S. War Department by U. S. linguists. As above, unit is idiom, phrase or sentence rather than word. English-Spanish and Spanish-English sections contain modern equivalents of over 18,000 sentences. Introduction and appendix as above. iv + 513pp.
20495-2 Paperbound $3.50

A PHRASE AND SENTENCE DICTIONARY OF SPOKEN RUSSIAN. Dictionary prepared for U. S. War Department by U. S. linguists. Basic unit is not the word, but the idiom, phrase or sentence. English-Russian and Russian-English sections contain modern equivalents for over 30,000 phrases. Grammatical introduction covers phonetics, writing, syntax. Appendix of word lists for food, numbers, geographical names, etc. vi + 573 pp. 6⅛ x 9¼.
20496-0 Paperbound $5.50

CONVERSATIONAL CHINESE FOR BEGINNERS, Morris Swadesh. Phonetic system, beginner's course in Pai Hua Mandarin Chinese covering most important, most useful speech patterns. Emphasis on modern colloquial usage. Formerly *Chinese in Your Pocket.* xvi + 158pp.
21123-1 Paperbound $1.75

How to Know the Wild Flowers, Mrs. William Starr Dana. This is the classical book of American wildflowers (of the Eastern and Central United States), used by hundreds of thousands. Covers over 500 species, arranged in extremely easy to use color and season groups. Full descriptions, much plant lore. This Dover edition is the fullest ever compiled, with tables of nomenclature changes. 174 full-page plates by M. Satterlee. xii + 418pp. 20332-8 Paperbound $3.00

Our Plant Friends and Foes, William Atherton DuPuy. History, economic importance, essential botanical information and peculiarities of 25 common forms of plant life are provided in this book in an entertaining and charming style. Covers food plants (potatoes, apples, beans, wheat, almonds, bananas, etc.), flowers (lily, tulip, etc.), trees (pine, oak, elm, etc.), weeds, poisonous mushrooms and vines, gourds, citrus fruits, cotton, the cactus family, and much more. 108 illustrations. xiv + 290pp. 22272-1 Paperbound $2.50

How to Know the Ferns, Frances T. Parsons. Classic survey of Eastern and Central ferns, arranged according to clear, simple identification key. Excellent introduction to greatly neglected nature area. 57 illustrations and 42 plates. xvi + 215pp. 20740-4 Paperbound $2.00

Manual of the Trees of North America, Charles S. Sargent. America's foremost dendrologist provides the definitive coverage of North American trees and tree-like shrubs. 717 species fully described and illustrated: exact distribution, down to township; full botanical description; economic importance; description of subspecies and races; habitat, growth data; similar material. Necessary to every serious student of tree-life. Nomenclature revised to present. Over 100 locating keys. 783 illustrations. lii + 934pp. 20277-1, 20278-X Two volumes, Paperbound $7.00

Our Northern Shrubs, Harriet L. Keeler. Fine non-technical reference work identifying more than 225 important shrubs of Eastern and Central United States and Canada. Full text covering botanical description, habitat, plant lore, is paralleled with 205 full-page photographs of flowering or fruiting plants. Nomenclature revised by Edward G. Voss. One of few works concerned with shrubs. 205 plates, 35 drawings. xxviii + 521pp. 21989-5 Paperbound $3.75

The Mushroom Handbook, Louis C. C. Krieger. Still the best popular handbook: full descriptions of 259 species, cross references to another 200. Extremely thorough text enables you to identify, know all about any mushroom you are likely to meet in eastern and central U. S. A.: habitat, luminescence, poisonous qualities, use, folklore, etc. 32 color plates show over 50 mushrooms, also 126 other illustrations. Finding keys. vii + 560pp. 21861-9 Paperbound $4.50

Handbook of Birds of Eastern North America, Frank M. Chapman. Still much the best single-volume guide to the birds of Eastern and Central United States. Very full coverage of 675 species, with descriptions, life habits, distribution, similar data. All descriptions keyed to two-page color chart. With this single volume the average birdwatcher needs no other books. 1931 revised edition. 195 illustrations. xxxvi + 581pp. 21489-3 Paperbound $5.00

AMERICAN FOOD AND GAME FISHES, David S. Jordan and Barton W. Evermann. Definitive source of information, detailed and accurate enough to enable the sportsman and nature lover to identify conclusively some 1,000 species and sub-species of North American fish, sought for food or sport. Coverage of range, physiology, habits, life history, food value. Best methods of capture, interest to the angler, advice on bait, fly-fishing, etc. 338 drawings and photographs. 1 + 574pp. 6⅝ x 9⅜.

22196-2 Paperbound $5.00

THE FROG BOOK, Mary C. Dickerson. Complete with extensive finding keys, over 300 photographs, and an introduction to the general biology of frogs and toads, this is the classic non-technical study of Northeastern and Central species. 58 species; 290 photographs and 16 color plates. xvii + 253pp.

21973-9 Paperbound $4.00

THE MOTH BOOK: A GUIDE TO THE MOTHS OF NORTH AMERICA, William J. Holland. Classical study, eagerly sought after and used for the past 60 years. Clear identification manual to more than 2,000 different moths, largest manual in existence. General information about moths, capturing, mounting, classifying, etc., followed by species by species descriptions. 263 illustrations plus 48 color plates show almost every species, full size. 1968 edition, preface, nomenclature changes by A. E. Brower. xxiv + 479pp. of text. 6½ x 9¼.

21948-8 Paperbound $6.00

THE SEA-BEACH AT EBB-TIDE, Augusta Foote Arnold. Interested amateur can identify hundreds of marine plants and animals on coasts of North America; marine algae; seaweeds; squids; hermit crabs; horse shoe crabs; shrimps; corals; sea anemones; etc. Species descriptions cover: structure; food; reproductive cycle; size; shape; color; habitat; etc. Over 600 drawings. 85 plates. xii + 490pp.

21949-6 Paperbound $4.00

COMMON BIRD SONGS, Donald J. Borror. 33⅓ 12-inch record presents songs of 60 important birds of the eastern United States. A thorough, serious record which provides several examples for each bird, showing different types of song, individual variations, etc. Inestimable identification aid for birdwatcher. 32-page booklet gives text about birds and songs, with illustration for each bird.

21829-5 Record, book, album. Monaural. $3.50

FADS AND FALLACIES IN THE NAME OF SCIENCE, Martin Gardner. Fair, witty appraisal of cranks and quacks of science: Atlantis, Lemuria, hollow earth, flat earth, Velikovsky, orgone energy, Dianetics, flying saucers, Bridey Murphy, food fads, medical fads, perpetual motion, etc. Formerly "In the Name of Science." x + 363pp.

20394-8 Paperbound $3.00

HOAXES, Curtis D. MacDougall. Exhaustive, unbelievably rich account of great hoaxes: Locke's moon hoax, Shakespearean forgeries, sea serpents, Loch Ness monster, Cardiff giant, John Wilkes Booth's mummy, Disumbrationist school of art, dozens more; also journalism, psychology of hoaxing. 54 illustrations. xi + 338pp.

20465-0 Paperbound $3.50

THE PRINCIPLES OF PSYCHOLOGY, William James. The famous long course, complete and unabridged. Stream of thought, time perception, memory, experimental methods—these are only some of the concerns of a work that was years ahead of its time and still valid, interesting, useful. 94 figures. Total of xviii + 1391pp.
20381-6, 20382-4 Two volumes, Paperbound $9.00

THE STRANGE STORY OF THE QUANTUM, Banesh Hoffmann. Non-mathematical but thorough explanation of work of Planck, Einstein, Bohr, Pauli, de Broglie, Schrödinger, Heisenberg, Dirac, Feynman, etc. No technical background needed. "Of books attempting such an account, this is the best," Henry Margenau, Yale. 40-page "Postscript 1959." xii + 285pp. 20518-5 Paperbound $3.00

THE RISE OF THE NEW PHYSICS, A. d'Abro. Most thorough explanation in print of central core of mathematical physics, both classical and modern; from Newton to Dirac and Heisenberg. Both history and exposition; philosophy of science, causality, explanations of higher mathematics, analytical mechanics, electromagnetism, thermodynamics, phase rule, special and general relativity, matrices. No higher mathematics needed to follow exposition, though treatment is elementary to intermediate in level. Recommended to serious student who wishes verbal understanding. 97 illustrations. xvii + 982pp. 20003-5, 20004-3 Two volumes, Paperbound $10.00

GREAT IDEAS OF OPERATIONS RESEARCH, Jagjit Singh. Easily followed non-technical explanation of mathematical tools, aims, results: statistics, linear programming, game theory, queueing theory, Monte Carlo simulation, etc. Uses only elementary mathematics. Many case studies, several analyzed in detail. Clarity, breadth make this excellent for specialist in another field who wishes background. 41 figures. x + 228pp. 21886-4 Paperbound $2.50

GREAT IDEAS OF MODERN MATHEMATICS: THEIR NATURE AND USE, Jagjit Singh. Internationally famous expositor, winner of Unesco's Kalinga Award for science popularization explains verbally such topics as differential equations, matrices, groups, sets, transformations, mathematical logic and other important modern mathematics, as well as use in physics, astrophysics, and similar fields. Superb exposition for layman, scientist in other areas. viii + 312pp.
20587-8 Paperbound $2.75

GREAT IDEAS IN INFORMATION THEORY, LANGUAGE AND CYBERNETICS, Jagjit Singh. The analog and digital computers, how they work, how they are like and unlike the human brain, the men who developed them, their future applications, computer terminology. An essential book for today, even for readers with little math. Some mathematical demonstrations included for more advanced readers. 118 figures. Tables. ix + 338pp. 21694-2 Paperbound $2.50

CHANCE, LUCK AND STATISTICS, Horace C. Levinson. Non-mathematical presentation of fundamentals of probability theory and science of statistics and their applications. Games of chance, betting odds, misuse of statistics, normal and skew distributions, birth rates, stock speculation, insurance. Enlarged edition. Formerly "The Science of Chance." xiii + 357pp. 21007-3 Paperbound $2.50

PLANETS, STARS AND GALAXIES: DESCRIPTIVE ASTRONOMY FOR BEGINNERS, A. E. Fanning. Comprehensive introductory survey of astronomy: the sun, solar system, stars, galaxies, universe, cosmology; up-to-date, including quasars, radio stars, etc. Preface by Prof. Donald Menzel. 24pp. of photographs. 189pp. 5¼ x 8¼.
21680-2 Paperbound $2.50

TEACH YOURSELF CALCULUS, P. Abbott. With a good background in algebra and trig, you can teach yourself calculus with this book. Simple, straightforward introduction to functions of all kinds, integration, differentiation, series, etc. "Students who are beginning to study calculus method will derive great help from this book." Faraday House Journal. 308pp.
20683-1 Clothbound $2.50

TEACH YOURSELF TRIGONOMETRY, P. Abbott. Geometrical foundations, indices and logarithms, ratios, angles, circular measure, etc. are presented in this sound, easy-to-use text. Excellent for the beginner or as a brush up, this text carries the student through the solution of triangles. 204pp.
20682-3 Clothbound $2.00

BASIC MACHINES AND HOW THEY WORK, U. S. Bureau of Naval Personnel. Originally used in U.S. Naval training schools, this book clearly explains the operation of a progression of machines, from the simplest—lever, wheel and axle, inclined plane, wedge, screw—to the most complex—typewriter, internal combustion engine, computer mechanism. Utilizing an approach that requires only an elementary understanding of mathematics, these explanations build logically upon each other and are assisted by over 200 drawings and diagrams. Perfect as a technical school manual or as a self-teaching aid to the layman. 204 figures. Preface. Index. vii + 161pp. 6½ x 9¼.
21709-4 Paperbound $2.50

THE FRIENDLY STARS, Martha Evans Martin. Classic has taught naked-eye observation of stars, planets to hundreds of thousands, still not surpassed for charm, lucidity, adequacy. Completely updated by Professor Donald H. Menzel, Harvard Observatory. 25 illustrations. 16 x 30 chart. x + 147pp.
21099-5 Paperbound $2.00

MUSIC OF THE SPHERES: THE MATERIAL UNIVERSE FROM ATOM TO QUASAR, SIMPLY EXPLAINED, Guy Murchie. Extremely broad, brilliantly written popular account begins with the solar system and reaches to dividing line between matter and nonmatter; latest understandings presented with exceptional clarity. Volume One: Planets, stars, galaxies, cosmology, geology, celestial mechanics, latest astronomical discoveries; Volume Two: Matter, atoms, waves, radiation, relativity, chemical action, heat, nuclear energy, quantum theory, music, light, color, probability, antimatter, antigravity, and similar topics. 319 figures. 1967 (second) edition. Total of xx + 644pp.
21809-0, 21810-4 Two volumes, Paperbound $5.75

OLD-TIME SCHOOLS AND SCHOOL BOOKS, Clifton Johnson. Illustrations and rhymes from early primers, abundant quotations from early textbooks, many anecdotes of school life enliven this study of elementary schools from Puritans to middle 19th century. Introduction by Carl Withers. 234 illustrations. xxxiii + 381pp.
21031-6 Paperbound $4.00

THE PHILOSOPHY OF THE UPANISHADS, Paul Deussen. Clear, detailed statement of upanishadic system of thought, generally considered among best available. History of these works, full exposition of system emergent from them, parallel concepts in the West. Translated by A. S. Geden. xiv + 429pp.

21616-0 Paperbound $3.50

LANGUAGE, TRUTH AND LOGIC, Alfred J. Ayer. Famous, remarkably clear introduction to the Vienna and Cambridge schools of Logical Positivism; function of philosophy, elimination of metaphysical thought, nature of analysis, similar topics. "Wish I had written it myself," Bertrand Russell. 2nd, 1946 edition. 160pp.

20010-8 Paperbound $1.50

THE GUIDE FOR THE PERPLEXED, Moses Maimonides. Great classic of medieval Judaism, major attempt to reconcile revealed religion (Pentateuch, commentaries) and Aristotelian philosophy. Enormously important in all Western thought. Unabridged Friedländer translation. 50-page introduction. lix + 414pp.

(USO) 20351-4 Paperbound $4.50

OCCULT AND SUPERNATURAL PHENOMENA, D. H. Rawcliffe. Full, serious study of the most persistent delusions of mankind: crystal gazing, mediumistic trance, stigmata, lycanthropy, fire walking, dowsing, telepathy, ghosts, ESP, etc., and their relation to common forms of abnormal psychology. Formerly *Illusions and Delusions of the Supernatural and the Occult.* iii + 551pp. 20503-7 Paperbound $4.00

THE EGYPTIAN BOOK OF THE DEAD: THE PAPYRUS OF ANI, E. A. Wallis Budge. Full hieroglyphic text, interlinear transliteration of sounds, word for word translation, then smooth, connected translation; Theban recension. Basic work in Ancient Egyptian civilization; now even more significant than ever for historical importance, dilation of consciousness, etc. clvi + 377pp. 6½ x 9¼.

21866-X Paperbound $4.95

PSYCHOLOGY OF MUSIC, Carl E. Seashore. Basic, thorough survey of everything known about psychology of music up to 1940's; essential reading for psychologists, musicologists. Physical acoustics; auditory apparatus; relationship of physical sound to perceived sound; role of the mind in sorting, altering, suppressing, creating sound sensations; musical learning, testing for ability, absolute pitch, other topics. Records of Caruso, Menuhin analyzed. 88 figures. xix + 408pp.

21851-1 Paperbound $3.50

THE I CHING (THE BOOK OF CHANGES), translated by James Legge. Complete translated text plus appendices by Confucius, of perhaps the most penetrating divination book ever compiled. Indispensable to all study of early Oriental civilizations. 3 plates. xxiii + 448pp. 21062-6 Paperbound $3.50

THE UPANISHADS, translated by Max Müller. Twelve classical upanishads: Chandogya, Kena, Aitareya, Kaushitaki, Isa, Katha, Mundaka, Taittiriyaka, Brhadaranyaka, Svetasvatara, Prasna, Maitriyana. 160-page introduction, analysis by Prof. Müller. Total of 670pp. 20992-X, 20993-8 Two volumes, Paperbound $7.50

JIM WHITEWOLF: THE LIFE OF A KIOWA APACHE INDIAN, Charles S. Brant, editor. Spans transition between native life and acculturation period, 1880 on. Kiowa culture, personal life pattern, religion and the supernatural, the Ghost Dance, breakdown in the White Man's world, similar material. 1 map. xii + 144pp.
22015-X Paperbound $1.75

THE NATIVE TRIBES OF CENTRAL AUSTRALIA, Baldwin Spencer and F. J. Gillen. Basic book in anthropology, devoted to full coverage of the Arunta and Warramunga tribes; the source for knowledge about kinship systems, material and social culture, religion, etc. Still unsurpassed. 121 photographs, 89 drawings. xviii + 669pp.
21775-2 Paperbound $5.00

MALAY MAGIC, Walter W. Skeat. Classic (1900); still the definitive work on the folklore and popular religion of the Malay peninsula. Describes marriage rites, birth spirits and ceremonies, medicine, dances, games, war and weapons, etc. Extensive quotes from original sources, many magic charms translated into English. 35 illustrations. Preface by Charles Otto Blagden. xxiv + 685pp.
21760-4 Paperbound $4.00

HEAVENS ON EARTH: UTOPIAN COMMUNITIES IN AMERICA, 1680-1880, Mark Holloway. The finest nontechnical account of American utopias, from the early Woman in the Wilderness, Ephrata, Rappites to the enormous mid 19th-century efflorescence; Shakers, New Harmony, Equity Stores, Fourier's Phalanxes, Oneida, Amana, Fruitlands, etc. "Entertaining and very instructive." *Times Literary Supplement*. 15 illustrations. 246pp.
21593-8 Paperbound $2.00

LONDON LABOUR AND THE LONDON POOR, Henry Mayhew. Earliest (c. 1850) sociological study in English, describing myriad subcultures of London poor. Particularly remarkable for the thousands of pages of direct testimony taken from the lips of London prostitutes, thieves, beggars, street sellers, chimney-sweepers, street-musicians, "mudlarks," "pure-finders," rag-gatherers, "running-patterers," dock laborers, cab-men, and hundreds of others, quoted directly in this massive work. An extraordinarily vital picture of London emerges. 110 illustrations. Total of lxxvi + 1951pp. 6⅝ x 10.
21934-8, 21935-6, 21936-4, 21937-2 Four volumes, Paperbound $16.00

HISTORY OF THE LATER ROMAN EMPIRE, J. B. Bury. Eloquent, detailed reconstruction of Western and Byzantine Roman Empire by a major historian, from the death of Theodosius I (395 A.D.) to the death of Justinian (565). Extensive quotations from contemporary sources; full coverage of important Roman and foreign figures of the time. xxxiv + 965pp. 20398-0, 20399-9 Two volumes, Paperbound $7.00

AN INTELLECTUAL AND CULTURAL HISTORY OF THE WESTERN WORLD, Harry Elmer Barnes. Monumental study, tracing the development of the accomplishments that make up human culture. Every aspect of man's achievement surveyed from its origins in the Paleolithic to the present day (1964); social structures, ideas, economic systems, art, literature, technology, mathematics, the sciences, medicine, religion, jurisprudence, etc. Evaluations of the contributions of scores of great men. 1964 edition, revised and edited by scholars in the many fields represented. Total of xxix + 1381pp. 21275-0, 21276-9, 21277-7 Three volumes, Paperbound $10.50

ADVENTURES OF AN AFRICAN SLAVER, Theodore Canot. Edited by Brantz Mayer. A detailed portrayal of slavery and the slave trade, 1820-1840. Canot, an established trader along the African coast, describes the slave economy of the African kingdoms, the treatment of captured negroes, the extensive journeys in the interior to gather slaves, slave revolts and their suppression, harems, bribes, and much more. Full and unabridged republication of 1854 edition. Introduction by Malcom Cowley. 16 illustrations. xvii + 448pp.　　　　　　　　　22456-2 Paperbound $3.50

MY BONDAGE AND MY FREEDOM, Frederick Douglass. Born and brought up in slavery, Douglass witnessed its horrors and experienced its cruelties, but went on to become one of the most outspoken forces in the American anti-slavery movement. Considered the best of his autobiographies, this book graphically describes the in-human treatment of slaves, its effects on slave owners and slave families, and how Douglass's determination led him to a new life. Unaltered reprint of 1st (1855) edition. xxxii + 464pp.　　　　　　　　22457-0 Paperbound $3.50

THE INDIANS' BOOK, recorded and edited by Natalie Curtis. Lore, music, narratives, dozens of drawings by Indians themselves from an authoritative and important survey of native culture among Plains, Southwestern, Lake and Pueblo Indians. Standard work in popular ethnomusicology. 149 songs in full notation. 23 draw-ings, 23 photos. xxxi + 584pp. 6⅝ x 9⅜.　　　　　21939-9 Paperbound $5.00

DICTIONARY OF AMERICAN PORTRAITS, edited by Hayward and Blanche Cirker. 4024 portraits of 4000 most important Americans, colonial days to 1905 (with a few important categories, like Presidents, to present). Pioneers, explorers, colonial figures, U. S. officials, politicians, writers, military and naval men, scientists, inven-tors, manufacturers, jurists, actors, historians, educators, notorious figures, Indian chiefs, etc. All authentic contemporary likenesses. The only work of its kind in existence; supplements all biographical sources for libraries. Indispensable to any-one working with American history. 8,000-item classified index, finding lists, other aids. xiv + 756pp. 9¼ x 12¾.　　　　　　21823-6 Clothbound $30.00

TRITTON'S GUIDE TO BETTER WINE AND BEER MAKING FOR BEGINNERS, S. M. Tritton. All you need to know to make family-sized quantities of over 100 types of grape, fruit, herb and vegetable wines; as well as beers, mead, cider, etc. Com-plete recipes, advice as to equipment, procedures such as fermenting, bottling, and storing wines. Recipes given in British, U. S., and metric measures. Accompanying booklet lists sources in U. S. A. where ingredients may be bought, and additional information. 11 illustrations. 157pp. 5⅝ x 8⅛.

　　　　　　　　　　　　　　22090-7　**Paperbound $2.00**

GARDENING WITH HERBS FOR FLAVOR AND FRAGRANCE, Helen M. Fox. How to grow herbs in your own garden, how to use them in your cooking (over 55 recipes included), legends and myths associated with each species, uses in medicine, per-fumes, etc.—these are elements of one of the few books written especially for Amer-ican herb fanciers. Guides you step-by-step from soil preparation to harvesting and storage for each type of herb. 12 drawings by Louise Mansfield. xiv + 334pp.

　　　　　　　　　　　　　　22540-2 Paperbound $2.50

INCIDENTS OF TRAVEL IN YUCATAN, John L. Stephens. Classic (1843) exploration of jungles of Yucatan, looking for evidences of Maya civilization. Stephens found many ruins; comments on travel adventures, Mexican and Indian culture. 127 striking illustrations by F. Catherwood. Total of 669 pp.

20926-1, 20927-X Two volumes, Paperbound $5.50

INCIDENTS OF TRAVEL IN CENTRAL AMERICA, CHIAPAS, AND YUCATAN, John L. Stephens. An exciting travel journal and an important classic of archeology. Narrative relates his almost single-handed discovery of the Mayan culture, and exploration of the ruined cities of Copan, Palenque, Utatlan and others; the monuments they dug from the earth, the temples buried in the jungle, the customs of poverty-stricken Indians living a stone's throw from the ruined palaces. 115 drawings by F. Catherwood. Portrait of Stephens. xii + 812pp.

22404-X, 22405-8 Two volumes, Paperbound $6.00

A NEW VOYAGE ROUND THE WORLD, William Dampier. Late 17-century naturalist joined the pirates of the Spanish Main to gather information; remarkably vivid account of buccaneers, pirates; detailed, accurate account of botany, zoology, ethnography of lands visited. Probably the most important early English voyage, enormous implications for British exploration, trade, colonial policy. Also most interesting reading. Argonaut edition, introduction by Sir Albert Gray. New introduction by Percy Adams. 6 plates, 7 illustrations. xlvii + 376pp. 6½ x 9¼.

21900-3 Paperbound $3.00

INTERNATIONAL AIRLINE PHRASE BOOK IN SIX LANGUAGES, Joseph W. Bátor. Important phrases and sentences in English paralleled with French, German, Portuguese, Italian, Spanish equivalents, covering all possible airport-travel situations; created for airline personnel as well as tourist by Language Chief, Pan American Airlines. xiv + 204pp.

22017-6 Paperbound $2.25

STAGE COACH AND TAVERN DAYS, Alice Morse Earle. Detailed, lively account of the early days of taverns; their uses and importance in the social, political and military life; furnishings and decorations; locations; food and drink; tavern signs, etc. Second half covers every aspect of early travel; the roads, coaches, drivers, etc. Nostalgic, charming, packed with fascinating material. 157 illustrations, mostly photographs. xiv + 449pp.

22518-6 Paperbound $4.00

NORSE DISCOVERIES AND EXPLORATIONS IN NORTH AMERICA, Hjalmar R. Holand. The perplexing Kensington Stone, found in Minnesota at the end of the 19th century. Is it a record of a Scandinavian expedition to North America in the 14th century? Or is it one of the most successful hoaxes in history. A scientific detective investigation. Formerly *Westward from Vinland*. 31 photographs, 17 figures. x + 354pp.

22014-1 Paperbound $2.75

A BOOK OF OLD MAPS, compiled and edited by Emerson D. Fite and Archibald Freeman. 74 old maps offer an unusual survey of the discovery, settlement and growth of America down to the close of the Revolutionary war: maps showing Norse settlements in Greenland, the explorations of Columbus, Verrazano, Cabot, Champlain, Joliet, Drake, Hudson, etc., campaigns of Revolutionary war battles, and much more. Each map is accompanied by a brief historical essay. xvi + 299pp. 11 x 13¾.

22084-2 Paperbound $7.00

ALPHABETS AND ORNAMENTS, Ernst Lehner. Well-known pictorial source for decorative alphabets, script examples, cartouches, frames, decorative title pages, calligraphic initials, borders, similar material. 14th to 19th century, mostly European. Useful in almost any graphic arts designing, varied styles. 750 illustrations. 256pp. 7 x 10.   21905-4 Paperbound $4.00

PAINTING: A CREATIVE APPROACH, Norman Colquhoun. For the beginner simple guide provides an instructive approach to painting: major stumbling blocks for beginner; overcoming them, technical points; paints and pigments; oil painting; watercolor and other media and color. New section on "plastic" paints. Glossary. Formerly *Paint Your Own Pictures.* 221pp.   22000-1 Paperbound $1.75

THE ENJOYMENT AND USE OF COLOR, Walter Sargent. Explanation of the relations between colors themselves and between colors in nature and art, including hundreds of little-known facts about color values, intensities, effects of high and low illumination, complementary colors. Many practical hints for painters, references to great masters. 7 color plates, 29 illustrations. x + 274pp.
20944-X Paperbound $3.00

THE NOTEBOOKS OF LEONARDO DA VINCI, compiled and edited by Jean Paul Richter. 1566 extracts from original manuscripts reveal the full range of Leonardo's versatile genius: all his writings on painting, sculpture, architecture, anatomy, astronomy, geography, topography, physiology, mining, music, etc., in both Italian and English, with 186 plates of manuscript pages and more than 500 additional drawings. Includes studies for the Last Supper, the lost Sforza monument, and other works. Total of xlvii + 866pp. 7⅞ x 10¾.
22572-0, 22573-9 Two volumes, Paperbound $12.00

MONTGOMERY WARD CATALOGUE OF 1895. Tea gowns, yards of flannel and pillow-case lace, stereoscopes, books of gospel hymns, the New Improved Singer Sewing Machine, side saddles, milk skimmers, straight-edged razors, high-button shoes, spittoons, and on and on . . . listing some 25,000 items, practically all illustrated. Essential to the shoppers of the 1890's, it is our truest record of the spirit of the period. Unaltered reprint of Issue No. 57, Spring and Summer 1895. Introduction by Boris Emmet. Innumerable illustrations. xiii + 624pp. 8½ x 11⅝.
22377-9 Paperbound $8.50

THE CRYSTAL PALACE EXHIBITION ILLUSTRATED CATALOGUE (LONDON, 1851). One of the wonders of the modern world—the Crystal Palace Exhibition in which all the nations of the civilized world exhibited their achievements in the arts and sciences—presented in an equally important illustrated catalogue. More than 1700 items pictured with accompanying text—ceramics, textiles, cast-iron work, carpets, pianos, sleds, razors, wall-papers, billiard tables, beehives, silverware and hundreds of other artifacts—represent the focal point of Victorian culture in the Western World. Probably the largest collection of Victorian decorative art ever assembled— indispensable for antiquarians and designers. Unabridged republication of the Art-Journal Catalogue of the Great Exhibition of 1851, with all terminal essays. New introduction by John Gloag, F.S.A. xxxiv + 426pp. 9 x 12.
22503-8 Paperbound $5.00

JOHANN SEBASTIAN BACH, Philipp Spitta. One of the great classics of musicology, this definitive analysis of Bach's music (and life) has never been surpassed. Lucid, nontechnical analyses of hundreds of pieces (30 pages devoted to St. Matthew Passion, 26 to B Minor Mass). Also includes major analysis of 18th-century music. 450 musical examples. 40-page musical supplement. Total of xx + 1799pp.
(EUK) 22278-0, 22279-9 Two volumes, Clothbound $25.00

MOZART AND HIS PIANO CONCERTOS, Cuthbert Girdlestone. The only full-length study of an important area of Mozart's creativity. Provides detailed analyses of all 23 concertos, traces inspirational sources. 417 musical examples. Second edition. 509pp.
21271-8 Paperbound $4.50

THE PERFECT WAGNERITE: A COMMENTARY ON THE NIBLUNG'S RING, George Bernard Shaw. Brilliant and still relevant criticism in remarkable essays on Wagner's Ring cycle, Shaw's ideas on political and social ideology behind the plots, role of Leitmotifs, vocal requisites, etc. Prefaces. xxi + 136pp.
(USO) 21707-8 Paperbound $1.75

DON GIOVANNI, W. A. Mozart. Complete libretto, modern English translation; biographies of composer and librettist; accounts of early performances and critical reaction. Lavishly illustrated. All the material you need to understand and appreciate this great work. Dover Opera Guide and Libretto Series; translated and introduced by Ellen Bleiler. 92 illustrations. 209pp.
21134-7 Paperbound $2.00

BASIC ELECTRICITY, U. S. Bureau of Naval Personel. Originally a training course, best non-technical coverage of basic theory of electricity and its applications. Fundamental concepts, batteries, circuits, conductors and wiring techniques, AC and DC, inductance and capacitance, generators, motors, transformers, magnetic amplifiers, synchros, servomechanisms, etc. Also covers blue-prints, electrical diagrams, etc. Many questions, with answers. 349 illustrations. x + 448pp. 6½ x 9¼.
20973-3 Paperbound $3.50

REPRODUCTION OF SOUND, Edgar Villchur. Thorough coverage for laymen of high fidelity systems, reproducing systems in general, needles, amplifiers, preamps, loudspeakers, feedback, explaining physical background. "A rare talent for making technicalities vividly comprehensible," R. Darrell, *High Fidelity.* 69 figures. iv + 92pp.
21515-6 Paperbound $1.35

HEAR ME TALKIN' TO YA: THE STORY OF JAZZ AS TOLD BY THE MEN WHO MADE IT, Nat Shapiro and Nat Hentoff. Louis Armstrong, Fats Waller, Jo Jones, Clarence Williams, Billy Holiday, Duke Ellington, Jelly Roll Morton and dozens of other jazz greats tell how it was in Chicago's South Side, New Orleans, depression Harlem and the modern West Coast as jazz was born and grew. xvi + 429pp.
21726-4 Paperbound $3.95

FABLES OF AESOP, translated by Sir Roger L'Estrange. A reproduction of the very rare 1931 Paris edition; a selection of the most interesting fables, together with 50 imaginative drawings by Alexander Calder. v + 128pp. 6½x9¼.
21780-9 Paperbound $1.50

POEMS OF ANNE BRADSTREET, edited with an introduction by Robert Hutchinson. A new selection of poems by America's first poet and perhaps the first significant woman poet in the English language. 48 poems display her development in works of considerable variety—love poems, domestic poems, religious meditations, formal elegies, "quaternions," etc. Notes, bibliography. viii + 222pp.
22160-1 Paperbound $2.50

THREE GOTHIC NOVELS: THE CASTLE OF OTRANTO BY HORACE WALPOLE; VATHEK BY WILLIAM BECKFORD; THE VAMPYRE BY JOHN POLIDORI, WITH FRAGMENT OF A NOVEL BY LORD BYRON, edited by E. F. Bleiler. The first Gothic novel, by Walpole; the finest Oriental tale in English, by Beckford; powerful Romantic supernatural story in versions by Polidori and Byron. All extremely important in history of literature; all still exciting, packed with supernatural thrills, ghosts, haunted castles, magic, etc. xl + 291pp.
21232-7 Paperbound $3.00

THE BEST TALES OF HOFFMANN, E. T. A. Hoffmann. 10 of Hoffmann's most important stories, in modern re-editings of standard translations: Nutcracker and the King of Mice, Signor Formica, Automata, The Sandman, Rath Krespel, The Golden Flowerpot, Master Martin the Cooper, The Mines of Falun, The King's Betrothed, A New Year's Eve Adventure. 7 illustrations by Hoffmann. Edited by E. F. Bleiler. xxxix + 419pp.   21793-0 Paperbound $3.00

GHOST AND HORROR STORIES OF AMBROSE BIERCE, Ambrose Bierce. 23 strikingly modern stories of the horrors latent in the human mind: The Eyes of the Panther, The Damned Thing, An Occurrence at Owl Creek Bridge, An Inhabitant of Carcosa, etc., plus the dream-essay, Visions of the Night. Edited by E. F. Bleiler. xxii + 199pp.
20767-6 Paperbound $2.00

BEST GHOST STORIES OF J. S. LEFANU, J. Sheridan LeFanu. Finest stories by Victorian master often considered greatest supernatural writer of all. Carmilla, Green Tea, The Haunted Baronet, The Familiar, and 12 others. Most never before available in the U. S. A. Edited by E. F. Bleiler. 8 illustrations from Victorian publications. xvii + 467pp.
20415-4 Paperbound $3.00

MATHEMATICAL FOUNDATIONS OF INFORMATION THEORY, A. I. Khinchin. Comprehensive introduction to work of Shannon, McMillan, Feinstein and Khinchin, placing these investigations on a rigorous mathematical basis. Covers entropy concept in probability theory, uniqueness theorem, Shannon's inequality, ergodic sources, the E property, martingale concept, noise, Feinstein's fundamental lemma, Shanon's first and second theorems. Translated by R. A. Silverman and M. D. Friedman. iii + 120pp.
60434-9 Paperbound $2.00

SEVEN SCIENCE FICTION NOVELS, H. G. Wells. The standard collection of the great novels. Complete, unabridged. *First Men in the Moon, Island of Dr. Moreau, War of the Worlds, Food of the Gods, Invisible Man, Time Machine, In the Days of the Comet.* Not only science fiction fans, but every educated person owes it to himself to read these novels. 1015pp.   (USO) 20264-X Clothbound $6.00

MATHEMATICAL PUZZLES FOR BEGINNERS AND ENTHUSIASTS, Geoffrey Mott-Smith. 189 puzzles from easy to difficult—involving arithmetic, logic, algebra, properties of digits, probability, etc.—for enjoyment and mental stimulus. Explanation of mathematical principles behind the puzzles. 135 illustrations. viii + 248pp.

20198-8 Paperbound $2.00

PAPER FOLDING FOR BEGINNERS, William D. Murray and Francis J. Rigney. Easiest book on the market, clearest instructions on making interesting, beautiful origami. Sail boats, cups, roosters, frogs that move legs, bonbon boxes, standing birds, etc. 40 projects; more than 275 diagrams and photographs. 94pp.

20713-7 Paperbound $1.00

TRICKS AND GAMES ON THE POOL TABLE, Fred Herrmann. 79 tricks and games— some solitaires, some for two or more players, some competitive games—to entertain you between formal games. Mystifying shots and throws, unusual caroms, tricks involving such props as cork, coins, a hat, etc. Formerly *Fun on the Pool Table.* 77 figures. 95pp.

21814-7 Paperbound $1.25

HAND SHADOWS TO BE THROWN UPON THE WALL: A SERIES OF NOVEL AND AMUSING FIGURES FORMED BY THE HAND, Henry Bursill. Delightful picturebook from great-grandfather's day shows how to make 18 different hand shadows: a bird that flies, duck that quacks, dog that wags his tail, camel, goose, deer, boy, turtle, etc. Only book of its sort. vi + 33pp. 6½ x 9¼.

21779-5 Paperbound $1.00

WHITTLING AND WOODCARVING, E. J. Tangerman. 18th printing of best book on market. "If you can cut a potato you can carve" toys and puzzles, chains, chessmen, caricatures, masks, frames, woodcut blocks, surface patterns, much more. Information on tools, woods, techniques. Also goes into serious wood sculpture from Middle Ages to present, East and West. 464 photos, figures. x + 293pp.

20965-2 Paperbound $2.50

HISTORY OF PHILOSOPHY, Julián Marias. Possibly the clearest, most easily followed, best planned, most useful one-volume history of philosophy on the market; neither skimpy nor overfull. Full details on system of every major philosopher and dozens of less important thinkers from pre-Socratics up to Existentialism and later. Strong on many European figures usually omitted. Has gone through dozens of editions in Europe. 1966 edition, translated by Stanley Appelbaum and Clarence Strowbridge. xviii + 505pp.

21739-6 Paperbound $3.50

YOGA: A SCIENTIFIC EVALUATION, Kovoor T. Behanan. Scientific but non-technical study of physiological results of yoga exercises; done under auspices of Yale U. Relations to Indian thought, to psychoanalysis, etc. 16 photos. xxiii + 270pp.

20505-3 Paperbound $2.50

Prices subject to change without notice.

Available at your book dealer or write for free catalogue to Dept. GI, Dover Publications, Inc., 180 Varick St., N. Y., N. Y. 10014. Dover publishes more than 150 books each year on science, elementary and advanced mathematics, biology, music, art, literary history, social sciences and other areas.